MOON HANDBOOKS®

ACAPULCO

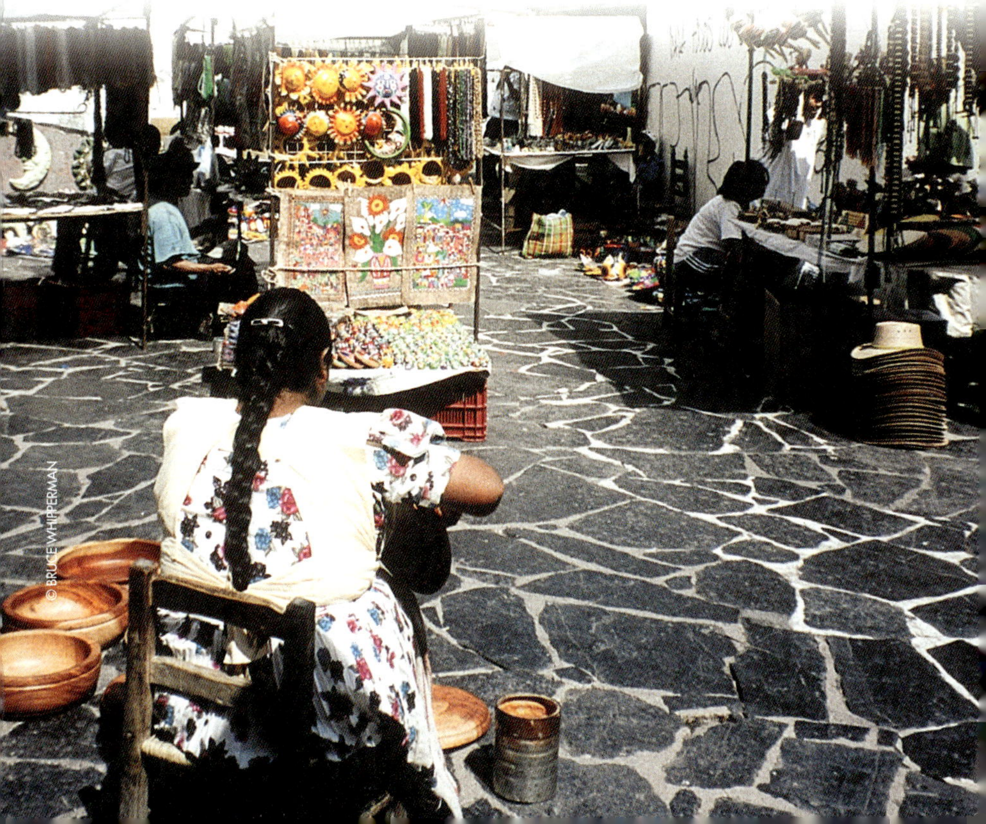

© BRUCE WHIPPERMAN

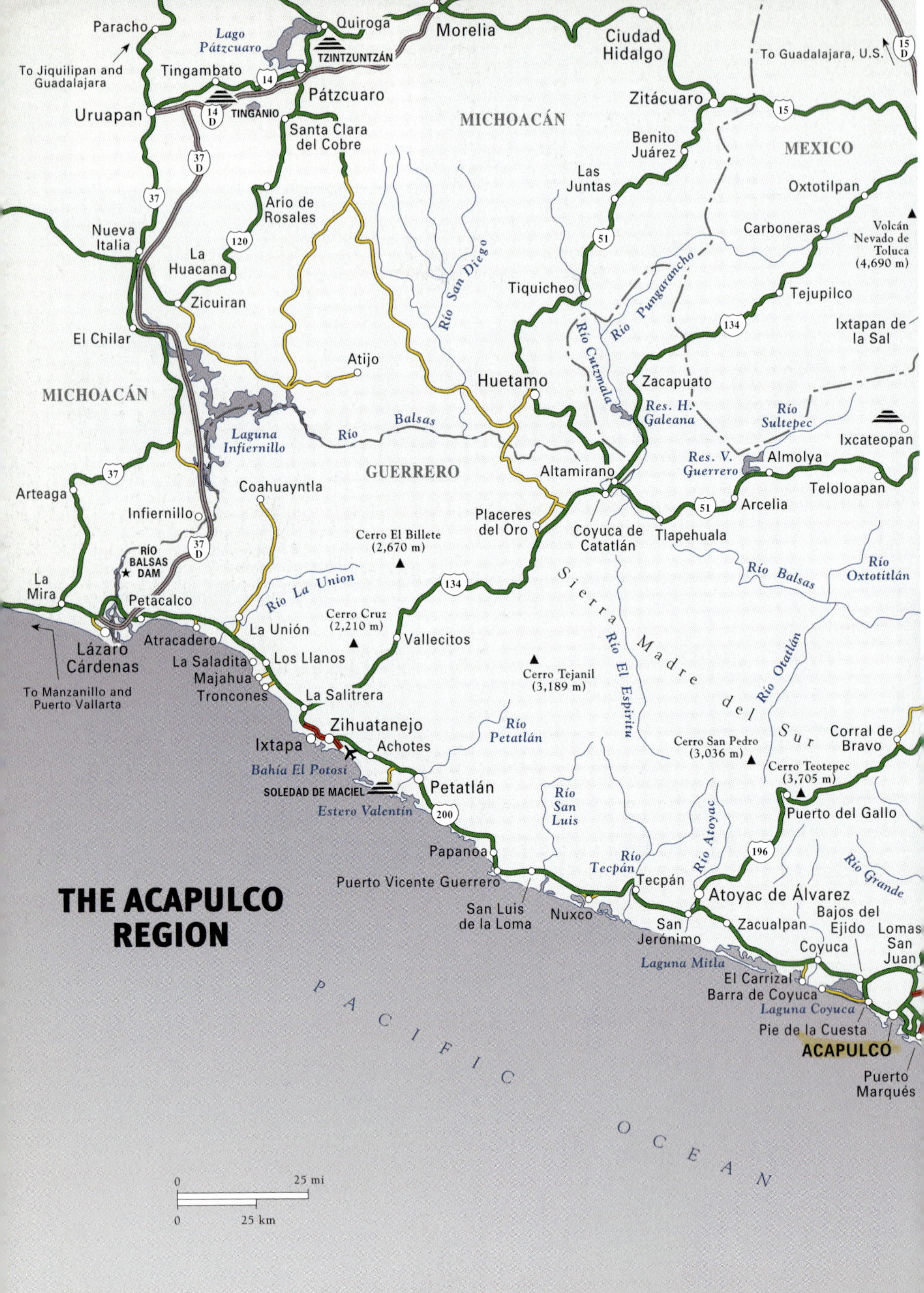
THE ACAPULCO REGION
MICHOACÁN
MEXICO
GUERRERO
PACIFIC OCEAN
Paracho
To Jiquilipan and Guadalajara
Lago Pátzcuaro
Quiroga
TZINTZUNTZÁN
Morelia
Ciudad Hidalgo
To Guadalajara, U.S.
Tingambato
Pátzcuaro
Uruapan
TINGANIO
Santa Clara del Cobre
Zitácuaro
Benito Juárez
Las Juntas
Oxtotilpan
Ario de Rosales
Carboneras
Volcán Nevado de Toluca (4,690 m)
Nueva Italia
La Huacana
Río San Diego
Tiquicheo
Río Pungarancho
Tejupilco
Zicuiran
Río Cutzmala
Ixtapan de la Sal
El Chilar
Atijo
Huetamo
Zacapuato
Laguna Infiernillo
Río Balsas
Res. H. Galeana
Río Sultepec
Ixcateopan
Res. V. Guerrero
Almolya
Arteaga
Coahuayntla
Altamirano
Teloloapan
Infiernillo
Placeres del Oro
Arcelia
Cerro El Billete (2,670 m)
Coyuca de Catatlán
Tlapehuala
RÍO BALSAS DAM
Río La Union
Sierra Madre del Sur
Río Oxtotitlán
La Mira
Petacalco
Cerro Cruz (2,210 m)
La Unión
Vallecitos
Lázaro Cárdenas
Atracadero
Los Llanos
Cerro Tejanil (3,189 m)
Río El Espiritu
Río Otatlán
To Manzanillo and Puerto Vallarta
La Saladita
Majahua
Troncones
La Salitrera
Zihuatanejo
Río Petatlán
Corral de Bravo
Ixtapa
Achotes
Cerro San Pedro (3,036 m)
Bahía El Potosí
Cerro Teotepec (3,705 m)
SOLEDAD DE MACIEL
Petatlán
Río San Luis
Puerto del Gallo
Estero Valentín
Río Atoyac
Papanoa
Río Tecpán
Río Grande
Puerto Vicente Guerrero
Tecpán
Atoyac de Álvarez
San Luis de la Loma
Nuxco
Bajos del Ejido
San Jerónimo
Zacualpan
Lomas San Juan
Laguna Mitla
Coyuca
El Carrizal
Barra de Coyuca
Laguna Coyuca
Pie de la Cuesta
ACAPULCO
Puerto Marqués
0 25 mi
0 25 km

To Queretaro, Monterrey, U.S., and Mex. 57D
MEXICO CITY
95 D
Texcoco
TLAXCALA
To Xalapa and Veracruz
Apizaco
Tlaxcala
136
Tequexquitla
Ixtapaluca
150 D
Toluca
Metepec
Chalco
Texmelucan
Zacatepec
140
San Salvador El Seco
95
D.F.
Coatepec
129
55 D
Tenango de Arista
106
Cholula
To Veracruz and Yucatán
Tepoztlán
Puebla
Tepeaca
Cuernavaca
Atlixco
150 D
XOCHICALCO
Tecamachalco
Miacatlán
Yautepec
Cuautla
160
Jantetelco
190
Río Atoyac
55
Cacahuamilpa
131 D
150
CAVES OF CACAHUAMILPA
Tlaltizapan
Zacatepec
Izucar de Matamoros
Tepexco
Jojutla
Tehuacán
Taxco
Puente de Ixtla
MORELOS
PUEBLA
Laguna Tuxpan
Tehuitzin
Huitzuco
135
Iguala
Res. V. Trujano
CUETLAJUCHITLÁN
Acatlán
Atenango del Río
95
95 D
125
93
Río Mixteco
Xalitla
Copalillo
TEOPANTECUANTLÁN
PUENTE MEZCALA
Xochihuehuetlán
HUAJUAPAN DE LEÓN
PUENTE MEZCALA SOLIDARIDAD
Río Mezcala
Huajuapan de León
131 D
Xochipala
Olinalá
LA ORGANERA XOCHIPALA
190
Zumpanga del Río
Atlixtac
Alpoyeca
Tonalá
Tamazulpan
Chilapa
Atenango
Tlapa
93
Chilpancingo
Tixtla
San Ángel
Atzacualoya
Tlatlauquitepec
To Oaxaca
CAVES OF JUXTLAHUACA
GUERRERO
Mazatlán
Colotlipa
Cerro San Marcos (3,100 m)
Acahuizotla
Mochitlán
Juxtlahuaca
Huamelulpan
Quechultenango
Cerro El Maguey (2,750 m)
Tlaxiaco
HUAMELULPAN
Río Azul
El Ocotito
125
Río Grande
Río Omitlán
Río Piedra Parada
95
Tierra Colorada
Río Quetzala
La Palma
Cerro Mexcaltepec (1,950 m)
Putla
Xaltianguis
OAXACA
95 D
Ayutla
Cerro El Violin (1,750 m)
Río Papagayo
Tecuanapa
Río Copala
Tlacoachistlahuaca
L. Tres Palos
San Marcos
Las Vigas
Acatlán
Chacalapa
Xochistlahuaca
MOON
Cruz Grande
Azoyu
Igualapa
Santa María Zacatepec
Tierra Blanca
Barra Vieja
Ometepec
Chautengo
Laguna Tecomate
Copala
San Pedro Amusgos
Marquelia
Cacahuatepec
Río Verde
Laguna Chautengo
Cuajinicuilapa
San Juan Colorado
San Nicolás
Playa Ventura
Barra de Tecoanapa
Tlacamama
Pinotepa Don Luis
200
Huaxpaltepec
Pinotepa Nacional
Jamiltepec
Puerto Maldonado
Huazolotitlán
Laguna Corralero
San Pedro Tututepec
To Puerto Escondido and Oaxaca
Río Grande

© BRUCE WHIPPERMAN

MOON HANDBOOKS®

ACAPULCO

FIRST EDITION

BRUCE WHIPPERMAN

AVALON
TRAVEL

MAPS

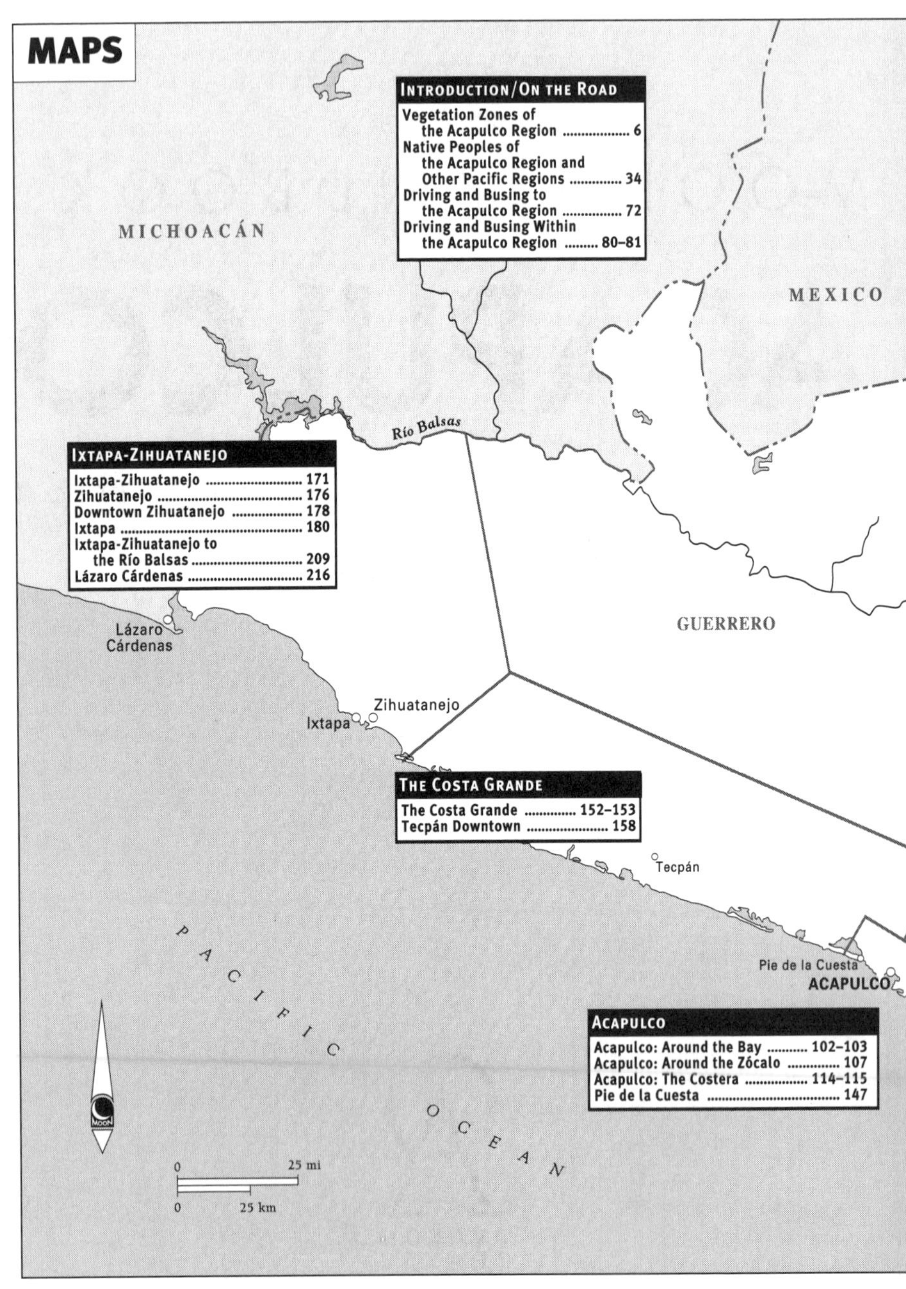
INTRODUCTION/ON THE ROAD
Vegetation Zones of the Acapulco Region 6
Native Peoples of the Acapulco Region and Other Pacific Regions 34
Driving and Busing to the Acapulco Region 72
Driving and Busing Within the Acapulco Region 80–81
MICHOACÁN
MEXICO
Río Balsas
IXTAPA-ZIHUATANEJO
Ixtapa-Zihuatanejo 171
Zihuatanejo 176
Downtown Zihuatanejo 178
Ixtapa 180
Ixtapa-Zihuatanejo to the Río Balsas 209
Lázaro Cárdenas 216
GUERRERO
Lázaro Cárdenas
Zihuatanejo
Ixtapa
THE COSTA GRANDE
The Costa Grande 152–153
Tecpán Downtown 158
Tecpán
Pie de la Cuesta
ACAPULCO
ACAPULCO
Acapulco: Around the Bay 102–103
Acapulco: Around the Zócalo 107
Acapulco: The Costera 114–115
Pie de la Cuesta 147
PACIFIC OCEAN
MOON
0 25 mi
0 25 km

GUERRERO UPCOUNTRY

Guerrero Upcountry 220–221
Chilpancingo 224–225
Chilpancingo Downtown 229
La Organera Xochipala Archaeological Zone 236
Chilapa 245
Olinalá 248
Iguala 252–253
Iguala Downtown 255
Taxco 265
Xochicalco Archaeological Zone 278–279

THE COSTA CHICA

The Costa Chica 284–285
Ometepec 290

Contents

© BRUCE WHIPPERMAN

Introduction 1

Four hundred years ago, the promise of treasure lured pirates to Acapulco's sun-drenched coast. Today's visitors are drawn to the region by its wealth of secluded beaches, mangrove-laden esteros, *lively crafts markets, and historic highland towns.*

Land and Sea **2;** Flora and Fauna **4;** History **13;** Economy and Government **30;** People **34**

On the Road 39

What's your vision of paradise? Whether it's finding the perfect surfing spot, figuring out where to string your hammock, or dining on fresh-caught fish under a shady palapa, *you'll find all the practical information you need right here.*

Sports and Recreation **39;** Festivals and Events **47;** Arts and Crafts **49;** Accommodations **55;** Food and Drink **60;** Shopping **65;** Getting There **66;** Getting Around **78;** Information and Services **84;** Health and Safety **93;** What to Take **98**

Acapulco 100

Its name long synonymous with palm-shaded beaches, good food, and merrymaking, Acapulco lives up to its reputation—and also surprises with its rich history and intimate, old-world neighborhoods. Just a few miles west, you'll find tranquillity in Pie de la Cuesta, where placid Laguna Coyuca is ideal for kayaking, sailboarding, and water-skiing.

Playa Larga; Barra Vieja and Laguna Tres Palos

PIE DE LA CUESTA 146

Laguna Coyuca

The Costa Grande 151

Stop along Guerrero's Big Coast for country living at its most serene, with colorful market towns, seaside hideaways, and breezy beaches just right for camping and surf fishing. Poke among sheltered tidepools near Piedra Tlalcoyunque, or join the fiesta in Petatlán, which comes alive in celebration of its beloved patrón, *Padre Jesús.*

Coyuca de Benítez and La Barra; El Carrizal; Laguna de Mitla; Camalote, Playa Paraíso, and San Jerónimo; Boca Chica and Tetitlán; Tecpán; San Luis de la Loma and Piedra Tlalcoyunque; Puerto Vicente Guerrero, Playa Escondida, and Playa Brisas del Mar; Papanoa; Playas Arroyo Seco, El Calvario, and Cayacal; Playa La Barrita and Las Salinas; Petatlán; Excursions from Petatlán: Ximalcota, Estero Valentín; Soledad de Maciel Archaeological Zone

Ixtapa-Zihuatanejo 170

Ixtapa and Zihuatanejo offer two distinct worlds only five miles apart. Zihuatanejo still resembles the easy-going seaside town visitors have enjoyed for years, while Ixtapa serves up luxury with high-rise hotels and stunning sunset vistas. To the north and south, idyllic fishing villages and wildlife-rich lagoons wait to be explored.

SOUTH OF IXTAPA-ZIHUATANEJO 208
Playa Las Pozas and Playa Blanca; Barra de Potosí

NORTH OF IXTAPA-ZIHUATANEJO 211
Troncones; Majahua; La Saladita, Atracadero, and the Río Balsas; Lázaro Cárdenas

Guerrero Upcountry 219

Venture into Guerrero's cool highland valleys to explore historic towns Chilpancingo and Iguala, shrines to Mexican independence. Nearby, you can wander through limestone caves, climb amid ancient ruins, and visit villages rich in handicrafts. All upcountry roads lead to colonial gem Taxco, with its cobbled hillside lanes and venerable silver-crafting tradition.

CHILPANCINGO 222
Excursions from Chilpancingo: Tixtla de Guerrero, La Organera Xochipala Archaeological Zone

RIVER COUNTRY 237
The Río Azul; Petaquillas, Mochitlán, and Quechultenango; The Caves of Juxtlahuaca; Colotlipa; The Río Papagayo

HANDICRAFTS COUNTRY 242
Chilapa; Olinalá

IGUALA 250
Excursions from Iguala: Tuxpan, Cuetlajuchitlán Archaeological Site, Teopantecuantlán Archaeological Site

TAXCO 263
Excursions from Taxco: Caves of Cacahuamilpa, Xochicalco Archaeological Zone, Ixcateopan

The Costa Chica 283

The Little Coast is not so little, running over 100 miles southeast of Acapulco into the state of Oaxaca. This is a land of diverse heritage, with centuries-old African Mexican communities and vibrant Mixtec and Amusgo market towns, where Spanish is often a foreign language.

San Marcos; Laguna Chautengo and Playa Ventura; Marquelia, Playa Las Peñitas, and Barra de Tecoanapa; Ometepec; Xochistlahuaca; Cuajinicuilapa and Puerto Maldonado; Pinotepa Nacional; Excursions North of Pinotepa: Pinotepa Don

Luis, San Juan Colorado, Cacahuatepec, San Pedro Amusgos; Excursions East of Pinotepa: Huaxpáltepec, Huazolotitlán, Jamiltepec

Resources

Resources 305
GLOSSARY 306
SPANISH PHRASEBOOK 309
SUGGESTED READING 316
INTERNET RESOURCES 322
INDEX 325

About the Author

Bruce Whipperman

© BRUCE WHIPPERMAN

In the early 1980s, the lure of travel drew Bruce Whipperman away from a 20-year career of teaching physics. The occasion was a trip to Kenya that included a total solar eclipse and a safari. He hasn't stopped traveling since.

With his family grown, he has been free to let the world's wild, beautiful corners draw him on: to the ice-clawed Karakoram, the Gobi Desert's trellised oases, the pink palaces of Rajasthan, Japan's green wine country, Bali's emerald terraces, and Pacific Mexico's palm-shaded beaches, colorful towns, and pine-scented highland valleys.

Bruce has always pursued his travel career for the fun of it. He started with slide shows and photo gifts for friends. Others wanted his photos, so he began selling them. Once, stranded in Ethiopia, he began to write. A dozen years later, after scores of magazine and newspaper feature stories, *Moon Handbooks Pacific Mexico* became his first book. Later, a second book, *Moon Handbooks Puerto Vallarta,* then a third, *Moon Handbooks Oaxaca,* a fourth, *Moon Handbooks Guadalajara,* and now a fifth, *Moon Handbooks Acapulco,* have brightened still more pathways for Mexico travelers.

Travel, after all, is for returning home, and that coziest of journeys always brings a tired but happy Bruce back to his friends, son, daughter, and wife, Linda, in Oakland, California.

For him, travel writing heightens his awareness and focuses his own travel experiences. He always remembers what a Nepali Sherpa once said: "Many people come, looking, looking; few people come, see."

Bruce invites readers of *Moon Handbooks Acapulco* likewise to "come see"—and discover and enjoy—Acapulco's delights with a fresh eye and renewed compassion.

Introduction

Contrary to popular outside perceptions, Acapulco offers much more than luxury living on golden beaches. Although it's true that modern Acapulco was built on its bayshore scarcely 50 years ago, there remains a historic old Acapulco that predates the Pilgrims at Plymouth Rock by half a century. It was in old Acapulco that intrepid Spanish seafarers fulfilled Christopher Columbus's old dream of a western trading route to Asia and, for more than four centuries, brought back a yearly trove of glittering Chinese silks, gold, lacquerware, and porcelain.

The bastion of old Acapulco—Fort San Diego—still stands proudly on the inner harbor shore, where it guarded the town from a dozen generations of foreign pirates. They lurked along the coast, waiting to capture the biggest prize of all, the renowned treasure-laden Manila galleon, that returned yearly across the Pacific to Acapulco.

History notwithstanding, the latter-day riches of the entire Acapulco region, which stretches up the coast to Ixtapa-Zihuatanejo, down the coast to Oaxaca, and upcountry to Taxco, flow from its millions of yearly vacationers. They arrive in the coastal resorts to enjoy multiple diversions—water sports and deep-sea fishing, nightlife and fine restaurants.

Visitors interested in quieter entertainments can explore the many hidden coastal beaches that few visitors know; watch a brilliant sunset;

traverse a tropical forest canopy; sunbathe in a secluded cove; camp, surf, beachcomb, and fish on a wild, open-ocean beach; or view flocks of birds by boat on a broad mangrove lagoon.

The shoreline alone would be enough but the Acapulco region offers much more. Within a half-day's ride are the oak- and pine-tufted highland valleys. Here, the historic colonial towns of Chilpancingo and Iguala, not unlike Philadelphia and Boston to Americans, stand as virtual shrines to Mexican independence. Not far from these centers, a host of active diversions—exploring monumental limestone caves, basking in crystalline springs, discovering ancient lost cities, and selecting from a treasury of handicrafts—reward travelers willing to venture from the well-worn route. And finally, all upcountry roads seem to lead to precious Taxco, the silver-rich colonial gem of the highlands.

So, although crowned by the celebrated big resorts of Acapulco and Ixtapa-Zihuatanejo, the Acapulco region offers even more. Whether you prefer glamour and luxury, the offbeat and rustic, or a little bit of both, this book will show the way.

Land and Sea

The Acapulco Region

Acapulco's influence extends far beyond its city limits, into the entire Acapulco region, an ethnically and geographically diverse domain that encompasses, broadly, the entire Mexican state of Guerrero.

The deep-south state of Guerrero (pop. 3,200,000, area 25,000 square miles, 65,000 square km) is about the same size of the U.S. state of West Virginia (or the European country of Austria). It stretches about 250 miles (400 km) along Mexico's south Pacific coast and extends about 150 miles (250 km) inland. In contrast to West Virginia and Austria, however, the Acapulco region covers a vastly diverse, ruggedly corrugated landscape of coastal plain, foothills, and high sierra, interspersed with a number of large and small upland valleys, many of which drain into the basin of the grand Río Balsas, Mexico's mightiest river.

Costa Chica and Costa Grande

Mountains notwithstanding, Acapulco's influence extends most strongly along the coast, and the Acapulco region has enough coastline for a pair of subregions, which Acapulco people call the Costa Chica (Little Coast) and Costa Grande (Big Coast), respectively. Labels aside, both coasts are big: the Costa Chica spreads 100 miles (160 km) east from Acapulco, to the state of Oaxaca border, while the Costa Grande spreads 150 miles (250 km) west, past Ixtapa-Zihuatanejo, to the great Río Balsas, which forms the border with the state of Michoacán.

LAGOONS, BAYS, COVES, AND BEACHES

Lagoons and Barrier Beaches

The land forms that define the entire Acapulco region spread north, east, and west from Acapulco Bay's sun-drenched shoreline. For example, arrivees, from their airplane windows, can enjoy an aerial view of one such feature, the blue expanse of a mangrove-lined lake, the Laguna Tres Palos, a minute before airport touchdown. This is only the beginning of a procession of such *lagunas* that dot the Acapulco region coastline: to the east, along the Costa Chica, after the Laguna Tres Palos, the Laguna Tecomate and the Laguna Chautengo; to the west, along the Costa Grande, first the Laguna Coyuca, then Laguna Mitla, Estero Valentín, and Laguna Potosí.

Although all of the lakes are accessible, Laguna Coyuca at Pie de la Cuesta, a few miles west of Acapulco, is most accessible and also very typical. All the Acapulco region's *lagunas* result from the opposing forces of surging water: of the ocean waves and currents pushing sand shoreward, against the flow of the rivers, coursing down from the sierra, depositing many millions of gallons of fresh water at the shoreline.

It's a seesaw struggle which the rivers temporarily win, if only during the summer-early fall wet season. Freshwater floods accumulated in the lagoons break though the shoreline sandbars and open channels to the ocean. Pacific waves rush in, carrying with them a bounty of sea creatures and nutrients, and for a spell during the summer the lagoons become slightly salty (brackish).

However, when the river flood abates in the early fall, the persistent ocean waves and currents deposit their burden of sand, closing the channels through the sandbars *(barras)*. Soon, the lagoons again become fresh, sweet, and clear.

On the ocean side of the lagoons lie the Acapulco region's hidden barrier beaches, with plenty of fine yellow sand, an abundance of fresh breezes, and seasonal driftwood, seashells, and sometimes even *palapa* restaurants and reusable shady palm-frond *ramadas,* awaiting new occupants. All are accessible, some easily, such as Playa Revolcadero and Barra Vieja, by road about 10 miles east of Acapulco; or farther afield east, San José de la Barra, by launch, from Laguna Chautengo. To the west, find Playa Pie de La Cuesta (by road) a few miles from Acapulco; the beach of Laguna de Mitla (by road); Playa Paraíso (by short launch trip); and Playa Boca Chica (by launch or road).

Bays and Coves

Gorgeous beaches also decorate many of the Acapulco region's plumy bays and coves. Besides the famous golden resort strands of Acapulco, Zihuatanejo, and Ixtapa, many other breeze-swept sandy coasts and small bays and coves hide lovely beaches. East along the Costa Chica and especially worth exploring are the petite resort beaches of Playa Ventura, Playa Las Peñitas, and Punta Maldonado. West along the Costa Grande, likewise gorgeous are El Carrizal, Playa Tlalcoyunque, Playa Escondida, Playa Barra de Potosí, and the coral-strewn gem, Playa Troncones.

COASTAL PLAIN, FOOTHILLS, AND SIERRA

Coastal Plain and Foothills

The Acapulco region's coastal plain, source of a major fraction of the region's agricultural wealth, concentrates along a relatively narrow strip. It begins at the lagoons' inland edges and, crossed by many south-flowing rivers, extends inland, only about 15 miles in the west along the Costa Grande, and broadening to about twice that, at the eastern, Oaxaca end of the Costa Chica.

North of the coastal strip, the cooler, lush, forested foothills, about equal in width to the coastal plain, gradually rise, from an elevation of about 1,000 feet to 3,000 feet (300 to 900 meters). Several tradition-rich foothill market towns, such as Petatlán and Atoyac, on the Costa Grande, and Ayutla, Acatlán and Ometepec, on the Costa Chica, are equally rich centers of lumber, produce—mangoes, papayas, tamarind, coffee, honey—and handicrafts.

The Sierra Madre del Sur

The foothills sharply give way to the Acapulco region's great mother of ranges, the Sierra Madre del Sur, a succession of gigantic, cloud-tipped mountains extending in an unbroken east-west line. Many of their jagged summits top 10,000 feet (3,000 meters). The line of rugged sentinels extends from Cerro Tejamil (10,460 feet, 3,190 meters) northeast of Zihatanejo, all the way east to Cerro San Marcos (10,170 feet, 3,100 meters), by the Oaxaca border. In the middle, tallest of all is mighty Cerro Teotepec, the Acapulco region's tallest summit, rising to 12,150 feet (3,705 meters), only 43 miles (70 km) as the crow flies northwest of Acapulco.

The Río Balsas and Other Rivers

As precipitously as the sierra rises in the south, it drops in the north, into the basin of the River Balsas, which drains a gigantic realm, including parts of five states—Jalisco, Michoacán, Morelos, Puebla, Oaxaca—and most of the Acapulco region.

The people of the Río Balsas basin are both victims and benefactors of the Sierra Madre and their Río Balsas. The mighty sierra forms a great rain shadow, blocking Pacific breeze–borne moisture and turning their homeland into the notorious Tierra Caliente: hot and desertlike most of the year. But the people, by their own ingenuity, and with a little government help, benefit from the waters of the river. Aided by dams and irrigation, they have created rich oases, of corn, cattle, cotton, mangoes, melons, bananas, and alfalfa by the riverbank.

Despite the dominance of the Río Balsas, many other rivers contribute to the Acapulco region. Without exception, from the Río San Cristóbal in the west, to the Río Quetzala in the east, they flow southward across the coastal plain, nurturing groves and fields and replenishing the wildlife-rich lagoons along the coast.

Most important of all these is the Río Papagayo, in the Acapulco region's center, which, joining its lovely spring-fed tributary, the Río Azul, winds southward through its precipitious, scenic canyon to the sea, at Lomas de Chapultepec Village, only 15 miles (25 km) east of Acapulco.

Climate

Nature has graced the Acapulco region with a microclimate tapestry. Although rainfall, offshore breezes, and vegetation introduce refreshing local variations, elevation provides the broad brush. The entire coastal strip where frost never bites (including the mountain slopes and plateaus up to 4,000 or 5,000 feet) luxuriates in the tropics.

The seashore is a land of perpetual summer. Winter days are typically warm and rainless, peaking at 80–85°F (27–30°C) and dropping to 60–70°F (16–21°C) by midnight.

Increasing elevation gradually decreases both temperature and humidity. In Chilpancingo (elev. 4,000 feet), you can expect warm, dry winter days 75–80°F (24–27°C) and cooler nights around 55–65°F (14–18°C).

Similar but sometimes cooler winter weather prevails in higher, 5,800-foot (1,800-meter) Taxco. Days will usually be balmy and springlike, climbing to around 75°F (24°C) by early afternoon, with nights dropping to a temperate 45–55°F (8–15°C); pack a sweater or light jacket.

On the other hand, Iguala, in the sunny and dry Río Balsas basin, will be at least warm year-round. In the winter expect 80–85°F (27–30°C) days and 65–70°F (19–21°C) nights.

The sunny, dry spring months of April and May are customarily the Acapulco region's warmest months. By mid-June, cooling rains arrive, moderating summer temperatures.

Summer days on the beaches are warm, humid, and sometimes rainy. July, August, and September forenoons are typically bright, warming to the high 80s or low 90s (around 33°C). By afternoon, however, clouds often gather and bring short, sometimes heavy, showers. By late afternoon, the clouds part, the sun dries the pavements, and the tropical breeze is just right for enjoying a sparkling sunset.

Chilpancingo and Taxco summers are delightful. Afternoon temperatures rise to the 80s (27–32°C) and cool to the balmy 70s (21–26°C), perfect for strolling during the evenings. In Iguala, however, late spring and summer temperatures are often hot, typically 85–95°F (30–36°C) during the dry April and May, but cooling a few degrees during the June–September rains.

Flora and Fauna

Abundant sun and summer rains nurture the vegetation of the Acapulco region. At some roadside spots, spiny bromeliads, pendulous passion fruits, and giant candelabra cactuses luxuriate, beckoning to admirers. Now and then visitors may stop, attracted by something remarkable, such as a riot of flowers blooming from apparently dead branches or what looks like grapefruit sprouting from the trunk of a roadside tree. More often, travelers pass by the long stretches of thickets, jungles, marshes, and dry uplands without stopping; however, a little knowledge of what to expect can blossom into recognition and discovery, transforming the humdrum into the extraordinary.

VEGETATION ZONES

Mexico's diverse landscape and fickle rainfall have sculpted its wide range of plant forms. Botanists recognize at least 14 major Mexican vegetation zones, seven of which occur in the Acapulco region.

© BRUCE WHIPPERMAN

The coconut, arguably the world's most useful tree, is a source of loads of products, ranging from lumber and roofing to oil and candy.

Directly along the coastal highway travelers often pass long sections of three of these zones: savanna, thorn forest, and tropical deciduous forest.

Savanna

Great swaths of pasturelike savanna stretch along Highway 200 between Acapulco and Zihuatanejo. In its natural state, savanna often appears as a palm-dotted sea of grass—green and marshy during the rainy summer, dry and brown by late winter.

Although grass rules the savanna, palms give it character. Most familiar is the **coconut,** the *cocotero (Cocos nucifera)*—the world's most useful tree—used for everything from lumber to candy. Coconut palms line the beaches and climb the hillsides—drooping, slanting, rustling, and swaying in the breeze like troupes of hula dancers. Less familiar, but with as much personality, is the Mexican **fan palm,** or *palma real (Sabal mexicana),* festooned with black fruit and spread flat like a señorita's fan.

The savanna's list goes on: the grapefruitlike fruit on the trunk and branches identify the **gourd tree,** or *calabaza (Crescentia alata).* The mature gourds, brown and hard, have been carved into *jícaros* (cups for drinking chocolate) for millennia.

Orange-sized, pumpkinlike gourds mark the **sand box tree,** or *jabillo (Hura polyandra),* so-named because they once served as desktop boxes full of sand for drying ink. The Aztecs, however, called it the exploding tree, because the ripe gourds burst their seeds forth with a bang like a firecracker.

The waterlogged seaward edge of the savanna nurtures lagoon-front forests of the **red mangrove,** or *mangle colorado (Rhizophora mangle),* short trees that seem to stand in the water on stilts. Their new roots grow downward from above; a time-lapse photo would show them marching, as if on stilts, into the lagoon.

Thorn Forest

Lower rainfall leads to the hardier growth of the thorn forest—domain of the pea family—the **legumes,** marked, in late winter and spring, by bursts of red, yellow, pink, and white flowers. Look closely at the blossoms and you will see they resemble the familiar wild sweet pea of North America. Even when the blossoms are gone, you can identify them by seed pods that hang from the branches. Local folks call them by many names. These include the ***tabachín,*** the scarlet Mexican bird of paradise; and its close relative the *flamboyán,* or **royal poinciana,** an import from Africa, where it's called the "flame tree."

Other spectacular members of the pea family (called "shower trees" in Hawaii) include the bright yellow ***abejón,*** which blooms nearly year-round; and the ***coapinol,*** marked by hosts of white blooms (March–July) and large, dark-brown pods. Not only colorful but useful is the **fishfuddle,** with pink flowers and long pods, from which fisherfolk derive a fish-stunning poison.

More abundant (although not so noticeable)

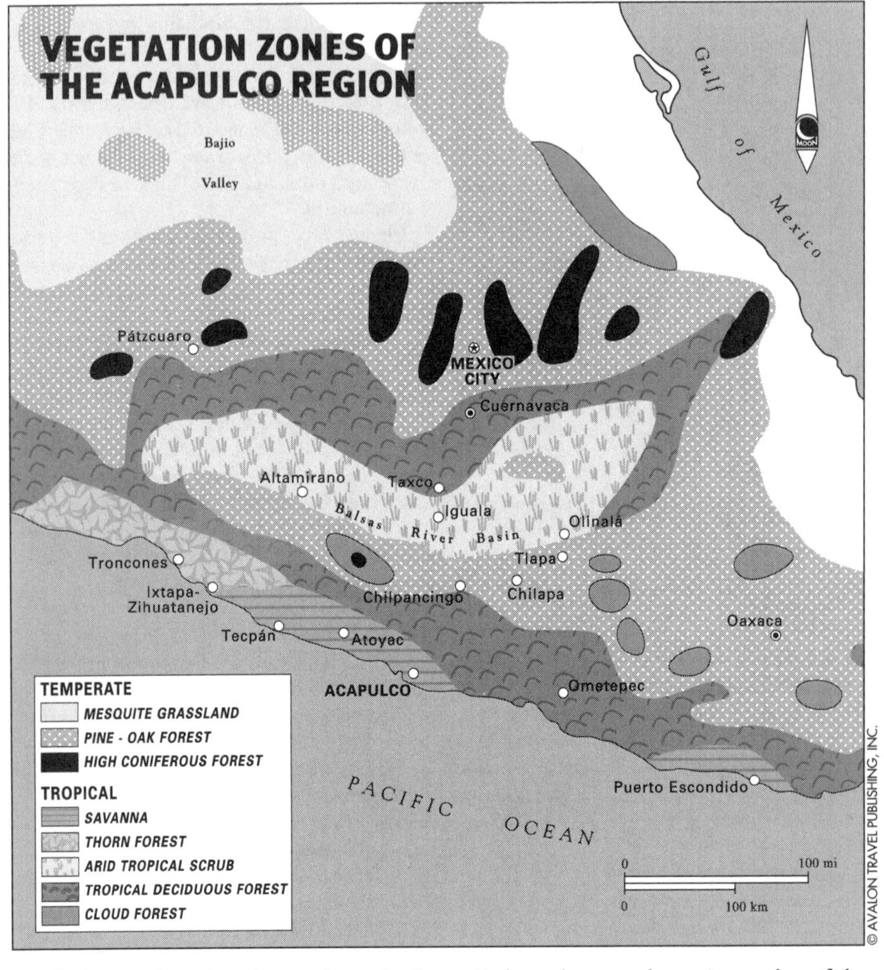

are the legumes' cousins, the **acacias** and **mimosas.** Long swaths of thorn forest sometimes grow right to the coastal highway and side-road pavements, so that the road appears tunnel like through a tangle of brushy acacia trees. Pull completely off the road for a look and you will spot the small yellow flower balls, ferny leaves, and long, narrow pods of the **boat spine acacia,** or *quisache tempamo (Acacia cochliacantha).* Take care, however, around the acacias; some of the long-thorned varieties harbor nectar-feeding, biting ants.

Perhaps the most dramatic member of the thorn community is the **morning glory tree,** or *palo blanco (Ipomoea aborescens),* which announces the winter dry season by a festoon of white trumpets atop its crown of seemingly dead branches.

The Mexican penchant for making fun of death shows in the alternate name for ***palo del muerto,*** or the tree of the dead. It is also called *palo bobo* (fool tree) in some locales because folks believe if you take a drink from a stream near its foot, you will go crazy.

© BRUCE WHIPPERMAN

The arid tropical scrub vegetation zone of the Río Balsas basin is home to dozens of cactus species, including the *órgano* (organ-pipe cactus).

Tropical Deciduous Forest

In rainier areas, the thorn forest grades into tropical deciduous forest. This is the "friendly" or "short-tree" forest, blanketed by a tangle of summer-green leaves that fall in the dry winter to reveal thickets of branches. Some trees show bright fall reds and yellows, later blossoming with brilliant flowers—spider lily, cardinal sage, pink trumpet, poppylike yellowsilk *(pomposhuti),* and mouse-killer *(mala ratón),* which swirl in the spring wind like cherry-blossom blizzards.

The tropical deciduous forest makes up the lush jungle coat that swathes much of the Acapulco region's coastal foothills. It is especially lush during the rainy summer, in the uplands along Highway 193, above Atoyac de Álvarez, northwest of Acapulco. Here, vine-strewn thickets overhang the road, like the edges of a lost prehistoric world, where at any moment you expect a dinosaur to rear.

The biological realities here are nearly as exotic. A four-foot-long green iguana, looking every bit as primitive as a dinosaur, slithers across the pavement. Beside the road, a spreading, solitary **strangler fig** *(Ficus padifolia)* stands, draped with hairy, hanging air roots (which, in time, plant themselves in the ground and support the branches). Its Mexican name, *matapalo* (killer tree), is gruesomely accurate, for strangler figs often entwine themselves in death embraces with less aggressive tree-victims.

Much more benign is the gentle giant of the Acapulco region's tropical deciduous forest, the **Mexican elm,** or *olmo (Chaetoptelea mexicana).* Probably Mexico's tallest tree, the *olmo* reaches a height of at least 285 feet (87 meters) (compared to the world's tallest, the California redwood, at 364 feet). It closely resembles its near relative, the American elm, notably in the shape of its serrated leaves and its hair-fringed fruit. Its tough, heavy wood, ideal for floors and door sills, makes it one of the Acapulco region's most valuable lumber trees.

Well-watered zones of the tropical deciduous forest have become home to a platoon of useful **introduced plants.** These include the common India-native **mango,** "king of fruit" (April–July); Asia-native bamboo, *bambu;* and Africa-native ***platano*** (banana). Also common but not so recognizable is the **coffee shrub,** or locally, *cafeto (Coffea arabica).* Coffee is widely grown in the Acapulco region, notably in the foothill forests, upcountry from Atoyac de Álvarez. Coffee shrubs grow unobtrusively, often in apparent wild "jungle" right next to the highway, beneath the shady canopy of taller trees. Farmers limit them to about five feet in height. They're recognizable by their bushy, camellia-bush appearance, with shiny, dark-green leaves, star-shaped white flowers, and red berries, in season.

Excursions by jeep or foot along shaded, off-highway tracks through the tropical deciduous forest can bestow delightful jungle scenes; however, unwary travelers must watch out for the poison-oaklike ***mala mujer,*** the "evil woman" tree. The oil on its large five-fingered leaves can cause an itchy rash.

Pine-Oak Forest

Along the upland highways (notably on the higher reaches of north-south Highway 95 and

POINSETTIA

Although this lovely red flowering plant only became known and appreciated by the wider world during the 1800s, the people of Mexico had enjoyed the poinsettia for millennia. It grows in gorgeous wild profusion in semitropical mountain zones of southwestern Mexico, especially in the Acapulco region and the neighboring states of Michoacán, Morelos, Oaxaca, and Chiapas.

The Aztecs, who called the poinsettia *cuetlaxochitle,* used its sap to control fevers and its crimson red petals (actually not petals, but colored leaves, called bracts) for dye. The emperor Moctezuma II (1466–1520) especially adored the *cuetlaxochitle.* He ordered caravans of them brought to his capital at Tenochtitlán to honor an Aztec goddess who was said to have died of a broken heart. The *cuetlaxochitle,* a legend recounted, had been born from one drop of the goddess's blood.

Most present-day Mexican folks know the poinsettia as the *flor de Nochebuena* (flower of Christmas Eve). It blooms during the late autumn and early winter, just in time for people to give birthday bouquets to the baby Jesus at churches all over Mexico on December 24.

An eminent German botanist, Karl Lugwig Wilenow, was among the first outsiders to study the poinsettia, from cuttings brought to him from central America. In 1800, recognizing it as a member of the grand Euphorbia family, Wilenow christened it *Euphorbiaceae pulcherrima,* meaning "most beautiful of the Euphoribias."

Although apt, this name has been largely forgotten because of the work of Joel Robert Poinsett, amateur botanist and U.S. ambassador to Mexico during the 1820s. Poinsett, keenly interested in identifying new species wherever he traveled in Mexico, noticed the spectacularly red plant growing beside the road. He brought specimens back to the United States and nurtured them in his South Carolina greenhouse. This led to the plant's spread and ultimate immense popularity all over North and South America, Europe, and most parts of the world.

In 1836, a group of Scottish botanists proposed to honor Poinsett's work by renaming his find *Poinsettia pulcherrima.* The name stuck, and now people everywhere enjoy holiday festoons of the charmingly divine plant known simply as the poinsettia.

the Chilpancingo-Chilapa-Olinalá Highway 93) the tropical forest gives way to temperate pine-oak forest. Here, many of Mexico's 112 oak and 39 pine species thrive. Oval two-inch cones and foot-long drooping needles (three to a cluster) make the ***pino triste,*** or sad pine *(Pinus lumholtzii),* appear in severe need of water. Unlike many of Mexico's pines, it produces neither good lumber nor much turpentine, although it *is* prized by guitar makers for its wood.

Much more regal in bearing and commercially important are the tall pines, including the **Mexican white pine** *(Pinus ayacahuite),* known locally as the *pinabete.* It grows to about 100 feet when mature and resembles the white pine of northern regions, with long, bluish-green needles, five to a bunch and pendulous, scaly 4-to-6-inch often reddish-brown cones that shed winged seeds. Equally notable is the **Montezuma pine** *(Pinus montezumae),* or the *ocote macho.* It likewise grows long (but gray) cones and needles, five to a bunch, but is distinguishable by its interesting, drooping needles.

Pines often grow in stands, mixed at lower elevations with **oaks,** which occur in two broad classifications—*encino* (evergreen, small-leafed) and *roble* (deciduous, large-leafed)—both much like the live oaks that dot California hills and valleys. Clustered on their branches and scattered in the shade, *bellota* (acorns) distinctly mark them as oaks.

Arid Tropical Scrub

This desertlike vegetation zone coincides with the semiarid Río Balsas basin, which sprawls for hundreds of miles east-west (reachable both along Highway 51 and north-south Highway 95) between Chilpancingo and Taxco. Although superficially appearing like the temperate deserts of the southwest United States and northern Mexico, the arid tropical scrub zone nurtures a botanic treasury of tropical, frost-sensitive plants, sculpted by extreme heat and drought.

The signature king of all these hardy plants is the spectacular **candelabra cactus,** *Lemaireocereus weberi,* or *candelabro.* Mature specimens, as wide and high as a four-story building, with a dozen or more 10-ribbed vertical columns, resemble a giant dining-table candelabra.

The candelabra's lookalike cousin is the **organ-pipe cactus,** *Marginatocereus marginatus,* or *órgano.* Distinguish it by its smaller but still formidable size (10–20 feet in height) and its five to seven ribs per vertical column.

At some spots, great forests of tall, pole-straight *tetetzo* cactuses, *Pachycereus ruficeps,* inhabit the arid tropical scrubland. Up to 50 feet tall, they resemble a grand army of cactus sentinels, guarding the rocky landscape.

Although not cactuses, many of the 300-odd members of the agave family thrive in dryer areas of the Acapulco region. Although some are cultivated (for beverages, fiber, soap, and more), others grow wild. One such is the charming **cabbage agave,** *Agave perryi,* which grows in families of neat, round, cabbagelike plants, up to three feet in diameter, with bluish-green, broad, spined leaves.

Cloud Forest and High Coniferous Forest

The Acapulco region's rarest and most exotic vegetation zones are removed from the coastal tourist centers. Adventurers who travel to certain high, dewy mountainsides, beginning around 5,000 feet, can explore the plant and wildlife community of the cloud forest. One such example lies along Highway 196, about 30 miles (50 km) uphill from Atoyac de Álvarez, past the village of El Paraíso. There, abundant cool fog nourishes a Pleistocene remnant forest of dripping tree ferns, liquid amber maples, lichen-draped pines and oaks, above a mossy carpet of orchids, bromeliads, and begonias.

About 20 miles (32 km) farther uphill along the same route, the Acapulco region's least accessible vegetation zone, the high coniferous forest, swathes the 10,000–12,000-foot slopes of Cerro Teotepec. This pristine alpine island, accessible only on horseback or by foot, nurtures stands of pines, spruce, and fir interspersed with grassy meadows, similar to the Rocky Mountain slopes in the United States and Canada. Here, besides the white and Montezuma pines, find hardy stands of **sacred fir,** *Abies religiosa* or *oyamel;* **Mexican cypress,** *Cupressa lusitanica;* and the high-altitude **alder,** *Alnus firmifolia.* (*Note:* Do not attempt the cloud forest and high coniferous forest explorations alone. Inquire at the Atoyac de Álvarez *presidencia municipal* for an experienced guide.)

For a wealth of details, consult M. Walter Pesman's delightful *Meet Flora Mexicana* (which is out of print, but major libraries often have a copy). Also informative is the popular paperback *Handbook of Mexican Roadside Flora,* by Charles T. Mason Jr. and Patricia B. Mason. (See Suggested Reading.)

WILDLIFE

Despite continued habitat destruction—forests are logged, wetlands filled, and savannas plowed—great swaths of the Acapulco region still abound with wildlife. Common in the temperate pine-oak forest highlands are mammals familiar to U.S. residents—such as the mountain lion *(puma),* coyote, fox *(zorro),* rabbit *(conejo),* and quail *(codorniz).*

However, the tropical coastal forests and savannas are home to fascinating species seen only in zoos north of the border. The reality of this dawns on travelers when they glimpse something exotic, such as raucous, screeching swarms of small green parrots rising from the roadside, or an armadillo or coati nosing in the sand just a few feet away from them at the forested edge of an isolated beach.

Population pressures have nevertheless decreased wild habitats, endangering many previously abundant animal species. If you are lucky, you may find a tracker who can lead you to a band of now-rare reddish-brown **spider monkeys** *(monos)* raiding a wild fruit tree. And deep in the mountain fastness, you may be led to a view of the endangered striped cat, the **ocelot** *(ocelotl)* or its smaller cousins, the **margay**

© BRUCE WHIPPERMAN

The mountain lion *(puma* or *león),* pictured here at Acapulco's Isla Roqueta zoo, still hunts in the Acapulco region's mountain and forest country.

(tigrillo) and the tan **jaguarundi** *(onza, leoncillo).* On such an excursion, if you are really fortunate, you may hear the "chesty" roar or catch a glimpse of a jaguar, the fabled *tigre.*

El Tigre

"Each hill has its own *tigre,*" a Mexican proverb says. With black spots spread over a yellow-tan coat, stretching five feet (1.5 meters) and weighing 200 pounds (90 kg), the typical jaguar resembles a muscular spotted leopard. Although hunted since prehistory, and now endangered, the jaguar lives on in the Acapulco region, where it hunts along thickly forested stream bottoms and foothills. Unlike the mountain lion, the jaguar will eat any game. Jaguars have even been known to wait patiently for fish in rivers and to stalk beaches for turtle and egg dinners. If they have a favorite food, it is probably the piglike wild peccary, *jabalí.* Experienced hunters agree that no two jaguars will have the same prey in their stomachs.

Although humans have died of wounds inflicted by cornered jaguars, there is little or no hard evidence that they eat humans, despite legends to the contrary.

Armadillos, Coatis, and Bats

Armadillos are cat-sized mammals that act and look like opossums but carry reptilianlike shells. If you see one, remain still, and it may walk right up and sniff your foot before it recognizes you and scuttles back into the woods.

A common inhabitant of the tropics is the raccoonlike coati *(tejón, pisote).* In the wild, coatis like shady stream banks, often congregating in large troops of 15–30 individuals. They are identified by their short brown or tan fur, small round ears, long nose, and straight, vertically held tail. With their endearing and inquisitive nature, coatis are often kept as pets; the first coati you see may be one on a string offered for sale at a local market.

Mexican bats *(murciélagos)* are widespread, with at least 126 species compared to 37 in the United States. In Mexico, as everywhere, bats are feared and misunderstood. As sunset approaches, many species come out of their hiding places and flit through the air in search of insects. Most people, sitting outside enjoying the early evening, will mistake their darting silhouettes for those of birds, who, except for owls, do not generally fly at night.

Bats are often locally called *vampiros,* even though only three relatively rare Mexican species actually feed on the blood of mammals—nearly always cattle—and of birds.

The many nonvampire Mexican bats carry their vampire cousins' odious reputation with forbearance. They go about their good works, pollinating flowers, clearing the air of pesky gnats and mosquitoes, ridding cornfields of mice, and dropping seeds, thereby restoring forests. Limestone caves, such as the Caves of Juxtlahuaca, are the best places to see bats. (See the Guerrero Upcountry chapter.)

BIRDS

The coastal lagoons of the Acapulco region lie astride the Pacific Flyway, one of the Americas' major north-south paths for migrating waterfowl. Many of the familiar American and Canadian species, including pintail, gadwall, baldpate, shoveler, redhead, and scaup, arrive Oct.–Jan., when their numbers will have swollen into the millions. They settle near food and cover—even at the borders of cornfields, to the frustration of farmers.

Besides the migrants, swarms of resident species—**herons** and **egrets** *(garzas),* cormorantlike **anhingas, lily-walkers** *(jacanas),* and hundreds more—stalk, nest, and preen in the same lagoons.

Few spots are better for observing seabirds than the beaches of the Acapulco region. **Brown pelicans** and black-and-white **frigate birds** are among the prime actors. When a flock of pelicans spots a school of favorite fish, they go about their routine deliberately. Singly or in pairs, they circle and plummet into the waves to come up, more often than not, with fish in their gullets. Each bird then bobs and floats over the swells for a minute or two, seeming to wait for its dozen or so fellow pelicans to take their turns. This continues until they've bagged a dinner of 10–15 fish apiece. Frigate birds, the scavengers par excellence of the Mexican Pacific coast, often profit by the labor of the teams of fisherfolk who haul in nets of fish on Acapulco region beaches. After they auction off the choice morsels of perch, tuna, red snapper, octopus, or shrimp to merchants, and the local villagers have scavenged everything else edible, the motley residue of small fish, sea snakes, skates, squid, slugs, and sharks is thrown to a screeching flock of frigate birds.

The wild blue mangrove lagoons of the Costa Chica and Costa Grande, east and west of Acapulco, nurture a trove of wildlife, especially birds, ripe for viewing on foot or by boat tours.

For more details on Mexico's mammals and birds in general, check out A. Starker Leopold's very readable classic, *Wildlife of Mexico,* and other works in Suggested Reading.

REPTILES AND AMPHIBIANS

Snakes, Gila Monsters, and Crocodiles

Mexico has 460-odd snake species, the vast majority shy and nonpoisonous; they will get out of your way if you give plenty of warning. In the Acapulco region poisonous snakes have been largely eradicated in city and tourist areas. In brush or jungle areas, carry a stick or a machete and beat the bushes ahead of you while watching where you put your feet. When hiking or rock-climbing in the country, don't put your hand in niches you can't see.

You might even see a snake underwater while swimming offshore at an isolated Acapulco region beach. The yellow-bellied sea snake, although rare and shy, can inflict fatal bites. If you see a yellow-and-black snake underwater, get away, pronto.

You might even see a snake underwater while swimming offshore at an isolated Acapulco region beach. The **yellow-bellied sea snake,** *Pelamis platurus* (to about two feet), although rare and shy, can inflict fatal bites. If you see a yellow-and-black snake underwater, get away, pronto.

Some eels, which resemble snakes but have gills like fish and inhabit rocky crevices, can inflict nonpoisonous bites and should also be avoided.

The Mexican land counterpart of the *Pelamis*

platurus is the **coral snake** *(coralillo),* which occurs as about two dozen species, all with multicolored bright bands that always include red. Although relatively rare, small, and shy, coral snakes occasionally inflict serious, sometimes fatal, bites.

More aggressive and generally more dangerous is the Mexican **rattlesnake** *(cascabel)* and its viper relative, the **fer-de-lance** *(Bothrops atrox).* About the same in size (to six feet) and appearance as the rattlesnake, the fer-de-lance is known by various local names, such as *nauyaca, cuatro narices, palanca,* and *barba amarilla.* It is potentially more hazardous than the rattlesnake because it lacks a warning rattle.

The Gila monster (confined in Mexico to northern Sonora) and its southern tropical relative, the yellow-spotted, black ***escorpión*** *(Heloderma horridum),* are the world's only poisonous lizards. Despite its beaded skin and menacing, fleshy appearance, the *escorpión* only bites when severely provoked; and, even then, its venom is rarely, if ever, fatal.

The **crocodile** *(cocodrilo, caimán),* once prized for its meat and hide, came close to vanishing in Mexican Pacific lagoons until the government took steps to ensure its survival; it's now officially protected. A few isolated breeding populations live on in the wild, while government and private hatcheries are breeding more for the eventual repopulation of lagoons where crocodiles once were common.

Two crocodile species occur in the Acapulco region. The true crocodile, *Crocodilus acutus,* has a narrower snout than its local cousin, *Caiman crocodilus fuscus,* a type of alligator *(lagarto).* Although past individuals have been recorded at up to 15 feet long, wild native crocodiles and alligators are usually young and only three feet or less in length.

Sea Turtles

The story of Mexican sea turtles is similar: they once swarmed ashore on Acapulco regional beaches to lay their eggs. Prized for their meat, eggs, hide, and shell, the turtles were severely devastated. Now officially protected, sea turtles are coming ashore in growing numbers at some isolated locations. Of the four locally occurring species, the **olive Ridley turtle** *(tortuga golfina)* and the **green turtle** *(tortuga negra* or *caguama)* are the most common. Green and olive Ridley, although officially endangered, have stabilized because of persistent government and volunteer efforts. The two other, relatively rare, locally occurring sea turtles are the **hawksbill** *(carey)* and the **leatherback** *(tortuga de cuero).* (For many more sea turtle details, see the sidebar "Saving Turtles" in The Costa Grande chapter.)

FISH AND MARINE MAMMALS

Shoals of fish abound in Acapulco's waters. Four billfish species are found in deep-sea grounds several miles offshore: **swordfish, sailfish,** and **blue** and **black marlin.** All are spirited fighters, though the sailfish and marlin are generally the toughest to bring in. The blue marlin is the biggest of the four; in the past, 10-foot specimens weighing more than 1,000 pounds were brought in at Pacific-coast marinas. Lately, four feet and 200 pounds for a marlin, and 100 pounds for a sailfish, are more typical. Progressive captains now encourage victorious anglers to return these magnificent "tigers of the sea" (especially the sinewy sailfish and blue marlin, which make for poor eating) to the deep after they've won the battle.

Billfish are not the only prizes of the sea, however. Serious fish lovers also seek varieties of tunalike **jack,** such as **yellowtail, Pacific amberjack, pompano, jack crevalle,** and the tenacious **roosterfish,** named for the "comb" atop its head. These, and the **yellowfin tuna, mackerel,** and ***dorado,*** which Hawaiians call mahimahi, are among the delicacies sought in Acapulco waters.

Accessible from small boats offshore and by casting from shoreline rocks are varieties of **snapper** *(huachinango, pargo)* and **sea bass** *(cabrilla).* Closer to shore, **croaker, mullet,** and **jewfish** can be found foraging along sandy bottoms and in rocky crevices.

Sharks and **rays** inhabit nearly all depths, with smaller fry venturing into beach shallows and lagoons. Huge **Pacific manta rays** appear to be frolicking, their great wings flapping like birds, not far off Acapulco shores. Just beyond the waves, local fisherfolk bring in **hammerhead, thresher,** and **leopard sharks.**

Also common is the **stingray,** which can inflict a painful wound with its barbed tail. Experienced swimmers and waders avoid injury by both shuffling (rather than stepping) and watching their feet in shallow waters with sandy bottoms. (For more fish talk and a chart of species encountered in Acapulco waters, turn ahead to Sports and Recreation in the On the Road chapter.)

Porpoises and Whales

The **California Gulf porpoise**—*delfín,* or *vaquita* (little cow)—is the smallest member of the whale family; it rarely exceeds five feet. Although more numerous in the Gulf of California (but now endangered), its playful diving and jumping antics can occasionally be observed from Acapulco region–based tour and fishing boats, and sometimes even from beaches.

Although the **California gray whale** has a migration pattern extending only to the southern tip of Baja California, occasional pods stray farther south, where deep-sea fishermen and cruise and tour boat passengers see them in deep waters offshore.

Larger whale *(ballena)* species, such as the **humpback** and **blue** whale, appear to enjoy tropical waters even more, ranging the north Pacific tropics from the southwest Mexican Pacific shore, west to Hawaii and beyond.

History

Once upon a time, maybe as long as 30,000 years ago, the first bands of hunters, perhaps following great game herds, crossed from Siberia to the American continent. They drifted southward, many of them eventually settling in the lush upland valleys and coastlines of present-day Mexico.

Much later, perhaps around 5000 B.C., these early people began gathering and grinding the seeds of a hardy grass that required only the summer rains to thrive. After generations of selective breeding, this grain, called *teocentli,* the sacred seed (which we call maize or corn), led to prosperity.

EARLY CIVILIZATIONS

With abundant food, villages grew into towns, and towns evolved into small cities. Leisure classes arose—artists, architects, warriors, and ruler-priests—who had time to think and create. With a calendar, they harnessed the constant wheel of the firmament to life on earth, defining the days to plant, harvest, feast, travel, and trade.

Of Mexico's early urban peoples, the Olmecs were foremost. Around 1500 B.C. they were establishing large ceremonial centers along the Gulf of Mexico Coast. At La Venta, in present-day Tabasco state, archaeologists have uncovered the Olmecs' most spectacular remains: giant stone heads, up to nine feet in height, with decidedly negroid features and football helmetlike caps. Other sculptures, many of lovely jade, show a strong jaguar cult influence, in the form of half-human, half-jaguar masklike faces.

The Olmec influence arrived early in the present-day Acapulco region. Olmec-style jaguar-motif art has been uncovered at Teopantecuantlán, an upland ceremonial center dating from around 1000 B.C. Moreover, Olmec-style wall paintings decorate caves, notably the Caves of Juxtlahuaca and Oxtotitlán, in lush highland valleys about 100 miles north of Acapulco.

Monte Albán, Teotihuacán, and Xochicalco

After the decline of the Olmecs, around 500 B.C., other civilizations rose. Monte Albán, in Oaxaca, which was flourishing around the time of Jesus, is thought by many experts to be Mexico's first true city. Later, Teotihuacán, north of present-day Mexico City, grew into one of the world's great metropolises, with a population of about 250,000, by A.D. 500.

Teotihuacán's epic monuments still stand: the towering Pyramid of the Sun, at the terminal of a grand avenue, faces a great Pyramid of the Moon. Along the avenue sprawls a monumental temple-court, surrounded by scowling effigies of Quetzalcoatl, the feathered serpent god of gods.

But, eventually both Monte Albán and Teotihuacán crumbled; they were all but abandoned by A.D. 700, leaving a host of former vassal city-states to tussle among themselves. In the Acapulco region, first among these was Xochicalco, near Taxco, 150 miles (250 km) north of present-day Acapulco.

The Living Quetzalcoatl

Xochicalco's wise men tutored a young noble who was to become a living legend. In A.D. 947, Topiltzín (literally, Our Prince) was born. Records recite Topiltzín's achievements. He advanced astronomy, agriculture, and architecture and founded the city-state of Tula in A.D. 968, north of old Teotihuacán.

© BRUCE WHIPPERMAN

Some of the earliest traces of high cultures in the Acapulco region are the Olmec-style cave paintings in the upcountry Caves of Juxtlahuaca.

Contrary to the times, Topiltzín opposed human sacrifice. He ruled benignly for two decades, becoming so revered that his people knew him as the living Quetzalcoatl, the plumed serpent god incarnate.

Bloodthirsty local priests, lusting for human victims, tricked him with alcohol, however; Topiltzín awoke groggily one morning, in bed with his sister. Devastated with shame, Quetzalcoatl banished himself. He headed east from Tula with a band of retainers in A.D. 987, vowing that he would return during the anniversary of his birth year, Ce Acatl. Legends say he sailed across the eastern sea and rose to heaven as the morning star.

The Aztecs

The civilization that Topiltzín founded, known to historians as the Toltec (People of Tula), was eventually eclipsed by others. These included the Aztecs, a collection of seven aggressive immigrant sub-tribes. Migrating around during the 11th century A.D., from a mysterious western land of Aztlán (Place of the Herons) into the lake-filled valley that Mexico City now occupies, the Aztecs survived by being forced to fight for every piece of ground they occupied.

Around the same time, another Aztec subtribe was migrating into the present-day Acapulco region. As did their Valley of Mexico cousins, they competed fiercely with the original inhabitants and finally rose to dominance by war and intermarriage over their defeated vassals. By A.D. 1100, their Náhuatl (Aztec-language) kingdom, called Coixcaltlapan, sprawled over both the central valleys of the Río Balsas basin and parts of the western coast, around Zacatula and Atoyac.

Meanwhile, to the north, the Valley of Mexico Aztecs, who called themselves the Méxica, had also clawed their way to dominion. In A.D. 1325 they founded their capital, Tenochtitlán, on an island in the middle of the valley-lake. From there, Aztec armies, not unlike Roman legions, marched out and subdued faraway kingdoms and returned with booty of gold, brilliant feathers, precious jewels, and captives, whom they enslaved and sacrificed by the thousands as food for their gods.

Among those gods they feared was Quetzalcoatl, who, legends said, was bearded and fair-skinned. It was a remarkable coincidence, therefore, that the bearded, fair-skinned Castilian Hernán Cortés landed on Mexico's eastern coast on April 22, 1519, during the year of Ce Acatl, exactly when Topiltzín, the Living Quetzalcoatl, had vowed he would return.

THE CONQUEST

Although a generation had elapsed since Christopher Columbus founded Spain's West Indian colonies, returns had been meager. Moreover, Columbus' original goal of reaching China by sailing west had eluded the Spanish explorers. Geographers and navigators realized that, instead of China, Columbus had discovered a new continent. Perhaps, explorers hoped, China lay only a bit farther west, tantalizingly just beyond the setting sun.

Hernán Cortés, a poor Spanish nobleman, then only 34, promoted an expedition of 11 small ships and 550 men and sailed westward from Cuba in February 1519. Upon landing near present-day Veracruz, he was in trouble. His men, mostly soldiers of fortune, hearing stories of a powerful Aztec empire west beyond the mountains, had realized the impossible odds they faced and became restive.

Cortés, however, cut short any thoughts of mutiny by burning his ships. As he led his grumbling but resigned band of adventurers toward the Aztec capital of Tenochtitlán, Cortés played Quetzalcoatl to the hilt, awing local chiefs. Coaxed by Doña Marina, Cortés's native translator-mistress, local chiefs began to add their warrior-armies to Cortés's march against their Aztec overlords.

Moctezuma, Lord of Tenochtitlán

Once inside the walls of Tenochtitlán, the Aztecs' Venicelike island-city, the Spaniards were dazzled by gardens of animals, gold and palaces, and a great pyramid-enclosed square where tens of thousands of people bartered goods gathered from all over the empire.

However, Moctezuma, the lord of that empire, was frozen by fear and foreboding, unsure if these figures truly represented the return of Quetzalcoatl. He quickly found himself hostage to Cortés and then died a few months later, during a riot against Spanish greed and brutality. On July 1, 1520, on what came to be called *noche triste* (the sad night), the besieged Cortés and his men broke out, fleeing for their lives along the lake causeway from Tenochtitlán, carrying Moctezuma's treasure. Many of them drowned beneath their burdens of gold booty, while the survivors hacked a bloody retreat through thousands of screaming Aztec warriors to safety on the lakeshore.

Aztec Defeat and Spanish Victory

Despite his grievous setback, Cortés regrouped and reinforced his small army with an armed sailboat fleet and 100,000 Indian warrior-allies and invaded Tenochtitlán a year later. The defenders, led by Cuauhtémoc, Moctezuma's nephew, refused to surrender, forcing Cortés to destroy the city to take it. Tenochtitlán fell on August 13, 1521.

MALINCHE AND CORTÉS

If it hadn't been for Doña Marina (received as a gift from a local chief), Hernán Cortés may have become a mere historical footnote. Doña Marina, speaking both Spanish and native tongues, soon became Cortés's interpreter, go-between, and negotiator. She persuaded a number of important chiefs to ally themselves with Cortés against the Aztecs. Clever and opportunistic, Doña Marina was a crucial strategist in Cortés's deadly game of divide and conquer. She eventually bore Cortés a son and lived in honor and riches for many years, profiting greatly from the Spaniards' exploitation of the Mexicans.

Latter-day Mexicans do not honor her by the gentle title of Doña Marina, however. They call her Malinche, after the volcano—the ugly, treacherous scar on the Mexican landscape—and curse her as the female Judas who betrayed her country to the Spanish. *Malinchismo* has become known as the tendency to love things foreign and hate things Mexican.

After his triumph, Cortés took former Emperor Cuauhtémoc captive. He forced Cuauhtémoc and his retainers to march with him on an ill-fated expedition to Honduras in 1523–1525. Tortured with foreboding that Cuauhtémoc and his compatriots were plotting against him, Cortés had Cuauhtémoc hanged on February 28, 1525.

But, unknown to Cortés, Cuauhtémoc's followers secretly took his remains hundreds of miles north and buried them at Ixcateopan, the home of Cuauhtémoc's mother, near present-day Taxco. There, 424 years later, on September 26, 1949, they were discovered and remain there in state to this very day. (See the sidebar "Cuauhtémoc: The Last Aztec Emperor" in the Guerrero Upcountry chapter.)

New Spain

With the Valley of Mexico firmly in his grip, Cortés sent his lieutenants south, north, and west to explore and extend the limits of his domain, which eventually expanded to more than a dozenfold the size of old Spain. In a letter to his king, Charles V, Cortés christened his empire "New Spain of the Ocean Sea," a label that remained Mexico's official name for 300 years.

THE SEARCH FOR CHINA

Even during his struggle with the Aztecs, Cortés continued to dream Columbus's old dream. Somewhere west lay China, and he was determined to find it. As early as 1520 Cortés began sending his lieutenants to Mexico's southern Pacific coast to look for safe, timber-rich harbors, where he would build the ships to China.

First on the Pacific shore was Gonzalo de Uribe, who, in 1520, arrived at Zacatula, at the mouth of the Río Balsas, west of Zihuatanejo. Besides bringing back gold samples, he told Cortés of a good harbor and plenty of big trees for building ships.

Discovery of Acapulco Bay

In 1522, conquistador Pedro de Alvarado founded the Acapulco region's first town, at Acatlán on the Costa Chica. Around the same time, Rodriguez de Villafuerte sailed into Acapulco Bay, which he named "Bahía de Santa Lucia," a label that persisted on maps for generations.

After reporting to Cortés of the bay's calm anchorage and abundance of shoreline trees, Villafuerte returned, and by 1530 had built two ships, the *San Miguel* and *San Marcos,* on the shore of Acapulco Bay. For his efforts, Villafuerte was awarded *encomienda* rights (see the Colonial Mexico section) over Acapulco and a big slice of the present Acapulco region.

Among the dozen-odd early Pacific expeditions (several of which were personally financed by Cortés), five set out from Acapulco. In 1532, Diego Hurtado de Mendoza sailed for China via the north Pacific and never returned. Another expedition, loaded with supplies for conquistador Pizarro in Peru, sailed in 1535; in the same year, Cortés himself sailed out, searching for treasure in Baja California. Then, in 1539, Cortés sent Francisco de Ulloa northwest to search for the fabled golden Seven Cities of Cibola, but he was never heard of again. Finally, in 1540, Domingo de Castillo set out to map Mexico's Pacific coast. He returned, with detailed charts and tantalizing hints of the location of Cibola.

Cortés's Monument

Disheartened by his failure to find China (or, at least, more golden cities), and discouraged with interference by his king's Mexican representatives, Cortés returned to Spain to reassert his authority at court. But mired down by lawsuits, a small war, and his daughter's marital troubles, he fell ill and died in Spain on December 2, 1547. Cortés's remains, according to his will, were eventually laid to rest in a vault at the Hospital de Jesús, which he had founded in Mexico City.

Since latter-day Mexican politics preclude memorials to the Spanish conquest, no monument anywhere in Mexico commemorates Cortés's remarkable achievements. His single monument, historians note, is Mexico itself.

The Manila Galleon

Although a handful of the early Spanish voyages of exploration did actually reach Asia, none had returned to Mexico until priest-navigator Andrés de Urdaneta discovered the north Pacific trade winds that pushed his ship *San Pedro* swiftly east back to America. He dropped anchor on October 8, 1565, with a trove of Chinese treasures in his ship's hold.

Thus, more than three generations after Columbus and 40 years of failed transpacific voyages from Mexico that lost dozens of ships and hundreds of lives, the western trade route to Asia was finally a reality.

Not long thereafter, authorities designated Acapulco as Mexico's sole Pacific trading port. Once a year, at least one silver-laden ship, known to the Spanish as the Nao de China, and to the English as the Manila galleon, set sail for the Spanish colony of Manila in the Philippines. It returned with an emperor's dream of rich silks, delicate porcelain, exquisite lacquerware, glittering gold, and rare spices.

For more than 250 years thereafter, merchants from all over Mexico and Peru gathered in Acapulco for a grand yearly trade fair. Bulging with bags of silver and a small mountain of trade goods, such as cochineal, cinnamon, jewels, and cacao, they camped out in Acapulco, eagerly awaiting the Manila galleon's return.

Pirate Threats

Attracted by the Manila galleon's treasures, Dutch, French, Portuguese, and English pirates, sometimes in squadrons of several heavily armed vessels, menaced the Mexican coast. The most famous was Francis Drake, known to the colonists as the feared El Draque. Drake raided a number of Spanish Pacific settlements during his 1578–1580 circumnavigation of the globe. After finishing with the South American colonies, Drake headed north, where he sacked Huatulco on April 13, 1579. He waited in vain for the Manila galleon outside of Acapulco, then continued northwest to California, then across the Pacific.

After a Dutch pirate fleet had attacked Acapulco in 1614, New Spain Viceroy Diego Fernandez de Córdoba decided to build a fort overlooking Acapulco Bay. It successfully deterred hostile attacks, until termites, hurricanes, old age, and finally an earthquake finished the old fort off, in 1776. A bigger stronger fort, the

FROM CONSTANTINOPLE TO CORTÉS

In a real sense, Acapulco's history trail leads from the opposite side of the world, from the ancient eastern Roman imperial capital of Constantinople, in present-day Turkey. For, on May 29, 1453, Muslim Turkish armies defeated the Christian rulers of Constantinople, thus cutting off European land-trade access to the treasured silks, spices, and porcelains of Asia.

The enterprising seafaring Portuguese spearheaded the subsequent furious European search for a sea route to Asia. Although Bartolomé Días, blazing the route east toward India in 1488, had rounded the south cape of Africa, Genoa-born Christopher Columbus thought he had a better idea. If the earth were indeed round (which nearly all scholars had believed for 1,000 years), maybe a shorter route to Asia lay to the west rather than to the east.

After four western voyages, from 1492 to 1502 (the latter three supported by an aggregate fleet of ships and many hundreds of sailors), Columbus plied the intricate coastline of a western land that he thought was China until the day he died. He believed so strongly that he had found Asia that he threatened his men with huge fines and loss of their tongues if they uttered the contrary.

But explorer Vasco Nuñez de Balboa, standing on a ridge in now-Panama in September 1513, proved Columbus wrong by glimpsing, then later swimming in, a grand southern ocean, later named the Pacific. Balboa's discovery thus shifted Columbus's old quest farther west, propelling Hernán Cortés to Mexico in 1519 in search of a water passage that would lead to the great southern "Ocean Sea" and China beyond.

© BRUCE WHIPPERMAN

Cannons of the Fuerte San Diego protected Acapulco from raiders for more than 200 years, from around 1614 until Mexican independence in 1821.

Fuerte San Diego, replaced it in 1783 and remains to the present day.

COLONIAL MEXICO

The Missionaries

Even while the conquistadores subjugated the Mexicans, missionaries began arriving to teach, heal, and baptize them. A dozen Franciscan brothers impressed natives and conquistadores alike by trekking the entire 300-mile stony path from Veracruz to Mexico City in 1523. Missionary authorities generally enjoyed a sympathetic ear from Charles V and his successors, who earnestly pursued Spain's Christian mission, especially when it coincided with its political and economic goals.

The King Takes Control

Increasingly after 1525, the crown, through the Council of the Indies, began to wrest power away from Cortés and his conquistador lieutenants, many of whom had been granted rights of *encomienda:* taxes and labor of a indigenous district. From the king's point of view, tribute pesos collected by *encomenderos* from their native serfs reduced the gold that would otherwise flow to the crown. Moreover, many *encomenderos* callously enslaved and sold their native wards for quick profit. Such abuses, coupled with European-introduced diseases, began to reduce the Native Mexican population at an alarming rate.

The king and his councillors, realizing that without their local labor force, New Spain would vanish, acted decisively, instituting new laws and a powerful viceroy, Don Antonio de Mendoza, to enforce them.

In 1542, the Council of the Indies, through Viceroy Mendoza, promulgated its liberal New Laws of the Indies. They rested on high moral ground: the only Christian justification for New Spain was the souls and welfare of the Native Mexicans. Slavery was outlawed and the colonists' *encomienda* rights over land and the Indians were to eventually revert to the crown.

Despite near-rebellion by the colonists, Mendoza and his successors kept the lid on New Spain. Although some *encomenderos* held their privileges into the 18th century, chattel slavery of Native Mexicans was abolished in New Spain 300 years before Lincoln's Emancipation Proclamation.

Peace reigned in Mexico for 10 generations. Viceroys came, served, and went; settlers put down roots; friars built country churches; and the conquistadores' rich heirs played while the natives worked.

In the port of Acapulco, as the Manila galleon departed and returned safely nearly every year, a small colony of merchants took up residence, built comfortable homes, and got fat on the labor of their native servants and the profits of the Manila galleon's increasingly rich trove of silks, spices, porcelain, lacquerware, and gold.

The Church

Apart from the missionaries, whose authority flowed directly from the pope in Rome, Mexican parish churches *(parroquias),* most of which re-

SIR FRANCIS DRAKE: THE PIRATE EL DRAQUE

The most renowned raider of the Spanish Main was Francis Drake, or the feared "El Draque," as the Spanish called him. The first European corsair to menace Spain's Pacific colonies, Drake left England in 1577, in command of five vessels and 166 men.

Supposedly headed on a trading mission to Africa, Drake's true purpose became clear when he ordered the attack and capture of a Portuguese merchant ship in the Eastern Atlantic. By the time he had crossed westward to South America, his disillusioned crew and merchant partners on board mutinied. Executing the leader of the mutineers, Drake abandoned two of his least seaworthy ships. Next, rallying the remainder of his men, he changed the name of his ship from the stodgy *Pelican* to the proud *Golden Hind.*

In attempting the westward passage through the stormy Strait of Magellan, at the extreme southern tip of South America, he lost two of his remaining three ships. Undaunted, Drake sailed his *Golden Hind* up the west coast of South America, raiding and sacking every possible port—Valparaíso, Lima, Arica—and capturing the royal treasure ship the *Cacafuego.*

Contrary to the Spaniards' worst fears, Drake's approach to robbery was very courtly. No one, Spanish or native, was intentionally harmed. Treasure seemed to be Drake's sole objective. During his last attack on the Pacific Coast, at Huatulco, on April 13, 1579, he even stole the church bell.

The ultimate prize, however, was the Manila galleon. He lurked offshore at Acapulco for a time, but seeing no treasure ship, Drake skipped northwest and dropped anchor and resupplied at undefended Zihuatanejo. He continued northwest for months, searching doggedly for the Manila galleon.

Finally, Drake stopped to rest at a safe anchorage probably somewhere on the present-day northern California coast, at a place with cliffs as white as those of Dover. He records in his log that he stayed for five weeks, traded with the native folks, repaired the *Golden Hind,* and erected his famous "plate of brass," yet to be found. On it he inscribed the claim, in the name of his queen, to the domain of "Nova Albion," now California.

The *Golden Hind* continued west across the Pacific, passing the Spice Islands and India and rounding the south Cape of Africa. Drake arrived in England on September 26, 1580, to a glorious welcome by Queen Elizabeth, having voyaged 35,000 miles and collected a booty of 50,000 pounds of silver.

main to the present day, were founded and controlled by local bishops. As did the missionaries, parish churches generally moderated the native Mexicans' toil. On feast days, the natives would dress up, parade their patron saint, drink *pulque,* and ooh and aah at the fireworks.

The church nevertheless profited from the status quo. The biblical tithe—one-tenth of everything earned—filled clerical coffers. By 1800, the church owned half of Mexico.

Moreover, both the clergy and the military were doubly privileged. They enjoyed the right of *fuero* (exemption from civil law) and could be prosecuted only by ecclesiastical or military courts.

Trade and Commerce

In trade and commerce, New Spain existed for the benefit of the mother country. For nearly the entire colonial era, exterior trade was funneled through only Veracruz on the Gulf and Acapulco on the Pacific. Trade was allowed only with Spain and certain Spanish colonies. As a result, colonists had to pay dearly for often-shoddy Spanish manufactures. The Casa de Contratación (the royal trade regulators) always ensured the colony's yearly payment deficit would be made up by bullion shipments from Mexican mines, from which the crown raked 10 percent off the top.

Despite its faults, New Spain, by most contemporary measures, was prospering in 1800. The native labor force was both docile and growing, and the galleons carried increasing tonnages of silver and gold to Spain. The authorities, however, failed to recognize that Mexico had changed in 300 years.

POPULATION CHANGES IN NEW SPAIN

	Early Colonial (1570)	Late Colonial (1810)
peninsulares	6,600	15,000
criollos	11,000	1,100,000
mestizos	2,400	704,000
indígenas	3,340,000	3,700,000
negros	22,000	630,000

Criollos—The New Mexicans

Nearly three centuries of colonial rule gave rise to a burgeoning population of more than a million criollos—Mexican-born, pure European descendants of Spanish colonists, many rich and educated—to whom power was denied.

High government, church, and military office always had been the preserve of a tiny minority of *peninsulares*—whites born in Spain. Criollos could only watch in disgust as unlettered, unskilled *peninsulares,* derisively called *gachupines* (wearers of spurs), were boosted to authority over them.

Mestizos, Indígenas, and African Mexicans

Upper-class luxury existed by virtue of the sweat of Mexico's mestizo, *indígena* (indigenous), and *negro* laborers and servants. African slaves were imported in large numbers during the 17th century after typhus, smallpox, and measles epidemics had wiped out most of the *indígena* population. Although the African Mexicans, whose communities are still concentrated around Veracruz and the Costa Chica east of Acapulco, contributed significantly (crafts, healing arts, dance, music, drums, and marimba), they had arrived last and experienced discrimination from everyone.

INDEPENDENCE

Although the criollos stood high above the mestizo, *indígena,* and *negro* underclasses, that seemed little compensation for the false smiles, deep bows, and costly bribes that *gachupines* demanded.

The chance for change came during the aftermath of the French invasion of Spain in 1808, when Napoléon Bonaparte replaced King Ferdinand VII with his brother Joseph on the Spanish throne. Most *peninsulares* backed the king; most criollos, however, inspired by the example of the recent American and French revolutions, talked and dreamed of independence. One such group, urged by a firebrand parish priest, acted.

El Grito de Dolores

"*¡Viva México! Death to the gachupines!*" Father Miguel Hidalgo cried passionately from the church balcony in the Guanajuato town of Dolores on September 16, 1810, igniting action. A mostly *indígena,* machete-wielding army of 20,000 coalesced around Hidalgo and his compatriots, Ignacio Allende and Juan Aldama. Their ragtag force raged out of control through central Mexico, massacring hated *gachupines* and pillaging their homes.

Hidalgo advanced on Mexico City but, unnerved by stiff royalist resistance, retreated and regrouped around Guadalajara. His rebels, whose numbers had swollen to 80,000, were no match for a disciplined, 6,000-strong royalist force. On January 17, 1811, Hidalgo (now "Generalisimo") fled north toward the United States but was soon apprehended, defrocked, and executed. His head and those of his comrades hung from the walls of the Guanajuato granary for 10 years in compensation for the slaughter of 138 *gachupines* by Hidalgo's army.

The 10-Year Struggle

Others carried on, however. Hidalgo's heroic efforts had immediately found crucial support in the Acapulco region. An African Mexican former student of Hidalgo, José María Morelos, journeyed south from central Mexico and recruited an entire rebel brigade in the countryside west and north of Acapulco. Attracted by the riches of the Manila galleon deposited at the port, the rebel army laid siege to Acapulco. Morelos avoided getting bogged down by the siege by splitting his force. He took half of his troops north, where he achieved signal victories, capturing Chilpancingo, Tixtla, and Chilapa, in the upcountry Acapulco region.

Buoyed by success, Morelos focused the independence movement in Chilpancingo, organizing the Congress of Anahuac that declared Mexican independence from Spain on November 6, 1813. Continuously threatened by Spanish counterattacks, Morelos successfully kept the Congress of Anahuac intact by moving the delegates, one step ahead of the Spanish troops, to a number of southern Mexico locations. Tragically, Morelos did not live to realize the fruits of his struggle; he was captured and executed by the Spanish in December 1815.

After Morelos's death, his compatriot, Vicente Guerrero, also of African Mexican descent, continued their hit-and-run war of attrition for five years. In 1821, a new liberal government (which included a new constitutional monarchy) in Spain pulled the rug out from beneath Mexican royalist conservatives, who began to defect to the cause of Mexican independence. The royalist commander in the south, Brigadier Agustín de Itúrbide, asked for a meeting with Guerrero. Guerrero was amazed at Itúrbide's proposal: that Mexico should become an independent constitutional monarchy, headed by the king of Spain, and based on "Three Guarantees"—the renowned Trigarantias: independence, Catholicism, and equality—that their army would enforce.

Mexico Wins Independence

On February 24, 1821, in the Acapulco-region town of Iguala, Guerrero and Itúrbide announced their proposal, which became known, famously, as the Plan of Iguala. The plan immediately gained wide support, and on September 21, 1821, Itúrbide rode triumphantly into Mexico City at the head of his Army of Trigarantias. Mexico was independent at last.

Independence, however, solved little except to expel the *peninsulares.* With an illiterate populace and no experience in self-government, Mexicans began a tragic 40-year love affair with a fantasy: the general on the white horse, the gold-braided hero who could save them from themselves.

The Rise and Fall of Agustín I

After the king of Spain refused titular reign over an independent Mexico, Itúrbide was crowned Emperor Agustín I by the bishop of Guadalajara on July 21, 1822. He soon lost his charisma, however. In a pattern that became sadly predictable for generations of topsy-turvy Mexican politics, an ambitious garrison commander issued a *pronunciamiento* or declaration of rebellion against him; old revolutionary heroes endorsed a plan to install a republic. Itúrbide, his braid tattered and brass tarnished, abdicated in February 1823.

The Disastrous Era of Santa Anna

The new Mexican republic, founded in 1824, teetered along, changing hands between

© BRUCE WHIPPERMAN

A monument memorializes Vicente Guerrero's immortal words, *"La patria es primero"* ("My country first"), at Tixtla, Guerrero's birthplace.

conservative and liberal control, for nine chaotic years. But, by 1833, the government was bankrupt; mobs demanded the ouster of conservative President Anastasio Bustamante, who had executed the rebellious old revolutionary hero, Vicente Guerrero.

Antonio López de Santa Anna, the ambitious military commander whose troops had defeated an abortive Spanish counterrevolution in Veracruz, issued a *pronunciamiento* against Bustamante; Congress obliged, elevating Santa Anna to "Liberator of the Republic" and naming him president in March 1833.

Like his contemporary, Abraham Lincoln, Juárez overcame his humble origins to become a lawyer, a champion of justice, and the president who held his country together during a terrible civil war. Like Lincoln, Juárez had little time to savor his triumph.

Santa Anna would pop in and out of the presidency like a jack-in-the-box 10 more times before 1855. First, he foolishly lost Texas to rebellious Anglo settlers in 1836; then he lost his leg (which was buried with full military honors) fighting the emperor of France.

Santa Anna's greatest debacle, however, was to declare war on the United States with just 1,839 pesos in the treasury. With his forces poised to defend Mexico City against a relatively small 10,000-man American invasion force, Santa Anna inexplicably withdrew and the United States Marines surged into the "Halls of Montezuma," Chapultepec Castle, where Mexico's six beloved Niños Héroes cadets fell in the losing cause on September 13, 1847.

In the subsequent treaty of Guadalupe Hidalgo, Mexico lost nearly half of its territory—the present states of New Mexico, Arizona, California, Nevada, Utah, and Colorado—to the United States.

Finally, Mexican leaders decided enough was enough. General Juan Álvarez (the first governor of the new state of Guerrero, founded in 1849) and Ignacio Comonfort denounced Santa Anna; in 1854, in Ayutla, on the Costa Chica, they proposed the Plan of Ayutla to get rid of him. With virtually all of his support eroded, Santa Anna fled into permanent exile in 1855.

REFORM, CIVIL WAR, AND INTERVENTION

While conservatives searched for a king to replace Santa Anna, liberals, led by Supreme Court Chief Justice Benito Juárez, plunged ahead with three controversial reform laws: the Ley Juárez, Ley Lerdo, and Ley Iglesias. These *reformas,* augmented by a new Constitution of 1857, directly attacked the privilege and power of Mexico's landlords, clergy, and generals. They abolished *fueros* (the separate military and church courts), reduced huge landed estates, and stripped the church of its excess property and power.

Conservative generals, priests, hacendados (landholders), and their mestizo and *indígena* followers revolted. The resulting War of the Reform (not unlike the U.S. Civil War) ravaged the countryside for three long years. The balance in Guerrero was tilted toward the liberal side by forces of General Juan Álvarez, whose brigades eventually won out over conservative General Miguel Miramón. Finally, the victorious army paraded triumphantly in Mexico City on New Year's Day 1861.

Later that year, at the urging of President Benito Juárez, the federal congress bestowed Mexico's highest honor, of "Benemérito de la Patria," on the old liberal soldier, Juan Álvarez.

Juárez and Maximilian

Benito Juárez, the leading *reformista,* had won the day. Like his contemporary, Abraham Lincoln, Juárez, of pure Zapotec native blood, overcame his humble origins to become a lawyer, a champion of justice, and the president who held his country together during a terrible civil war. Like Lincoln, Juárez had little time to savor his triumph.

Imperial France invaded Mexico in January 1862, initiating the bloody five-year imperialist struggle known infamously as the French Intervention. After two costly years, the French pushed Juárez's liberal army into the hills and installed the king that Mexican conservatives thought the country needed. Austrian Archduke Maximilian and his wife, Carlota, the very models of modern Catholic monarchs, were crowned emperor and empress of Mexico in June 1864.

The naive Emperor Maximilian I was surprised that some of his subjects resented his presence. Meanwhile, Juárez refused to yield, stubbornly performing his constitutional duties in a somber black carriage one jump ahead of the French occupying army. The climax came in May 1867, when the liberal forces besieged and defeated Maximilian's army at Querétaro. Juárez, giving no quarter, sternly ordered Maximilian's execution by firing squad on June 19, 1867.

RECONSTRUCTION AND THE PORFIRIATO

Juárez worked day and night at the double task of reconstruction and reform. He won reelection but died, exhausted, in 1872.

The death of Juárez, the stoic partisan of reform, signaled hope to Mexico's conservatives. They soon got their wish: General Don Porfirio Díaz, the "Coming Man," was elected president in 1876.

Pax Porfiriana

Don Porfirio is often remembered wistfully, as old Italians remember Mussolini: "He was a bit rough, but, dammit, at least he made the trains run on time."

Although Porfirio Díaz's humble Oaxaca mestizo origins were not unlike Juárez's, Díaz was not a democrat: when he was a general, his officers took no captives; when he was president, his country police, the *rurales,* shot prisoners in the act of "trying to escape."

Order and Progress, in that sequence, ruled Mexico for 34 years. Foreign investment flowed into the country; new railroads brought the products of shiny factories, mines, and farms to modernized Gulf and Pacific ports. Mexico balanced its budget, repaid foreign debt, and became a respected member of the family of nations.

The human price was high. Don Porfirio allowed more than a hundred million acres—one-fifth of Mexico's land area (including most of the arable land)—to fall into the hands of his friends and foreigners. Poor Mexicans suffered the most. By 1910, 90 percent of the *indígenas* had lost their traditional communal land. In the spring of 1910, a smug, now-cultured, and elderly Don Porfirio anticipated with relish the centennial of Hidalgo's Grito de Dolores.

REVOLUTION AND STABILIZATION

¡No Reelección!

Porfirio Díaz himself had first campaigned on the slogan. It expressed the idea the president should step down after one term. Although Díaz had stepped down once in 1880, he had gotten himself reelected for 26 consecutive years. In 1910, Francisco I. Madero, a short, squeaky-voiced son of rich landowners, opposed Díaz under the same banner.

Although Díaz had jailed him before the election, Madero refused to quit campaigning. From a safe platform in the United States, he called for a revolution to begin on November 20, 1910.

Villa and Zapata

Not much happened, but soon the millions of poor Mexicans who had been going to bed hungry began to stir. In Chihuahua, followers of Francisco (Pancho) Villa, an erstwhile ranch hand, miner, peddler, and cattle rustler, began attacking the *rurales,* dynamiting railroads, and raiding towns. Meanwhile, in the south, horse trader, farmer, and minor official Emiliano Zapata and his *indígena* guerrillas were terrorizing rich hacendados and forcibly recovering stolen ancestral village lands. Zapata's movement gained steam and by May had taken the Morelos state capital, Cuernavaca. Meanwhile, Madero crossed the Río Grande and joined with Villa's forces, who took Ciudad Juárez.

The *federales,* government army troops, began deserting in droves, and on May 25, 1911, Díaz submitted his resignation.

As Madero's deputy, General Victoriano

Huerta, put Díaz on his ship of exile in Veracruz, Díaz confided, "Madero has unleashed a tiger. Now let's see if he can control it."

The Fighting Continues

Emiliano Zapata, it turned out, was the tiger Madero had unleashed. Meeting with Madero in Mexico City, Zapata fumed over Madero's go-slow approach to the "agrarian problem," as Madero termed it. By November, Zapata had denounced Madero. "*¡Tierra y Libertad!*" ("Land and Liberty!") the Zapatistas cried, as Madero's support faded. The army in Mexico City rebelled; Huerta forced Madero to resign on February 18, 1913, and then murdered him four days later.

The rum-swilling Huerta ruled like a Chicago mobster; general rebellion, led by the "Big Four"—Villa, Alvaro Obregón, and Venustiano Carranza in the north, and Zapata in the south—soon broke out. Pressed by the rebels and refused U.S. recognition, Huerta fled into exile in July 1914.

Fighting sputtered on for three years as authority see-sawed between revolutionary factions. Finally Carranza, whose forces ended up controlling most of the country by 1917, got a convention together in Querétaro to formulate political and social goals. The resulting Constitution of 1917, while restating most ideas of the Reformistas' 1857 constitution, additionally prescribed a single four-year presidential term, labor reform, and subordinated private ownership to public interest. Every village had a right to communal *ejido* land, and subsoil wealth could never be sold away to the highest bidder.

The Constitution of 1917 was a revolutionary expression of national aspirations and, in retrospect, represented a social and political agenda for the entire 20th century. In modified form, it has lasted to the present day.

Obregón Stabilizes Mexico

On December 1, 1920, General Alvaro Obregón legally assumed the presidency of a Mexico still bleeding from 10 years of civil war. Although a seasoned revolutionary, Obregón was also a pragmatist who recognized peace was necessary to implement the goals of the revolution. In four years, his government pacified local uprisings, disarmed a swarm of warlords, executed hundreds of *bandidos,* obtained U.S. diplomatic recognition, assuaged the worst fears of the clergy and landowners, and began land reform.

All this set the stage for the work of Plutarco Elías Calles, Obregón's Minister of Gobernación (Interior) and handpicked successor, who won the 1924 election. Aided by peace, Mexico returned to a semblance of prosperity. Calles brought the army under civilian control, balanced the budget, and shifted Mexico's social revolution into high gear. New clinics vaccinated millions against smallpox, new dams irrigated thousands of previously dry acres, and campesinos received millions of acres of redistributed land.

By single-mindedly enforcing the pro-agrarian, pro-labor, and anti-clerical articles of the 1917 constitution, Calles made many influential enemies. Infuriated by the government's confiscation of church property, closing of monasteries, and deportation of hundreds of foreign priests and nuns, the clergy refused to perform marriages, baptisms, and last rites. As members of the Cristero movement, militant Catholics crying "*¡Viva Cristo Rey!*" armed themselves, torching public schools and government property and murdering hundreds of innocent bystanders.

Simultaneously, Calles threatened foreign oil companies, demanding they exchange their titles for 50-year leases. A moderate Mexican supreme court decision over the oil issue and the skillful arbitration of American Ambassador Dwight Morrow smoothed over both the oil and church troubles by the end of Calles's term.

Calles, who started out brimming with revolutionary fervor and populist zeal, became increasingly conservative and dictatorial. Although he bowed out peaceably in favor of Obregón (the constitution had been amended to allow one six-year nonsuccessive term), Obregón was assassinated two weeks after his election in 1928. Calles continued to rule for six more years through three puppet-presidents: Emilio Portes Gil (1928–1930), Pascual Ortíz Rubio (1930–1932), and Abelardo Rodríguez (1932–1934).

For the 14 years since 1920, the revolution had first waxed, then waned. With a cash surplus in 1930, Mexico skidded into debt as the Great Depression deepened and Calles and his cronies lined their pockets. In blessing his minister of war, General Lázaro Cárdenas, for the 1934 presidential election, Calles expected more of the same.

Lázaro Cárdenas, President of the People

The 40-year-old Cárdenas, former governor of Michoacán, immediately set his own agenda, however. He worked tirelessly to fulfill the social prescriptions of the revolution. As morning-coated diplomats fretted, waiting in his outer office, Cárdenas ushered in delegations of campesinos and factory workers and sympathetically listened to their petitions.

In his six years of rule, Cárdenas moved public education and health forward on a broad front, supported strong labor unions, and redistributed 49 million acres of farmland, more than any president before or since.

Cárdenas's resolute enforcement of the constitution's Artículo 123 brought him the most renown. Under this pro-labor law, the government turned over a host of private companies to employee ownership and, on March 18, 1938, expropriated all foreign oil corporations.

In retrospect the oil corporations, most of which were British, were not blameless. They had sorely neglected the wages, health, and welfare of their workers while ruthlessly taking the law into their own hands with private police forces. Although Standard Oil cried foul, U.S. President Franklin Roosevelt did not intervene. Through negotiation and due process, the U.S. companies eventually were compensated with $24 million, plus interest. In the wake of the expropriation, President Cárdenas created Petróleos Mexicanos (Pemex), the national oil corporation that continues to run all Mexican oil and gas operations.

Manuel Avila Camacho

Manuel Avila Camacho, elected in 1940, was the last general to be president of Mexico. His administration ushered in a gradual shift of Mexican politics, government, and foreign policy as Mexico allied itself with the U.S. cause during World War II. Foreign tourism, initially promoted by the Cárdenas administration, ballooned. Good feelings surged as Franklin Roosevelt became the first U.S. president to officially cross the Río Grande when he met with Camacho in Monterrey in April 1943.

In both word and deed, moderation and evolution guided President Camacho's policies. *"Soy creente"* ("I am a believer"), he declared to the Catholics of Mexico as he worked earnestly to bridge Mexico's serious church-state schism. Land-policy emphasis shifted from redistribution to utilization as new dams and canals irrigated hundreds of thousands of previously arid acres. On one hand, Camacho established IMSS (Instituto Mexicano de Seguro Social) and on the other, trimmed the power of labor unions.

As World War II moved toward its 1945 conclusion, both the United States and Mexico were enjoying the benefits of four years of governmental and military cooperation and mutual trade in the form of a mountain of strategic minerals that had moved north in exchange for a similar mountain of U.S. manufactures that moved south.

CONTEMPORARY MEXICO

The Mature Revolution

During the decades after World War II, beginning with moderate President Miguel Alemán (1946–1952), Mexican politicians gradually honed their skills of consensus and compromise as their middle-aged revolution bubbled along under liberal presidents and sputtered haltingly under conservatives. Doctrine required of all politicians, regardless of stripe, that they be "revolutionary" enough to be included beneath the banner of the PRI (Partido Revolucionario Institucional), Mexico's dominant political party.

Mexico's revolution hasn't been very revolutionary about women's rights, however. The PRI didn't get around to giving Mexican women, millions of whom fought and died during the revolution, the right to vote until 1953.

Adolfo Ruíz Cortínes, Alemán's secretary of the interior, was elected overwhelmingly in 1952. He fought the corruption that had crept into government under his predecessor, continued land reform, increased agricultural production, constructed new ports, eradicated malaria, and built a number of automobile assembly plants.

Women, voting for the first time in a national election, kept the PRI in power by electing liberal Adolfo López Mateos in 1958. Resembling Lázaro Cárdenas in social policy, López Mateos redistributed 40 million acres of farmland, forced automakers to use 60 percent domestic components, built thousands of new schools, and distributed hundreds of millions of new textbooks. *"La electricidad es nuestra"* ("Electricity is ours"), Mateos declared as he nationalized foreign power companies in 1962.

Despite his left-leaning social agenda, unions were restive under López Mateos. Protesting inflation, workers struck; the government retaliated, arresting Demetrios Vallejo, the railway union head, and renowned muralist David Siqueiros, former communist party secretary.

Troubles notwithstanding, López Mateos climaxed his presidency gracefully in 1964 as he opened the celebrated National Museum of Anthropology, appropriately located in Chapultepec Park, where the Aztecs had first settled 20 generations earlier.

In 1964, as several times before, the outgoing president's interior secretary succeeded his former chief. Dour, conservative Gustavo Díaz Ordaz immediately clashed with liberals, labor, and students. The pot boiled over just before the 1968 Mexico City Olympics. Reacting to a student rebellion, the army occupied the National University; shortly afterward, on October 2, government forces opened fire with machine guns on a downtown protest, killing and wounding hundreds of demonstrators.

Maquiladoras

Despite its serious internal troubles, Mexico's relations with the United States were cordial. President Lyndon Johnson visited and unveiled a statue of Abraham Lincoln in Mexico City. Later, Díaz Ordaz met with President Richard Nixon in Acapulco.

Meanwhile, bilateral negotiations produced the Border Industrialization Program. Within a 12-mile strip south of the U.S.-Mexico border, foreign companies could assemble duty-free parts into finished goods and export them without any duties on either side. Within a dozen years, a swarm of such plants, called maquiladoras, were humming as hundreds of thousands of Mexican workers assembled and exported billions of dollars worth of shiny consumer goods—electronics, clothes, furniture, pharmaceuticals, and toys—worldwide.

Concurrently, in Mexico's interior, Díaz Ordaz pushed Mexico's industrialization ahead full steam. Foreign money financed hundreds of new plants and factories. Primary among these was the giant Las Truchas steel plant at the new industrial port and town of Lázaro Cárdenas at the Pacific mouth of the Río Balsas, at the western border of the Acapulco region.

Discovery, in 1974, of gigantic new oil and gas reserves along Mexico's Gulf coast added fuel to Mexico's already rapid industrial expansion. During the late 1970s and early 1980s billions in foreign investment, lured by Mexico's oil earnings, financed other major developments—factories, hotels, power plants, roads, airports—all over the country.

Economic Trouble of the 1980s

The negative side to these expensive projects was the huge dollar debt required to finance them. President Luis Echeverría Alvarez (1970–1976), diverted by his interest in international affairs, passed Mexico's burgeoning financial deficit to his successor, José López Portillo. As feared by some experts, a world petroleum glut during the early 1980s burst Mexico's ballooning oil bubble and plunged the country into financial crisis. When the 1982 interest came due on its foreign debt, Mexico's largest holding company couldn't pay the $2.3 billion owed. The peso plummeted more than fivefold, to 150 per U.S. dollar. At the same time, prices doubled every year.

But by the mid-1980s, President Miguel de la Madrid (1982–1988) was straining to get Mexico's economic house in order. He sliced government and raised taxes, asking rich and poor alike to tighten their belts. Despite getting foreign bankers to reschedule Mexico's debt, de la Madrid couldn't stop inflation. Prices skyrocketed as the peso deflated to 2,500 per U.S. dollar, becoming one of the world's most devalued currencies by 1988.

Salinas de Gortari and NAFTA

Public disgust led to significant opposition during the 1988 presidential election. Billionaire PAN (National Action Party) candidate Michael Clothier and liberal National Democratic Front candidate Cuauhtémoc Cárdenas ran against the PRI's Harvard-educated technocrat Carlos Salinas de Gortari. The vote was split so evenly that all three candidates claimed victory. Although Salinas eventually won the election, his showing, barely half of the vote, was the worst ever for a PRI president.

Salinas nevertheless climaxed his presidency by negotiating the North American Free Trade Agreement (NAFTA) with U.S. President George Bush and Canadian Prime Minister Brian Mulrooney in 1992.

But, on the very day in early January 1994 that NAFTA took effect, rebellion broke out in the poor, remote state of Chiapas. A small but well-disciplined campesino force, calling itself Ejército Zapatista Liberación Nacional (Zapatista National Liberation Army or EZLN), or "Zapatistas," captured a number of provincial towns and held the former governor of Chiapas hostage.

To further complicate matters, while Salinas de Gortari's chief negotiator, Manuel Camacho Solís, was attempting to iron out a settlement with the Zapatista rebels, Luis Donaldo Colosio, Salinas's handpicked successor, was gunned down just months before the August balloting. However, instead of disintegrating, the nation united in grief; opposition candidates eulogized their fallen former opponent and later earnestly welcomed his replacement, stolid technocrat Ernesto Zedillo, in Mexico's first presidential election debate.

In a closely watched election relatively unmarred by irregularities, Zedillo piled up a solid plurality against his PAN and PRD opponents. By perpetuating the PRI's 65-year hold on the presidency, the electorate had again opted for the PRI's familiar although imperfect middle-aged revolution.

New Crisis, New Recovery

Zedillo, however, had little time to savor his victory. The peso, after having been pumped up a thousand-fold by Salinas's free and easy monetary policies, crashed, losing half of its value in the few months around Christmas 1994. Mexican financial institutions were in danger of defaulting on their obligations to international investors. To stave off a worldwide financial panic, U.S. President Clinton, in February 1995, secured an unprecedented multibillion dollar loan package for Mexico.

Although disaster was temporarily averted, the cure for the country's ills was another painful round of inflation and belt-tightening for poor Mexicans. During 1995, inflation soared, wages dropped, and malnutrition soared sixfold, while Third-World diseases, such as cholera and dengue fever, resurged in the countryside.

Meanwhile, as negotiations with the rebel Zapatistas sputtered on and off in Chiapas, popular discontent erupted in Guerrero, leading to the massacre of 17 unarmed campesinos at Aguas Blancas, in the hills west of Acapulco, by state police in June 1995. One year later, at a demonstration protesting the massacre, a new, well-armed revolutionary group, Ejército Popular Revolucionario (People's Revolutionary Army, or EPR), appeared. A few months later, EPR guerrillas killed two dozen police and soldiers at several locations, mostly in southwestern Mexico. Although President Zedillo's immediate reaction was moderate, platoons of soldiers were soon scouring rural Guerrero, Oaxaca, Michoacán, and other states, searching homes and arresting suspected dissidents. Public response was mostly negative, though some locals felt that they were far better off in the hands of the army than those of state or federal police.

Mexican democracy got a much-needed boost when notorious Guerrero governor Ruben Figueroa, who had tried to cover up the Aguas Blancas massacre with a bogus videotape, was forced from office. At the same time, the Zedillo government gained momentum in addressing the Zapatistas' grievances in Chiapas, even as it decreased federal military presence, built new rural electrification networks, and refurbished health clinics.

Moreover, Mexico's economy began to improve. By mid-1996, inflation had slowed to a 20 percent annual rate, investment dollars were flowing back into Mexico, the peso had stabilized at about 7.5 to the U.S. dollar, and Mexico had paid back half the borrowed U.S. bailout money.

Economic Recovery and Political Reforms

The best news for which the Zedillo administration could justly claim credit was the dramatically improving national economy. By mid-1998, annual inflation had dropped below 15 percent, investment dollars continued to pour into Mexico, the peso was stable at about 8 to the U.S. dollar, and Mexico had paid back every penny of the money from the 1995 U.S. bailout.

Moreover, in the political arena, although the justice system generally left much to be desired, a pair of unprecedented events signaled an increasingly open political system. In the 1997 congressional elections, voters elected a host of opposition candidates, depriving the PRI of an absolute congressional majority for the first time since 1929. A year later, in early 1998, Mexicans were participating in their country's first primary elections—in which voters, instead of politicians, chose party candidates.

Although President Zedillo had had a rough ride, he entered the twilight of his 1994–2000 term able to take credit for an improved economy, some genuine political reforms, and relative peace in the countryside. The election of 2000 revealed, however, that the Mexican people were not satisfied.

End of an Era: Vicente Fox Unseats the PRI

During 1998 and 1999 the focal point of opposition to the PRI's three-generation rule had been shifting from lackluster left-of-center Cuauhtémoc Cárdenas to relative newcomer Vicente Fox, former president of Coca-Cola Mexico and clean former PAN governor of Guanajuato.

Fox, who had announced his candidacy for president two years before the election, seemed an unlikely challenger. After all, the minority PAN had always been the party of wealthy businessmen and the conservative Catholic right. But blunt-talking, six-foot-five Fox, who sometimes campaigned in cowboy boots and a ten-gallon hat, preached populist themes of coalition building and "inclusion." He backed up his talk by carrying his campaign to hardscrabble city *barrios,* dirt-poor country villages, and traditional outsider groups, such as Jews.

Meanwhile, as the campaign heated up in early 2000, PRI candidate Francisco Labastida, ex-Interior Secretary and governor of the drug-plagued state of Sinaloa, sounded the usual PRI themes to gatherings of party loyalists. At the same time, dour PRD liberal Cuauhtémoc Cárdenas, resigning from a mediocre term as mayor of Mexico City, faded to a weak third place.

In a closely monitored election, on July 2, 2000, Fox decisively defeated Labastida, 42 percent to 38 percent, while Cárdenas received only 17 percent. Fox's win also swept a PAN plurality (223/209/57) into the 500-seat Chamber of Deputies lower house (although the Senate remained PRI-dominated).

Nevertheless, in removing the PRI from the all-powerful presidency after 71 consecutive years of domination, Fox had ushered Mexico into a new, much more Democratic era.

Despite stinging criticism from his own ranks, President Zedillo, who historians were already judging as the real hero behind the new democratic era, made an unprecedented, early appeal, less than a week after the election, for all Mexicans to unite behind Fox.

On the eve of his December 1 inauguration, Mexicans awaited Fox's speech with hopeful anticipation. He did not disappoint them. Although acknowledging that he couldn't reverse 71 years of PRI entrenchment in one six-year term, he vowed to ride the crest of reform, revamping the tax system, and reduce poverty by 30 percent, by creating a million new jobs a year through new private investment in electricity and oil production and by forming a new common market with Latin America, the United States, and Canada.

He promised, moreover, to secure Mexican democracy by a much-needed reform of police, the federal attorney general, and the army. Perhaps most difficult of all, Fox called for the formation of an unprecedented "Transparency Commission" to investigate a generation of past grievances, including the 1968 massacre of student demonstrators and assassinations of, among others, a Roman Catholic cardinal in 1993 and a presidential candidate in 1994.

Vicente Fox, President of Mexico

Wasting little time getting started, President Fox first headed to Chiapas to confer with indigenous community leaders. Along the way, he shut down Chiapas military bases and removed dozens of military roadblocks. Back in Mexico City, he sent the long-delayed peace plan, including the indigenous bill of rights, to Congress. Zapatista rebels responded by journeying en masse from Chiapas to Mexico City, where, in their black masks, they addressed Congress, arguing for indigenous rights. Although by mid-2001, Congress had passed a modified version of the negotiated settlement, and the majority of states had ratified the required constitutional amendment, indigenous leaders condemned the legislation plan as watered down and unacceptable, while proponents claimed it was the best possible compromise between the Zapatistas' demands and the existing Mexican constitution.

On the positive side, by mid-2002, Vicente Fox could claim credit for cracking down on corruption and putting drug lords in jail, negotiating a key immigration agreement with the United States, keeping the peso stable, clamping down on inflation, and attracting a record pile of foreign investment dollars.

Furthermore, Fox continued to pry open the door to democracy in Mexico. In May 2002, he signed Mexico's first freedom of information act, entitling citizens to timely copies of all public documents from federal agencies. Moreover, Fox's long-promised "Transparency Commission" was taking shape. In July 2002, federal attorneys were taking unprecedented action. They were questioning a list of 74 former government officials, including ex-President Luís Echeverría, about their roles in government transgressions, notably political murders and the University of Mexico massacres during the 1960s and 1970s.

But, Mexico's economy, reflecting the U.S. economic slowdown, began to sour in 2001, losing half a million jobs and cutting annual growth to 2.5 percent, down from the 4.5 percent that the government had predicted. Furthermore, a so-called "Towelgate" furor (in which aides had bought dozens of $400 towels for the presidential mansion) weakened Fox's squeaky-clean image.

During 2002 and 2003 the Mexican economy continued its lackluster performance, increasing public dissatisfaction. In the July 7, 2003, congressional elections, voters took their frustrations out on the PAN and gave its plurality in the Chamber of Deputies to the PRI. When the dust settled the PRI total had risen to 225 seats, while the PAN had slipped to 153. The biggest winner, however, was the PRD, which gained more than 40 seats, for a total of about 100.

On balance, in mid-2003, pundits were writing that "Fox is running out of time" to accomplish what he promised. Mexican men and women in the street were seeing little improvement in their lives and were increasingly impatient with Fox's efforts to remake the economy and political system. However, most still believed that unseating the PRI was good for Mexico, and that even Fox couldn't completely undo in six years what 71 years of PRI dominance created.

And regardless of how history will judge Vicente Fox, it's important to remember the prime fact of July 2, 2000: that, in pushing out the PRI after 71 years and cleanly electing an opposition president, Mexicans have taken a crucial, irreversible step in their long journey toward democracy and justice for all.

Economy and Government

THE MEXICAN AND GUERRERO ECONOMIES

Post-Revolutionary Gains

By many measures, Mexico's 20th-century revolution appears to have succeeded. Since 1910, illiteracy has plunged from 80 percent to 10 percent, life expectancy has risen from 30 years to nearly 70, infant mortality has dropped from a whopping 40 percent to about 2 percent, and, in terms of caloric intake, and Mexicans are eating about twice as much as their forebears at the turn of the 20th century.

Decades of steady economic growth account for rising Mexican living standards. The Mexican economy has repeatedly rebounded from recessions, by virtue of its plentiful natural resources, notably oil and metals; diversified manufacturing, such as cars, electronics, and petrochemicals; steadily increasing tourism; exports of fruits, vegetables, and cattle; and its large, willing, low-wage workforce.

Recent Mexican governments, moreover, have skillfully exploited Mexico's economic strengths. The Border Industrialization Program has led to millions of jobs in thousands of border maquiladora factories, from Tijuana to the mouth of the Rio Grande. The increased manufacturing output has produced manifold economic benefits, including reduced dependency on oil exports and burgeoning foreign trade as Mexico joined in the General Agreement on Tariffs and Trade (GATT) in 1986 and NAFTA in 1994. Consequently, Mexico has become a net exporter of goods and services to the United States, its largest trading partner. Although Mexico suffered a peso collapse of about 50 percent (in relation to the U.S. dollar) in 1995, the Zedillo administration acted quickly. Belt-tightening measures brought inflation, which had initially surged, down to 20 percent per year, and foreign investment flowed back into Mexico by mid-1996.

The Fox administration continued its predecessor's prudent economic course, which further reduced inflation to a low of about 6 percent in 2003 and stabilized the peso at between 10 and 11 per dollar during the 2001–2003 period. The bad news, however, is that, in 2001–2003, the U.S. economic slowdown decreased demand for Mexican products; consequently, Mexico lost many hundreds of thousands of jobs, forcing economic growth down to a weak 2.5 percent for 2001 and even less for 2002 and 2003.

Guerrero Economic Challenges

Many of Mexico's latter 20th-century economic gains have bypassed Mexico's poor southern states of Chiapas, Oaxaca, and Guerrero. Of the three, Guerrero perennially ranks low in most indicators of quality of life, such as income, infant mortality, malnutrition, and illiteracy.

Although rich in sunshine, mountainous Guerrero lacks arable land and needs more water and capital to irrigate what arable land exists. Under the right conditions, bountiful crops of sesame, corn, tomatoes, citrus, mangoes, peanuts, alfalfa, soy, and *chiles* sprout quickly from bottomland fields.

A potentially valuable crop in Guerrero is coffee, now cultivated by thousands of farmers in the vine-draped lower slopes of the coastal mountains. However, as all over the developing world, growing a crop is the easiest part of trying to make a living from it. Isolation, quality control, and access to markets has kept Guerrero coffee farmers poor. To make matters even worse, the bottom has fallen out of worldwide coffee prices during recent years. It seems patently unjust that farmers can get only about $.50 per pound for the same coffee that, after transport and roasting, sells in United States and European grocery stores for $6 or $7 per pound.

The bright part of the Guerrero economy is tourism, which accounts, both directly and indirectly, for most of the earnings of half of Guerrero families. If it weren't for the resorts of Acapulco, Ixtapa-Zihuatanejo, and Taxco, most Guerrero people would be even poorer than they are now.

But, reason for hope exists. In 2000 the Mexican government launched a renewable six-year

Hard times force many Mexicans to take every possibility to earn a living. Here, musicians play their *marimba* for spare change on a Chilpancingo streetfront.

investment strategy, Development Plan for the Mexican South, which provides money for irrigation, education, roads, utilities, telecommunications, and more, with an eye toward lifting the economies of Guerrero and its poor neighboring states closer to those of the rest of Mexico.

Long-Term Economic Challenges

Despite huge gains, Mexico's Revolution of 1910 is nevertheless incomplete. Improved public health, education, income, and opportunity have barely outdistanced Mexico's population, which has increased nearly sevenfold—from 15 million to 100 million—between 1910 and 2000. For eample, although the illiteracy rate has decreased, the actual number of Mexican people who can't read, about 10 million, has remained about constant since 1910.

Moreover, the land reform program, once thought to be a Mexican cure-all, has long been a disappointment. The *ejidos* of which Emiliano Zapata dreamed have become mostly symbolic. The fields are typically small and unirrigated. Furthermore, *ejido* land, being communal, is not easily accepted by banks as loan collateral. Capital for irrigation networks, fertilizers, and harvesting machines is consequently lacking. Communal farms are typically inefficient; the average Mexican field produces about *one-quarter* as much corn per acre as a U.S. farm. Mexico must accordingly use its precious oil dollar surplus to import millions of tons of corn—originally indigenous to Mexico—annually.

The triple scourge of overpopulation, lack of arable land, and low farm income has driven millions of campesino families to seek better lives in Mexico's cities and the United States. Since 1910, Mexico has evolved from a largely rural country, where 70 percent of the population lived on farms, to an urban nation where 70 percent of the population lives in cities. Fully one-fifth of Mexico's people now live in Mexico City.

Nevertheless, the future appears bright for many privately owned and managed Mexican farms, concentrated largely in the northern border states. Exceptionally productive, they typically work hundreds or thousands of irrigated acres of crops, such as tomatoes, lettuce, *chiles,* wheat, corn, tobacco, cotton, fruits, alfalfa, chickens, hogs, and cattle, just like their counterparts across the border in California, New Mexico, Arizona, and Texas.

Staples—wheat for bread, corn for tortillas, milk, and cooking oil—are all imported and consequently expensive for the typical working-class Mexican family, which must spend half or more of its income (typically $500 per month) for food. Recent inflation has compounded the problem, particularly for the millions of families on the bottom half of Mexico's economic ladder.

Although average gross domestic product figures for Mexico—about $9,000 per capita (much less for Guerrero) compared to about $35,000 for the United States—place it above nearly all other developing countries, averages, when applied to Mexico, mean little. A primary socioeconomic reality of Mexican history remains: the richest one-fifth of Mexican families earns about 10 times the income of the poorest one-fifth. A relative handful of people own a large hunk of Mexico, and they don't seem inclined to share much of it with the less fortunate. As for the poor, the typical Mexican family in the bottom one-third income bracket often owns neither car nor refrigerator, and the children typically do not finish elementary school.

GOVERNMENT AND POLITICS

The Constitution of 1917

Mexico's governmental system is rooted in the Constitution of 1917, which incorporated many of the features of its reformist predecessor of 1857. The 1917 document, with amendments, remains in force. Although drafted at the behest of conservative revolutionary Venustiano Carranza by his handpicked Querétaro "Constitucionalista" congress, it was greatly influenced by liberal Álvaro Obregón and generally ignored by Carranza during his subsequent three-year presidential term.

Although many articles resemble those of its United States model, the Constitution of 1917 contains provisions that stem directly from Mexican experience. Article 27 addresses the question of land. Private property rights are qualified by societal need; subsoil rights are public property, and foreigners and corporations are severely restricted in land ownership. Although the 1917 constitution declared *ejido* (communal) land inviolate, 1994 amendments allow, under certain circumstances, the sale or use of communal land as loan security.

Article 23 severely restricts church powers. In declaring that "places of worship are the property of the nation," it stripped churches of all title to real estate, without compensation. Article 5 and Article 130 banned religious missionary orders, expelled foreign clergy, and denied priests and ministers all political rights, including voting, holding office, and even criticizing the government.

Article 123 establishes the rights of labor: to organize, bargain collectively, strike, work a maximum eight-hour day, and receive a minimum wage. Women are to receive equal pay for equal work and be given a month's paid leave for childbearing. Article 123 also establishes social security plans for sickness, unemployment, pensions, and death.

On paper, Mexico's constitutional government structures appear much like their U.S. prototypes: a federal presidency, a two-house Congress, and a Supreme Court, with their counterparts in each of the 32 states. Political parties field candidates, and all citizens vote by secret ballot.

Mexico's presidents, however, have traditionally enjoyed greater powers than their U.S. counterparts. They need not seek legislative approval for many cabinet appointments, can suspend constitutional rights under a state of siege, can initiate legislation, veto all or parts of bills, refuse to execute laws, and replace state officers. The federal government, moreover, retains nearly all taxing authority, relegating the states to a role of merely administering federal programs.

Although ideally providing for separation of powers, the Constitution of 1917 subordinates both the legislative and judicial branches, with the courts being the weakest of all. The Supreme Court, for example, can only, with repeated deliberation, decide upon the constitutionality of legislation. Five separate individuals must file successful petitions for writs *amparo* (protection) on a single point of law to affect constitutional precedent.

Democratizing Mexican Politics

Reforms in Mexico's stable but top-heavy "Institutional Revolution" came only gradually. Characteristically, street protests were brutally put down at first, with officials only later working to address grievances. Generations of dominance by the PRI, the "Institutional Revolutionary Party," led to widespread cynicism and citizen apathy. Regardless of who gets elected, the typical person on the street used to say, the officeholder was bound to retire with his or her pockets full.

Nevertheless, by 1985, movement toward more justice and pluralism seemed be in store for Mexico. During the subsequent dozen years, minority parties increasingly elected candidates to state and federal office. Although none captured a majority of any state legislature, the strongest non-PRI parties, such as the conservative pro-Catholic Partido Acción Nacional (PAN) or National Action Party and the liberal-left Partido Revolucionario Democratico (PRD), elected governors. In 1986, minority parties were given federal legislative seats, up to a maximum of 20, for winning a minimum of 2.5 percent of the national presidential vote. In the 1994 election, minority parties received public campaign financing, depending upon their fraction of the vote.

After his 1994 inaugural address, in which he called loudly and clearly for more reforms, President Ernesto Zedillo quickly began to produce results. He immediately appointed a respected member of the PAN opposition party as attorney general—the first non-PRI cabinet appointment in Mexican history. Other Zedillo firsts were federal Senate confirmation of both Supreme Court nominees and the attorney general, multiparty participation in the Chiapas peace negotiations, and congressional approval of the 1995 financial assistance package received from the United States. Zedillo, moreover, organized a series of precedent-setting meetings with opposition leaders that led to a written pact for political reform and the establishment of permanent working groups to discuss political and economic questions.

Perhaps most important was Zedillo's campaign and inaugural vow to separate both his government and himself from PRI decision-making. He kept his promise, becoming the first Mexican president, in as long as anyone could remember, who did not choose his successor.

A New Mexican Revolution

Finally, in 2000, like a Mexican Gorbachev, Ernesto Zedillo, the man most responsible for Mexico's recent democratic reforms, watched as PAN opposition reformer Vicente Fox swept Zedillo's PRI from the presidency after a 71-year rule. Moreover, despite severe criticism from his own party, Zedillo quickly called for the country to close ranks behind Fox. Millions of Mexicans, still dazed but buoyed by Zedillo's statesmanship and Fox's epoch-making victory, eagerly awaited Fox's inauguration address on December 1, 2000.

He promised nothing less than a new revolution for Mexico and backed it up with concrete proposals: reduce poverty by 30 percent with a million new jobs a year from revitalized new electricity and oil production, a Mexican Silicon Valley, and free trade between Mexico, all of Latin America, and the United States and Canada. He promised justice for all, through a reformed police, army, and the judiciary. He promised conciliation and an agreement with the Zapatista rebel movement in the south, including a bill of rights for Mexico's native peoples. With all of Mexico listening, Fox brought his speech to a hopeful conclusion: "If I had to summarize my message today in one sentence, I would say: Today Mexico has a future, but we have lost much time and wasted many resources. Mexico has a future, and we must build that future starting today."

People

Let a broad wooden chopping block represent Mexico; imagine hacking it with a sharp cleaver until it is grooved and pocked. That fractured surface resembles Mexico's central highlands, where most Mexicans, divided from each other by high mountains and yawning *barrancas,* have lived since before history.

The Mexicans' deep divisions, in large measure, led to their downfall at the hands of the Spanish conquistadores. The Aztec empire that Hernán Cortés conquered was a vast but fragmented collection of tribes. Speaking more than 100 mutually alien languages, those original Mexicans viewed each other suspiciously, as barely human barbarians from strange lands beyond the mountains. And even today the lines Mexicans draw between themselves—of caste, class, race, wealth—are the result, to a significant degree, of the realities of their mutual isolation.

POPULATION

The Spanish colonial government and the Roman Catholic religion provided the glue that through 400 years has welded Mexico's fragmented people into a burgeoning nation-state. Mexico's population, nearly 100 million by the year 2000, increased during the '90s, but at a rate diminished to about half that of previous decades. Increased birth control and emigration largely account for the slowdown.

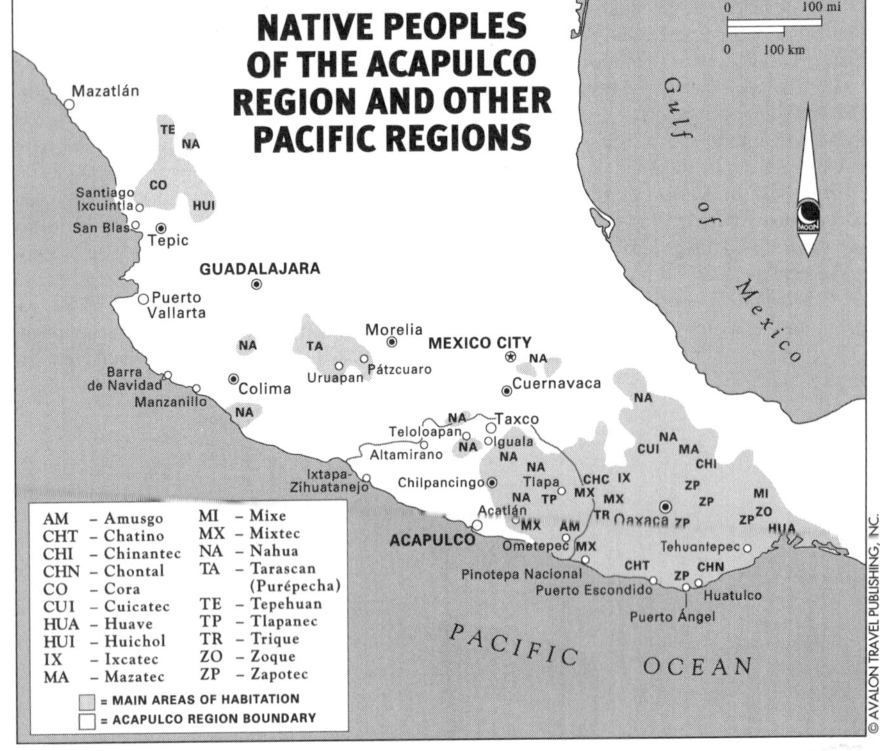

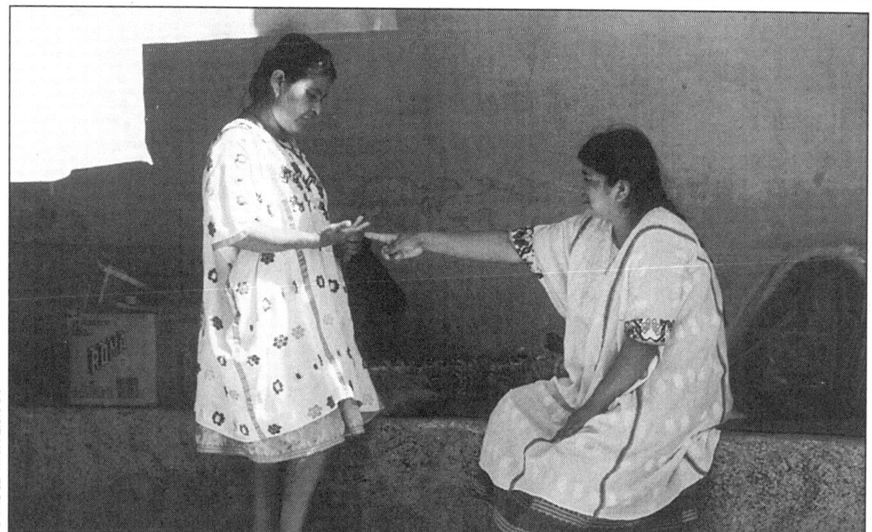

© BRUCE WHIPPERMAN

The design woven into her cotton *huipil* marks an indigenous woman's neighborhood or town, as shown by these Amusgo women on a Xochistlahuaca streetfront.

Mexico's population has not always been increasing. Historians estimate that European diseases, largely measles and smallpox, wiped out as many as 25 million—perhaps 95 percent—of the *indígena* population within a few generations after Cortés stepped ashore in 1519. The Mexican population dwindled from an estimated 20 million at the eve of the conquest to a mere one million inhabitants by 1600. It wasn't until 1950, four centuries after Cortés, that Mexico's population recovered to its preconquest level of about 20 million.

Mestizos, Indígenas, Criollos, and African Mexicans

Although by 1950 Mexico's population had recovered, it was completely transformed. The mestizo, a Spanish-speaking person of mixed blood, had replaced the pure Native Mexican, the *indígena* (een-DEE-hay-nah), as the typical Mexican.

The trend continues. Perhaps three of four Mexicans would identify themselves as mestizo: that class whose part-European blood elevates them, in the Mexican mind, to the level of *gente de razón* (people of "reason" or "right"). And there's the rub. The *indígenas* (or, mistakenly but much more commonly, Indians), by the usual measurements of income, health, or education, squat at the bottom of the Mexican social ladder.

The typical *indígena* family lives in a small adobe house in a remote valley, subsisting on corn, beans, and vegetables from its small, unirrigated *milpa* (cornfield). They usually have chickens, a few pigs, and sometimes a cow, but no electricity; their few hundred dollars a year in cash income isn't enough to buy even a small refrigerator, much less a truck.

The usual mestizo family, on the other hand, enjoys most of the benefits of the 21st century. They typically own a modest concrete house in town. Their furnishings, simple by developed-world standards, will often include an electric refrigerator, washing machine, propane stove, television, and car or truck. The children go to school every day, and the eldest son sometimes looks forward to college.

Sizable *negro* communities, descendants of 18th-century African slaves, live in the Gulf states and along the Guerrero-Oaxaca Pacific coastline.

MEXICAN NAMES

Foreign visitors, confounded by long handles such as Doña Juana María López de Díaz, wonder how Mexican names got so complicated.

The preceding "Doña Juana" example is especially complicated, because it's a typical woman's name, which is generally more complex than that of a typical man.

So, let's explain a man's name first. Take the national hero, Vicente Ramón Guerrero Saldaña. Vicente is his first given name; Ramón, the second given name, corresponding to the "middle" name in the United States. The third, Guerrero, is customarily the father's first surname, and the last, Saldaña, his mother's first surname. Only on formal occasions are men referred to with all four of their names. Simply, "Vicente Guerrero" would do most of the time.

Now, back to "Doña Juana." I threw a curve at you by introducing "Doña." It's an honorific, used as "Dame," for a distinguished woman. ("Don" is the corresponding honorific for Spanish men.)

So, skipping the honorific, women's names start out like men's: first given name, Juana; second given name María, and father's first surname López.

Now, things get more complicated. For unmarried women, the naming is the same as for men. But when a woman gets married, she customarily replaces her second surname with her husband's first surname, preceded by "de," meaning "of." So in the example, Juana is evidently a married woman, who has substituted "de Díaz" (her husband's first surname being Díaz) for her second surname, all adding up to "Juana María López de Díaz."

Thankfully, however, informal names for women also are simplified. Juana, above, would ordinary shorten her name to her first given name, followed by her husband's first surname: simply Juana Díaz.

All of the above notwithstanding, many Mexican women do not go along with this male-dominated system at all and simply use their maiden names as they were known before they were married.

Last to arrive, the *negros* experience discrimination at the hands of everyone else and are integrating very slowly into the mestizo mainstream.

Above the mestizos, a small criollo (Mexican-born white) minority, a few percent of the total population, inherits the privileges—wealth, education, and political power—of its colonial Spanish ancestors.

THE INDÍGENAS

Although anthropologists and census takers classify them according to language groups (such as Náhuatl, Mixtec, and Zapotec), *indígenas* generally identify themselves as residents of a particular locality rather than by language or ethnic grouping. And although, as a group, they are referred to as *indígenas* (native, or aboriginal), individuals are generally uncomfortable at being labeled as such.

While the mestizos are the emergent self-conscious majority class, the *indígenas,* as during colonial times, remain the invisible people of Mexico. They are politically conservative, socially traditional, and tied to the land. On market day, the typical *indígena* family might make the trip into town. They bag tomatoes, squash, or peppers, and tie up a few chickens or a pig. The rickety country bus will often be full and the mestizo driver may wave them away, giving preference to his friends, leaving them to trudge stoically along the road.

Their lot, nevertheless, has been slowly improving. *Indígena* families now almost always have access to a local school and a clinic. Improved health has led to a large increase in their population. Official census figures, however, are probably low. *Indígenas* are traditionally suspicious of government people, and census takers, however conscientious, seldom speak the local language.

Recent figures, however, indicate at least 8 percent of Mexicans are *indígenas*—that is, they speak one of Mexico's 50-odd native languages. Of these, a quarter speak no Spanish at all. These fractions are changing only slowly. Many *indígenas* prefer the old ways. If present trends continue, the year 2019, 500 years after the Spanish arrival, will mark the return of the Mexican indigenous population to the preconquest level of 20 million.

Indígena Language Groups

The Maya speakers of Yucatán and the aggregate of the Náhuatl (Aztec language) speakers of the central plateau are Mexico's most numerous *indígena* groups, totaling three million (one million Maya, two million Nahua).

Official figures, which show that the Acapulco region's indigenous population amounts to about 370,000, or about 14 percent of the region's total population, may be misleading. Official counts often do not measure the droves of transient folks—migrants and new arrivals—who sleep in vehicles, shantytowns, behind their crafts stalls, and with friends and relatives. Although they are officially invisible, you will see them in Acapulco and Ixtapa or Zihuatanejo, walking along the beach, for example, laden with their for-sale fruit or handicrafts—men in sombreros and scruffy jeans, women in homemade full-skirted dresses with aprons much like your great-great-grandmother may have worn.

Immigrants in their own country, indigenous people flock to cities and tourist resorts from hardscrabble rural areas. Although of pure native blood, they will not acknowledge it or will even be insulted if you ask them if they are *indígenas.* It would be more polite to ask them where they're from. If from Michoacán, they'll usually speak Tarasco (more courteously, say Purépecha: poo-RAY-pay-chah); if from Oaxaca, the answer will probably be Zapateco, Mixteco, or Chatino; or from Guerrero, the answer will probably be Náhuatl, Tlapaneco, Mixteco, or Amusgo.

As immigrants always have, they come seeking opportunity. If you're interested in what they're selling, bargain with humor. And if you err, let it be on the generous side. They are proud, honorable people who prefer to walk away from a sale rather than to lose their dignity.

Dress

Country markets are where you're most likely to see people in traditional dress. There, some elderly men still wear the white cottons that blend Spanish and native styles. Absolutely necessary for men is the Spanish-origin straw sombrero (literally, shade-maker) on their heads, loose white cotton shirt and pants, and leather huaraches on their feet.

Women's dress, by contrast, is more colorful. It can include a *huipil* (long, sleeveless dress) embroidered in bright floral and animal motifs and a handwoven *enredo* (wraparound skirt that identifies the wearer with a locality). A *faja* (waist sash) and, in winter, a *quechquemitl* (shoulder cape) complete the ensemble.

RELIGION

"God and Gold" was the two-pronged mission of the conquistadores. Most of them concentrated on gold, while missionaries tried to shift the emphasis to God. They were famously successful; more than 90 percent of Mexicans profess to be Catholics.

Catholicism, spreading its doctrine of equality of all people before God and incorporating native gods into the church rituals, eventually brought the *indígenas* into the fold. Within 100 years, nearly all Native Mexicans had accepted the new religion, which raised the universal God of humankind over local tribal deities.

The Virgin of Guadalupe

Conversion of the *indígenas* was sparked by the vision of Juan Diego, a humble farmer. On the hill of Tepayac north of Mexico City in 1531, Juan Diego saw a brown-skinned version of the Virgin Mary enclosed in a dazzling aura of light. She told him to build a shrine in her memory on that spot, where the Aztecs had long worshipped their "earth mother," Tonantzín. Juan Diego's brown virgin told him to go to the cathedral and relay her instruction to Archbishop Zumárraga.

The archbishop, as expected, turned his

DUENDES: SPIRITS OF MEXICO

Once upon a time, most everyone believed that the world was full of spirits that inhabited every object in creation: trees, rocks, animals, mountains, even the wind and the stars. World mythology is replete with examples, from the leprechauns of Ireland and the fairies of Mount Tirich Mir in Pakistan, to the spirits who haunt old Hawaiian *heiaus* (temples) and the *duendes* of Mexico.

Eventually many a campesino will take his children to his mountainside cornfield to introduce them to the *duendes,* the elfin beings that folks sometimes glimpse in the shadowed thickets where they hide from mortals.

At the upper end of his field, the campesino father addresses the *duendes:* "With your permission we clear your brush and use your water because it is necessary to nourish our corn and beans. Please allow us, for otherwise, we would starve."

Modernized city Mexicans, generations removed from country village life, often scoff at such antique beliefs. That is, until the family doctor fails to cure their weakened spouses or sick children. Then they often run to a *curandero* or *curandera* folk healer.

"Enduendado" (affliction by an angry *duende*), the curandero sometimes diagnoses. Often the cure is simple and savvy: teas and poultices of forest-gathered herbs; other times it is mystical, such as "purifying," by passing an egg all over the afflicted one's body to draw out the illness, and then breaking the egg into a bowl. The shape the broken yolk takes, maybe of a snake, might determine the treatment, which could be long and intricate: massage with lotions of herbs and oils, followed by a *temazcal* (sweat bath) rubdown with rough maguey fibers, all consummated by intense prayers to the Virgin of Guadalupe to force the *duende* to cease the affliction.

Many times the folk cure fails; other times, however, it succeeds, and with enough frequency to convince millions of Mexicans of the power of the village folk healer to purge a *duende*'s poisonous spell.

nose up at Juan Diego's story. The vision returned, however, and this time Juan Diego's brown virgin realized that a miracle was necessary. She ordered him to pick some roses at the spot where she had first appeared to him (a true miracle, since roses had been previously unknown in the vicinity) and take them to the archbishop. Juan Diego wrapped the roses in his rude fiber cape, returned to the cathedral, and placed the wrapped roses at the archbishop's feet. When he opened the offering, Zumárraga gasped: imprinted on the cape was an image of the brown virgin herself—proof positive of a genuine miracle.

In the centuries since Juan Diego, the brown virgin—La Virgen Morena, or Nuestra Señora La Virgen de Guadalupe—has blended native and Catholic elements into something uniquely Mexican. In doing so, she has become the virtual patroness of Mexico, the beloved symbol of Mexico for *indígenas,* mestizos, *negros,* and criollos alike.

In the summer of 2002, Pope John Paul journeyed to Mexico to perform a historic gesture. Before millions of joyous faithful, on July 31, 2002, the frail aging pontiff elevated Juan Diego to sainthood, thus making him Latin America's first indigenous person to be so honored.

With few exceptions, every Acapulco regional town and village celebrates the cherished memory of its Virgin of Guadalupe on December 12. This celebration, however joyful, is but one of the many fiestas that Mexicans, especially the *indígenas,* live for. Each village holds its local fiesta in honor of its patron saint, who is often a thinly veiled sit-in for a local preconquest deity. Themes appear Spanish—Christian vs. Moors, devils vs. priests—but the native element is strong, sometimes dominant.

On the Road

Sports and Recreation

BEACHES

Their soft sand, gentle waves, and south-seas ambience have made the golden shores of Acapulco, Ixtapa, and Zihuatanejo a magnet for a generation of seekers of paradise. And while those brilliant strands are justly renowned, travelers are increasingly discovering the many small beach hideaways, such as Pie de la Cuesta, Troncones, Barra de Potosí, Playa Escondida, El Carrizal, Playa Ventura, and Playa Las Peñitas, that beckon beyond the famous resorts.

Other travelers take adventure a step further and set up camp to enjoy the solitude and the rich wildlife of even more pristine shorelines. They explore beaches that vary from pristine driftwood-strewn barrier dunes and wildlife-rich jungle lagoons to foamy tidepools and sand of seemingly innumerable colors and consistencies.

Sand makes the beach—and the Acapulco region has plenty—from warm golden quartz to cool, velvety white coral. Some beaches drop steeply to turbulent, close-in surf, fine for fishing. Others are level, with gentle, rolling breakers, made for surfing and swimming.

Beaches are fascinating for the surprises they yield. The Acapulco region's beaches, especially the hidden strands near resorts and the dozens of miles of wilderness beaches and tidepools, yield

© BRUCE WHIPPERMAN

© BRUCE WHIPPERMAN

Silky Playa La Ropa, on the protected shore of Zihuatanejo Bay, is a favorite of both Mexican and international vacationers.

troves of shells and treasures of flotsam and jetsam for those who enjoy looking for them. Beachcombing is more rewarding during the summer-fall storm season, when big waves deposit acres of fresh shells—among them conch, scallop, clams, combs of Venus, whelks, limpets, olives, cowries, starfish, and sand dollars.

During the summer rainy season, beaches near river mouths are often fantastic outdoor galleries of wind- and water-sculpted snags and giant logs deposited by the downstream flood.

Viewing Wildlife

Wildlife-watchers should keep quiet and always be on the alert. Animal survival depends on their seeing you first. Occasional spectacular offshore sights, such as whales, porpoises, and manta rays, or an onshore giant constrictor, beached giant squid or Pacific octopus, crocodile, or even a jaguar looking for turtle eggs are the reward of those prepared to recognize them. Don't forget your binoculars and Steve Howell's *Bird-Finding Guide to Mexico* (see Suggested Reading).

(For notes on good hiking, tidepooling, wildlife-viewing, and shell-browsing spots, see the destination chapters.)

WATER SPORTS

Swimming, surfing, sailboarding, snorkeling, scuba diving, kayaking, sailing, and personal watercraft riding are the Acapulco region's water sports of choice. (For details on local favorite spots, conditions, rental shops, equipment, see the Acapulco and Ixtapa-Zihuatanejo destination chapters.)

Safety First

Viewed from Acapulco region beaches, the Pacific Ocean usually lives up to its name. Many protected inlets, safe for child's play, dot the coastline. Unsheltered shorelines, on the other hand, can be deceiving. Smooth water in the calm forenoon often changes to choppy in the afternoon; calm ripples that lap the shore in March can grow to hurricane-driven walls of water in November. Such storms can wash away sand, temporarily changing a wide, gently sloping beach into a

WHEN TO GO TO ACAPULCO

Although temperatures and rainfall are crucial in deciding when to visit the Acapulco region, they don't tell the whole story. Crowds, high-priced high seasons, and low-priced low seasons are also factors. The first thing to consider is that the Acapulco region has two sharply defined seasons: wet summer-fall and dry winter-spring. For folks arriving from the U.S. west coast, the summer contrast is sharp. The change from dust-dry California in August to the tropical-moist Acapulco region can be exotically refreshing.

But the Acapulco region is too hot in the summer, people say. This, however, isn't necessarily the case. In fact, increased summer cloud cover and showers can actually push average daily July, August, and September temperatures lower than bright and clear April, May, and June. And being near the coast, Acapulco region nights never get warmer than balmy, even during the summer.

The other summer plus is the vegetation. If you like lush, green landscapes, the summer-fall may be your season. This is true everywhere, but especially in the highlands, where myriads of multicolored wildflowers decorate the roadsides and the clouds seem to billow into a 1,000-mile-high blue sky.

By contrast, during the admittedly sunnier and more temperate winter, by February it hasn't rained for months. In natural areas trees are bare of leaves, grass is brown, and cacti seem to be the only green plants. The landscape continues dry and dusty during February through April, turning hot in April and May, until the rains arrive and green breaks out again by late June.

Crowding and high prices are also another factor. If you want to avoid both, don't go to the Acapulco region resorts during the high Christmas to New Year's rush (Dec. 20–Jan. 3) or the Semana Santa pre-Easter week up through and including Easter Sunday.

Well, then when should you go? If you shun crowds but like the sunny, temperate winter, January, a low-occupancy miniseason, is a good bet, especially on the beach. The landscape still retains some green and hotels often offer discounts.

September through mid-December are also good months to go. Hotel prices are cheapest, the landscape is lush and green, it's cooler and not so rainy as July and August. However, in September, Ixtapa-Zihuatanejo is too empty for folks who enjoy lots of company. Although beaches are beautifully uncrowded, your favorite restaurants and entertainments may be closed down until mid-October. The pace picks up, however, during November through mid-December, when moderate temperatures, blue skies, low prices, and enough company create the best of all possible worlds in the Acapulco region.

steep one plagued by turbulent waves and treacherous currents.

Undertow, whirlpools, cross-currents, and occasional oversized waves can make ocean swimming a fast-lane adventure. Getting unexpectedly swept out to sea or hammered onto the beach bottom by a surprise breaker are potential hazards.

Never attempt serious swimming when tipsy or full of food; never swim alone where someone can't see you. Always swim beyond big breakers (which come in sets of several, climaxed by a huge one, which breaks highest and farthest from the beach). If you happen to get caught in the path of such a wave, avoid it by *diving directly toward and under it,* letting it roll harmlessly over you. If you are unavoidably swept up in a whirling, crashing breaker, try to roll and tumble with it, as football players tumble, to avoid injury.

Look out for other irritations and hazards. Now and then swimmers get a nettlelike (but usually harmless) jellyfish sting. Be careful around coral reefs and beds of sea urchins; corals can sting (like jellyfish) and you can additionally get infections from coral cuts and sea-urchin spines. *Shuffle* along sandy bottoms to scare away stingrays before stepping on one. If you're unlucky, its venomous tail-spines may inflict a painful wound.

Snorkeling and Scuba Diving

A number of exciting clear-water sites, especially around Ixtapa and Zihuatanejo, and offshore Isla Roqueta in Acapulco, await both beginner and expert scuba divers. Veteran divers usually arrive during the dry winter and early spring when river outflows are mere trickles, leaving offshore waters clear. In Acapulco, Ixtapa, and Zihuatanejo, professional dive shops rent equipment, provide lessons and guides, and transport divers to choice sites.

While convenient, rented equipment is often less than satisfactory. To be sure, serious divers bring their own gear. This should probably include wetsuits in the winter, when many swimmers begin to feel cold after an unprotected half-hour in the water.

Surfing, Sailing, Sailboarding, and Kayaking

Although Acapulco Bay itself seldom if ever offers any good surfing opportunities, nearby Playa Revolcadero does. Moreover, a few good surfing spots sprinkle the Ixtapa-Zihuatanejo area. Farther afield, a number of crystalline strands, such as Troncones, Piedra Tlacoyunque, Playa Escondida, Playa Cayaquitos, Playa El Calvario, Playa Ventura, and Punta Maldonado, offer good seasonal surfing breaks. (See the destination chapters for details.)

The surf everywhere is highest and best during the July–Nov. hurricane season, when big swells from storms far out at sea attract platoons of surfers to favored beaches (except at crowded Acapulco Bay, where surfing is off-limits).

Sailboarders, sailboaters, and kayakers—who, by contrast, require more tranquil waters—do best in the Acapulco region's winter or spring. Aquatics shops rent sailboarding outfits, sailboats, and kayaks at a number of resort hotel beaches on both Acapulco and Zihuatanejo Bays and Ixtapa's main beach.

The Acapulco region's many coastal lagoons offer fine sailboating and kayaking opportunities. Very accessible examples are Laguna Coyuca at Pie de la Cuesta, just west of Acapulco, and Laguna Barra de Potosí east of Zihuatanejo. (Bring your own equipment, however; few if any rentals are available.)

© BRUCE WHIPPERMAN

Rivers and crystal springs, especially those of the Río Azul (like at Coxcamila, above), are delightful family retreats most any day and especially on Sundays.

While beginners can have fun with the equipment available from rental shops, serious surfers, sailboarders, sailboaters, and kayakers should pack their own gear.

POWER SPORTS

Acapulco and to a lesser extent, Ixtapa, have long been centers for motorboating, water-skiing, parasailing, and personal watercraft riding. Crowded conditions on Acapulco Bay have fortunately pushed most water-skiing to spacious Laguna Coyuca (at Playa Pie de la Cuesta) east of town. There, a few well-equipped providers offer equipment and lessons for about $100 per hour.

In parasailing, a motorboat pulls while a parachute lifts you, like a soaring gull, high over the ocean. After five or 10 minutes the driver deposits you—usually gently—back on the sand.

Personal watercraft ("wave-runners") are like snowmobiles except that they operate on water, where, with a little practice, beginners can quickly learn to whiz over the waves.

Although Acapulco and Ixtapa resort hotels' aquatic shops generally provide experienced power sports crews and equipment, crowded conditions increase the hazard to both participants and swimmers. You, as the patron, are paying plenty for the privilege; you have a right to expect that your providers and crew are well-equipped, sober, and cautious.

Beach Buggies and ATVs

Some visitors enjoy racing along the beach and rolling over dunes in beach buggies and ATVs (all-terrain vehicles—*motos* in Mexico), balloon-tired, three-wheeled motor scooters. While certain resort rental agencies cater to the growing use of such vehicles, limits are in order. Of all the proliferating high-horsepower beach pastimes, these are the most intrusive. Noise, exhaust, and gasoline pollution, injuries to operators and bystanders, scattering of wildlife and destruction of their habitats have led (and I hope will continue to lead) to the restriction of dune buggies and ATVs on beaches.

TENNIS AND GOLF

Most Mexicans are working too hard to be playing much tennis and golf. Consquently, nearly all courses and courts are private. Acapulco golfers enjoy one public *campo de golf* (golf course) and at least two plush private ones. In Ixtapa, one public and one private course serve golfers.

As for tennis, plenty of private courts are available in both Acapulco and Ixtapa. If you are planning on a lot of golf and tennis, check into (or inquire about court rental at) one of the many hotels with these facilities. Use of hotel tennis courts is often, but not always, included in your hotel tariff. If not, fees will run about $10 per hour. Golf greens fees, which begin at about $50 for 18 holes, are always extra.

(See the Acapulco and Ixtapa-Zihuatanejo destination chapters for plenty of golf and tennis listings.)

FISHING AND HUNTING

Experts agree the Acapulco region (and increasingly Zihuatanejo) is a world-class deep-sea and

An adventuring parasailor enjoys a soft landing on Playa del Palmar, Ixtapa's main resort beach.

surf fishing ground. Sportspeople routinely bring in dozens of species from among the hundreds that have been hooked in Acapulco region waters.

Surf Fishing

Most good fishing beaches away from the immediate resort areas will typically have only a few locals (mostly with nets) and fewer visitors. Mexicans typically do little sportfishing. Most either make their living from fishing, or they do none at all. Consequently, few shops sell sportfishing equipment in the Acapulco region; plan to bring your own surf-fishing equipment, including hooks, lures, line, and weights.

Your best general information source before you leave home is a good local bait-and-tackle shop. Tell the folks there where you're going, and they'll often know the best lures and bait to use and what fish you can expect to catch with them.

© BRUCE WHIPPERMAN

Most Mexicans who fish on local beaches use nets.

In any case, the cleaner the water, the more interesting your catch. On a good day, your reward might be *sierras, cabrillas,* porgies, or pompanos pulled from the Acapulco region surf.

You can't have everything, however. Foreigners cannot legally take Mexican abalone, coral, lobster, clams, rock bass, sea fans, shrimp, turtles, or seashells. Neither are they supposed to buy them directly from fishermen.

Deep-Sea Fishing

Zihuatanejo and Acapulco have long been world-class sportfishing grounds. A deep-sea boat charter generally includes the boat and crew for a full or half day, plus equipment and bait for two to six people, not including food or drinks. The full-day price depends upon the season. Around Christmas and New Year and before Easter (when reservations will be mandatory) a boat can run $400 and up at Acapulco and Zihuatanejo. During low season, however, you might be able to bargain a captain down to as low as $200.

Renting an entire big boat is not the only choice. Winter sportfishing is sometimes so brisk at Acapulco and Zihuatanjeo that travel agencies can make reservations for individuals for about $60 per person per day.

Pangas, outboard launches seating 2–6 passengers, are available for as little as $50, depending on the season. Once, six of my friends hired a *panga* for $50, had a great time, and came back with a boatload of big tuna, jack, and mackerel. A restaurant cooked them as a banquet for a dozen of us in exchange for the extra fish, and I discovered for the first time how heavenly fresh *sierra veracruzana* can taste.

Bringing Your Own Boat

If you're going to do lots of fishing, your own boat may be your most flexible and economical option. One big advantage is that you can go to the many excellent fishing grounds the charter boats do not frequent. Keep your equipment simple, scout around the dock, and keep your eyes peeled and ears open for local regulations and customs, plus tide, wind, and fish-edibility information.

FISH

A bounty of fish darts, swarms, jumps, and wriggles in the Acapulco region's surf, reefs, lagoons, and offshore depths. While many make delicious dinners (albacore, *dorado*, pompano, red snapper, roosterfish), others are tough (sailfish), bony (bonefish), and even poisonous (puffers). Some grow to half-ton giants (marlin, jewfish), while others are diminutive reef-grazers (parrot fish, damselfish, angelfish) whose bright colors delight snorkelers and divers. Here's a sampling of what you might find underwater or on your dinner plate.

albacore *(albacora, atún):* 2–4 feet in size; blue; deep waters; excellent taste

angelfish *(ángel):* one foot; yellow, orange, blue; reef fish*

barracuda *(barracuda, picuda):* two feet; brown; deep waters; good taste

black marlin *(marlin negro):* six feet; blue-black; deep waters; good taste

blue marlin *(marlin azul):* eight feet; blue; deep waters; poor taste

bobo *(barbudo):* one foot; blue, yellow; surf; fair taste

bonefish *(macabi):* one foot; blue or silver; inshore; poor taste

bonito *(bonito):* two feet; black; deep waters; good taste

butterfly fish *(muñeca):* six inches; black, yellow; reef fish*

chub *(chopa):* one foot; gray; reef fish; good taste

croaker *(corvina):* two feet; brownish; inshore bottoms; rare and protected

damselfish *(castañeta):* four inches; brown, blue, orange; reef fish*

dolphinfish, mahimahi *(dorado):* three feet; green, gold; deep waters; good taste

grouper *(garropa):* three feet; brown, rust; offshore and in reefs; good taste

grunt *(burro):* eight inches; black, gray; rocks, reefs*

jack *(toro):* 1–2 feet; bluish-gray; offshore; good taste

mackerel *(sierra):* two feet; gray with gold spots; offshore; good taste

mullet *(lisa):* two feet; gray; sandy bays; good taste

needlefish *(agujón):* three feet; blue-black; deep waters; good taste

Pacific porgy *(pez de pluma):* 1–2 feet; tan; sandy shores; good taste

parrot fish *(perico, pez loro):* one foot; green, pink, blue, orange; reef fish*

pompano *(pómpano):* one foot; gray; inshore bottoms; excellent taste

puffer *(botete):* eight inches; brown; inshore; poisonous

red snapper *(huachinango, pargo):* 1–2 feet; reddish pink; deep waters; excellent taste

roosterfish *(pez gallo):* three feet; black, blue; deep waters; excellent taste

sailfish *(pez vela):* five feet; blue-black; deep waters; poor taste

sardine *(sardina):* eight inches; blue-black; offshore; good taste

sea bass *(cabrilla):* 1–2 feet; brown, ruddy; reef and rock crevices; good taste

shark *(tiburón):* 2–10 feet; black to blue; in- and offshore; good taste

snook *(robalo):* 2–3 feet; black-brown; brackish lagoons; excellent taste

spadefish *(chambo):* one foot; black-silver; sandy bottoms; reef fish*

swordfish *(pez espada):* five feet; black to blue; deep waters; good taste

triggerfish *(pez puerco):* 1–2 feet; blue, rust, brown, black; reef fish; excellent taste

wahoo *(peto, guahu):* 2–5 feet; green to blue; deep waters; excellent taste

yellowfin tuna *(atún amarilla):* 2–5 feet; blue, yellow; deep waters; excellent taste

yellowtail *(jurel):* 2–4 feet; blue, yellow; offshore; excellent taste

*generally too small to be considered edible

Fishing Licenses and Boat Permits

Anyone 16 or older who is either fishing or riding in a fishing boat in Mexico is required to have a fishing license. Although Mexican fishing licenses are obtainable from certain travel and insurance agents or at government fishing offices everywhere along the coast, save yourself time and trouble by getting both your fishing licenses and boat permits by mail ahead of time from the Mexican Department of Fisheries. Call at least a month before departure (tel. 619/233-6956, fax 619/233-0344) and ask for applications and the fees (which are reasonable but depend upon the period of validity and the fluctuating exchange rate). On the application, fill in the names (exactly as they appear on passports) of the people requesting licenses. Include a cashier's check or a money order for the exact amount, along with a stamped, self-addressed envelope. Address the application to the Mexican Department of Fisheries (Oficina de Pesca), 2550 5th Ave., Suite 101, San Diego, CA 92103-6622.

© BRUCE WHIPPERMAN

Despite gradual depletion of stocks, boats still bring in big billfish like marlin, swordfish, and sailfish to the Acapulco sportfishing dock.

BULLFIGHTING

It is said there are two occasions for which Mexicans arrive on time: funerals and bullfights.

Bullfighting is a recreation, not a sport. The bull is outnumbered seven to one and the outcome is never in doubt. Even if the matador (literally, killer) fails in his duty, his assistants will entice the bull away and slaughter it in private beneath the stands.

La Corrida de Toros

Moreover, Mexicans don't call it a "bullfight"; it's the *corrida de toros,* during which six bulls are customarily slaughtered, beginning at 5 P.M. (4 in the winter). After the beginning parade, featuring the matador and his helpers, the picadores and the banderilleros, the first bull rushes into the ring in a cloud of dust. Clockwork *tercios* (thirds) define the ritual: the first, the *puyazos* (stabs), requires that two picadores on horseback thrust lances into the bull's shoulders, weakening it. During the second *tercio,* the banderilleros dodge the bull's horns to stick three long, streamered darts into its shoulders.

Trumpets announce the third *tercio* and the appearance of the matador. The bull—weak, confused, and angry—is ready for the finish. The matador struts, holding the red cape, daring the bull to charge. Form now becomes everything. The expert matador takes complete control of the bull, which rushes at the cape, past its ramrod-erect opponent. For charge after charge, the matador works the bull to exactly the right spot in the ring—in front of the judges, a lovely señorita, or perhaps the governor—where the matador mercifully delivers the precision *estocada* (killing sword thrust) deep into the drooping neck of the defeated bull.

Most sizable Acapulco region towns, including Zihuatanejo, Taxco, Chilpancingo, Iguala, and Ometepec, stage *corridos de toros.*

In Acapulco, *corridas de toros* are staged Sunday at 5:30 P.M. seasonally, usually Jan.–March, at the arena (here called a *frontón*) near west-side Playa Caletilla.

Festivals and Events

Mexicans love a party. Urban families watch the calendar for midweek national holidays that create a *puente* or "bridge" to the weekend and allow them to squeeze in a three- to five-day minivacation. Visitors should likewise watch the calendar. Such holidays (especially Christmas and Semana Santa, pre-Easter week) mean packed buses, roads, and hotels, especially around the Acapulco region's beach resorts.

Country people, on the other hand, await their local saint's or holy day. The name of the locality often provides the clue. For example, in San Marcos, on the Costa Chica, 30 miles west of Acapulco, expect a celebration in late April, around April 25, the feast day of St. Mark. People dress up in their traditional best, sell their wares and produce in a street fair, join a procession, get tipsy, and dance in the plaza.

FIESTAS

The following calendar lists national and notable Acapulco region holidays and festivals. Dates may vary. If you want to attend a specific local fiesta, contact a local travel agent or tourism bureau for information. (But, if you happen to be where one of these is going on, get out of your car or bus and join in!)

Jan. 1: **¡Feliz Año Nuevo!** (New Year's Day; national holiday).

Jan. 6: **Día de los Reyes** (Day of the Kings; traditional gift exchange).

Jan. 17–18: **Fiesta de Santa Prisca** in Taxco; families bring their pet animals for blessing at the church. The next day, pilgrims arrive at the *zócalo* for *mañanitas* (dawn Mass) in honor of the saint, then head for folk dancing inside the church.

Jan. 20–21: **Fiesta de San Sebastián;** townsfolk honor the saint martyred in Rome in A.D. 288.

Jan. 23–Feb. 2: **Fiesta de la Virgen de la Salud;** processions, dancing, food, and fireworks.

Feb. 2: **Día de Candelaria** (plants, seeds, and candles blessed; processions and bullfights).

February: During the four days before Ash Wednesday (*Miercoles de Ceniza,* 46 days before Easter Sunday), usually in late February, many towns and villages stage **Carnaval** (Mardi Gras) extravaganzas; especially in Teloloapan, near Iguala.

March 10–17: **Fiesta de San Patricio** (St. Patrick's Day festival).

Fifth Friday before Easter Sunday: **Fiesta del Señor del Perdón,** grand pilgrimage festival, in Igualapa, near Ometepec.

Fourth Friday before Easter Sunday: **Fiesta de Jesús el Nazareno** (in Huaxpáltepec; traditional Dance of the Conquest; big native country fair).

March 19: **Día de San José** (Day of St. Joseph).

March 21: **Birthday of Benito Juárez,** the "Hero of the Americas" (national holiday).

April 1–7: **Feria de Café** (Coffee Fair in Atoyac de Álvarez; coffee farmers sell their best; also plenty of horse trading, handicrafts, country food, and bull riding and roping).

April 1–19: **Fiesta de Ramos** (Palm Sunday); local area crafts fair, food, dancing, mariachis; especially in Jamiltepec.

April: **Good Friday,** two days before Easter Sunday.

April: **Semana Santa** (pre-Easter Holy Week, culminating in Domingo Gloria, Easter Sunday national holiday), especially in Taxco, Pinotepa Nacional, Teloloapan, Petatlán, Ometepec, Iguala, Olinalá, and Jamiltepec.

May 1: **Fiesta del Primer de Mayo,** in Atliaca, near Tixtla. Age-old indigenous rite; sacrifices, praying for rain, and traditional dances at the sacred site, the Sótano (Sinkhole) de Oztotempa.

May 1: **Labor Day** (national holiday).

May 3: **Fiesta del Día de la Santa Cruz** (Holy Cross). Processions to hilltops and sacred sites; many towns, but especially in Ometepec.

May 3–15: **Fiesta of St. Isador the Farmer** (blessing of seeds, animals, and water; agricultural displays, competitions, and dancing).

May 5: **Cinco de Mayo** (defeat of the French at Puebla in 1862; national holiday).

May 10: **Mother's Day** (national holiday).

June 24: **Fiesta de San Juan Bautista** (Festival of St. John the Baptist; fairs and religious festivals, playful dunking of people in water, especially in Chilapa).

June 29: **Día de San Pablo y San Pedro** (Day of St. Peter and St. Paul).

July 20–30: **Fiesta de Santiago Apóstol** (St. James the Apostle); in many locations, but especially in Pinotepa Nacional, Quechultenango, and Ometepec.

Aug. 6–7: **Fiesta del Padre Jesús.** Grand pilgrimage celebration of Petatlán's beloved *patrón,* accompanied by plenty of merrymaking, traditional dances, country food, and fireworks.

Aug. 9: **Fiesta de Vicente Guerrero.** In Tixtla, folks celebrate, with cultural events, music, and traditional dances, the birthday of their celebrated native son, Vicente Guerrero.

Aug. 14–15: **Fiesta de la Virgen de la Asunción** (Virgin of the Assumption). The celebration of the ascension of Mother Mary into heaven, especially in Chilapa.

Sept. 1–8: **Fiesta de la Natividad de María.** Indigenous folks flood into Tixtla to sell handicrafts, get tipsy, and watch their favorite traditional dances.

Sept. 9–11: **Fiesta de San Nicolás Tolentino,** in Ometepec.

Sept. 14: **Charro Day** (Cowboy Day all over Mexico; rodeos).

Sept. 15–16: **Dias Patrias** (Patriotic Days, national holiday). Mayors everywhere reenact Father Hidalgo's 1810 Grito de Dolores from city hall balconies at 11 P.M. on the night of 15 September; especially in Teloloapan and Ometepec.

Sept. 27–Oct. 2: **Fiesta de San Miguel,** often with the Danza de los Cristianos y Moros (Dance of the Christians and Moors).

Oct. 4: **Día de San Francisco** (Day of St. Francis of Assisi), especially in Iguala and Olinalá.

Oct. 12: **Día de la Raza** (Day of the Race, national holiday that commemorates the union of the races).

Nov. 1: **Día de Todos Santos** (All Souls' Day, in honor of the souls of children). The departed descend from heaven to eat sugar skeletons, skulls, and treats on family altars.

Nov. 2: **Día de los Muertos** (Day of the Dead; in honor of ancestors). Families visit cemeteries and decorate graves with flowers and favorite food of the deceased. Especially colorful in Iguala and Taxco.

Monday after the Day of the Dead: **Fiesta de los Jumiles.** In Taxco, folks collect and feast on raw or roasted *jumiles* (small crickets), along with music and plenty of fixings.

Nov. 7–30: **Feria de la Nao de China** in Acapulco; fair celebrating the galleon trade that linked colonial Acapulco with China via the Philippines.

Nov. 20: **Revolution Day** (anniversary of the Revolution of 1910–1917; national holiday).

Nov. 28–Dec. 5: **National Silver Fair** in Taxco; Mexico's most skilled silversmiths compete for prizes amid a whirl of concerts, dances, and fireworks.

Dec. 1: **Inauguration Day** (national government changes hands every six years: 2006, 2012, 2018 . . .).

Dec. 8: **Día de la Purísima Concepción** (Day of the Immaculate Conception).

Dec. 12: **Día de Nuestra Señora de Guadalupe,** Festival of the Virgin of Guadalupe, patroness of Mexico; processions, music, and dancing nationwide, and especially around the Acapulco *zócalo,* and the adjacent Pozo de la Nación neighborhood.

Dec. 16–24: **Christmas Week** (week of *posadas* and piñatas; midnight Mass on Christmas Eve).

Dec. 24–Jan. 8: **Feria de San Mateo, la Navidad, y el Año Nuevo.** In Chilpancingo, the festivities kick off with the *teopancolaquio,* a ritual honoring the birth of God on Earth. Subsquently folks celebrate with favorite traditional dances, bullfights, carnival, fireworks, cockfights, and plenty of food.

Dec. 25: **¡Feliz Navidad!** (Christmas Day; Christmas trees and gift exchange; national holiday).

Dec. 31: **New Year's Eve.**

Arts and Crafts

Mexico is so stuffed with lovely, reasonably priced handicrafts (*artesanías,* ar-tay-sah-NEE-ahs) that many crafts devotees, if given the option, might choose Mexico over heaven. A sizable fraction of Acapulco region families still depend upon homespun items—clothing, utensils, furniture, native herbal remedies, religious offerings, adornments, toys, musical instruments—which either they or their neighbors craft at home. Many such traditions reach back thousands of years, to the beginnings of Mexican civilization. The accumulated knowledge of manifold generations of artisans has, in many instances, resulted in finery so prized that whole villages devote themselves to the manufacture of a certain class of goods.

Mexico is so stuffed with lovely, reasonably priced handicrafts that many crafts devotees, if given the option, might choose Mexico over heaven.

In the Acapulco region, handicrafts shoppers who venture away from the coastal resorts to the source towns and villages will most likely benefit from lower prices, wider choices, and, most important, the privilege of encountering the artisans themselves.

The Acapulco region's three prime handicrafts source towns are **Taxco,** renowned for silver jewelry; **Olinalá,** for fine lacquerware, furniture, and jaguar masks; and **Chilapa,** for a swarm of handicrafts that folks bring in from outlying villages and sell at the Sunday crafts market. Items in Chilapa that you might be able to buy include trinkets of **horn** *(cuerno):* mescal bottles, combs, pen holders, ash trays, and lampshades; **ironwork** *(hierro):* hachets, daggers, swords, and knives; **maguey fiber** *(ixtle):* handpainted bags and purses; **embroidery** *(bordado):* napkins, tablecloths, and shawls *(rebozos);* **basketry and woven fiber** *(cestería):* palm sombreros, reed baskets, purses, mats *(petates),* and palm baskets *(tenates);* **wood** *(madera):* masks, lacquerware, miniature human and animal figurines, furniture; **leather** *(cuero):* purses, belts, wallets; and **pottery** *(alfarería).* (For access details, see the Guerrero Upcountry chapter.)

BASKETRY AND WOVEN CRAFTS

Weaving straw, leaves, palm fronds, and reeds is among the oldest of Mexican crafts traditions. Mat and basketweaving methods and designs 5,000 years old survive to the present day. In the dry sierra and Río Balsas basin of northeastern Guerrero, people weave *petates* (straw mats) upon which vacationers stretch out on the beach and which local folks use for everything, from keeping tortillas warm to shielding babies from the sun. Palm-leaf weaving is a near-universal occupation. The craft spills over to Acapulco and the Costa Chica, where you might see a person waiting for a bus or even walking down the street while weaving creamy white palm leaf strands into a coiled basket. (Despite appearances, the product, if made of palm leaf, is not strictly a basket—*canasta* in Spanish—which is made of reeds, but instead a *tenate,* which has no handle, like a basket does, but a woven tumpline that folks loop over their foreheads when carrying a load.)

Not unlike the origami paper-folders of Japan, folks who live around Lake Pátzcuaro in neighboring Michoacán have taken basketweaving to its ultimate by crafting virtually everything—from toy turtles and Christmas bells to butterfly mobiles and serving spoons—from the reeds they gather along the lakeshore.

Hatmaking has likewise attained high refinement in Mexico. Many of the same Guerrero palm-leaf weavers who craft *petates* and *tenates* also craft sombreros. Also, in Sahuayo, Michoacán (near the southeast shore of Lake Chapala), and due east across Mexico, in Becal, Campeche, workers also craft so-called "Panama" hats, or *jipis* (HEE-pees), of palm leaf. The measure of a fine palm leaf hat is its softness and flexibility—so pliable that you can stuff one into your purse or pants pocket without damage.

CLOTHING AND EMBROIDERY

Although ***traje*** (ancestral tribal dress) has nearly vanished in urban Mexico, significant numbers of Mexican women, especially in remote districts of Michoacán, Guerrero, Oaxaca, Chiapas, and Yucatán, make and wear *traje.* Most common is the *huipil,* a full, square-shouldered, short- to mid-sleeved dress, often hand-embroidered with animal and floral designs. Notable *huipil* designs come from Xochistlahuaca, Guerrero, and San Pedro de Amusgos, Oaxaca (Amusgo tribe: white cotton, often embroidered with abstract colored animal and floral motifs); San Andrés Chicahuaxtla, Oaxaca (Trique tribe: white cotton, richly embroidered red stripes, interwoven with green, blue, and yellow, and hung with colored ribbons); Tehuantepec, Oaxaca (Zapotec tribe: white cotton, with bright multicolored flowers embroidered along two or four vertical seams). Beyond the Pacific coast, Yucatán Maya *huipiles* are among the most prized. They are of white cotton, embellished with big, brilliant machine-embroidered flowers around the neck and shoulders.

Shoppers sometimes can buy other, less common types of *traje,* such as a *quechquémitl* (shoulder cape), often made of wool and worn as an overgarment in winter. The *enredo,* a full-length skirt, wraps around the waist and legs like a Hawaiian sarong. Mixtec women on the Guerrero-Oaxaca border around Pinotepa Nacional commonly wear the *enredo,* known locally as the *pozahuanco* (poh-sah-oo-AHN-koh) below the waist, and when at home, go bare-breasted. When wearing their *pozahuancos* in public, they usually tie a *mandil,* a wide calico apron, around their front side. Women weave the best *pozahuancos* using cotton thread dyed a light purple with secretions of tidepool-harvested snails, *Purpura patula pansa,* and silk dyed deep red with cochineal, extracted from the dried bodies of a locally cultivated scale insect, *Dactylopius coccus.* On a typical day, two or three women will be selling handmade *pozahuancos* at the Pinotepa Nacional market. (For details, see The Costa Chica chapter.)

Colonial-era Spanish styles have blended with native *traje,* producing a wider class of dress, known generally as ***ropa típica.*** Lovely embroidered blouses *(blusas),* shawls *(rebozos),* and dresses *(vestidos)* fill boutique racks and market stalls all over the Acapulco region. Among the most popular is the so-called Oaxaca wedding dress, made of cotton with a crochet-trimmed riot of diminutive flowers hand-stitched about the neck and yoke. Some of the finest examples are made in San Antonino Castillo, just north of Ocotlán in the Valley of Oaxaca.

In contrast to women, only a small fraction of Mexican men—members of remote groups, such as Amusgos in Xochistlahuaca, Guerrero (see the Costa Chica chapter), Huichol, Cora, and Tarahumara in northwest Mexico, and Maya and Lacandón in the southeast—wear *traje.* Nevertheless, shops offer some fine men's *ropa típica,* such as wool jackets and serapes for northern or highland winter wear, and *guayaberas,* hip-length, pleated tropical dress shirts.

Fine embroidery *(bordado)* embellishes much traditional Mexican clothing, tablecloths *(manteles),* and napkins *(servilletas).* As everywhere, women define the art of embroidery. Although some still work by hand at home, cheaper machine-made factory lace and needlework is more commonly available in shops.

LEATHER

Acapulco region shops offer an abundance of leather goods, which, if not manufactured locally, are shipped from the renowned leather centers. These include Guadalajara, Mazatlán, and Oaxaca (sandals and huaraches), and León (shoes, boots, and saddles). For unique and custom-designed articles you'll probably have to confine your shopping to the expensive tourist resort shops. For the more usual though still attractive leather items such as purses, wallets, belts, coats, and boots, veteran shoppers go to local city markets.

FURNITURE

Although furniture is usually too bulky to carry back home with your airline luggage, low Mexican prices allow you to ship your purchases home and enjoy beautiful, unusual pieces for a fraction of what you would pay—if you could find them—at home.

A number of classes of furniture (*muebles,* moo-AY-blays) are crafted in villages near the sources of raw materials—either wood, leather, reeds, bamboo, or wrought iron.

Sometimes it seems as if every house in Mexico is furnished with wood **colonial-style furniture.** The basic design of much of it dates at least back to the Middle Ages. Although variations exist, most colonial-style furniture is heavily built. Table and chair legs are massive, often lathe-turned; chair backs are usually straight and vertical. Although usually varnished, colonial-style tables, chairs, and chests sometimes shine with inlaid wood or tile, or animal and flower designs. Family shops turn out good furniture, usually in the highlands, where suitable wood is available. Products from shops in Guadalajara's Tonalá and Tlaquepaque villages, Lake Pátzcuaro (especially Tzintzuntzan), and Taxco and Olinalá in the Acapulco region, are among the best known.

A second, very distinctive class of Mexican furniture is ***equipal,*** usually roundish tables, chairs, and sofas, made of brown pigskin or cowhide stretched over wooden frames. Factories are mostly in Guadalajara and nearby Tlaquepaque and Tonalá villages.

It is intriguing that **lacquered furniture,** in both process and design, has much in common with lacquerware produced half a world away in China. Moreover, Mexican lacquerware tradition both predated the conquest and was originally practiced only on the Pacific, where legends persist of preconquest contact with Chinese traders. Consequently, a number of experts believe that the Mexicans learned the craft of lacquerware from Chinese artists, centuries before Columbus.

Today, artisan families in and around Pátzcuaro, Michoacán, and Olinalá, Guerrero (see the Guerrero Upcountry chapter), carry on the tradition. The process, which at its finest resembles cloisonné manufacture, involves carving and painting intricate floral and animal designs, followed by repeated layerings of lacquer, clay, and sometimes gold and silver to produce satiny, jewel-like surfaces.

A few villages produce furniture made of plant fiber, such as reeds, raffia, and bamboo. In some cases, entire communities, such as Ihuatzio (near Pátzcuaro), and Villa Victoria (in Mexico state, west of Toluca), have long harvested the bounty of local lakes and marshes as the basis for their products.

Wrought iron, produced and worked according to Spanish tradition, is used to produce tables, chairs, and benches. Ruggedly fashioned in a riot of baroque scrollwork, pieces often decorate garden, patio, and park settings. Many colonial cities, notably San Miguel de Allende, Toluca, Guanajuato, Guadalajara, and Oaxaca are wrought-iron manufacturing centers.

GLASS AND STONEWORK

Glass manufacture, unknown in pre-Columbian times, was introduced by the Spanish. Today, factories scattered all over the country turn out mountains of *burbuja* (boor-BOO-hah) bubbled glass tumblers, goblets, plates, and pitchers, usually in blue, green, or red. Finer glass is manufactured in Guadalajara; especially suburban Tlaquepaque and Tonalá villages, you can watch artisans blow glass into a number of shapes, notably, paper-thin balls in red, green, or blue.

Artisans work stone, usually near sources of supply. Puebla, Mexico's main source of onyx (*onix,* OH-neeks), is the manufacturing center for the galaxy of mostly rough-hewn, cream-colored items, from animal charms and chess pieces to beads and desk sets, that crowd curio shop shelves throughout the country. *Cantera,* a volcanic tufa stone occurring in pastel shades from pink to green, is used similarly.

For a keepsake from a truly ancient Mexican tradition, don't forget the hollowed-out stone metate (may-TAH-tay), a corn-grinding basin, and the three-legged *molcajete* (mohl-kah-HAY-tay), a mortar for grinding *chiles.*

HUICHOL ART

Growing demand, especially around Guadalajara and Puerto Vallarta, has greatly stimulated the supply of Huichol art. Originally produced by shamans for ritual purposes, pieces such as beaded masks, *cuadras* (rectangular yarn paintings), gourd rattles, arrows, and yarn *cicuri* (God's eyes) have a ritual symbolism. Eerie beaded masks of wood often represent the Huichols' earth mother, Tatei Urianaka. The larger *cuadras,* of colored acrylic yarn painstakingly glued in intermeshing patterns to a plywood base, customarily depict the drama of life being played out between the main actors of the Huichol pantheon. For example, as Tayau (Father Sun) radiates over the land, alive with stylized cactus, flowers, peyote buds, snakes, and birds, antlered "Brother Deer" Kauyumari heroically battles the evil sorcerer Kieri, while nearby, Tatei Urianaka gives birth.

JEWELRY

Gold and silver were once the basis for Mexico's wealth. Her Spanish conquerors plundered a mountain of gold—religious offerings, necklaces, pendants, rings, bracelets—masterfully crafted by a legion of native metalsmiths and jewelers. Unfortunately, much of that indigenous tradition was lost because the Spanish denied access to precious metals to the Mexicans for generations while they introduced Spanish methods. Nevertheless, a small goldworking tradition survived the dislocations of the 1810–1821 War of Independence and the 1910–1917 revolution. Silvercrafting, moribund during the 1800s, was revived in the Acapulco region in Taxco, principally through the joint efforts of architect-artist William Spratling and the local community.

Today, spurred by the tourist boom, jewelry-making is thriving in Mexico. Taxco, where a swarm of local families, guilds, and cooperatives produce sparkling silver and gold adornments, is the acknowledged center. Scores of Taxco shops display the results—shimmering ornamental butterflies, birds, jaguars, serpents, turtles, and fish from ancient native tradition. Pieces, mostly in silver, vary from humble but attractive trinkets to glittering necklaces, silver candelabras, and place settings for a dozen, sometimes embellished with precious stones.

WOODCARVING AND MUSICAL INSTRUMENTS

Masks

Spanish and Native Mexican traditions have blended to produce a multitude of masks—some strange, some lovely, some scary, some endearing, all interesting. The tradition flourishes in the strongly indigenous southern Pacific states of Michoacán, Guerrero (especially in Chilapa and Olinalá), Oaxaca, and Chiapas, where campesinos gear up all year for the village festivals—especially Semana Santa (Easter week), early December (Virgin of Guadalupe), and the festival of the local patron, whether it be San José, San Pedro, San Pablo, Santa María, Santa Barbara, or one of a host of others. Every local fair has its favored dances, such as the Dance of the Conquest, the Christians and Moors, the Old Men, or the Jaguar, in which masked villagers act out age-old allegories of fidelity, sacri-

In ancient times, ceremonial jaguar masks were believed to imbue the wearer with mystical powers of the jaguar god.

fice, faith, struggle, sin, and redemption. (For a singularly fascinating display of Acapulco region masks, be sure to visit the House of Masks—Casa de la Máscara—in Acapulco.)

Although masks are made of many materials—from stone and ebony to coconut husks and paper—wood, where available, is the medium of choice. For the entire year, village master carvers cut, shave, sand, and paint to ensure that each participant will be properly disguised for the festival.

The popularity of masks has led to an entire made-for-tourist mask industry of mass-produced duplicates, many cleverly antiqued. Examine the goods carefully; if the price is high, don't buy unless you're convinced it's a real antique.

Alebrijes

Tourist demand has made zany wooden animals *(alebrijes)* a Oaxaca growth industry. Virtually every family in certain Valley of Oaxaca villages—notably Arrazola and San Martin Tilcajete—runs a factory studio. There, piles of *copal* wood, which men carve and women finish and intricately paint, become whimsical giraffes, dogs, cats, iguanas, gargoyles, dragons, and most of the possible permutations in between. The farther from the source you get, the higher the *alebrije* price becomes; in Arrazola, what costs $5 will probably run about $10 in the Acapulco region and $30 in the United States or Canada.

Others commonly available are the charming colorfully painted wooden fish carved mainly in Guerrero, and the burnished, dark hardwood animal and fish sculptures of desert ironwood from the state of Sonora.

Musical Instruments

The great majority of Mexico's guitars and other stringed instruments are made in Paracho in neighboring Michoacán. There, scores of cottage factories turn out guitars, violins, mandolins, *viruelas,* ukuleles, and a dozen more variations every day. They vary widely in quality, so look carefully before you buy. Make sure that the wood is well cured and dry; damp, unripe wood instruments are more susceptible to warping and cracking.

METALWORK

Bright copper, brass, and tinware, sturdy ironwork, and razor-sharp knives and machetes are made in a number of regional centers. Copperware, from jugs, cups, and plates to candlesticks—and even the town lampposts and bandstand—all comes from Santa Clara del Cobre, a few miles south of Pátzcuaro, Michoacán.

Although not the source of brass itself, Tonalá, in the Guadalajara eastern suburb, is the place where brass is most abundant and beautiful, appearing as menageries of brilliant, fetching birds and animals, sometimes embellished with shiny nickel highlights.

A number of Oaxaca family factories turn out fine cutlery—swords, knives, machetes—scrolled cast-iron grillwork, and a swarm of bright tinware or *(hojalata)* mirror frames, masks, and glittering Christmas decorations.

Be sure not to miss the miniature *milagros,* one of Mexico's most charming forms of metalwork. Usually of brass, they are of homely shapes—a horse, dog, or baby, or an arm, head, or foot—which, accompanied by a prayer, the faithful pin to the garment of their favorite saint whom they hope will intercede to cure an ailment or fulfill a wish.

PAPER AND PAPIER-MÂCHÉ

Papier-mâché has become a high art in Tonalá, Jalisco, where a swarm of birds, cats, frogs, giraffes, and other animal figurines are meticulously crafted by building up repeated layers of glued paper. The result—sanded, brilliantly varnished, and polished—resembles fine sculpture rather than the humble newspaper from which it was fashioned.

Other paper goods you shouldn't overlook include piñatas (durable, inexpensive, and as Mexican as you can get), available in every town market; colorful decorative cutout-banners (string overhead at your home fiesta) from San Salvador Huixcolotla, Puebla; and *amate,* wild fig tree bark paintings in animal and flower motifs, from Xalitla and Ameyaltepec, Guerrero.

POTTERY AND CERAMICS

Although Mexican pottery tradition is as diverse as the country itself, some varieties stand out. Among the most prized is the so-called Talavera (or Majolica), the best of which is made by a few family-run shops in Puebla. The labels Talavera and Majolica derive from Talavera, the Spanish town from which the tradition migrated to Mexico; before that it originated on the Spanish Mediterranean island of Mayorca (thus Majolica), from a combination of still older Arabic, Chinese, and African ceramic styles. Shapes include plates, bowls, jugs, and pitchers, hand-painted and hard-fired in intricate bright yellow, orange, blue, and green floral designs. So few shops make true Talavera these days that other, cheaper, look-alike grades, made around Guanajuato, are more common, selling for as little as one-tenth of the price of the genuine article.

More practical and nearly as prized is the hand-painted, high-fired stoneware from Tonalá in Guadalajara's eastern suburbs. Although made in many shapes and sizes, such stoneware is often sold as complete dinner place settings. Decorations are usually in abstract floral and animal designs, hand-painted over a reddish clay base.

From the same tradition come the famous *bruñido* pottery animals of Tonalá. Round, smooth, and cuddly as ceramic can be, the Tonalá animals—very commonly doves and ducks, but also cats and dogs and sometimes even armadillos, frogs, and snakes—each seems to embody the essence of its species.

Some of the most charming Mexican pottery, made from a ruddy low-fired clay and crafted following pre-Columbian traditions, comes from western Mexico, especially Colima. Charming figurines in timeless human poses—flute-playing musicians, dozing grandmothers, fidgeting babies, loving couples—and animals, especially Colima's famous playful dogs, decorate the shelves of a sprinkling of shops.

The Acapulco region also sustains a vibrant pottery tradition. In crafts shops everywhere you'll find the humble but very attractive unglazed brightly painted animals—cats, ducks, fish, and many others—that folks bring to resort centers from their village family workshops.

Much more acclaimed are certain types of pottery from the valley surrounding the city of Oaxaca. The village of Atzompa is famous for its tan, green-glazed clay pots, dishes, and bowls. Nearby San Bártolo Coyotepec village

Uncomplicated and low tech is still the rule for ceramic creations in the Acapulco region.

has acquired equal renown for its black pottery, sold all over the world. Doña Rosa, now deceased, pioneered the crafting of big round pots without using a potter's wheel. Now made in many more shapes by Doña Rosa's descendants, the pottery's exquisite silvery black sheen is produced by the reduction (reduced air) method of firing, which removes oxygen from the clay's red (ferric) iron oxide, converting it to black ferrous oxide.

Although most latter-day Mexican potters have become aware of the health dangers of lead pigments, some for-sale pottery may still contain lead. The hazard comes from low-fired pottery in which the lead has not been firmly melted into the glaze. Acids in foods such as lemons, vinegar, and tomatoes dissolve the lead pigments, which, when ingested, eventually result in lead poisoning. In general, the hardest, shiniest pottery, which has been twice fired—such as the high-quality Tonalá stoneware used for dishes—is the safest.

WOOLEN WOVEN GOODS

Mexico's finest wool weavings come from Teotitlán del Valle, in the Valley of Oaxaca, less than an hour's drive east of Oaxaca city. The weaving tradition, carried on by Teotitlán's Zapotec-speaking families, dates back at least 2,000 years. Many families still carry on the arduous process, making everything from scratch. They gather the dyes from wild plants and the bodies of insects and sea snails. They hand-wash, card, spin, and dye the wool and even travel to remote mountain springs to gather water. The results, they say, *vale la pena* (are worth the pain): intensely colored, tightly woven carpets, rugs, and wall hangings that retain their brilliance for generations.

Rougher, more loosely woven blankets, jackets, and serapes come from other parts, notably mountain regions, especially around San Cristóbal Las Casas, in Chiapas, and Lake Pátzcuaro in Michoacán.

Accommodations

The Acapulco region has many hundreds of lodgings to suit every style and pocketbook: world-class resorts, small beachside hotels, homey *casas de huéspedes* (guesthouses), palm-shaded trailer parks, and many dozens of miles of pristine beaches, ripe for camping.

HIGH AND LOW SEASONS

Acapulco region high seasons depend on whether the visitors are international or domestic: international visitors, mostly from the United States, Canada, and Europe begin arriving in droves around December 20 and remain in significant numbers through Easter. Mexican vacationers, on the other hand, concentrate in the resorts during holidays, especially Christmas-New Year and Semana Santa (pre-Easter week), and weekends, especially during *puentes* (long weekends) around national holidays, and July and August.

As for resort preferences, the new-town district of Acapulco is most popular with international visitors; the old town with Mexicans. Ixtapa and Zihuatanejo are mostly popular with international visitors, less so with Mexicans. Taxco, on the other hand, is mostly popular with Mexicans, especially during holidays and weekends.

So, make sure you arrive with reservations in Ixtapa-Zihuatanejo and Acapulco during the winter-spring season and Taxco during Christmas-New Year, pre-Easter week, weekends, and July and August. (For more details, see the sidebar "When to Go to Acapulco.")

PICKING A HOTEL

The hundreds of accommodations described in this book are positive recommendations—checked out in detail—good choices, from which you can pick according to your taste and purse.

Hotel Rates

The rates listed in the destination chapters are U.S. dollar equivalents of peso prices, taxes included, as quoted by the hotel management at the time of writing. Where many hotels are available—Acapulco, Ixtapa-Zihuatanejo, and Taxco—hotels are listed in ascending order of high-season, double-occupancy rate. Both low- and high-season rates are quoted whenever possible and are intended as a general guide only. Since rates fluctuate sharply according to local demand, quoted figures will probably only approximate the asking rate when you arrive. (Some readers, unfortunately, try to bargain by telling desk clerks that, for example, the rate should be $30 because they read it in this book. This is unwise, because it makes hotel managers and clerks reluctant to quote rates for fear readers might hold their hotels responsible for such quotes years later.)

In the Acapulco region, hotel rates depend strongly upon inflation and season. To cancel the effect of relatively steep Mexican inflation, rates are reported in U.S. dollars. However, when settling your hotel bill, *you should always pay in pesos.*

Saving Money

The hotel prices quoted in this book are rack rates, the maximum tariff, exclusive of packages and promotions, that you would pay if you walked in and rented an unreserved room for one day. Savvy travelers seldom pay the maximum. Always inquire if there are any discounts or packages (*descuentos o paquetes,* des-koo-AYN-tohs OH pah-KAY-tays). At most times other than the super-high Christmas to New Year and Easter weeks, you can get at least one or two free days for a one-week stay. Promotional packages available during slack seasons may include free extras such as breakfast, a car rental, a boat tour, or a sports rental. A travel agent or travel website can be of great help in shopping around for such bargains.

You nearly always save additional money if you deal in pesos only. Insist on both booking your lodging for an agreed price in pesos and paying the resulting hotel bill in the same pesos, rather than dollars. The reason is that dollar rates quoted by hotels are often based on the hotel desk exchange rate, which is customarily about 5 percent, or even as much 15 percent, less than bank rates. For example, if the clerk tells you your hotel bill is $1,000, instead of handing over the dollars, or having him mark $1,000 on your credit card slip, ask him how much it is in pesos. Using the desk conversion rate, he might say something like 10,000 pesos (considerably less than the 11,000 pesos that the bank might give for your $1,000). Pay the 10,000 pesos in cash or make sure the clerk marks 10,000 pesos on your credit card slip, and save yourself $100.

For stays of more than two weeks, you'll most likely save money and add comfort with an apartment or condominium rental. Monthly rates range $500–1,500 (less than half the comparable hotel per diem rate) for comfortable one-bedroom furnished kitchenette units, often including resort amenities such as pool and sundeck, beach club, and private view balcony. (See the Acapulco and Ixtapa-Zihuatanejo destination chapters and Internet Resources for apartment and condominium rental details.)

Airlines regularly offer air/hotel packages, which, by combining your hotel and air fees, may save you lots of pesos. Accommodations are usually, but not exclusively, in luxury resorts. See a travel website, a travel agent, or contact the airlines directly. (See the sidebar "Airlines to the Acapulco Region" for airline phone numbers and websites; see Internet Resources for travel websites.)

GUESTHOUSES AND LOCAL HOTELS

As did most of the celebrated Mexican Pacific coast resorts, both Acapulco and Zihuatanejo began with an old town, which expanded to a new *zona hotelera* (hotel strip) where big hostelries rise along a golden strand. In the old town, near the piquant smells, sights, and sounds of traditional Mexico, are the *casas de huéspedes* and smaller local hotels where rooms are often arranged around a plant-decorated patio.

Such lodgings vary from scruffy to spic-and-span, and humble to semideluxe. At minimum, you can expect a plain room, a shared toilet and hot-water shower, and plenty of atmosphere for your money. High-season rates, depending on the resort, run between about $15 and $40 for two, depending upon amenities. Discounts are often available for long-term stays. *Casas de hués-*

pedes will rarely be near the beach, unlike many of the medium-to-high-end local hotels.

Medium-to-High-End Local Hotels

Locally owned and operated hotels make up most of the recommendations of this book. Many veteran travelers find it hard to understand why people come to Mexico and spend $200–400 a day for a hotel room when good alternatives run between $40 and $100, high season, depending upon the resort.

Many locally run hostelries are right on the beach, sharing the same velvety sand and golden sunsets as their much more expensive international-class neighbors. Local hotels, which depend as much on Mexican tourists as foreigners, generally have clean, large rooms, often with private view balconies, ceiling fans, and toilet and hot-water bath or shower. What they often lack are the plush extras—air-conditioning, cable TV, phones, tennis courts, exercise gyms, and golf courses—of the luxury resort hotels.

Booking these hotels is straightforward. All can be dialed direct (from the United States, dial 011-52, then the local area code and number) for information and reservations; like the big resorts, many have websites, are contactable by email, and some even have U.S. and Canada toll-free 800 information numbers. Always ask about money-saving packages *(paquetes)* and promotions *(promociones)* when reserving.

INTERNATIONAL-CLASS RESORTS

The Acapulco region has many beautiful, well-managed international-class resort hotels. They spread along the pearly strands of Acapulco Bay, Zihuatanejo, and Ixtapa. Their super-deluxe amenities, moreover, need not be overly expensive. During the right time of year you can vacation at many of the big-name spots, such as Barceló (formerly Sheraton), Fairmont, Melia, Las Brisas, Hyatt, Fiesta Americana, NH Krystal, Best Western—for surprisingly little. While high-season room tariffs ordinarily run $150–350, low-season (May–Nov., and to a lesser degree, Jan.–Feb.) packages and promotions can cut these prices to as low as $100. Shop around for savings via your Sunday newspaper travel section, travel agents,

Many comfortable, medium-priced resort hotels, such as the Hotel Bali Hai (shown), accommodate Acapulco visitors.

RESORT TOLL-FREE NUMBERS AND WEBSITES

These luxury resorts have branches (** = outstanding, * = recommended) at Acapulco (AC) and Ixtapa-Zihuatanejo (IX).

Barceló, formerly Sheraton (IX*); tel. 800/346-5454, www.barcelo.com or www.mexico-travelnet.com
Best Western (IX**); tel. 800/528-1234, www.bestwestern.com
Camino Real (AC); tel. 800/7CAMINO (800/722-6466), www.caminoreal.com
Club Med (IX**); tel. 800/CLUBMED (800/258-2633), www.clubmed.com
Fairmont Acapulco Princess (AC**); tel. 800/866-5577 or 800/257-7544, www.fairmont.com
Fiesta Americana (AC**); tel. 800/FIESTA1 (800/343-7821), www.fiestaamericana.com.mx
Holiday Inn (IX, AC); tel. 800/HOLIDAY (800/465-4329), www.sixc.com
Hyatt (AC**); tel. 800/228-9000, www.hyatt.com
La Casa Que Canta (IX**); tel. 888/523-5050, www.lacasaquecanta.com
Las Brisas Hotels (IX**, AC); tel. 888/559-4329, www.lasbrisas.com
Melia (IX); tel. 800/336-3542, www.solmelia.com
Mexico Boutique Hotels, Villa del Sol (IX**) and Villa Vera (AC**); U.S. tel. 877/278-8018, Can. tel. 866/818-8342, www.mexicoboutiquehotels.com
NH Krystal (IX**); tel. 800/231-9860, www.nh-hoteles.com
Qualton Club (IX, AC); tel. 866/297-0100, www.qualton.com
Vidafel, Mayan Palace (AC**); tel. 800/843-2335, www.mayan-palace.com.mx

and by contacting the hotels directly through their toll-free 800 numbers or websites.

APARTMENTS, BUNGALOWS, CONDOMINIUMS, AND VILLAS

For longer stays, many visitors prefer the convenience and economy of an apartment or condominium or the luxurious comfort of a villa vacation rental. Choices vary, from spartan studios to deluxe beachfront suites and rambling, view homes big enough for entire extended families. Prices depend strongly upon season and amenities, from $500 per month for the cheapest to at least 10 times that for the most luxurious.

A Mexican variation on the apartment style of accommodation is called a bungalow, although, in contrast to English-language usage, it does not usually imply a detached dwelling. Common in Zihuatanejo, a bungalow accommodation generally means a motel-type kitchenette-suite with less service, but with more space and beds. For families or for long stays by the beach, where you want to save money by cooking your own meals, such an accommodation might be ideal.

At the low end, you can expect a clean, furnished apartment within a block or two of the beach, with kitchen and regular maid service. More luxurious condos, very common in Acapulco and Ixtapa (which usually rent for $500 per week and up), are typically high-rise ocean-view suites with hotel-style desk services and resort amenities, such as a pool, whirlpool tub, sundeck, and beach-level restaurant.

Higher up the scale, villas and houses vary from moderately luxurious homes to sky's-the-limit beach-view mansions, blooming with built-in designer luxuries, private pools and beaches, tennis courts, and gardeners, cooks, and maids.

Shopping Around

You'll generally find the most economical apartment, condo, and house rental deals through on-the-spot local contacts, such as the tourist newspaper want ad section, neighborhood "for rent" signs, or local listing agents.

If you prefer making rental arrangements before arrival, you can usually write, fax, email, or telephone managers—many of whom speak English—directly, using the numbers given in the destination chapters of this book.

Many additional rentals are available through agents (see the Acapulco and Ixtapa-Zihuatanejo destination chapters) who will make long-distance rental agreements. Moreover, such rentals are becoming increasingly available through the Internet. (For many lodging rental sources, see the Internet Resources section and the Acapulco and Ixtapa-Zihuatanejo destination chapters.)

Yet another fertile vacation rental source is the Sunday travel section of a major metropolitan daily, such as the *Los Angeles Times* or the *San Francisco Chronicle,* which routinely list Acapulco region vacation rentals. Also, local real estate agents such as Century 21, which specializes in nationwide and foreign contacts, sometimes list (or know someone who does) Acapulco region vacation rentals.

Home Exchange and Renting Out Your Own House

You may also want to consider using the services of a home exchange agency/website whereby you swap homes with someone in the Acapulco region for an agreed-upon time. (At this writing, home-exchange websites and toll-free numbers—see Internet Resources—revealed few Acapulco region homeowners looking for a swap. You may try listing your home, however, and see if you get a bite.)

It may be easier to rent or lease your own house and use the income to rent a house or apartment in the Acapulco region. (Although some people find this strategy successful, talk to someone who's done it to find out if it's your cup of tea.)

CAMPING AND TRAILER PARKS

Beach Camping

Informal beach camping is popular among middle-class Mexican families, especially during the Christmas to New Year week and during Semana Santa, the week before Easter. The crowds even

Many local vacationers enjoy camping on the beach, right next to *palapa* restaurants.

overflow on to the resort beaches of Acapulco, Zihuatanejo Bay, and Ixtapa, where folks set up tents or simply sleep under the stars.

On nearly all other Acapulco region beaches plenty of camping space is always available. The good spots, such as Playa Ventura, Playa Las Peñitas, Playa Escondida, Playa El Carrizal, Playa Puerto Maldonado, and dozens more typically have a shady palm grove for camping and at least one *palapa* (palm-thatched) restaurant that serves drinks and fresh seafood. (Heads up for falling coconuts, especially in the wind.) Cost for parking and tenting is often minimal, typically only the price of food at the restaurant.

Days are often perfect for swimming, strolling, and fishing, and nights are balmy—too warm for a sleeping bag, but fine for a hammock (which allows the air circulation that a tent does not). However, good tents keep out mosquitoes and other pesties, which may be further discouraged by a good bug repellent. Tents can get hot, requiring only a sheet or very light blanket for sleeping cover.

As for camping on isolated beaches, opinions vary, from dire warnings of *bandidos* to bland assurances that all is peaceful along the coast. The truth is somewhere in between. Trouble is most likely to occur in the vicinity of towns, where a few local thugs sometimes harass isolated campers.

When scouting out an isolated beach for camping, a good rule is to arrive early enough in the day to get a feel for the place. Buy a soda at the *palapa* or store and take a stroll along the beach. Say *"Buenos días"* to the people along the way; ask if the fishing is good *("¿Pesca buena?")*. Above all, use your common sense and intuition. If the people seem friendly, ask if it's *seguro* (safe). If so, ask permission: *"¿Es bueno acampar acá?"* ("Is it okay to camp around here?"). You'll rarely be refused.

Camping Upcountry

Scenic river canyons provide some of the most inviting camping opportunities in the Acapulco region's vast upcountry hinterland. One of the best is at Campamento Santa Fe on the spring-fed Río Azul (Blue River) about 20 miles east of Chilpancingo. Other promising spots are on the Papagayo River on Highway 95, about 30 miles south of Chilpancingo, and the San Pedro River, near Xochistlahuaca. (For the Río Azul and Río Papagayo, see the Guerrero Upcountry chapter; for the Río San Pedro, see The Costa Chica chapter.)

You can enjoy one of the most informative and entertaining discussions of camping in Mexico in the *The People's Guide to Mexico.* (See Suggested Reading.)

Trailer Parks

Campers who prefer company to isolation usually stay in trailer parks. Trailer parks sprinkle the Acapulco region's beach resorts. Northwest to southeast, you'll find a total of five formal trailer parks: in Troncones, Zihuatanejo, and three in Pie de la Cuesta, just west of Acapulco. (See the Ixtapa-Zihuatanejo and Acapulco destination chapters for details.)

Food and Drink

Some travel to the Acapulco region for the food. True Mexican food is old-fashioned, home-style fare requiring many hours of loving preparation. Such food is short on meat and long on corn, beans, rice, tomatoes, onions, eggs, and cheese.

Mexican food is the unique product of thousands of years of native tradition. It is based on corn—*teocentli,* the Aztec "holy food"—called *maíz* (mah-EES) by present-day Mexicans. In the past, a Mexican woman spent much of her time grinding and preparing corn: soaking the grain in lime water, which swells the kernels and removes the tough seed-coat, and grinding the bloated seeds into meal on a stone metate. Finally, she patted the meal into tortillas and cooked them on a hot, baked mud griddle.

Sages (men, no doubt) wistfully imagined that gentle pat-pat-pat of women all over Mexico to be the heartbeat of Mexico, which they feared would cease when women stopped making tortillas.

Fewer women these days make tortillas by hand. The gentle pat-pat-pat has been replaced by the whir and rattle of the automatic tortilla-making machine in myriad *tortillerías,* where women and girls line up for their family's daily kilo-stack of tortillas.

Tortillas are to the Mexicans as rice is to the Chinese and bread to the French. Mexican food is invariably some mixture of sauce, meat, beans, cheese, and vegetables wrapped in a tortilla, which becomes the culinary be-all: the food, the dish, and the utensil wrapped into one.

If a Mexican man has nothing to wrap in his lunchtime tortilla, he will content himself by rolling a thin filling of salsa (*chile* sauce) in it.

Hot or Not?

Much food served in Mexico is not "Mexican." Eating habits, as most other customs, depend upon social class. Upwardly mobile Mexicans typically shun the corn-based *indígena* fare in favor of the European-style food of the Spanish colonial elite: chops, steaks, cutlets, fish, clams, omelettes, soups, pasta, rice, and potatoes.

Such fare is often as bland as Des Moines on a summer Sunday afternoon. *No picante*—not spicy—is how the Mexicans describe bland food. *Caliente,* the Spanish adjective for "hot" (as in hot water), does not, in contrast to English usage, imply spicy, or *picante.*

Vegetarian Food

Although the availability of healthy food is increasing, strictly vegetarian (vegan, VAY-gahn) cooking is the exception in Mexico, as are macrobiotic restaurants, health-food stores, and organic produce. Meat is such a delicacy for most Mexicans that they can't understand why people would give it up voluntarily. If, as a vegetable-lover, you can manage with corn, beans, cheese, eggs, *legumbres* (vegetables), and fruit, Mexican cooking will suit you fine.

Seafood

Early chroniclers wrote that Aztec Emperor Moctezuma employed a platoon of runners to bring fresh fish 300 miles every day from the sea to his court. In the Acapulco region, fresh seafood is fortunately much more available from many dozens of shoreline establishments, varying from thatched beach *palapas* to five-star hotel restaurants.

Despite the plenty, Acapulco region seafood prices reflect high worldwide demand, even at the humblest seaside *palapa.* The freshness and variety, however, make even the typical dishes seem bargains at any price.

CATCH OF THE DAY

Ceviche (say-VEE-chay): A chopped raw fish appetizer as popular on Acapulco region beaches as sushi is on Tokyo sidestreets. Although it can contain anything from conch to octopus, the best ceviche consists of diced young shark *(tiburón)* or mackerel *(sierra)* fillet and plenty of fresh tomatoes, onions, garlic, and *chiles,* all doused with lime juice.

Filete de pescado (fish fillet): Sautéed *al mojo* (ahl-MOH-hoh)—with butter and garlic.

Pescado frito (pays-KAH-doh FREE-toh): Fish, pan-fried whole; if you don't specify that it be cooked lightly *(a medio),* the fish may arrive well done, like a big, crunchy french fry.

Pescado veracruzana: A favorite everywhere. Best with red snapper *(huachinango),* smothered in a savory tomato, onion, *chile,* and garlic sauce. *Pargo* (snapper), *mero* (grouper), and *cabrilla* (sea bass) are also popularly used in this and other specialties.

Shellfish: These abound: *ostiones* (oysters) and *almejas* (clams) by the dozen; *langosta* (lobster) and *langostina* (crayfish) *asado* (broiled), *al vapor* (steamed), or fried. Pots of fresh-boiled *camarones* (shrimp) are sold on the street by the kilo; cafés will make them into *cóctel,* or prepare them *en gabardinas* (breaded) at your request.

Fruits and Juices

Squeezed vegetable and fruit juices (*jugos,* HOO-gohs) are among the widely available delights of the Acapulco region. Among the

MEXICAN FOOD

On most Mexican-style menus, diners will find variations on a number of basic themes:

Carnes (meats): ***Carne asada*** is grilled beef, usually chewy and well-done. Something similar you might see on a menu is *cecina* (say-SEE-nah), dried salted beef, grilled to a shoe-leather-like consistency. Much more appetizing is ***birria,*** a Guadalajara specialty. Traditional *birrias* are of lamb or goat, often wrapped and pit-roasted in maguey leaves, with which it is served, for authenticity. In addition to *asada,* meat cooking styles are manifold, including *guisado* (stewed), *al pastor* (spit barbecue), and *barbacoa* (grill barbecued). Cuts include *lomo* (loin), *chuleta* (chop), *milanesa* (cutlet), and *albóndigas* (meatballs).

Chiles rellenos: Fresh roasted green chiles, usually stuffed with cheese but sometimes with fish or meat, coated with batter, and fried. They provide a piquant, tantalizing contrast to tortillas.

Enchiladas and **tostadas:** variations on the filled-tortilla theme. Enchiladas are stuffed with meat, cheese, olives, or beans and covered with sauce and baked, while tostadas consist of toppings served on crisp, open-faced tortillas.

Guacamole: This luscious avocado, onion, tomato, lime, and salsa mixture remains the delight it must have seemed to its Aztec inventors centuries ago. In nontourist Mexico, it's

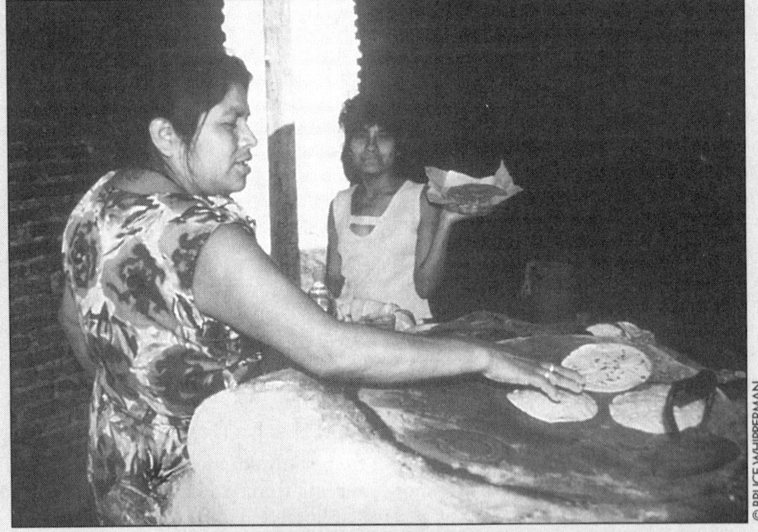

The foundation of Mexican food is corn, usually consumed via the tortilla, shown being grilled on a traditional mud-brick oven griddle.

served sparingly as a garnish, rather than in appetizer bowls as is common in the U.S. Southwest (and Mexican resorts catering to North Americans). (Similarly, in nontourist Mexico, burritos and fajitas, both stateside inventions, seldom if ever appear on menus.)

Moles (MOH-lays): uniquely Mexican specialties. *Mole poblano,* a spicy-sweet mixture of chocolate, *chiles,* and a dozen other ingredients, is cooked to a smooth sauce, then baked with chicken (or turkey, a combination called *mole de pavo*). So *típica* it's widely regarded as the national dish.

Quesadillas: made from soft flour tortillas, rather than corn, quesadillas resemble tostadas and always contain melted cheese.

Sopas: Soups consist of vegetables in a savory chicken broth, and are an important part of both *comida* (afternoon) and *cena* (evening) Mexican meals. *Pozole,* a rich steaming stew of hominy, vegetables, and pork or chicken, often constitutes the prime evening offering of small side street shops. *Sopa de taco,* an ever-popular country favorite, is a medium-spicy cheese-topped thick *chile* broth served with crisp corn tortillas.

Tacos or **taquitos:** tortillas served open or wrapped around any ingredient.

Tamales: as Mexican as apple pie is American. This savory mixture of meat and sauce imbedded in a shell of corn dough and baked in a wrapping of corn husks is rarely known by the singular, however. They're so yummy that one tamale invariably leads to more tamales.

Tortas: the Mexican sandwich, usually hot meat with fresh tomato and avocado, stuffed between two halves of a crisp *bolillo* (boh-LEE-yoh) or Mexican bun.

Tortillas y frijoles refritos: cooked brown or black beans, mashed and fried in pork fat, and rolled into tortillas with a dash of vitamin-C-rich salsa to form a near-complete combination of carbohydrate, fat, and balanced protein.

Beyond the Basics

Mexican food combinations seem endless. Mexican corn itself has more than 500 recognized culinary variations, all from indigenous tradition. This has led to a myriad of permutations on the taco, such as *sopes* (with small and thick tortillas), *garnacho* (flat taco), *chilaquile* (shredded taco), and *chalupa* (like a tostada).

Taking a lesson from California nouveau cuisine, avante-garde Mexican chefs are returning to traditional ingredients. They're beginning to use more and more *chiles*—habanero, poblano, jalapeño, and more—prepared with many variations, such as chipotle, ancho, *piquín,* and *mulato.* Squash flowers *(flor de calabaza)* and cactus (nopal) leaves are increasingly finding their way into soups and salads.

More often chefs are serving the wild game—*venado* (venison), *conejo* (rabbit), *guajalote* (turkey), *codorniz* (quail), *armadillo,* and *iguana*—that country Mexicans have always depended upon. As part of the same trend, *cuitlacoche* (corn mushroom fungus), *chapulines* (french-fried small grasshoppers), and *gusanos de maguey* (maguey worms) are being increasingly added as ingredients in fancy restaurants.

many establishments—restaurants, cafés, and *loncherías*—willing to supply you with your favorite *jugo,* the juice bars *(jugerías)* are often the most fun. Colorful fruit piles usually mark *jugerías.* If you don't immediately spot your favorite fruit, ask anyway; it might be hidden in the refrigerator.

Besides your choice of pure juice, a *jugería* will often serve *licuados.* Into the juice, they whip powdered milk, your favorite fruit, and sugar to taste for a creamy afternoon pick-me-up or evening dessert. One big favorite is a cool banana-chocolate *licuado,* which comes out tasting like a milk shake minus the calories.

Alcoholic Drinks

The Aztecs sacrificed anyone caught drinking alcohol without permission. The later, more lenient, Spanish attitude toward getting *borracho* (soused) has led to a thriving Mexican renaissance of native alcoholic beverages: tequila, mescal, Kahlúa, pulque, and *aguardiente.* Tequila and mescal, distilled from the fermented juice of the maguey, originated in Oaxaca, where the best are still made. Quality tequila (named after the Guadalajara-area distillery town) and mescal come 76 proof (38 percent alcohol) and up. A small white worm, endemic to the maguey, is customarily added to each bottle of factory mescal for authenticity.

Pulque, although also made from the sap of the maguey, is locally brewed to a modest alcohol content between that of beer and wine. The brewing houses are sacrosanct preserves, circumscribed by traditions that exclude women and outsiders. The brew, said to be rich in nu-

A TROVE OF FRUITS AND NUTS

Besides carrying the usual temperate fruits, *jugerías* and especially markets are seasonal sources of a number of exotic (followed by an *) varieties:

avocado (*aguacate*—ah-wah-KAH-tay): Aztec aphrodisiac

banana *(platano):* many kinds—big and small, red and yellow

chirimoya* *(chirimoya):* green scales, white pulp, sometimes called an *anona*

***ciruela**:** looks like (but tastes better than) a small yellow-to-red plum

coconut *(coco):* coconut "milk," called *agua coco,* is a wonderful and healthy thirst quencher

grapes *(uvas):* Aug.–Nov. season

***guanabana**:** looks, but doesn't taste, like a green mango

guava *(guava):* delicious juice, widely available canned

lemon (*limón*—lee-MOHN): uncommon and expensive; use lime instead

lime (*lima*—LEE-mah): sometimes called *limón verde;* douse salads with it

mamey* (*mamey*—mah-MAY): yellow, juicy fruit, excellent for jellies and preserves

mango *(mango):* king of fruit, in a 100 varieties June–November

orange (*naranja*—nah-RAHN-ha): greenish skin but sweet and juicy

papaya *(papaya):* said to aid digestion and healing

peach (*durazno*—doo-RAHS-noh): delicious and widely available as canned juice

peanut (*cacahuate*—kah-kah-WAH-tay): home roasted and cheap

pear *(pera):* fall season

pecan *(nuez):* for a treat, try freshly ground pecan butter

***piña anona**:** looks like a thin ear of corn without the husk; tastes like pineapple

pineapple *(piña):* huge, luscious, and cheap

strawberry (*fresa*—FRAY-sah): local favorite

tangerine *(mandarina):* common around Christmas

watermelon (*sandía*—sahn-DEE-ah): perfect on a hot day

zapote* (sah-POH-tay): yellow, fleshy fruit, said to induce sleep

***zapote colorado**:** brown skin, red, puckery fruit, like persimmon; commonly, but incorrectly, called *mamey*

trients, is sold to local *pulquerías* and drunk immediately. If you are ever invited into a *pulquería,* it is an honor you cannot refuse.

Aguardiente, by contrast, is the notorious fiery Mexican "white lightning," a locally distilled, dirt-cheap ticket to oblivion for poor Mexican men.

While pulque comes from age-old indigenous tradition, beer (introduced by 19th-century German brewers) is the beverage of modern mestizo Mexico. More full-bodied than "light" U.S. counterparts, Mexican beer enjoys an enviable reputation.

Those visitors who indulge usually know their favorite among the many brands, from light to dark: Superior, Corona, Pacífico, Tecate (served with lime), Carta Blanca, Modelo, Dos Equis, Bohemia, Tres Equis, and Negro Modelo. Nochebuena, a hearty dark brew, becomes available only around Christmas.

Mexicans have yet to develop much of a taste for *vino tinto* or *vino blanco* (red or white table wine), although some domestic wines (such as the Baja California labels Cetto and Domecq and the boutique Monte Xanic) are at least very drinkable and at best, excellent.

Bread and Pastries

Excellent locally baked bread is a delightful surprise to many first-time visitors to the Acapulco region. Small bakeries everywhere put out trays of hot, crispy-crusted *bolillos* (rolls) and sweet *panes dulces* (pastries). The pastries vary from simple cakes, muffins, cookies, and doughnuts to fancy fruit-filled turnovers and puffs. Half the fun occurs before the eating: grab a tray and tongs, peruse the goodies, and pick out the most scrumptious. With your favorite dozen or so finally selected, you take your tray to the cashier, who deftly bags everything up and collects a few pesos (two or three dollars) for your entire mouthwatering selection.

Shopping

What to Buy

Although bargains abound in Mexico, savvy shoppers are selective. Steep import and luxury taxes drive up the prices of foreign-made goods such as cameras, computers, sports equipment, and English-language books. Instead, concentrate your shopping on locally made items: leather, jewelry, cotton resort wear, Mexican-made designer clothes, and the galaxy of handicrafts for which Mexico is renowned.

Handicrafts

The upcountry towns of Chilapa, Olinalá, and Taxco are the Acapulco region's renowned sources of handicrafts. And, although most crafts are not made in the resorts of Acapulco and Ixtapa-Zihuatanejo, each has dozens of good private handicrafts stores and several crafts markets where local folks maintain stalls stuffed with their homemade crafts. Moreover, the rich cornucopia of crafts from other Mexican centers, such as Oaxaca, around Guadalajara, and the Lake Pátzcuaro region of Michoacán, spills over to the Acapulco region. (For many more details, see the destination chapters and the Arts and Crafts section in this chapter.)

Bargaining

Bargaining will stretch your money even further. It comes with the territory in Mexico and needn't be a hassle. On the contrary, if done with humor and moderation, bargaining can be an enjoyable way to meet Mexican people and gain their respect, even friendship.

The local crafts market is where bargaining is most intense. For starters, try offering half the asking price. From there on, it's all psychology: you have to content yourself with not having to have the item. Otherwise, you're sunk; the vendor will probably sense your need and stand fast. After a few minutes of good-humored bantering, ask for *el último precio* (the final price), in which, if it's close, you may have a bargain.

Buying Silver and Gold Jewelry

Silver and gold jewelry, the finest of which is crafted in Taxco, fills dozens of shops there and a number of shops in Acapulco and Ixtapa-Zihuatanejo.

Moreover, Iguala, half an hour's drive south of Taxco, is a center of gold jewelry.

One hundred percent pure silver is rarely sold because it's too soft. Silver (sent from processing mills in the north of Mexico to be worked in Taxco shops) is nearly always alloyed with 7.5 percent copper to increase its durability. Such pieces, identical in composition to sterling silver, should have ".925," together with the initials of the manufacturer, stamped on their back sides. Other, less common grades, such as "800 fine" (80 percent silver), should also be stamped.

If silver is not stamped with the degree of purity, it probably contains no silver at all and is an alloy of copper, zinc, and nickel, known by the generic label "alpaca," or "German" silver. Once, after haggling over the purity and prices of his offerings, a street vendor handed me a shiny handful and said, "Go to a jeweler and have them tested. If they're not real, keep them." Calling his bluff, I took them to a jeweler, who applied a dab of hydrochloric acid to each piece. Tiny, tell-tale bubbles of hydrogen revealed the cheapness of the merchandise, which I returned the next day to the vendor.

Some shops price sterling silver jewelry simply by weighing, which typically translates to about $1 per gram. If you want to find out if the price is fair, ask the shopkeeper to weigh it for you.

Iguala, an hour's drive south of Taxco, is a center of gold jewelry. People prize pure gold, partly because, unlike silver, it does not tarnish. Gold, nevertheless, is rarely sold pure (24 karat); for durability, it is alloyed with copper. Typical purities, such as 18 karat (75 percent) or 14 karat (58 percent), should be stamped on the pieces. If not, chances are they contain no gold at all.

Getting There

BY AIR

From the United States and Canada

The vast majority of travelers reach the Acapulco region by air. Flights are frequent and reasonably priced. Competition sometimes shaves prices down as low as $300 for an Acapulco or Ixtapa-Zihuatanejo round-trip.

Air travelers can save lots of money by shopping around. Don't be bashful about asking for the cheapest price. Make it clear to the airline or travel agent you're interested in a bargain. Ask the right questions: are there special-incentive, advance-payment, night, midweek, tour package, or charter fares? Peruse the ads in the Sunday newspaper travel section for bargain-oriented travel agencies. Check airline and travel websites, such as www.orbitz.com, www.expedia.com, and www.travelocity.com.

Although some agents charge booking fees and don't like discounted tickets because their fee depends on a percentage of ticket price, many will nevertheless work hard to get you a bargain, especially if you book an entire air-hotel package with them.

Although few airlines fly directly to the Acapulco region from the northern United States and Canada, many charters do. In locales near Vancouver, Calgary, Ottawa, Toronto, Montreal, Minneapolis, Chicago, Detroit, Cleveland, and New York, consult a travel agent or website for charter flight options. Be aware that charter reservations, which often require fixed departure and return dates and provide minimal cancellation refunds, decrease your flexibility. If available charter choices are unsatisfactory, then you might choose to begin your vacation with a connecting flight to one of the Acapulco region gateways, such as Seattle, San Francisco, Los Angeles, Phoenix, Dallas, Houston, or Chicago.

You may be able to save money by booking an air/hotel package through one of the airlines that routinely offer them from their Acapulco region gateway cities:

Mexicana: tel. 866/263-9732
Alaska: tel. 800/468-2248
America West: tel. 800/356-6611
American: tel. 800/321-2121
Aeroméxico: tel. 800/245-8585
Continental: tel. 800/634-5555
World of Vacations (Canada charter): tel. 800/661-8881
Delta: tel. 800/872-7786

From Europe, Latin America, and Australasia

A few airlines fly across the Atlantic directly to Mexico City. These include **Lufthansa,** which connects directly from Frankfurt, and **Aeroméxico,** which connects directly from Paris and Madrid. In Mexico City, several connections with the Acapulco region are available, mostly via Mexicana and Aeroméxico airlines.

From Latin America, **Aeroméxico** connects directly with Mexico City, from Sao Paulo, Brazil; Santiago, Chile; and Lima, Peru. A number of other Latin American flag carriers also fly directly to Mexico City.

Very few flights cross the Pacific directly to Mexico, except for **Japan Airlines,** which connects Tokyo to Mexico City, via Vancouver. More commonly, travelers from Australasia routinely transfer at Seattle, San Francisco, Los Angeles, or Phoenix, for the Acapulco region.

Baggage, Insurance, "Bumping," and In-Flight Meals

The tropical Acapulco region makes it easy to pack light. (See the "Packing Checklist.") Use it at the last minute to make certain that you're not leaving something important behind. Veteran tropical travelers condense their luggage to carry-ons only. Airlines routinely allow one carry-on (not exceeding 45 inches in combined length, width, and girth), a small book bag, and a purse. Thus relieved of heavy burdens, your trip will become much simpler.

Even if you can't avoid checking luggage, loss of it needn't ruin your vacation. *Always carry your irreplaceable items in the cabin with you.* These should include all money, credit cards, traveler's checks, keys, tickets, cameras, passport, prescription drugs, and eyeglasses.

At the X-ray security check, insist that your film and cameras be hand-inspected. Regardless of what attendants claim, repeated X-ray scanning will fog any undeveloped film, especially the sensitive ASA 400, 800, and 1600 high-speed varieties.

Travelers packing lots of expensive baggage, or who (because of illness, for example) may have to cancel a nonrefundable flight or tour, might consider buying travel insurance. Travel agents routinely sell packages that include baggage, trip cancellation, and default insurance. Baggage insurance covers you beyond the (typically $1,000 domestic, $500 international, check with your carrier) liability limits.

Trip cancellation insurance pays if you must cancel your prepaid trip, while default insurance protects you if your carrier or tour agent does not perform as agreed. Travel insurance, however, can be expensive. Traveler's Insurance Company, for example, offers $1,000 of baggage insurance per person for two weeks for about $50. (For more information, see the travel websites in the Internet Resources section or call a travel agent.) Weigh your options and the cost against benefits carefully before putting your money down.

It's wise to reconfirm both departure and return flight reservations, especially during the busy Christmas and Easter seasons. This is a useful strategy, as is prompt arrival at check-in, against getting "bumped" (losing your seat) by the tendency of airlines to overbook the rush of high-season vacationers. For further protection, always try to get your seat assignment and boarding pass included with your ticket.

Airlines generally try hard to accommodate travelers with dietary or other special needs. When booking your flight, inform your travel agent or carrier of the necessity of a low-sodium, low-cholesterol, vegetarian, or lactose-reduced meal, or other requirements. (Seniors, travelers with disabilities, and parents traveling with children, see Specialty Travel.)

BY BUS

As air travel rules in the United States, bus travel rules in Mexico. Hundreds of gleaming luxury- and first-class buses with names such as Elite, Turistar, Futura, Omnibus de Mexico, Primera Plus, Transportes Pacífico, and White Star (Estrella Blanca) depart the border daily, headed for Acapulco region.

Since North American bus lines ordinarily terminate just north of the Mexican border, you must usually disembark, walk to the Mexican

AIRLINES TO THE ACAPULCO REGION

A number of airlines offer direct flights to Acapulco (AC) or Ixtapa-Zihuatanejo (IX), or Mexico City (MX), where air or bus connections with Acapulco and Ixtapa-Zihuatanejo may be made. The airlines with the most flights, in approximate descending order of activity, are **Mexicana, Aeroméxico, American, Delta, Aviacsa, Continental, America West, Alaska,** and **Air Canada.** Others offering flights are Azteca, Aerocalifornia, Allegro, and Canadian World of Vacations charter. Some flights may be seasonal (usually winter-spring) only.

Airline	Origin	Destinations
Mexicana tel. 800/531-7921 www.mexicana.com	Los Angeles	MX
	San Francisco	MX
	Oakland	MX
	San Jose	MX
	Las Vegas	MX
	Portland	MX
	Tijuana	MX
	Denver	MX
	San Antonio	MX
	Chicago	AC, MX
	Newark	MX
	Miami	MX
	Toronto	MX
	Montreal	MX
	Vancouver	MX
Aeroméxico tel. 800/237-6639 www.aeromexico.com	Los Angeles	MX
	San Diego	MX
	Ontario	MX
	Tijuana	MX
	Phoenix	MX
	Houston	MX
	Dallas	MX
	Chicago	MX
	New York	MX
	Miami	MX
	Atlanta	MX
American tel. 800/433-7300 www.aa.com	Dallas	AC, MX
	Chicago	MX
	Miami	MX
Delta tel. 800/221-1212 www.delta.com	Los Angeles	MX
	Dallas	MX
	Atlanta	MX
	New York	MX

Airline	Origin	Destinations
Aviacsa tel. 800/758-2188 www.aviacsa.com.mx	Los Angeles	MX
	Las Vegas	MX
	Houston	MX
	Chicago	MX
Continental tel. 800/231-0856 www.continental.com	Houston	AC, IX, MX
	Newark	MX
America West tel. 800/363-2597 www.americawest.com	Phoenix	IX, AC, MX
Alaska Airlines tel. 800/426-0333 www.alaskaair.com	Seattle	IX
	San Francisco	IX
	Los Angeles.	IX
Air Canada tel. 888/247-2262 www.aircanada.com	Toronto	MX
	Montreal	MX
	Calgary	IX
Azteca agent tel. 305/223-9820 www.reservaciones.com/ airlines/azteca.shtml	Dallas	MX
	Laredo	MX
	El Paso	MX
Aerocalifornia tel. 800/237-6225 (no website)	Los Angeles	MX
	Tijuana	MX
Allegro tel. 877/443-7585 www.allegroair.net	Oakland	MX
	Las Vegas	MX
World of Vacations charter tel. 800/661-8881 www.worldofvacations.com	Toronto	AC, IX
	Vancouver	IX
	Calgary-Edmonton	IX

immigration *(migración)* office just across the border. After having completed the necessary but very simple paperwork, proceed to the nearby taxi stand *(sitio taxi)* and hire a taxi (agree upon the price before getting in) to take you the few miles to the *camionera central* (central bus station).

First- and luxury-class bus service in Mexico is much cheaper and more frequent than in the United States. Tickets for comparable trips in Mexico cost a fraction (as little as $50 for a 1,000-mile trip, compared to $150 in the United States).

Nevertheless, in Mexico, as on United States buses, you often have to take it as you find it. *Asientos reservados* (seat reservations), *boletos* (tickets), and information must generally be obtained in person at the bus station, and credit cards and traveler's checks are not often accepted. Neither are reserved bus tickets typically refundable, so don't miss the bus. On the other hand, plenty of buses roll south almost continually.

From California and the West

Cross the border to Tijuana, Mexicali, or Nogales, where you can ride one of several bus lines south along the Mexican Pacific coast route (National Highway 15): Estrella Blanca subsidiaries—first-class Elite (which connects the whole way to Ixtapa-Zihuatanejo and Acapulco), deluxe-class Turistar, second-class Transportes Norte de Sonora; or first-class independent Transportes del Pacífico.

At Mazatlán or Tepic, depending on the line, you transfer or continue on the same bus, west via Guadalajara, or south via Puerto Vallarta (the longer but more scenic option). If you choose Guadalajara, transfer there to the Estrella Blanca affiliate Acapulco-direct bus (Turistar at this writing) that bypasses Mexico City, via Toluca and Taxco to Acapulco, thence to Ixtapa-Zihuatanejo. If however, you choose to go via Puerto Vallarta, continue south through Manzanillo, along the gorgeously scenic Michoacán coast, to Ixtapa-Zihuatanejo and/or Acapulco. Allow a minimum of two full 24-hour days for either option. Carry liquids and food (which might only be minimally available en route) with you.

Instead of doing the trip in one big bite, you might stop overnight or more for a rest in Guadalajara (go to semideluxe Hotel La Serena, $35 d, tel. 33/3600-0910, fax 33/3600-1974, adjacent to the bus station) or in Puerto Vallarta (Hotel Rosita, $45, tel./fax 322/223-2000, tel. 322/223-2177, on the beach) en route.

From the U.S. Midwest, South, and East

From the U.S. Midwest, cross the border from El Paso to Ciudad Juárez and ride one of the Estrella Blanca subsidiaries (luxury-class Turistar or Transportes Chihuahuenses) via Chihuahua and Torreón, to either Mexico City Norte (North), or preferably, the Mexico City Sur (South) bus terminal.

From the Sur (sometimes known as Taxqueña) terminal, many buses connect directly with Taxco (Futura, Estrella de Oro), Acapulco via Chilpancingo (independent Estrella de Oro, or Estrella Blanca deluxe-class affiliates Turistar or Futura and second-class Transportes Cuauhtémoc) and Zihuatanejo. If you go from the Norte terminal, ride Estrella Blanca affiliates Turistar or Futura, or independent Estrella de Oro to Acapulco or Ixtapa-Zihuatanejo. For the entire trip, allow at least two full days to Acapulco, a few hours longer for Ixtapa-Zihuatanejo.

From U.S. South and East (and alternatively from the Midwest), cross the border at Laredo, Texas, to Nuevo Laredo and ride one of Estrella Blanca deluxe-class subsidiaries Turistar, Elite, or Futura to the Mexico City Norte (or possibly Sur) terminal. Continue south, exactly as described above. Allow a minimum of a day and a half (36 hours) for the trip to Acapulco.

BY CAR OR RV

If you're adventurous, like going to out-of-the-way places, but still want to have all the comforts of home, you may enjoy driving your car or RV to the Acapulco region. On the other hand, consideration of cost, risk, wear on both you and your vehicle, and the congestion hassles in towns may change your mind.

Mexican Car Insurance

Mexico does not recognize foreign insurance.

When you drive into Mexico, Mexican auto insurance is at least as important as your passport. At the busier crossings, you can get it at insurance "drive-ins" just north of the border. The many Mexican auto insurance companies are government-regulated; their numbers keep prices and services competitive.

Many Mexico insurance agents' long-hours offices line the border just north of the big crossings, especially at Tijuana, Mexicali, Nogales, Ciudad Juárez, Nuevo Laredo, and Matamoros. Although these are convenient, it may be wiser and even more convenient to get your car insurance ahead of time.

Sanborn's Mexico Insurance, one of the best-known agencies, certainly seems to be trying hardest. Besides insurance, Sanborn's offers a number of books and services, including the *Recreational Guide to Mexico* (see Suggested Reading), a good all-Mexico road map, "smile-by-mile" *Travelog* guide to "every highway in Mexico," hotel discounts, and more. Much of the above is available to members of Sanborn's "Sombrero" Club. Sign up for membership, buy insurance using your credit card, and order books through Sanborn's toll-free number, tel. 800/222-0158. For other queries, call tel. 956/682-7433, write Sanborn's Mexico, P.O. Box 310, McAllen, TX 78502, or log on to www.sanbornsinsurance.com.

Alternatively, look into **Vagabundos del Mar,** an RV-oriented Mexico fishing and travel club that offers memberships that include a newsletter, caravaning opportunites, discounts, insurance, and much more. Call tel. 800/474-2252 for a free information packet or look at www.vagabundos.com.

Mexican car insurance runs from a bare-bones rate of about $5 a day to a more typical $10 a day for more complete coverage ($50,000/$40,000/$80,000 public liability/property damage/medical payments) on a vehicle worth $10,000–15,000. On the same scale, insurance for a $50,000 RV and equipment runs about $30 a day. These daily rates decrease sharply for six-month or one-year policies, which run from about $200 for the minimum to $400–1,600 for complete, high-end coverage.

If you get broken glass, personal effects, and legal expenses coverage with these rates, you're lucky. Mexican policies don't usually cover them.

You should get something for your money, however. The deductibles should be no more than $300–500, the public liability/medical payments should be about double the ($25,000/$25,000/$50,000) legal minimum, and you should be able to get your car fixed in the United States and receive payment in U.S. dollars for losses. If not, shop around.

A Sinaloa Note of Caution

Although *bandidos* no longer menace Mexican roads (loose burros, horses, and cattle still do), be cautious in the infamous marijuana- and opium-growing region of Sinaloa state north of Mazatlán. It's best not to stray from Highway 15 between Culiacán and Mazatlán or from Highway 40 between Mazatlán and Durango. Curious tourists have been assaulted in the hinterlands adjacent to these roads.

The Green Angels

The Green Angels have answered many motoring tourists' prayers in Mexico. Bilingual teams of two, trained in auto repair and first aid, help distressed tourists along main highways. They patrol fixed stretches of road twice daily by truck. To make sure they stop to help, pull completely off the highway and raise your hood. You may want to hail a passing trucker to call them for you (toll-free Mex. tel. 800/903-9200 for the tourism hotline, who might alert the Green Angels for you).

If, for some reason, you have to leave your vehicle on the roadside, don't leave it unattended. Hire a local teenager or adult to watch it for you. Unattended vehicles on Mexican highways are quickly stricken by a mysterious disease, the symptoms of which are rapid loss of vital parts.

Mexican Gasoline

Pemex, short for Petroleos Mexicanos, the government oil monopoly, markets diesel fuel and two grades of unleaded gasoline: 92-octane *premio* (PRAY-mee-oh) and 89-octane Magna (MAHG-nah). Magna is good gas, yielding performance similar to that of U.S.-style regular unleaded gasoline. (My car, whose manufacturer

ON THE ROAD

DRIVING AND BUSING TO THE ACAPULCO REGION

From Western U.S.
From Central U.S.
From Central or Eastern U.S.
UNITED STATES
Gulf of Mexico
GUATEMALA
PACIFIC OCEAN
Sea of Cortez
Baja California

San Diego
Tijuana
159/193 3:15
Mexicali
Calexico
165/266 3:45
Sonoyta
Tucson
262/422 5:30
Nogales
173/279 3:15
Hermosillo
161/260 3:00
Ciudad Obregón
15D
137/220 2:40
Los Mochis
Topolobampo
15/24 0:30
Ferry Lines
8:00
18:00
Culiacan
139/224 2:30
Mazatlán
El Paso
Juárez
233/375 5:00
Chihuahua
284/457 6:30
45D
Torreon
157/253 3:30
Durango
198/318 6:00
220/354 5:30
45
174/280 3:45
40D
Monterrey
143/230 2:30
85
Nuevo Laredo
Laredo
McAllen
Reynosa
53/85 1:00
Saltillo
155/250 3:15
Matehuala
112/180 2:30
57
San Luis Potosí
129/208 2:50
Queretaro
133/215 2:30
57D
40/64 1:00
54
230/370 5:45
Zacatecas
198/318 5:45
54
Guadalajara
224/361 5:45
15D
Morelia
154/248 4:30
Toluca
74/119 2:15
Taxco
MEXICO CITY
197/317 4:30
Ciudad Victoria
180/290 4:15
Tampico
227/366 7:30
150 D
Tehuácan
350/564 8:00
131 D
Oaxaca
148/238 6:15
Puerto Ángel
291/469 8:15
259/417 5:15
95D
ACAPULCO
150/242 4:00
Ixtapa-Zihuatanejo
76/122 2:30
Playa Azul
200
195/314 6:15
Manzanillo
195/311 4:30
54D
141/227 3:00
Tepic
182/293 4:00
Puerto Vallarta
104/167 3:00
172/276 4:30
1
159/740 9:00
Guerrero Negro
263/424 6:00
Loreto
225/362 4:50
La Paz
Cabo San Lucas
0 150 mi
0 150 km
MOON

NOTE: DISTANCES ARE SHOWN AS MILES/KILOMETERS. APPROXIMATE DRIVING TIMES ARE SHOWN AS HOURS:MINUTES.

ROAD SAFETY

Hundreds of thousands of visitors enjoy safe Mexican auto vacations every year. Their success is due in large part to their frame of mind: Drive defensively, anticipate and adjust to danger before it happens, and watch everything—side roads, shoulders, the car in front, and cars far down the road. The following tips will help ensure a safe and enjoyable trip:

- **Don't drive at night.** Range animals, unmarked sand piles, pedestrians, one-lane bridges, cars without lights, and drunken drivers are doubly hazardous at night.
- Although **speed limits** are rarely enforced, *don't break them.* Mexican country roads are often narrow and shoulderless. Poor markings and macho drivers who pass on curves are best faced at a speed of 40 mph (64 kph) rather than 75 mph (120 kph).
- **Don't drive on sand.** Even with four-wheel-drive, you'll eventually get stuck if you drive often or casually on beaches. When the tide comes in, who'll pull your car out?
- **Slow down** at the *topes* (speed bumps) at the edges of towns and for *vados* (dips), which can be dangerously bumpy and full of water.
- Extending the **courtesy of the road** goes hand-in-hand with safe driving. Both courtesy and machismo are more infectious in Mexico; on the highway, it's much safer to spread the former than the latter.
- For maximum speed and safety, use Mexico's ***cuota autopistas*** (toll expressways) when convenient. (See the maps: color frontispiece, Driving and Busing to the Acapulco Region, and Driving and Busing Within the Acapulco Region.)

recommended 91-octane, ran well on Magna.) It runs about $.50 per liter (or about $2.40 per gallon). On main highways, Pemex makes sure that major stations (typically spaced about 30 miles apart in the countryside) stock Magna.

Gas Station Thievery

Although the problem has abated considerably in recent years (by the hiring of female attendants), boys who hang around gas stations to wash windows are notoriously light-fingered. When stopping at the *gasolinera,* make sure that your cameras, purses, and other moveable items are out of reach. Also, make sure that your car has a lockable gas cap. If not, insist on pumping the gas yourself, or be super-watchful as you pull up to the gas pump to make certain that the pump reads zero before the attendant pumps the gas.

A Healthy Car

Preventive measures spell good health for both you and your car. Get that tune-up (or that long-delayed overhaul) *before,* rather than after, you leave.

Carry a stock of spare parts, which will be more difficult to get and more expensive in Mexico than at home. Carry an extra tire or two, a few cans of motor oil and octane enhancer, oil and gas filters, fan belts, spark plugs, tune-up kit, ignition points, and fuses. Be prepared with basic tools and supplies, such as screwdrivers, pliers including Vice-Grip, lug wrench, jack, adjustable wrenches, tire pump and patches, tire pressure gauge, steel wire, and electrical tape. For breakdowns and emergencies, carry a folding shovel, a husky rope or chain, a gasoline can, and flares.

Car Repairs in Mexico

The American big three—General Motors, Ford, and Chrysler—as well as Nissan and Volkswagen are represented by extensive dealer networks in Mexico. Latecomers Toyota and Honda are also represented, although to a much lesser extent. Getting your car or truck serviced at such agencies is straightforward. While parts will probably be higher in price, shop rates run about half U.S.

prices, so repairs will generally come out cheaper than back home.

The same is not true for repairing other makes, however. Mexico has few, if any, other car or truck dealers; consequently, officially certified mechanics for other Japanese, British, and European makes are hard to find.

Nevertheless, many clever Mexican independent mechanics can fix any car that comes their way. Their humble repair shops *talleres mecánicos* (tah-YER-ays may-KAH-nee-kohs) dot town and village roadsides everywhere.

Although most mechanics are honest, beware of unscrupulous operators who try to collect double or triple their original estimate. If you don't speak Spanish, find someone who can assist you in negotiations. *Always* get a cost estimate, including needed parts and labor, in writing, even if you have to write it yourself. Make sure the mechanic understands, then ask him to sign it before he starts work. Although this may be a hassle, it might save you a much nastier hassle later. Shop labor at small, independent repair shops should run $10–20 per hour. For much more information, and for entertaining anecdotes of car and RV travel in Mexico, consult Carl Franz's *The People's Guide to Mexico.*

Bribes (Mordidas)

The usual meeting ground of the visitor and Mexican police is in the visitor's car on a highway or downtown street. To the tourists, such an encounter may seem mild harassment by the police, accompanied by vague threats of going to the police station or impounding the car for such-and-such a violation. The tourist often goes on to say, "It was all right, though . . . we paid him $20 and he went away. . . . Mexican cops sure are crooked, aren't they?"

And, I suppose, if people want to go bribing their way through Mexico, that's their business. But calling Mexican cops crooked isn't exactly fair. Police, like most everyone else in Mexico, have to scratch for a living, and they have found that many tourists are willing to slip them a $20

DISASTER AND RESCUE ON A MEXICAN HIGHWAY

My litany of Mexican driving experiences came to a climax one night when, heading north from Tepic, I hit a cow at 50 mph head-on. The cow was knocked about 150 feet down the road, while I and my two friends endured a scary impromptu roller-coaster ride. When the dust settled, we, although in shock, were grateful that we hadn't suffered the fate of the poor cow, which had died instantly from the collision.

From that low point, our fortunes soon began to improve. Two buses stopped and about 20 men got out to move my severely wounded van to the shoulder. The cow's owner, a rancher, arrived to cart off the cow's remains in a jeep. Then the police—a man and his wife in a VW bug—pulled up. *"Pobrecita camioneta"* ("Poor little van"), the woman said, gazing at my vehicle, which now resembled an oversized, crumpled accordion. They gave us a ride to Mazatlán, found us a hotel room, and generally made sure we were okay.

If I hadn't had Mexican auto insurance I would have been in deep trouble. Mexican law—based on the Napoleonic Code—presumes guilt and does not bother with juries. It would have kept me in jail until all damages were settled. The insurance agent I saw in the morning took care of everything. He called the police station, where I was excused from paying damages when the cow's owner failed to show. He had my car towed to a repair shop, where the mechanics banged it into good enough shape so I could drive it home a week later. Forced to stay in one place, my friends and I enjoyed the most relaxed time of our entire three months in Mexico. The *pobrecita camioneta,* all fixed up a few months later, lasted 14 more years.

bill for nothing. Rather than crooked, I would call them hungry and opportunistic.

Instead of paying a bribe, do what I've done a dozen times: remain cool, and if you're really guilty of an infraction, calmly say, "Ticket, please." *("Boleto, por favor.")* After a minute or two of stalling, and no cash appearing, the officer most likely will not bother with a ticket, but will wave you on with only a warning. If, on the other hand, the officer does write you a ticket, he will probably keep your driver's license, which you will be able to retrieve at the *presidencia municipal* (city hall) the next day in exchange for paying your fine.

Crossing the Border

Squeezing through the border traffic bottlenecks during peak holidays and rush hours can be time-consuming. Avoid crossing 7–9 A.M. and 4:30–6:30 P.M.

Highway Routes from the United States

If you decide to drive to the Acapulco region, you have your choice of three general routes. Maximize comfort and safety by following the broad toll *(cuota)* expressways that often parallel the old narrow nontoll *(libre)* routes. Despite the increased cost (about $150 total to Acapulco for a car, double or triple that for a motorhome) the *cuota* expressways will save you at least a day, probably two (including the extra food and hotel tariffs) and wear and tear on both your vehicle and your nerves. Most folks in passenger cars should allow at least three (more likely four or five, depending on the route) full south-of-the-border driving days to Acapulco or Ixtapa-Zihuatanejo. Larger RVs and motorhomes should allow at least a day or two more.

From the U.S. Pacific Coast and West, follow National Highway 15 (called 15 D as the toll expressway) from the border at Nogales, Sonora, an easy hour's drive south via I-19 south, from Tucson, Arizona. (California drivers, unless you have some special reason for doing so, *do not cross the border farther west at Tijuana or Mexicali;* access to Nogales and Highway 15 via Tucson is half a day quicker than the corresponding two-lane south-of-the-border route.)

From Nogales, Highway 15 D continues southward smoothly, leading you through cactus-studded mountains and valleys, which turn into lush farmland and tropical coastal plain and forest by the time you arrive at Mazatlán. Watch for the peripheral bypasses *(periféricos)* and truck routes that guide you past the congested downtowns of Hermosillo, Guaymas, Ciudad Obregón, Los Mochis, and Culiacán. Between these centers, you speed along, via the *cuota* (toll) expressway, all the way to Mazatlán. If you prefer not to pay the high tolls (about $60 Nogales-Mazatlán for a car, much more for motor home), stick to the old *libre* (free) highway. Hazards, bumps, and slow going might force you to reconsider, however.

From Mazatlán, continue along the narrow (but soon to be replaced) two-lane route to Tepic. There, you can either fork left, east, along Highways 15 or 15 D (east) to Guadalajara, or fork right, south, along Highway 200, to Puerto Vallarta.

If you opt for the Guadalajara route, continue east past Tepic along the easy toll expressway 15 D to Guadalajara. There, you link eastward, via crosstown expressway (watch for signs) Avenida Lázaro Cárdenas to Mexico City–bound expressway 15 D on the east side of town. Continue east on 15 D past Morelia, to Toluca, where you *do not continue ahead for Mexico City.* Instead, connect, on the southeast side of town, with Highway 55 (Boulevard José M. Pino Suárez to Metepec) that, after continuing several miles southeast, connects directly with southbound toll expressway 55 D to spa resort Ixtapan del Sal. Continue south on Highway 55 and connect directly with either old Highway 95 to Taxco and Iguala, or expressway 95 D south, via Chilpancingo, to Acapulco. (Total about 1,700 miles, 2,730 km, minimum 36 hours at the wheel to Acapulco, 40 hours to Ixtapa-Zihuatanejo.)

Although slower, the Puerto Vallarta route to the Acapulco region is more scenic and easier to follow. From Tepic, simply continue south, via two-lane Highway 200, through the palmy coastal resorts of Puerto Vallarta, Manzanillo, and the spectacularly scenic Michoacán coast, to Ixtapa-Zihuatanejo and Acapulco. (Total about

1,600 miles, 2,580 km, minimum 36 hours at the wheel, to Zihuatanejo, 40 hours to Acapulco.)

Although choosing between the Puerto Vallarta and Guadalajara options appears to be a tossup, the Guadalajara route, via expressway nearly all the way, allows for safer driving more hours per day. In effect, this might amounts to as little as four days of south-of-the border traveling, in comparison to about five or six days via Puerto Vallarta. However, the extra day or two required by the Puerto Vallarta option might be well worth the scenery and the opportunity to stop in beautiful ocean-front spots along the way. But never mind, you can have it both ways: go one way coming and the way other going. (For details of many of the towns along both the Puerto Vallarta and Guadalajara routes, check out my *Moon Handbooks Pacific Mexico,* listed in the Resources section.)

From the U.S. Midwest, South, and East, a number of routes are possible. Probably fastest and most direct is via the southern Texas Laredo-Nuevo Laredo border crossing. Continue south via toll *(cuota)* expressways 85 D, 40 D, and 57 D to Mexico City, thence to Acapulco via toll expressway 95 D. Along the way, keep an eye out for the "Mexico" (meaning Mexico City) signs that mark suburban bypasses (commonly labeled *libramiento* or *periférico*): before Monterrey (*periférico* Highway 40 or 40 D); before Saltillo (*libramiento* Highway 57 or 57 D); before San Luis Potosí (Highway 57 or 57D); before Querétaro (Highway 57 D).

At the Mexico City northern outskirt, bypass the congested Mexico City downtown the same way by following the right fork Cuernavaca- or Acapulco-direction *periférico* bypass; after several miles also fork right along Boulevard Avila Camacho *periférico* bypass, until finally you see the sign for toll *(cuota)* Cuernavaca/Acapulco Highway 95 D. From there, you can breeze all the way to Acapulco either direct, or via the smooth, wide, and scenic two-lane Taxco-Iguala Highway 95 toll cutoff.

Also, make sure that you're not in Mexico City on your forbidden day, determined by the last digit of your car license. (See the sidebar "Mexico City Driving Restrictions" in the Acapulco chapter.)

BY FERRY

An alternative, but longer, route to the Acapulco region is by ferry from the southern tip of Baja California. Bus travelers should cross the border at Tijuana or Mexicali and ride Autobuses Blanca Coordinados (ABC) through the long desert to La Paz (about 20 hours). Car travelers also cross at Tijuana or Mexicali and follow good, two-lane Mexico National Highway 1 (900 miles, 1,500 km) south to La Paz.

At La Paz (a pleasant Mexican town during the winter, although often very hot during the late spring and summer), you have your choice of two ferry lines. **Baja Ferries** takes passengers (about $50 per adult) and vehicles (car $100, motorhomes $300–400) across to Topolobambo, near Los Mochis, in northern Sinaloa, swiftly in about six hours. The boat, the big, shiny *California Star,* which accommodates about 200 vehicles and 1,000 passengers, departs La Paz Mon.–Fri. at 4 P.M. and Saturday at midnight. For more information and reservations (recommended, especially Christmas and Easter holidays), visit www.bajaferries.com or dial its La Paz office direct (in Spanish only), tel. 612/123-0200, fax 612/123-0504.

The other choice is to go via the pricier and slower former government, now privatized, **Sematur** boats to either Topolobampo or 300 miles farther south to Mazatlán. The Mazatlán crossing takes about 18 hours and costs a minimum of about $80 per adult passenger and about $200–400 for a car, more for a motorhome. Sleeping cabins are available for an additional $90 and up. The Mazatlán boat departs La Paz (actually the ferry slip at Pichilingue) Mon.–Sat. at about 3 P.M. From the United States, contact its La Paz office direct (in Spanish only) for information at tel. 612/125-5117 or 612/125-5717. From Mexico, for information and reservations, call toll-free Mex. tel. 800/718-9581. For more information and reservations, visit www.sematur.com.mx.

All things being equal, the above choices seem to be about a toss-up. The cheaper prices of the Baja Ferries option are balanced by the extra night hotel stay probably required on the mainland around Los Mochis and, for drivers, the tolls on Highway 15 D (or for bus travelers the bus fare) between Los Mochis and Mazatlán.

During recent years, ferry service has been in a state of flux and subject to change. Be sure to check through the contact numbers and/or websites for the newest ferry information before making the long desert trip south to La Paz.

BY TOUR, CRUISE, AND SAILBOAT

For travelers on a tight time budget, prearranged tour packages can provide a hassle-free route for sampling the attractions of Acapulco region coastal resorts and upcountry towns and cities. If, however, you prefer a self-paced vacation, or desire thrift over convenience, you should probably defer tour arrangements until after arrival. Many Acapulco region travel and tour agencies are as close as your hotel telephone or front lobby tour desk and can customize a tour for you. Options vary from city highlight tours and bay snorkeling adventures to shopping in inland colonial cities and sightseeing overnights to boat adventures through wildlife-rich mangrove jungle hinterlands. (For local possibilities, guides, and tour agencies, see the Acapulco, Ixtapa-Zihuatanejo, and Upcountry Guerrero destination chapters.)

By Cruise or Sailboat

Travel agents and websites advertise many cruises that include Acapulco and/or Ixtapa-Zihuatanejo on their itineraries. Vacationers who enjoy being pampered with lots of food and ready-made entertainment (and who don't mind paying for it) can have great fun on cruises. Accommodations on a typical 10-day winter tour or cruise (which would include several days in Ixpata-Zihuatanejo and Acapulco) can run as little as $100 per day per person, double occupancy, to as much as $1,000 or more.

If, however, you want to get to know Mexico and the local people, a cruise is not for you. Included lodging, food, and entertainment are the main events of a cruise; shore sightseeing excursions, which generally cost plenty extra, are a sideshow.

Sailboats, on the other hand, offer an entirely different kind of sea route to the Acapulco region. **Ocean Voyages,** a California-based agency, arranges passage on a number of sail and motor vessels that regularly depart to Ixtapa-Zihuatanejo and Acapulco from ports such as San Diego, Los Angeles, San Francisco, Seattle, and Vancouver, British Columbia. It offers customized itineraries and flexible arrangements that can vary from complete round-trip voyages to weeklong coastal idylls between Acapulco region ports of call. Some captains allow passengers to save money by signing on as crew. For more information, contact Ocean Voyages, 1709 Bridgeway, Sausalito, CA 94965, tel. 415/332-4681 or 800/299-4444, fax 415/332-7460, sail@oceanvoyages.com, www.oceanvoyages.com.

Getting Around

BY BUS

The bus is the king of the Mexican road. Dozens of lines connect virtually every town in the Acapulco region. Three distinct levels of service—deluxe, first-class, and second-class—are generally available. **Deluxe-class** (called Turistar, Futura, Diamante, and Primera Plus, depending upon the line) express coaches speed between major towns, seldom stopping en route. In exchange for relatively high fares (about $30 Acapulco-Zihuatanejo or $40 Acapulco-Taxco, for example), passengers often enjoy rapid passage and airline-style amenities: plush reclining seats, air-conditioning, an on-board toilet, video, and aisle attendant.

Although less luxurious, for about half the price **first-class** service is frequent and always includes reserved seating. Additionally, passengers enjoy soft reclining seats and air-conditioning (if it is working). Besides their regular stops at or near most towns and villages en route, first-class bus drivers, if requested, will usually stop and let you off anywhere along the road. (For information on routes and bus station locations, refer to the destination chapters.)

Second-class bus seating is unreserved. In outlying parts of the Acapulco region, there is even a class of bus beneath second-class, but given the condition of many second-class buses, it seems as if third-class buses wouldn't run at all. Such buses are the stuff of travelers' legends: the recycled old GMC, Ford, and Dodge schoolbuses that stop everywhere and carry everyone and everything to even the smallest villages tucked away in the far mountains. As long as there is any kind of a road, the bus will most likely go there.

Now and then you'll read a newspaper story of a country bus that went over a cliff somewhere in Mexico, killing the driver and a dozen unfortunate souls. The same newspapers, however, never bother to mention the half million safe passengers for whom the same bus provided trips during its 15 years of service before the accident.

Second-class buses are not for travelers with weak knees or stomachs. Often, you will initially have to stand, cramped in the aisle, in a crowd of campesinos. They are warm-hearted but poor people, so don't tempt them with open, dangling purses or wallets bulging in back pockets. Stow your money safely away. After a while, you will be able to sit down. Such privilege, however, comes with obligation, such as holding an old woman's bulging bag of carrots or a toddler on your lap. But if you accept your burden with humor and equanimity, who knows what favors and blessings may flow to you in return.

Tickets, Seating, and Baggage

Mexican bus lines do not usually publish schedules or fares. You have to ask someone who knows (such as your hotel desk clerk), or call the bus station. Not many travel agents bother handling bus tickets. If you don't want to spend the time to get a reserved ticket yourself, hire someone trustworthy to do it for you. Another option is to get to the bus station early enough on your traveling day to ensure that you'll get a bus to your destination.

Although some lines accept credit cards and issue computer-printed tickets at their major stations, most reserved bus tickets are sold for cash and handwritten, with a specific seat number *número de asiento,* on the back. If you miss the bus, you lose your money. Furthermore, airlines-style automated reservations systems have not yet arrived at many Mexican bus stations. Consequently, you can generally buy reserved tickets only at the local departure *(salida local)* station. (An agent in Puerto Vallarta, for example, cannot ordinarily reserve you a ticket on a bus that originates in Tepic, 100 miles up the road.)

Request a reserved seat, if possible, with numbers 1–25 in the front *(delante)* to middle *(medio)* of the bus. The rear seats are often occupied by smokers, drunks, and rowdies. At night, you will sleep better on the right side *(lado derecho)* away from the glare of oncoming traffic lights.

Baggage is generally secure on Mexican buses. Label it, however. Overhead racks are generally too cramped to accommodate airline-sized carry-ons. Carry a small bag with your money and irreplaceables on your person; pack clothes and less-essentials in your checked luggage. For peace of mind, watch the handler put your checked baggage on the bus and watch to make sure it is not mistakenly taken off the bus at intermediate stops.

If your baggage gets misplaced, remain calm. Bus employees are generally competent and conscientious. If you are patient, recovering your luggage will become a matter of honor for many of them. Baggage handlers are at the bottom of the pay scale; a tip for their mostly thankless job is very much appreciated.

On long trips, carry food, beverages, and toilet paper. Station food may be dubious, and the sanitary facilities may be ill-maintained.

If you are waiting for a first-class bus at an intermediate *salida de paso* (passing station), you have to trust to luck that there will be an empty seat. If not, your best option may be to ride a more frequent second-class bus.

BY CAR OR RV

Driving your own car in Mexico may or may not be for you. (See the Getting There section).

Rental Car

Car and jeep rentals are an increasingly popular transportation option for Acapulco region travelers. They offer mobility and independence for local sightseeing and beach excursions. In the resorts, most of the gang's there: Hertz, Avis, Alamo, and Budget, plus several local outfits. They generally require drivers to have a valid driver's license, passport, a major credit card, and may require a minimum age of 25. Some local companies do not accept credit cards, but offer lower rates in return.

Base prices of international agencies such as Hertz and Avis are not cheap. With a 17 percent value-added tax and mandatory insurance, rentals run more than in the United States. The cheapest possible rental car, usually a used, stick-shift VW Beetle, runs $40–60 per day or $250–450 per week, depending on location and season. Prices are highest during Christmas and pre-Easter weeks. Before departure, use the international agencies' toll-free numbers and websites for availability, prices, and reservations. During nonpeak seasons, you may save lots of pesos by waiting until arrival and renting a car through a local agency. Shop around, starting with the agent in your hotel lobby or with the local Yellow Pages (under *"Automoviles, renta de"*).

Car insurance that covers property damage, public liability, and medical payments is an absolute "must" with your rental car. If you get into an accident without insurance, you will be in deep trouble, probably jail. Narrow, rough roads and animals grazing at roadside make driving in Mexico more hazardous than back home. (For important car safety and insurance information, see By Car or RV under Getting There.)

BY TAXI, LOCAL TOUR, AND HITCHHIKING

Taxis

The high prices of rental cars make taxis a viable option for local excursions. Cars are luxuries, not necessities, for most Mexican families. Travelers might profit from the Mexican money-saving practice of piling everyone in a taxi for a Sunday outing. You may find that an all-day taxi and driver, who, besides relieving you of driving, will become your impromptu guide, will cost no more than a rental car.

The magic word for saving money by taxi is *colectivo:* a taxi you share with other travelers. The first place you'll practice getting a taxi will be at either the Acapulco or Ixtapa-Zihuatanejo airport, where *colectivo* tickets are routinely sold from booths at the terminal door.

If, however, you want your own private taxi, ask for a *taxi especial,* which will run about three or four times the individual tariff for a *colectivo.*

Your airport experience will prepare you for in-town taxis, which rarely, if ever, have meters. You must establish the price before getting in. Bargaining comes with the territory in Mexico, so don't shrink from it, even though it seems a hassle. If you get into a taxi without an agreed-upon price, you are letting yourself in for a more serious and potentially nasty hassle later. If your driver's price is too high, he'll probably come to his senses as soon as you hail another taxi.

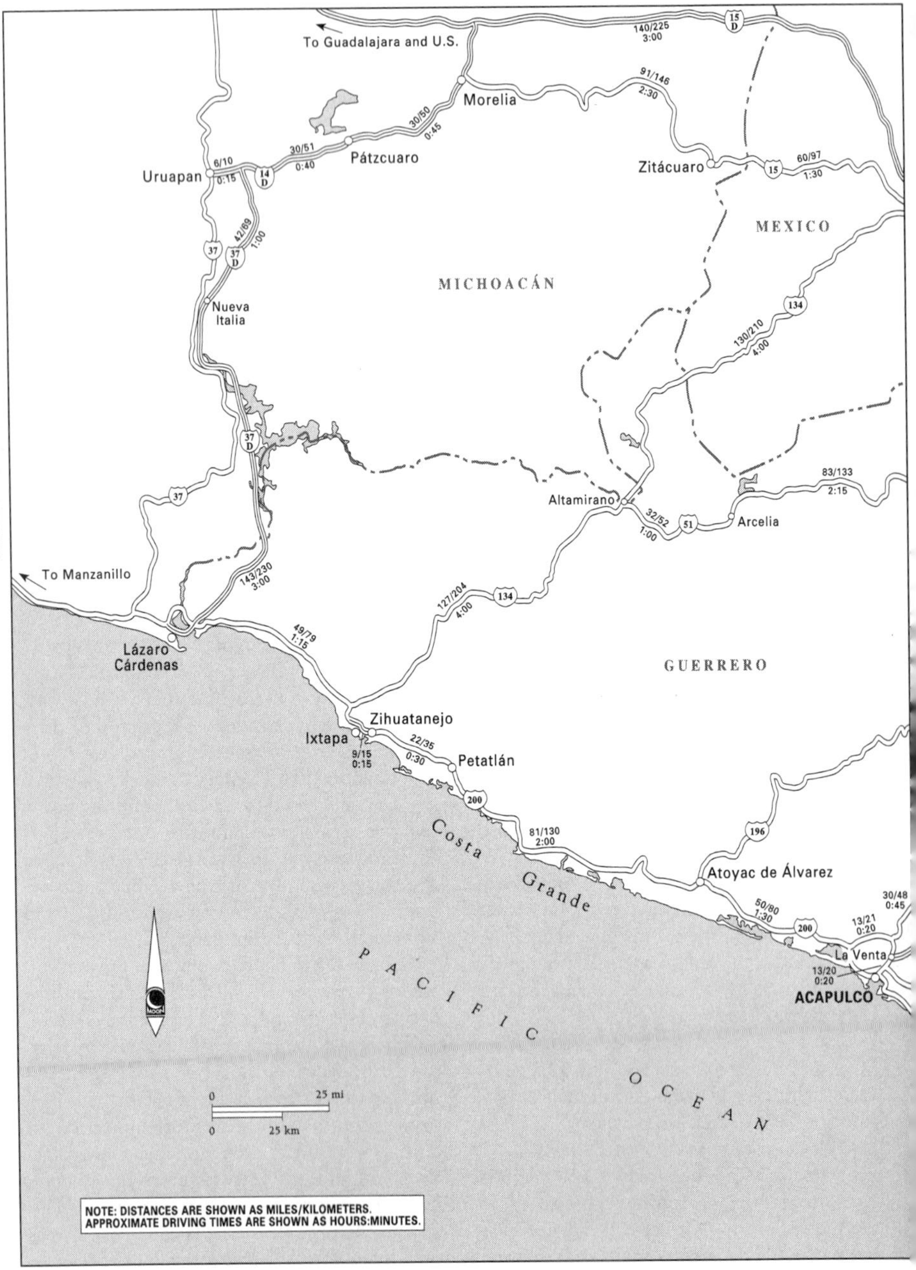

To Guadalajara and U.S.
140/225
3:00
15 D
91/146
2:30
Morelia
30/50
0:45
Pátzcuaro
30/51
0:40
6/10
0:15
Uruapan
14 D
Zitácuaro
15
60/97
1:30
MEXICO
42/69
1:00
37
37 D
MICHOACÁN
Nueva
Italia
134
130/210
4:00
37 D
83/133
2:15
Altamirano
32/52
1:00
51
Arcelia
37
To Manzanillo
143/230
3:00
127/204
4:00
134
49/79
1:15
Lázaro
Cárdenas
GUERRERO
Zihuatanejo
Ixtapa
9/15
0:15
22/35
0:30
Petatlán
200
Costa
Grande
81/130
2:00
196
Atoyac de Álvarez
50/80
1:30
200
30/48
0:45
13/21
0:20
La Venta
13/20
0:20
ACAPULCO
PACIFIC
OCEAN
0
25 mi
0
25 km
NOTE: DISTANCES ARE SHOWN AS MILES/KILOMETERS.
APPROXIMATE DRIVING TIMES ARE SHOWN AS HOURS:MINUTES.

DRIVING AND BUSING WITHIN THE ACAPULCO REGION
To Queretaro and U.S.
MEXICO CITY
Toluca
D.F.
Tlaxcala
Puebla
Cuernavaca
Cuautla
MORELOS
Izucar de Matamoros
PUEBLA
Tehuacán
Taxco
Iguala
Olinalá
Huajuapan de León
Chilapa
Chilpan-cingo
Tlapa
Tierra Colorada
Ayutla
Cruz Grande
Ometepec
Cuajinicuilapa
Pinotepa Nacional
OAXACA
To Oaxaca
Costa Chica
To Puerto Escondido
TOLL
78/126 2:00
30/48 0:45
55/89 1:30
74/119 2:15
42/67 1:00
76/123 1:30
29/47 1:00
38/61 1:00
64/105 1:45
22/36 0:30
39/63 1:00
51/82 1:30
89/143 2:30
57/91 2:00
65/105 1:45
95/153 1:45
40/64 1:15
35/57 1:15
71/115 2:30
22/35 1:00
171/275 6:00
32/51 0:35
37/60 1:00
29/46 0:40
54/87 2:00
20/33 0:45
63/102 2:00
10/16 0:20
48/78 1:30
16/26 0:30
32/52 1:00

ON THE ROAD

WHICH BUSES GO WHERE

Destinations (arranged in approximate north to south order)	**Bus Lines**
Guadalajara (new terminal)	EL, ETN, FU, OM, PP, TC, TN, TP
Mexico City West *(poniente)*	EB, ETN, FU, OM, PAR, PP, TP
Mexico City South (*sur* or "Tasqueña")	EB, EO, FR
Mexico City North *(norte)*	EB, FU, OM, TC, TN
Pátzcuaro, Mich.	EL, FA, GA, PAR, RP
Lázaro Cárdenas, Mich.	ACU, EL, FA, FU, GA, PAR, RP
Taxco, Gro.	EB, EO, FR
Iguala, Gro.	EB, EO, FR
Chilpancingo, Gro.	EB, EO, FR
Chilapa, Gro.	EB
Tlapa de Comonfort, Gro.	EB, SUR
Olinalá, Gro.	EB, SUR
Zihuatanejo, Gro.	ACU, EL, FA, GA, GAC, PAR, RP
Tecpán de Galeana, Gro.	EL, EO
Acapulco, Gro.	EL, EO, FR, FU, GAC, TUR
Ometepec, Gro.	EB
Cuajinicuilapa, Gro.	EL
Oaxaca, Oax.	ADO, AU, CC, ERS, EV, FP, OP, SUR
Pinotepa Nacional, Oax.	CC, EL, ERS, EV, FP, FR, OP
Puerto Escondido, Oax.	CC, EL, ERS, EV, OP
Pochutla-Puerto Angel, Oax.	CC, EL, ERS, EV, FP, OP
Huatulco, Oax.	CC, EL, EV, OP

After a few days, getting taxis around town will be a cinch. You'll find that you don't have to take the more expensive taxis lined up in your hotel driveway. If the price isn't right, walk toward the street and hail a regular taxi.

In town, if you can't find a taxi, it may be because taxis are waiting for riders at the local stand, called a taxi *sitio.* Ask someone to direct you to it: *"Disculpe. ¿Dónde está el sitio taxi, por favor?"* ("Excuse me. Where is the taxi stand, please?")

Local Tours and Guides

For many Acapulco region travelers, locally arranged tours offer a hassle-free alternative to rental car or taxi sightseeing. Hotels and travel agencies, many of whom maintain front-lobby travel and tour desks, offer a bounty of sightseeing, water sports, bay cruise, fishing, and wildlife-viewing tour opportunities. (For details, see the Acapulco, Ixtapa-Zihuatanejo, and Guerrero Upcountry destination chapters.)

Bus Key

ACU	Autotransportes Cuauhtemoc (subsidiary of EB)
ADO	Autobuses del Oriente
AU	Autobuses Unidos
CC	Cristóbal Colón
EB	Estrella Blanca
EL	Elite (subsidiary of EB)
EO	Estrella de Oro
ERS	Estrella Roja del Sureste
ETN	Enlaces Transportes Nacionales
EV	Estrella del Valle
FA	Flecha Amarilla
FP	Fletes y Pasajes
FR	Flecha Roja (subsidiary of EB)
FU	Futura (subsidiary of EB)
GA	Galeana (subsidiary of FA)
GAC	Gacela
OM	Omnibus de Mexico
OP	Oaxaca-Pacifico
PAR	Parhikuni
PP	Primera Plus (subsidiary of FA)
RP	Ruta Paraíso
SUR	Autotransportes del Sur
TC	Transportes Chihuahuenses (subsidiary of EB)
TN	Transportes del Norte (subsidiary of EB)
TNS	Transportes Norte de Sonora (subsidiary of EB)
TP	Transportes del Pacífico
TUR	Turistar

Hitchhiking

Most everyone agrees hitchhiking is not the safest mode of transport. If you're unsure, don't do it. Hitchhiking doesn't make for a healthy steady travel diet, nor should you hitchhike at night.

The recipe for trouble-free hitchhiking requires equal measures of luck, savvy, and technique. The best places to catch rides are where people are arriving and leaving anyway, such as bus stops, highway intersections, gas stations, and on the highway out of town.

Male-female hitchhiking partnerships seem to net the most rides (although it is technically illegal for women to ride in commercial trucks). The more gear you and your partner have, the fewer rides you will get. Pickup and flatbed truck owners often pick up passengers for pay. Before hopping onto the truck bed, ask how much the ride will cost.

Information and Services

PASSPORTS, TOURIST CARDS, AND VISAS

Your Passport

Your passport (or birth or naturalization certificate) is your positive proof of national identity; without it, your status in any foreign country is in doubt. Don't leave home without one. United States citizens may obtain passports (allow four to six weeks) at local post offices. For-fee private passport agencies can speed this process and get you a passport within a week, maybe less.

Entry into Mexico

For U.S. and Canadian citizens, entry by air into Mexico for a few weeks could hardly be easier. Airline attendants hand out tourist cards *(tarjetas turísticas)* en route and officers make them official by glancing at passports and stamping the cards at the immigration gate. Business travel permits for 30 days or fewerr are handled by the same simple procedures.

Entry is not entirely painless, however. The Mexican government charges an approximate $20 fee per person for a tourist card. For air and bus travelers, this is no problem, since the fee is automatically included in the fare. The entry fee can be a bit of a hassle for drivers, however. At this writing the government does not allow collection of the fee by border immigration officers. Instead, the officers issue a form that you must take to a bank, where you pay the fee. For multiple entries this can get complicated and time-consuming.

In addition to the entry fee, Mexican border immigration officials require that all entering U.S. citizens 15 years old or over must present proper identification—either a valid U.S. passport, original or a notarized copy of your birth certificate, military ID, or state driver's license, while naturalized citizens must show naturalization papers (or a laminated naturalization card) or valid U.S. passport.

Canadian citizens must show a valid passport or original birth certificate. Nationals of other countries (especially those such as Hong Kong, which issue more than one type of passport) may be subject to different or additional regulations. For advice, consult your regional Mexico Tourism Board office or consulate. For more Mexico-entry details, call the Mexico Tourism Board at toll-free U.S. tel. 800/44-MEXICO (800/446-3942) or visit www.visitmexico.com.

More Options

For more complicated cases, get your tourist card early enough to allow you to consider the options. Tourist cards can be issued for multiple entries and a maximum validity of 180 days; photos are often required. If you don't request multiple entry or the maximum time, your card will probably be stamped single entry, valid for some shorter period, such as 90 days. If you are not sure how long you'll stay in Mexico, request the maximum (180 days is the absolute maximum for a tourist card; long-term foreign residents routinely make semiannual "border runs" for new tourist cards).

Student and Business Visas

A visa is a notation stamped and signed on your passport showing the number of days and entries allowable for your trip. Apply for a student visa at the Mexican consulate nearest your home well in advance of your departure; the same is true if you require a business visa of longer than 30 days. One-year renewable student visas are available (sometimes with considerable red tape). An ordinary 180-day tourist card may be the easiest option, if you can manage it.

Entry for Children

Children under 15 can be included on their parents' tourist cards, but complications occur if the children (by reason of illness, for example) cannot leave Mexico with both parents. Parents can avoid such red tape by getting a passport and a Mexican tourist card for each of their children.

In addition to passport or birth certificate, minors (under age 18) entering Mexico without parents or legal guardians must present a notarized letter of permission signed by both parents or legal guardians. Even if accompanied by one parent, a notarized letter from the other must be presented. Divorce or death certificates must also be presented, when applicable. Airlines will require the name, address, and telephone number of the person meeting unaccompanied minors upon arrival in Mexico.

Acapulco region travelers should hurdle all such possible delays far ahead of time in the cool calm of their local Mexican consulate rather than the hot, hurried atmosphere of a border or airport immigration office.

Entry for Pets

A pile of red tape can delay the entry of dogs, cats, and other pets into Mexico. Be prepared with veterinary-stamped health and rabies certificates for each animal. Contact your regional Mexico Tourism Board, call toll-free U.S. tel. 800/44-MEXICO (800/446-3942), or visit www.visitmexico.com for assistance.

Don't Lose Your Tourist Card

If you do, be prepared with a copy of the original, which you should present to the nearest federal Migración (Immigration) office (on duty long hours at the Acapulco and Ixtapa-Zihuatanejo international airports) and ask for a duplicate tourist permit. Lacking this, you might present some alternate proof of your date of arrival in Mexico, such as a stamped passport or airline ticket. Savvy travelers carry copies of their tourist cards with them, while leaving the originals safe in their hotel rooms or hotel desk safes.

Car Permits

If you drive to Mexico, you will need a permit for your car. Upon entry into Mexico, be ready with originals and copies of your proof-of-ownership or registration papers (state title certificate, registration, or notarized bill of sale), current license plates, and current driver's license. The auto permit fee runs about $25, payable only by non-Mexican bank MasterCard, Visa, or American Express credit cards. (The credit-card-only requirement discourages those who sell or abandon U.S.-registered cars in Mexico without paying customs duties.) Credit cards must bear the same name as the vehicle proof-of-ownership papers.

The resulting car permit becomes part of the owner's tourist card and receives the same length of validity. Vehicles registered in the name of an organization or person other than the driver must be accompanied by a notarized affidavit authorizing the driver to use the car in Mexico for a specific time.

Border officials generally allow you to carry or tow additional motorized vehicles (motorcycle, another car, large boat) into Mexico but will probably require separate documentation and fee for each vehicle. If a Mexican official desires to inspect your trailer or RV, go through it with him or her.

Accessories, such as a small trailer, boat shorter than six feet, CB radio, or outboard motor, may be noted on the car permit and must leave Mexico with the car.

For updates and details on documentation required for taking your car into Mexico, call toll-free U.S. tel. 800/446-3942 or visit www.visitmexico.com. For more details on motor vehicle entry and what you may bring in your baggage to Mexico, consult the AAA (American Automobile Association) *Mexico TravelBook.*

Since Mexico does not recognize foreign automobile insurance, you must buy Mexican automobile insurance. (For more information on this and other details of driving in Mexico, see Getting There.)

Crossing the Border and Returning Home

Squeezing through border bottlenecks during peak holidays and rush hours can be time-consuming. Avoid crossing 7–9 A.M. and 4:30–6:30 P.M.

Just before returning across the border with your car, park and have a customs *(aduana)* official *remove and cancel the holographic identity sticker that you received on entry.* If possible, get a receipt *(recibo)* or some kind of verification that it's been canceled *(cancelado).* Tourists have been fined hundreds of dollars for inadvertently carrying uncanceled car entry stickers on their windshields.

At the same time, return all other Mexican permits, such as tourist cards and hunting and fishing licenses. Also, be prepared for Mexico exit inspection, especially for cultural artifacts and works of art, which may require exit permits. Certain religious and pre-Columbian artifacts, legally the property of the Mexican government, cannot be taken from the country.

If you entered Mexico with your car, you cannot legally leave without it except by permission from local customs authorities, usually the Aduana (Customs House) or the Oficina Federal de Hacienda (Federal Treasury Office). (For local details, see Information and Services in the destination chapters.)

All returnees are subject to U.S. immigration and customs inspection. These inspections have become generally more time-consuming since September 11, 2001. The worst bottlenecks are at busy border crossings, especially Tijuana and to a lesser extent, Mexicali, Nogales, Ciudad Juárez, Laredo, and Brownsville, all of which should be avoided during peak hours.

United States law allows a fixed value (at present

MEXICO TOURISM BOARD OFFICES

More than a dozen Mexico Tourism Board (Consejo de Promoción Turístico de Mexico) offices and scores of Mexican government consulates operate in the United States, Canada, Europe, and South America. Consulates generally handle questions of Mexican nationals abroad, while Mexico Tourism Boards serve travelers heading for Mexico.

For straightforward questions and Mexico regional information brochures, call toll-free U.S./Can. tel. 800/44-MEXICO (800/446-3942) or Europe tel. 800/11-2266, or visit www.visitmexico.com. Otherwise, contact one of the North American regional, European, or South American Mexico Tourism Boards for guidance:

In North America

From Arizona, California, Colorado, Hawaii, Idaho, Montana, Nevada, New Mexico, and Utah, contact **Los Angeles:** 2401 W. 6th St., 5th Floor, Los Angeles, CA 90057, tel. 213/351-2069, fax 213/351-2074, losangeles@visitmexico.com.

From Alaska, Washington, Oregon, Idaho, Wyoming, and Montana and the Canadian provinces of British Columbia, Alberta, Yukon, Northwest Territories, and Saskatchewan, contact **Vancouver:** 999 W. Hastings St., Suite 1110, Vancouver, British Columbia V6C 2W2, tel. 604/669-2845, fax 604/669-3498, mgto@telus.net.

From Texas, Oklahoma, and Louisiana, contact **Houston:** 4507 San Jacinto, Suite 308, Houston TX 77004, tel. 713/772-2581, fax 713/772-6058, houston@visitmexico.com.

From Alabama, Arkansas, Florida, Georgia, Mississippi, Tennessee, North Carolina, and South Carolina, contact **Miami:** 5975 Sunset Dr. #305, Miami, FL 33143, tel. 786/621-2909, fax 786/621-2907, miami@visitmexico.com.

From Illinois, Indiana, Iowa, Kansas, Michigan, Minnesota, Missouri, Nebraska, North Dakota, Ohio, South Dakota, and Wisconsin, contact **Chicago:** 300 N. Michigan Ave., 4th Floor, Chicago, IL 60601, tel. 312/606-9252, fax 312/606-9012, chicago@visitmexico.com.

From Connecticut, Delaware, Kentucky, Maine, Maryland, Massachusetts, New Hampshire, New Jersey, New York, Pennsylvania, Rhode Island, Vermont, Virginia, Washington, D.C., and West Virginia, contact **New York:** 375 Park Ave., Suite 1905, New York, NY 10152, tel. 212/308-2110, ext. 105, newyork@visitmexico.com.

$400) of duty-free goods per returnee. This may include no more than one liter of alcoholic spirits, 200 cigarettes, and 100 cigars. A flat 10 percent duty will be applied to the first $1,000 (fair retail value, save your receipts) in excess of your $400 exemption. You may, however, mail packages (up to $50 value each) of gifts duty-free to friends and relatives in the United States. Make sure to clearly write "unsolicited gift" and a list of the value and contents on the outside of the package. Perfumes (over $5), alcoholic beverages, and tobacco may not be included in such packages.

Improve the security of such mailed packages by sending them by Mexpost class, similar to U.S. Express Mail service. Even better (but much more expensive), send them by Federal Express or DHL international couriers, which maintain offices in Acapulco and Ixtapa-Zihuatanejo.

For more information on U.S. customs regulations important to travelers abroad, write for a copy of the useful pamphlet *Know Before You Go,* from the U.S. Customs Service, 1300 Pennsylvania Avenue, Washington, DC 20229. You may also order by dialing the Customs

From Ontario and Manitoba, contact **Toronto:** 2 Bloor St. W, Suite 1502, Toronto, Ontario M4W 3E2, tel. 416/925-0704, fax 416/925-6061, toronto@visitmexico.com.

From New Brunswick, Newfoundland, Nova Scotia, Prince Edward Island, and Quebec, contact **Montreal:** 1 Place Ville Marie, Suite 1931, Montreal, Quebec H3B2C3, tel. 514/871-1052 or 514/871-1103, fax 514/871-3825, montreal@visitmexico.com.

In Europe

In Europe, travelers may use the tourism information number, all-Europe toll-free Mex. tel. 800/11-2266, visit the website www.visitmexico.com, or contact the local offices directly:

London: Wakefield House, 41 Trinity Square, London EC3N 4DT, England, UK, tel. 207/488-9392, fax 207/265-0704, uk@visitmexico.com.

Frankfurt: Taunusanlage 21, 60325 Frankfurt-am-Main, Deutschland, tel. 69/253509, fax 69/253755, germany@visitmexico.com.

Paris: 4, Rue Notre-Dame des Victoires, 75002 Paris, France, tel. 1/428-96122, 1/428-69213, fax 1/428-60580, france@visitmexico.com.

Madrid: Calle Velázquez 126, 28006 Madrid, España, tel. 91/561-3520, 91/561-1827, fax 91/411-0759, spain@visitmexico.com.

Rome: Via Barbarini 3-piso 7, 00187 Roma, Italia, tel. 06/487-4698, fax 06/487-3630, fax 06/420-4293, italy@visitmexico.com.

In South America

Contact the Mexico Tourism Board in either Argentina or Chile:

Buenos Aires: Av. Santa Fe 920, 1054 Buenos Aires, Argentina, tel. 1/4393-7070 or 1/4393-8235, fax 1/4393-6607, argentina@visitmexico.com.

Santiago: Bucarest 162, Providencia, Santiago, Chile, tel. 562/234-5899, fax 562/234-5898, chile@visitmexico.com.

Service at tel. 202/354-1000. For more information, visit www.customs.gov.

Additional U.S. rules prohibit importation of certain fruits, vegetables, and domestic animal and endangered wildlife products. Certain live animal species, such as parrots, may be brought into the United States, subject to 30-day agricultural quarantine upon arrival, at the owner's expense. For more details on agricultural product and live animal importation, write for the free booklet *Travelers' Tips,* by the U.S. Department of Agriculture, Washington, D.C. 20250, tel. 202/720-2791.

For more information on the importation of endangered wildlife products, contact the Fish and Wildlife Service, 1849 C. Street NW, Washington, DC 20240, tel. 202/208-4717.

MONEY

The Peso: Down and Up

Overnight in early 1993, the Mexican government shifted its monetary decimal point three places and created the "new" peso, which now trades at around 11 per U.S. dollar. Since the peso value sometimes changes rapidly, U.S. dollars have become a much more stable indicator of Mexican prices; for this reason they are used in this book to report prices. You should, nevertheless, always use pesos to pay for everything in Mexico.

Since the introduction of the new peso, the centavo (one-hundredth of a new peso) has reappeared, in coins of 5, 10, 20, and 50 centavos. Incidentally, the dollar sign, "$," also marks Mexican pesos. Peso coins (*monedas*) in denominations of 1, 2, 5, 10, and 20 pesos, and bills, in denominations of 20, 50, 100, 200, and 500 pesos, are common. Since banks like to exchange your traveler's checks for a few crisp large bills rather than the often-tattered smaller denominations, ask for some of your change in 50- and 100-peso notes. A 500-peso note, while common at the bank, may look awfully big to a small shopkeeper, who might be hard-pressed to change it.

Banks, ATMs, and Money Exchange Offices

Mexican banks, like their North American counterparts, have lengthened their business hours. Banco Internacional (BITAL), maintains the longest hours: as long as Mon.–Sat. 8 A.M.–7 P.M. Banamex (Banco Nacional de Mexico), generally the most popular with local people, usually posts the best in-town dollar exchange rate in its lobbies; for example: *Tipo de cambio: venta 10.615, compra 10.720,* which means the bank will sell pesos to you at the rate of 10.615 per dollar and buy them back for 10.720 per dollar.

ATMs (automated teller machines) *(Cajeros Automáticos,* kah-HAY-rohs ahoo-toh-MAH-tee-kohs) are rapidly becoming the money source of choice in Mexico. Virtually every bank has a 24-hour ATM, accessible (with proper PIN identification code) by a swarm of U.S. and Canadian credit and ATM cards. *Note:* Some Mexican bank ATMs will "eat" your ATM card if you don't retrieve it within about 15 seconds of completing your transaction. Retrieve your card *immediately* after getting your cash.

Although one-time bank charges, typically about $2 per $100, for ATM cash remain small, the pesos you can usually get from a single card is limited to about $300 or less per day.

Even without an ATM card, you don't have to go to the trouble of waiting in long bank service lines. Opt for a less-crowded bank, such as Bancomer, Banco Serfín, Banco Internacional, or a private money-exchange office *(casa de cambio).* Often most convenient, such offices often offer long hours and faster service than the banks for a fee (as little as $.50 or as much as $3 per $100).

Keeping Your Money Safe

Traveler's checks, the traditional prescription for safe money abroad, are widely accepted in the Acapulco region. Even if you plan to use your ATM card, buy some U.S. dollar traveler's checks (a well-known brand such as American Express or Visa) as an emergency reserve. Canadian traveler's checks and currency are not as widely accepted as U.S. traveler's checks, European and Asian even less. Unless you like signing your name or paying lots of per-check commissions, buy denominations of $100 or more.

In the Acapulco region, as everywhere, thieves circulate among the tourists. Keep valuables in your hotel *caja de seguridad* (security box). If you don't particularly trust the desk clerk, carry what you cannot afford to lose in a money belt. Pickpockets love crowded markets, buses, and airport terminals where they can slip a wallet out of a back pocket or dangling purse in a blink. Guard against this by carrying your wallet in your front pocket, and your purse, waist pouch, and daypack (which clever crooks can sometimes slit open) on your front side.

Don't attract thieves by displaying wads of money or flashy jewelry. Don't get sloppy drunk; if so, you may become a pushover for a determined thief.

Don't leave valuables unattended on the beach; share security duties with trustworthy-looking neighbors, or leave a secure bag with a shopkeeper nearby.

Tipping

Without their droves of visitors, Mexican people would be even poorer. Deflation of the peso, while it makes prices low for outsiders, makes it rough for Mexican families to get by. The help at your hotel typically get paid only a few dollars a day. They depend on tips to make the difference between dire and bearable poverty. Give the *camarista* (chambermaid) and floor attendant 20 pesos every day or two. And whenever uncertain of what to tip, it will probably mean a lot to someone—maybe a whole family—if you err on the generous side.

In restaurants and bars, Mexican tipping customs are similar to those in the United States: tip waiters, waitresses, and bartenders about 15 percent for satisfactory service.

Credit Cards

Credit cards, such as Visa, MasterCard, and to a lesser extent, American Express and Discover, are widely honored in the hotels, restaurants, handicrafts shops, and boutiques that cater to foreign tourists. You will generally get better bargains, however, in shops that depend on local trade and do not so readily accept credit cards. Such shops sometimes offer discounts for cash sales.

Whatever the circumstance, your travel money will usually go much further in Acapulco region than back home. Despite the national 15 percent ("value added" IVA) sales tax, local lodging, food, and transportation prices will often seem like bargains compared to the developed world. Outside of the pricey high-rise beachfront strips, pleasant, palmy hotel room rates often run $40 or less.

COMMUNICATIONS

Using Mexican Telephones

Although Mexican phone service has improved in the last decade, it's still sometimes hit-or-miss. If a number doesn't get through, you may have to redial it more than once. When someone answers (usually *"Bueno"*) be especially courteous. If your Spanish is rusty, say, *"¿Por favor, habla inglés?"* (¿POR fah-VOR, AH-blah een-GLAYS?). If you want to speak to a particular person (such as María), ask, *"¿María se encuentra?"* (¿mah-REE-ah SAY ayn-koo-AYN-trah?).

Since November 2001, when telephone numbers were standardized, Mexican phones operate pretty much the same as in the United States and Canada. In Acapulco, for example, a complete telephone number is generally written like this: 744/485-4709. As in the United States, the "744" denotes the telephone area code *(lada)* (LAH-dah) and the 485-4709 is the number that you dial locally. If you want to dial this number long-distance *(larga distancia),* first dial "01" (like "1" in the United States), then 744/485-4709. All Mexican telephone numbers, with only three exceptions, begin with a three-digit *lada,* followed by a seven-digit local number. (The exceptions are Monterrey, Guadalajara, and Mexico City, which have two-digit *ladas* and eight-digit local numbers. The Mexico City *lada* is 55; Guadalajara's is 33, Monterrey's is 81. (For example, a complete Guadalajara phone number would read 33/6897-2253.)

In Acapulco region towns and cities, direct long-distance dialing is the rule—from hotels, public phone booths, and efficient private Computel telephone offices. The cheapest, often most convenient way to call is by buying and using a public telephone Ladatel card. Buy them in 20-, 30-, 50-, and 100-peso denominations at the many outlets—minimarkets, pharmacies, liquor stores—that display the blue and yellow Ladatel sign.

Calling Mexico and Calling Home

To call Mexico direct from the United States, first dial 011 (for international access), then 52 (for Mexico), followed by the Mexican area code and local number.

For station-to-station calls to the United States from Mexico, dial 001 plus the area code and the local number. For calls to other countries, ask your hotel desk clerk or see the easy-to-follow directions in the local Mexican telephone directory.

Another convenient way (although a more expensive one) to call home is via your personal telephone credit card. Contact your U.S. long-distance operator by dialing 001-800/462-4240 for AT&T; 001-800/674-7000 for MCI; or 001-800/877-8000 for Sprint.

Yet another (although expensive) way of calling home is collect. You can do this in one of two ways. Simply dial 09 for the local English-speaking international operator, or dial the AT&T, MCI, and Sprint numbers listed above.

Beware of certain private "To Call Long Distance to the U.S.A. Collect and Credit Card" telephones installed prominently in airports, tourist hotels, and shops. Tariffs on these phones often run as high as $10 per minute (with a three-minute minimum), for a total of $30, whether you talk three minutes or not. Always ask the operator for the rate, and if it's too high, take your business elsewhere.

In smaller towns, you must often do your long-distance phoning in the *larga distancia* (local phone office). Typically staffed by a young woman and often connected to a café, the *larga distancia* becomes an informal community social center as people pass the time waiting for their phone connections.

© BRUCE WHIPPERMAN

Street telephones, operable with readily purchasable Ladatel phone cards, are an economical and handy communications option in larger towns of the Acapulco region.

Post, Telegraph, and Internet Access

Mexican *correos* (post offices) operate similarly, but more slowly and less securely, than their counterparts in the developed world. Mail services usually include *lista de correo* (general delivery, address letters *"a/c lista de correo"), servicios filatelicas* (philatelic services), *por avión* (airmail), *giros* (postal money orders), and Mexpost secure and fast delivery service, usually from separate Mexpost offices.

Mexican ordinary mail is sadly unreliable and pathetically slow. If, for mailings within Mexico, you must have security, use the efficient, reformed government Mexpost (like U.S. Express Mail) service. For international mailings, check the local yellow pages for widely available DHL or Federal Express courier service.

Telégrafos (telegraph offices), usually near the post office, send and receive *telegramas* (telegrams) and *giros*. Telecomunicaciones (Telecom), the new high-tech telegraph offices, add telephone and public fax to the available services.

Internet service, including personal email access, has arrived in the Acapulco region's cities and larger towns. Internet "cafés" are becoming increasingly common, especially in the Acapulco and Ixtapa-Zihuatanejo. Online rates average about $3 per hour.

Electricity and Time

Mexican electric power is supplied at U.S.-standard 110 volts, 60 cycles. Plugs and sockets are generally two-pronged, nonpolar (like the pre-1970s U.S. ones). Bring adapters if you're going to use appliances with polar two-pronged or three-pronged plugs. (A two-pronged polar plug has different-sized prongs, one of which is too large to plug into an old-fashioned nonpolar socket.)

The Acapulco region operates on central time, just like Mexico City and most of the rest of the country, except for the northwest states of Sinaloa, Nayarit, and Sonora, which operate on mountain time, and Baja California Norte, which operates on Pacific time.

SPECIALTY TRAVEL

Bringing the Kids

Children are treasured like gifts from heaven in Mexico. Traveling with kids will ensure your welcome most everywhere. On the beach, take extra precautions to make sure they are protected from the sun.

A sick child is no fun for anyone. Fortunately, clinics and good doctors are available even in small towns. When in need, ask a storekeeper or a pharmacist, *"¿Dónde hay un doctor, por favor?"* (¿DOHN-day eye oon doc-TOHR por fah-VOHR?). In most cases, within five minutes you will be in the waiting room of the local physician or hospital.

Children who do not favor typical Mexican fare can easily be fed with always available eggs, cheese, *hamburguesas,* milk, oatmeal, corn flakes, bananas, cakes, and cookies.

Your children will generally have more fun if they have a little previous knowledge of Mexico and a stake in the trip. For example, help them select some library picture books and magazines so they'll know where they're going and what to expect, or give them responsibility for packing and carrying their own small travel bag.

Be sure to mention your children's ages when making air reservations; child discounts of 50 percent or more are often available. Also, if you can arrange to go on an uncrowded flight, you can stretch out and rest on the empty seats.

For more details on traveling with children, check out *Adventuring with Children* by Nan Jeffrey. (See Suggested Reading.)

Travel for People with Disabilities

Mexican airlines and hotels are becoming increasingly aware of the needs of travelers with disabilities. Open, street-level lobbies and large, wheelchair-accessible elevators and rooms are available in most Acapulco region resort hotels.

United States law forbids travel discrimination against otherwise qualified people with disabilities. As long as your disability is stable and not liable to deteriorate during passage, you can expect to be treated like any passenger with special needs.

Make reservations far ahead of departure and ask your agent to inform your airline of your needs, such as boarding wheelchair or in-flight

© BRUCE WHIPPERMAN

Mexican authorities and citizens are becoming increasingly aware of the needs of people with disabilities.

oxygen. Be early at the gate to take advantage of the preboarding call.

For many helpful details to smooth your trip, get a copy of *Traveling Like Everyone Else: A Practical Guide for Disabled Travelers* by Jacqueline Freeman and Susan Gerstein. Get it from the publisher, Lambda Publishing, 3709 13th Ave., Brooklyn, NY 11218, tel. 718/972-5449. Also useful is the book *The Wheelchair Traveler,* by Douglas R. Annand. Yet another helpful publication is *New Horizons,* available from the United States Department of Transportation or the Paralyzed Veterans of America; call tel. 888/860-7244, or visit www.pva.org.

Certain organizations both encourage and provide information about travel for those with disabilities. One with many Mexican connections is **Mobility International USA,** P.O. Box 10767, Eugene, OR 97440, tel. 541/343-1284 voice/TDD, fax 541/343-6812, www.miusa.org. A $35 membership gets you a semiannual newsletter and referrals for international exchanges and homestays.

Similarly, **Partners of the Americas,** 1424 K St. NW, Suite 700, Washington, D.C. 20005, tel. 202/628-3300 or 800/322-7844, fax 202/628-3306, info@partners.net, with chapters in 45 U.S. states, works to improve understanding of disabilities and facilities in Mexico and Latin America. It maintains lists of local organizations and individuals whom handicapped travelers with disabilities may contact at their destinations. For more information see www.partners.net.

Travel for Senior Citizens

Age, according to Mark Twain, is a question of mind over matter: If you don't mind, it doesn't matter. Mexico is a country where entire extended families, from babies to great-grandparents, live together. Elderly travelers will benefit from the respect and understanding Mexicans accord to older people. Besides these encouragements, consider the number of retirees already in havens in the Acapulco region.

Certain organizations support senior travel. Leading the field is **Elderhostel,** 11 Ave. de Lafayette, Boston, MA 02111-1746, tel. 877/426-8056, www.elderhostel.org, which publishes extensive U.S. and international catalogs of special tours, study, homestays, and people-to-people travel programs.

A number of newsletters publicize Acapulco region vacation and retirement opportunities. Among the best is ***Adventures in Mexico,*** published six times yearly and filled with pithy hotel, restaurant, touring, and real estate information for independent travelers and retirees seeking the "real" Mexico. For information, write Adventures in Mexico, c/o Lloyd Guadalajara, P.O. Box 437090, San Ysidro, CA 92143-7090; or, in Mexico, P.O. Box 31-70, Guadalajara, Jalisco 45050. Back issues are $2; one-year subscription $16, Canadian $19.

Equally worthy is the ***Mexico File*** monthly newsletter that, besides featuring pithy stories by Mexico travelers and news updates, offers an opportunity-packed classified section of Mexico rentals, publications, services, and much more. Subscribe ($39/year) at Simmonds Publications, 5580 La Jolla Blvd., #306, La Jolla, CA 92037, tel./fax 858/456-4419, tel. 800/563-9345 (voice mail), mf@mexicofile.com, www.mexicofile.com.

Houston-based Vacation Publications offers yet more possibilities. Check out the book ***Special Report for Discount Travelers,*** which lists a plethora of hotel, travel club, cruise, air, credit card, single, and off-season discounts. Also useful is the magazine ***Where to Retire.*** For information, a catalog, and to order, contact Vacation Publications, 1502 Augusta, Suite 415, Houston, TX 77057, tel. 713/974-6903, www.vacationsmagazine.com.

Health and Safety

STAYING HEALTHY

In the Acapulco region, as everywhere, prevention is the best remedy for illness. For those visitors who confine their travel to the beaten path, a few basic common-sense precautions will ensure vacation enjoyment.

Resist the temptation to dive headlong into Mexico. It's no wonder that people get sick—broiling in the sun, gobbling peppery food, guzzling beer and margaritas, then discoing half the night—all in their first 24 hours. An alternative is to give your body time to adjust. Travelers often arrive tired and dehydrated from travel and heat. During the first few days, drink plenty of bottled water and juice, and take siestas.

It's no wonder that people get sick—broiling in the sun, gobbling peppery food, guzzling margaritas, then discoing half the night—all in their first 24 hours. Give your body time to adjust. During the first few days, drink plenty of bottled water and juice, and take siestas.

Immunizations and Precautions

A good physician can recommend the proper preventatives for your Acapulco region trip. If you are going to stay pretty much in town, your doctor will probably suggest little more than updating your basic typhoid, diphtheria-tetanus, and polio shots.

For camping or trekking in remote tropical areas—below 4,000 feet or 1,200 meters—doctors often recommend a gamma-globulin shot against hepatitis A and a schedule of chloroquine pills against malaria. While in back-country areas, use other measures to discourage mosquitoes—and fleas, flies, ticks, no-see-ums, "kissing bugs" (see Chagas' Disease and Dengue Fever), and other tropical pesties—from biting you. Common precautions include sleeping under mosquito netting, burning *espirales mosquito* (mosquito coils), and rubbing on plenty of pure DEET (n,n dimethyl-meta-toluamide) "jungle juice," mixed in equal parts with rubbing (70 percent isopropyl) alcohol. Although super-effective, 100 percent DEET dries and irritates the skin.

Sunburn

For sunburn protection, use a good sunscreen with a sun protection factor (SPF) rated 15 or more, which will reduce burning rays to one-fifteenth or less of direct sunlight. Better still, take a shady siesta-break from the sun during the most hazardous midday hours. If you do get burned, applying your sunburn lotion (or one of the "caine" creams) after the fact usually decreases the pain and speeds healing.

Safe Water and Food

Although municipalities have made great strides in sanitation, food and water are still potential sources of germs in some parts of the Acapulco region. Although it's probably safe most everywhere, except in a few upcountry localities, it's still probably best to drink bottled water only. Hotels, whose success depends vitally on their customers' health, generally provide *agua purificada* (purified bottled water). If, for any reason, the available water is of doubtful quality, add a water purifier, such as "Potable Aqua" brand (get it at a camping goods stores before departure) or a few drops per quart of water of *blanqueador* (household chlorine bleach) or *yodo* (tincture of iodine) from the pharmacy.

Pure bottled water, soft drinks, beer, and fresh fruit juices are so widely available it is easy to avoid tap water, especially in restaurants. Ice and *paletas* (iced juice-on-a-stick) may be risky, especially in small towns.

Washing hands before eating in a restaurant is a time-honored Mexican ritual that visitors should religiously follow. The humblest Mexican eatery will generally provide a basin to *lavar las manos* (wash the hands). If it doesn't, don't eat there.

Hot, cooked food is generally safe, as are peeled fruits and vegetables. Milk and cheese these days in Mexico are generally processed under sanitary conditions and sold pasteurized (ask, "*¿Pasteurizado?*") and are typically safe. Mexican ice cream used to be both bad-tasting and of dubious safety, but national brands available in supermarkets are so much improved that it's no longer necessary to resist ice cream while in town.

In recent years, much cleaner public water and increased hygiene awareness have made salads—once shunned by Mexico travelers—generally safe to eat in tourist-frequented Acapulco region cafés and restaurants. Nevertheless, lettuce and cabbage, particularly in country villages, are more likely to be contaminated than tomatoes, carrots, cucumbers, onions, and green peppers. In any case, you can try dousing your salad in vinegar *(vinagre)* or plenty of sliced lime *(limón)* juice, the acidity of which kills some but not all bacteria.

© BRUCE WHIPPERMAN

Latter-generation Acapulco region authorities and citizens have made great strides in public health. Here, a small-town health clinic advertises the connection of larva and mosquitoes to dengue fever.

First-Aid Kit

In the tropics, ordinary cuts and insect bites are more prone to infection and should receive immediate first aid. A first-aid kit with aspirin, rubbing alcohol, hydrogen peroxide, water-purifying tablets, household chlorine bleach or iodine for water purifying, swabs, bandages, gauze, adhesive tape, Ace bandage, chamomile *(manzanilla)* tea bags for upset stomachs, Pepto-Bismol, acidophilus tablets, antibiotic ointment, hydrocortisone cream, mosquito repellent, knife, and good tweezers is a good precaution for any traveler and mandatory for campers.

HEALTH PROBLEMS

Traveler's Diarrhea

Traveler's diarrhea (known in Southeast Asia as "Bali Belly" and in Mexico as turista or "Montezuma's Revenge") sometimes persists, even among prudent vacationers. You can suffer turista for a week after simply traveling from California to Philadelphia or New York. Doctors say the familiar symptoms of runny bowels, nausea, and sour stomach result from normal local bacterial strains to which newcomers' systems need time to adjust. Unfortunately, the dehydration and fatigue from heat and travel reduce your body's natural defenses and sometimes lead to a persistent cycle of sickness at a time when you least want it.

Time-tested protective measures can help your body either prevent or break this cycle. Many doctors and veteran travelers swear by Pepto-Bismol for soothing sore stomachs and stopping diarrhea. Acidophilus, the bacteria found in yogurt, is widely available in the United States in tablets and aids digestion. Warm *manzanilla* (chamomile) tea, used widely in Mexico (and by Peter Rabbit's mother), provides liquid and calms upset stomachs. Temporarily avoid coffee and alcohol, drink plenty of *manzanilla* tea, and eat bananas and rice for a few meals until your tummy can take regular food.

Although powerful antibiotics and antidiarrhea medications such as Lomotil and Imodium are readily available over *farmacia* counters, they may involve serious side effects and should not be taken in the absence of medical advice. If in doubt, consult a doctor.

Chagas' Disease and Dengue Fever

Chagas' disease, spread by the "kissing" (or, more appropriately, "assassin") bug, is a potential hazard in the Mexican tropics. Known locally as a *vinchuca,* the triangular-headed, three-quarter-inch (two-centimeter) brown insect, identifiable by its yellow-striped abdomen, often drops upon its sleeping victims from the thatched ceiling of a rural house at night. Its bite is followed by swelling, fever, and weakness and can lead to heart failure if left untreated. Application of drugs at an early stage can, however, clear the patient of the trypanosome parasites that infect victims' bloodstreams and vital organs. See a doctor immediately if you believe you're infected.

Most of the precautions against malaria-bearing mosquitoes also apply to dengue fever, which does occur (although uncommonly) in outlying tropical areas of Mexico. The culprit here is a virus carried by the mosquito species *Aedes aegypti.* Symptoms are acute fever, with chills, sweating, and muscle aches. A red, diffuse rash frequently results, which may later peel. Symptoms abate after about five days, but fatigue may persist. A particularly serious, but fortunately rare, form, called dengue hemorrhagic fever, afflicts children and can be fatal. See a doctor immediately. Although no vaccines or preventatives, other than deterring mosquitoes, exist, you should nevertheless see a doctor immediately.

For more good tropical preventative information, get a copy of the excellent pamphlet distributed by the International Association of Medical Advice to Travelers (IAMAT). (See Medical Care.)

Scorpions and Snakes

While camping or staying in a *palapa* or other rustic accommodation, watch for scorpions, especially in your shoes, which you should shake out every morning. Scorpion stings and snakebites are rarely fatal to an adult but are potentially very serious for a child. Get the victim to a doctor calmly but quickly. (For more snakebite details, see Reptiles and Amphibians under Flora and Fauna in the general Introduction.)

Sea Creatures

While snorkeling or surfing, you may suffer a coral scratch or jellyfish sting. Experts advise you to wash the afflicted area with ocean water and pour alcohol (rubbing alcohol or tequila) over the wound, then apply hydrocortisone cream available from the *farmacia.*

Injuries from sea urchin spines and stingray barbs are painful and can be serious. Physicians recommend similar first aid for both: remove the spines or barbs by hand or with tweezers, then soak the injury in as-hot-as-possible fresh water to weaken the toxins and provide relief. Another method is to rinse the area with an antibacterial solution—rubbing alcohol, vinegar, wine, or ammonia diluted with water. If none are available, the same effect may be achieved with urine, either your own or someone else's in your party. Get medical help immediately.

Tattoos

All health hazards don't come from the wild. A number of Mexico travelers have complained of complications from black henna tattoos. When enhanced by the chemical dye PPD, an itchy rash results that can lead to scarring. It's best to play it safe: if you must have a vacation tattoo, get it at an established, professional shop.

MEDICAL CARE

For medical advice and treatment, let your hotel (or if you're camping, the closest *farmacia*) refer you to a good doctor, clinic, or hospital. Mexican doctors, especially in medium-sized and small towns, practice like private doctors in the United States and Canada once did before health insurance, liability, and group practice. They will come to you if you request it; they often keep their doors open even after regular hours and charge reasonable fees.

You will receive generally good treatment at the many local hospitals in the Acapulco region's tourist centers. If you must have an English-speaking, American-trained doctor, the International Association for Medical Assistance to

MEDICAL TAGS AND AIR EVACUATION

Travelers with special medical problems might consider wearing a medical identification tag. For a reasonable fee, **Medic Alert,** P.O. Box 1009, Turlock, CA 95381, toll-free U.S. tel. 800/344-3226, www.medicalert.org, provides such tags, as well as an information hotline that will provide doctors with your vital medical background information.

For life-threatening emergencies, **Critical Air Medicine,** Montgomery Field, 4141 Kearny Villa Rd., San Diego, CA 92123, tel. 619/571-0482, toll-free U.S. tel. 800/247-8326 or (reachable from Mexico 24 hours) 800/010-0268, provides high-tech jet ambulance service from any Mexican locale to the United States. For a fee averaging about $15,000, it promises to fly you to the right U.S. hospital in a hurry.

Alternatively, for similar services, consider **Medjet Assistance,** toll-free U.S. tel. 800/963-3538. In emergencies worldwide, call U.S. tel. 205/595-6626 collect. For more information, visit www.medjetassistance.com.

Travelers (IAMAT) publishes an updated booklet of qualified member physicians, several of whom practice in Acapulco and Ixtapa-Zihuatanejo. (See the destination chapters for doctor and hospital details.) IAMAT also distributes a very detailed *How to Protect Yourself Against Malaria* guide, together with worldwide malaria risk and communicable disease charts. Contact IAMAT, at 417 Center Street, Lewiston, NY 14092, tel. 716/754-4883, or in Canada at 40 Regal Road, Guelph, ON N1K 1B5, tel. 519/836-0102, or 1287 St. Clair Ave. West, Toronto, Ontario M6E 1B8, tel. 416/652 0137. You may also contact it at info@iamat.org or www.iamat.org.

For more useful information on health and safety in Mexico, consult Dr. William Forgey's *Traveler's Medical Alert Series: Mexico, A Guide to Health and Safety* (Merrillville, IN: ICS Books), or Dirk Schroeder's *Staying Healthy in Asia, Africa, and Latin America* (Emeryville, CA: Avalon Travel Publishing).

CONDUCT AND CUSTOMS

Safe Conduct

Mexico is an old-fashioned country where people value traditional ideals of honesty, fidelity, and piety. Crime rates are low; visitors are often safer in Mexico than in their home cities.

Even though four generations have elapsed since Pancho Villa raided the U.S. border, the image of a Mexico bristling with *bandidos* persists. And similarly for Mexicans: despite the century and a half since the *yanquis* invaded Mexico City and took half their country, the communal Mexican psyche still views gringos (and, by association all white foreigners) with revulsion, jealousy, and wonder.

Fortunately, the Mexican love-hate affair with foreigners does not usually apply to individual visitors. Your friendly *"buenos dias"* ("good morning") or *"por favor"* ("please"), when appropriate, is always appreciated, whether in the market, the gas station, or the hotel. The shy smile you will most likely receive in return will be your small, but not insignificant, reward.

Women

Your own behavior, despite low crime statistics, largely determines your safety in Mexico. For women traveling solo, it is important to realize that the double standard is alive and well in Mexico. Dress and behave modestly and you will most likely avoid embarrassment. Whenever possible, stay in the company of friends or acquaintances; find companions for beach, sightseeing, and shopping excursions. Ignore strange men's solicitations and overtures. A Mexican man on the prowl will invent the sappiest romantic overtures to snare a gringa. He will often interpret anything but a firm "no" as a "maybe," and a "maybe" as a yes.

Men

For male visitors, alcohol often leads to trouble. Avoid bars and cantinas; and if, given Mexico's excellent beers, you can't abstain completely, at least maintain soft-spoken self-control in the face of challenges from macho drunks.

The Law and Police

While Mexican authorities are tolerant of alcohol,

they are decidedly intolerant of other substances such as marijuana, psychedelics, cocaine, and heroin. Getting caught with such drugs in Mexico usually leads to swift and severe results.

Equally swift is the punishment for nude sunbathing, which is both illegal in public and offensive to Mexicans. Confine your nudist colony to very private locations.

Although with decreasing frequency lately, traffic police in Acapulco and Ixtapa-Zihuatanejo sometimes seem to watch foreign cars with eagle eyes. Officers seem to inhabit busy intersections and one-way streets, waiting for confused tourists to make a wrong move. If they whistle you over, stop immediately or you will really get into hot water. If guilty, say *"Lo siento"* ("I'm sorry") and be cooperative. Although the officer probably won't mention it, he or she is usually hoping that you'll cough up a $20 *mordida* (bribe) for the privilege of driving away.

Don't do it. Although he may hint at confiscating your car, calmly ask for an official *boleto* (written traffic ticket, if you're guilty) in exchange for your driver's license (have a copy), which the officer will probably keep if he writes a ticket. If after a few minutes no money appears, the officer will most likely give you back your driver's license rather than go to the trouble of writing the ticket. If not, the worst that will usually happen is you will have to go to the *presidencia municipal* (city hall) the next morning and pay the $20 to a clerk in exchange for your driver's license.

MACHISMO

I once met an Acapulco man who wore five gold wristwatches and became angry when I quietly refused his repeated invitations to get drunk with him. Another time, on the beach near San Blas, two drunk campesinos nearly attacked me because I was helping my girlfriend cook a picnic dinner. Outside Taxco I once spent an endless hour in the seat behind a bus driver who insisted on speeding down the middle of the two-lane highway, honking aside oncoming automobiles.

Despite their wide differences (the first was a rich criollo, the campesinos were *indígenas,* and the bus driver, mestizo), the common affliction shared by all four men was machismo, a disease that seems to possess many Mexican men. Machismo is a sometimes reckless obsession to prove one's masculinity, to show how macho you are. Men of many nationalities share the instinct to prove themselves. Japan's *bushido* samurai code is one example. Mexican men, however, often seem to try the hardest.

When confronted by a Mexican braggart, male visitors should remain careful and controlled. If your opponent is yelling, stay cool, speak softly, and withdraw as soon as possible. On the highway, be courteous and unprovocative; don't use your car to spar with a macho driver. Drinking often leads to problems. It's best to stay out of bars or cantinas unless you're prepared to deal with the macho consequences. Polite refusal of a drink may be taken as a challenge. If you visit a bar with Mexican friends or acquaintances, you may be heading for a no-win choice of a drunken all-night *borrachera* (binge) or an insult to the honor of your friends by refusing.

For women, machismo requires even more cautious behavior. In Mexico, women's liberation is long in coming. Although a handful of Mexican women have risen to positions of political or corporate power, they constitute a small minority.

Machismo requires that female visitors obey the rules or suffer the consequences. Keep a low profile; wear bathing suits and brief shorts only at the beach. Follow the example of your Mexican sisters: Make a habit of going out, especially at night, in the company of friends or acquaintances. Mexican men believe an unaccompanied woman wants to be picked up. Ignore such offers; any response, even refusal, might be taken as a "maybe." If, on the other hand, there is a Mexican man whom you'd genuinely like to meet, the traditional way is an arranged introduction through family or friends.

Mexican families, as a source of protection and friendship, should not be overlooked—especially on the beach or in the park, where, among the gaggle of kids, grandparents, aunts, and cousins, there's room for one more.

Pedestrian and Driving Hazards

Although the Acapulco region's potholed pavements and "holey" sidewalks won't land you in jail, one of them might send you to the hospital if you don't watch your step, especially at night. "Pedestrian beware" is especially good advice on Mexican streets, where it is rumored that some drivers speed up rather than slow down when they spot a tourist stepping off the curb. Falling coconuts, especially frequent on windy days, constitute an additional hazard to unwary campers and beachgoers.

Driving Mexican country roads, where slow trucks and carts block lanes, campesinos stroll the shoulders, and horses, burros, and cattle wander at will, is hazardous—doubly so at night.

Socially Responsible Travel

Latter-day jet travel has brought droves of vacationing tourists to developing countries largely unprepared for the consequences. As the visitors' numbers swell, power grids black out, sewers overflow, and roads crack under the strain of accommodating more and larger hotels, restaurants, cars, buses, and airports.

Worse yet, armies of vacationers drive up local prices and begin to change native customs. While visions of tourists as sources of fast money replace traditions of hospitality, television wipes out folk entertainments, Coke and Pepsi substitute for fruit drinks, and prostitution and drugs flourish.

Some travelers have said enough is enough and are forming organizations to encourage visitors to travel with increased sensitivity to native people and customs. They have developed travelers' codes of ethics and guidelines that encourage visitors to stay at local-style accommodations, use local transportation, and seek alternative vacations and tours, such as language-study and cultural programs and people-to-people work projects.

What to Take

"Men wear pants, ladies be beautiful" was once the dress code of one of the Mexican Pacific's classiest hotels. Men in the casual Acapulco region can get by easily without a jacket, women with simple skirts and blouses.

Loose-fitting, hand-washable, easy-to-dry clothes make for trouble-free tropical vacationing. Synthetic or cotton-synthetic-blend shirts, blouses, pants, socks, and underwear will fit the bill practically always on the Acapulco region's balmy coast. For breezy nights, bring a lightweight windbreaker. If you're going upcountry (Chilpancingo, Iguala, Taxco), add a medium-weight jacket.

In all cases, leave showy, expensive clothes and jewelry at home. Stow items that you cannot lose in your hotel safe or carry them with you in a sturdy zipped purse or a waist pouch on your front side.

Packing

What you pack depends on how mobile you want to be. If you're staying the whole time at a self-contained resort, you can take the two suitcases and one carry-on allowed by airlines. If, on the other hand, you're going to be moving around a lot, you'd do better to condense everything to one easily carried bag with wheels that doubles as luggage and soft backpack. Experienced travelers accomplish this by packing prudently and tightly, choosing items that will do double or triple duty.

Campers will have to be super-careful to accomplish this. Fortunately, camping along the tropical coast requires no sleeping bag. Simply use a hammock (buy it in Mexico) or, if sleeping on the ground, a sleeping pad and a sheet for cover. In the winter, at most, you may have to buy a light blanket. A compact tent that you and your partner can share is a must against bugs, as is mosquito repellent. A first-aid kit is absolutely necessary.

PACKING CHECKLIST

Necessary Items
__ camera, film (expensive in Mexico)
__ comb
__ guidebook, reading books
__ inexpensive watch, clock
__ keys, tickets
__ lightweight clothes, hat for sun
__ money, ATM card, and/or traveler's checks
__ mosquito repellent
__ prescription eyeglasses
__ prescription medicines and drugs
__ purse, waist-belt carrying pouch
__ sunglasses, sunscreen
__ swimsuit
__ toothbrush, toothpaste
__ tourist card, visa
__ windbreaker

Useful Items
__ address book
__ birth control
__ checkbook, credit cards
__ contact lenses
__ dental floss
__ earplugs
__ first-aid kit
__ flashlight, batteries
__ immersion heater
__ lightweight binoculars
__ portable radio/cassette player
__ razor
__ travel booklight
__ vaccination certificate

Necessary Items for Campers
__ collapsible gallon plastic bottle
__ dish soap
__ first-aid kit
__ hammock (buy in Mexico)
__ insect repellent
__ lightweight hiking shoes
__ lightweight tent
__ matches in waterproof case
__ nylon cord
__ plastic bottle, quart
__ pot scrubber/sponge
__ sheet or light blanket
__ Sierra Club cup, fork, and spoon
__ single-burner stove with fuel
__ Swiss army knife
__ tarp
__ toilet paper
__ towel, soap
__ two nesting cooking pots
__ water-purifying tablets or iodine

Useful Items for Campers
__ compass
__ dishcloths
__ hot pad
__ instant coffee, tea, sugar, powdered milk
__ moleskin (Dr. Scholl's)
__ plastic plate
__ poncho
__ short (votive) candles
__ whistle

Acapulco

Acapulco (pop. 1.5 million) retains its renown as the "Queen of Mexican Beach Resorts," still Mexico's favorite and as sunny and breezy as ever. By day, viewed either from the shore or an airy hilltop, Acapulco's golden strand curves around its picture-perfect half-moon bay. At night, myriad twinkling city lights decorate the same space, bordered below by the bay's ebony darkness and above by the starry firmament.

In Acapulco as in its latter-day metropolitan cousins, Hollywood and Las Vegas, the new, the brash, the loud, and the bright far outshine the many quiet, charming Acapulcos that few visitors know.

But despite the hullabaloo you can discover and enjoy Acapulco's hidden feast of old-Mexico diversions: intimate, old-world neighborhoods around the *zócalo* with their upcountry traditional food restaurants, fascinating museums, such as Fuerte San Diego and Casa de la Máscara, and manifold outdoor diversions, including sunning on the beaches, glass-bottomed boat rides, exploring rock hieroglyphs, and soaking up the sunset at Hotel Los Flamingos.

With more time, you can adventure beyond the edges of the Acapulco metropolis and discover more hidden Acapulcos: the breezy, driftwood-strewn strands of Playa Larga; plumy south-seas islands, such as Isla Montosa, in wildlife-rich Laguna Coyuca; and the palmy, charmingly out-of-date downscale resort village of Pie de la Cuesta.

© BRUCE WHIPPERMAN

History

IN THE BEGINNING

Experts believe that Acapulco Bay, with its trove of seafood ripe for the picking, was home to bands of hunter-gatherers beginning at least 4,000 years ago. They left mute testimony, rock paintings of their gods at Puerto Marqués, Pie de la Cuesta, and the newly opened site at Palma Sola, uphill from present-day Acapulco town. Moreover, these earliest inhabitants left direct evidence of their daily life, stone metates and pottery utensils at seaside sites, that experts have dated to around 2500 B.C.

Acapulco's bounty eventually led to more leisure and more sophistication. At Las Sabanas, at the northern edge of the Acapulco suburb, archaeologists unearthed a trove of fetching female statuettes, reminiscent of early Polynesian and Asian artifacts. Such discoveries have added credence to widespread legends of early Chinese influences on the Mexican Pacific coast long before Columbus.

Highland Influences

Evidence of far-flung influences is equally intriguing. Among the most fascinating of finds are the ancient paintings at the caves of Juxtlahuaca, not far from Chilpancingo, in the mountains north of Acapulco. Here, deep in a regal limestone-draped grotto, captivating multicolored Olmec-origin paintings decorate the cavern walls. Although a trove of similar finds all over the state of Guerrero lead historians to the conclusion that Acapulco's early inhabitants were undoubtedly influenced by Mexico's high civilizations—Olmec, Mixtec, Zapotec, and Aztec—and frequented by their traders, the same experts believe that Acapulco never came under their direct control but instead remained the domain of a fiercely tenacious tribe, known as the Yopes until the Spanish conquest.

CONQUEST AND COLONIZATION

Enter Hernán Cortés, who in 1519 sailed in command of a small fleet west from Cuba. He didn't find the elusive passage to China, but, hearing of a grand kingdom in the mountains to the west, marched overland and boldly took the Aztec Emperor Moctezuma captive. Nearly immediately, Cortés asked Moctezuma about Mexico's southern coast and dispatched expeditions west and south, founding villages and shipbuilding ports, in Oaxaca, at Huatulco and Tehuantepec, and in the Acapulco region, at Zacatula and Acapulco.

One of the earliest of those expeditions, commanded by Juan Rodríguez de Villafuerte, landed at Acapulco Bay on the feast day of Santa Lucia in 1523. Following Spanish custom, Villafuerte christened his discovery the Bahía de Santa Lucia, a name it retained for years. A safe anchorage, good fresh water, and an abundance of big trees led Villafuerte to establish an outpost and shipbuilding port by the latter 1520s. Word got back to the authorities, and by royal decree, in 1528, "Acapulco and her land . . . where the ships of the south will be built . . ." passed directly into the hands of the Spanish Crown.

Voyages of discovery set sail from Acapulco for Peru, the Gulf of California, and Asia. None returned from across the Pacific, however, until navigator-priest Father Andrés de Urdaneta discovered the northern Pacific tradewinds, which propelled him and his ship, loaded with Chinese treasure, to Acapulco in October 1565.

The Manila Galleon

From then on, for more than 250 years, a special yearly trading ship, renowned in Mexico as the Nao de China and in England as the Manila galleon, set sail exclusively from Acapulco for Asia. Tensely anticipating the Manila galleon's return, Acapulco authorities sent ships to scan the northwestern horizon. Runners and signal fires brought the news to Acapulco and Mexico City, setting in motion a long line of Acapulco-bound traders.

The galleon's arrival sparked an annual trade fair, swelling Acapulco's population with merchants from not only all Mexico, but from as far

ACAPULCO: AROUND THE BAY

To Mex. 200, Chilpancingo, Taxco, and Mexico City
95
AV. ADOLFO RUÍZ CORTINEZ
RESTAURANT EL CAMPANARIO
AV. FARALLÓN
AV. CUAUHTÉMOC
COMERCIAL MEXICANA
ESTRELLA DE ORO (1ST CLASS BUS)
WILFRIDO MASSIEU
200
DIANA TRAFFIC CIRCLE
Playa Condesa
La Redonda
Playa Morro
ESTRELLA BLANCA (1ST CLASS BUS)
Parque Papagayo
Playa Hornitos
El Morro
AV. NIÑOS HÉROES
AV. CONSTITUYENTES
Farallón de San Lorenzo
GIGANTE
Playa Hornos
Morro Chico
AMAL ESPINA
M. ALEMÁN
HOTEL EL CID
HOTEL CASTILLO REAL
HOTEL ACA BAY
CLUB TROPICANA
CLUB COPACABANA
Bahía de Acapulco
CALLE DE EJIDO
MARKET
AV. DE MENDOZA
ESCUDERO
AV. COSTERA
ESTRELLA BLANCA (1ST AND 2ND CLASS BUSES)
200
To Pie de la Cuesta, The Costa Grande, and Ixtapa-Zihuatanejo
PIE DE LA CUESTA
HOTEL LAS HAMACAS
Playa Hamacas
COMERCIAL MEXICANA
FUERTE SAN DIEGO
MALECÓN STEAMSHIP DOCK
SEE "ACAPULCO: AROUND THE ZÓCALO" MAP
ZÓCALO
Piedra del Elefante
Playa Tlacopanocha
CAMINO DE LA PINZONA
HOTEL TORRE EIFEL
SUITES ETEL
HOTEL MAJESTIC
GRAN VIA TROPICAL
Playas
SPORT FISHING AND SCUBA DOCK
CASA DE DOLORES OLMEDO
SUITES ALBA
LA QUEBRADA (CLIFFDIVERS)
Playa Manzanillo
MARINA ACAPULCO
BUCEOS (DIVE SHOP)
CLUB DE YATES
las
AV. LOPES MATEOS
Playa Angosta
RESTAURANT COYUCA 22
HOTEL ACAMAR BEACH RESORT
LA CABAÑA
HOTEL GRAND MEIGAS ACAPULCO
SINFONIA DEL SOL (SUNSET VIEW)
de
Playa Caleta
MÁGICO MUNDO
Playa Caletilla
Peninsula
HOTEL BOCA CHICA
SUBMARINE VIRGIN
La Yerba Buena
Playa Marín
HOTEL LOS FLAMINGOS
AV. LÓPEZ MATEOS
Canal Boca Chica
Playa Roqueta
Isla Roqueta
RESTAURANT PALAO
EL FARO (LIGHTHOUSE)
Trail

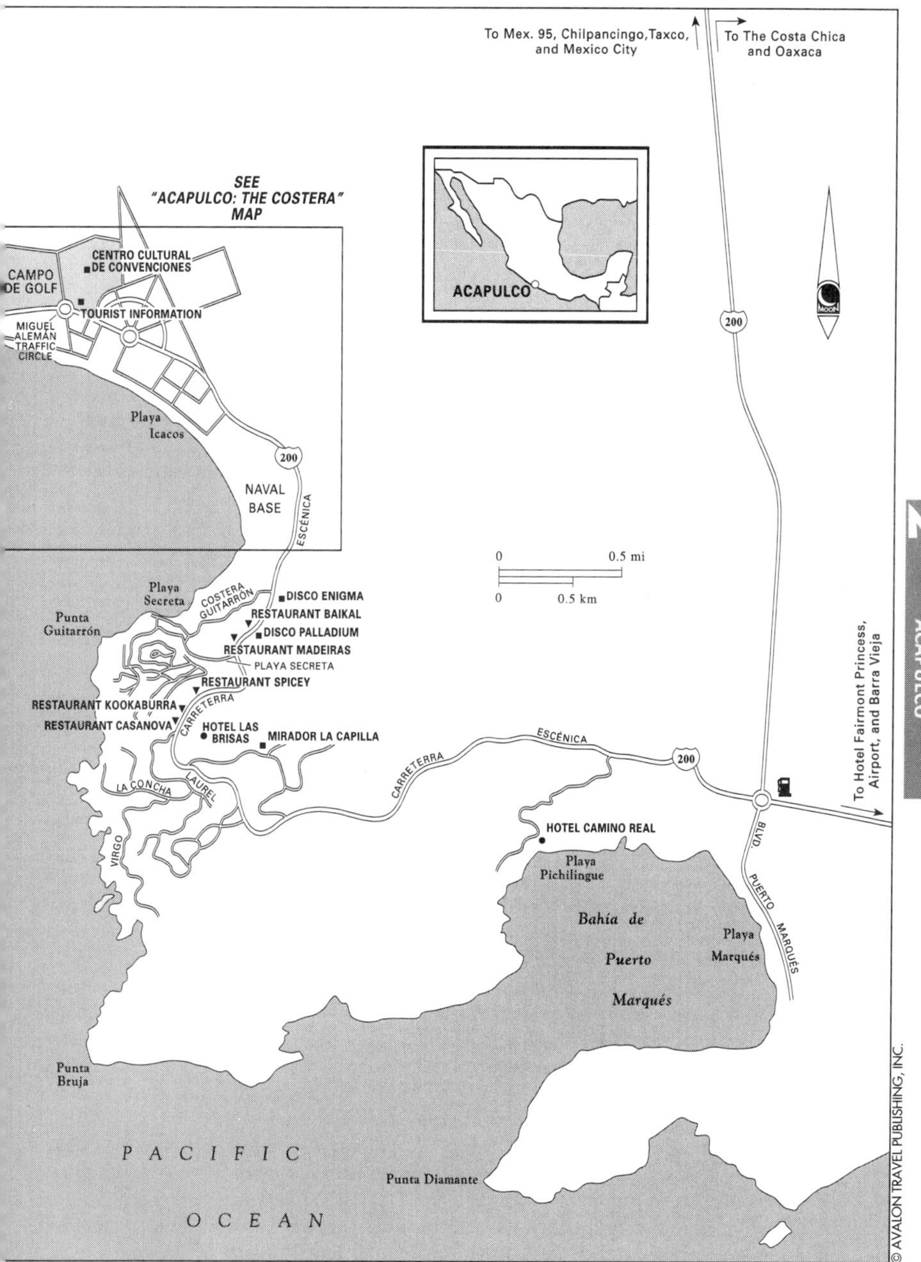
To Mex. 95, Chilpancingo, Taxco, and Mexico City
To The Costa Chica and Oaxaca
ACAPULCO
200
SEE "ACAPULCO: THE COSTERA" MAP
CAMPO DE GOLF
CENTRO CULTURAL DE CONVENCIONES
TOURIST INFORMATION
MIGUEL ALEMÁN TRAFFIC CIRCLE
Playa Icacos
NAVAL BASE
ESCÉNICA
0 0.5 mi
0 0.5 km
Playa Secreta
COSTERA GUITARRÓN
DISCO ENIGMA
RESTAURANT BAIKAL
DISCO PALLADIUM
RESTAURANT MADEIRAS
PLAYA SECRETA
Punta Guitarrón
RESTAURANT SPICEY
RESTAURANT KOOKABURRA
RESTAURANT CASANOVA
CARRETERRA
HOTEL LAS BRISAS
MIRADOR LA CAPILLA
ESCÉNICA
CARRETERRA
LA CONCHA
LAUREL
VIRGO
HOTEL CAMINO REAL
BLVD. PUERTO MARQUÉS
To Hotel Fairmont Princess, Airport, and Barra Vieja
Playa Pichilingue
Bahía de Puerto Marqués
Playa Marqués
Punta Bruja
PACIFIC OCEAN
Punta Diamante
© AVALON TRAVEL PUBLISHING, INC.
ACAPULCO

THE LEGEND OF ACAPULCO

The *Codex Mendoza* records that, in 1499, en route south from their capital of Tenochtitlán, Aztec commanders and their armies first gazed downward at the blue sweep of Acapulco Bay. Motivated by their need for tropical treasures, such as exotic bird feathers and cacao—so valuable that cacao seeds served as the Aztecs' currency—Aztec forces tried but failed to subdue the fierce Yope tribes that ruled the Acapulco coast.

Nevertheless, the Aztec-origin name, Acapulco, from *acatl,* the Náhuatl (Aztec-language) word for reed, remained. Although translations for "Acapulco" vary, the meaning "place where the reeds are destroyed," appears most credible. First of all, the Aztec hieroglyph for Acapulco shows a pair of hands, one of which is shown breaking a reed. Moreover, there is the Yope legend of Acapulco that tells the story of Acatl, the son of the Aztec commander. It seems that Acatl fell hopelessly in love with Quiahuitl, comely daughter of the Yope chieftain. When his father forbade him to marry Quiahuitl, Acatl screamed with sorrow. His tears flowed so profusely that they melted him, transforming Acatl into a pond bordered by a reed thicket. Meanwhile, Quiahuitl, vaporized by her all-consuming grief, rose to the heavens as a cloud, condemned to float aimlessly over land and sea. But the lovers nevertheless received fulfillment every year during the summer rains, when Quiahuitl would float over Acapulco and rain upon Acatl's pond, uniting the lovers with so much ardor that the downpour flattened and drowned the reeds lining the pond.

as Spain and Peru. Loaded down with gold-filled purses, the traders jostled to bargain for the Manila galleon's shiny trove of silks, satins, damasks, porcelain, gold, ivory, and lacquerware. Fortunes were not only exchanged at trading; they were also gained and lost at gambling at raucous cockfights and exciting horseraces, in which African Mexicans soon became the star riders.

Pirates and Forts

Acapulco's yearly treasure soon attracted marauders. In 1579, Francis Drake, during his circumnavigation of the globe, and blessed by England's Queen Elizabeth, threatened the Spanish Pacific coast from Chile to California. One of his most notorious raids was at Huatulco, on April 13, 1579, when he even stole the church bell. Drake waited fruitlessly for the Manila galleon as far north as Cape Mendocino, before continuing west across the Pacific.

Later, corsair Thomas Cavendish managed similar mischief, burning Huatulco in 1586. He continued northwest, where, off Cabo San Lucas, Cavendish was the first to capture the Manila galleon, the *Santa Ana.* The cash booty alone, 1.2 million gold pesos, severely depressed the London gold market.

On October 11, 1614, a five-ship Dutch fleet, consisting of the *Sun, Moon, Pechelinga, Jager* and *Meeuve,* attacked the unfortified village of Acapulco. Already weakened by scurvy and hunger, the Dutch sailors called off the attack and, for food and water, traded two dozen hostages they had captured in Peru.

Such attacks pushed Viceroy Diego Fernandez de Córdoba to build a fort overlooking Acapulco Bay. In 1615, he commissioned, ironically, Dutch architect Adrian Bott, who completed the citadel, called Fuerte San Diego, with five sturdy crenellated ramparts, arranged in a formidable pentagonal array. Although the fort was mostly symbolic, it limited subsequent attacks on Acapulco throughout the 16th and 17th centuries to a few unsuccessful attempts. In reality, sun, termites, and earthquakes posed the fort's most serious hazards. Repairs seemed to be constantly necessary until a terrible earthquake in 1776 finished the old fort off.

It was resurrected in grand style by military engineers Miguel Costanzo, who drew the plans, and Ramón Panón, who supervised the construction. The entire job, completed in July 1783, cost about 600,000 gold pesos, which would amount to many tens of millions of U.S. dollars today. Now serving as a distinguished museum, the Fuerte San Diego, austere and grand, still proudly stands guard over Acapulco Bay.

INDEPENDENCE AND MODERN ACAPULCO

Scarcely a month after Miguel Hidalgo's impassioned *grito* that inspired revolt against Spain, Hidalgo's *insurgente* compatriot, José María Morelos, was leading a rebel regiment against the royalist garrison in Acapulco. Attracted by the Manila galleon wealth he assumed was hidden there, Morelos besieged the Fuerte San Diego. Although he squeezed down on the fort, eventually surrounding it after a several-month siege, the royalist garrison broke out and scattered Morelos's soldiers. Consequently, the Manila galleon was able to land more or less annually until 1820, when rebel forces cut off all support from Mexico City, stopping the Manila galleon forever.

At the end of the war for Independence, in 1821, Acapulco was nearly completely in ruins. Most of its 3,000 inhabitants, the majority poor African Mexicans, were hungry and ill-clothed. Housing consisted nearly entirely of grass huts, except for the 30 or 40 stone or adobe homes of Acapulco's business and professional gentry.

By the mid-1800s, Acapulco's fine natural harbor began to turn its fortunes around. After 1850, Acapulco became a stopover for a flotilla of steamships, filled with San Francisco-bound gold-rush adventurers. Subsequently Acapulco also served as a coaling station for British, American, and French navy steamers that were plying the Pacific in increasing numbers.

Modern Acapulco

On November 11, 1927, the Mexican government blasted through the first Mexico City-Acapulco automobile road; the first cars shortly began arriving (after a six-day trip, however). The first luxury hotel, the Mirador, at La Quebrada, went up in 1933; soon airplanes began arriving.

During the late 1940s, Mexican President Miguel Alemán fell in love with Acapulco and thought everyone else should have the same opportunity. He built new boulevards, power plants, and modern Highway 95, which cut the Mexico City driving time to six hours. Investors responded with a lineup of high-rise hotels. Finally, in 1959, Presidents Dwight Eisenhower and Adolfo López Mateos convened their summit conference in a grand Acapulco hostelry.

Movie stars such as Elvis Presley and Lana Turner began coming, staying for weeks, and buying homes. Elizabeth Taylor married movie magnate Michael Todd in the posh new Hotel Villa Vera overlooking the new Acapulco. International jet service began in 1964.

Thousands of Mexicans flocked to fill jobs in the shiny hotels and restaurants. They built shantytowns, which climbed the hills and spilled over into previously sleepy communities nearby. The government responded with streets, drainage, power, housing, and schools.

However, by the 1980s overdevelopment was beginning to tarnish Acapulco's luster. Hotels had aged; some had become run-down. Untreated sewage was beginning to pollute Acapulco's once-pristine bay.

Fortunately, the government acted to reverse Acapulco's decline. New sewage works were built, clearing up the pollution. New streets and parks were constructed, and dozens of middle-aged hotels were returned to their former grandeur.

By the year 2000 Acapulco had been largely restored and was attracting new investments. Its sky was again blue, its azure waters were again clean, and it was a magnet for millions of yearly visitors, foreign and domestic.

Sights

GETTING ORIENTED AND GETTING AROUND

Getting Oriented

In one tremendous sweep, Acapulco curves around its dazzling half-moon bay. Face the open ocean and you are looking due south. West will be on your right hand, east on your left. (The Pacific Ocean lies to the south, not the west? Unexpected but true. Remember that everywhere on earth, the sun sets in the west, and then notice where the sun sets in Acapulco: not out to sea, as in San Francisco or Seattle, but in a direction approximately parallel to the shoreline.)

One continuous beachfront boulevard, appropriately named the **Costera Miguel Alemán** (the "Costera," for short), unites old (pre-1950) Acapulco, west of the Parque Papagayo amusement zone, with new Acapulco, the lineup of big beach hotels that stretches around the bay to the Las Brisas condo headland. There, during the night, a big cross glows and marks the hilltop lookout, Mirador La Capilla, above the bay's east end.

On the opposite, old-town side of Parque Papagayo, the Costera curves along the palmy, uncluttered *playas* Hornos and Hamacas to the steamship dock. Here the Costera, called the *malecón* as it passes the *zócalo* (town plaza), continues to the mansion-dotted hilly jumble of Peninsula de las Playas.

Getting Around

Buses run nearly continuously along the Costera. Fare averages the equivalent of about $.30. Bus routes—indicated by such labels as Base (BAH-say, the naval base on the east end), Centro (*zócalo*), Caleta (the beach, at the far west end), Cine (movie theater near the beach before the *zócalo*), and Hornos (the beach near Parque Papagayo)—run along the Costera.

Taxis, on the other hand, cost between $1.50 and $5 for any in-town destination. They are not metered, so agree upon the price *before* you get in. If the driver demands too much, hailing another taxi often solves the problem.

AROUND OLD ACAPULCO

In old Acapulco, traffic slows and people return to traditional ways. Couples promenade along the *malecón* dockfront, fishing boats leave and return, while in the adjacent *zócalo,* families stroll past the church, musicians play, and tourists and businesspeople sip coffee in the shade of huge banyan trees.

Start your walk beneath those *zócalo* trees. Under their pendulous air roots, browse the bookstalls, relax in one of the cafés; at night, watch the clowns perform, listen to a band concert, or join in a pitch-penny game. Take a look inside the mod-style **cathedral** dedicated to Our Lady of Solitude. Admire its angel-filled sky-blue ceiling and visit the Virgin to the right of the altar.

Outside, cross the boulevard to the *malecón*

© BRUCE WHIPPERMAN

As viewed from the Acapulco Costera shoreline, the Pacific Ocean lies due south, beyond the bay.

ACAPULCO

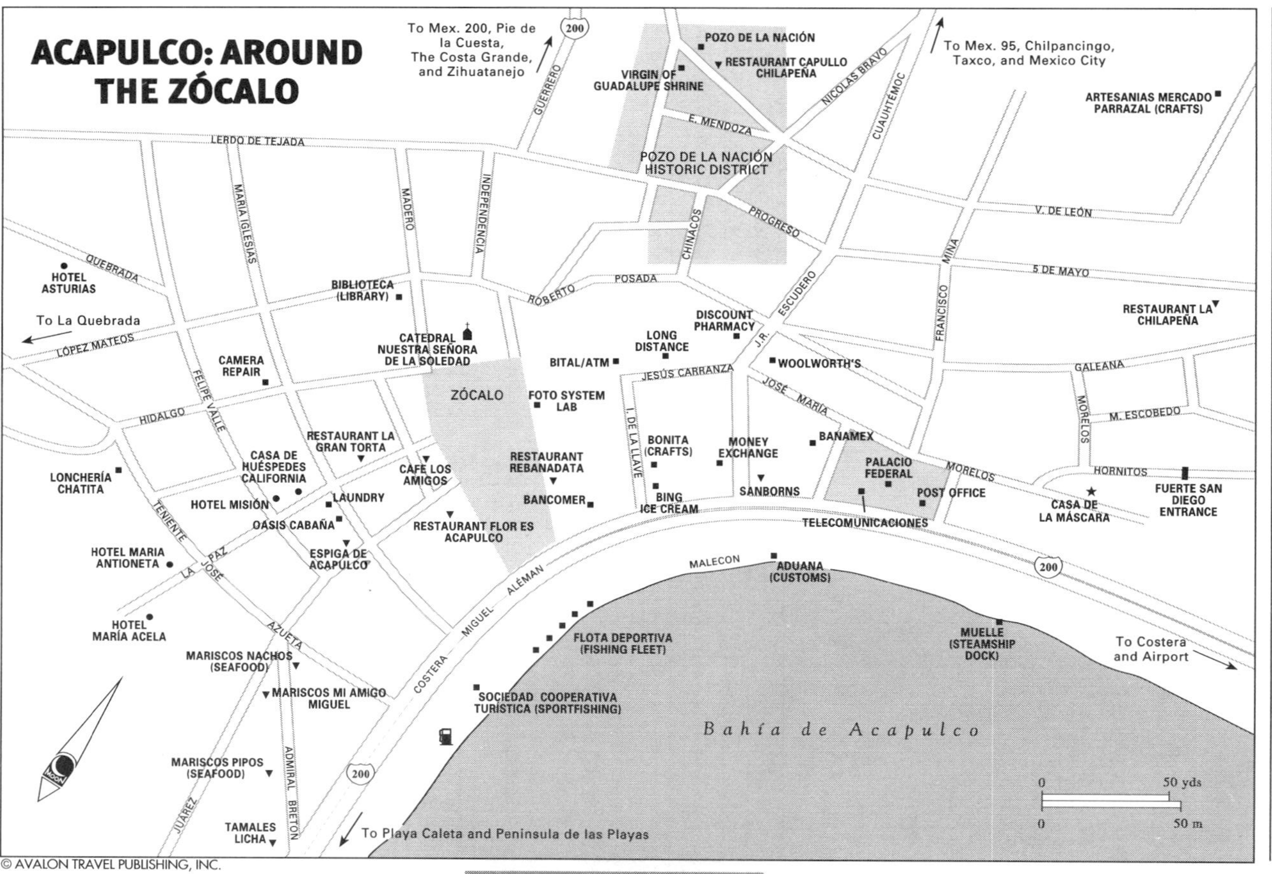
ACAPULCO: AROUND THE ZÓCALO
To Mex. 200, Pie de la Cuesta, The Costa Grande, and Zihuatanejo
To Mex. 95, Chilpancingo, Taxco, and Mexico City
To La Quebrada
To Costera and Airport
To Playa Caleta and Peninsula de las Playas
Bahía de Acapulco
POZO DE LA NACIÓN
RESTAURANT CAPULLO CHILAPEÑA
VIRGIN OF GUADALUPE SHRINE
POZO DE LA NACIÓN HISTORIC DISTRICT
ARTESANIAS MERCADO PARRAZAL (CRAFTS)
RESTAURANT LA CHILAPEÑA
HOTEL ASTURIAS
BIBLIOTECA (LIBRARY)
CATEDRAL NUESTRA SEÑORA DE LA SOLEDAD
DISCOUNT PHARMACY
LONG DISTANCE
BITAL/ATM
WOOLWORTH'S
CAMERA REPAIR
ZÓCALO
FOTO SYSTEM LAB
RESTAURANT LA GRAN TORTA
BONITA (CRAFTS)
MONEY EXCHANGE
BANAMEX
PALACIO FEDERAL
POST OFFICE
TELECOMUNICACIONES
SANBORNS
BING ICE CREAM
CASA DE HUÉSPEDES CALIFORNIA
CAFE LOS AMIGOS
RESTAURANT REBANADATA
BANCOMER
LONCHERÍA CHATITA
HOTEL MISIÓN
LAUNDRY
OASIS CABAÑA
RESTAURANT FLOR ES ACAPULCO
ESPIGA DE ACAPULCO
HOTEL MARIA ANTIONETA
HOTEL MARÍA ACELA
CASA DE LA MÁSCARA
FUERTE SAN DIEGO ENTRANCE
ADUANA (CUSTOMS)
MALECON
MUELLE (STEAMSHIP DOCK)
FLOTA DEPORTIVA (FISHING FLEET)
SOCIEDAD COOPERATIVA TURÍSTICA (SPORTFISHING)
MARISCOS NACHOS (SEAFOOD)
MARISCOS MI AMIGO MIGUEL
MARISCOS PIPOS (SEAFOOD)
TAMALES LICHA
COSTERA MIGUEL ALEMAN
200
GUERRERO
LERDO DE TEJADA
E. MENDOZA
NICOLAS BRAVO
CUAUHTÉMOC
MARÍA IGLESIAS
MADERO
INDEPENDENCIA
CHINACOS
PROGRESO
V. DE LEÓN
QUEBRADA
ROBERTO
POSADA
ESCUDERO
MINA
5 DE MAYO
FRANCISCO
LÓPEZ MATEOS
J.R.
JESÚS CARRANZA
JOSÉ MARÍA
GALEANA
FELIPE VALLE
HIDALGO
I. DE LA LLAVE
MORELOS
M. ESCOBEDO
HORNITOS
TENIENTE JOSÉ LA PAZ
AZUETA
ADMIRAL BRETON
JUAREZ
0 50 yds
0 50 m
© AVALON TRAVEL PUBLISHING, INC.

© BRUCE WHIPPERMAN

At nighttime, especially on weekends, clowns entertain folks who crowd the *zócalo*. Here, two clowns rest between performances.

dockside; in midafternoon, you may see huge marlin and swordfish being hauled up from the boats.

Fuerte San Diego

Head out of the *zócalo* and left along the Costera. At the big intersection and signal (at Sanborns) head inland a block, and turn right at Jesús Carranza (at Woolworth's). Continue about three blocks to the 18th-century fort, **Fuerte San Diego,** atop its bayside hill; open Tues.–Sun. 10:30 A.M.–4:30 P.M. Engineer Miguel Costanzo completed the massive, five-pointed maze of moats, walls, and battlements in 1783.

Inside, galleries within the original fort storerooms, barracks, chapel, and kitchen illustrate local pre-Columbian, conquest, and colonial history. The excellent, unusually graphic displays include much about pirates (such as Francis Drake, Thomas Cavendish, and John Hawkins, known as "admirals" to the English-speaking world); Spanish galleons, their history and construction; and famous visitors, notably Japanese Ambassador Hasekura Tsunenaga, who in 1613 built a ship and sailed from Sendai, Japan, to Acapulco; thence he continued overland to Mexico City, by sea to Spain, to the pope in Rome, and back again through Acapulco to Japan.

If you'd like to learn still more of Acapulco history, visit the **Naval Historical Museum of Acapulco,** recently relocated within the Fuerte San Diego. Exhibits detail famous voyages, display historic nautical maps and charts, ship models, and memorabilia of the Manila galleons.

Fuerte San Diego puts on a *spectaculo* **sound and light show,** using symphonic melodies and dramatic projection upon curtains of water and the old fortress walls themselves to recount Acapulco's remarkable history. Showtimes are at 7 P.M. Saturday low season, Thurs.–Sat. high, admission $10; times may vary, confirm the schedule (*horario*) at the museum, tel. 744/482-3828 or at the tourist information office, tel. 744/484-4416 or 744/484-4583.

Casa de la Máscara

As you exit the Fuerte San Diego, continue along the lane that begins just past (west) of the museum parking lot. In half a block, you'll arrive at Casa de la Máscara. Inside, enjoy six rooms decorated with trove of fascinating indigenous masks, all handcrafted for the myriad traditional *fiestas* celebrated in towns and villages all over the state of Guerrero.

Besides the well-known examples, such as the clownish Viejitos (old ones), grinning red devils, scary jaguars, and angelic cherubs, be sure to see the masks that poke fun (such as three eyes, double noses, bald heads, big ears) at the Spanish colonials.

Although in modern society masks serve merely theatrical and celebratory functions, in parts of rural Mexico certain masks retain their pre-Columbian function and significance. The belief was (and in some remote villages, still is) that by donning a mask, a person soaks up the supernatural power of the god that the mask depicts. Jaguar masks, for example, are a remnant of the jaguar cult, common in Mesoamerican tradition. Many ancient Mexican and Central American stone glyphs and paper or bark codices show half human-half jaguar personages, which anthropologists commonly interpret as depictions of priests in jaguar mask and costume and who are thus elevated to the powerful realm of the gods.

Before leaving, be sure to visit the room of masks exotically reminiscent of West Africa, made by the *costeños,* African Mexicans, most of whom now live along the Guerrero-Oaxaca coast east of Acapulco.

The Casa de la Máscara is open 10 A.M.–4 P.M. Tues.–Sunday. Although the museum has no phone, you can confirm its schedule via email: clara_bono@hotmail.com.

Pozo de la Nación Historic District

Pozo de la Nación, Acapulco's oldest permanent neighborhood, where the merchants that prospered from the Manila galleon trade built their homes, spreads uphill, behind the cathedral, north from the *zócalo.* The heart of the several-square-block district is the small intersection-square, at the corner of Calles Allende and Alarcón. (See the map Acapulco: Around the Zócalo.) A monument at the square's north, uphill, corner marks the ***pozo*** (well), for which the district is named. In 1850, governor Juan Álvarez ordered the well dug to furnish a clean water source and alleviate the devastating local cholera epidemic.

Acapulco people remember that wise and kindly act, especially around January 12, when droves of folks arrive to pay homage at the illuminated shrine to the Virgin of Guadalupe across the square from the *pozo.*

Behind the Guadalupe shrine, pause (especially if it's a warm day) in the cool shade beneath the great **Árbol del Fraile** (Tree of the Friar), brought from Peru as a seedling centuries ago. Local people enjoy the sweet yellow fruit that it drops from its spreading branches during the month of June.

Another good place to pause, especially if you're hungry, is at the clean *comedor* **El Nuevo Capullo Chilapeño,** adjacent to (behind, to the right) the *pozo* monument. Afternoons are best to enjoy the four-course *comida corrida* set lunch ($3–4); evenings, go for the upcountry Guerrero specialties, Chilapa-style *antojitos* and *pozole.* Thursday, a regiment of regular customers crowds in for the super-specialty, *pozole verde.* Open 7:30 A.M.–midnight daily, tel. 744/482-4311, at Alarcón 16.

La Quebrada

Head back to the *zócalo* and continue west from the cathedral-front. After three short blocks to Avenida López Mateos, continue uphill to the La Quebrada diver's point, marked by the big parking lot at the hillcrest. There, Acapulco's energy focuses five times a day (at 1 P.M. and evenings hourly 7:30–10:30 P.M.) as tense crowds watch the divers plummet more than 100 feet to the waves below. Admission is about $2, collected by the divers' cooperative. Performers average less than $100 per dive from the proceeds. The adjacent Hotel Mirador charges about $5 cover to view the dives from its terrace.

Casa de Dolores Olmedo

Celebrated muralist and painter Diego Rivera (1886–1957), whose renown has received a boost from the latter-day fame of his second wife, Frida Kahlo, spent the last years of his life with his friend and late grand dame of Acapulco, Dolores Olmedo. Señora Olmedo, who herself died

THE EPIC VOYAGE OF AMBASSADOR HASEKURA TSUNENAGA

By 1600, competition with the Portuguese and Dutch for missionary and trade concessions in east Asia pushed Spanish authorities toward closer ties with Japan. In 1602, Rodrigo de Vivero, acting governor of the Philippines, initiated contact with Shogun Tokugawa Ieyasu (of *Shogun* movie and novel fame).

Vivero's efforts were successful, but literally by accident. During his return to Acapulco in 1609, Vivero's ship, the galleon *San Francisco,* was wrecked on the Japanese coast near Edo (now Tokyo). Fortunately for the Spanish this incident coincided with a serious deterioration in relations between the Tokugawa government and the Dutch trade mission. To their own detriment, the Dutch had issued impossibly stiff rules for buying Japanese silk and added insult to injury by trying to hog all Japanese foreign trade for themselves.

Vivero must have impressed the shogun, for Tokugawa ended up giving him an entire new ship (built by English samurai William Adams, also of *Shogun* movie fame), a small fortune in gold to fit out and operate the ship, a Spanish-Japanese trade treaty, and a request to the king of Spain for an exchange of ambassadors. Vivero, in his new ship, christened the *San Buenaventura,* sailed on August 1, 1610, and landed safely in Acapulco three months later.

This set the stage for one of history's most remarkable odysseys. In reciprocation for the requested Spanish ambassador, explorer Sebastián Vizcaíno, who arrived from Acapulco on June 10, 1610, the Japanese authorities designated nobleman Hasekura Tsunenaga as ambassador-elect to the Spanish court in Madrid.

How Hasekura accomplished his task is one of history's great little-known but epic adventures. First, he needed an oceangoing ship (few if any of which were available in Japan) to carry him across the entire Pacific and return. With the enthusiastic backing of the *daimyo* (baron) of Sendai in northwest Japan, a sturdy vessel christened the *San Sebastián* was built by 7,000 workers in a mere six months, and it sailed from Sendai (where, to this day, a monument marks the event) on October 27, 1613.

Hasekura's reception in Acapulco three months later was a celebration long remembered. To the multiple booms of cannon salutes, an array of blasting harquebuses, and the rhythm of drums, fifes, and trumpets, port authorities escorted Tsunenaga's entourage of 78 (including his entire family) to "lodgings that were ordered to be as luxurious as possible."

in July 2002, was perhaps the world's foremost collector of Rivera works. One of the most visible decorates the front wall of Olmedo's former home compound, on a quiet side street in the upscale Peninsula de las Playas neighborhood, not far from La Quebrada.

The work is a rainbow-hued mosaic, dynamically depicting some of Rivera's favorite prime actors of Mexican mythology. Foremost is the feathered serpent god Quetzalcoatl, who writhes along more than half the entire 100-foot length of the mosaic. Also present is the beloved Mexican hairless dog, Xoloitzciutle.

Rivera, weakened by age, toiled for a year and a half during 1956 and 1957 to complete the mosaic. Loyal to his own communist idealogy, he included a red hammer and sickle; but, in response to a government request, Rivera removed it before he died.

Rising behind the mural is Dolores Olmedo's former house, where Rivera stayed and worked, covering the inside chamber walls with a treasury of stunning murals. It's to be hoped that Señora Olmedo's heirs will continue her former practice of allowing public viewing tours of some of the inside rooms. For more information, contact the Guerrero Turismo at tel. 744/484-4583 or 744/484-4416.

Get there most easily by taxi. If you don't mind (or would welcome) a short but steep hike

After a short Acapulco stay, Hasekura pushed ahead. His entire entourage, which had swollen to hundreds, continued to Mexico City, where they were likewise received with due tumult and honor and where all of the Japanese accepted baptism.

They continued to Veracruz, pushed eastward to Cuba, and finally arrived in Spain on October 5, 1614. After being feted at a number of towns, notably Seville, along the way, Hasekura continued to Madrid and presented his credentials to King Phillip III on January 30, 1615. He accepted a second baptism, this time taking the name of Felipe Francisco (in honor of both the Spanish king and the Franciscan order), on February 17. Continuing to Rome, via Barcelona and Genoa, Hasekura was declared a Roman citizen by the city fathers and received by Pope Paul V on November 3, 1615.

Despite all of the honors, pageantry, and polite talk, Hasekura's mission accomplished virtually nothing. He received no promises of trade from the Spanish authorities nor support from the pope. The reason was a feisty combination of economics and politics. Many, including rich Christian merchants in India, Macao, and the Philippines, were opposed to Spanish-Japanese trade. The Spanish Jesuits, who already had a bishop in Japan, were opposed to Hasekura because his Christian support came from the rival Franciscans. Perhaps most devastating were the machinations of the shogun, who suspected that Spanish incursion into Japan might lead to domination. He was persecuting Japanese Christians and expelling a crowd of Spanish priests from Japan at the very moment Hasekura was conducting negotiations in Spain.

Disheartened, ill with fever, and nearly broke, Hasekura left Rome and returned quickly west. Without even stopping in Madrid, he and his entourage left Spain in July 1617, continuing via their reverse route through Mexico. They departed from Acapulco in late 1617 in the *San Sebastián* and arrived in the Philippines in February 1618. In the Philippines, Hasekura renewed efforts on behalf of Japanese-Spanish trade and diplomatic contacts, but to no avail. He returned in August 1620, to a Japan increasingly hostile to any foreign trade or Christian missions. During the next dozen years, thousands of Japanese Christian converts were burned at the stake and all external trade, except for a trickle limited to the Dutch, was forbidden. Thus Japan remained a hermit empire, with virtually all foreign contact punishable by death, for 230 years.

(best mornings or late afternoon), go from La Quebrada (see the map Acapulco: Around the Bay). Cross busy Avenida López Mateos and continue south, heading up steep, winding Camino de la Pinzona. Turn right at the first street (after about a quarter mile), Camino de la Inalambrica, and continue another quarter mile to the Olmedo house, and mosaic, on the right, at Inalambrica 6.

Palma Sola Archaeological Site

On a high hillside, above Acapulco's west-side neighborhood, a trove of recently excavated petroglyphs have been excavated for public viewing. The site, at an elevation of about 1,200 feet, adjacent to ridgetop El Veladero ecological park, displays a number of big (3–20 feet) geometric-, animal- and human-form petroglyphs. Created by an ancient people, known generically as "Los Yopes," the stone carvings date from between 200 B.C. and A.D. 600. Get there most easily by taxi, up Avenida Palma Sola to road's end before the hilltop, where a path leads you the last few hundred yards. Take a hat, water, and walking shoes. Local guides will most likely be available on-site. You may also want to arrange a tour through a travel agent, such as American Express, tel. 744/469-1121 through 744/469-1124. For more information, contact the tourist information office, tel. 744/484-4416.

BEACHES

Old Town Beaches

These start not far from the *zócalo.* At the foot of the Fuerte San Diego, the sand of **Playa Hamacas** begins, changing to **Playa Hornos** (Ovens) and curves northeasterly a mile to a rocky shoal-line called Farallón de San Lorenzo. Hornos is the Sunday favorite of Mexican families, where boats buzz beyond the very tranquil waves and retirees stroll the wide, yellow sand while vendors work the sunbathing crowd.

Moving south past the *zócalo* and the fishing boats, you'll find **Playa Tlacopanocha,** a petite strip of sand beneath some spreading trees. Here, bay-tour launches wait for passengers, and kids play in the glassy water, which would be great for swimming if it weren't for the refuse from nearby fishing boats.

From there, cross the Costera and hop onto a bus marked Caleta to gemlike **Playa Caleta** and its twin **Playa Caletilla** on the far side of the hilly peninsula (named, appropriately, Peninsula de las Playas). With medium-coarse yellow sand and blue ripples for waves, Caleta and Caletilla are for people who want company. They are often crowded, sometimes nearly solid on Sundays and holidays. Boats offer banana-tube rides, and snorkel gear is rentable from beach concessionaires. Dozens of stalls and restaurants serve food and refreshments. Prominent among them is the stall of Arturo "Chocolate" Castro and his oyster divers, who serve their own catch-of-the-day mussels, oysters, and octopus right on the west end of the beach.

Mágico Mundo water park, tel. 744/483-1215—with an aquarium, museum, restaurant, water slides, cascades, and more—perches on the little peninsula between the beaches. Open daily 9 A.M.–5 P.M.; admission $3 adult, $2 child.

Isla Roqueta

A Roqueta Island ticket tout will often try to snare you as you get off the Caleta bus. The round-trip, which runs around $3, is usually in a boat with a glass bottom, through which you can peer at the fish as they peer back from their aqua underwater world. On the other side, you can relax on sunny little Playa Roqueta and have lunch at one of several beachside *palapas.*

© BRUCE WHIPPERMAN

Playa Caleta, at the west end of Acapulco's Peninsula de las Playas, is an Acapulco family favorite, for its soft sand and good, moderately priced hotels.

© BRUCE WHIPPERMAN

The little dab of sand called Playa Angosta (Narrow Beach) offers one of Acapulco's only beachfront sunset views.

Later, you might visit the small hillside **zoo,** in the forest above the beach. Animals include some of the endangered local species, such as spider monkey, jaguar, mountain lion, coatimundi, *javelín* (peccary), crocodile, and ocelot.

Other Isla Roqueta options include hiking the midisland trail uphill from Playa Roqueta a few hundred yards through the shady mixed acacia-deciduous hillside forest to the **lighthouse** (*faro*) at the island summit. Afterward, you could cool off with a swimming, snorkeling, and sunning excursion at one of the island's intimate hidden beaches. For example, on the island's east side past the zoo, a trail climbs to the hillcrest and leads steeply downhill to tiny, secluded **Playa Marin,** where you can loll to your heart's content in the waves that funnel into the narrow channel. (Be prepared to avoid sunburn, however.)

A **boat tour** from Playa Tlacopanocha is another way to get to Isla Roqueta. Glass-bottomed boats leave several times daily for 90-minute tours (about $5 per person). Trips include viewing underwater life, shoreline vistas, the *Virgen Submarina* (a statue submerged in the Isla Roqueta channel), a stop on the island, and snorkeling. Beer and soft drinks are sold onboard.

Playa Angosta

Back on the mainland, you can visit another hidden beach nearby, Playa Angosta (Narrow Beach), the only Acapulco strand with an unobstructed sunset horizon. A breezy dab of a beach, sandwiched between a pair of sandstone cliffs, Angosta's ocean waves roll in, swishing upon the sand. A food *palapa* occupies one side of the beach and a few fishing launches and nets are on the other. With caution, swimming, bodysurfing, and boogie boarding are sometimes possible here; otherwise, Angosta is best for scenery and picnics.

Just uphill, a few hundred yards along the southbound cliffside Avenida López Mateos, is **Sinfonia del Sol** sunset amphitheater. Here, local folks begin gathering around 5 P.M. daily during the winter (6:30 P.M. in the summer) to enjoy the sun's oft-spectacular twilight performance.

Costera Beaches

These are the hotel-lined golden shores where affluent Mexicans and foreign visitors stay and play in the sun. They are variations on one continuous curve of sand. Beginning at the west end with **Playa Hornitos** (also known as Playa Papagayo), they continue, changing names from **Playa Morro** to **Playa Condesa** and finally, **Playa Icacos,** which curves and stretches to its sheltered east end past the naval base. All of the same semicoarse golden silica sand, the beaches begin with fairly broad 200-foot-wide Playas Papagayo and Morro. They narrow sharply to under 100 feet at Playa Condesa, then broaden again to more than 200 feet along Playa Icacos.

Their surf is mostly gentle, breaking in one- or two-foot waves near the beach and receding with moderate undertow. This makes for safe swimming within float-enclosed beachside areas, but waves break generally break too near the beach for bodysurfing, boogie boarding, or surfing. Beyond the swimming floats, motorboats hurry along, pulling parasailors and banana-tube riders, while personal watercraft cavort and careen over the swells.

Such motorized hubbub lessens the safety and enjoyment of quieter sports off most new town

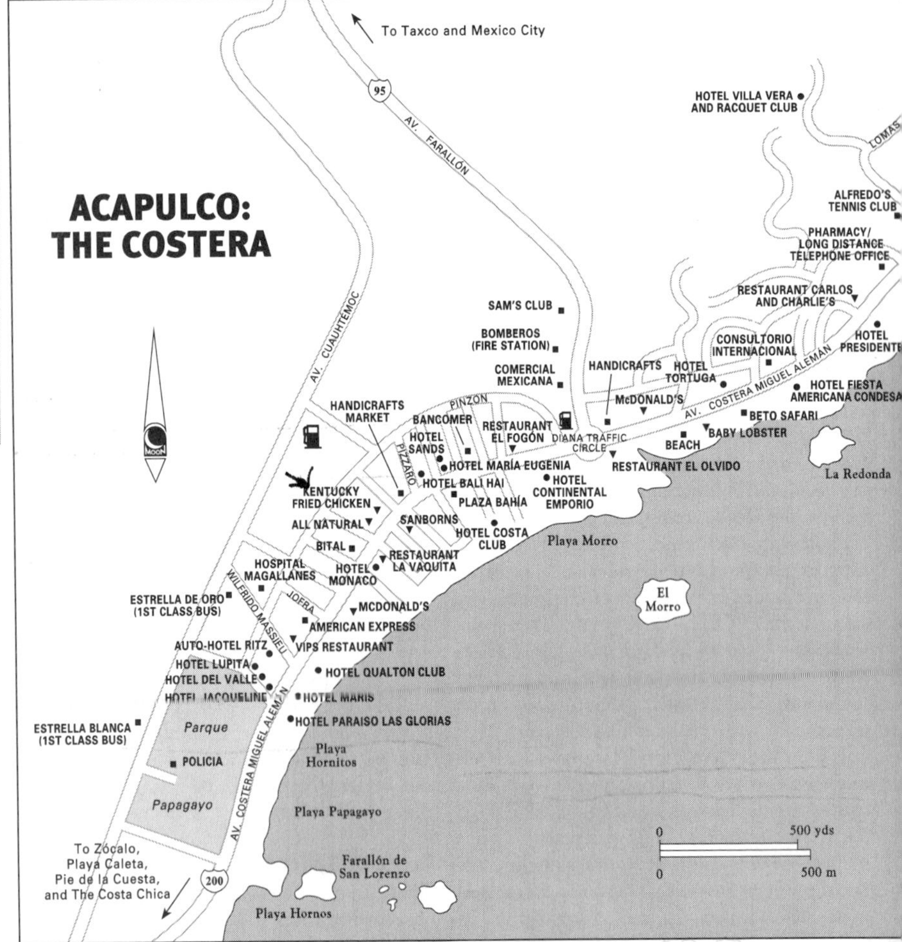

beaches. Sailboaters and sailboarders with their own equipment might try the remote, more tranquil east end of Playa Icacos, however.

Water-skiing, officially restricted to certain parts of Acapulco Bay, has largely moved to Coyuca Lagoon northwest of the city. Coyuca Lagoon also has enough space for many good motorboat-free spots for sailboaters and sailboarders (see Pie de la Cuesta at the end of this chapter).

Rocky outcroppings along Playas Papagayo, Morro, and Condesa add interest and intimacy to an already beautiful shoreline. The rocks are good for tidepooling and fishing by pole-casting (or by net, as locals do) above the waves.

Beaches Southeast of Town

Ride a Puerto Marqués- or Lomas-marked bus or drive along the Costera eastward. Past the naval base entrance on the right, the road climbs the hill, passing a number of panoramic bay viewpoints. After the Las Brisas condo-hotel complex, the road curves around the hill shoulder and heads downward past picture-perfect vistas of **Bahía de Puerto Marqués.**

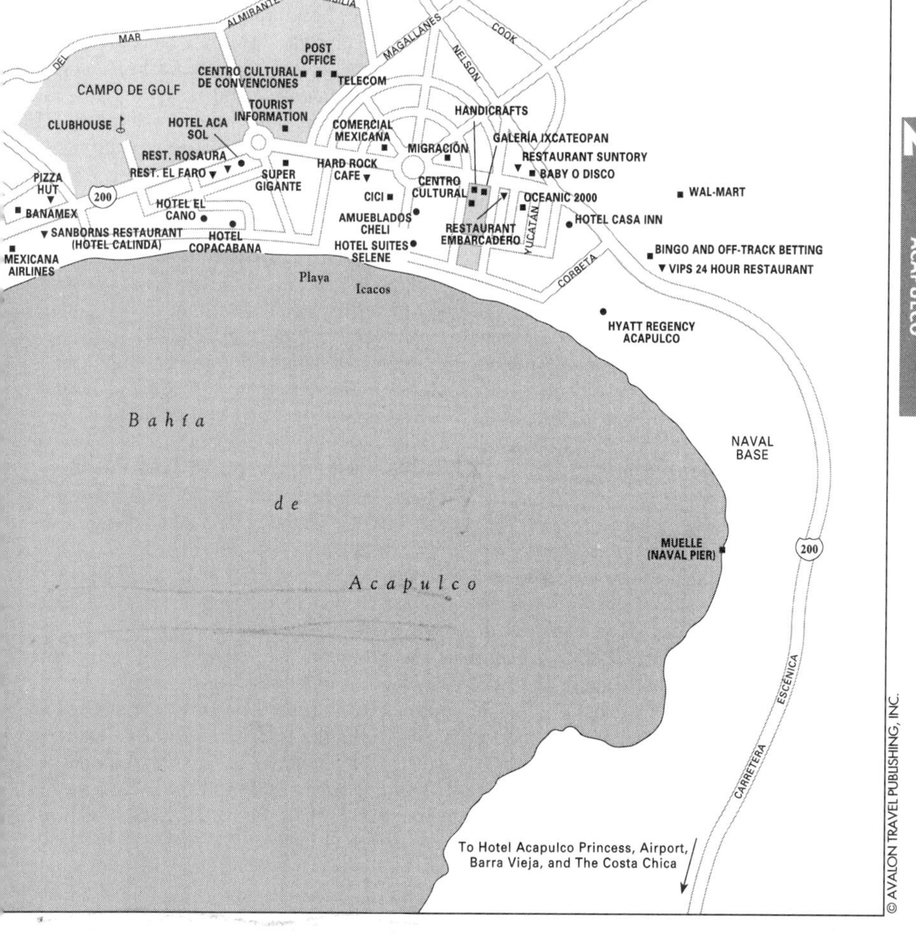

ACAPULCO

At the bottom-of-the-hill intersection and overpass, a road branches right to Puerto Marqués.

The little bayside town is mainly a Sunday seafood and picnicking retreat for Acapulco families. Dozens of *palapa* restaurants line its motorboat-dotted sandy beach. One ramshackle hotel, at the far south end of the single main beachfront street, offers lodgings.

If you're driving, mark your odometer at the hill-bottom intersection and head east toward the airport. If traveling by bus, continue via one of the Lomas buses, which continue east from Acapulco about once an hour. About a mile farther, a turn-off road goes right to the Fairmont Acapulco Princess and the Pierre Marques hotels and golf course on Playa Revolcadero.

Beach access is by side roads or by walking directly through the hotel lobbies. If you come by bus, hail a taxi from the highway to the Hotel Princess door for the sake of a good entrance.

Playa Revolcadero, a broad, miles-long, yellow-white strand, has the rolling open-ocean billows that Acapulco Bay doesn't. The sometimes-rough waves are generally good for boogie boarding, bodysurfing, and even surfing, especially near the shoals on the northwest end. Because of the waves and sometimes hazardous currents, the hotel provides lifeguards for safety. The Playa Revolcadero breeze is also brisk enough for sailing and sailboarding with your own boat or board. Some rentals may be available from the hotel beach concession.

Playa Larga

About seven miles (11 km) from the Puerto Marqués traffic intersection, the Barra Vieja road forks right and heads along breezy, wild Playa Larga. About two miles from the fork, you will pass the lovely retreat Villas San Vicente, a collection of five small villas and two studio cottages, all nestled in their own palmy, private beachside park. (For details and rental information, see Out of Town Hotels in the Accommodations section.)

For the past several years a hardy group of ecovolunteers has patrolled Playa Larga (Long Beach), Playa Revolcadero's dozen-mile-long eastern extension to Barra Vieja. Recently, they've been camping at around 10 miles (16 km) from the fork for the summer-fall turtle season at their "Campamento Tortuguero Playa Larga." If you see them, stop and say a word of encouragement and perhaps donate some food or money to help them sustain their lonely vigil. Even better, set up your own tent nearby and volunteer your help recovering, incubating, and finally releasing the turtle hatchlings.

If you do camp, you'll be able to share in enjoying the wide, breezy strand, whose rolling waves, with ordinary precautions, appear to be good for boogie boarding, bodysurfing, and possibly surfing. The sun sets on an unobstructed horizon, and the crab-rich beach is good for surf fishing (or by boat if you launch during morning calm). Additionally, the firm, level sand is excellent for jogging, walking, and beachcombing.

About 18 miles (32 km) from the traffic intersection (11 miles from the fork) a weathered sign marks the former Playa Encantada resort and restaurant, which unfortunately is returning to ruin. Let's hope someone will restore this little paradise to its previous condition: an airy downscale beachside restaurant beside a big blue pool, garden, and large parking lot, with camping space along the beach beneath the palms. (For the present, however, the beachside palm grove appears inviting for picnicking and overnight tenting. Be prepared to offer a watchman—I didn't see anybody—10 or 20 pesos for the privilege.)

Barra Vieja and Laguna Tres Palos

About a mile farther on, the stores (groceries and long-distance phone) and modest houses of fishing village Barra Vieja dot the roadside. Many seafood *palapas* line the beach side. The better among them include Don Beto's and Gloria del Mar, both with pools.

In addition to the beach, Barra Vieja visitors enjoy access to the vast Laguna Tres Palos mangrove wetland from the *estero* at the east end of town before the bridge. From there, boatmen (ask for José Organes or Felipe Sala) take parties on fishing and wildlife-viewing excursions for about $25 per hour for six. Horseback rides are also available, for about $17/hour.

Despite its steady flow of Sunday tourists, this sleepy lagoonside hamlet remains an Acapulco few people know—like a faraway South Seas village—with drowsy palms, rolling waves, pleasant breezes, and fisherfolk who live by the ancient rhythms of sun and tide.

The road (which maps routinely show going through to Highway 200) crosses a rickety lagoon bridge and ends about two miles farther east at scruffy Lomas de Chapultepec village.

Accommodations

Location largely determines the price and style of Acapulco hotels. Most of the budget hotels are in old Acapulco, near the *zócalo.* None of them are near a beach, and with only one deluxe exception, none of them have wheelchair access. Nevertheless, their doors lead directly to a nearby feast of old-Mexico sights and sounds, and their prices are certainly right.

Old Acapulco does offer beachfront hotel options, however. A number of good, moderately priced beachfront hotels are available in the Peninsula de las Playas on Caleta and Caletilla beaches and on Playa Los Hornos, east of the *zócalo.* Here, guests enjoy semideluxe resort amenities and luscious ocean vistas.

New Acapulco hotels, by contrast, lie along the Costera Miguel Alemán either right on the beach or within a block or two of it. Guests at the fancier beachfront hostelries enjoy a wealth of resort amenities and luxury view rooms at correspondingly luxurious prices. Most have wheelchair access.

Many Acapulco lodgings, however, defy categorization. Acapulco offers numerous choices to suit individual tastes and pocketbooks. Moreover, *Acapulco occupancy is highly seasonal.* In the new town luxury hotels, Americans and Canadians crowd in during the winter. In old Acapulco, popular with middle- and working-class Mexican families, high season is during July and August. All hotels are full during the major Christmas–New Year and *Semana Santa* pre-Easter week holidays. During the low seasons, you can usually save money by requesting package (*paquete,* pah-KAY-tay) and four-night, weekly, or monthly discounts (*descuentos,* dees-kooh-AYN-tohs). For high-season lodgings, always call, email, fax, or write (use global priority mail) early for reservations. More information about the hotels listed here is available at their websites.

(*Note:* Addresses along Acapulco's main boulevard, Costera Miguel Alemán, do not correspond with location. Instead, numbers seem to have been mostly assigned chronologically.)

OLD ACAPULCO HOTELS

Hotels near the Zócalo

A number of clean, budget-to-moderately priced hotels cluster in the colorful working-class neighborhood between the *zócalo* and La Quebrada divers' point. In ascending order of price:

Under $50: Three blocks west of the *zócalo* on the quiet cul-de-sac end of Avenida La Paz stands the spartan three-story **Hotel María Acela,** Av. La Paz 19, Acapulco, Guerrero 39300, tel. 744/482-0661, fax 744/484-3121, anava99@prodigy.net.mx. Its family management lends a homey atmosphere more like a guesthouse than a hotel. The austerely furnished rooms, although clean enough (but not immaculate), lack hot water. Guests enjoy a small lobby library of paperback books. The 21 rooms rent for a bargain $8 s, $12 d, with fan.

Also on quiet side-street La Paz stands good budget buy **Casa de Huéspedes California,** at La Paz 12, Acapulco, Guerrero 39300, tel. 744/482-2893. Guests enjoy about 20 plainly decorated but clean rooms, in two stories, around a quiet inner tropical patio. Rentals run about $9 s, $18 d low season, $10 and $20 high.

One block farther away from the *zócalo,* the 1960s-modern **Hotel María Antioneta** fronts the busy store- and restaurant-lined Av. Azueta, at Teniente Azueta 17, Acapulco, Guerrero 39300, tel. 744/482-5024. The 34 plainly furnished, somewhat worn rooms are nevertheless light, especially on the upper floor. Bathrooms could use a good scrubbing, however. Most rooms are fortunately recessed along the leafy inner courtyard,

OWNING PARADISE

Droves of repeat visitors have fled their northern winters and bought or permanently rented a part of their favorite Mexican Pacific paradises. They happily live all or part of the year in beachside developments that have mushroomed, especially around Acapulco, Ixtapa-Zihuatanejo, Manzanillo, and Puerto Vallarta. Deluxe vacation homes, which foreigners can own through special trusts, run upward from $100,000; condos begin at about half that. Time-shares, a type of rental, start at about $5,000.

Trusts

In the past, Mexicans have feared, with some justification, that foreigners were out to buy their country. As a consequence, present laws prohibit foreigners from holding direct title to property within 30 miles (50 km) of a beachfront or within 60 miles (100 km) of a national border.

However, Mexican law does permit *fideicomisos* (trusts), which substitute for outright foreign ownership. Trusts allow you, as the beneficiary, all the usual rights to the property, such as use, sale, improvement, and transfer, in exchange for paying an annual fee to a Mexican bank, the trustee, which holds nominal title to the property. Trust ownership has been compared to owning all the shares of a corporation, which in turn owns a factory. While not owning the factory in name, you have legal control over it.

Although some folks have been bilked into buying south-of-the-border equivalents of the Brooklyn Bridge, Mexican trust ownership is a happy reality for growing numbers of American, Canadian, and European beneficiaries who simply love Mexico. Take note, however, that *the great majority of Mexican real estate sales are cash only.* Real estate mortgage loans in Mexico, while not unheard of, are definitely the exception.

Bienes raíces (bee-AY-nays rah-EE-says) (real estate) in Mexico works a lot like it does in the United States and Canada. Agents handle multiple listings, show properties, assist negotiations, track paperwork, and earn commissions for sales completed. If you're interested in buying a Mexican property, work with one of the many honest and hardworking agents in Mexico, preferably recommended through a reliable firm back home or trustworthy, property-savvy friends in Mexico.

Once you find a good property and have a written sales agreement in hand, your agent should

away from street noise. Guests have the use of a handy communal kitchen and an unfurnished but potentially attractive upstairs terrace (that I suggested to the manager would be greatly improved with some tables and chairs). Rates run about $17 d low season, $22 high, with hot water and fans. Credit cards are not accepted.

The **Hotel Asturias,** Quebrada 45, Acapulco, Guerrero 39300, tel./fax 744/483-6548, cerardoancera@aol.com, on Avenida Quebrada a few blocks uphill from the *zócalo,* offers a relaxing atmosphere at budget rates. Its two stories of plain but tidy rooms surround a plant-decorated pool and patio with chairs for sunning. Get an upper room for more light and privacy. Rates for the 15 rooms are about $9 s, $18 d, $26 t low season, $13, $26, and $34 high, with fans; four short blocks west of the cathedral, between Ramírez and Ortiz.

Farther west uphill above and south of the La Quebrada parking lot is **Hotel Torre Eifel,** Inalambrica 110, Acapulco, Guerrero 39300, tel. 744/482-1683. Above a hillside garden overlooking the La Quebrada diver's point tourist mecca, guests enjoy 25 simply but comfortably furnished rooms overlooking an inviting pool-patio. Guests in the uppermost rooms enjoy breezy sea views and a sunset horizon. Rooms rent for a bargain-basement $10 s, $15 d, $20 t low season, and $15, $30, $45 high, with fans, hot water, and parking. (*Note:* The hotel's Inalambrica address is misleading: you'll find it at the corner of Avenida Pinzona, one block uphill, on the right from the La Quebrada parking lot.)

$50–100: Arguably the most charming of *zócalo*-area hotels is the authentically colonial-era **Hotel Misión,** Felipe Valle 12, Acapulco, Guerrero 39300, tel. 744/482-3643, fax 744/482-2076, corner of La Paz, two blocks west of the

recommend a *notaria pública* (notary) who, unlike a U.S. notary public, is an attorney skilled and licensed in property transactions.

A Mexican notary, functioning much as a title company does in the United States, is the most important person in completing your transaction. The notary traces the title, ensuring that your bank-trustee legally receives it, and makes sure the agreed-upon amounts of money get transferred between you, seller, bank, agent, and notary.

You and your agent should meet jointly with the notary early on to discuss the deal and get the notary's computation of the closing costs. For a typical trust-sale, closing costs (covering permit, filing, bank, notary, and registry fees) are considerable, typically 8–10 percent of the sale amount. After that, you will continue to owe property taxes and an approximately 1 percent annual fee to your bank-trustee.

Time-Sharing

Started in Europe, time-sharing has spread all over the globe. A time-share is a prepaid rental of a condo for a specified time period per year. Agreements usually allow you to temporarily exchange your time-share rental for similar lodgings throughout the world.

Your first contact with time-sharing will often be someone on a resort street corner who offers you a half-price tour for "an hour of your time." Soon you'll be attending a hard-sell session offering you tempting inducements in exchange for a check written on the spot. The basic appeal is your investment—say $10,000 cash for a two-week annual stay in a deluxe beach condo—will earn you a handsome profit if you decide to sell your rights sometime in the future. What isn't mentioned is that time-shares have become increasingly difficult to sell and the interest or dividends you could get for your $10,000 cash would go far toward renting an equally luxurious vacation condo every year without entailing as much risk.

And risk there is, because you would be handing over your cash for a promise only. Read the fine print. Shop around, and don't give away anything until you inspect the condo you would be getting and talk to others who have invested in the same time-share. It may be a good deal, but don't let anyone rush you into paradise.

zócalo. The owner, María Elena Sayago, relates the history of her hotel-home. From 1930 to 1966, it was a school, the Colegio Acapulco. When she began repairs several years ago, her workers uncovered broken antique Chinese porcelain, most likely brought from Asia by the colonial-era Manila galleons. Before the 1910–1917 Revolution, she says, the place housed army offices, and before that, it was a banklike *estango* (depository) for valuables. The front-section walls and rooms were preserved in the original adobe, and the columns in the original stone.

Most of the guest rooms, however, she had rebuilt, in two stories around a plant-decorated patio, shaded by a spreading mango tree. When the mangoes ripen in April guests get their fill of the fragrant fruit. Her 24 attractively decorated rooms rent for about $20 s, $40 d, low season, $25 and $50 high. With fans, hot water, and parking in an adjacent lot.

Five blocks west of the *zócalo,* up winding Avenida Pinzona, the **Hotel Etel Suites** perches on the view hillside above old Acapulco, at Av. Pinzona 92, Acapulco, Guerrero 39390, tel. 744/482-2240 or 744/482-2241, etelsuites@terra.com.mex. Well managed by friendly owner Etel Sutter Álvarez (great-granddaughter of renowned California-Swiss pioneer Johann A. Sutter) and her daughter, the three-building complex stair-steps downhill to a luxurious view garden and pool. Its airy hillside perch lends the Etel Suites a tranquil, luxurious ambience unusual in a moderately priced lodging. Chairs and sofas in a small street-level lobby invite relaxed conversation with fellow guests. The primly but thoughtfully furnished and well-maintained rooms vary from singles to multibedroom view apartments. The dozens of rooms and suites rent from about $30 s or d low season, $50 high, with fans, a/c, and hot water. Completely furnished view apartments with kitchens go for about $50 low season, $70 high, with discounts negotiable for monthly rentals. With some parking, and credit cards are accepted. (*Note:* If you arrive in Acapulco on a crowded high-season weekend without a reservation, the Etel Suites will probably be the last decent place in town likely to have a room.)

Over $100: At the cliff end of Calle Quebrada stands the *zócalo* area's only upscale hostelry, the **Hotel El Mirador Acapulco.** Acapulco's first deluxe hotel, El Mirador was built in the early 1930s, at Plazoleta La Quebrada 72, Acapulco, Guerrero, 39300, tel. 744/483-1155, toll-free Mex. tel. 800/021-7557 or U.S./Can. tel. 800/53SUITE (800/537-8483), fax 744/482-4564, mirador@hotelmiradoracapulco.com, www.hotelmiradoracapulco.com. The El Mirador appropriately uses the La Quebrada diver in its logo. Directly below the hotel restaurant-bar, the divers accomplish their feat to the acclaim of hundreds of spectators five times daily. The hotel has much more to recommend than spectacle, however. Guests choose from a collection of about 50 semidetached picturesquely perched hillside lodgings. Inside, they are attractively furnished in dark masculine tones, shiny rustic floor tiles, decorator reading lamps, and deluxe bathrooms. Two airy, sunset-view restaurants, bars, and three swimming pools complete the attractive picture. All this for about $100 d standard, $115 deluxe, $130 d large suite with private view balcony and kitchenette; all rooms with cable TV, a/c, some wheelchair access, and parking. Ask for a four-night "honeymoon" package, which runs about $105 per night, with private view, whirlpool tub, and breakfast. Reserve via telephone or email.

Peninsula de las Playas Hotels

Many of old Acapulco's mid- to high-end lodgings are spread along one continuous boulevard that winds through the plush Peninsula de las Playas neighborhood. The boulevard starts as the Costera Miguel Alemán as it heads past the *zócalo.* A couple of miles farther southwest, the boulevard curves left as the Gran Via Tropical, rounding the Peninsula de las Playas clockwise. Passing Caleta and Caletilla beaches, the boulevard changes to Avenida López Mateos and continues along the peninsula's sunset (southwest) side past Playa Angosta and La Quebrada diver's point before ending back in the *zócalo* neighborhood.

$50–100: A quartet of highly recommendable semideluxe hotels decorate the peninsula's luscious south-side oceanfront. Least expensive is the **Hotel Grand Meigas Acapulco,** Cerro San Martin 225, Playa Caleta, Acapulco, Guerrero 39300, tel. 744/483-9334, 744/483-9234, or 744/483-9140, toll-free Mex. tel. 800/716-2159, fax 744/483-9125, meigaca@prodigy.net.mx, www.meigashoteles.com, on the east headland bordering Playa Caleta. Hotel guests enjoy a big blue pool and view sundeck, an intimately private (but sometimes trash-strewn) rock-enfolded open-ocean beach, lush green garden, and comfortable rooms, with private panoramic view balconies. Although renovated in the mid-1990s, the hotel is now showing a bit of wear around the edges. Nevertheless, prices for the 260 rooms are very reasonable, at about $60 d, rising to $85 during holidays and July and August. All-inclusive rates run $60 per person low-season double occupancy, $85 high, including all meals, drinks, and in-house sports and entertainment. All with a/c, phones, cable TV, some wheelchair access, and parking; credit cards are accepted.

A block farther east, right on the beach, stands the **Acamar Beach Resort** (formerly Hotel Playa Caleta), at Costera M. Alemán 26, Fracc. Las Playas, Acapulco, Guerrero 39390, tel. 744/482-0570 through 744/482-0573, toll-free Mex. tel. 800/719-3684, fax 744/482-2119, rentas@acamaracapulco.com, www.acamaracapulco.com. The hotel's popularity among middle-class Mexican vacationers flows from its semideluxe amenities and lovely beachfront location, all at moderate prices. Above the 1950s-genre but attractively renovated lobby-restaurant-bar rise six floors of 136 rooms, invitingly decorated in white stucco, with shiny marble floors, cheery tropical-bright bedspreads, polished rattan furniture, and modern-standard shower baths. Reserve an upper (floors 4, 5, or 6) for more quiet, light, and a gorgeous ocean view. Rentals ordinarily run about $40 d, $47 t, street view only, or $66 d, $75 t, with ocean view. Add $18 for kitchenette (stove, sink, dishes and utensils, without refrigerator, however.) Rates rise 20–40 percent during pre-Easter week, Christmas and New Year, and July and August. For a splurge, treat yourself to a corner suite, with panoramic 270-degree view, about $90 d. Amenities include cable TV, a/c, beachfront pool-patio, some wheelchair access, parking ($2/day), and credit cards accepted. Reserve directly through the hotel desk telephone, the toll-free number, or email.

Two blocks farther west along the beach, guests of the **Hotel Boca Chica** enjoy an enviable beach vantage and semideluxe amenities, at Playa Caletilla s/n, Acapulco, Guerrero 39300, tel./fax 744/483-6601 or 744/483-6741, bocach@acabtu.com.mx. Here, views of Playa Caletilla on one hand and the green Isla Roqueta beyond an azure channel on the other are stunning. The hotel perches on a rocky point, invitingly close to the sand and clear aqua water from the pool deck and surrounding garden paths. The light, comfortably furnished rooms vary; if you have the option, look at two or three before you choose. Early reservations year-round are strongly recommended. Rates for the 45 rooms with phones and a/c run about $64 d low season, $70 high, with breakfast, some wheelchair access; credit cards are accepted, and parking is available.

Half a mile farther west uphill, a different but equally attractive option is available at the **Hotel Los Flamingos,** P.O. Box 70, Acapulco, Guerrero 39300, tel. 744/482-0690, 744/482-0691, or 744/482-0692, fax 744/483-9806, flamingo@acabtu.com.mx. The Los Flamingos is the place where oldsters reminisce and youngsters find out who John Wayne, Johnny Weissmuller, and Rory Calhoun were. Personable owner-manager and musician Adolfo Santiago González enjoys playing his guitar and relating his experiences with his famous guests of yesteryear. Vintage Hollywood photos decorate the open-air lobby walls, while pathways lead through a hilltop jungle of palm, hibiscus, and spreading mangoes. The 40-odd rooms, several with private, ocean-view balconies, perch on a cliffside that plummets into foaming breakers hundreds of feet below. Soft evening guitar music in an open-air sunset-view restaurant and a luxurious clifftop pool and patio complete the lovely picture. The rooms, in standard, superior, and junior suite grades, run about $70, $82, and $93 d low season, respectively; and $80, $100, and $112 high season; add about $30 for an extra person. The hotel also rents **Casa Redonda,** a luxurious cliffside view house, the former Acapulco home-away-from-home of Johnny Weissmuller (the most famous *Tarzan*), who died in 1984. All with parking, some a/c; credit cards are accepted. Owner Adolfo says show your copy of *Moon Handbooks Acapulco* or *Pacific Mexico* and get a 10 percent discount.

(*Note:* Playas Caleta and Caletilla are customarily crowded with local picnickers and vacationers all holidays and most weekends, especially Sunday. If noise is a problem for you, you had better stay at the Acamar Beach Resort or the Hotel Boca Chica weekdays only; or alternatively stay at the Hotels Los Flamingos or Grand Meigas Caleta, both with more spacious grounds and removed from the beachfront hubbub.)

Over $100: On the peninsula's east side, apartment-style **Suites Alba,** Gran Via Tropical 35, Acapulco, Guerrero 39390, tel. 744/483-0073, fax 744/483-8378, alba@suitesalba.com.mx, www.suitesalba.com.mx, rambles through its well-kept hilltop garden of palms and pools. The mostly Canadian and American middle-class guests enjoy many facilities, including a pair of pools, a whirlpool tub, a restaurant, a minimart, some wheelchair access, and a bayside beach club with its own saltwater pool. The 292 comfortably furnished apartments have kitchenettes, a/c, and private garden-view balconies. Rentals begin at about $85 d low season, $140 high, with discounts available for monthly rentals; credit cards are accepted, and parking is available.

Playa Los Hornos Hotels

As Acapulco development moved eastward around the bay during the 1940s and 1950s, a row of comfortable, multifloored hotels were built, across the Costera boulevard from the long, plumy Playa Los Hornos beachfront grove, now midway between the *zócalo* and new Acapulco. Many of these hotels, recently renovated, remain popular, especially with Mexican weekenders and savvy budget-conscious foreign vacationers, who enjoy airy, uncluttered panoramic bay views from upper-floor rooms.

$50–100: One of the best is the very worthy **Hotel Castillo Real,** at Av. Costera Miguel Alemán 265, Fracc. Hornos, Acapulco, Guerrero 39350, tel./fax 744/486-2300, toll-free Mex. tel. 800/711-4609, hotelcastilloreal@yahoo.com.mx. This middle-aged but well-maintained, locally owned hostelry offers 10 floors of 135 rooms, about half with panoramic ocean views. Rooms are all the same high standard: immaculate and comfortably furnished with two double beds, modern wood furniture, a wall-mounted reading lamp, and a smallish but attractively tiled modern shower bath. Other amenities include a spare but sunny top-floor pool-patio, fine for lap swimming. Rentals, Mon.–Thurs., go for about $60 s or d, $67 t, $75 q; weekends, holidays, and July–August $66, $76, and $86. With either fans or a/c, cable TV, parking, and credit cards accepted. Reserve by telephone or email.

Next door, find another excellent choice, **Hotel Aca Bay,** at Av. Costera Miguel Alemán 266, Fracc. Hornos, Acapulco, Guerrero 39350, tel. 744/485-8228, toll-free Mex. tel. 800/714-2762 or U.S./Can. tel. 877/400-9302, fax 744/485-0774, acabay@prodigy.net.mx, www.hotel-acabay.com.mx. This modern, modest resort-style hotel offers 118 rooms in 20 floors. Four room grades are available: standard for one or two people; double for up to four; junior suite, with more room for up to six; and larger, choicer master suites, all immaculate and comfortably furnished, with attractive wood furniture, reading lamps, marble floors, shiny shower baths, and most with panoramic bay views. Normal (other than holidays and July–August) per-room prices run, respectively, about $75, $90, $110, and $130. Get a 20 percent discount (to about $60, $72, $92, or $115) by reserving directly through the hotel (instead of through an agent). Rooms vary; look at more than one. Get an upper-floor room (above the 10th story) for more quiet and a better view. All with cable TV, telephones, restaurant, bar, ocean view pool-patio, kiddie pool, some wheelchair access, parking, and credit cards accepted.

Other Los Hornos longtime beachfront hotels that might be worth checking out include the **Las Hamacas,** tel. 744/482-2861, fax 744/483-0575, on the Costera a couple of blocks east of the Fuerte San Diego; and **El Cid,** tel. 744/485-1312, fax 744/485-1312 or 744/485-1387, about five blocks farther east, just east of the corner of Capitán Mal Espina.

NEW ACAPULCO HOTELS

Costera—West End

With few exceptions, these hostelries line both beach and inland sides of the busy boulevard Costera Miguel Alemán, east of Papagayo amusement park. Hotels are nearly all either right on or just a short walk from the beach.

Under $50: Among the most economical is the modest **Hotel del Valle,** G. Gomez Espinosa 8, Acapulco, Guerrero 39670, tel. 744/485-8336 or 744/485-8388, www.travelbymexico.com/guer/hotel del valle, across the street from Papagayo amusement park. Two motel-style floors of plain but clean rooms border a small but inviting pool-patio. On a side street away from the noisy boulevard, the del Valle is a tranquil winter headquarters for retirees and youthful budget travelers. The 20 rooms rent for about $35 s or d low season, $45 high, with hot water; add about $10 for a more deluxe a/c-equipped room.

If the Hotel del Valle is full, you might try its equally budget-priced (but without pools) petite next-door neighbors, the **Hotel Jacqueline,** tel./fax 744/485-9338, and the **Amueblados Lupita,** tel. 744/485-9412.

$50–100: Farther east, check out best-buy **Hotel Sands,** Costera Miguel Alemán 178, P.O. Box 256, Acapulco, Guerrero 39670, tel. 744/484-2261, 744/484-2262, 744/484-2263, or 744/484-2264, toll-free Mex. tel. 800/710-9800, fax 744/484-1053, sands@sands.com.mx, www.sands.com.mx. In addition to a pool-patio and restaurant next to the main 1960s-modern building, the hotel's spacious grounds encompass a shady green park in the rear that leads to an attractive hidden cluster of garden cabanas. Of the main building rooms, the uppers are best; many have been redecorated with light, comfortable furnishings. Cabana guests, on the other hand, enjoy tasteful browns, tile decor, and big win-

© BRUCE WHIPPERMAN

Although on the inland side of the busy Costera, the garden of the moderately priced Hotel Sands provides a tranquil haven from the Acapulco hubbub.

dows looking out into a leafy garden. Cabanas 1–8 are the most secluded. The 59 rooms and 34 cabanas run about $47 d low season, $55 high, holidays such as Christmas and Easter even higher. Low-season discounts weekdays and for longer stays may be available; be sure to ask. All with a/c, cable TV, and phones. Parking and use of squash courts are included; credit cards are accepted. Reserve by telephone or email.

On the beach side of the street, east of McDonald's, the petite, three-story **Hotel Monaco,** Av. Costera Miguel Alemán 137, Acapulco, Guerrero 39670, tel./fax 744/485-6467, 744/485-6415, or 744/485-6518, offers a tropical miniretreat from the Costera noise and bustle. Past the small lobby, a big, round blue pool, decorated with shade umbrellas and edged by palms and leafy greenery, invites relaxation. (The patio's attractiveness, however, leads to its drawback: for peace and quiet, spend your time here on the beach during the weekends, when families love to frolic in the pool. Weekdays by the pool are usually more tranquil.) Upstairs, the rooms are plain but clean, with the basics: hot showers and two double beds. Tariffs run about $46 d low season, $59 high, with a/c, phone, TV, and parking; it's close to everything, just a block from the beach.

Just east of the Hotel Sands stands the compact but nevertheless worthy and kid-friendly **Hotel Hacienda María Eugenia,** at Costera Miguel Alemán 176, Acapulco, Guerrero 39670, tel. 744/481-2989 or 744/481-2990, toll-free Mex. tel. 800/712-6628, fax 744/481-2991, haciendamariaeugenia@prodigy.net.mx, www.haciendamariaeugenia.com.mx. Only a block and a half from the beach, guests can choose from about 50 rooms in three storiess, around a petite, leafy pool-patio, embellished with a meandering kiddie pool, small water slide, and playground equipment. A modest but well-managed boulevard-front restaurant offers a hearty, economical breakfast buffet. Upstairs, rooms are invitingly furnished, with two double beds, attractive rustic wooden furniture and floor tiles and modern-standard shower baths. Light, however, usually must be artificial, since rooms face exterior corridors, where curtains must be drawn for privacy. (However, a number of kitchenette-equipped rooms have doors opening to private side balconies, and thus more light.) Rentals (excluding holidays) normally go from about $62 d, two kids free with parents, with cable TV, a/c, parking, and credit cards accepted. The standard promotion runs $267 for three nights, fourth night free, including breakfast buffet. Reserve via email or telephone.

The renovated, longtime **Auto-Hotel Ritz,** near the west end, stands just a block from the beach, at the corner of Costera M. Alemán and Wilfrido Massieu, Acapulco, Guerrero 39670, tel. 744/486-2081, toll-free Mex. tel. 800/715-4054, fax 744/484-0984, panorami@aca-novenet.com.mx. The downstairs, with its chandeliered but dowdy lobby, leads nevertheless to an invitingly tropical pool and patio, climaxed by plumy, exotic fan palms. The rooms (get an upstairs one for more privacy) are likewise attractive: light and clean, with big double beds, marble baths, and airy, private patio-view balconies. Rates run a reasonable $50 d low season, $90 high, with a/c, cable TV, and parking.

Over $100: Just a block from Papagayo amusement park and right on the beach stands the midrise **Hotel Maris,** Av. Costera M. Alemán 59, Acapulco, Guerrero 39670, tel. 744/485-8440, fax 744/485-8492. Here, guests enjoy spacious rooms with private view balconies for surprisingly reasonable rates. Lobby-level amenities include a small pool above the beach club *palapas,* with bar and restaurant. (You may want to ask someone to turn down the TV volume.) Rates for the 85 rooms run about $70 d low season, $110 high; with a/c, TV, and phones. Street parking only.

Several blocks farther east on the inland side, the lovely, low-rise **Hotel Bali Hai,** at Costera Miguel Alemán 186, Acapulco, Guerrero 39670, tel. 744/485-6622 or 744/485-6336, fax 744/485-7972, balihai@balia.com.mx, www.balihai.com.mx, offers a bit of class at reasonable rates. The superbly maintained hotel offers 108 motel-style rooms in two floors, all enfolding a palmy interior parking-pool-patio. A pair of designer pools (one of them shallow and kid-friendly) furnished with a collection of chaise lounges set the relaxing tone. Furthermore, the hotel layout, set far back from the boulevard, produces a surprisingly tranquil ambience, shielded from the Costera traffic hubbub. Inside, the rooms themselves, spotless marble and tile, handsome Polynesian-mode wood furniture, and modern standard baths complete the inviting picture. The only blot on this lovely portrait is that rooms often must be artifically lit, since they face outward on to the corridor and drapes must be drawn for privacy. Reserve an upper room in the rear for more quiet and privacy. Rooms come in two grades: standard are large and deluxe, sleeping up to four. Superior are larger and more deluxe, sleeping up to six. Rates begin at about $120 d for standard for one night, decreasing to $85 d for the second, third, and fourth nights. The hotel sometimes offers 3–4-night packages for a nightly rate of about $75 per night. Add about 20 percent for superior rooms. All with a/c, cable TV, refrigerator, parking, bar, and quiet a/c restaurant out front. Reserve by calling the hotel directly or by email.

Return to the beachside and the **Hotel Maralisa,** which nestles among its towering beachfront condo neighbors, at Alemania s/n, Acapulco, Guerrero 39670, tel. 744/485-6677, fax 744/485-9228, maralisa@aca-novenet.com.mx. The Maralisa is a luxuriously simple retreat, where guests, after their fill of sunning beside the palm-lined pool-patio, can step down onto the sand for a jog or stroll along the beach. Later, they might enjoy a light meal in the hotel's beachside café and go out for dancing in nearby resort hotels. Several of the Maralisa's 90 comfortable rooms, tastefully decorated in whites and warm pastels, have private balconies. Standard rooms rent for about $60 d low season, $150 high; be sure to ask for a discount or package. Up to two kids under 12 stay free; with a/c, cable TV, phones, and parking; credit cards are accepted. (At this writing, some parts of the common areas and some rooms need repairs, such as the badly leaking toilet that I pointed out to the bellman who showed me around.) Check your room to see if everything works before moving in.

A mile farther east, the super-popular longtime luxury **Hotel Fiesta Americana Condesa,** Av. Costera M. Alemán 1220, Acapulco, Guerrero 39690, tel. 744/484-2828, toll-free U.S./Can.

tel. 800/FIESTA-1 (800/343-7821), fax 744/484-1828, resfaca@posadas.com, www.fiestamericana.com, presides atop its rocky shoreline perch smack in the middle of the Costera action. Boulevard traffic roars nonstop past the front door and nightclubs rock (on the west side; the east side is quiet) nearby. By day during the winter ranks of middle-class American and Canadian vacationers sun on the hotel's spacious pool deck and downstairs at its *palapa*-shaded beach club. Resort facilities include multiple restaurants and bars, nightly live music, shops, auto rental, golf nearby, and all aquatic sports. Rooms, most with private bay-view balconies, are furnished in luscious pastels, rattan, and designer lamps. Rooms rent from about $200 d low season, $250 high, with a/c, cable TV, phones, parking, and full wheelchair access; credit cards are accepted. Low-season promotions or discounts may be available. Reserve by telephone, fax, or email.

In exclusive isolation several blocks uphill, guests at the **Hotel Villa Vera Spa and Racquet Club** enjoy what seems like their own Acapulco country club, at Lomas del Mar 35, P.O. Box 3964, Acapulco, Guerrero 39690, tel. 744/484-0333 or 744/484-0334, toll-free Mex. tel. 800/710-9300 or U.S./Can. tel. 888/554-2361, fax 744/484-7479, www.clubregina.com. The Villa Vera still basks in its glory days, when Lana Turner stayed for weeks, Elvis Presley swam up to the world's first swim-up bar, and Elizabeth Taylor married movie magnate Mike Todd in one of its villas. Overlooking the entire city and bay, the hotel's luxuriously spacious villas and deluxe rooms and bungalows nestle in a manicured garden above an elegant hillside pool and terrace restaurant. The lodgings, which vary from one-room doubles to suites and villas, are decorated in creams, pastels, and earth tones and tastefully appointed with handicrafts and one-of-a-kind wall art. No children under 18 are admitted, however. Lodgings come in three grades: superior rooms, suites, and villas. Rates for the 48 rooms and suites run about $200 d low season, $220 d high for all superior grade rooms; $220 and $240, respectively, for suites; villas around $1,000. All with a/c, cable TV, phones, parking, clay tennis courts, airy gourmet restaurant, massage, and sauna; credit cards are accepted. Reserve by telephone or the website listed above; for more information, visit the website www.acapulco.com/en/hotels/villavera. Get there, from the Costera, about half a mile east of the Hotel Fiesta Americana, via the street that separates the Pizza Hut and the golf course, continuing uphill at each fork. The Villa Vera gate will appear on the left after about four blocks.

Costera—East End

East of the golf course stretches the newest, shiniest part of Acapulco, where seemingly every enterprise, including Wal-Mart and McDonalds, Hooters and Hyatt Regency, has strained to locate during the recent past. Despite the hubbub, corners of tranquillity do exist, especially among many of the high-rise hostelries and condominiums that occupy the golden beachfront.

Under $50: A few vintage east-side remnants of Acapulco "the way it used to be" live on, seemingly oblivious to the fast-lane world around them. At the CICI water park corner, walk straight toward the beach, along Calle Cristóbal Colón. Just before the beach, on the left, you'll find **Suites Selene,** at Colón 175, Acapulco, Guerrero 39860, tel./fax 744/484-2977 or 744/484-3643, suitesselene@hotmail.com, www.acapulco-travel.com/hotels/selene. Here, just half a block from the beach, by a shady street's-end park, stands a complex of 24 modest apartments. Exterior amenities include a leafy garden, a blue pool and patio, and parking sensitively situated in the rear, away from the garden and apartments. Most of the somewhat worn but clean units have one bedroom with two double beds, a living-dining room, bathroom, and a kitchenette, with stove, refrigerator, utensils and dishes, and purified water in a five-gallon *garafón* (demijohn) for cooking. The remaining six units have everything but the kitchenette. Excepting holidays, rentals usually go for about $41 per day without kitchenette, $49 with. Discounts are customarily available for weekly or monthly rentals. Reserve by telephone, fax, or email.

Walk away from the beach two doors and find neighboring complex **Amueblados Cheli,** also scarcely a block from the beach, at Colón

155, Acapulco, Guerrero, tel. 744/484-3160 or 744/484-2019. The complex (titled Amueblados, meaning, literally, Furnished) consists of about 20 apartments in two floors, set around a lovingly tended tropical garden and parking patio. On the south, beach side of the apartments is an inviting pool-patio for guest use. The whole place is set behind a sturdy security fence, probably mostly to keep beachgoers from wandering in at all hours. The only possible drawback here might be the music and noise from the CICI water park (open daily 10 A.M.–6 P.M.) across the street. Although most apartments are rented by the month, vacant rentals are often rented by the day, for about $45. (Although the manager wasn't available to show me individual apartments, judging from the well-tended look of the place, Amueblados Cheli would certainly be worth checking out.) Contact via telephone (in Spanish).

$50–100: For a very worthy, moderately priced alternative, just a block and a half from the beach, return directly back to the Costera and classy small **Hotel Aca Sol,** at Costera Miguel Alemán 53B, Acapulco, Guerrero 39690, tel. 744/484-3091 or 744/484-2782, fax 744/484-0977, intersol@wspanmex.com.mx. Enter the petite but invitingly chic lobby and continue to an airy, palm-decorated rear pool-patio. To one side, an attractive small restaurant, shielded from street noise, serves guests. Upstairs, the 35 rooms in four floors enfold the patio. Inside, rooms are white, marbled, and squeaky clean. Yet another hotel plus is the excellent Rossaura restaurant (see Food) next door. Guests in most rooms enjoy exterior balconies. Get a room overlooking Almendro, the adjacent quiet side street. Rentals, excluding Easter, Christmas, and July and August, usually run about $70 s or d, fourth night free, with a/c, parking, cable TV, telephones, and credit cards accepted. Reserve by telephone, fax, or email.

Over $100: On the other hand, those who hanker for a party can have it on the beach, at **Hotel Copacabana,** at Tabachines 2, Fracc. Club Deportivo, Acapulco, Guerrero 39690, tel. 744/484-3260 or 744/484-3155, tel./fax 744/484-6268, toll-free Mex. tel. 800/710-9888, acapulco@hotelcopacabana.com, www.hotelcopacabana.com. Past the midsized, attractive lobby, guests enjoy a live music restaurant-bar, a beachview pool deck, and a squadron of private beachfront *palapas.* Everywhere inside, the marble, brass and rattan are polished, the guests are youngish, and the mood is upbeat. Upstairs, the 18 floors of 400-plus rooms are deluxe, comfortable, marble-floored, and cheerily decorated in yellows and whites, with bamboo furniture and bedsteads. All this for the standard promotional rate (except holidays and July and August) of about $117 d (third and fourth person free), with a/c, cable TV, parking, credit cards accepted, and boogie boards, kayaks, water polo, aerobics, and volleyball at no extra cost. Other downstairs amenities include shops, travel agent, and business center. Reserve by telephone or email.

Moving several blocks farther east along the Costera, find the **Casa Inn,** Costera M. Alemán 2310, Acapulco, Guerrero 39860, tel. 744/435-2000 or 744/435-2037, reserva@acabtu.com.mx, www.casainnacapulco.com, a less refined but still best-buy hostelry, especially during low season. The youngish, mostly single clientele also like the lively late-night bar and the big pool deck where they can rest and recover during the day. The 279 light and comfortable rooms come with a/c, TV, views, and phones. Rooms, most with kitchenettes, rent, for one through four people, for about $65 low season, $150 high. Be sure to ask for a discount or a package. Parking is available, and credit cards are accepted. Reserve by telephone, email, or website.

Favorite among lovers of peace and quiet is the grand, dignified **Hotel Elcano,** two blocks removed—and with rooms facing away from the Costera traffic, at Av. Costera Miguel Alemán 75, Acapulco, Guerrero 39690, tel./fax 744/435-1500 or 744/484/2230, toll-free U.S. tel. 800/917-4901 or Can. tel. 877/260-1765, elcano@hotel-elcano.com.mx, www.hotel-elcano.com.mx. The hotel was named after Ferdinand Magellan's navigator, Sebastián Elcano (who actually was the one who first circumnavigated the globe; Magellan died en route but got the credit). Hotel Elcano is austerely luxurious, hued in shades of nautical blue, from the breezy, gracefully columned lobby and the spacious turquoise beachside pool to the 180 immaculate, marble-tiled view rooms. Unlike some of Acapulco's beachfront hostelries, the Elcano has plenty of space for guests to enjoy its load of extras, which include two restaurants, three bars, poolside hot tub, beach club, kiddie pool, gym, nine-hole golf course three blocks away, and video games center. Rooms, all with private ocean-view balconies, rent for a very reasonable $105 d low season, $200 high. Be sure to ask for possible promotional packages, or midweek or weekly rates.

Towering over the Costera's east end is the 20-story high-rise of the **Hyatt Regency Acapulco,** Costera M. Alemán 1, Acapulco, Guerrero 39869, tel. 744/469-1234, toll-free Mex. tel. 800/091-2300 or U.S./Can. tel. 800/223-1234, fax 744/484-3087, reservehyatt@prodigy.net.mx, www.acapulco.regency.hyatt.com. Its lavish beachfront facilities include spacious gardens, blue lagoon swimming pool, a Tarzan jungle waterfall, a squadron of personal beach *palapas,* restaurants, bars, frequent live music, shops, all aquatic sports, tennis, and golf nearby. The 690 rooms, all with private view balconies, are large and luxurious. Standard rooms rent from about $210 d low season, $360 high, with a/c, cable TV, phones, parking, and full wheelchair access; credit cards are accepted. (Low-season promotional prices, however, can range as low as $125 d. When reserving, don't forget to ask for a package or discount.) Reserve via telephone or email.

OUT-OF-TOWN HOTELS

Pie de la Cuesta

For many more budget beachfront lodgings, check out the sleepy Pie de la Cuesta downscale beach resort village on placid Coyuca Lagoon (about six miles by the oceanfront Highway 200 northwest from the Acapulco *zócalo*). There, you'll find plenty of inexpensive palm-shaded shoreline hotels and bungalows. Drive, taxi (about $10), or ride a Pie de la Cuesta–marked bus from Avenida Escudero in front of Sanborn's and Woolworth's near the *zócalo.* (For many more details, see the Pie de la Cuesta section.)

Hotels East of Town

A number of luxury hostelries spread along the Playa Revolcadero shore, on the beach side of the airport road.

Over $100: One of the most reasonably priced yet most heavenly is the **Villas San Vicente,** a miniparadise for lovers of peace and quiet. Plenty of space, sweeping green lawns, swaying palms, and a long gorgeous strand, where seekers of peace and quiet can have it all: afternoons in splendid isolation, reading by the pool, long walks on the beach, savoring the tropical breeze, and watching the sun go down. Guests in the five spacious, super-deluxe minivillas enjoy two bedrooms, with king-sized beds, and two baths, designer living-dining room, completely equipped kitchen, hot tub, a/c, and a small private pool. The two smaller units are more modest but still comfortable studios, with bath, kitchenette, and a/c, set at the upper edge of the property, a bit farther from the beach. All residents share a lusciously inviting main pool and patio, with bar, tennis courts, and parking, all on about 10 palm-shaded beachfront acres. High-season (January 3 through Easter) rentals run about $120 for the studios, upward from $220 to about $300 for the minivillas, depending on location and amenities. Low-season rates are about 30 percent less. Reservations (mandatory high season, strongly recommended low) are available by contacting the Villas' Acapulco office, Casas y Villas Real Estate, Centro Comercial Flamboyant, 180 Costera Miguel Alemán, Acapulco, Guerrero 39300, tel. 744/484-7600, 744/484-2500, or 744/466-2040, fax 744/484-8500, casas@casasyvillas.com.mx, www.casasyvillas.com.mx. You may also contact the Villas San Vicente directly, tel. 744/462-0149 or 744/462-0120. Get to Villas San Vicente by following the airport road, eastbound about seven miles (11 km) past the hill-bottom Puerto Marqués traffic interchange. Instead of heading straight ahead to the airport, fork right, toward Barra Vieja. After a mile or two, you'll reach the Villas San Vicente gate, on the right.

Closer in (only about a mile east of the Puerto Marqués interchange) along the airport road, the showplace **Hotel Fairmont Acapulco Princess** provides an abundance of resort facilities (including an entire 18-hole golf course), spreading from luscious beachfront garden grounds at Playa Revolcadero, P.O. Box 1351, Acapulco, Guerrero 39300, tel. 744/469-1000, toll-free U.S./Can. tel. 800/866-5577, fax 744/469-1016, aca.reservations@fairmont.com. Although the hotel centers on a pair of hulking neopyramids (1,019-room total), the impression from the rooms themselves is of super luxury; from the garden it is of Edenlike jungle tranquillity—meandering pools, gurgling cascades, strutting flamingos, swaying palms—which guests seem to soak up with no trouble at all. Rooms, all deluxe with a plethora of up-to-date amenities, rent from about $200 d low season, $400 high, including breakfast and dinner high season; guests enjoy a host of facilities, all sports, and full wheelchair access, and credit cards are accepted. Reserve via telephone, fax, or email.

Alternatively, consider the **Vidafel Mayan Palace** about a mile farther along the beach from the Fairmont Acapulco Princess. Here, in a palace like the Maya kings never had, you can have an 18-hole golf course, 12 clay tennis courts, a kilometer-long swimming pool (no kidding), five bars, three restaurants, fountains, waterfalls, and an entire blue lagoon, all overlooking a gorgeous, breezy beach. Hotel rates run from about $350 d, high season, for a luxurious and spacious marble and pastel room with everything. Ask for a discount or promotional package. For information and reservations, contact Vidafel Mayan Palace, Av. Costera del las Palmas, Fracc. Playa Diamante, Acapulco, Guerrero 39300, tel./fax 744/469-0201, toll-free U.S./Can. tel. 800/VIDAFEL (800/843-2335) or 800/996-2926, mayanp@mayan-palace.com.mx, www.mayan-palace.com.mx.

LONG-TERM RENTALS

Probably the best source of Acapulco long-term rentals is the website **www.acabtu.com,** electronic descendant of the former community newspaper *Acapulco Heat.* (Curiously, "btu" refers to the "British thermal unit" commonly used to measure quantity of heat energy.) Click on the real estate *(bienes raices)* selection for links for both individual villa, condo, and house rentals and agencies (including Casa y Villas, recommended under Villas San Vicente) that maintain their own rental listings.

For folks unconnected to the Internet, the most useful rental sources appear to be **Bachur Real Estate,** specializing in condos, at Av. Costera Miguel Aleman 20, Hotel Tropicana, Fracc. Costa Azul, Acapulco, Guerrero 39300, tel./fax 744/484-1333, and **Erika Real Estate,** at Av. Comandante Carreon 175, Fracc. Costa Azul, Acapulco, Guerrero 39300, tel./fax 744/484-2764.

Some U.S. and Canadian real estate networks have Acapulco branches. One of the most active is the Century 21 local branch, **Century 21 Realty Mex** in the eastern Costera neighborhood, at Calle Alonso Martín 43, Fracc. Magellanes, Acapulco, Guerrero 39670, tel. 744/485-9090 or 744/486-6110, fax 744/486-4187. Although it specializes in condominiums, with a listing of about two dozen condominiums, the staff also may be able to get you a house or villa rental (or suggest someone who can). For more information, email c21realtymex@prodigy.net.mx, or visit the Mexico-based website www.century21mexico.com and click through to the website of Century 21 Realty Mex.

Another potentially useful Internet site is **www.mexonline,** which links to some individual Acapulco rentals and at least one agency, selectable through www.mexonline as "Se Renta Acapulco." You can also contact "Se Renta Acapulco" directly at its U.S. address, 1605 B Pacific Rim Ct., Suite 9-265, San Diego, CA 92154, toll-free U.S. tel. 800/445-0206, or www.acapulcoluxuryvillas.com.

Finally, don't forget the three moderately priced apartment complexes recommended under Accommodations in this chapter: **Hotel Etel Suites,** in the Hotels near the Zócalo section, and the **Amueblados Cheli** and **Suites Selene,** in the Costera—East End section.

TRAILER PARKS AND CAMPING

Although condos and hotels have crowded out virtually all of Acapulco's in-town trailer parks, good prospects exist nearby. The best are the Acapulco Trailer Park and the KOA campground, right on the beach in Pie de la Cuesta, six miles by the coast highway northwest of the Acapulco *zócalo.* (For details, see the Pie de la Cuesta section.)

And although development and urbanization have likewise squeezed out in-town camping, possibilities exist in the trailer parks in Pie de la Cuesta and on Playa Larga near Barra Vieja. (See Beaches.)

Food

SNACKS AND BREAKFAST

Near the Zócalo

Eat well for under $3 at **Lonchería Chatita,** Avenida Azueta, corner of Hidalgo, open daily 8 A.M.–10 P.M., where a friendly female kitchen squad serves mounds of wholesome, local-style specialties. On a typical day, these may include savory *chiles rellenos,* rich *puerco mole de Uruapan, pozole* (savory hominy soup), or potato pancakes.

Something fancier is available at **Flor Es Acapulco** (formerly Restaurant La Parroquia) on the upstairs balcony, overlooking the *zócalo,* good for a snack or a light lunch as you soak in the scene below.

For something creamy and cool, go to **Bing** ice cream, open daily 9 A.M.–11 P.M., one block from the *zócalo* toward the steamship dock.

Continue another block to **Sanborns,** *malecón* at the corner of Escudero, open daily 7:30 A.M.–11 P.M., where you can escape the heat and enjoy home-style ham and eggs, hamburgers, roast beef, and apple pie, although prices are fairly high ($4–10).

Woolworth's, one block from the Costera, behind Sanborn's, also offers air-conditioned ambience and similar fare at more reasonable prices.

Finally, for dessert, head back over to the opposite side of the *zócalo* to **La Espiga de Acapulco** bakery, for a tasty tart or piece of cake (about $1). On Juárez, tel. 744/482-2699, a block west of the *zócalo* open daily 7 A.M.–10 P.M.

Costera

Snack food concentrates in Acapulco, as in many places, around **McDonald's,** with at least two branches, the original one, at the corner of Esclavo and Avenida Costera M. Alemán, a few blocks east of the landmark Qualton Club; and also farther east, on the Costera, east of the Diana fountain and traffic circle. Here, you have it all, from breakfast Egg McMuffins to Chicken McNuggets and the Big Mac, priced about a third higher than back home. Open daily 8 A.M.–11 P.M.

For an interesting contrast, visit **Taco Tumbra** across the adjacent street from the original McDonald's. Here, piquant aromas of barbecued chicken, pork, and beef and strains of Latin music fill the air. For a treat, order three of the delectable tacos ($2) along with a refreshing fruit juice *(jugo)* ($1.50) or fruit-flavored *agua* ($1). Open Sun.–Thurs. 6:30 P.M.–2 A.M., Fri.–Sat. 6:30 P.M.–4 A.M.

About two blocks east, **La Vaquita** (Little Cow), corner of Costera M. Alemán and Sandoval, despite its soaring modern canopy, takes pride in its country Mexican cooking, served with a flourish that makes even a bowl of *pozole* seem like a party. If you're hankering for something a bit out of the ordinary, try the house specialty, nopales *en molcajete* (mohl-kah-HAY-tay)—a stone bowl draped with succulent cooked nopales (cactus leaves) and filled with big green onions and savory stewed beef, pork, or chicken. Enough for two ($3–6). Open daily about 9 A.M.–midnight.

Sanborns (formerly Denny's), tel. 744/485-5360, next door provides a blessedly cool, refined, and thoroughly modern Mexican refuge from the street. Here, around the clock daily, you can sample an international menu of either North American favorites (eggs, pancakes, bacon, and bottomless coffee), or hearty Mexican specialties ($4–10). Sanborn's also offers a rack of

American magazines, such as *Time, Glamour,* and *National Geographic.*

100% Natural, open daily 7 A.M.–11 P.M., tel. 744/485-3982, in competition directly across the Costera from Sanborn's, offers appropriately contrasting fare: many veggie and fruit drinks (try the Conga—made of papaya, guava, watermelon, pineapple, lime, and spinach), several egg breakfasts, breads, sandwiches, tacos, and enchiladas ($3–6). You can also find 100% Natural branches in at least two more locations: mid-Costera, next door to Carlos'n Charlie's, tel. 744/484-6447, across from Hotel Presidente; and, on the east side, next to Baby O disco, tel. 744/484-8440.

Two miles farther along the Costera, at Hotel Calinda, the **Sanborns** central Costera branch, tel. 744/481-2426, offers the same Sanborn's refined atmosphere, good food, and a big book and gift store, open daily 6:30–1 A.M.

RESTAURANTS

Zócalo and Peninsula de las Playas

Even though Acapulco has seemingly zillions of restaurants, only a fraction may suit your expectations. Local restaurants come and go like the Acapulco breeze, though a handful of solid long-time eateries continue, depending on a steady flow of repeat customers.

For plain good eating and homey sidewalk atmosphere morning and night, try outdoor **Cafe Los Amigos,** Calle La Paz, a few steps off the *zócalo.* Shady umbrellas beneath a spreading green tree and many familiar favorites, from tuna salad and chili to waffles, T-bone steak, and breaded shrimp, attract a friendly club of Acapulco Canadian and American longtimers ($3–6). Open daily 8:30 A.M.–10 P.M.

Meanwhile, on the *zócalo's* opposite, east side, **La Rebanadata** (Big Slice) pizza and Italian restaurant profits from the abundant *zócalo* foot traffic. Here, you can choose between cool inside seating and umbrella-shaded outdoor tables. Select from several styles of pizza (veggie to seafood, $4–10), four salad choices ($3–5), many pastas ($4–6), and more. Open daily except Tuesday 11–3 A.M., tel. 744/482-5555.

La Gran Torta at La Paz 6, one block west from the *zócalo,* tel. 744/483-8476, is an old town headquarters for hearty local-style food at local-style prices. Specialties here are *tortas* (hearty sandwiches), often of *pierna* (roast pork), *chorizo* (spicy sausage), or *pollo* (chicken) with tomato and avocado stuffed in a *bolillo* bun ($2–4). Additional favorites include hearty *pozole* Thursday and Friday ($3–4). Open daily 8 A.M.–11 P.M.

Although the very clean, strictly local-style **Restaurant La Chilapeña,** at Cinco de Mayo 36, requires a walk of a few blocks east from the *zócalo,* it's worth it. Friendly owner Consuela Araiz de Rosario welcomes everyone to sample her Guerrero-style *antojitos* cooked the way she learned from her mother years ago in upcountry Chilapa. It's best to organize a party so you can sample everything. Besides the tostadas, tacos, enchiladas, and *chalupas* ($2–4), be sure to order the house specialty, *pozole* ($3–4)—which Señora Consuela claims was invented in Chilapa; see the *Origin of Pozole* wall painting—complete with its bountiful vegetable plate. Additionally, Señora Consuela is very proud of her *pata* (leg of pork vinaigrette) with carrots *zanahoria* ($2). Get to La Chilapeña (see the map Acapulco: Around the Zócalo) from the *zócalo* by walking east two blocks to the Avenida Escudero corner (at Sanborns). Turn left and walk along the east side of the street (passing Woolworth's) three blocks north to Cinco de Mayo. Turn right and walk a block and a half to Restaurant La Chilapeña on the right. Open daily 10 A.M.–11 P.M., tel. 744/482-0498.

For more good local eating, Señora Consuela recommends nearby **Restaurant La Chilapeña III,** at 3 Calle Petaquillas (continue west along Cinco de Mayo, turn right at the next corner, Calle Galeana, and walk a few steps to Calle Petaquillas and the restaurant). Similar and also highly recommended is the **Restaurant Capullo Chilapeño,** in the Pozo de la Nación district, described in the Around Old Acapulco section under Sights.

For another very popular variation on local-style cooking go two blocks west of the *zócalo,* at Costera M. Alemán 322, corner of Almirante

Breton, to **Tamales Licha,** tel. 744/482-2021. Here, appetizing south-of-the-border specialties—succulent tamales, savory *pozole,* crunchy tostadas, and tangy enchiladas—reign supreme ($2–4). Portions are generous, ambience is relaxed, and hygiene standards are impeccable. Open nightly 6–11 P.M.

Good, reasonably priced seafood restaurants are unexpectedly hard to come by in Acapulco. An important exception is the lineup of local-style seafood eateries along Avenida Azueta three blocks west from the *zócalo.* Situated right where the boats come in, they get the freshest morsels first. Local longtimers swear by the excellence of seafood served at **El Amigo Miguel,** at the corner of Juárez and Azueta, where continuous patronage assures daily fresh shrimp, prawns, half a dozen kinds of fish ($5–10), and lobster (big, $14, smaller, $10). Open daily 10 A.M.–9:30 P.M. (Similarly successful is rival **Mariscos Nachos,** across the street, open about the same hours.)

If you prefer something a bit fancier, head a block farther from the *zócalo* to tourist favorite **Mariscos Pipos,** at 3 Almirante Breton, tel. 744/482-2237. The freshest of everything, cooked and served to please, runs $6–14. Open daily around noon–9 P.M.

Continue west to the Peninsula de las Playas for rave-review seafood at **La Cabaña** on Playa Caleta, next to landmark white beachfront Acamar Beach Resort. Part of the fun here is the luscious view (arrive while it's still light) location, where you can choose from a number of delicious specialties. Favorites are the thick mahimahi (*dorado*) fillet ($10), *cazuela de mariscos* (seafood stew) ($8), or whole fish ($8), red snapper recommended. Open daily 9:30 A.M.–8 P.M., tel. 744/482-5007 or 744/483-7121.

Many visitors' Acapulco vacations wouldn't be complete without a dinner at the luxuriously scenic clifftop *palapa* restaurant at the **Hotel Los Flamingos,** Av. López Mateos s/n, tel. 744/482-0690, about a mile uphill, west from Playa Caleta. Here all the ingredients for a memorable evening—attentive service, tasty seafood, chicken, and meat entrées ($5–12), airy sunset view, and soft strumming of guitars—come together. Open daily 8 A.M.–10:30 P.M.; credit cards are accepted. Coat not necessary (but on breezy winter evenings a windbreaker might feel cozy).

Costera

Moving east, first find **VIPs,** on the Costera, a block past Papagayo Amusement Park, tel. 744/486-8574, where you can glimpse the Mexico of the future. Here, Mexican middle-class families flock to a south-of-the-border-style Denny's that beats Denny's at its own game. Inside, the air is as fresh as a spring breeze; the windows, water glasses, and utensils shine like silver; the food is tasty and reasonably priced ($4–10); and the staff is both amiable and professional. Open Sun.–Thurs. 7 A.M.–midnight, Fri.–Sat. 7–2 A.M.; credit cards are accepted. (Also, visit VIPs newer Costera locations, beach side, near the Hotel Calinda, and far east side, across the boulevard from the Hyatt Regency.)

Although these days sometimes overlooked, enduring open-air terrace **Restaurant El Olvido** (The Forgotten One), on the mid-Costera, rear of Plaza Marbella, beach side of the Diana Circle, remains one of Acapulco's best. It seems the model by which some of Acapulco's now-trendy eateries were created. What's remarkable is that such a tranquil tropical mini-island could exist so close to the smoggy roar of the Costera traffic. By day, guests enjoy a palm-tufted airy bay view and by night an ebony star-studded sky bordered below by myriad twinkling city lights. The excellent cuisine, however, provides the main attraction. Choose from a very recognizable menu of lots of pasta ($5–8), meat ($6–15), and fish ($8–18), including a number of nouveau international specialties. For example, start off with Boston lettuce with watercress and strawberries ($6), continue with black fettuccine with smoked Norwegian salmon ($13) or quail with honey and pineapple ($14), and finish off with tiramisu ($5). Open daily 6 P.M.–2 A.M., reservations recommended, tel. 744/481-0214 or 744/481-0236, especially on weekends.

No tour of Acapulco restaurants would be complete without a stop at **Carlos'n Charlie's,** which, like all of the late Carlos Anderson's worldwide chain, specializes in the zany. On the Costera, across from and a block east of the Hotel

Fiesta Americana Condesa, tel. 744/484-0039. The fun begins with the screwy decor, continues via the good-natured, tongue-in-cheek antics of the staff, and climaxes with the food and drink, which is organized on the menu by categories, such as "Slurp," "Munch," "Peep," "Moo," and "Zurts," and is very tasty ($6–18). Open daily 6 A.M.–midnight; credit cards are accepted.

Refined and relaxed, but completely without pretension, is **Restaurant Villa Rossaura,** in Hotel Arbela, beach side of the Costera, across from the eastern end of the golf course. Here, the fun begins with the big gratis *botana* (appetizer) plate, accompanied by a quartet of luscious salsas. Taste gingerly. Next, pick from an innovative, Mexican-gourmet-international menu, including soups (for, example Puebla-style dry noodle, with cheese and sour cream, $3); salads (three lettuce, with goat cheese dressing, ask for the dressing on the side, $6); entrées (black *mole* Oaxaca style, on chicken breast, $8, or Vizcaina codfish, $14). For an extra-special treat, arrive Tuesday night around 8 and enjoy the music of the Afro-Cuban trio. Call ahead, tel. 744/481-2333, to confirm. Open daily 8 A.M.–11 P.M.

Another successful culinary experiment is the Acapulco branch of the worldwide **Suntory** Japanese restaurant chain, across from the Oceanic 2000 building, east end of the Costera, tel. 744/484-8088. Although a Japanese restaurant in Mexico is as difficult to create as a Mexican restaurant in Japan, Suntory, the giant beer, whiskey, and wine manufacturer, carries it off with aplomb. From the outside, the clean-lined wooden structure appears authentically classic Japanese, seemingly lifted right out of 18th-century Kyoto. The impression continues in the cool interior, where patrons enjoy a picture-perfect tropical Zen garden, complete with moss, a stony brook, sago palm, and feathery festoons of bamboo. Finally comes the food, from a host of choices—vegetables, rice, fish, and meat—which chefs (who, although Mexican, soon begin to look Japanese) individually prepare for you on the grill built into your table ($8–20). Open daily 2–11 P.M.; credit cards are accepted.

The Acapulco bent for restaurant fantasy continues right across the street, at **El Embarcadero,** tel. 744/484-8787. Inside, you enter a dim, Disneyesque world. A jungle waterfall cascades behind you while a rickety bridge leads you over a misty lagoon, where at any moment, you fear that a crocodile or a pirate is going to grab you. If you cross over safely your reward will be a cool salad bar and a choice of several intriguing specialties, such as Siamese chicken ($8), Blackbeard's shrimp ($12), or alligator steak ($20). Credit cards are accepted. Open 7 P.M.–midnight.

Splurge Restaurants

Acapulco visitors and well-to-do residents enjoy a number of fashionable, top-of-the-line restaurants, renowned for their super-scenic locations, fine cuisine, or both. Here's a sampling of the worthy, west to east:

Longtime favorite **Coyuca 22** is both the name and the address of the restaurant so exclusive and popular it manages to close half the year. The setting is a spacious hilltop garden, where tables spread down an open-air bay- and city-view terrace. Arrive early (around 5:30 P.M. winter, 7 P.M. late spring-early summer) to enjoy the sunset sky lighting up and painting the city ever-deepening colors, ending in a deep rose as finally the myriad lights shimmer and stars twinkle overhead. After that, the food (specialties such as prime rib and lobster tails, $20–30) and wines seem like dessert. Find it on Calle Coyuca (a side-street off Av. López Mateos on the Peninsula de las Playas), no. 22. Open daily 7–10:30 P.M. Nov. 1–April 30; credit cards are accepted. Reservations are required, tel. 744/482-3468 or 744/483-5030.

Another super-romantic cocktail-dinner spot is the showplace **El Campanario,** commanding a second-to-none view of all of Acapulco. Here, owners have converted a former mansion into a regal bar and restaurant, leading through a princely, arched stone hall to airy vista terraces and a luxuriously inviting pool and patio outside. House specialties are red snapper Azteca, with *cuitlacoche* sauce, rolled fillet of beef with spinach, and Chambertine chicken in mushroom sauce ($15–30). Open daily 7 P.M.–midnight, closed May–December. Call tel. 744/484-8830 for reservations.

Restaurant El Faro (The Lighthouse), of Hotel Elcano, has raised Acapulco to new heights of culinary fantasy, at least equal to that of its rotating beacon high above the Costera. The cool subdued interior is reminiscent of a 1940s Hollywood supper club, tinted in suave greens and blues. The numerous nautical accents climax in an overhead stained glass submarine mural. The total impression is as if you and your fellow diners are inhabitants of a grand aquarium, visible only to the poor exterior denizens through the street-level porthole windows. The cuisine is no less than you'd expect: mostly seafood, some exotic, such as *koktoxas* of grouper (fish cheeks, $20), or more recognizable, such as cod a la Vasque ($22) or grilled shrimp with vegetables and wild rice, sauteed in sesame oil ($20). Meat lovers, neverthless, will do quite well, with entrées such as lusciously tender rib eye steak ($25) or lamb ribs in their own juice ($18), marinated in oils of wild grass, apple puree, and shallots. Open daily noon–11 P.M., high-season reservations recommended, tel. 744/435-3100.

The east-end bayview Las Brisas district has acquired an exclusive sprinkling of stylish restaurants. Among them, one of the places to be seen is **Kookaburra's,** where, among the beautiful people, you can gaze out on yet another view of Acapulco. In the cool of the evening, from afar, the heat, fumes, and congestion of the Costera give way to a curtain of twinkling lights, like a galaxy, sliced by the curving ebony line of the bay. The food (for example, start with crab cakes, $10, continue with roast duck with mandarin sauce, $25, finish with almond cake, $6) simply embellishes the effect. Open daily 6 P.M.–midnight. Reservations, tel. 744/446-6020 or 744/446-6039, are mandatory.

Acapulco's latest "must do" restaurant among the rich and famous is **Baikal,** right in the middle of the Las Brisas bayview strip, at Carretera Escenica 22, across from landmark Palladium disco. Join the well-heeled mostly Mexico City crowd and soak in the relaxed elegance—massive white columns, draped windows, looking out on the gleaming galaxy of the Acapulco night—all to the soothing strains of live jazz. Start off with a fine overview of the entire scene, accompanied by appetizers, at the upper bar, then take a main-floor table for your entrée and dessert.

After such an introduction, the food may seem like an afterthought. For example, for appetizer, try fresh mussels, $16; for salad, arugula with pear, $13; and entrée, salmon in honey and balsamic vinaigrette, $25. Find it open daily 6 P.M.–midnight. Reservations, tel. 744/446-6867, strongly recommended any time.

Nearby, at Italian-style **Casanova,** at 5236 Carretera Escenica Las Brisas, you can enjoy either a cool inside section or the same starry, panoramic view outside, while sampling from a long list of tasty salads, pastas, meats, chicken, and seafood specialties ($15–30). The house especially recommends its super-fresh shrimp fettuccine ($22). Open daily 7 P.M.–midnight; reservations mandatory, closed low season, tel. 744/446-6237, 744/446-6238, or 744/446-6239.

Entertainment and Recreation

ENTERTAINMENT AND EVENTS

Strolling and Sidewalk Cafés

The old *zócalo* is the best place for strolling and people-watching. Bookstalls, vendors, band concerts, and, on weekend nights especially, pitch-penny games, mimes, and clowns are constant sources of entertainment. When you're tired of walking, take a seat at a sidewalk café, such as La Flor Es Acapulco (upstairs balcony) or Cafe Los Amigos, and let the scene pass *you* by for a change.

Movies

The best cinemas are the Costera multiplexes. As you move eastward, past Papagayo Park, first comes Cineapolis, in the shopping plaza next to VIPs restaurant, corner of the Costera and Wilfrido Massieu.

Next comes Cinema 5, admission $3, on the third floor of the Plaza Bahía shopping center, next to the Hotel Costa Club, tel. 744/485-5124. Screenings include first-run American drama and comedy.

Finally, in the east-end Oceanic 2000 plaza, you'll get about the same at the newest *cine* in town, tel. 744/481-0646, across from Baby O disco.

Tourist Shows

The **Mexican Fiesta,** Acapulco's dance performance extravaganza, goes on two, three, or four days a week, depending on the season, at the plaza-stage, behind the sprawling Centro Cultural de Convenciones convention center just east of the golf course. The all-Mexico sombrero and whirling-skirt folkloric dance show is often highlighted by a replica performance of the wheeling Papantla flyers. Tickets can include the show with open bar only ($25), or open bar and buffet ($42); kids get the buffet for half price. The food is customarily served around 7 P.M., followed by the performance at 8:15. Book your tickets through a travel or tour agent, or call the Mexican Fiesta box office directly, tel. 744/484-3218.

© BRUCE WHIPPERMAN

The *zócalo,* shaded by giant *higuera* (banyan) trees, is one of Acapulco's favorite strolling and people-watching grounds.

Sunsets

West-side hills block Acapulco Bay's sunset horizon. Sunset connoisseurs remedy the problem by gathering at ocean-view points on the west-side Peninsula de las Playas, such as the Sinfonia del Sol sunset amphitheater (see Playa Angosta), La Quebrada, Playa Angosta, and especially the cliffside restaurant and gazebo/bar of the Hotel Flamingos (see Accommodations) before sunset.

Far east-side beach locations around the Hotel Hyatt Regency and hilltop viewpoints, such as restaurant-bar El Campanario and the east-end Las Brisas Scenic Highway (Carretera Escenica) restaurants (see Splurge Restaurants) also provide unobstructed sunset-viewing horizons.

Bay Cruise Parties

One popular way to enjoy the sunset and a party at the same time is via a cruise aboard the steel excursion ship *Bonanza.* It leaves from its bayside dock on the Costera half a mile (toward the Peninsula de las Playas) from the *zócalo.* Although cruise schedules vary seasonally, offerings can include midday (11 A.M.–2 P.M.), sunset (4:30–7 P.M.), and moonlight (10:30 P.M.–1 A.M.) cruises. Tickets are available from hotels, travel agents, or at the dock, tel. 744/483-1803. Tickets run about $17 per person, kids 1.4 meters (about four feet, nine inches) tall and under go for half price.

Bullfights

Bullfights are staged every Sunday at 5:30 P.M. seasonally, usually January through March, at the arena (here called a *frontón*) near Playa Caletilla. Avoid congestion and parking hassles by taking a taxi. Get tickets (about $25) through a travel agent or the ticket office, tel. 744/483-9561.

Jai-Alai, Bingo, and Offtrack Betting

About $10 gains you entrance to Acapulco's big jai-alai *frontón,* an indoor stadium—look for the Bingo sign—on the Costera, east end, across from the Hyatt Regency, open Tues.–Sun. 9 P.M.–1 A.M. Here, it's hard not to ooh and aah at the skill of players competing in the ancient

Basque game of jai-alai. With a long, narrow, curved basket tied to one arm, players fling a hard rubber ball, at lethal speeds, to the far end of the court, where it rebounds like a pistol shot and must be returned by an opposing player. You can place wagers on your favorite player, or, downstairs, bet on horse races and other sports events taking place far away.

Music and Dancing

Several of the Costera hotels have live music for dancing at their lobby bars. As you move east along the Costera, the better possibilities are: the **Hotel Costa Club,** tel. 744/485-9050; the **Hotel Fiesta Americana Condesa,** tel. 744/4842-828; and the **Hyatt Regency,** tel. 744/469-1234. Call to verify times.

A number of restaurant/bars along the Costera have nightly dance music, both recorded and live. A pair of favorites of both longtime tourists and local people are the **Tropicana** (on the beach side, across the Costera from Cine Hornos), tel. 744/485-3050, and the **Copa Cabana** (on the beach side, near the corner of Amal Espina), tel. 744/485-1051. Both have cocktails and live Latin (sometimes called "tropical") music for dancing till around 3 A.M. Call ahead to verify times.

A lively band also plays nightly during the high season (Friday, Saturday, and Sunday 3–10 P.M., low season) at the restaurant/club **Paradise** (across from the Hotel Romano), on the Costera beachside entertainment strip west of the Hotel Fiesta Americana Condesa. Zany waiters, a lively and varied musical repertoire, and good-enough food all spell happy times at the Paradise, tel. 744/484-5988.

On the other hand, lovers of quieter music enjoy the piano bar evenings, from 6:30 P.M., at the **Hotel Tortuga,** Restaurant Pacífico, on the mid-Costera, between the Diana Circle and the Hotel Fiesta Americana Condesa, tel. 744/484-8889.

The same is approximately true at **Escala** view piano bar, across the east-side highway from Hotel Las Brisas.

Discos and Hangouts

Discotheques usually monitor their entrances carefully and are consequently safe and pleasant places for a night's entertainment (provided you are either immune to the noise or bring earplugs). They open their doors around 10 P.M. and play relatively low-volume music and videos for starters until around 11 P.M., when fogs descend, lights flash, and the thumping begins, continuing sometimes till dawn. Admission runs about $7 to $15 or more for the tonier joints.

Acapulco's discos and dance hangouts concentrate in two major east-side spots. As you move east, between the Diana Circle and the Fiesta Americana Condesa, a solid lineup of clubs, hangouts, and discos occupies the Costera's beach side. During peak seasons, the dancing crowds spill onto the street. Stroll along and pick out the style and volume that you like.

Of the bunch, **Beach** disco is the loudest, brashest, and among the most popular. For the entrance fee of $5, the music and the lights go till dawn. Other neighboring discos, such as Mammy's, Baby Lobster, Blackbeard's, Crazy Lobster, and Beto Safari, while sometimes loud, are nevertheless subdued in comparison.

Another mile east, Planet Hollywood and Hard Rock Cafe, both of which actually serve food, signal the beginning of a second lineup on both sides of the street of about a dozen live-music or disco clubs. The energy they put out trying to outdo each other with brighter lights, louder music, and larger and flashier facades is exceeded only by the frequency at which they seem to go in and out of business. More or less permanently fixed are **Planet Hollywood,** with recorded music and videos, 10 P.M.–2 A.M., no cover, tel. 744/484-0717; **Hard Rock Cafe,** "Save the Planet," live music, 10:30 P.M.–2 A.M., no cover, tel. 744/484-0047; **Baby O** disco and concert hall, "There's only one Acapulco and only one Baby O," 10 P.M.–4 A.M., $12 cover, tel. 744/484-7474; and **Nina's** night club, "guaranteed fun," 10 P.M.–4 A.M., moderate cover, tel. 744/484-2400.

Reigning above all of these lesser centers of discomania is **Palladium,** visible everywhere around the bay as the pink neon glow on the east-side Las Brisas hill. Go there, if only to look, though call for a reservation beforehand, tel. 744/446-5490, or you might not be let in. Inside, the impression is of ultramodern fantasy—a giant spaceship window facing outward on a galactic star carpet—while the music explodes, propelling you, the dancing traveler, through inner space. A mere $35 cover (women $20) gets you through the door; inside, cocktails are around $10, while French champagne runs upward of $300 a bottle. Open Tuesday, Thursday, Friday, and Saturday low season, Mon.–Sat. high.

Child's Play

CICI (short for Centro Internacional de Convivencia Infantil) is the biggest of Acapulco's water parks. An aquatic paradise for families, CICI has acres of liquid games, where you can swish along a slippery toboggan run, plummet down a towering kamikaze slide, or loll in a gentle wave pool. Other pools contain performing whales, dolphins, and sea lions. Sea mammal performances occur at 12:30, 3:30, and 5:30 P.M. Patrons also enjoy a restaurant, a beach club, and much more. CICI is on the east end of the Costera between the golf course and the Hyatt Regency; open daily 10 A.M.–6 P.M., adult admission $6, kids $3, tel. 744/484-8210.

Mágico Mundo, tel. 744/483-1215, Acapulco's other water park, is on the opposite side of town at Playa Caleta. It includes an aquarium, museum, restaurant, water slides, cascades, and more; open daily 9 A.M.–5 P.M., admission $3 adult, $2 child.

SPORTS AND RECREATION

Walking and Jogging

The most interesting beach walking in Acapulco is along the two-mile stretch of beach between the Hotel Fiesta Americana Condesa and the rocky point at Parque Papagayo. Avoid the midday heat by starting early for breakfast along the Costera (a good choice is Sanborn's Restaurant, tel. 744/481-2426, at the Hotel Calinda) and walking west along the beach with the sun to your back. Besides the beach itself, you'll pass rocky outcroppings to climb on, tidepools to poke through, plenty of fruit vendors, and *palapas* to rest in from the sun. Bring a hat, shirt, and sunscreen and allow two or three hours. If you get tired, ride a taxi or bus back. You can do the reverse walk just as easily in the afternoon after about 3 P.M. from Playa Hamacas just past the steamship dock after lunch on the *zócalo* (try the Cafe Los Amigos).

Soft sand and steep slopes spoil most jogging prospects on Acapulco Bay beaches. However, the green open spaces surrounding the Centro Cultural de Convenciones, just east of the golf course, provide a good in-town substitute.

Tennis and Golf

Acapulco's tennis courts are all private and mostly at the hotels. Try the Costa Club, tel. 744/485-9050 ($6/hour days, $9 nights); Acapulco Park, tel. 744/485-5437, $5 an hour days, $10 nights, on the Costera near the Hotel Costa Club; Villa Vera, tel. 744/484-0333 (hard surface and clay courts, $9 by day only); Presidente, tel. 744/484-1700. Lessons by in-house teaching pros customarily run $20–30 an hour.

One of the coziest places for tennis in town is **Alfredo's Tennis Club,** the home of the late former tennis champion Alfredo Millet. His family continues the tradition, renting their two night-lit courts for $8 per hour by day, $12 at night, including towel, refreshment, and use of their swimming pool. Lessons run about $5 extra per hour. At Av. Prado 29, tel. 744/484-0004 (call ahead of time); get there via Avenida Deportes, next to the Pizza Hut. Go uphill one block, then left another to Alfredo's, at the corner of Prado.

The Acapulco **Campo de Golf** course, tel. 744/484-0781 or 744/484-0782, right on the mid-Costera, is open to the public on a first-come, first-served basis, daily 6:30 A.M.–5:30 P.M. Exceptions are Wednesday and Saturday after 1 P.M., when the course is limited to foursomes. Greens fee is about $40 for nine holes and $55 for 18 holes. Caddy costs $9, club rental $15.

Much more exclusive are the fairways at the **Club de Golf** of hotels Fairmont Acapulco Princess and Pierre Marques, tel. 744/469-1000, about five miles past the southeast edge of town. Here, the 18-hole greens fee runs about $80.

The **Vidafel Mayan Palace,** farther east past the Fairmont Acapulco Princess, also has a luxury beachfront golf course. For more information, call tel. 744/469-0201.

Swimming, Surfing, and Boogie Boarding

Acapulco Bay's tranquil (if not pristine) waters usually allow safe swimming from hotel-front beaches. The water is often too tranquil for surf sports, however. Strong waves off open-ocean Playa Revolcadero southeast of the city often give good rides. Be aware; the waves can be dangerous. The Fairmont Acapulco Princess on the beach provides lifeguards. Check with them before venturing in. Bring your own equipment; rentals may not be available.

Snorkeling and Scuba Diving

The best local snorkeling is off **Isla Roqueta.** Closest access point is by boat from the docks at Playa Caleta and Playa Tlacopanocha. Such trips usually run about $20 per person for two hours, equipment included. Snorkel trips can also be arranged through beachfront aquatics shops at hotels such as the Ritz, Hotel Costa Club, Hotel Fiesta Americana Condesa, the Hyatt Regency, and the scuba shops below.

Although local water clarity is often not ideal, especially during the summer-fall rainy season, Acapulco does have a few professional dive shops. Contact instructor José Vasquez's **Acapulco Scuba Center** near the Bonanza tour boat dock, about half a mile west, past the old-town *zócalo,* tel. 744/482-9474.

Another option, near the same old-town dockfront location, is the very professional, safety-conscious **Divers de Mexico,** tel. 744/482-1398 or 744/483-6020.

Sailing and Sailboarding

Close-in Acapulco Bay waters (except off west-end Playa Icacos) are generally too congested with motorboats for tranquil sailing or sailboarding. Nevertheless, some beach concessionaires at the big hotels, such as the Hotel Costa Club and Hyatt Regency, do rent (or take people sailing in) simple sailboats from $15 per hour.

Outside of town, tranquil **Laguna Coyuca,** on the coast about 20 minutes' drive northwest of the *zócalo,* offers good sailboarding and sailing prospects.

Personal Watercraft Riding, Water-Skiing, and Parasailing

Power sports are very popular on Costera hotel beaches. Concessionaires—recognized by their lineup of beached minimotorboats—operate from most big hotel beaches, notably around the Qualton Club, Hotel Costa Club, Hotel Fiesta Americana Condesa, and the Hyatt Regency. Prices run about $60 per hour for personal watercraft, $50 per hour for water-skiing, and $20 for a 10-minute parasailing ride.

Shotover Jet Ecoadventuring

The Shotover Jet, a jet boat excursion company that originated in New Zealand, offers breezy, spray-laced jet boat excursions from its Papagayo River canyon base 40 miles (66 km) north of Acapulco, off Highway 95, near Tierra Colorada. The tariff runs about $60, including transportation, from the Hotel Continental Emporio, on the central Costera. From the same base, which they have named "Bravo Town" they also offer a menu of adventures, including hiking, camping, caving, rappeling, climbing, and rafting. For more information, call tel. 744/484-1155, fax 744/484-2648, or visit www.shotoverjet-acapulco.com. For more Papagayo River options, see the River Country section in the Guerrero Upcountry chapter.

Sportfishing

Fishing boats line the *malecón* dockside across the boulevard from the *zócalo.* Activity centers on the dockside office of the 20-boat blue and white fleet of fishing boat cooperative **Sociedad Cooperativa Servicios Turístico,** whose dozens of licensed captains regularly take visitors for big-game fishing trips. Although some travel agents may book you individually during high season, the Sociedad Cooperativa Turísticas office, open daily 8 A.M.–6 P.M., tel. 744/482-1099 (managed by Captain Daniel Romero, home tel. 744/483-4822), rents only entire, captained boats, including equipment, and bait.

Rental prices and catches depend on the season. Drop by the dock after 2 P.M. to see what the boats are bringing in. During good times, boats might average one big marlin or sailfish apiece.

© BRUCE WHIPPERMAN

A fisherman carves fillets from a sailfish at the Acapulco sportfishing dock in front of the *zócalo*.

Best months for sailfish *(pez vela)* are said to be November, December, and January; for marlin, February and March.

Big 40-foot boats with five or six fishing lines rent from $250 per day. Smaller boats, with three or four lines and holding five or six passengers, rent from around $200. All of the Cooperativa boats are radio-equipped, with toilet, life preservers, tackle, bait, and ice. Customers usually supply their own food and drinks. Although the Cooperativa is generally competent, look over the boat and check its equipment before putting your money down.

You can also arrange fishing trips through a travel agent or your hotel lobby tour desk.

Sailfish and marlin are neither the only nor necessarily the most desirable fish in the sea. Competently captained *pangas* can typically haul in three or four large 15- or 20-pound excellent-eating *robalo* (snook), *huachinango* (snapper), or *atún* (tuna) in two hours just outside Acapulco Bay.

Such lighter boats are rentable from the cooperative for about $20 per hour or from individual fishermen on Playa Las Hamacas (past the steamship dock at the foot of Fort San Diego).

A number of independent sportfishing captains operate from the excursion ship Bonanza dock about a mile west of the *zócalo*. One who is English savvy is **Fish-R-Us,** tel. 744/482-8282 or 744/487-8787, toll-free Mex. tel. 800/FISHRUS (800/347-4787) or U.S. tel./fax 877-3FISHRUS (877/334-7478), reservation@fish-r-us.com, www.fish-r-us.com, which offers fully equipped fishing yachts and scuba diving or advanced and beginners. For more information and reservations, call, email, or visit the website.

Marina and Boat Docking

A safe place to dock your boat is the 150-slip **Marina Acapulco** on the Peninsula de las Playas's sheltered inner shoreline, Av. Costera M. Alemán 215, Fracc. Las Playas, Acapulco, Guerrero 39300, tel. 744/483-7498, fax 744/483-7436. Boat launching (30-foot maximum) runs about $25 per day. The slip rate is around $.65 per foot per day, including 110/220-volt power ($.20 per kilowatt-hour extra), potable water, pump-out, toilets, showers, ice, restaurant, hotel, repair facilities, customs and immigrations paperwork, and access to the marina pool except weekends and holidays. Get there via the driveway past the suspension bridge over the Costera about a mile southeast of the *zócalo*.

Other Practicalities

SHOPPING

Market

Acapulco, despite its modern glitz, has a very colorful traditional market, which is fun for strolling through even without buying anything. It is open daily, dawn to dusk. Vendors arrive here with grand intentions: mounds of neon-red tomatoes, buckets of nopales (cactus leaves), towers of toilet paper, and mountains of soap bars. As you wander through the sunlight-dappled aisles, past big gaping fish, bulging rounds of cheese, and festoons of huaraches, don't miss **Piñatas Amanda,** one of the market's friendliest shops. You may even end up buying one of Amanda's charming paper Donald Ducks, Snow Whites, or Porky Pigs. The market is at the corner of Mendoza and Constituyentes, a quarter mile inland from Hornos Beach. Ride a Mercado-marked bus or take a taxi.

Supermarkets and Department Stores

In the *zócalo* area, **Woolworth's** is a good source of a little bit of everything at reasonable prices, on Escudero, corner of Morelos, behind Sanborn's; open daily 9:30 A.M.–8:30 P.M. Its lunch counter, furthermore, provides a welcome refuge from the midday heat.

Comercial Mexicana, with three Acapulco branches, is a big Mexican Kmart, which, besides the expected film, medicines, cosmetics, and housewares, also includes groceries and a bakery. Its locations are: on the Costera, at Cinco de Mayo, just east of the Fuerte San Diego; on Farallones, a couple of blocks uphill from the Costera's Diana Circle; and two miles farther, across from CICI water park. All open daily 9 A.M.–9 P.M.

If you can't find what you want at Comercial Mexicana, try the huge **Sam's Club,** just uphill from the Farallones Comercial Mexicana, and the giant **Wal-Mart,** at the far east end, across from the Hyatt Regency.

Photography

Acapulco visitors enjoy the services of a number of photo stores. On the Costera, several outlets have come and gone during the past few years. However, **Foto System Lab** (and Internet access), tel. 744/482-2112, seems to be fixed on the *zócalo* supplying photofinishing, a few cameras and accessories, and several popular film varieties. Open daily 8 A.M.–10 P.M. on the corner of J. Carranza, right side as you enter the *zócalo* from the Costera.

Also near the *zócalo,* get your **camera repaired** at experienced **Foto y Mechanica,** corner of Iglesia and Hidalgo, one block west of the *zócalo.*

On the east side of the Costera, among the several photo stores try **Foto Diamante,** open daily 8 A.M.–9 P.M., half a block west of McDonald's restaurant, for one-hour film developing and a fair stock of film, accessories, and point-and-shoot cameras.

Handicrafts

Despite much competition, asking prices for Acapulco handicrafts are relatively high. Bargaining is usually necessary to bring them down to size. **Sanborns,** tel. 744/482-4095, two blocks from the *zócalo* at Costera M. Alemán and Escudero, is open daily 8 A.M.–11 P.M., with bookstore and restaurant. The all-Mexico selection includes, notably, black Oaxaca *barra* pottery, painted gourds from Uruapan, Guadalajara leather, Taxco silver jewelry, colorful plates from Puebla, and Tlaquepaque pottery and glass.

With Sanborns' prices in mind, head one block toward the *zócalo* to **Bonita** handicrafts store, where, in the basement of the big old Edificio Oviedo, glitters an eclectic fiesta of Mexican jewelry. Find it at I. de la Llave and Costera M. Alemán, local 1, tel. 744/482-0590 or 744/482-5240; open Mon.–Sat. 9 A.M.–7 P.M., Sunday (seasonally only) 9 A.M.–3 P.M. Never mind if the place is empty; cruise-line passengers regularly fill the aisles. Here you'll be able to see artisans adding to the acre of gleaming silver, gold, copper, brass, fine carving, and lacquerware around you.

Don't forget to get your free margarita (or soft drink) before you leave.

Another bountiful handicrafts source near the *zócalo* is the artisans' market **Mercado de Parrazal.** From Sanborns, head away from the Costera a few short blocks to Vasquez de León and turn right one block. There, a big plaza of semipermanent stalls offers a galaxy of Mexican handicrafts: Tonalá and Tlaquepaque papier-mâché, brass, and pottery animals; Bustamante-replica eggs, masks, and humanoids; Oaxaca wooden animals and black pottery; Guerrero masks; and Taxco jewelry. Sharp bargaining is necessary, however, to lower the excessive asking prices.

A number of handicrafts shopping centers line the new town Costera. Check out the pair of handicrafts arcades, **Dalia** and **Pueblito,** across the Costera from the Plaza Bahía shopping mall (just west of the Hotel Costa Club). Stalls along shady interior walkways display a host of moderately priced leather, silver, hand-embroidered dresses, *huipiles,* bedspreads, napkins, and ceramics, glass, stoneware, and much more.

For a grand selection of largely inexpensive, but still attractive, native-made handicrafts, go to the large indigenous **mercado de artesanías** warren of stalls, on the mid-Costera, just east of the Diana Circle, inland side.

Not far from the Costera's eastern end, the state of Guerrero operates **Casa Artesanal Guerrerense** handicrafts store, in the shady mango grove-now-park a couple of blocks east of the CICI water park. Step inside and peruse the modest all-Guerrero handicrafts selection, which usually includes Taxco bright silver, fierce jaguar masks from Chilapa, shiny lacquerware from Olinala, and fetching *huipiles* from Xochistlahuaca. Find it open daily 10 A.M.–8 P.M.

In the same park, about half a block farther east, visit the for-sale art **Galería Ixcateopan,** which exhibits paintings and sculpture of prominent local artists. Open daily 9 A.M.–9 P.M.

The above-mentioned handicrafts store and gallery are part of the **Centro Cultural Guerrerense** that encompasses the entire park. Additional facilities, hidden in the shady rear section, away from the boulevard, are the student library, open daily 9 A.M.–9 P.M., and the auditorium, venue for a cultural program of dance, plays, music, and more every Saturday at 7 P.M.

A final long-time handicrafts source that displays a moderately priced all-Mexico selection is the streetfront store a block east of Galería Ixcateopan, in front of **El Embarcadero** restaurant. It's open approximately noon until 10 P.M.

INFORMATION

Tourist Information and Travel Agents

An easily accessible local tourist information office is the *modulo,* in front of the convention center, two blocks east of the golf course, tel. 744/484-4416 or 744/484-4583. Here, workers staff a small crafts shop, money exchange office, daily 9 A.M.–9 P.M.

Acapulco is stuffed with travel agents. Probably you're best to start at your hotel travel desk. Alternatively, some of the most experienced local travel agents include **Acuario Tours,** in mid-Costera, by American Express, at Costera Miguel Aleman 48, tel. 744/485-6100; **American Express,** same address, tel. 744/484-3109; or **San Diego Tours,** at Francisco Pizarro 45, tel. 744/484-3637.

Publications

The best new-book sources in town are the three branches of **Sanborns:** as you move west to east, you'll find the *zócalo* branch, tel. 744/482-4095, open daily 7 A.M.–11 P.M., on the Costera across from the steamship dock. Alternatively, try the mid-Costera branch, tel. 744/482-2426, at the Hotel Calinda. Finally, the east-Costera branch is on the ground floor of the Oceanic 2000 shopping plaza, beach side of the Costera, a few blocks from the east end, tel. 744/484-2035, open daily 7:30–1 A.M.

English-language international newspapers, such as the Mexico City *News,* the *Los Angeles Times,* and *USA Today,* are often available in the large hotel bookshops, especially the Fiesta Americana Condesa, and the Hyatt Regency. In old town, newsstands around the *zócalo* regularly sell the *News* from Mexico City.

Pick up the commercial but handy and widely available American Express–sponsored tourist booklet *Acapulco Passport* free at a hotel, store, or travel agency.

Acapulco's former expatriate and tourist English-language newspaper *Acapulco Heat* has gone completely electronic as the website www.acabtu.com.mx. It provides a number of useful links to mostly midscale hotels, restaurants, community events and organizations, travel activities, and entertainments.

Public Library

The small, friendly Acapulco *biblioteca* is near the *zócalo* adjacent to the cathedral, at Madero 5, corner of Quebrada, tel. 744/482-0388. Its collection, used mostly by college and high school students in the airy reading room, is nearly all in Spanish. Open Mon.–Fri. 9 A.M.–9 P.M., Saturday 9 A.M.–2 P.M.

Language Instruction

Get Spanish language instruction at the reputable private Universidad Americana on the Costera, approximately across from the Hotel Costa Club. For more information, contact coordinator Elba Molina at the university at Costera Miguel Alemán 1756, Fracc. Magellanes, Acapulco 39670, tel. 744/486-5618, ext. 122, or 744/486-5619, ext. 122, uamerica@aca.uamericana.mx, www.uaa.edu.mx.

Service Club

The Friends of Acapulco charitable club holds fund-raising fiestas and fashion shows to support the Acapulco Children's Home and other local good works. For information, write P.O. Box C-54, Acapulco, Guerrero 39300.

SERVICES

Money Exchange

In the *zócalo* neighborhood, long-hours **Banco Internacional** is the best bet, tel. 744/483-5722, open Mon.–Sat. 8 A.M.–7 P.M., at no. 8 Jesús Carranza, the one-block side street, tucked near the *zócalo*'s northeast corner. Alternatively, go to **Bancomer,** fronting the Costera, tel. 744/484-8055, to change U.S. cash or traveler's checks only (Mon.–Fri. 9 A.M.–4 P.M., Saturday 10 A.M.–2 P.M. Although the lines at **Banamex,** tel. 744/483-6425, nearby, two blocks from the *zócalo* next to Sanborn's, are usually longer, it exchanges major currencies Mon.–Fri. 9 A.M.–4 P.M. You can avoid the lines by using the bank **ATMs,** which are routinely connected with international networks.

On the new side of town, also change money at **Banco Internacional** across from McDonald's, open Mon.–Sat. 8 A.M.–7 P.M., tel. 744/485-5309; or at **Bancomer,** a few blocks west of the Glorieta Diana (Diana Circle), tel. 744/484-7245, open Mon.–Fri. 9 A.M.–4 P.M., Saturday 9 A.M.–2 P.M. for U.S. and Canadian currency and traveler's checks.

After hours on the Costera, the **Consultorio International,** tel. 744/484-3108, in Galería Picuda shopping center, across the street and a block west from the Hotel Fiesta Americana Condesa, exchanges currency and traveler's checks Mon.–Sat. 9 A.M.–7 P.M., Sunday 9 A.M.–3 P.M.

American Express Office

The Acapulco American Express branch, at Costera M. Alemán 1628, tel. 744/469-1121, 744/469-1122, 744/469-1123, 744/469-1124, Costera west end, across from McDonald's, cashes American Express traveler's checks at near-bank rates and provides member financial services and travel agency services. It's open Mon.–Fri. 10 A.M.–7 P.M., Saturday 10 A.M.–2 P.M. although check-cashing hours may be shorter.

Communications

The Acapulco main ***correo*** (post office) is in the Palacio Federal across the Costera from the steamer dock three blocks from the *zócalo.* It provides Mexpost fast, secure mail and philatelic services, Mon.–Sat. 8 A.M.–8 P.M. A branch post and telegraph office at the Estrella de Oro bus terminal, Cuauhtémoc and Massieu, is open Mon.–Fri. 9 A.M.–8 P.M., Saturday 9 A.M.–noon.

Telecomunicaciones, tel. 744/482-2622 or 744/482-2621, next to the main post office, provides money order, telegram, and fax services, Mon.–Fri. 8 A.M.–8 P.M. and Sat.–Sun. 9 A.M.–noon.

In mid-Costera, go to the small branch post, tel. 744/484-8029, and Telecom, tel. 744/484-6976, offices at the Centro de Convenciones (convention center), both open Mon.–Fri. 9 A.M.–3 P.M.

For lowest phone rates, use the widely available **Ladatel** cards in the many public street telephones. First dial 001 for long distance to the United States and Canada and 01 for Mexico. Otherwise, near the *zócalo* you can call ***larga distancia*** daily 8 A.M.–10 P.M. from either the small office on J. Carranza at Calle de la Llave, or on the *zócalo*'s other side, next to Restaurant Los Amigos, Mon.–Fri. 9 A.M.–9 P.M., Sat.–Sun. 9 A.M.–2 P.M. and 4–9 P.M.

Health and Emergencies

If you get sick, ask your hotel to call a doctor for you or contact the **Hospital Magellanes,** one of Acapulco's most respected private hospitals, for both office calls or round-the-clock emergencies. Facilities include a lab, 24-hour pharmacy, and an emergency room with many specialists on call, at W. Massieu 2, corner of Colón, one block from the Costera and the Hotel Qualton Club; tel. 744/485-6544 or 744/485-6597, ext. 119 for the pharmacy.

A group of American-trained **IAMAT physicians** (International Association for Medical Assistance to Travelers) offers medical consultations in English. Contact them at the medical department, Hotel Fairmont Acapulco Princess, tel. 744/469-1000, ext. 1309.

For routine medications near the *zócalo* go to one of many pharmacies, such as at **Sanborns,** corner of Escudero and the Costera, tel. 744/482-6167, or the big **Farmacia Discuento** (discount pharmacy), tel. 744/482-0804, open daily 8 A.M.–10 P.M., at Escudero and Carranza, across the street from Woolworth's.

For police emergencies, contact one of the many **tourist police** (on the Costera, in safari pith helmets), tel. 744/485-0650 or 744/486-8220, or call the officers at the municipal police Papagayo station, tel. 744/485-0490, at the end of Avenida Camino Sonora, on the inland side of Papagayo Park.

In case of fire, call the ***bomberos,*** tel. 744/484-4122, on Avenida Farallón, behind Comercial Mexicana, two blocks off the Costera from the Glorieta Diana.

Immigration and Customs

If you lose your tourist card go to **Migración,** at the airport (sufficiently early on your day of departure) or on the Costera, across the traffic circle from Comercial Mexicana, same side of the Costera, tel. 744/484-9022, open Mon.–Fri. 9 A.M.–1 P.M. Bring proof of your identity and some proof (such as your stamped passport, airline ticket, or a copy of your lost tourist card) of your arrival date in Mexico. If you try to leave Mexico without your tourist card, you may face trouble and a fine. Also report to Migración if you arrive in Acapulco by yacht.

The **Aduana** (Customs) office, tel. 744/466-9005, on the Costera, *zócalo* area, at the dock across from Sanborn's, is open Mon.–Fri. 8 A.M.–3 P.M. If you have to temporarily leave your car in Mexico, check to see what paperwork, if any, must be completed.

Consulates

Acapulco has several consular agents and officers. The offices of the **U.S. consular officer,** Alexander Richards, tel. 744/481-1699, 744/484-0300, or 744/481-0100, fax 744/484-0300, consular@prodigy.net.mx, Mon.–Fri. 10 A.M.–2 P.M., are in the Hotel Continental Emporio. He's a busy man, and he asks that you kindly have your problem written down, together with a specific request for information or action. In emergencies only, contact him at tel. 744/431-0094.

The **Canadian consul,** Diane McLean de Huerta, tel. 744/484-1305, fax 744/484-1306 or 744/481-1349, holds office hours Mon.–Fri. 9 A.M.–5 P.M. at the Centro Comercial Marbella, suite 23. After hours, in an emergency, call toll-free Mex. tel. 800/706-2900.

For the **British consul,** Lorraine Bajas, call 744/484-1735. Contact the **German consul,** Mario Wichtendahl, at Antone de Alamino 26, tel. 744/484-1860. The **Netherlands consul,** Ángel Díaz, can be reached by dialing tel. 744/486-6179.

For additional information and assistance, the consulates maintain a joint **Consular Corps** office, open Mon.–Fri. 9 A.M.–2 P.M., in the Centro de Convenciones (convention center) just east of the golf course, tel. 744/481-2533.

Laundry

Near the *zócalo,* get your laundry done at **Lavandería Laradin,** open Mon.–Sat. 8 A.M.–10 P.M., at the corner of Iglesias and La Paz, one block west of the *zócalo.*

Auto Mechanic

If something goes haywire with your car, contact (or ask your hotel desk to contact in Spanish) skilled and reliable Hugo Wilson, tel. 744/484-0570. Find him at his house (and garage) at Calle Rivadavia 4. Get there just past the Acapulco Convention Center (on the Costera just east of the golf course). Follow Magellanes, the street that borders the convention center's east side. After three blocks, turn left at Rivadavia. His house is less than half a block farther, on the right.

GETTING THERE AND AWAY

By Air

Several airlines connect the **Acapulco airport** (code-designated ACA, officially the Juan N. Álvarez International Airport) with U.S. and Mexican destinations.

Aeroméxico flights connect directly with Houston via Mexico City, Monterrey, Tijuana, and Guadalajara. For reservations, contact Aeroméxico at tel. 744/485-1625 or 744/485-1600. For flight information, call the airport at tel. 744/466-9296 or 744/466-9109.

Mexicana Airlines flights connect five times daily with Mexico City. For reservations, call tel. 744/486-7586 or 744/486-7587, or toll-free Mex. tel. 800/502-2000; for flight information, call the airport at tel. 744/466-9136 or 744/466-9138.

America West Airlines flights connect with Phoenix; for reservations and information, call a local travel agent, such as American Express, tel. 744/469-1124 or toll-free U.S. tel. 800/235-9292.

Continental Airlines flights connect with Houston. For reservations from Mexico, call a travel agent or toll-free Mex. tel. 800/900-5000; for flight information, call tel. 744/466-9063.

American Airlines flights connect with Dallas during the winter season. For reservations, call a travel agent or toll-free Mex. tel. 800/904-6000; for flight information, call the airport at tel. 744/466-9227.

Aviacsa Airlines flights connect with Guadalajara, Mexico City, and Cuernavaca. For reservations, call tel. 744/486-0002 or 744/486/5630; for flight information, call the airport at tel. 744/466-9013.

Delta Air Lines Aéromexico affiliate charter flights connect with Los Angeles, Portland, and Dallas during the winter season. For reservations, call a travel agent or Delta at toll-free Mex. tel. 800/902-2100.

Canadian **World of Vacations** charter flights connect with Winnipeg and Toronto during the winter-spring season. For reservations, call a travel agent, such as American Express, tel. 744/469-1124, or the local Canadian agent, tel. 744/446-5716.

Air Arrival and Departure

After the usually quick immigration and customs checks, Acapulco arrivees enjoy airport car rentals, efficient transportation for the 15-mile trip to town, post box (*buzon*), and ATMs.

Local car rental agents often available for arriving flights include Hertz, tel. 744/485-8947 or 744/485-6889; Avis, tel. 744/466-9190 or 744/466-0075; Alamo, tel. 744/466-9444 or 744/484-3305; Budget, tel. 744/481-2433; Quick, tel. 744/486-3420 or 744/486-2197; and SAAD jeep rentals, tel. 744/484-3445, 744/484-5325, or 744/466-9179. You can ensure availability and often save money by bargaining for a reservation with agencies via their national toll-free numbers.

Tickets for **ground transport** to town are sold by agents near the terminal exit. Options include a *colectivo* GMC Suburban station wagon (about $8), which deposits passengers at individual hotels. *Taxis especiales* run about $11 to $22, depending on distance. GMC Suburbans can be hired *"especial"* as private taxis for $35–45 for up to seven passengers.

On your departure day, save money by sharing a taxi with fellow departees. Don't get into the taxi until you settle the fare. Having already arrived, you know what the airport ride should cost. If the driver insists on greed, hail another taxi.

Simplify your departure by saving $17 or its peso equivalent for your international (or $12 national) departure tax, if your ticket doesn't already cover it. If you lost your tourist permit (which immigration stamped upon your arrival) either go to Migración, tel. 744/484-9022 (see Services) before your departure date, or arrive early enough at the airport to iron out the problem with airport Migración officials, tel. 744/446-9025, before departure. Bring some proof of your date of arrival, either a stamped passport, airline ticket copy, or a copy of your lost tourist permit.

The Acapulco air terminal building has a number of shops upstairs for last-minute handicrafts purchases, a *buzón* (mailbox), stamp vending machine, long-distance telephones (be sure to ask the operator for the price before completing a call), and a restaurant.

By Bus

Major competitors Estrella Blanca and Estrella de Oro operate three separate long-distance *centrales de autobús* (central bus terminals), one (Estrella Blanca—the Ejido—station) on the west side and two (both Estrella Blanca and Estrella de Oro) stations on the east side of town.

Estrella Blanca, tel. 744/469-2028, 744/469-2029, or 744/469-2030, coordinates the service of its subsidiary lines Elite, Flecha Roja, Autotransportes Cuauhtémoc, Turistar, Futura, and Gacela at two separate terminals. Credit cards are accepted. Most first- or luxury-class departures use the big west-side **Ejido** terminal at Av. Ejido 47. The airy station is so clean you could sleep on the polished onyx floor and not get dirty; bring an air mattress and blanket. Other conveniences include left-luggage lockers, food stores across the street, a deluxe and midscale hotel booking agency, and Sendatel 24-hour *larga distancia* and fax office open daily 6 A.M.–10 P.M.

Also from the Ejido station, scores of Estrella Blanca *salidas locales* (local departures) connect with destinations in three directions: northern interior, Costa Grande (northwest), and Costa Chica (southeast) coastal destinations. Most connections are first-class Elite, Turistar, and Futura. Specific northern interior connections include Mexico City (dozens daily, some via Taxco), Toluca, Morelia via Chilpancingo and Altamirano (six daily), and Guadalajara (three daily).

Many first-class (about 10 per day) and second-class (hourly) departures connect northwest with Costa Grande destinations of Zihuatanejo and Lázaro Cárdenas and many intermediate points. Southeast Costa Chica connections with Puerto Escondido, some continuing to Huatulco and Salina Cruz, include four first-class daily (one via Ometepec) and several second-class connections per day.

Also from the Avenida Ejido Estrella Blanca terminal, one or two daily departures connect with the U.S. border (Mexicali and Tijuana) via the entire Pacific coast route, through Zihuatanejo, Manzanillo, Puerto Vallarta, and Mazatlán. Other departures connect with the U.S. border at Ciudad Juárez, via San Luis Potosí, Zacatecas, Torreón, and Chihuahua.

Many additional first- and luxury-class buses depart from Estrella Blanca's separate west-side big **Papagayo** terminal, on Avenida Cuauhtémoc, tel. 744/469-2028 and 744/469-2029, about five blocks west of the Estrella de Oro Terminal. Facilities and services include an a/c waiting room, left-luggage service, fax service (744/485-8331), a snack bar, and hotel reservations. From the Papagayo terminal, luxury-class and first-class buses connect with northeast Mexico and the U.S. border, via Querétaro, San Luis Potosí, Monterrey, and Nuevo Laredo. Other departures connect northwest, with Guadalajara, Leon, Celaya, and Irapuato; and north with Puebla and Mexico City bus stations Norte and Sur; and northwest, with Zihuatanejo.

The busy, modern **Estrella de Oro** bus terminal on the east side of town, at Cuauhtémoc and Massieu, tel. 744/485-8758, 744/485-8705, or 744/485-9360, provides connections with the Mexico City corridor (Chilpancingo, Iguala, Taxco, Cuernavaca, Mexico City) and northwest Costa Grande destinations via Zihuatanejo with Lázaro Cárdenas. Services include left-luggage lockers, but no food except sweets, chips, and drinks. *Correo* (post) and *telecomunicaciones* (telephone, fax, and money orders), offices, open Mon.–Sat. 8 A.M.–9 P.M. are on the outside upstairs walkway, west end.

Estrella de Oro departures include dozens of first- and luxury-class with Mexico City and intermediate points. Several connect directly through Taxco and Iguala. Four departures connect daily with the Costa Grande, three with Zihuatanejo, one only with Lázaro Cárdenas. Estrella de Oro offers no Costa Chica (Ometepec-Oaxaca) connections southeast.

MEXICO CITY DRIVING RESTRICTIONS

To reduce smog and traffic gridlock, authorities have limited which cars can drive on which days in Mexico City, depending upon the last digit of their license plates. If you violate these rules, you risk getting an expensive ticket. On Monday, no vehicle may be driven with final digits 5 or 6; Tuesday, 7 or 8; Wednesday, 3 or 4; Thursday, 1 or 2; Friday, 9 or 0. Weekends, all vehicles may be driven.

By Car or RV

Good highways connect Acapulco north with Mexico City, northwest with the Costa Grande and Michoacán, and southeast with the Costa Chica and Oaxaca.

The Mexico City Highway 95 *cuota* (toll) superhighway would make the initial leg connection via Chilpancingo (83 miles, 133 km, about two hours) easy if it weren't for the Acapulco congestion. (Go by the toll tunnel.) The uncluttered superhighway toll (*cuota*) extension (125 miles, 201 km) to Cuernavaca is a breeze in 2.5 hours. For Iguala and Taxco, leave the superhighway at the Chilpancingo north end and follow the winding but scenic Highway 95 northwest *libre* (nontoll) cutoff 75 miles (120 km) to Iguala, continuing 22 miles (35 km) to Taxco. From Cuernavaca, the over-the-mountain leg to Mexico City (53 miles, 85 km) would be simple except for possible Mexico City gridlock, which might lengthen it to two hours. Better allow a minimum of around 5.5 driving hours for the entire 261-mile (420-km) Acapulco-Mexico City trip. Make sure you arrive on a day permitted by the last digit of your license plate.

The Costa Grande section of Highway 200 northwest toward Zihuatanejo is generally uncluttered and smooth (except for occasional bumps and potholes). Allow about four hours for the 150-mile (242-km) trip.

The same is true for the Costa Chica stretch of Highway 200 southeast to Ometepec (122 miles, 197 km), Pinotepa Nacional (157 miles, 253 km) and Puerto Escondido (247 miles, 398 km total). Allow about three driving hours to Ometepec, four to Pinotepa, and about 6.5 hours total to Puerto Escondido.

Acapulco's most congested ingress-egress bottleneck used to be the over-the-hill leg of Highway 95 from the middle of town. Although this route has been speeded up by an expensive (about $6) one-mile toll tunnel, the scenery is much prettier if you drive east along the Costera past Hotel Las Brisas as if you were heading to the airport. At the big cloverleaf intersection downhill, near Puerto Marqués, head north. When you reach Highway 200, head right for the Costa Chica, or left for Highway 95 and northern points.

Pie de la Cuesta

The translation of the name Pie (pee-YAY) de la Cuesta (Foot of the Hill) aptly describes this downscale resort village. Tucked around the bend a few miles northwest of Acapulco, between a wide open-ocean beach and placid Laguna Coyuca, Pie de la Cuesta appeals to those who want the excitement the big town offers and the tranquillity it doesn't.

Although tranquil, Pie de la Cuesta offers plenty of outdoor activities, such as mangrove jungle boat tours, Barra de Coyuca village, water-skiing, jet-boating, beachcombing, boat and kayak launching, and swimming in the lagoon.

Laguna Coyuca, kept full by the sweet waters of the Río Coyuca, has long been known for its fish, birdlife, and tranquil, palm-lined shores. During the early 1400s, the Purépecha kings (who ruled from the Michoacán highlands) established a provincial capital near the town of Coyuca. After the Aztecs drove out the Purépecha a century later (and the Aztecs in turn were defeated by the Spanish), Pie de la Cuesta and its beautiful Laguna Coyuca slumbered in the shadow of Acapulco.

SIGHTS

Laguna Coyuca is a large sandy-bottomed lake, lined by palms and laced by mangrove channels. It stretches 10 miles along the shoreline, west from Pie de la Cuesta, which occupies the southeast (Acapulco) side. The barrier sandbar, wide Playa Pie de la Cuesta, separates the lagoon from the ocean. It extends a dozen miles west to the river outlet, which is open to the sea only during the rainy season. A road runs along the beach west the length of Laguna Coyuca to the tourist hamlet of Barra de Coyuca. There, *palapas* line the beach and serve seafood to busloads of Sunday visitors.

Playa Pie de la Cuesta, a seemingly endless, 100-yard-wide stretch of yellow sand, is fine for surf fishing, beachcombing, jogging, and long sunset walks. However, its powerful open-ocean waves are unsuited for surfing and frequently hazardous for swimming. They often break thunderously near the sand and recede with strong, turbulent undertow.

On the other side of the bar, the tranquil Acapulco (east) end of Laguna Coyuca is an embarkation point for lagoon tours and the center for water-skiing and personal watercraft riding. Among the best equipped of the shoreline clubs that offer powerboat services is the **Restaurant and Club de Skis Tres Marias.** Besides a pleasant lake-view shoreline *palapa* restaurant, it offers water-skiing at about $43/hour and personal watercraft riding for about $75/hour.

If you want to launch your own boat, you can do so easily at Club Tres Marias and others for about $15. The boat traffic, which confines itself mostly to midlagoon, does not deter swimming in the lagoon's clear waters. Slip on your bathing suit and jump in anywhere along the sandy shoreline.

Lagoon tours begin from several landings dotting the Pie de la Cuesta end of the lagoon. Half-day regular excursions (maximum 10 people, about $10 per person) push off daily around 11 A.M., noon, and 1:30 P.M. Along the way, they pass islands with trees loaded with nesting cormorants, herons, and pelicans. In midlake, gulls dip and sway in the breeze behind your boat while a host of storks, ducks, avocets, and a dozen other varieties paddle, preen, and forage in the water nearby. Other times, your boat passes through winding channels hung with vines and lined with curtains of great mangrove roots. At midpoint, tours usually stop for a bite to eat at **Isla Montosa.** (Ask ahead of time, because you shouldn't miss it.) Here, roosters crow, pigs root, bougainvillea blooms, and a colony of fishing families live, unencumbered by 21st-century conveniences, beneath their majestic shoreline palm grove.

On another day, drive your car or ride one of the frequent buses that head from Pie de la Cuesta to **Barra de Coyuca** village at the west end of the lagoon. Along the way, you will pass several scruffy hamlets and a parade of fenced lots, some still-open meadows where horses graze while others are filled with trees and big houses.

Lack of potable water, local residents complain, is a continuing problem on this dry sandbar.

At road's end, 10 miles from Pie de la Cuesta, a few tourist stores, a platoon of T-shirt vendors, and hammock-equipped beach *palapa* restaurants serve holiday crowds. Boats head for tours from lagoonside, where patrons at the **Restaurant Dos Vistas** enjoy a double view of both beach and lagoon.

(Mobile travelers can also continue west from here, by cross-lagoon launch to La Barra, thence to Costa Grande points west. See Getting There and Away in this section.)

ACCOMMODATIONS AND FOOD

Hotels and Bungalows

Approximately 20 basic accommodations line Pie de la Cuesta's single beachside road. Competition keeps rooms clean, management sharp, and prices low. They all cluster along a one-mile roadfront, enjoying highly visible locations right on the beach. Telephone, fax, or email for reservations, especially for the winter season and holidays. Many have tepid, room-temperature bath water only and do not accept credit cards; exceptions are noted below.

Note: Some unscrupulous Acapulco taxi drivers are trying to squeeze commissions from Pie de la Cuesta lodgings in return for bringing customers to their doorsteps. Typical tactics include outright refusing to take customers to places that don't pay commissions, or telling customers that the hotel they request *"no sirve"* ("is not running"). You can combat this on the spot by making sure, before you get into the taxi, that the driver agrees to take you to the hotel of your choice, and, once in Pie de la Cuesta, insisting that he follows through or don't pay. Daytime taxi fares from Acapulco shouldn't run more than about $5 from old town, $7 from the Costera; nighttime tariffs should be no more than double those amounts. Plenty of daytime buses run there for less than half a dollar. All lodgings recommended below are marked on the Pie de la Cuesta map.

Under $50: Cooperating on-site owner-managers account for the relaxed atmosphere of the combined yet distinct **Villa Nirvana** and **Villa Roxana,** at 302 Playa Pie de la Cuesta, P.O. Box 950, Acapulco, Guerrero 39300. Guests get to choose which they prefer between the two equally attractive options. Facilities of both hotels are shared by all. Pluses include two pools, at the inner and beach ends, respectively, of a lovely

ACAPULCO

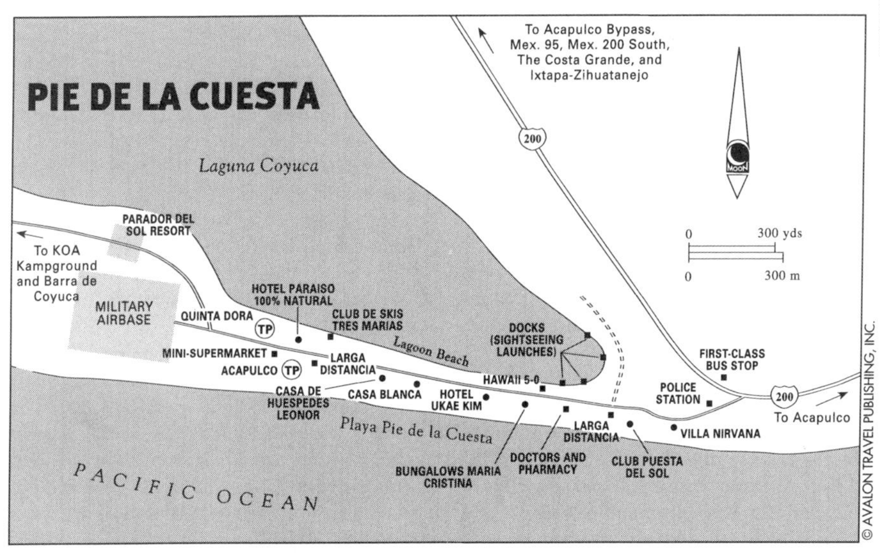

high-fenced garden and *palapa* restaurant compound. Cars park in an adjacent lot. Rooms in both complexes occupy two-floor tiers bordering the garden, upper floors being more private. The Villa Nirvana, tel. 744/460-1631, nirvana@acabtu.com, is operated by Daniel Reams and Pamela Fox, with help from the former owner's son Tomás. It occupies the beachfront half of the property. Their 14 clean, comfortable rooms rent from about $20 s or d low season, $35 high. Discounts for monthly rentals run about 15 percent. The original owner, Roxana, with her daughter Alexis, manage the Villa Roxana, tel. 744/460-3252. Their 14 clean and comfortable rooms rent for about $20 d, low season, $25 high, except for four rooms with kitchenettes, which go for about $25 d low, $35 high.

Very popular with a loyal cadre of Canadian winter returnees is **Casa de Huéspedes Playa Leonor,** 63 Carretera Pie de la Cuesta, Guerrero 39900, tel. 744/460-0348. Guests enjoy camaraderie around the tables of the *palapa* restaurant that occupies the beachside end of a large parking-lot garden. The several breezy, more private, upper-floor, plain but clean units are most popular. All 10 accommodations have two beds, showers, and fans, and rent for about $25 d low season, $30 high, with approximately 20 percent discount for monthly rentals.

The most spacious and prettiest grounds of Pie de la Cuesta beach accommodations belong to the **Hotel Club Puesta del Sol,** Manzana 57, Pie de La Cuesta, Guerrero 39900, tel. 744/460-0412, where guests enjoy a beachfront *palapa* dining area, a gorgeous blue pool, and a rough (but playable) tennis court within a sculpture-decorated garden. Tasty food from the kitchen of the amiable co-managers Alba Garcia and Nestor Cisneros and hours spent socializing, relaxing, and reading around the restaurant tables account for the hotel's loyal North American, European, and Mexican clientele. The 24 spartan but clean rooms are spread among two double-story buildings, one at beachfront. Doubles by the beach go for about $25 low season and $30 high; away from the beach, the same run $20 and $25. Kitchen-equipped beachside apartments for six rent for about $40 low season, $60 high. All accommodations come with fans and include parking.

Guests at the **Hotel and Restaurant Casa Blanca,** Av. Fuerza Aerea 370, Pie de la Cuesta, Guerrero 39900, tel. 744/460-0324 or 744/460-4028, casablanca@prodigy.net.mx, enjoy a tranquil, car-free tropical garden, small blue beachfront pool and restaurant, and new French management. Rents for the approximately 15 very clean and comfortable rooms, all with toilets and hot-water showers and a/c, run around $30 for one to four people, all year round. Discounts may be available for monthly or low season (May–Oct.) rentals. Credit cards are accepted.

Equally comfortable are the **Bungalows María Cristina,** P.O. Box 607, Acapulco, Guerrero 39300, tel. 744/460-0262, with eight units (four rooms, four kitchen-equipped bungalows) set between a streetside parking lot and a palmy beachside restaurant/garden. The clean, fixed-up and painted rooms with toilets and hot-water showers rent for about $30 d low season, $35 high. The kitchenettes, most of which face the ocean, run about $60 low season, $70 high, for up to four people. Negotiate for long-term discounts.

Also worthy is **Paraíso 100% Natural,** a project of the Acapulco family that runs several "100% Natural" restaurants. They offer eight clean, comfortable rooms with bath on the luscious lagoon-front, across the road from the Acapulco Trailer Park. Rates run about $40 d, with fans, good restaurant, and an inviting lakeview pool and patio. Reserve at Pie de la Cuesta 410, Guerrero, tel. 744/460-2577.

$50–100: Trying hard to be deluxe is the **Hotel Ukae Kim,** Av. de Fuerza Aerea 356, Pie de la Cuesta 39900, tel./fax 744/460-2187. Unfortunately, the builder crammed the 21 rooms into a small, albeit palmy space, rendering them private but generally dark. Amenities include a smallish but inviting pool and patio and *palapa* restaurant at the hotel's beachfront end. The clean, tastefully decorated rooms with hot water and a/c go, low season, for about $40 s or d, $60 for ocean view, $100 with ocean view and hot tub. Corresponding high season rates are about $60, $80, and $120. Credit cards are accepted.

Pie de la Cuesta's only upscale lodging is the roomy low-rise all-inclusive **Hotel Parador del Sol** on the west-side road past the air base. (See the description under Entertainment and Events.)

Trailer Parks and Camping

RV-equipped Pie de la Cuesta vacationers have three recommendable trailer park choices. First to consider is the homey and popular **Acapulco Trailer Park,** with about 60 densely packed palm-shaded spaces at beachfront and roomier choice lagoonside spaces, with all hookups, P.O. Box 1, Acapulco, Guerrero 39300, tel. 744/460-0010, fax 744/460-2457, acatrailerpark@hotmail.com. A congenial atmosphere, good management, and many extras, including a secure fence and gate, keep the place full most of the winter. Facilities include a boat ramp, blue pool, a store, a security guard, and clean restrooms and showers. The spaces rent for about $15 or $300 per month; tent spaces, $10. Get your winter reservation in early.

The security guard at the Acapulco Trailer Park is a reminder of former times, when muggings and theft were occurring with some frequency on Playa Pie de la Cuesta. Although bright new night lights on the beach (which soldiers patrol while local police patrol the streets) have greatly reduced the problem, some (but not all) local folks still warn against camping or walking on the beach at night.

Next in line is homey **Quinta Dora Trailer Park,** tel. 744/460-1138 or 744/460-0600, across the road from the Acapulco Trailer Park. Its pluses are an azure, palm-shaded lagoonfront location and boat ramp. Spaces rent for about $9 with electricity and water only, no sewer connection. Owners do welcome campers for the same daily rate.

KOA Kampgrounds has come to Pie de la Cuesta, in the form of a large park, about a mile out of the Pie de la Cuesta village, along the west-bound Barra de Coyuca road. Undoubtedly the best-equipped, the KOA Kampground, tel./fax 744/444-4062, tel. 744/483-7830, 744/483-2281, or 744/444-4277, koaaca@acabtu.com.mx, offers some shade in a big lot, with most spaces not right on the beach. Nevertheless, everyone is a stone's throw from the long, silky Pie de la Cuesta beach,

Tenters and RV campers at the Pie de la Cuesta KOA Kampground enjoy lavish beachfront facilities, including an inviting palmy pool area.

fine for shells, beachcombing, and surf fishing. Facilities include a snack restaurant, ministore, security fence, laundry, playground, pool, and kiddie pool. Big motor home spaces with all hookups run $30 by the beach, $22 in the shade away from beach, tent spaces go for $16; all get a 20 percent discount for monthly rentals. Tents rent for $15. For more information, visit www.koa.com.

Food

A number of restaurants have appeared in Pie de la Cuesta during recent years. Nearly all, however, are nondescript beachfront *palapas.* Of the few restaurants along the Pie de la Cuesta road, the class act is the lakeview *palapa* of the **Restaurant and Club de Skis Tres Marias.** Also, the open-air dining room of the **Hotel Casablanca,** the beachfront *palapa* of the **Villa Nirvana** (see above), and the poolside beachfront **Hotel Ukae Kim** are good prospects for a relaxing light meal.

ENTERTAINMENT AND EVENTS

Pie de la Cuesta's big fiesta honors the local patron, the **Virgin of Guadalupe,** with Masses, processions, fireworks, and dances on December 10, 11, and 12. The fiesta's climax, de rigueur for visitors, is the mass pilgrimage around the lake by boat.

At least one local discotheque, **Hawaii 5-O,** fires up seasonally and occasionally on weekends. Brightly painted signs on the roadside at mid-illage make it impossible to miss.

The deluxe **Parador del Sol** all-inclusive resort (about a mile west of Pie de la Cuesta village—turn right at the Barra de Coyuca fork before the air base) invites visitors to buy day and/or evening guest memberships for about $35 per adult (kids 4–11, half price) per eight-hour day session (10 A.M.–6 P.M.) and evening session (7 P.M.–2 A.M.). Day guests enjoy breakfast (10–11 A.M.), lunch (1–2 P.M.), open bar, and free use of the pools, beach club, kiddie playground, exercise gym, and basketball, volleyball, minigolf course, and tennis courts. The evening program kicks off at 7, with sports (including night-lit tennis) and swimming, continuing with supper (8:30–9:30 P.M.), open bar, and dancing at the discotheque until after midnight. If after a day you haven't had your fill, you might want to accept the resort's invitation to stay overnight for about $80 per person, double occupancy, low season, $100 high. For details, inquire at the front desk, at tel./fax 744/444-4050 or 744/444-4125, or check www.acabtu.com.mx/parador.

SERVICES

Although most services are concentrated half an hour away in Acapulco, Pie de la Cuesta nevertheless provides a few essentials. For medical consultations, see either Doctora Patricia Villalobos or her husband, Dr. Luis Amados Rios, tel. 744/460-0923, at their pharmacy where the lagoon begins, right in the middle of the village. Between them, they understand both English and French.

A scattering of minimarkets supply food. Two public long-distance phones are available, one in front of the Acapulco Trailer Park and the other on the highway by the doctors' pharmacy. In emergencies, go to the *policía,* at the small station near the intersection of the Pie de la Cuesta road and the highway to Acapulco.

GETTING THERE AND AWAY

Pie de la Cuesta is accessible via the fork from Highway 200 near Km 10, six miles (10 km) northwest of the Acapulco old town *zócalo* by car, taxi ($5), or local bus. The same road fork is also 144 miles (232 km) southwest of Zihuatanejo. First-class buses drop passengers at the roadside, where they can either walk, taxi, or ride one of the very frequent local minibuses.

Alternatively, mobile travelers can travel west toward the Costa Grande via local bus from Pie de la Cuesta west to Barra de Coyuca, thence by launch northwest across the Laguna Coyuca to La Barra and points west. (See La Barra in the Costa Grande chapter.)

The Costa Grande

The Costa Grande, the "Big Coast" of the state of Guerrero, stretches 150 miles northwest from Acapulco to Zihuatanejo. Before the highway came during the 1960s, this was a land of corn, coconuts, fish, and fruit. Although it's still that, the road added a new ingredient: a trickle of visitors seeking paradise in Zihuatanejo, a sleepy fishing village on a beautiful bay.

Now, however, that trickle of visitors is increasingly enjoying the host of country delights along the way. These include historic market towns, such as Tecpán de Galeana; a beloved pilgrimage shrine at Petatlán; the fascinating archaeological zone of Soledad de Maciel; breezy beaches for camping, beachcombing, and surf fishing, such as Laguna de Mitla, Arroyo Seco, Playa Brisas del Mar; and petite resort hideaways such as El Carrizal and Playa Escondida.

History

Long before Zihuatanejo's latter-day popularity, people had been attracted to the Costa Grande. Their oldest remains, pottery dating from around 3000 B.C., decorates the displays at the Zihuatanejo archaeological museum. Later, around 1000 B.C., the Olmecs (famous for their monumental

© BRUCE WHIPPERMAN

Gulf coast sculptures) left their unmistakable mark on regional pottery.

After them came waves of settlers, including the barbaric Chichimecs (Drinkers of Blood), the agricultural Cuitlatecs, and an early invasion of Aztecs, perhaps wandering in search of their eventual homeland in the Valley of Mexico.

None of those peoples were a match for the armies of Tarascan emperor Hiripan, who during the late 14th century A.D. invaded the Costa Grande from his Michoacán highland capital and established a coastal province, headquartered at the present town of Coyuca de Benítez, less than an hour's drive west of Acapulco.

Three generations later the star of the Aztec emperor Tízoc was rising over Mexico. His armies invaded the Costa Grande and pushed out the Tarascans. By 1500 the Aztecs ruled the coast from their provincial town capital at Cihuatlán, the "Place of Women" not far from present-day Zihuatanejo.

Along the Road

By bus, go by first- or second-class (whose drivers,

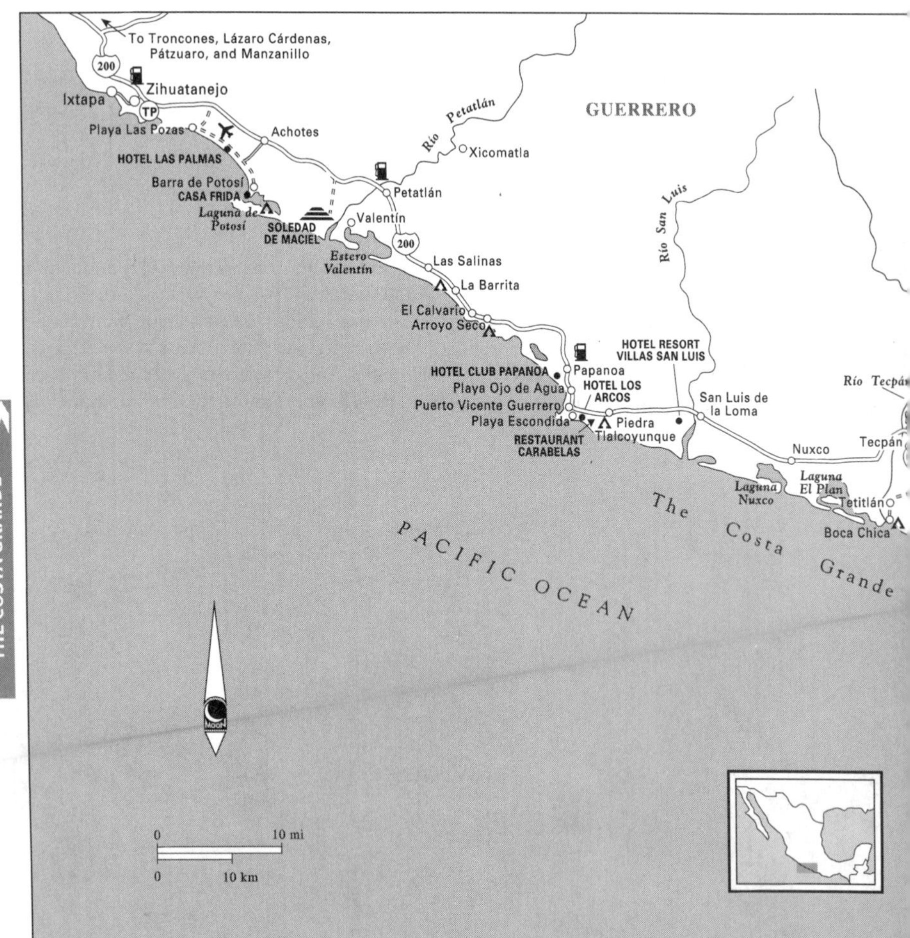

if asked, will let you off most anywhere) from the Estrella Blanca northwest-side Avenida Ejido terminal.

Drivers, follow Avenida Ejido (see the map Acapulco: Around the Bay), bear right at the Avenida Pie de la Cuesta "T" and continue northwest along the coastal Highway 200. Let the many highway signs and kilometer markers (both at roadside and painted on the highway asphalt highway itself, all measured from the Acapulco old-town *zócalo*) be your guide to the many palmy paradises along the way.

(For the laid-back downscale beach resort of Pie de la Cuesta just northwest of Acapulco, see the end of the Acapulco chapter. For the mini-paradises of Playa Las Pozas, Playa Blanca, and Barra de Potosí, see South of Ixtapa-Zihuatanejo in the Ixtapa-Zihuatanejo chapter.)

COYUCA DE BENÍTEZ AND LA BARRA

Coyuca de Benítez, pop. about 20,000, 20 miles (32 km) from Acapulco, is the market and service

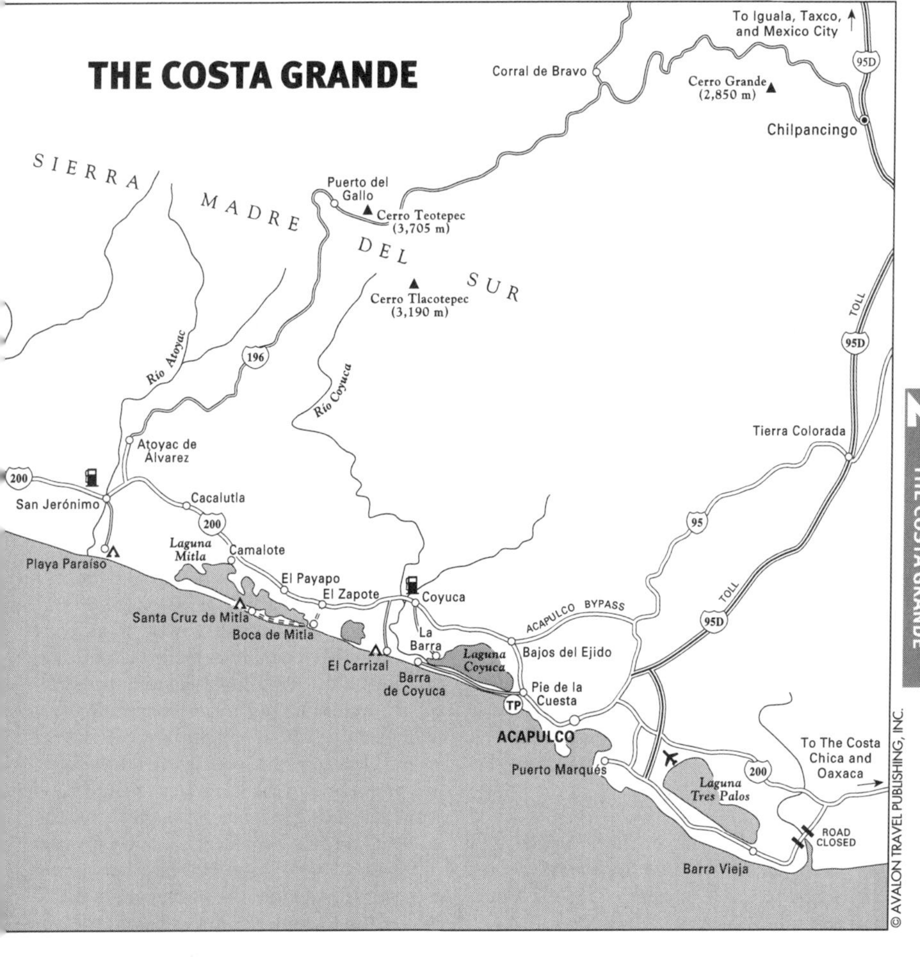

center of the southwest Costa Chica. Besides being a trading center for the produce of upcountry *fincas cafelatera* (coffee farms) and the *copra* of coastal coconut plantations, Coyuca is famous for its Easter celebration, when folks from all over the Costa Chica crowd in for the fun. Locally known as the **Fiesta de la Palmera,** the festival climaxes the few days before Easter Sunday, with pageants of the Passion of Jesus, and a carnival of food, rides, games, fireworks, bull-roping and riding *(jaripeo)* and cockfights *(peleas de gallos).*

Traffic slows to a crawl at the stall-crowded heart of town, marked by the corner bus station, tel. 781/452-0238, on the north side of the street.

Accommodations and Food

The most comfortable nearby hotel accommodations are at beach resort El Carrizal. In town, the best hotel is the **Posada Coyuca,** at Las Palmeras 6, tel. 781/452-0569, right on the highway, north side, a block east of the town center. The dozen-odd rooms are plainly decorated but very clean and reasonably priced, at $15 s or d in one double bed, $25 d, t, q in two double beds, all with fans, TV and restaurant downstairs. Add $10 for a/c. For more quiet and privacy, get an upstairs rear room, away from the highway. In an emergency, check out the hotels Imperio and Provinciano, tel. 781/452-0243, near the town plaza.

As for **camping** either go to the Laguna Coyuca at La Barra or the beach at El Carrizal or check out the shady informal campsite possibilities along the Coyuca River, at the west edge of town.

Coyuca is well-known for its good seafood. Two restaurants are especially recommended. Try either **La Brasa,** on the east, Acapulco side of the town center, or the airy *palapa* **Coyuca 33,** perched above the river at the west end of town.

Get your groceries and fruits and vegetables at the **market,** big every day, that sprawls over several town blocks north and south of the highway.

Services

Beyond the market stalls, on the north side, find the town plaza, with the *presidencia municipal,* tel. 781/452-1131, *telegrafos,* tel. 781/452-0017, and post office.

Back on the main street, services include a bank, Banamex, open Mon.–Fri. 9 A.M.–4 P.M., with 24-hour ATM, *abarrotes* (groceries), *farmacias* (pharmacies), and street telephones. Alternatively, go to the *caseta larga distancia* (long-distance telephone office), in the center of town, south side, across from the Farmacia de Jesús.

Also nearby, find an *agencia de viajes* (travel agent), on Guerrero, corner of Reforma, tel. 781/452-0034, a *centro de salud* (health clinic), Domínguez 36, tel. 781/452-0515, and Red Cross ambulance, on the highway, tel. 781/452-0515. For police and information, visit the small but well-marked roadside office, tel. 781/452-1164, a couple blocks east of the town center.

La Barra

This breezy lakefront boating, kayaking, fishing, and wildlife-viewing haven is reachable directly by car, taxi, or *colectivo* minibus, via the paved road south from the Coyuca town-center corner of Highway 200 and Calle Guadencia Parra.

If driving, mark your odometer. At Mile 1.7 (Km 2.7) pass through Las Lomas village (stores, pharmacy); at Mile 3.8 (Km 6.1), pass palmy, riverfront *palapa* Restaurant Dos Vistas. Arrive at the breezy boat jetty and local-style waterfront *palapa* restaurant Polita, at Mile 4.1 (Km 6.6)

From La Barra, the broad mangrove-fringed freshwater Laguna Coyuca spreads both a mile south across the river estuary to Barra de Coyuca ocean beach and east 10 miles to downscale Pie de la Cuesta resort village, on the edge of Acapulco.

The most popular La Barra activity is the boat ride, roaring directly across the lagoon ($1 per person in collective boat; $5 one way, by private boat) a mile to the Barra de Coyuca tourist village restaurants and beach. Alternatively, and with more tranquillity, try fishing (with your own equipment) and/or viewing (about $50 per boat per day) the trove of birds and other wildlife that prowl, perch, and preen among the lake's lacy channels and palmy islets. Bring your binoculars, bird book, hat, repellent, and sunscreen. Along the way, you might visit an island or two, especially the drowsy south-sea haven Isla Montosa and restaurant, in the lagoon, about four miles east of La Barra.

On the other hand, adventurers might do much the same, with their own boat or kayak. It's best to hire a guide; offer $10–20.

Camping or RV parking is a fertile possibility nearby. The best spots appear to be on the shady Coyuca River estuary-front, by the Restaurant Dos Vistas, by the road, a quarter-mile back toward Coyuca.

EL CARRIZAL

You know you may be in for something special when you see the "Zona Ecoturística" sign near the Km 37 marker three miles west of Barra de Coyuca. At the end of the road, you can have all the pleasures of easy country beach living.

If you're on foot, hire a taxi or ride a *colectivo* minivan from the highway. If by car, mark your odometer at the highway just before turning south. At Mile 4.1 (Km 6.6) pass through Epinarillo village, with a sprinkling of stores and a pharmacy or two.

At Mile 4.6 (Km 7.4), arrive at the beach, a gorgeous miles-long medium-steep golden-yellow fine-sand shoreline with powerful, close-in breaks. Flocks of seabirds skitter along the sand, glide over the billows, and dive for fish offshore. Waves seasonally deposit shells and driftwood. The surf, although unsuitable for surfing and generally too rough for swimming, appears excellent for wading and surf fishing. Boat launching, although not impossible, appears difficult at best.

At the beach, you can either go right or left. Go right, for a miles-long breezy strand, ripe for tenting or RV camping. Go left for a long lineup of permanent, family-friendly *palapa* restaurants and cabana lodgings.

A few of the beachfront establishments stand out. Immediately, find inviting **Restaurant Dunas** and adjacent, away from the beach, **Bungalows El Carrizal,** tel. 781/452-1869. Owned and operated by personable Virginia Díaz, the five small, spartan but clean rooms rent for about $20 s or d, $30 weekends and holidays, with hot-water showers, TV, fans, and shaded parking. Señora Díaz also runs a snack restaurant (separate from neighbor Restaurant Dunas) whose menu features plenty of fruit, vegetables, yogurt, and granola.

At El Carrizal, folks can enjoy both the freshwater Laguna Coyuca and the open ocean beach a short walk behind the line of palms.

Continue east along the beach road a few hundred yards, passing a number of *palapas,* to the inviting and popular family-friendly beach **Resort and Restaurant Nautilus,** tel. 781/452-1933 or 781/452-1933. Managers rent five plain but clean cabanas, two with private bath, $20; three with shared bath, $15, next to their large, beachview *palapa* restaurant and blue pool. Although weekdays (except Christmas, Easter, July, and August) would generally be quiet here, seekers of peace and quiet on a weekend better stay elsewhere. Nevertheless, tent camping is customary, for a nominal fee, in the shade on the beach, right in front of the restaurant.

The Nautilus's friendly owner, Amado Fajardo Colixto, takes parties of up to eight people on lagoon tours in the adjacent Coyuca Lagoon for about $20 per hour. He also sells lots for homes along the beach. (In all property transactions, work through a well-established real estate agent; see the sidebar "Owning Paradise" in the Acapulco chapter.)

Continue east to the palmy, picturesque road's end, at Mile 6.3 (Km 10.1), where boats line docks, ready to whisk visitors on lagoon wildlife-viewing and restaurant excursions.

Here, lagoon-front **Hotel Paraíso Playa Azul** offers the only deluxe local accommodations, in a cluster of modern rooms around a invitingly grassy pool-patio. Rooms, however, are unfortunately dark (without turning on the lights) and make little use of the beautiful lagoonside setting. Nevertheless, rooms are comfortable, each with a pair of soft double beds, hot-water shower bath, and small refrigerator. They rent for $40 weekends and holidays (offer $30 weekdays), with a/c, cable TV, a shaded sitting area overlooking the leafy lagoon, and massage at extra cost. The gorgeous beach is only a few steps away across the road. Relaxing, ocean- and lagoon-view *palapa* restaurants are also nearby. For information and reservations, call the hotel directly, tel. 744/431-9485 or toll-free Mex. tel. 800/713-4621. By the time you read this the hotel may have a website and email; log on an Internet search engine and type in the hotel name and see what comes up.

LAGUNA DE MITLA

Curiosity alone might drive adventurous lovers of tropical Mexico to explore the reaches of the grand, freshwater Laguna de Mitla. Its 25-mile (40-km) high-water length makes it the longest natural lake in Guerrero, so big that it has enough room for three separate bays along its north-side shoreline. The rewards along the road are a lush, freshwater swimming lagoon, beachfront seafood *palapa* restaurants, local fisherfolk willing to guide parties on fishing and wildlife-viewing trips, and a long, pristine, breeze-swept wild (but largely shadeless) beach, ready for camping or RV parking, surf-fishing, and beachcombing. At the end of the road, you'll even find a small community museum and a small store with a freshwater well.

Get there from Highway 200, at El Zapote, 30 miles (48 km) from Acapulco. Drivers, mark your odometer. Hikers, hire a taxi, thumb a ride, or simply walk the 1.2 miles (2 km) to **Boca de Mitla.** There, cross the bridge over the channel that connects the east and west branches of the Laguna de Mitla.

You may not want to go any farther. Mangroves decorate the river, a few *lanchas* and *canoas* rest on the bank, men, waist-deep, cast nets into the water, and kids splash downstream nearby. You might either hire a *lancha* and guide, or launch your own boat or kayak for your private fishing or bird-watching expedition. Be equipped, however, with a hat, binoculars, repellent, bottled water, and fishing tackle.

Continue less than half a mile to the beach at Mile 1.6 (Km 2.6). Beachfront **Restaurant Sirenita** (Little Mermaid) perches on the sand, ready for customers. A fine golden-sand beach appears to stretch endlessly, both west and east. Powerful waves break suddenly along long fronts and recede with strong undertow. Tiny crabs, sandpipers, and plovers scurry along the sand, sun-bleached driftwood lies for the taking, and a few unused temporary palm-frond shelters await new occupants. With the restaurant nearby and plenty of room to spread out, beach tenting or RV parking could hardly be better here.

Continue along the beachfront road west. At

Mile 3.1 (Km 5) the scene is similarly inviting, at seafood *palapa* **Yenifer** right on the beach. Farther along, at Mile 3.4 (Km 5.5), pass the local aquaculture cooperative where workers tend ponds of fish (tilapia), prawns, and shrimp. Moreover, they offer tours in the adjacent Laguna Mitla. Continue to Mile 4 (Km 6.4), passing a small store that can probably furnish, at least, some staples and water.

The gravel road bumps along, paralleling the beach, through miles of short scrub and cactus. Occasional houses, remnants of a moribund "Acapulco Pacifico" second-home development, dot the flat, sandy landscape. Finally, at Mile 8.1 (Km 13), head inland, away from the beach, to the Santa Cruz de Mitla village plaza, store, and kiosk, labeled "Santa Cruz de Mitla Museo Comunitario." Inside, the village exhibits ancient, locally discovered pottery artifacts. Nearby, beneath some trees, the store offers a few vital canned goods and staples and also maintains a well, which is said to provide fresh water.

© BRUCE WHIPPERMAN

At Playa Paraíso, a hanging bridge leads across a small lagoon to car-free, family-friendly Hacienda de Cabaña miniresort.

CAMALOTE, PLAYA PARAÍSO, AND SAN JERÓNIMO

Visit each of these little places and fill entirely different needs: Camalote for seafood, boating, and camping; Playa Paraíso for a picnic and a cooling swim and snooze in the shade; and San Jerónimo for a hotel room and essential services.

Camalote

Reach this lagoon-shore refuge 36 miles (58 km) northwest of Acapulco. Follow the signed dirt turnoff road about a half mile to the pair of permanent country-style restaurants on the airy east shoreline of the freshwater Laguna de Mitla.

This pretty spot offers easy boating, fishing, and kayaking on the broad lagoon. Some shady sites beneath lakefront trees also invite tenting and RV parking. However, you may have to start by cleaning a bit of trash from your site. Moreover, if you require tranquillity, confine your camping to nonholiday weekdays, since this spot is popular with local families (with their radios and CD players) on weekend outings.

Playa Paraíso

Formerly known as "Playa Paraíso Perdido" (Lost Paradise Beach), this place has now been found, and for good reason: Local folks love it for its gorgeous swimming-picnicking-camping ground and the breezy boat rides across the Rio Atoyac lagoon to good seafood restaurants and a long open-ocean beach.

Get there via the Highway 200 turnoff signed Hacienda de Cabaña, near the Km 81 highway marker, 50 miles northwest of Acapulco (and two miles before San Jerónimo). After about five miles (8 km) along a good paved road, arrive at family-friendly **Hacienda de Cabaña** resort. Cross over on its picturesque hanging bridge and enjoy a swim, a picnic, or an overnight in the walk-in palm-shaded campground.

Continue to the adjacent estuary-front boat landing that, on weekends and holidays, buzzes with motorboats that whisk families to the restaurants and long open-ocean beach on the other side. Alternatively, rent a launch for fishing tilapia, *robalo* (snook), or *pez gallo* (roosterfish), or launch your own boat or kayak.

San Jerónimo

The small market town of San Jerónimo, pop. 10,000, on Highway 200, 52 miles (84 km) east of Acapulco, offers a modicum of services and lodging.

At the highway-center of town, find the bus station. On the town plaza nearby is a *telecomunicaciones,* with public telephone, money orders, and fax. Nearby, also find a post office, a pharmacy, *centro de salud,* and a pair of modest emergency hotels, the Posada San Francisco and the Hotel and Restaurant Villa del Mar.

BOCA CHICA AND TETITLÁN

For the fun and adventure of it, visit Boca Chica, a beach village accessible sometimes by boat only. Here, camping is de rigueur, since even permanent residents are doing it. It makes no sense to pour concrete on a sandbar where palm fronds are free and the next wave may wash everything away anyway.

The jumping-off spot is near Km 98 (88 miles, 142 km southeast of Zihuatanejo and 61 miles, 98 km northwest of Acapulco), where a sign marks the road to Tetitlán (pop. 2,000). In about three miles, turn left at the T intersection at the town plaza (with long-distance phone, pharmacy, groceries) and continue a couple of miles along a bumpy, but negotiable when dry, road to the Laguna Tecpán, which, during the dry season, may have narrowed to a river or dried completely. Here, launches will ferry you (or you can walk) the mile across to the village on the sandbar. Bargain the *viaje redondo* (return-trip) price with your boatman before you depart.

On the other side, the waves thunder upon the beach and sand crabs guard their holes, while the village's four separate societies—people, dogs, pigs, and chickens—each go about their distinct business. Shells and driftwood decorate the sand, and surf fishing with bait from the lagoon couldn't be better.

Most visitors come for the eating only: superfresh seafood charcoal-broiled in one of the dozen *palapas* along the beach. If, however, you plan to camp overnight, bring drinking water, a valuable Boca Chica commodity.

During the summer rainy season, the Tecpán River, which feeds the lagoon, breaks through the bar. Ocean fish enter the lagoon, and the river current sometimes washes Boca Chica, *palapas* and all, out to sea.

TECPÁN

The major service center of the central Costa Grande, Tecpán de Galeana (pop. 25,000), commonly shortened to Tecpán, is the birthplace of celebrated independence hero Hermanegildo Galeana (1762–1814). Galeana, son of a prominent farming family, successfully operated his family's hacienda until he joined the *insurgente* cause in 1811, at the age of 49.

According to scholars, the town's name has two interpretations, both from the Náhuatl (Aztec language): either from *tetl* (stone) and *pan* (atop or on), meaning "atop the stone"; or from *tecutli* (lord) and *pan* (place of), meaning "place of the lord."

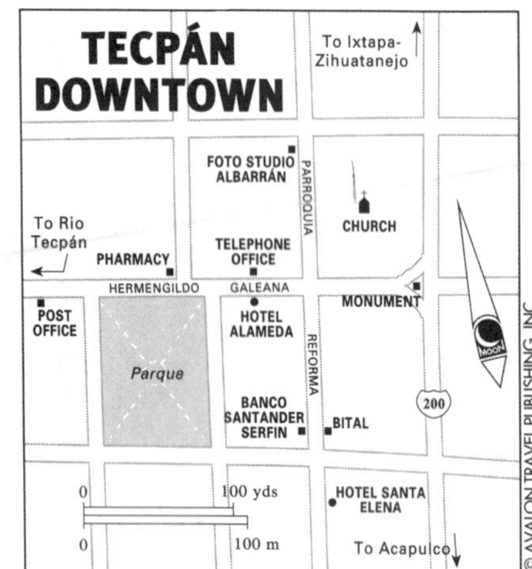

HERMANEGILDO GALEANA: GENTLEMAN REBEL

Hermanegildo (air-mah-nay-HEEL-doh) Galeana (1762–1814) wasted little time in rallying to Father Miguel Hidalgo's cry for Mexican independence. A well-to-do Mexican-born *hacendado,* Galeana resented having to bow to the arrogant *peninsulares* who were elevated to Mexico's ruling upper crust by the sole virtue of having been born in Spain.

He was born in Tecpán, on April 13, 1762, of a criollo mother and an English sea captain father who established a successful farm in the fertile Río Tecpán valley. As a youth, Hermanegildo benefited from the modicum of advantages that his landed criollo class enjoyed.

During most of his adult years, Galeana enjoyed the life of a country gentleman, successfully managing his family estate, Hacienda El Zanjón, while fathering a brood of children by a succession of six wives.

All that changed drastically when rebel priest José María Morelos, under direct orders from Hidalgo, marched into Tecpán in front of his newly recruited rebel brigade. Drawn by Morelos's charismatic determination, Galeana, along with his two brothers, joined Morelos's force, bringing with them dozens of their workers and a swarm of their Tecpán friends and followers. Thus, at the late age of 49, Hermanegildo Galeana launched the final heroic chapter of his life.

Soon the Galeanas rose to field command rank, joining Morelos's circle of most trusted adjutants. The Spanish challenged them right away, with little success. On January 4, 1811, the Galeanas fought bravely, achieving a rebel victory at El Veledero, which won them 800 prisoners and a trove of captured arms and ammunition.

From then on, Hermanegildo Galeana fought side by side with Morelos, bravely orchestrating a series of signal victories, including the triumph at Tixtla, Vicente Guerrero's hometown. Buoyed by success, Morelos led his triumphant army north, quickly capturing Cuautla, in the present state of Morelos. However, Galeana's severest challenge came when Spanish forces counterattacked and laid a 73-day siege upon the rebels. The siege climaxed when the Spanish attackers penetrated the rebels' perimeter, flanking Morelos and Galeana. A royalist colonel got near Morelos and fired his pistol but missed. Galeana returned fire with his rifle at point-blank range, saving Morelos's life.

Galeana fought on, commanding a victorious battalion in Huajuapan, Oaxaca, in July 1812. In 1813, back south on the coast, Galeana and his men surprised a Spanish force entrenched on Roqueta Island, an action that led to the rebel capture of Acapulco.

By mid-1814, Galeana was riding a wave of victories. He had won the admiration of his men, who called him, affectionately, "Tata" (Daddy) Gildo, for his selfless, heroic devotion to them and the *insurgente* cause.

But his days were numbered. On June 27, 1814, royalist General Calleja's soldiers ambushed and killed Galeana at Salitral, near Tecpán. Aviles, the royalist commander, ordered Galeana's head cut off, placed on the point of a lance, and exhibited in the Tecpán town plaza. But, because of the riot that such barbarous action ignited, Aviles had Galeana's head taken down and buried with his body inside the Tecpán church. Later, a pair of Galeana's soldiers buried his remains in a secret location to avoid further mutilation.

The independence cause for which Galeana had fought finally prevailed. The new republican government of an independent Mexico elevated beloved "Tata Gildo" to the revered national rank of Benemérito de la Patria, on July 19, 1823.

Orientation and Sights

Tecpán spreads along the west bank of the broad south-flowing Río Tecpan. Highway 200, approaching westerly from Acapulco, bends north and continues for two miles through the town before turning west again and crossing the river.

A modern abstract stone monument on the highway's west side marks the center of town. It also marks Tecpán's main east-west street, appropriately named Hermanegildo Galeana. If from that point you head west, away from the highway, you pass the church, on your right (north side), at Calle Parroquia, which continues south as Calle Reforma. After another block, you arrive at the red and pink-adorned town parque that harmonizes cheerily with its bougainvillea floral decor.

Accommodations and Food

Tecpán has four or five simple hotels. On Galeana, just east of the park, try the **Hotel Alameda,** tel. 742/425-0616, with about half a dozen plainly decorated upstairs rooms for $20 d, with a/c.

Alternatively nearby, around the corner, on Reforma, past the bank, check out the similarly modest **Hotel Santa Elena,** tel. 742/425-0091.

Tecpan's most highly recommended restaurant is the clean, Mexican-style family **Restaurant Fogata** (Campfire). Find it on the through-town highway, about two blocks north of Galeana, tel. 742/425-0033.

Services

Several service establishments are handily within a block or two of the park: the *correo* (post office), one block west; *farmacia* del Centro, tel. 742/425-2858, open daily 9 A.M.–9 P.M. across Galeana from the park; long-distance telephone, across Galeana and half a block east; Banco Internacional, east and around the corner, on Reforma, open Mon.–Sat. 8 A.M.–7 P.M., or across the street, Banco Santander Serfin, both with ATMs; and photo and film, at Foto Studio Albarrán, on Calle Parroquia, across from the church, open daily 8 A.M.–8 P.M., tel. 742/425-2323.

A number of doctors—gynecologist, internist, pediatrician, and traumatologist—are available at the Centro de Especialidades medical offices, tel. 742/425-0258, a few blocks south, on the highway downtown. After medical office hours, go to the town Centro de Salud, tel. 742/425-0030.

SAN LUIS DE LA LOMA, HOTEL RESORT VILLAS SAN LUIS, AND PIEDRA TLALCOYUNQUE

San Luis de la Loma

Nearby, two miles east, the pleasant little market town of San Luis de la Loma (pop. 5,000) runs along a hilltop main street that angles off Highway 200 near Km 140. Besides a number of groceries, fruit stalls, and pharmacies, San Luis has a guesthouse—Hotel Hermanos Ruiz—a post office, a health center, a *larga distancia,* a dentist, and a doctor, gynecologist José Luis Barrera Garcia, tel. 742/427-0193 and 742/427-0025, on the plaza, three blocks from the highway. First-class buses also stop and pick up passengers at the main street-highway intersection.

Hotel Resort

Little was spared to embellish this pretty hacienda-like corner of a big mango, papaya, and coconut grove. It appears as if the owner, tiring of all work and no play, built a park to entertain his friends. Now, his project blooms with lovely swimming and kiddie pools, a big *palapa* restaurant, a smooth *palapa*-covered dance floor, a small zoo, basketball and volleyball courts, and an immaculate hotel.

Ideal for a lunch/swim break or an overnight rest, the 40 immaculate and attractively furnished hotel rooms rent for about $50 s or d, with a/c and hot water included; credit cards are not accepted. Add about 10 percent during holidays. If you'll be arriving on a weekend or holiday, write, phone, or fax for a reservation: Hotel Resort Villas San Luis, Carretera Zihuatanejo-Acapulco, Km 143, Buenavista de Juárez, Guerrero 40906, tel. 742/427-0228, fax 742/427-0235.

Find it on the westbound side of the road near Km 142, 61 miles (98 km) southeast of Zihuatanejo, 89 miles (143 km) northwest of Acapulco.

Piedra Tlalcoyunque

At Km 150 (56 miles, 90 km from Zihuatanejo or 94 miles, 151 km from Acapulco) a signed side road heads seaward to Piedra Tlalcoyunque and the Carabelas Restaurant. About a mile down the paved road, the restaurant appears, perching on a bluff overlooking a monumental sandstone rock, Piedra Tlalcoyunque. Below, a wave-tossed strand, ripe for beachcombing and surf fishing, stretches for miles. Powerful breakers with fine right-hand surfing angles roll in and swish up the steep beach.

For fishing, buy some bait from the net fishermen on the beach and try some casts beyond the billows crashing into the south side of the Piedra. Later, stroll through the garden of eroded rock sea stacks on the north side. There you can poke among the snails and seaweeds in a big sheltered tidepool, under the watchful guard of the squads of pelicans roosting on the surrounding pinnacles.

The *palapa* house (currently in need of repair) on the beach is the seasonal headquarters of the **Campamento Playa Piedra de Tlalcoyunque,** whose mission is to rescue, incubate, and hatch as many turtle eggs as possible. Several staff members patrol the beach during the summer-fall hatching (and egg-poaching) season. Although they are dedicated to their task, their vigil is a lonely one, and they generally welcome visitors and contributions of drinks and food.

At the Carabelas Restaurant on the bluff above, you can take in the whole breezy scene while enjoying the recommended catch of the day. The name Carabelas (Caravels) comes from the owner's admiration of Christopher Columbus. He christened his restaurant's three petite ocean-view gazebos after Columbus's three famous caravels: the *Niña,* the *Pinta,* and the *Santa María.*

For an overnight or a short stay, ask the restaurant owners if you can set up your tent or park your (self-contained) RV in the restaurant lot or by the beach below the restaurant. For shower and dishwashing water, drop your bucket down into their well, at the bottom of the rise, before the restaurant.

PUERTO VICENTE GUERRERO, PLAYA ESCONDIDA, AND PLAYA BRISAS DEL MAR

Puerto Vicente Guerrero, a small workaday fishing port and naval training center, 97 miles (156 km) from Acapulco and 52 miles (84 km) from

A forest of angular sea rocks, tidepools, foaming surf, and perching sea birds attract visitors to Playa Piedra Tlalcoyunque.

SAVING TURTLES

Sea turtles were once common on the beaches of the Acapulco region. Times have changed, however. Now a determined corps of volunteers literally camps out on isolated beaches, trying to save the turtles from extinction. This is a tricky business, because their poacher opponents are invariably poor, determined, and often armed. Since turtle tracks lead right to the eggs, the trick is to get there before the poachers. The turtle-savers dig up the eggs and hatch them themselves, or bury them in secret locations where they hope the eggs will hatch unmolested. The reward—the sight of hundreds of new hatchlings returning to the sea—is worth the pain for this new generation of Mexican ecoactivists.

Once featured on dozens of Acapulco restaurant menus, turtle meat, soup, and eggs are now illegal commodities. Though not extinct, the Mexican Pacific's main sea turtle species—including the green, olive ridley, hawksbill, and leatherback—have dwindled to a small fraction of their previous numbers.

green turtle

BOB RACE

Turtle activists point out that poaching is only one of the hazards that have driven sea turtles to the edge of extinction. Beach habitat loss, ingestion of floating debris, such as plastic bags and tar balls, disease, and accidental capture by trawler nets continue to take deadly tolls.

The **green turtle** *(Chelonia mydas)*, the second-largest sea turtle species, is named for the color of its fat (although in Mexico it's called the *tortuga negra* or *caguama)*. Officially endangered, the prolific green turtle nevertheless remains relatively numerous. Female green turtles can return to shore up to eight times during the year, depositing 500 eggs in a single season. When not mating or migrating, the vegetarian greens can be spotted often in lagoons and bays, nipping at seaweed with their beaks. Adults, usually three or four feet long and weighing 200–300 pounds, are easily identified out of water by the four big plates on either side of their shells. Green turtle meat was once prized as the main ingredient of turtle soup.

The **olive ridley** *(Lepidochelys olivacea)*, or locally,

Zihuatanejo, hides a pearl of a beach, appropriately known as Playa Escondida, beyond its southeast headland.

Playa Escondida

Two miles from the signed highway turnoff, continue through the port village, bearing left (east), uphill, at the village-center road fork overlooking the harbor. Pass the naval training center at the road's summit, and continue ahead a few blocks downhill to the Playa Escondida beach.

Beyond the several permanent *palapa* restaurants that populate the beachfront spreads a wide yellow-sand beach, sheltered on both sides by rocky headlands. Strong waves break and roll in along a nearly level shoreline, receding with only mild undertow.

Playa Escondida (also known locally as Playa Secreta) appears ideal for every kind of beach entertainment, from kiddie play and beachcombing, to intermediate surfing and scuba diving. The beach even has ample room for tent camping, especially on the east side.

New lodgings are receiving a growing number of visitors. Most prominent is **Hotel and Restaurant Los Arcos,** Mex. cell tel. 044-742/424-5916, outside Mexico 742/424-5916. Its dozen-odd modern, light, and comfortably furnished rooms encircle an inviting pool and parking patio. On the beach side, guests also enjoy an airy beachview restaurant restaurant. Room rentals run about $35 s, $40 d, $50 t, with hot-water shower baths, a/c, and cable TV.

Folks interested in sportfishing and other water sports might want to take a look at the **Bahía la Tortuga Fishing Lodge,** tel.

golfina, turtle population, thanks to persistent government and local volunteer efforts, seems to be stabilizing, at several hundred thousand worldwide. Olive ridleys (so-named for their dull green shells) nest in significant numbers at isolated Acapulco region beaches, notably Playa Revolcadero, east of Acapulco, and Playa Piedra Tlalcoyunque, west on the Costa Grande. Among the smaller of sea turtles, olive ridley (80–100 pounds, with two-foot-long shells at maturity) come ashore to nest, customarily during summer. They lay clutches of around 80–100 eggs, which they bury with their flippers, and quickly return to the sea. They hunt most of the year near shorelines for shellfish, crabs, fish, and squid.

By contrast, the severely endangered **hawksbill** *(Eretmochelys imbricata)* has vanished from many Mexican Pacific beaches. Known locally as the *tortuga carey* (kah-RAY), it was the source of both meat and the lovely translucent tortoiseshell that has been supplanted largely by plastic. Adult *careys,* among the smaller of sea turtles, run two to three feet in length and weigh 30–100 pounds. Their usually brown shells are readily identified by shinglelike overlapping scales. During late summer and fall, females come ashore to lay clutches of eggs (around 100) in the sand. *Careys,* although preferring fish, mollusks, and shellfish, will eat almost anything, including seaweed. When attacked, *careys* can be plucky fighters, inflicting bites with their eagle-sharp hawksbills.

BOB RACE

hawksbill turtle

You'll be fortunate indeed if you glimpse the rare **leatherback** *(Dermochelys coriacea),* the world's largest turtle. Experts have learned much about the leatherback *(laut* or *tortuga de cuero)* in recent years. About 100,000 female leatherbacks are thought to nest on their favorite breeding ground, the Mexican Pacific coast. Tales of the leatherback—of fisherfolk catching seven- or eight-foot individuals weighing nearly a ton—are legend. If you see even a small one you'll recognize it immediately by its back of leathery skin, creased with several lengthwise ridges.

742/424-5795, www.escapeixtapa.com, which has recently opened on the beach. Owner-operators John and Angélica Lorenz advertise three night–four day packages for two, beginning at $450, including two days sportfishing, one meal daily, and airport pickup. They also offer kayaking, snorkeling, scuba diving, surfing lessons, and whale- and turtle-watching, in season.

One or two bed-and-breakfasts and local homeowners also rent rooms. Follow their signs, posted along the street above Hotel Los Arcos.

One especially recommended local **scuba diving** site is El Morro, the big rock island visible off the coast northwest around Papanoa town. Although no dive shop is operating locally, experienced divers might get there with John Lorenz of the Bahía la Tortuga Fishing Lodge or Juan Barnard Avila of Zihuatanejo Scuba Center, tel./fax 755/554-3873, 755/554-8156, or 755/554-2147, divemexico@email.com.

Playa Brisas del Mar

Scarcely more than a mile on the Acapulco side from Puerto Vicente Guerrero, this breezy gem of a beach spreads west from the point where Highway 200 skirts the oceanfront, at Km 154.

A dirt side road leads 100 yards to the few houses and *palapa* restaurants (notably, Restaurant Robert's) that line the near (west) end of the beach. The dirt road forks left, passing the restaurants, and continues east along the beach, a pristine 200-foot-wide golden strand with rollers that break gradually about 100 yards out. All beach diversions, including surfing, boogie boarding, kiddie play, beachcombing, surf fishing, and boat launching (provided you can negotiate the soft sand) appear promising here. Although no shade is available, at least one abandoned beach *palapa* appears ready for new occupants. Tenting and RV parking also appear customary. Out of courtesy, ask at Restaurant Robert's if camping is permitted.

© BRUCE WHIPPERMAN

Its leafy garden, blue pool, and uncrowded beach beyond are good reasons to stop at Hotel Club Papanoa.

PAPANOA AND PLAYA OJO DE AGUA

Papanoa

The small town of Papanoa (pop. 3,000) straddles the highway 103 miles (165 km) northwest of Acapulco, and 47 miles (75 km) south of Zihuatanejo. Local folks tell the tongue-in-cheek story of its Hawaiian-sounding name. It seems that there was a flood, and the son of the local headman had to talk fast to save his life by escaping in a *canoa.* Instead of saying "Papa . . . canoa," the swift-talking boy shortened his plea to "Papa . . . noa."

At least two hotels offer rooms. At the Zihuatanejo end of town, a block or two from the bus station, find the barely mentionable bare-bones Auto Hotel Papanoa. Expect to pay about $15 d for a plain, worn, bare-bulb room. Much more comfortable, however, is Papanoa's resort-style lodging, the **Hotel Club Papanoa,** Papanoa, Guerrero 40907, tel. 742/422-0150. Near the beach about a mile southeast of town, the hotel offers about 30 large rooms, a restaurant, and a big pool set in spacious ocean-view garden grounds. Built to be luxurious but now a bit frayed around the edges, the hotel is full during holidays and nearly empty most other times. Rooms rent for about $40 s or d low season, $50 high. All with a/c. Ask for a discount.

The hotel grounds adjoin the beach, **Playa Cayaquitos.** The wide, breezy, yellow-gray strand stretches for two miles, washed by powerful open-ocean rollers with good left and right surfing breaks. Additional attractions include surf fishing beyond the breakers and driftwood along the sand. Beach access is via the off-highway driveway just north of the hotel. At the beach, a parking lot borders a seafood restaurant. Farther on, the road narrows (but is still motor-home accessible) through a defunct beachside home development, past several brush-bordered informal RV parking or tent camping spots.

A pair of clean restaurants, the **Annel** and the **Cabaña,** in the town center, south side of the highway, serve passable country-style food.

As for services, Papanoa offers a doctor, friendly Salvador Zarate, tel. 742/422-0046 with pharmacy, a photo shop, tel. 742/422-0276, a *gasolinera,* first-class bus stops, a long-distance telephone, and Ladatel card-operated public phones.

Playa Ojo de Agua

Nestled in the little nook between the headlands, about half a mile southeast of the Hotel Club Papanoa, is the petite half-moon beach, named Playa Ojo de Agua for its cooling and cleansing fresh-water spring. Local families flock here on weekend afternoons to play in the surf, eat fresh seafood at the beachfront *palapas,* and rinse themselves in the community spring (*ojo de agua,* literally eye of water) that trickles from the hillside above the beach.

PLAYAS ARROYO SECO, EL CALVARIO, AND CAYACAL

Between Km 178 and Km 183, Highway 200 veers spectacularly close to the ocean. Here, three long beaches, Arroyo Seco, Calvario, and Cayacal, join in one continuously scenic sweep of sand, sea, and sky. From the Acapulco end, first comes long, wild Playa Arroyo Seco; then Playa El Calvario, stunningly viewable from any one of several clifftop *palapa* restaurants, and finally golden Playa Cayacal, seemingly extending forever west.

Between Km 178 and Km 183, Highway 200 veers spectacularly close to the ocean. Here, three long beaches, Arroyo Seco, Calvario, and Cayacal, join in one continuously scenic sweep of sand, sea, and sky.

Along this entire stretch, conditions seem perfect for a day or a week of beach diversions. Waves, fine for boogie boarding or surfing, roll in gradually with little undertow. Seasonal storms deposit a few shells and a bit of driftwood. Rock outcroppings provide resting spots for resident gulls, pelicans, boobies, and cormorants, while a sprinkling of visitors stroll the sand and play in the surf.

Playa Arroyo Seco

Get the best view of this breezy, palm-lined strand at headland Mirador El Calvario by clifftop Restaurant El Mirador, near Km 181. Below the restaurant, look along the long Arroyo Seco beach below to the petite palm grove and abandoned *palapa* restaurant at the bottom of the cliff. At this writing it appears ripe for RV parking or tenting. (With no one around, though, security might be questionable. Check at the restaurant to be sure.) You could also set up your tent or park your RV in the parking lot by the restaurant.

Check out Playa Arroyo Seco close-up via at least two access roads. Either try the dirt road (easy by high-clearance truck or SUV, difficult by ordinary car) at the bottom of the bluff, at Km 180.5; or more easily, reach Playa Arroyo Seco via the dirt road, on the west, Zihuatanejo side of the Río Arroyo Seco, at around Km 183. Pass through the village of the same name to the palm-lined beach after about a mile.

Playa Calvario

In contrast to secluded Playa Arroyo Seco, Playa El Calvario is well-frequented, especially by the dozens of daily visitors who stop at one of its several clifftop restaurants perched above the beach. Playa Calvario, although especially fine for surfing and nearly everything else (except maybe surf fishing because of the flat shallows), isn't good for camping because it's only about 100 feet wide and vulnerable to flooding at high tide. Instead, camp on Playa Arroyo Seco or Playa Cayacal at either end (or stay at the hotels in Papanoa or Puerto Vicente Guerrero).

Nevertheless, Playa Calvario is an irresistible spot to stop and take in the gorgeous scene. Gulls soar, pelicans dive, waves carry surfers shoreward, and cormorants preen and cackle on the Piedras Calvarios rocks, visible at the Acapulco end, and Piedra Fierre, in the middle.

Furthermore, at the Playa Calvario clifftop, the sun, at dawn and sunset, graphically demonstrates why the Spanish explorers called the Pacific Ocean the Mar del Sur, the "Southern Sea." Here, from the clifftop in late afternoon, you can see the sun (which everywhere rises in the east and sets in the west), shining along a line parallel to the beach line. Thus, the direction south, perpendicular to the east-west beach line, must point straight out toward the ocean.

PLAYA LA BARRITA AND LAS SALINAS

These two little roadside spots are interesting for completely different reasons. Playa La Barrita is a lovely beachside miniparadise, while at Las Salinas, people continue to make their living from technology whose origin is lost in time.

Playa La Barrita

Of the several small *palapa* restaurants that decorate the beach, Playa La Barrita, around

Km 188, none has such an attractive setting as Restaurant Paraíso Escondido (Paradise Lost). Although the food (shrimp, octopus, fish, prawns) is good enough, the site is stunning. The fine, yellow-sand beach stretches for about a mile in both directions, and waves wash in from about 100 yards out with little undertow. Surfing, boogie boarding, and surf fishing and boat launching appear distinctly possible. For tots, the restaurant even has a blue kiddie pool out front.

Best of all, however, are the luscious camping prospects by the restaurant's shady, forested lagoon (which also makes a fine swimming hole). What's more, the owner welcomes campers, for no more than the price of a meal or two in his restaurant. (The only drawback is the popularity of this place, especially on weekends and holidays, when, if you must have tranquillity, you had better stay in a hotel or camp down the beach a way.)

Las Salinas

Families of Las Salinas village (pop. 500) of salt harvesters use the inner flats of the neighboring arm of the ocean, Estero El Cuajo, to make their living. Pause by the highway around Km 197 to see how they do it. With long-handled wooden trowels, workers fashion diked ponds, about 10 feet (three meters) square, from the dried mud of the lagoon. They surface the ponds' bottoms with lime, which soon hardens into an impervious basin.

The salt workers channel the seawater into the ponds. The sun evaporates the water and the salt crystallizes on the edges. The workers scoop the salt crystals to small piles outside the ponds, where, dried by the sun, the salt is taken to the warehouse and bagged.

Along Highway 200 in the village, around Km 192, you can see the results of all this. Instead of waiting by the roadside, villagers let their salt bags do the waiting, perched on posts, like roadside mailboxes, for someone to stop and leave a dollar for a one-kilo sack. People don't mind doing this. The loss of an occasional dollar is small compared to long hours of waiting. And besides, every dollar they make this way is one they didn't have in the first place.

© BRUCE WHIPPERMAN

At Las Salinas, villagers use an ingenious system of channels and ponds to evaporate seawater into pure white salt, useful for dozens of industrial and domestic purposes.

PETATLÁN

The town of Petatlán (pop. about 25,000), only 22 miles (35 km) east of Zihuatanejo, besides being Guerrero's most cherished pilgrimage site, has a distinguished pre-Columbian heritage that is only recently being appreciated.

Sights

All roads seem to lead to Petatlán's inviting central *parque municipal,* a fraction of a mile north of Highway 200, around Km 207. Here, near the bright pink *kiosko* bandstand, stand a pair of intriguing **monoliths,** excavated and brought from Soledad de Maciel (see the Soledad de Maciel Archaeological Zone section) to save them from looters. One is a circular stone ring, undoubtedly used in the pre-Columbian ceremonial ball game. The other, protected beneath a covered structure nearby, is a carved disk-shaped monolith, said to represent the god Tlaltecutli.

While in the *parque,* be sure to step inside the adjacent **Parroquia de Padre Jesús,** hallowed ground for the many thousands of pilgrims who arrive yearly from all over Guerrero and Mexico. Inside the innovative parabolic-arched nave, the faithful pay their respects to the venerated wooden image, known affectionately as "Papa Chuy," that arrived under miraculous circumstances as the gift of a mysterious but grateful "Christian Pirate," around 1600. The Petatlán townsfolk fete their beloved Papa Chuy at least twice a year, during the pre-Easter Semana Santa celebration and the August 6 and 7 Fiesta del Padre Jesús. During both occasions the *parque* is awash with merrymakers, watching folkloric dances, eating

THE LEGEND OF PADRE JESÚS

Sometime during the late 1500s, a priest was assigned to minister to the people of Petatlán. Upon arrival, the priest sympathized with the people's sorry state. For years they had endured both the terrible ravages of smallpox and the greed and cruelty of the Spanish soldiers and colonists. Nevertheless, the priest taught them and helped heal them, and, after a few years he had gained their confidence.

During the yearly Semana Santa celebration the priest saw that the people had been carrying an old rickety image of San Antonio for the reenactment of the Stations of the Cross. In a church meeting, he convinced his congregation to take up a collection to obtain a true image of Jesus for the upcoming Semana Santa celebration.

Although the collection amounted to only a few small coins, the priest prepared to journey somewhere to get an appropriate new image of Jesus.

Meanwhile, a great storm had been blowing off the coast. Unknown to the priest and the people of Petatlán, a pirate ship, dismasted and waterlogged, was in danger of sinking. On the ship was an image of Jesus, to which the pirate sailors prayed to save their ship. The pirate captain vowed that, if they were saved, he would take the image to the nearest town and donate it to the local people.

It turned out that they were saved. The storm drove them aground on the Bahía de Potosí's sandy shoreline. The pirate captain, true to his vow, with two of his crew took the image ashore.

The priest, meanwhile, had been in a quandary; he did not know where he could find a suitable image of Jesus for the few coins that he had collected. Late one night, as he was praying for guidance, the priest was startled by a hard knock on his door. It was the pirate captain, who told the priest that he had the image of Jesus that the priest was looking for. Then, without further explanation, the pirate disappeared into the night.

Barely able to believe the mysterious man who became known as the "Christian Pirate," the priest nevertheless delayed his trek to find a new image.

Easter Sunday came, and the promised image had not appeared. The priest was relating the story of Jesus's death and resurrection to his congregation when a poor woodcutter pushed himself through the assembly and cried out that Jesus with a cross had appeared to him nearby.

The people followed the woodcutter to a clear stream where, under a great tree, was the sculpture of Padre Jesús. The people joyfully carried Padre Jesús back their church, where he remains in Petatlán to this day.

The preceding is a synopsis of the story of Padre Jesús, as researched and written by Petatlán's official historian, Señor Agapito Galeana.

traditional sweets, and thrilling to the boom and flash of fireworks overhead.

During your downtown stroll, be sure to visit the **Mercado de Oro** (Gold Market) lineup of stalls offering a trove of bright solid golden necklaces, amulets, chains, bracelets, and much more.

Accommodations and Services

A dozen-odd modest downtown hotels accommodate overnight guests. They include the Camino del Mar Centro, tel. 758/538-2255; Tapatías Juárez, tel. 758/538-3300; Comerciante, at F.J. Mina 105, tel. 758/538-2084; and the California, at Allende 113, tel. 758/538-2349.

While downtown, you can avail yourself of a number of services. These include a bank, Bancomer, open Mon.–Fri. 9 A.M.–4 P.M., tel. 758/538-2977; a *correo* (post office); Ladatel card-operated street telephones; a travel agent (Agencia de Viajes Mayte), at Benito Juárez 16, tel. 758/538-2047; the police, tel. 758/538-4040, at the Presidencia Municipal; and a doctor, Saul Enríquez Garcia, at Bravo 42, tel. 758/538-2321.

Excursions from Petatlán

Adventurers might go for an upcountry side trip to **Ximalcota** (shee-mahl-KOH-tah) to enjoy picnicking, hiking, and other diversions possible on the bank of the cascading mountain Río Petatlán. These include cooling off in a cascade, paddling in a swimming hole decorated with friendly rocks, smoothed through eons of the river's flow. Nearby, visit a tree so old and large that it requires a dozen people holding hands to encircle its base. Get there by car, taxi, or guide (contact the travel agent in town), about eight miles (12 km) via the country road from Petatlán's north side. (*Note:* This trip is best enjoyed during the drier months from September to May, when the river runs clear, in contrast to the rainy months of June, July and August, when the river runs an unappetizing brown.)

In the opposite, southerly direction, consider an excursion to the freshwater mangrove lake **Estero Valentín,** for fresh seafood, wildlife-watching, turtle rescuing, pristine beach camping, fishing, and more. Drive or taxi the country road south from Highway 200 in mid-Petatlán. The three families in charge offer seafood dinners at their palm-shadowed lagoon-front *palapa.* Nearby, from their rustic dockfront, they take visitors on wildlife-watching tours on the mangrove-fringed expanse of Estero Valentín. During the turtle season, be sure to visit their government-sponsored **turtle sanctuary,** and, if you're equipped, camp on the pristine, boat-accessible-only barrier beach that separates the estuary from the ocean.

SOLEDAD DE MACIEL ARCHAEOLOGICAL ZONE

Find this important archaeological site, five miles (8 km) south of Highway 200, via the good signed side road at Km 214, about 31 miles east

An ancient ball ring, found at the nearby Soledad de Maciel archaeological zone, stands on the south side of Highway 200, at the edge of Petatlán.

of Zihuatanejo. It was first explored by INAH (National Institute of Archaeology and History) investigators around 1925. From time to time excavations have continued, although none of the structures has been yet restored. It is only recently that local folks (who call their site El Chole) have begun to benefit from it. They now welcome visitors to their small artifact museum, introduce them to the monumental "King of Chole" monolith, and offer tours.

Investigators identify a classic-era (circa A.D. 300) habitation and ceremonial zone that extends over at least a square mile (2 or 3 square km) around the present Soledad de Maciel village. Identified structures include three pyramids, ceremonial mounds and courtyards, a ball court, and extensive former habitation zones. Many artifacts have been uncovered; examples include pottery, on display at the Zihuatanejo archaeological museum, the two monoliths at the Petatlán downtown *parque,* and two ball rings beside Highway 200 in town.

Other artifacts are also on display at the modest village museum, also the point of departure for the local tour (in Spanish, of course). Find the museum on the right at the first intersection in the village. The major village artifact is the "King of Chole" monolith, in front of the village church, adjacent to the museum. It represents a personage with two faces, looking in opposite right and left directions. One face, representing death, is emaciated, the other, representing life, is vital.

Guides offer their services for a one- or two-hour tour of the environs. Highlight of the tour is the 200-foot, forested **Cerro de las Peñas,** "Hill of the Rocks." On the way up, ask your guide to point out the plants along the way. These include the wild, plumlike *ciruela,* the *cuachalalope* tree, with buds on the trunk, which are boiled for a rejuvenating tonic, the *cacahuanache* tree, whose boiled bark makes a good shampoo, and the *paniko* tree, which makes a sedative tonic.

At the airy summit, the broad hinterland of corn and tobacco (for locally made cigars) fields and communal coconut groves spreads to the ocean, visible on the southern horizon. Also uphill, you will find a monumental *organo* (organ cactus), some petroglyphs (of the "Lord of the Hill"), and a small cave, complete with bats and more petroglyphs. Bring a flashlight. Among the best qualified of the local guides is Adan Belez Romero, available at the museum or local cell tel. 755/551-4851. Offer $10–20 for a two-hour tour.

Ixtapa-Zihuatanejo

The resort pair of Ixtapa and Zihuatanejo present an irresistible opportunity for a season of relaxed vacationing. The choices seem nearly endless. You can sun to your heart's content on luscious beaches, choose from a feast of delicious food, and shop from a trove of fine, all-Mexico handicrafts. Furthermore, outdoor lovers can enjoy their fill of unhurried beachwalking and snorkeling, bicycling, horsebacking, kayaking, surfing, scuba diving, caving, and forest canopy adventuring.

First, be sure to visit some intimate beaches, such as Playa Las Gatas and Isla Ixtapa, for some sunning and snorkeling; enjoy some good restaurants; stretch out with some exercise such as bicycling to Playa Linda and back; browse some good handicrafts shops, such as Casa Marina, Cerámicas Tonalá, and Casa Maya.

© BRUCE WHIPPERMAN

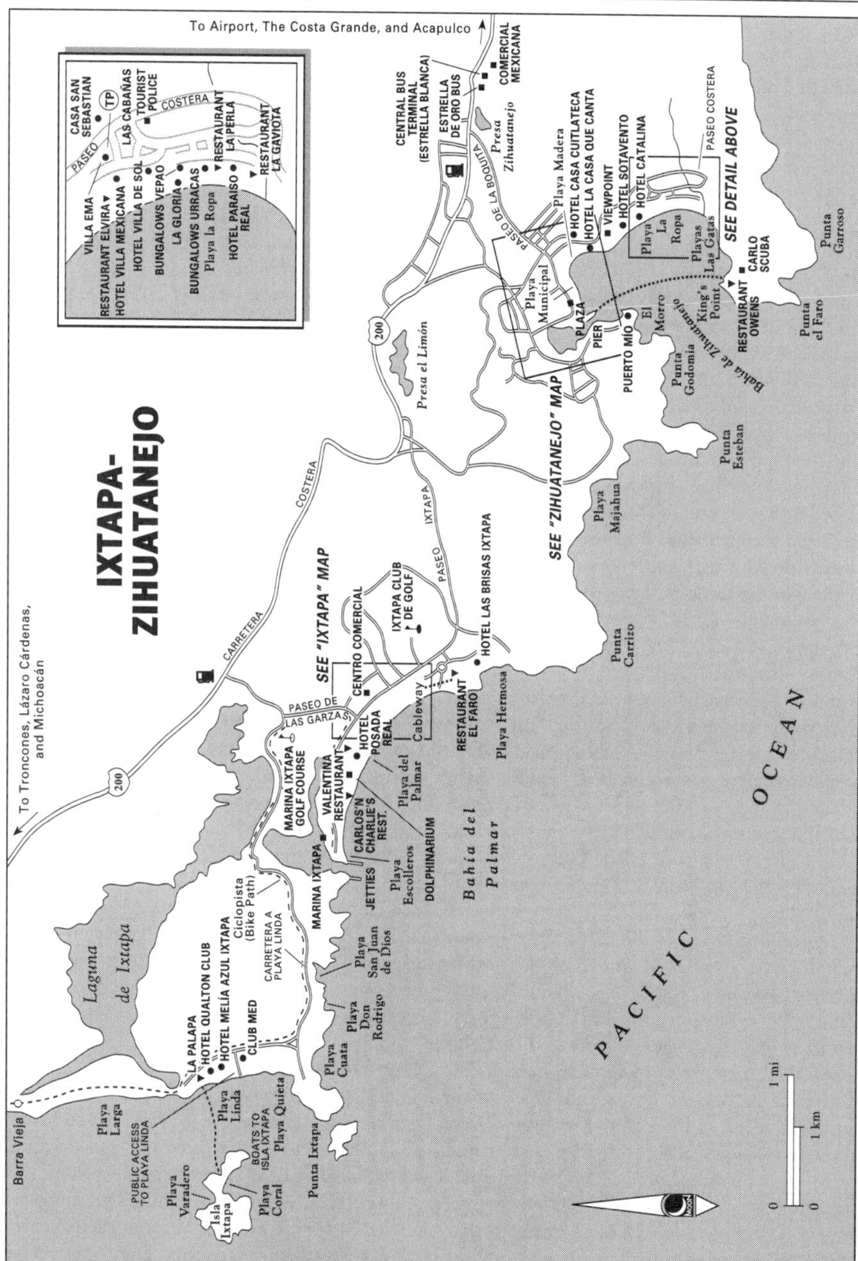
IXTAPA-ZIHUATANEJO
To Airport, The Costa Grande, and Acapulco
To Troncones, Lázaro Cárdenas, and Michoacán
CARRETERA
COSTERA
200
CASA SAN SEBASTIAN
TP
LAS CABAÑAS
TOURIST POLICE
PASEO
COSTERA
VILLA EMA
RESTAURANT ELVIRA
HOTEL VILLA MEXICANA
HOTEL VILLA DE SOL
BUNGALOWS VEPAO
LA GLORIA
BUNGALOWS URRACAS
Playa la Ropa
HOTEL PARAISO REAL
RESTAURANT LA PERLA
RESTAURANT LA GAVIOTA
CENTRAL BUS TERMINAL (ESTRELLA BLANCA)
ESTRELLA DE ORO BUS
COMERCIAL MEXICANA
Presa Zihuatanejo
PASEO DE LA BOQUITA
Playa Madera
HOTEL CASA CUITLATECA
HOTEL LA CASA QUE CANTA
VIEWPOINT
HOTEL SOTAVENTO
HOTEL CATALINA
PASEO COSTERA
SEE DETAIL ABOVE
Playa La Ropa
Playas Las Gatas
CARLO SCUBA
Punta Garroso
Playa Municipal
PLAZA
PIER
PUERTO MÍO
El Morro
King's Point
RESTAURANT OWENS
Punta el Faro
Bahía de Zihuatanejo
Punta Godomia
Punta Esteban
SEE "ZIHUATANEJO" MAP
Presa el Limón
Playa Majahua
PASEO IXTAPA
HOTEL LAS BRISAS IXTAPA
IXTAPA CLUB DE GOLF
CENTRO COMERCIAL
SEE "IXTAPA" MAP
Punta Carrizo
PASEO DE LAS GARZAS
HOTEL POSADA REAL
Cableway
RESTAURANT EL FARO
Playa Hermosa
VALENTINA RESTAURANT
MARINA IXTAPA GOLF COURSE
CARLOS'N CHARLIE'S REST.
Playa del Palmar
DOLPHINARIUM
Bahía del Palmar
MARINA IXTAPA
JETTIES
Playa Escolleros
Laguna de Ixtapa
Ciclopista (Bike Path)
CARRETERA A PLAYA LINDA
HOTEL QUALTON CLUB
HOTEL MELÍA AZUL IXTAPA
LA PALAPA
CLUB MED
Playa San Juan de Dios
Playa Don Rodrigo
Playa Cuata
Barra Vieja
Playa Larga
PUBLIC ACCESS TO PLAYA LINDA
Playa Linda
BOATS TO ISLA IXTAPA
Playa Quieta
Playa Varadero
Isla Ixtapa
Playa Coral
Punta Ixtapa
PACIFIC OCEAN
1 mi
1 km
0
0
MOON

With more days, head out of town south to Barra de Potosí for wildlife viewing on the Laguna de Potosí or north to Troncones for cave exploring and a forest canopy adventure and linger a few nights at a comfortable bed-and-breakfast lodging.

HISTORY

In the Beginning

The ancient underwater rock-walled enclosure off Las Gatas beach, across the bay from Zihuatanejo town, gives substance to an oft-told local legend. The story goes that the emperor of the Purépecha people (who still inhabit the highlands of Michoacán) around A.D. 1400 built a royal bathing pool and resort on the shore of Zihuatanejo Bay. The emperor had the pool enclosed by a rock wall to reassure his many wives and retainers that they'd be safe from attack by the colony of (in fact harmless) small whiskered sharks who swam offshore. Although the emperor is long gone, the sharks continue to swim off Playa Las Gatas (The Cats), named for the sharks' whiskers.

The Purépecha, who were relative latecomers, were preceded by waves of immigrants to Zihuatanejo. The local archaeological museum displays ancient pottery made by Zihuatanejo artisans as long as 5,000 years ago. Later, more sophisticated artists, influenced by the renowned Olmec mother-culture of the Gulf of Mexico coast, left their indisputable mark on local pottery styles.

By the beginning of the Christian era, local people had developed more sophisticated lifestyles. Instead of wandering and hunting and gathering their food, they were living in permanent towns and villages, surrounded by fields where they grew most of what they needed. Besides their staple corn, beans, and squash, these farmers, called Cuitlatecs by the Aztecs, were also cultivating tobacco, cotton for clothes, and cacao for chocolate. Attracted by the Cuitlatecs' rich produce, the highland Aztecs, led by their emperor Tizoc, invaded the coast during the late 1400s and extracted a small mountain of tribute yearly from the Cuitlatecs.

Conquest and Colonization

Scarcely months after Hernán Cortés conquered the Aztecs, he sent an expedition to explore the "Southern Sea" and find the long-sought route to China. In November 1522 Captain Juan Álvarez Chico set sail with boats built on the Isthmus of Tehuántepec and reconnoitered the Zihuatanejo coast all the way northeast to at least the Río Balsas, planting crosses on beaches and claiming the land for Spain.

Cortés, encouraged by the samples of pearls and gold that Chico brought back, built more ships and outfitted more expeditions. At a personal cost of 60,000 gold pesos (probably several million dollars today) Cortés had three ships built at Zacatula, at the mouth of the Río Balsas. He commissioned Captain Alvaro Saavedra Cerón to command the first expedition to find the route to Asia. Saavedra Cerón set off from Zihuatanejo Bay on October 31, 1527. He commanded a modest force of about 110 men, with 30 cannons, in three small caravels, the *Florida,* his flagship, accompanied by the *Espíritu Santo* and the *Santiago.* The *Florida,* Saavedra Cerón's sole vessel to survive the fierce Pacific typhoons, reached present-day Guam on December 29, 1527, and the Philippines on February 1, 1528. As he did not know any details of the Pacific Ocean and its winds and currents, it is not surprising that Saavedra Cerón failed to return to Mexico. He died at sea in October 1529 in search of a return route to Mexico.

No fewer than seven more attempts were needed (from Acapulco, 1532, 1539, and 1540; Tehuantepec, 1535; and Barra de Navidad, two in 1542 and one in 1564) until finally, in 1565, navigator-priest Andrés de Urdaneta coaxed Pacific winds and currents to give up their secret and returned, in triumph, to Acapulco, from Asia.

The Manila Galleon

Thereafter, for more than 250 years, the yearly trading ship called the Manila galleon sailed from Acapulco for Asia. It returned to Acapulco within a year, laden with a fortune in spices, silks, gold, and porcelain. Although Acapulco's prominence all but shut down all other Mexican Pacific ports, the Manila galleon would from time to time stop off at Zihuatanejo. The same was true for the

PIRATES OF ZIHUATANEJO

For 10 generations, from the late 1500s to independence in 1821, corsairs menaced the Mexican Pacific coast. They often used Zihuatanejo Bay for repair and resupply.

The earliest was the renowned and feared English privateer Sir Francis Drake (see the sidebar "Sir Francis Drake: The Pirate El Draque" in the Introduction). During his circumnavigation of 1577–1580, Drake raided a number of Spanish Pacific ports.

The biggest prize, however, was the Manila galleon, for which he searched the Mexican coast for months. Finally, low on water and food, he dropped anchor and resupplied briefly at Zihuatanejo Bay before continuing northwest.

Enter the Dutch

Dutch corsairs also scoured the seas for the Manila galleon. In October 1624, a Dutch squadron, commanded by Captain Hugo Schapenham, grouped in a semicircle outside Acapulco Bay to intercept the departing galleon. Port authorities, however, delayed the sailing, and the Dutch began running out of food and water. They tried to trade captives for supplies, but the Spanish refused, offering only inedible gold for the captives. In desperation, Schapenham tried to attack the Acapulco fort directly, but his vessels were damaged and driven off by the fort's effective artillery fire.

The starving Dutch sailors retreated up the coast to Zihuatanejo Bay where, after a few weeks, rested and resupplied, they set sail for Asia on November 29, 1624.

Although most of them arrived in the Moluccas Islands in the East Indies, they disbanded. Most of them, including Schapenham, who was dead by the end of 1625, never returned to Europe.

Dampier and Anson

A much more persistent and fortunate galleon hunter was English captain William Dampier (1652–1715), who, besides accumulating a fortune in booty, was renowned as a navigator and mapmaker. Lying in wait for the Manila galleon, Dampier anchored in Zihuatanejo Bay in 1704. On December 7, Dampier came upon the Manila galleon *Nuestra Señora del Rosario.* However, a ferocious Spanish defense forced Dampier's squadron to retreat.

Six years later, commanding another squadron jointly with captain Woodes Rogers, Dampier captured both the galleon *Encarnación* and the *Nuestra Señora de Begoña* between January 1 and January 5, 1710. Rogers and Dampier returned triumphantly to England in the *Encarnación,* which they had rechristened the *Batchelor.*

Luckiest of all Manila galleon treasure hunters was George Anson (1697–1762), who volunteered for the English navy at the age of 15 and rose rapidly, attaining the rank of captain at the age of 25.

He arrived off Acapulco, in command of a small fleet of ships and many hundreds of sailors, on March 1, 1742. After waiting three weeks for the galleon to sail, and running low on food and water, Anson sailed northwest, resupplied at Zihuatanejo, and then departed west across the Pacific. On July 1, 1743, off Guam, Anson's forces caught up with and captured the galleon *Nuestra Señora de Covdonga,* with 1.3 million pieces of eight, 35,000 ounces of silver, and a trove of jewels.

Although suffering from the loss of 90 percent of his men, Anson finally returned to England in command of his last remaining ship, carrying booty worth 800,000 pounds sterling, a fortune worth many tens of millions of dollars today.

occasional pirate ship (or fleet) that lurked along the coast, hungry to capture the galleon's riches.

The most famous corsair was Francis Drake, who landed in Zihuatanejo in 1579. Later came the Dutch fleet of Hugo Schapenham in 1624. English Captain William Dampier entered Zihuatanejo Bay in 1704, recording that the shoreline village had about 40 grass huts, inhabited by about 100 unfriendly people who vigorously discouraged his disembarkation. The luckiest of all the corsairs was Captain George Anson, who, in 1715, captured the Manila galleon and returned to England with booty then worth 800,000 pounds sterling and upward of $50,000,000 today.

On one occasion, no one knows when exactly, a galleon evidently lost some of its precious silk cargo, which washed ashore on one of Zihuatanejo's beaches, now known as Playa La Ropa (Clothes Beach).

Independence

In 1821, Mexico became independent, stopping the Manila galleon forever. Deprived even of an occasional galleon or pirate, Zihuatanejo went to sleep and didn't wake up for more than half a century. The occasion was the arrival of ex-President Lerdo de Tejada, who, during the 1870s, embarked from Zihuatanejo for exile in the United States.

By the 20th century, some of the maritime prosperity of Acapulco, which benefited from the stream of California-bound steamers, spilled over to Zihuatanejo. During the 1920s, nearby resources were exploited, and now-Playa Madera (Wood Beach) earned its label as a loading point for fine hardwood timber exports.

Modern Zihuatanejo

Recognition of Zihuatanejo's growing importance came on November 30, 1953, when the Guerrero state legislature decreed the formation of the Zihuatanejo *municipio,* whose governmental center was established at the budding town on the bay of the same name.

In the 1960s, a new airport, suitable for propeller passenger airplanes, and the paved highway, which arrived from Acapulco around the same time, jolted Zihuatanejo from its final slumber. No longer isolated, Zihuatanejo's headland-rimmed aqua bay began to attract a small colony of seekers of paradise on earth.

Tourism grew steadily. Small hotels and restaurants were built to accommodate them. Zihuatanejo had a population of perhaps 5,000 by the late 1970s when Fonatur, the government tourism-development agency, decided to develop Zihuatanejo Bay. Local folks, however, objecting that the proposed lineup of high-rise hotels would block the view of their beautiful bay, squelched the plan.

Fonatur regrouped and alternatively proposed Ixtapa (often translated as White Place, but it more likely means White Top for the several guano-topped offshore islets) five miles north of Zihuatanejo as a perfect site for a world-class resort. Investors agreed, and the infrastructure—drainage, roads, and utilities—was installed. The jetport was built, hotels rose, and by 2000, the distinct but inseparable twin resorts of Ixtapa and Zihuatanejo (combined pop. 80,000) were attracting a steady stream of Mexican and foreign vacationers.

Sights

Getting Oriented

Both Ixtapa and Zihuatanejo are small and easy to know. Zihuatanejo's little Plaza de Armas town square overlooks the main beach, Playa Municipal, that fronts the palm-lined pedestrian walkway, Paseo del Pescador. From the plaza looking out toward the bay, you are facing south. On your right is the pier (*muelle,* moo-AY-yay), and on the left, the bay curves along the outer beaches Playas La Ropa, Madera, and finally Las Gatas beneath the far Punta El Faro (Lighthouse Point).

Turning around and facing inland (north), you see a narrow but busy waterfront street, Juan Álvarez, running parallel to the beach past the plaza, crossing the main business streets (actually tranquil shady lanes) Cuauhtémoc and Guerrero. A third street, bustling Benito Juárez, one block to the right of Guerrero, conducts traffic several blocks to and from the shore, passing the market and intersecting a second main street, Avenida Morelos, about 10 blocks inland from the beach. There, a right turn will soon bring you to Highway 200 and, within five miles, Ixtapa.

Most everything in Ixtapa lies along one three-mile-long boulevard, Paseo Ixtapa, which parallels the main beach, hotel-lined Playa del Palmar. Heading westerly, arriving from Zihuatanejo, you first pass the Club de Golf Ixtapa, then the big Hotel Barceló on the left, followed by a succession of other high-rise hotels. Soon comes the Zona Comercial shopping malls and the Paseo de las Garzas corner on the right. Turn right for either Highway 200 or the outer beaches, Playas Cuata, Quieta, Linda, and Larga. At Playa Linda, boats continue to heavenly Isla Ixtapa.

If, instead, you continued straight ahead back at the Paseo de las Garzas corner, you would soon reach the Marina Ixtapa condo development and yacht harbor.

Getting Around

In downtown Zihuatanejo, shops and restaurants are within a few blocks' walking distance of the plaza. For the beaches, walk along the beachfront *andador* (walkway) to Playa Madera, take a taxi ($3) to Playa La Ropa, and a launch from the pier ($5) to Playa Las Gatas.

For Ixtapa or the outer beaches, take a taxi (about $5) or ride one of the very frequent minibuses, labeled by destination, which leave from both Juárez, across from the market, and the northeast downtown corner of Juárez and Morelos, a few blocks farther north from the beach. In Ixtapa itself, walk or ride the minibuses that run along Paseo Ixtapa.

Museo Arqueología de la Costa Grande

Zihuatanejo's smallish but interesting archaeological museum authoritatively details the prehistory of the Costa Grande. Professionally prepared maps, paintings, dioramas, and artifacts—many donated by local resident and innkeeper Anita Rellstab—illustrate the development of local cultures, from early hunting and gathering to agriculture and, finally, urbanization by the time of the conquest. Find it at the east end of Álvarez, beach side; open Tues.–Sun. 9 A.M.–8 P.M.

Beaches Around Zihuatanejo Bay

Ringed by forested hills, edged by steep cliffs, and laced by rocky shoals, Zihuatanejo Bay would be beautiful even without its beaches. Five of them line the bay. On the west side is narrow, tranquil **Playa el Almacén** (Warehouse Beach), mostly good for fishing from its nearby rocks. Moving past the pier toward town comes the colorful, bustling **Playa Municipal.** Its sheltered waters are fine for wading, swimming, and boat launching (which fishermen, their motors buzzing, regularly do) near the pier end.

For maximum sun and serenity, walk away from the pier along Playa Municipal past the usually dry creek outlet where a concrete *andador* winds about 200 yards along the beachfront rocks that mark the beginning of Playa Madera. If you prefer, you can also hire a taxi to take you to Playa Madera, about $3.

Playa Madera (Wood Beach), once a loading point for lumber, stretches about 300 yards,

ZIHUATANEJO

To Mex. 200 South, Airport, and Acapulco
To Mex. 200 North and Ixtapa
COLEGIO MILITAR
IMMIGRATION
TELECOM
POST OFFICE
CLINICA MACIEL
PASEO DEL PALMAR
COCINA ECONÓMICA DOÑA LICHA
KYOTO
PLAZA
Canal (Seasonally Dry)
PASEO DE LA BOQUITA
MICROBUS-STOP TO IXTAPA
SUPER DE ZIHUATANEJO
MARKET
FARMACIA AND SUPER ROSY
BENITO JUÁREZ
GLOB'S CAFE
BANCO SERFIN
BANCOMER
NAVA
GONZÁLES
EJIDO
BRAVO
ECONOMY RESTAURANTS
ARCHAEOLOGY MUSEUM
Footbridge
GUERRERO
SHOE REPAIR
PANADERIA FRANCES
LAVANDERÍA EXPRESS
GALERÍA MAYA
RAMIREZ
PLAZA DE ARMAS
AV. MORELOS
ALTIMIRANO
GALEANA
LAUNDRY SUPER CLEAN
FOTO EXPRESS
CUAUHTÉMOC
LIBRARY
CAMERA REPAIR
LAVANDERÍA PREMIUM
INTERNET CAFE
ÁLVAREZ
CHURCH
ASENCIO
WHISKEY WATERWORLD (SPORTFISHING)
5 DE MAYO
SEE "DOWNTOWN ZIHUATANEJO" MAP
ARTISAN TOURIST MARKET
HOTEL RAOÚL TRES MARÍAS CENTRO
CASA DE HUÉSPEDES ELVIRA
RESTAURANT CASA ELVIRA
PESCA DEPORTIVA (SPORTFISHING)
SIRENA GORDA
NAVAL COMPOUND
PLAYA LAS GATOS BOAT TICKETS
CAPTAIN OF THE PORT
SOCIEDAD COOPERATIVA TENIENTE AZUETA (SPORTFISHING)
SERVICIOS SOCIEDAD COOPERATIVA (SPORTFISHING)
MUELLE
Playa Municipal
Las Salinas (Lagoon)
Footbridge
HOTEL RAOÚL TRES MARÍAS
AV. NORIA
Playa el Almacén
Boats to Playa las Gatas
To Puerto Mío (Hotel and Marina)
Bahía de Zihuatanejo
Andador (Walkway)
Playa Madera
Cerro Madera
CASA AZUL
CASA LAGARTIJA
EVA SAMANO DE LÓPEZ MATEOS
BUNGALOWS PACÍFICO
BUNGALOWS SOTELO
BUNGALOWS ALLEC
BUNGALOWS LEY AND CASA LEIGH AND LOROS
HOTEL BRISAS DEL MAR
HOTEL VILLAS MIRAMAR
BUNGALOWS MILAGRO
To Playa la Ropa
HOTEL PALACIO
HOTEL IRMA
RESTAURANT KAU KAN
RESTAURANT IL MARE
0 200 yds
0 200 m

decorated with rocky nooks and outcroppings, and backed by the lush hotel-dotted hill, **Cerro Madera.** The beach sand is fine and gray-white. Swells enter the facing bay entrance, breaking suddenly in two- or three-foot waves, which roll in gently and recede with little undertow. Madera's usually calm billows are good for child's play and easy swimming. Bring your mask and snorkel for glimpses of fish in the clear waters. Beachside restaurant/bars Kau Kan, La Bocana, and the Hotel Irma, above the far east end, serve drinks and snacks. (Lately, some pollution overflow has fouled Playa Madera; authorities, however, are at work enlarging waste-treatment facilities.)

Zihuatanejo Bay's favorite resort beach is **Playa La Ropa** (Clothes Beach), a mile-long crescent of yellow-white sand washed by oft-gentle surf. The beach got its name centuries ago from the apparel that once floated in from a galleon wrecked offshore. From the bay's best *mirador* (viewpoint) at the summit of **Paseo Costera,** the La Ropa approach road, the beach sand, relentlessly scooped and redeposited by the waves, appears as an endless line of half-moons.

On the 100-foot-wide beach, vacationers bask in the sun, personal watercraft buzz beyond the breakers, rental sailboats ply the waves, and sailboard outfits recline on the sand. The waves, generally too gentle and quick-breaking for surf sports, break close-in and recede with only mild undertow. Joggers come out mornings and evenings. Restaurants at the several beachfront hotels provide food and drinks.

Secluded **Playa Las Gatas** (Cat Beach), reachable by very rough shoreline rock-hopping or easily by launch from the town pier, lies sheltered beneath the south-end Punta El Faro headland. Once a walled-in royal Tarascan bathing pool, the beach got its name from a species of locally common, small, whiskered nurse sharks. Generally calm and quiet, often with super-clear offshore waters, Playa Las Gatas is both a snorkeling haven and a jumping-off spot for dive trips headed for prime scuba sites. Beach booths rent gear for beach snorkelers, and a professional dive shop, **Carlo Scuba** right on the beach, instructs and guides both beginner and experienced scuba divers. (For many more diving details, see Sports and Recreation.)

© BRUCE WHIPPERMAN

Playa Madera (Wood Beach) graces the tranquil inner edges of Zihuatanejo Bay, continuing as the main Zihuatanejo town beach.

For a treat (high season only, however), pass the beach restaurant lineup and continue to **Owen's** *palapa* restaurant, visible on **King's Point,** the palm-shaded outcropping past the far curve of the beach. There, enjoy some refreshment, watch the surfers glide around the point, and feast on the luscious beach, bay, and hill view.

Ixtapa Beaches

Ixtapa's 10 distinct beaches lie scattered like pearls along a dozen miles of creamy, azure coastline. As you move from the Zihuatanejo direction, **Playa Hermosa** comes first. The elevators of the super-luxurious clifftop Hotel Brisas Ixtapa make access to the beach very convenient. At the bottom you'll find a few hundred yards of

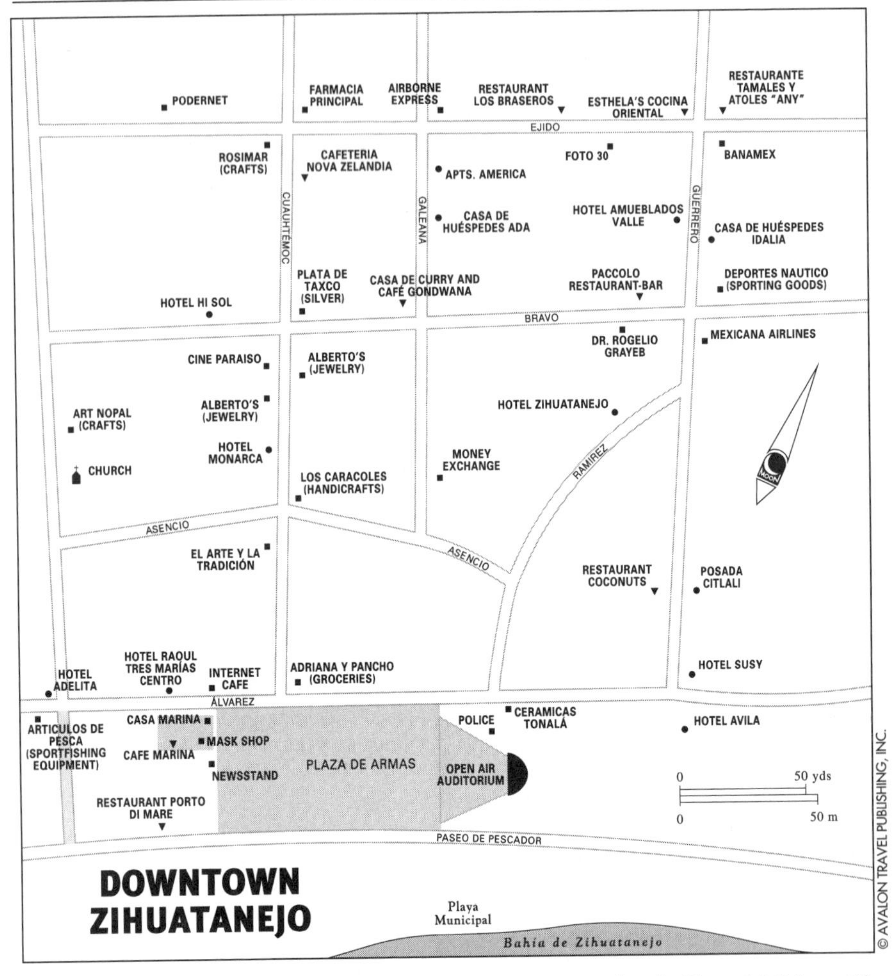

seasonally broad white sand, with open-ocean (but often gentle) waves usually good for most water sports except surfing. Good beach-accessible snorkeling is possible off the shoals at either end of the beach. Extensive rentals are available at the beachfront aquatics shop. A poolside restaurant serves food and drinks. Hotel access is only by car or taxi.

For a sweeping vista of Ixtapa's beaches, bay, and blue waters, ride the ***teleférico*** (cable tramway, open daily 7 A.M.–7 P.M.) to El Faro restaurant, tel. 755/553-1027, at the south end of Ixtapa's main beach, Playa del Palmar. It's open daily 8 A.M.–10 P.M. (hours may be seasonally shortened).

Long, broad, and yellow-white, **Playa del Palmar** could be called the "Billion-Dollar Beach" for the investment money it attracted to Ixtapa. The confidence seems justified. The broad strand stretches for three gently curving miles. Even though it fronts the open ocean, protective offshore rocks, islands, and shoals keep the surf gentle most of the time. Here, most sports are of the high-powered variety—parasailing ($20), personal watercraft riding and water-skiing ($40), banana-boating ($10)—although boogie boards are rentable for $5 an hour on the beach.

Challenging surfing breaks roll in consistently off the jetty at **Playa Escolleros,** at Playa del Palmar's far west end. Bring your own board.

Ixtapa Outer Beaches

Ixtapa's outer beaches spread among the coves and inlets a few miles northwest of the Hotel Zone. Drive, bicycle (rentals by bank Bital, in front of the Hotel Riviera), taxi, take a "Playa Linda" minibus along the Paseo de las Garzas (drivers, turn right just past the shopping mall), then fork left again after less than a mile. After the Marina Golf Course (watch out for crocodiles crossing the road, no joke), the road turns toward the shoreline, winding past a trio of development-blocked beach gems, **Playa San Juan de Dios, Playa Don Rodrigo,** and **Playa Cuata.**

Mangrove-fringed Laguna de Ixtapa is becoming an attraction. The lagoon's star actors are crocodiles that often sun and doze in the water and along the bank beneath the bridge.

Although Mexican law theoretically allows free public oceanfront access, guards might try to shoo you away from Playa Cuata, on the open-ocean side, even if you arrive by boat. If somehow you manage to get there, you will discover a cream-yellow strip of sand, nestled between rocky outcroppings, with oft-gentle waves and correspondingly moderate undertow for good swimming, bodysurfing, and boogie boarding. Snorkeling and fishing are equally good around nearby rocks and shoals.

On the peninsula's sheltered northern flank, **Playa Quieta** (Quiet Beach) is a place that lives up to its name. A ribbon of fine yellow sand arcs around a smooth inlet dotted by a regatta of Club Med kayaks and sailboats plying the water. Get there via the north-end access stairway from the parking lot, signed Playa Quieta Acceso Público. Stop by the beachfront restaurant for refreshment or fresh seafood lunch.

Playa Linda

Playa Linda, an open-ocean yellow-sand beach, extends for miles beyond the road's end. Flocks of sandpipers and plovers skitter at the surf's edge; pelicans and cormorants dive offshore, while gulls, terns, and boobies skim the wavetops. Driftwood and shells decorate the sand beside a green-tufted palm grove that seems to stretch endlessly to the north.

In addition to the beach, mangrove-fringed **Laguna de Ixtapa,** an arm of which extends south to the bridge before the Playa Linda parking lot, is becoming an attraction. The lagoon's star actors are crocodiles that often sun and doze in the water and along the bank beneath the bridge.

Officially, the bicycle path ends at the bridge, but you can continue on foot or by bicycle about 1.5 miles to Barra Vieja village. Take a hat, water, insect repellent, your binoculars, and your bird-identification book. (For more bicycling information, see the Sports and Recreation section.)

The friendly downscale **La Palapa** beach restaurant, at pavement's end, offers beer, sodas, and seafood, plus showers, toilets, and free parking. Neighboring stable **Rancho Playa Linda,** managed by friendly "Spiderman" Margarito, provides horseback rides at about $15 per hour.

The flat, wide Playa Linda has powerful rollers often good for surfing. Boogie boarding and bodysurfing—with caution, don't try it alone—are also possible. Surf fishing yields catches, especially of *lisa* (mullet), which locals have much more success netting than hooking.

Isla Ixtapa

Every few minutes a boat heads from the Playa Linda embarcadero to mile-long Ixtapa Island daily 9 A.M.–5 P.M.; $3 round-trip. Upon arrival, you soon discover the secret to the preservation of the island's pristine beaches, forests, and natural underwater gardens. "No trash here," the *palapa* proprietors say. "We bag it up and send it back to the mainland."

It shows. Great fleshy green orchids and bromeliads hang from forest branches, multicolored fish dart among offshore rocks, shady

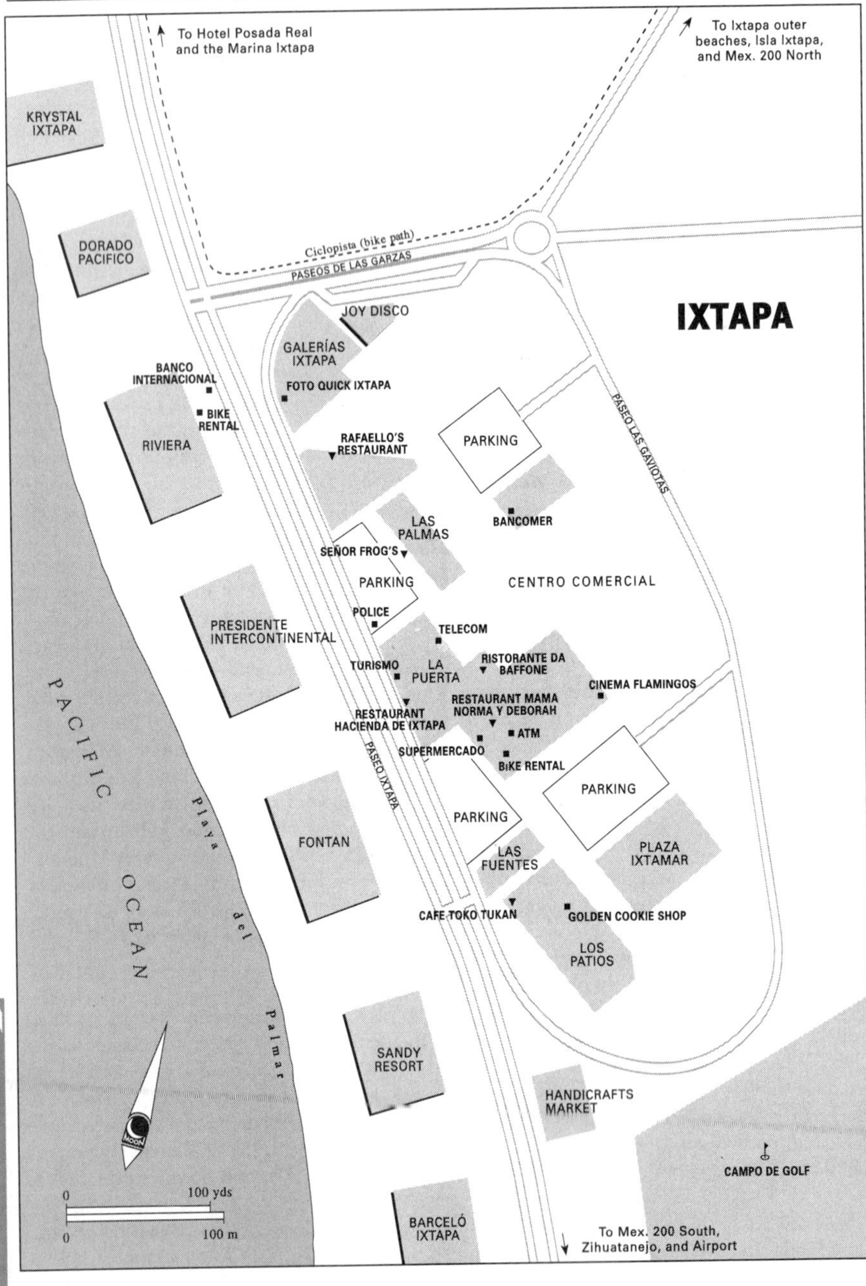

To Hotel Posada Real and the Marina Ixtapa
To Ixtapa outer beaches, Isla Ixtapa, and Mex. 200 North
KRYSTAL IXTAPA
DORADO PACIFICO
Ciclopista (bike path)
PASEOS DE LAS GARZAS
IXTAPA
JOY DISCO
GALERÍAS IXTAPA
BANCO INTERNACIONAL
FOTO QUICK IXTAPA
BIKE RENTAL
RIVIERA
RAFAELLO'S RESTAURANT
PARKING
PASEO LAS GAVIOTAS
BANCOMER
LAS PALMAS
SEÑOR FROG'S
PARKING
CENTRO COMERCIAL
POLICE
PRESIDENTE INTERCONTINENTAL
TELECOM
RISTORANTE DA BAFFONE
TURISMO
LA PUERTA
CINEMA FLAMINGOS
RESTAURANT MAMA NORMA Y DEBORAH
RESTAURANT HACIENDA DE IXTAPA
ATM
SUPERMERCADO
BIKE RENTAL
PACIFIC OCEAN
PASEO IXTAPA
PARKING
PARKING
Playa del Palmar
FONTAN
LAS FUENTES
PLAZA IXTAMAR
CAFE TOKO TUKAN
GOLDEN COOKIE SHOP
LOS PATIOS
SANDY RESORT
HANDICRAFTS MARKET
MOON
CAMPO DE GOLF
0 100 yds
0 100 m
BARCELÓ IXTAPA
To Mex. 200 South, Zihuatanejo, and Airport
© AVALON TRAVEL PUBLISHING, INC.

Isla Ixtapa, just a short boat ride from the Ixtapa mainland, is a restful haven of intimate beaches, rustic seafood restaurants, and pristine coastal forest.

native acacias hang lazily over the shell-decorated sands of the island's little beaches. Boats from Playa Linda arrive at **Playa Cuachalatate** (koo-ah-chah-lah-TAH-tay), the island's most popular beach, named for a local tree whose bark is said to relieve liver ailments. Many visitors stay all day, splashing, swimming, and eating fresh fish, shrimp, and clams cooked at any one of a dozen beachfront *palapas.* Visitors also enjoy the many sports rentals: water skis, banana boat rides, boats for fishing, aquatic bicycles ($6/hour), snorkel gear ($3/hour), and kayaks ($5/hour).

For a change of scene, follow the short concrete walkway over the west-side (right as you arrive) forested knoll to **Playas Varadero** and **Coral** on opposite flanks of an intimate little isthmus. Varadero's yellow-white sand is narrow and tree-shaded, its waters are calm and clear. Behind it lies Playa Coral, a steep coral-sand beach fronting a rocky blue bay. Playa Coral is a magnet for beach lovers, snorkelers, and the scuba divers who often arrive by boat to explore the waters around the offshore coral reef.

Scuba diving is so rewarding here that a dive shop, **Oliverio,** is operated by the sons of the late founder, near the west end of Playa Cuachalatate. Other shops in Zihuatanejo (see Sports and Recreation) are better equipped to provide the same services, however.

Isla Ixtapa's fourth and smallest beach, secluded **Playa Carey,** is named for the sea-turtle species (see the sidebar "Saving Turtles" in The Costa Grande chapter). For access, hire a boat from Playa Cuachalatate.

Accommodations and Food

ACCOMMODATIONS

Ixtapa-Zihuatanejo is one of the Mexican Pacific Coast's loveliest but also most highly seasonal resorts. Hotels and restaurants are most likely to be full during the winter-spring sunny high season, customarily beginning about December 20 and running through Easter week. Low season begins during the oft-hot dry months of May and June and continues until early December. Some restaurants even shut down during September and October. Nevertheless, for those who crave peace and quiet, bargain hotel prices, just-right balmy weather, and lush green verdure, late fall—mid-October through mid-December—is an excellent time to visit.

Zihuatanejo Downtown Hotels

Zihuatanejo's hotels divide themselves by location (and largely by price) between the budget to moderate downtown and more expensive Playa Madera and Playa La Ropa. For more information and updates on most of the following lodgings, visit the excellent websites www.zihuatanejo.net and www.ixtapa-zihuatanejo.com. Although Zihuatanejo hotels (with the few exceptions noted) provide little or no wheelchair access, all Ixtapa hotels described in the Ixtapa Hotels section do.

Under $50: Right in the middle of the downtown beachfront action is **Casa de Huéspedes Elvira,** Paseo del Pescador 9, Zihuatanejo, Guerrero 40880, tel. 755/554-2061, operated since 1956 by its founder, Elvira R. Campos. Every day, Elvira looks after her little garden of flowering plants, feeds rice to her birds—both wild and caged—and passes the time of day with friends and guests. She tells of the "way it used to be" when all passengers and supplies arrived from Acapulco by boat, local *almejas* (clams) were as big as cabbages, and you could pluck fish right out of the bay with your hands. Her petite eight-room lodging divides into an upstairs section, with more light and privacy, and a lower, with private baths. The leafy, intimate lower patio leads upward, via a pair of quaint, plant-decorated spiral staircases to the airy upper level. The rooms themselves are small, authentically rustic, and clean. The four upper rooms share a bathroom and toilet. Rates run about $10 s or d, $20 t low season, $11 $15, $22 high. If nighttime noise bothers you, bring earplugs; TV and music from Elvira's adjoining restaurant continues until about 11 P.M. most evenings during the winter high season.

A few blocks north and west, find unpretentious guesthouse **Casa de Huéspedes Idalia,** at Guerrero 9, tel. 755/554-2062. The grandmotherly owner offers two floors of about a dozen

IXTAPA OR ZIHUATANEJO?

Your choice of local lodging sharply determines the tone of your stay. Zihuatanejo still resembles the colorful seaside village that visitors have enjoyed for years. Fishing *pangas* decorate its beach side, while *panaderías, taquerías,* and *papelerías* line its narrow shady lanes. Many of its hotels—budget to moderate, with spartan but clean fan-only rooms—reflect the tastes of the bargain-conscious travelers who "discovered" Zihuatanejo during the 1960s.

Ixtapa, on the other hand, mirrors the fashionwise preferences of new-generation Mexican and international vacationers. A broad boulevard fronts your Ixtapa hotel, while on the beach side, thatch-shaded chairs on a wide strand, a palmy garden, blue pool, and serene outdoor restaurant are yours to enjoy. Upstairs, your air-conditioned room—typically in plush pastels, with private sea-view balcony, marble bath, room service, and your favorite TV shows by satellite—brings maximum convenience and comfort to a lush tropical setting.

Actually, you needn't be forced to choose. Split your hotel time between Ixtapa and Zihuatanejo and enjoy both worlds.

plain but clean rooms, with room-temperature-only shower baths. Idalia's guests enjoy an airy upstairs corridor-view porch, furnished with hammocks, rocking chairs, and shelves of thick paperback books. Rentals go for $15 s, $20 d, with fans only, or $35 s or d, with a/c and TV.

On the west side, across the lagoon-mouth by footbridge from the end of Paseo del Pescador, is the **Hotel Raoúl Tres Marias,** at Noria 4, Colonia Lázaro Cárdenas, Zihuatanejo, Guerrero 40880, tel. 755/554-2191, fax 755/554-2591. Its longtime popularity derives from its (formerly) low prices and the colorful lagoonfront boat scene, visible from porches outside some of its 25 rooms. Otherwise, facilities are strictly bare-bones, with only tepid room-temperature water. Rooms rent for a modest $15 s, $20 d, $25 t, low season, and $25, $35, $40, high season, with fans and most with private baths.

Another good choice, if you don't mind a bit of morning noise from the adjacent school, is the popular **Posada Citlali** (Star in Náhuatl), at Guerrero 3, tel./fax 755/554-2043. The hotel rises in a pair of three-story tiers, around a shady, plant-decorated inner courtyard. The 20 plain, rather small, but clean rooms are all thankfully removed from direct street traffic hubbub. Guests on the upper floors experience less corridor traffic and consequently enjoy more privacy. Reservations are mandatory during the high winter season and strongly recommended at other times. Rates run about $25 s, $30 d, $35 t low season, $30 s, $35 d, $40 t high, with hot water and fans.

Next door, **Hotel Susy,** corner of Guerrero and Álvarez, Zihuatanejo, Guerrero 40880, tel. 755/554-2339, fax 755/554-4739, viajesbravo@yahoo.com, across Álvarez, has three floors of rooms around a shady inner patio. The seven upper-floor bayside rooms have private view balconies. Inside corridors unfortunately run past room windows, necessitating closing curtains for privacy, a drawback in these fan-only rooms. Avoid traffic noise by requesting an upper-floor room away from the street. The 20 clean but plain rooms go for $25 s, $30 d, $40 t low season, and $30, $40, $50 high, including fans and hot water.

Right in the middle of the downtown action is compact **Hotel Monarca,** at Cuauhtémoc 13, tel./fax 755/554-2030. Choose from six attractive kitchenette (microwave oven only) studios in three floors. Units are clean, airy and comfortable; two have private view balconies. They accommodate two to four people with combinations of double and single beds. Rentals run a reasonable $40 d per day, $1,000 per month, all with TV, refrigerator, fans, and coffeemaker.

On a quiet midtown east-side lane, find the big **Hotel Zihuatanejo Centro,** favorite of Mexican families, at Ramírez 2, tel. 755/554-2669, 755/554-5330, or 755/554-5340, fax 755/554-6897, zihuacenter@prodigy.net.mx, www.ixtapa-zihuatanejo.com/zihuacenter. Hotel guests are sheltered from the town hubbub by rooms that face inward on to an inviting inner pool-courtyard. The approximately 75 rooms rising in four floors are clean and simply but comfortably furnished in pastels and vinyl floor tile. Some rooms have two double beds, others have one king- or queen-sized bed. For more air and light, ask for a room with a balcony. Rates run about $40 d year-round, with a/c, fans, TV, hot-water showers, parking, and restaurant; credit cards are accepted.

Not far away stands **Hotel Amueblados Valle,** at Guerrero 33, tel. 755/554-2084, fax 755/554-3220. Inside the front door, find eight units in three floors around an inviting inner patio. The apartments themselves, all with kitchenettes and either one or two bedrooms and shower baths, are clean, spacious, and comfortably furnished. Upper units are breezier and lighter. One-bedroom units go for about $40 s or d; two bedrooms about $50 d or t, or $60 for four or five. Discounts are possible for monthly rentals. All with TV, fans, but no parking included.

Nearby, owner Ada Aburto Pineda's modest guesthouse, **Casa de Huéspedes Ada,** fronts a tranquil, shady traffic-free street mall, at Galeana 14, tel. 755/554-2186, nos@prodigy.net.mx. Her seven rentals differ markedly. Downstairs, she offers three plain, dark, small but clean rooms, two with fans, one with a/c. Her four upstairs accommodations are much larger and lighter. Two are airy, multiroom kitchenette apartments, with fans, accommodating up to four or five people. They open to a spacious, leafy front porch overlooking the shady street scene below. The two remaining upstairs units are in the rear and are smaller but still comfortable and clean, with fans and double beds. The larger of the two has a kitchenette. The three downstairs rooms go for $20 d; the big upstairs apartments, $50 d, or $900/month. The smaller upstairs kitchenette goes for $40 d, the nonkitchenette, $30 d. All units come with private baths, TV, and parking.

Next door, **Apartments America** shares the same choice location at Galeana 16, tel. 755/554-4337, fax 755/554-4338, zihuatanejoamerica7@hotmail.com. The 10 one- and two-bedroom kitchenette apartments, stacked in two floors around an inner patio-corridor, are plainly but comfortably furnished with tile floors, bedspreads, curtains, and well-maintained shower baths. Choose an upstairs apartment for more light and air. The one-bedroom apartments, sleeping one or two adults, rent for about $40/day, $450 per month. The two-bedroom units, sleeping up to six, go for about $70/day, $700/month. Add $10/day for a/c. All with TV, fans, and parking included.

$50–100: Its location near the pier draws many fishing enthusiasts to the **Hotel Raoúl Tres Marias Centro,** at Juan Álvarez and Cinco de Mayo, Zihuatanejo, Guerrero 40880, tel./fax 755/554-6706, garroboscrew@prodigy.net.mx. Some of the 18 rooms have private balconies looking out on the street below. Newcomers might pick up some local fishing pointers after dinner at the hotel's restaurant, Los Garrobos. Rooms go for about $40 s or d, $47 t low season, $50 and $57 high, with hot water and a/c.

Also popular with fishing parties is the **Hotel Hi-Sol,** at Bravo 120, tel./fax 755/554-0595, three blocks from the beach. The hotel offers two floors of around a dozen spacious, clean, semideluxe rooms. All have shiny shower baths and are invitingly decorated with tile and cheery yellow-blue motif bedspreads and curtains. All rooms open to airy, private street-view balconies. Rates run about $65 s or d, $80 t, and $95 q high season; $55, $70, and $80 low, with TV, fans, and telephone.

Hotel Ávila, at Juan Álvarez 8, Zihuatanejo, Guerrero 40880, tel. 755/554-2010, fax 755/554-8592, downtown Zihuatanejo's only beachfront hostelry, is popular for its location. Rooms, although simply decorated, are comfortable. Guests in the hotel's several beachfront rooms enjoy luxurious private-patio bay and beach views. If possible avoid taking a room on the noisy streetfront side. The 27 rooms rent, low season, for about $65 s or d with view and $40 without. Corresponding high season rates are about $70 with view, $50 without. All rooms have fans, TV, a/c, phones, and hot water. Credit cards are accepted.

Zihuatanejo Playa Madera Hotels

Another sizable fraction of Zihuatanejo's lodgings spreads along and above Playa Madera on the east side of the bay, most easily reachable on foot from the town plaza, via the scenic beachfront *andador* (walkway). Many of the lodgings line the summit of Cerro Madera, the bayfront hill just east of town.

Because of Zihuatanejo's one-way streets (which fortunately direct most noisy traffic away from downtown), getting to Cerro Madera by car is a bit tricky. The key is Plaza Kyoto, the traffic circle-intersection of Paseo de la Boquita and Paseo del Palmar a quarter mile east of downtown. Drivers, keep a sharp eye out and follow the small "Zona Hotelera" signs. At Plaza Kyoto, marked by a big Japanese *torii* gate, bear right across the canal bridge and turn right at the first street, Señora de los Remedios. Continue for another block to Avenida Adelita, address of several Playa Madera hotels, which runs along the base of Cerro Madera. At Adelita, continue straight uphill to the lane, Calle Eva Samano de López Mateos, that runs atop Cerro Madera.

Guests in all Cerro Madera lodgings enjoy direct beach access by simply walking about a block downhill to luscious Playa Madera.

Under $50: Playa Madera's only beachfront low-end lodging is the circa-1960s **Bungalows Allec,** at Cerro Madera, Calle Eva Samano de López Mateos, Zihuatanejo, Guerrero 40880, tel./fax 755/554-2002, bun_allec@hotmail.com, www.ixtapa-zihuatanejo.net/bun_allec. Comfortable, light, and spacious, although worn, the 12 clean fan-only apartments have breezy bay views from private balconies. Six of the units are very large, sleeping up to six, with kitchenettes. The others are smaller doubles without kitchenette. No pool, but Playa Madera is a few steps downhill. The kitchenette apartments go for about $50 low season, $150 high; the smaller doubles are about $25 low, $40 high. Long-term discounts may be available.

A couple of blocks inland downhill, find the downscale but homey **Bungalows El Milagro,** Av. Marina Nacional s/n, P.O. Box 71, Playa Madera, Zihuatanejo, Guerrero 40880, tel. 755/554-3045, the project of Dr. Niklaus Bührer and his wife, Lucina Gomes. A haciendalike walled compound of cottages and apartments clustering around a shady pool, the Bungalows El Milagro is winter headquarters for a cordial group of German longtime returnees. The friendly atmosphere and the inviting pool and garden account for the El Milagro's success, rather than the plain but clean kitchenette lodgings, which vary in style from rustic to 1940s motel. Look at several before you choose. The 17 units rent, high season, between about $45/day ($500/month) for two for the smaller rooms to about $90/day ($1,100/month) for the larger, six-person suites. All have kitchenettes, hot water, fans, pool, and parking.

$50–100: On Avenida Adelita, right above the beach, is the longtime Mexican family-run **Hotel Palacio,** Av. Adelita, Playa Madera, P.O. Box 57, Zihuatanejo, Guerrero 40880, tel./fax 755/554-2055, a beachfront maze of rooms connected by meandering, multilevel walkways. Room windows along the two main tiers face corridor walkways, where curtains must be drawn for privacy. Upper units fronting the quiet street avoid this drawback. The rooms themselves are clean, renovated, brightly decorated, and comfortable, with fans or a/c and hot water. Guests enjoy a small but very pleasant bay-view pool, kiddie pool, and sundeck, which perches above the waves at the hotel beachfront. High season rentals run about $45 s, $55 d with fan, $50 and $62 with a/c, but street parking only. Low season rates run about 20 percent less.

Back uphill on Cerro Madera, consider a pair of home-in-a home-type lodgings. First, find **Casa Lagartijas,** named for the *lagartijas* (geckos) that benignly inhabit tropical area houses, at Calle Eva Samano 43, tel. 755/554-9391, larbym41@bigplanet.com, www.casa-lagartija.com. Personable owner Joan Rubaloff rents two clean, spacious, and comfortable two-bedroom fan-only apartments for two to six people, with kitchen, living-dining room, and full bath. Rentals go for about $60 d low season, $70 d high. Add $10 for each additional person.

A few doors away, **Casa Azul,** tel. 755/554-3534, marsha_gould@msn.com, www.mexonline.com/sucasita, offers a similar value. Owner Marsha Gould likewise rents two apartments, an upper and a lower. The upper is a tropical hideaway for two or three, with a luxurious *palapa* roof, kitchenette, loft bedroom with king-sized bed, and an airy bay view from both the shower and the private balcony. The larger apartment, downstairs, is equally comfortable, but darker, with two bedrooms, sleeping up to six, with bath, living room-dining room, and a back garden town-view hammock patio. The upper rents for $85 d, the lower for $70 d; add $5 for each extra person. All nonsmoking, please. Marsha closes down from about May 1 until mid-October, when you can contact her in Denver, Colorado, at tel. 303/458-8630. (She also rents a deluxe view condo, Casa Buenavista, for about $95 d, on the same quiet street. Visit her website and click through to Casa Buenavista.)

Several bungalow complexes cluster along the same scenic Cerro Madera hilltop street. Although their details differ, their basic layouts—which stair-step artfully downhill to private beachfront gardens—are similar. First comes **Bungalows Sotelo,** at Calle Eva Samano de López Mateos 13, Zihuatanejo, Guerrero 40880, tel./fax 755/554-6307. Guests in a number of the clean stucco-and-tile apartments enjoy spacious private or semiprivate terraces with deck lounges and bay views. Rents for the smaller units without kitchenette run about $40 d low season, $60 high; larger one- and two-bedroom kitchenette suites rent for about $60 d low season, $80 high (for one bedroom) and $100 low season, $140 high (for two bedrooms). Some readers have reported that the Bungalows Sotelo management leaves something to be desired.

Rentals vary; look at more than one before moving in. No pool, street parking only, but with a/c; get your winter reservations in early.

A few doors farther east is yet another Cerro Madera option, **Hotel Brisas del Mar,** at Calle Eva Samano de López Mateos s/n, Cerro Madera, Zihuatanejo, Guerrero 40880, tel./fax 755/554-8332, 755/554-2142, brisamar@prodigy.net.mx, www.brisasdelmar.net. Owners have completely renovated the original hotel and have added a big new wing of a dozen spacious, rustic-chic, native Mexico decor, view suites to the original 20 apartments. The bright spot of this entire complex, besides the sweeping bay views, is the hotel's lovely beach club, with its shady *palapas,* lounge chairs, and big blue pool. Brisas del Mar rents its original (but upgraded) apartments for about the same rates as its neighbors: about $60 d low season, $70 high, with hot water and fans. For the spacious new-wing junior suites, expect to pay about $95 low season (ask for a discount), $110 high, all with a/c and cable TV.

The **Hotel Irma,** Av. Adelita, Playa Madera, Zihuatanejo, Guerrero 40880, tel./fax 755/554-3738, a few hundred yards east of Cerro Madera, remains a favorite of longtime lovers of Zihuatanejo, if for no reason other than its location. Guests enjoy very comfortable renovated deluxe rooms, a passably pleasant sunset-view terrace restaurant and bar, and a pair of blue pools perched above the bay. A short walk downhill and you're at creamy Madera beach. Best of all, many of the front-tier rooms have private balconies with just about the loveliest view on Playa Madera. The 70 rooms rent for about $60 s or d low season, $80 high, with view ($45 and $60 without view), all with a/c, TV, and hot water. Low-season packages and discounts may be available May–June and Sept.–November. Hotel Irma rooms are reservable through the agency Mexico Condo Reservations at toll-free U.S./Can. tel. 800/262-4500, info@mcrx.com. For more information, visit www.mexicocondores.com/zihuatanejo/hotelirma.

Two doors downhill, the **Hotel Villas Miramar,** Playa Madera, Av. Adelita, P.O. Box 211, Zihuatanejo, Guerrero 40880, tel. 755/554-2106, fax 755/554-2149, villasm@prodigy.net.mx, clusters artfully around gardens of pools, palms, and leafy potted plants. The gorgeous, manicured layout makes maximum use of space, creating both privacy and intimacy in a small setting. The designer rooms have high ceilings, split levels, built-in sofas, and large, comfortable beds. The street divides the hotel into two different but both lovely sections, each with its own pool. The restaurant, especially convenient for breakfast, is in the shoreside section but still serves guests who sun and snooze around the luxurious, beach-view pool-patio on the other side of the street. The garden rooms rent for about $60 d low season, $80 high; the ocean-view apartments, about $75 low, $95 high; all have phones and a/c, some have wheelchair access; and credit cards are accepted. Additional discounts may be available during May–Dec. 15 low seasons. Reservations strongly recommended during the winter season.

Back atop Cerro Madera, find **Bungalows Pacífico,** the enterprise of longtime local resident Anita Rellstab Hahner, at Cerro Madera, P.O. Box 12, tel./fax 755/554-2112, bungalowspacifico@yahoo.com. Her guests can choose from six spartan but spacious hillside furnished apartments with broad bay-view patios, including kitchenettes and daily maid service. Anita, herself an amateur archaeologist, ecologist, bird-watcher, and community leader, is a forthright and knowledgeable hostess. No matter for lack of a pool; lovely Playa Madera is a short walk down the leafy front slope. Get your reservations in early, especially for winter. The apartments rent for about $58 d low season, $82 high, with hot water, fans only, and street parking; monthly discount possible during the May 1–Dec. 15 low season. (If at all possible, make reservations; some guests have complained that Anita has been grouchy when they arrived unexpectedly.)

Also atop Cerro Madera, consider the spiffy **Bungalows Ley,** at Calle Eva Samano de López Mateos s/n, Playa Madera, P.O. Box 466, Zihuatanejo, Guerrero 40880, tel. 755/554-4087, fax 755/554-4563, bungalowsley@prodigy.net.mx. Here, several white stucco studio apartments stair-step directly downhill to heavenly Playa Madera. Their recent decorations show nicely. Bathrooms shine with flowery Mexican tile, hammocks hang in spacious, rustic-chic, *palapa*-roofed view patios, and bedrooms glow with wall art, native wood details, and soothing pastel bedspreads. Except for a two-bedroom kitchenette unit at the top, all are kitchenette studios. No pool, but the beach is straight down the steps from your door. The fan-only studios run about $75 d low season, $92 high. The beautiful two-bedroom unit with a/c runs $150 low season, $170 high. Long-term low-season discounts (of 15–30 percent for 6–21 night stays) are available.

Over $100: Perched atop Bungalows Ley, with the same address, but completely separate, is upscale **Casa Leigh y Loros,** the lovely life project of friendly California resident Leigh Roth and her pet parrot, Loros. Casa Leigh y Loros, which Leigh rents when she's away, is a multilevel, art-decorated, white-stucco-and-tile, two-bedroom, two-bath villa with roof garden, airy bay-view balconies, and up-to-date kitchen appliances. High winter season (except Christmas) rent runs about $250/day, $1,500/week; during low season, Leigh charges $175/day, $1,150/week. With a/c, fans, TV, and daily maid service; cooking is available at extra charge. Leigh also rents a number of smaller but similarly luxurious apartments from about $95/day, $570/week low season ($175/day, $1,000/week high) in villa **Casa San Sebastián** on the hillside, a mile away, above Playa La Ropa. For a more economical option, ask Leigh (or Lila, as she's known locally) about **Casa de Bambu,** which she also rents, across the street from Casa Leigh y Loros. Contact her or her agent at tel. 755/554-3755, zihua01@earthlink.net, or visit www.zihuatanejo-rentals.com. She also acts as agent for a number of small luxury hotels, bed-and-breakfasts, and villas, mostly along Playa Madera and Playa Ropa.

A few hundred yards farther east along the Paseo Costera, follow the signed uphill driveway to **Casa Cuitlateca,** P.O. Box 124, Zihuatanejo, Guerrero 40880, tel. 755/554-2448, fax 755/554-7934, casa@altahotelgroup.com, www.cascuitlateca.com. Builders have spared little to create this luxuriously tropical bed-and-breakfast hideaway, charmingly perched above Zihuatanejo Bay. You know you're in for something special as you enter by the hanging bridge. Guests enjoy a choice of four luxuriously rustic suites, invitingly decorated in white tile and stucco, highlighted by attractive one-of-a-kind handcrafted art. Bathrooms are large and super-luxurious, likewise tiled in white. Three of the suites have panoramic bay views. The lavish amenities include bar, restaurant (dinner by reservation only) exotically lush garden, an overflow panoramic- view pool, and a sumptuous tip-top *palapa*-shaded terrace with whirlpool tub for all-guest use. Rates run about $400 d high season, $250 low (June 1–Nov. 15), with full breakfast, cable TV, phone, a/c, and parking. Reserve by phone or email.

Just across the road, **La Casa Que Canta,** Camino Escénico a Playa La Ropa, Zihuatanejo, Guerrero 40880, tel. 755/555-7030, toll-free Mex. tel. 800/710-9345 or U.S. tel. 888/523-5050, fax 755/554-7040, info@lacasaquecanta.com, www.lacasaquecanta.com, is as much a work of art as a hotel. The pageant begins at the lobby, a luxurious soaring *palapa* that angles gracefully down the cliffside to an intimate open-air view dining-room. Suite-clusters of natural adobe sheltered by thick *palapa* roofs cling artfully to the craggy precipice decorated with riots of bougainvillea and gardens of cactus. From petite pool terraces perched above foamy shoals, guests enjoy a radiant aqua bay panorama in the morning and brilliant ridge-silhouetted sunsets in the evening. The 18 art-bedecked, rustic-chic suites, all with private view balconies, come in three grades: super deluxe "terrace" rooms, more spacious "grand suited," and even more spacious and luxurious "master suites," the latter two options with their own small pools. Rentals run about $450, $580, and $800; low-season discounts may be available. All come with a/c, fans, and phone, but no TV, and no kids under 16 allowed. Make winter reservations very early. (*Note:* Casa Que Canta now offers the best of all possible upscale worlds all within its present grounds: El Murmullo super-private 10,000-square-foot four-villa inner sanctum compound, built for a maharaja, with complete all-exclusive staff, from gardener, chambermaids, and butler, to waiters, kitchen staff, and gourmet chefs, all for only $4,000 daily.)

Zihuatanejo Playa La Ropa Hotels

$50–100: Luscious Playa La Ropa begins at **Hotel Sotavento,** P.O. Box 2, Zihuatanejo, Guerrero 40880, tel. 755/554-2032 or 755/554-2024, toll-free U.S./Can. tel. 888-523/5050, fax 755/554-2975, info@beachresortsotavento.com.mx, www.beachresortsotovento.com.mx. Good hands-on owner management keeps the rambling complex, which perches on a leafy bayview hillside, healthy. The Sotavento is a 70-room mod-style warren that stair-steps five stories down the slope. Each floor of rooms opens to a broad, hammock-hung communal terrace overlooking the beach and bay. Inside, the Sotavento's rooms are spartan 1960s-style, clean and comfortable, most opening onto the view terrace, with king- or queen-sized beds and ceiling fans. High-season rates begin at about $52 d for a nonview, $58 d for view, rising to about $100 for the largest deluxe family-sized bungalows. Subtract about 20 percent during the post-Easter–Dec. 15 low season. (*Note:* Views, light, and shade depend on your room's vertical position in the layout. Guests in upper-level rooms enjoy expansive bay and sunset vistas, while guests in less pricey lower-level rooms nevertheless enjoy intimate tropical verdure-framed sunset vistas of the bay beyond. Look at both kinds of rooms before choosing.) The Hotel Sotavento's amenities include a beachside pool, room fans, parking, restaurants, and a beach aquatics shop, but no elevator or wheelchair access; credit cards are accepted.

By contrast, the 30 cabanas of the neighboring **Catalina Beach Resort** next door are scattered picturesquely beneath shady hillside trees all the way down to the beach. The Catalina's comfortably appointed tropical-rustic cabanas maximize privacy, being mostly separate units with individual view terraces and hammocks. Lodgings vary, from huge through simply large to smaller economy units. Look until you find the one that most suits you and your budget. At the bottom of the hill, a beach aquatics shop offers sailing, sailboarding, snorkeling, and other rentals; those who want to simply rest enjoy chairs beneath the shady boughs of a beachside grove. A trio of restaurants, accessible by clients of both the Sotavento and Catalina, include an ordinary breakfast-lunch cafeteria at the beach level, a fancier dinner restaurant upstairs, and an airy upper-level terrace restaurant-bar. The Catalina's high-season rates range upward from economy room

© BRUCE WHIPPERMAN

Hotel Villa del Sol guests enjoy lavish beachfront facilities on lovely Playa La Ropa.

$60 d, standard room $80 d, casita $120, deluxe housekeeping bungalow $140; low season, the same run $55, $65, $77, and $90. Reserve at tel. 755/554-2137, 755/554-9321 through 755/554-9325, or toll-free Mex. tel. 800/640-1111, U.S. tel. 877/287-2411, Can. tel. 866/485-4312, or Germany tel. 0800/181-5405, fax 755/554-9327, info@catalinabeachresort.com, www.catalina beachresort.com.

A dozen-odd hotels, bungalow complexes, and restaurants spread a mile farther along La Ropa Beach. Nearby, a block from the beach, **Villas Ema** perches at the top of a flowery hillside garden. Here, the enterprising husband-wife owners of downtown Posada Citlali have built kitchenette apartments, beautifully furnished with white tile floors, matching floral drapes and bedspreads, modern-standard shower baths, plenty of windows for light, and sliding doors leading to private view porches for reading and relaxing. Amenities include a/c or fans, hot water, a beautiful blue pool, and the murmur of the waves on Playa La Ropa nearby. Rates for the nine smaller units, with kitchen in common, run about $60 d low season, $90 high. The three top-level units, although sunnier (and consequently warmer), have the best views and and most privacy. A pair of ground-level larger "villitas," each with its own kitchen and patio, sleeping four, rent for about $100 low season, $120 high. For reservations, highly recommended in winter, contact the owners through Posada Citlali, Av. Guerrero 3, Zihuatanejo, Guerrero 40880, tel./fax 755/554-2043, or at home (in Spanish) at tel. 755/554-4880. To avoid confusion, be sure to specify your reservation is for Villas Ema.

A pair of good housekeeping bungalow-type complexes share the same luxuriously lovely beachfront as the renowned upscale Hotel Villa del Sol, but at greatly reduced prices. One of these is **Bungalows Vepao,** address simply Playa La Ropa, Zihuatanejo, Guerrero 40880; reserve by calling either owner Gonzalo Ramírez, tel. 755/554-3619 (in Spanish), or manager Margarita Castro, tel. 755/554-2631. Here they have created your basic clean and pleasant beach lodging, simply but architecturally designed, with floor-to ceiling drapes, modern-standard kitchenettes, tiled floors, shower baths, white stucco walls, and pastel bedspreads and shaded lamps. Guests in each apartment enjoy front patios (upper ones have some bay view) that lead right to the hotel's private beachfront row of *palapas* a few steps away. Rates run about $50 d low season, $65 high, with parking, fans, and long-term discounts possible.

The same owner also rents four apartments in **Casa La Gloria,** a designer white stucco beachfront house, on the same property. Each of the deluxe units (two upstairs and two down) is attractively decorated with native rustic tile floors, bright floral tile baths, and whimsical hand-painted wall designs at the head of the two queen-sized beds. Each unit has its own kitchenette on an outdoor beachview patio. For more breeze and privacy, ask for one of the top-floor units. Rentals run about $85 low season, $105 high, with parking and fans. For reservations, see the Bungalows Vepao contacts. For more information, visit www.ixtapa-zihuatanejo.com or www.zihuatanejo.net.

Nearby, but as distinct as day from night, is **Bungalows Urracas,** about 15 petite brick cottages, like proper rubber planter's bungalows out of Somerset Maugham's *Malaysian Stories,* nestling in a shady jungle of leafy plants, trees, and vines. Inside, the illusion continues: dark, masculine wood furniture, spacious bedrooms, shiny tiled kitchenettes and baths, and overhead, rustic beamed ceilings. From the bungalows, short "jungle" paths lead to the brilliant La Ropa beachfront. About eight additional bungalows occupy beachfront view locations in front. Amenities include private, shady front porches (use insect repellent in the evenings), hot water, and fans. Rentals run a bargain $60 d low season, $70 high. Ask for a long-term discount. Get your winter reservations in early. Write Bungalows Urracas, Playa La Ropa, Zihuatanejo, Guerrero 40880, call tel. 755/555-2053, or fax 755/554-2049.

Go to the end of the road at Playa La Ropa and you'll find the **Hotel Paraíso Real,** the personal project of the friendly husband-wife team of scuba master Juan Barnard Avila and his wife, Margo. Their example reveals their strong commitment to sustainable ecotourism. In the mid-1990s, Juan and Margo renovated an old hotel, cleaned up the adjacent mangrove lagoon, and nurtured its wildlife (dozens of bird species and a number of crocodiles) back to health. They added 14 units around a rear jungle-garden and pool-patio. They run a combined hotel, restaurant, and scuba center, where guests may stay and relax for a week or a season, enjoy wholesome food and friendly people, perhaps get a massage, and sample the good snorkeling, scuba diving, kayaking, turtle hatching, and fishing available right from the beach. Choose your room from one of two sections: beachview in front, or garden view in back. All rooms are immaculate and simply but comfortably furnished with handsomely handcrafted wooden beds, lamps, and cabinets. Rentals cost about $90 d year-round, with hot water, parking, and fans. For reservations (mandatory in winter) contact Hotel Paraíso Real, Playa La Ropa, Zihuatanejo, Guerrero, 40880, tel./fax 755/554-3873, 755/554-8156, or 755/554-2147, divemexico@email.com, or for more information, visit www.divemexico.com.

Over $100: The **Hotel Villa Mexicana,** Playa La Ropa, Zihuatanejo, Guerrero 40880, tel./fax 755/554-3776 or 755/554-3636, seems to be popular for nothing more than its stunning location right in the middle of the sunny beach hubbub. Its 75 rooms, comfortable and air-conditioned, are packed in low-rise stucco clusters around an inviting beachfront pool-patio-restaurant. This seems just perfect for the mostly North American winter package-vacation clientele, who ride personal watercraft, parasail, and boogie board from the beach, snooze around the pool, and socialize beneath the *palapa* of the beachside restaurant. High-season rates begin at about $100 d ($145 d for a room with private view balcony). Low-season package three-night rates run about $200 d. Some rooms have wheelchair access. Parking is available; credit cards are accepted. Rooms are reservable either directly or through the Internet agency Mexico Condo Hotel reservations, toll-free U.S./Can. tel. 800/262-4500, info@mcrx.com, www.mexicocondores.com/zihuatanejo/hotelirma.

German expatriate Helmut Leins sold out in Munich and came to create paradise on Playa La Ropa in 1978. The result is Playa La Ropa's luxury **Hotel Villa del Sol,** Playa La Ropa, P.O. Box 84, Zihuatanejo, Guerrero 40880, tel. 755/555-5500 or 755/554-3239, fax 755/554-2758 or 755/554-4066, hotel@villasol.com.mx. Here, in Helmut's exquisite beachside mini-Eden, a corps of well-to-do North American, European, and Mexican clients return yearly to enjoy tranquillity and the elegance of the Villa del Sol's crystal-blue pools, palm-draped patios, and classic *palapas.* The lodgings vary, from luxuriously spacious at the high end to large at the low end; all have rustic-chic floor tile, handcrafted wall art, and big, soft beds. The plethora of extras includes restaurants, bars, pools, night tennis courts, a newsstand, art gallery boutique, beauty salon, and meeting room. The least expensive of the approximately 90 accommodations begin at $300 s or d, low season, $450 high. Super-plush room options include more bedrooms and baths, ocean views, and small private whirlpool tubs for around $600 and up. All lodgings come with cable TV, phone, a/c, and parking; some have wheelchair access. Credit cards are accepted, but children in two-bedroom suites only. For reservations, call toll-free U.S./Can. tel. 888/389-2645 or contact its agent, Mexico Boutique Hotels, at toll-free U.S. tel. 877/278-8018 or Can. tel. 866/818-8342, villadelsol@mexicoboutiquehotels.com. For more information, visit www.hotelvilladelsol.com or www.mexicoboutiquehotels.com/villadelsol.

Ixtapa Hotels

Ixtapa's dozen-odd hotels line up in a luxurious strip between the beach and boulevard Paseo Ixtapa. Guests in all of them enjoy deluxe resort-style facilities and wheelchair access. All are high end (more than $100/day) hostelries.

Over $100: Best buy of them all is the Best Western **Hotel Posada Real,** Paseo Ixtapa s/n, Ixtapa, Guerrero 40880, tel. 755/553-1625 or 755/553-1745, fax 755/553-1805, pr1ixt@prodigy.net.mx, at Paseo Ixtapa's far west end. Get there via the street, beach side, just past the big corner restaurant on the left. With a large grassy soccer field instead of tennis courts, the hotel attracts a seasonal following of soccer enthusiasts. Other amenities include a large

© BRUCE WHIPPERMAN

Hotel Las Brisas Ixtapa's room terraces stairstep down to the tower where guests ride an elevator down to an intimate, wave-washed white coral-sand beach.

airy beachfront restaurant and two luscious pools. Although the 110 (rather small) rooms are clean and comfortable, many lack ocean views. Rooms rent for about $117 d low season, $140 high, often with extended-stay or low-season discounts, such as third night free. Kids under 12 with parents stay free; with a/c, satellite TV, phones, wheelchair access, and parking; credit cards are accepted. Reserve by Best Western toll-free U.S./Can. tel. 800/528-1234 or visit www.bestwestern.com.

Right in the middle of the hotel zone stands the **Hotel Dorado Pacífico,** Paseo Ixtapa s/n, P.O. Box 15, Ixtapa, Guerrero 40880, tel. 755/553-2025, fax 755/553-0126, reserv@doradopacifico.com.mx, www.doradopacifico.com.mx, next door. Here, three palm-shaded blue pools, water slides, a swim-up bar, and three restaurant/bars seem to keep guests happy. Upstairs, the rooms, all with sea-view balconies, are pleasingly decorated with sky-blue carpets and earth-tone designer bedspreads. The 285 rooms rent from $145 d low season, $180 high, with a/c, phones, and TV. Low-season and extended stay discounts may be available. Other extras include tennis courts, parking, and wheelchair access; credit cards are accepted.

The **Hotel Barceló Ixtapa,** Paseo Ixtapa s/n, Ixtapa, Guerrero 40880, tel. 755/555-0000, fax 755/553-2438, reservas@barceloixtapa.com.mx, www.barcelo.com, across from the golf course at the east end of the beach, rises around a soaring lobby/atrium. The Barceló, formerly the Sheraton, offers a long list of resort facilities, including pools, all sports, an exercise gym, several restaurants and bars, cooking and arts lessons, nightly dancing, and a Fiesta Mexicana. The 330-odd rooms in standard (which include inland-view balconies only), ocean view, and junior suite grades, are spacious and tastefully furnished in designer pastels and include a/c, phones, wheelchair access, and satellite TV. The Barceló operates both on a room only or all-inclusive basis. Room-only tariffs run about $162 d low season, $180 high, including breakfast, kids under 12 free; all-inclusive (all drinks, food, and entertainment) $220 d low, $250 d high, kids 6–12 $33. For reservations, call toll-free U.S./Can. tel. 800/BARCELO (800/227-2356).

Back near the west end, consider the European-owned **Hotel NH Krystal Ixtapa,** Paseo Ixtapa s/n, Ixtapa, Guerrero 40880, tel. 755/553-0333, fax 755/553-0216, nhkrystalixtapa@nh-hoteles.com.mx, www.nh-hoteles.com. The hotel, which towers over its spacious garden compound, has an innovative wedge design that ensures an ocean view from each room. A continuous round of activities—a table-tennis tournament, handicrafts and cooking classes, and aerobics and scuba lessons—fills the days, while buffets, theme parties, and dancing fill the nights. Unscheduled relaxation centers on the blue pool, where guests enjoy watching each other slip from the water slide and duck beneath the waterfall all day. The 260 tastefully appointed deluxe rooms and suites have private view balconies, satellite TV, a/c, wheelchair access, and phones. Rooms rent from a low of about $92 d low season to about $320 high. Check for additional discounts through extended-stay or other packages. Extras include tennis courts, racquetball, an exercise gym, parking. Credit cards are accepted. For reservations, dial toll-free U.S./Can. tel. 800/231-9860.

From the east-end jungly hilltop, the **Hotel Las Brisas Ixtapa,** Paseo de la Roca, P.O. Box 97, Ixtapa, Guerrero 40880, tel. 755/553-2121, fax 755/553-0751, www.brisas.com.mx, slopes downhill to the shore like a latter-day Aztec pyramid. The monumentally stark hilltop lobby, open and unadorned except for a clutch of huge stone balls, contrasts sharply with its surroundings. The hotel's severe lines immediately shift the focus to the adjacent jungle. The fecund forest aroma wafts into the lobby and the terrace restaurant, where, at breakfast, during the winter and early spring, guests sit watching iguanas munch hibiscus blossoms in the nearby treetops. The hotel entertains guests with a wealth of luxurious resort facilities, including pools, four tennis courts, a gym, aerobics, an intimate shoal-enfolded beach, restaurants, bars, and nightly piano bar music. The standard rooms, each with its own spacious view patio, are luxuriously spartan, floored with big designer tiles, furnished in earth tones, and equipped with big TVs, small refrigerators, phones, wheelchair access, and a/c. More luxurious options include suites with individual pools and hot tubs. The 427 rooms begin at about $210 for a standard low-season double, $340 high, and run about twice that for super-luxury suites. June–Oct., bargain packages can run as low as $160 d per night. For reservations, dial toll-free Mex. tel. 800/227-4727 or U.S./Can. tel. 866/226-3161.

Ixtapa Playa Linda Hotels

A trio of all-inclusive resort hotels decorate the luscious, tranquil Playa Linda shoreline about five miles northwest of the main Ixtapa Hotel Zone.

The original of the three is the **Club Med Ixtapa,** which, as its long-time clients have acquired families, has become kid-friendly. Besides deluxe rooms, the usual good Club Med food and a plethora of included activities, from sailboating and surfing to water aerobics and chess, children can also enjoy a full supervised program of kid-appropriate activities. At Club Med, the usual lodging arrangement is for a minimum of one week, paid in advance. Typical winter (nonholiday) weekly rates run about $700 per adult, double occupancy, discounts for kids. For more information, call toll-free U.S. tel. 800/CLUBMED (800/258-2633), visit www.clubmed.com, or contact a travel agent or travel website (sometimes offering discount packages.)

Alternatively, you might consider the Club Med's worthy neighbors, the **Hotel Melia Azul Ixtapa** and the **Hotel Qualton Club.** They offer comparable deluxe amenities, food, and activities, sometimes at reduced prices. Contact them respectively at toll-free U.S./Can. tel. 866/297-0100 or 800/336-3542, or at www.qualton.com or www.melia.com.

Trailer Parks and Camping

Ixtapa-Zihuatanejo has one small, very basic trailer park. At south-end **Trailer Park Las Cabañas,** a block from La Ropa Beach, P.O. Box 197, Zihuatanejo, Guerrero 40880, tel. 755/554-4718, you can find out what it's like to park or camp in someone's shady backyard. Friendly, retired owner-managers María Elena and Hernán Cabañas, to make ends meet, decided to rent out their front and back yards. The result is enough space for a dozen tents or four medium-sized RVs in back, and one in front, with electricity, water, showers, and toilets. The price is certainly right—about $4 per person for tents, RVs $12—and it's only a block from one of the loveliest resort beaches on the Mexican Pacific coast.

If Trailer Park Las Cabañas is too small for you, go to El Burro Borracho at Playa Troncones. (See the Troncones section in this chapter.)

House, Apartment, and Condo Rentals

Zihuatanejo residents sometimes offer their condos and homes for temporary lease through agents. Among the most experienced and highly recommended is **Judith Whitehead,** tel. 755/554-6226, cell tel. 044-755/557-0078, fax 755/553-1212, jude@prodigy.net.mx, www.paradiseproperties.com.mx.

Also, owner-agent **Francisco Ibarra,** tel. 755/554-4924, fax 755/554-0595, donfrancisco@zihua.net, www.donfranciscoproperties.com, rents several moderately priced condos and houses on La Ropa Beach.

For many more house, condo, and apartment rentals, visit website www.zihuatanejo.net and click "rentals."

For modestly priced rentals, don't forget the **Hotel Monarca, Casa de Huéspedes Ada, Apartments America,** and **Hotel Amueblados Valle** in the Zihuatanejo Downtown Hotels section.

FOOD

Zihuatanejo Snacks, Bakeries, and Breakfasts

For something cool in Zihuatanejo, stop by the **Paletería y Nevería Michoacana** ice shop across from the plaza. Besides ice cream, popcorn, and safe *nieves* (ices), it offers delicious *aguas* (fruit-flavored drinks, $.50), which make nourishing, refreshing non-Pepsi alternatives.

Downtown Zihuatanejo has at least two good bakeries. The long-time standby is **Panadería Francesa,** tel. 755/554-2742, tucked away on Galeana, the lane paralleling Cuahtémoc, a few doors north (uphill) from Gonzales, which turns out a daily acre of fresh goodies, from *pan integral* (whole-wheat) and black bread loaves to doughnuts and rafts of Mexican-style cakes, cookies, and tarts. It's open Mon.–Sat. 7 A.M.–9 P.M., Sunday 7 A.M.–2 P.M. Alternatively, sample the offerings of bakery **Buen Gusto,** at Guerrero 11, on the east side of the street, a few doors up the street from Coconuts Restaurant. Choose from a simply delicious assortment of fruit and nut tarts and cakes: pineapple, coconut, peach, strawberry, pecan, with coffee to go with them all. Open daily 8 A.M.–10 P.M.

Tasty, promptly served breakfasts are the specialty of the downtown **Cafetería Nova Zelandia** on Cuauhtémoc, corner of Ejido. Favorites include hotcakes, eggs any style, fruit, juices, and espresso coffee. Nova Zelandia serves lunch and supper also. Open daily 8 A.M.–10 P.M.

For hot sandwiches and good pizza on the downtown beach, try the **Cafe Marina** on Paseo del Pescador, just west of the plaza. The friendly, hardworking owner features a spaghetti party—either bolognesa, pesto, or primavera ($3–4)—Wednesday night and chili ($4) on Friday. The shelves of books for lending or exchange are nearly as popular as the food. Open Mon.–Sat. noon–10 P.M., closed approximately June to mid-September.

A local vacation wouldn't be complete without dropping in to the **Sirena Gorda** (Fat Mermaid), daily except Wednesday, 9 A.M.–11 P.M., near the end of Paseo del Pescador across from the naval compound, tel. 755/554-2687. Here the fishing crowd relaxes, trading stories after a tough day hauling in the lines. The other unique attractions, besides the well-endowed sea nymphs who decorate the walls, are tempting shrimp-bacon and fish tacos, juicy hamburgers, fish *mole,* and conch and nopal (cactus leaves, minus the spines) plates, ranging between $4 and $7.

Zihuatanejo Restaurants

Local chefs and restaurateurs, long accustomed to foreign tastes, operate a number of good local restaurants, mostly in Zihuatanejo (where, in contrast to Ixtapa, most of the serious eating occurs *outside* of hotel dining rooms). Note, however, that a number of the best restaurants are closed during low-season months of September and October.

Local folks swear by **Cocina Economica Doña Licha,** on Calle Diamante, an east-side lane. (From Plaza Kyoto, follow the canal east one block, turn left on to Diamante.) The reason is clear: tasty local-style food, served promptly in an airy, spic and span setting. Here customers have it all: for breakfast *huevos Mexicanos* ($3) or pancakes ($2); for *lonche,* go for the four-course *comida corrida* set lunch ($5); for *cena* (supper), try tacos, enchiladas, *chiles rellenos,* and *pozole* ($2–5). Open daily 7 A.M.–11 P.M.

All expatriate trails seem to lead to **Glob's Restaurant,** on the east side of downtown, corner of Juárez and Ejido, three blocks from the beach. Here the cool, coffee-shop atmosphere is refined but friendly, and the food is strictly for comfort—good American breakfasts, hamburgers, spaghetti, and salads. Most entrées $4–8. Open daily 8 A.M.–9 P.M. year-round.

Equally popular, **Esthela's Cocina and Express** a block west, corner of Ejido and Guerrero, offers the uniquely personal cooking of friendly, knowledgeable owner, Esthela Buenaventura. Her entrées consist of variations of stir-fried vegetables, to which she can add meat or fish for an additional price at your choice. For starters, Esthela offers such goodies as *lumpia* (Philippine-style spring rolls, $4), cucumber salad ($2), Buddha's Delight ($3), and much more. Find her open daily 1:30–10 P.M., cell tel. 044-755/557-9672.

Zihuatanejo has a pair of good, genuinely local-style restaurants in the downtown area. Right across the street from Esthela's, **Tamales y Atoles "Any,"** tel. 755/554-7303, Zihuatanejo's clean, well-lighted place for Mexican food, is the spot to find out if your favorite Mexican restaurant back home is serving the real thing. Tacos, tamales, quesadillas, enchiladas, *chiles rellenos* ($4–8) and such goodies are called *antojitos* in Mexico. At Tamales y Atoles "Any," they're savory enough to please even demanding Mexican palates. Open daily 9 A.M.–11 P.M., corner Guerrero and Ejido. Incidentally, "Any" (AH-nee) is the co-owner, whose perch is behind the cash register, while her friendly husband cooks and tends the tables.

Restaurant Los Braseros, half a block along Ejido, at Ejido 21, between Cuauhtémoc and Guerrero, tel. 755/554-4858, is similarly authentic and popular. Waiters are often busy after midnight even during low season serving seven kinds of tacos ($3) and specialties such as Gringa, Porky, and Azteca ($3–5), from a menu it would take three months of dinners (followed by a six-month diet) to fully investigate. Open daily 4 P.M.–1 A.M.

In the preface to their menu, the English owners of **Casa de Curry and Café Gondwana,** write that "in ancient times the European and Asian continents were part of one larger continent called Gondwana. And we are re-uniting the continents together again through our cooking." And they're making a good show of it. Indian-food lovers will easily recognize and enjoy the result, which seems a major achievement here in Zihuatanejo so far from Madras and Mumbai. Typical entrées run between $6 and $10. They also provide some familiar international specialties for those who do not indulge, for about the same prices. Find them at the corner of Bravo and Galeana, two blocks from the beach; open daily 4 P.M.–midnight, tel. 755/554-6016.

Longtime **Casa Elvira,** on waterfront Paseo del Pescador, by the naval compound, tel. 755/554-2061, founded long ago by now-octogenarian Elvira Campos, is as popular as ever, still satisfying the palates of a battalion of loyal Zihuatanejo longtimers. Elvira's continuing popularity is easy to explain: a palm-studded beachfront, strumming guitars, whirling ceiling fans, and a list of super-fresh salads and soups ($4–6), fish ($6–10), meat ($4–9), and Mexican specialties ($4–8), expertly prepared and professionally served. Open daily 1–10 P.M.; reservations recommended during the high season.

If Elvira's is full, an excellent alternative would be **Porto de Mare,** also on the beach, half a block east. It's the labor of love of its Italian architect owner, who designed and crafted its elegant open-air interior himself. As would be expected, his specialties are Italian-style pastas blended with the superbly fresh local seafood (entrées $8–18). Open daily noon–11 P.M.

No guide to Zihuatanejo restaurants would be complete without mention of **Coconuts** restaurant, on Guerrero, a block from the beach, across from Posada Citlali, tel. 755/554-2518. Here, the food, whether it be light (pasta primavera, $12) or hearty (rib eye steak, $24), appears to be of importance equal to the airy garden setting and good cheer generated among the droves of longtimers who return year after year. Open daily in season noon to midnight; closed approximately July–October.

Restaurant Kau Kan, on the clifftop road east and above Playa Madera, tel. 755/554-8446, continues to be popular for both its romantic view location and its excellent food and service. While music plays softly and bay breezes gently blow, waiters scurry, bringing savory appetizers ($5–12) Caesar salad ($7), and cooked-to-perfection *dorado,* lobster, steak, and shrimp ($12–25). Open daily noon–6 P.M. and 7 P.M.–midnight; high-season reservations mandatory, closed Sept.–October.

Right next door and equally worthy is Mediterranean boutique **Restaurant Il Mare.** Enter and let the luscious ambience—soothing Italian arias, waves crashing against the rocks far below, the golden setting sun—transport you somewhere to the southern Amalfi coast: *O! Sole mio!* The menu extends the impression: start with *bruschetta alla Romagna* ($4); follow with soup *brodetta di pesce* ($7); salad *pomodoro cipolla rossa con gorgonzola* ($6); and *scampi al vino bianco* ($20), accompanied by a bottle of good Chilean Sendero chardonnay ($19). Finish off with lemon liqueur *Sogna di Sorrento* ($5). Find it open daily noon–midnight high season, 4 P.M. to midnight, low. Reservations recommended in high season, tel. 755/554-9067.

Ixtapa Bakery and Breakfasts

The perfume wafting from freshly baked European-style yummies draws dozens of the faithful to the nearby **Golden Cookie Shop,** brainchild of local longtimers Helmut and Esther Walter. He, a German, and she, an East Indian from Singapore, satisfy homesick palates with a continuous supply of scrumptious cinnamon rolls, pies, and hot buns, and hearty American-style breakfasts daily ($4–6). In recent years, Helmut and Esther have served an authentic German buffet ($10) every Friday; call tel. 755/553-0310 to confirm. Open Mon.–Fri. 8 A.M.–3 P.M., Saturday 8 A.M.–1 P.M., on the inner patio, upper floor of the Los Patios shopping complex.

For breakfast, the **Cafe Toko Tucán,** tel. 755/553-0717, offers a refreshing alternative to hotel breakfasts. White cockatoos and bright toucans in a leafy patio add an exotic touch as you enjoy the fare, which, besides the usual juices, eggs, hotcakes, and French toast, includes lots of salads, veggie burgers, and sandwiches, from about $3 to $6. Open daily 9 A.M.–10 P.M., on the west front corner of the Los Patios shopping complex, across the boulevard from Hotel Sandy Resort.

Ixtapa Restaurants

Restaurants in Ixtapa have to be exceptional to compete with the hotels. One such, the **Bella Vista,** tel. 755/553-2121, *is* in a hotel, being the Las Brisas Ixtapa's view-terrace café. Breakfast is the favorite time to watch the antics of the iguanas in the adjacent jungle treetops. These black, green, and white miniature dinosaurs crawl up and down the trunks, munch flowers, and sunbathe on the branches. The food and service, incidentally, are quite good. Open daily 7 A.M.–11 P.M. Breakfast buffet runs $12, à la carte lunch $6–12, dinner entrées, $10–20. Call ahead to reserve a terrace-edge table; credit cards are accepted.

An Ixtapa restaurant that has customers when most others don't is **Restaurant Mama Norma and Deborah,** in La Puerta shopping center, in the rear, by Da Baffone Italian restaurant, tel. 755/553-0274, www.restaurantmamanorma.com. Canadian expatriate proprietor Deborah Thompson manages with aplomb, working from a menu of delicious specialties familiar to North American and European palates. Whatever your choice, be it Greek salad ($7), lobster ($15), steak ($10–15), or *fettuccine Alfredo* ($10), Deborah makes sure it pleases. Open Mon.–Sat. 11 A.M.–11 P.M., Sunday 3–11 P.M.

Those hankering for Italian-style pastas and seafood walk next door to **Ristorante Da Baffone.** The friendly owner, a native of the Italian isle of Sardinia, claims his restaurant is the oldest in Ixtapa. He's most likely right: he served his first meal here in 1978, simultaneous with the opening of Ixtapa's first hotel. While Mediterranean-Mex decor covers the walls, marinara-style shrimp ($12), clams with linguini ($10), calamari, ricotta- and spinach-stuffed cannelloni ($12), and glasses of Chianti and chardonnay ($5) load the tables. Open daily about noon–midnight during high season; call for reservations, tel. 755/553-1122.

If Da Baffone is full or closed, try the highly recommended gourmet Italian restaurant **Becco Fino** in the Marina Ixtapa. Reservations, tel. 755/553-1770, are usually necessary. Figure spending at least $30 per person.

(Other Ixtapa restaurants, popular for their party atmosphere, are described under Entertainment and Events.)

Entertainment and Recreation

ENTERTAINMENT AND EVENTS

In Zihuatanejo, visitors and residents content themselves mostly with quiet pleasures. Afternoons, they stroll the beachfront or the downtown shady lanes and enjoy coffee or drinks with friends at small cafés and bars. As the sun goes down however, folks head to Ixtapa for its sunset vistas, happy hours, shows, clubs, and dancing.

Sunsets

Sunsets are tranquil and often magnificent from the **Restaurant/Bar El Faro,** tel. 755/553-1027, which even has a cableway, south end of the Ixtapa beach, open 7 A.M.–7 P.M., leading to it. Many visitors stay to enjoy dinner and the relaxing piano bar. The restaurant is open daily around 5:30–10 P.M.; reservations are recommended winter and weekends. Drive or taxi via the uphill road toward the Hotel Las Brisas Ixtapa, east of the golf course; at the first fork, head right for El Faro.

For equally brilliant sunsets in a lively setting, try either the lobby bar or Bella Vista terrace restaurant of the **Las Brisas Ixtapa.** Lobby bar happy hour runs 6–7 P.M.; live music begins around 7:30 P.M. Drive or taxi, following the signs, along the uphill road at the golf course, following the signs to the crest of the hill just south of the Ixtapa beach.

The west-side headland blocks most Zihuatanejo sunset views, except for spots at the far end of Playa La Ropa. Here, guests at the longtime favorite **Restaurant La Perla,** open 4–10 P.M., tel. 755/554-8700, and especially **Restaurant Elvira,** tel. 755/554-2588, at the opposite, inner, end of the beach, delight in Zihuatanejo's most panoramic sunset vistas.

Sunset and Sunshine Cruises

Those who want to experience a sunset party while at sea ride the trimaran ***Tri Star,*** which leaves from the Zihuatanejo pier daily around 5 P.M., returning around 7:30 P.M. The tariff runs about $40 per person, including open bar.

The *Tri Star* also heads out daily on a Sunshine Cruise around 10 A.M., returning around 2:30 P.M. Included are open bar, lunch, and snorkeling, for about $50 per person. Book tickets for both of these cruises, which customarily include transportation to and from your hotel, through a hotel travel agent, such as American Express, tel. 755/553-0853, at Hotel NH Krystal in Ixtapa. Tickets are also available at the *Tri Star* office, tel. 755/554-2694, ydelsol@prodigy.net.mx, at Puerto Mío, the small marina about half a mile across the bay from town. Get there via the road that curves around the western, right-hand shore of Zihuatanejo Bay.

Movies

Head over to the petite **Cine Paraíso,** on Cuauhtémoc, three blocks from the beach in downtown Zihuatanejo, to escape into American pop, romantic comedy, and adventure. About the same is available daily from 4:30 P.M. at **Cine Flamingos,** tel. 755/553-2490, in the shopping plaza, behind Señor Frog's, across the boulevard from the Hotel Presidente Intercontinental.

Tourist Shows

Ixtapa hotels regularly stage **Fiesta Mexicana**

ZIHUATANEJO, "PLACE OF WOMEN"

An oft-told Costa Grande story says that when Captain Juan Álvarez Chico was exploring at Zihuatanejo, he looked down on the round tranquil little bay, lined with flocks of seabirds and women washing clothes in a freshwater spring. His Aztec guide told him that this place was called Cihuatlán, the "Place of Women." When Chico described the little bay, Cortés tacked *"nejo"* (little) on the name, giving birth to "Zihuatlanejo," which later got shortened to the present Zihuatanejo.

Investigators have offered a pair of intriguing alternative explanations of the "Place of Women" name, a handle that evokes visions of a land of Amazons. They speculate that either Isla Ixtapa or the former royal bathing resort at Playa Las Gatas may have given rise to the name. The bathing resort, founded by the Purépecha emperor, was most probably a carefully guarded preserve of the emperor's dozens of wives and female relatives. If not that, Isla Ixtapa may have been used as a refuge for the isolation and protection of women and children against the Aztec invaders who thus attached the label "Place of Women" to the locality.

extravaganzas, which begin with a sumptuous buffet and go on to a whirling skirt-and-sombrero folkloric ballet. After that, the audience becomes part of the act, with piñatas, games, cockfights, dancing, while enjoying drinks from an open bar. In the finale, fireworks often boom over the beach, painting the night sky in festoons of reds, blues, and greens.

Entrance runs about $30–40 per person, with kids under 12 usually half price. The most reliable and popular shows are staged (often seasonally only) at the **Presidente Intercontinental,** tel. 755/553-0018; **Dorado Pacífico,** tel. 755/553-2025 (Tuesday); and **Barceló,** tel. 755/555-0000 (Wednesday). Usually open to the public; call ahead for confirmation and reservations.

Clubs and Hangouts

Part restaurant and part wacky seasonal nightspot, **Carlos'n Charlie's,** tel. 755/553-0085, is as wild and as much fun as all of the other Carlos Anderson restaurants from Puerto Vallarta to Paris. Here in Ixtapa you can have your picture taken on a surfboard in front of a big wave for $3, or have a fireman spray out the flames from the chili sauce on your plate. You can also enjoy the food, which, if not fancy, is innovative and tasty. Loud rock music ($10 minimum) goes on 10 P.M.–4 A.M. during the winter season. The restaurant serves daily noon–midnight entrées, $8–16. It's on the beachfront about half a block on the driveway road west past the Hotel Posada Real.

For more of the same, but even more loud and outrageous, go to **Señor Frog's** in the shopping plaza, across from the Hotel Presidente Intercontinental.

In Zihuatanejo, at **Paccolo** bar, Bravo 38, just west of the corner of Guerrero, tel. 755/554-9116, a guitarist plays jazz melodies, from about 7 P.M. Thurs.–Sat. in season.

Dancing and Discoing

Many Ixtapa hotel lobbies blossom with dance music from around 7 P.M. during the high winter season. Year-round, however, good medium-volume groups usually play for dancing nightly from about 7 P.M. at the **Dorado Pacífico,** tel. 755/553-2025; the **Presidente Intercontinental,** tel. 755/553-0018; the **Barceló,** tel. 755/555-0000; and the **Las Brisas,** tel. 755/553-2121. Programs change, so call ahead to confirm.

Christine, Ixtapa's big-league discotheque in the Hotel NH Krystal, offers fantasy for a mere $10 cover charge. From 10 P.M., the patrons warm up by listening to relatively low-volume rock, watch videos, and talk while they can still hear each other. That stops around 11:30 P.M., when the fogs descend, the lights begin flashing, and the speakers boom forth their 200-decibel equivalent of a fast freight train roaring at trackside. Call to verify times, tel. 755/553-0333.

SPORTS AND RECREATION

Walking and Jogging

Zihuatanejo Bay is strollable from the Playa Madera all the way west to Puerto Mío. A relaxing half-day adventure could begin by taxiing to the Hotel Irma, Avenida Adelita, on Playa Madera, for breakfast. Don your hats and follow the stairs down to Playa Madera and walk west toward town. At the end of the Playa Madera sand, head left along the ***andador*** (walkway) that twists along the rocks, around the bend toward town. Continue along the beachfront Paseo del Pescador; at the west end, cross the lagoon bridge, head left along the bayside road to **Puerto Mío** for a drink at the hotel café and perhaps a dip in the pool. Allow three hours, including breakfast, for this two-mile walk; do the reverse trip during late afternoon for sunset drinks or dinner at the Irma.

Playa del Palmar, Ixtapa's main beach, is good for similar strolls. Start in the morning with breakfast at the Restaurant/Bar El Faro, atop the hill at the south end of the beach; open daily, mornings 6–11 A.M. (low season, 8:30–11 A.M., evenings 6–10 P.M. Ride the cableway or walk downhill. With the sun at your back stroll the beach, stopping for refreshments at the hotel pool-patios en route. The entire beach stretches about three miles to the marina jetty, where you can often watch surfers challenging the waves and where taxis and buses return along Paseo Ixtapa. Allow about four hours, including breakfast. The reverse walk would be equally enjoyable during the afternoon. Time yourself to arrive at the El Faro cableway (call ahead, tel. 755/553-1027, to make sure the cableway is running) about half an hour before sundown to enjoy the sunset over drinks or dinner. Get to El Faro by driving or taxiing via Paseo de la Roca, which heads uphill off the Zihuatanejo road at the golf course. Follow the first right fork to El Faro.

Adventurers who enjoy ducking through underbrush and scrambling over rocks might enjoy exploring the acacia forest and pristine beaches of the uninhabited west side of **Isla Ixtapa.** Take water, lunch, and a good pair of walking shoes.

Joggers often practice their art either on the smooth, firm sands of Ixtapa's main beachfront or on Paseo Ixtapa's sidewalks. Avoid crowds and midday heat by jogging early mornings or late afternoons. For even better beach jogging, try the flat, firm sands of uncrowded Playa Quieta about three miles by car or taxi northwest of Ixtapa. Additionally, mile-long Playa La Ropa can be enjoyed by early morning and late afternoon joggers.

Golf and Tennis

Ixtapa's 18-hole, professionally designed **Campo de Golf** is open to the public. In addition to its manicured, 6,898-yard course, patrons enjoy full facilities, including pool, restaurant, pro shop, lockers, and tennis courts. Greens fee runs $50, cart $30, club rental $22, 18 holes with caddy $16, and golf lessons $25 an hour. Play goes on daily 7 A.M.–3 P.M. The clubhouse, tel. 755/553-1062, is off Paseo Ixtapa, across from the Barceló. No reservations are accepted; morning golfers, get in line early during the high winter season.

The **Marina Golf Course,** tel. 755/553-1410 or 755/553-1424, offers similar services (greens fee $73, cart $68 for two, club rental $25, caddy $20) for higher prices.

Ixtapa has nearly all of the local **tennis** courts, all of them private. The Campo de Golf has some of the best. Rentals run about $5/hour days, $9 nights. Reservations, tel. 755/553-1062, may be seasonally necessary. A pro shop rents and sells equipment. A teaching professional offers lessons for about $25 per hour.

Several hotels also have tennis courts, equipment, and lessons. Call the **Barceló,** tel. 755/555-0000; **Dorado Pacífico,** tel. 755/553-2025; **NH Krystal,** tel. 755/553-0333; and the **Las Brisas,** tel. 755/553-2121, for information.

Horseback Riding

Rancho Playa Linda on Playa Linda rents horses daily for beach riding for about $15 per hour. Travel agencies and hotels offer the same, though for higher prices.

Bicycling

Ixtapa's hot new activity is bicycling along the new 10-mile round-trip *ciclopista* bike path to Playa Linda. Rental stations are along Paseo Ixtapa: in front of the Hotel Riviera by Banco Internacional, and east a couple of blocks, at the Las Fuentes shopping center parking lot, across from Hotel Fontana. Bargain for a discount from the steep $10/hour asking rate.

The *ciclopista* takes off north, across the street from the Banco Internacional rental station, at the Paseo Las Garzas intersection. Officially the *ciclopista* ends five miles west, at the wooden bridge and crocodile-viewing point at the Playa Linda parking lot, but you can go another 1.5 miles to Barra Vieja village at the lagoon's edge. Be sure to take a hat, water, and insect repellent.

Swimming and Surfing

Calm Zihuatanejo Bay is fine for swimming and sometimes good for boogie boarding and bodysurfing at Playa Madera. On Playa La Ropa, however, waves generally break too near shore for either bodysurfing or boogie boarding. Surfing is generally good at Playa Las Gatas, where swells sweeping around the south-end point give good, rolling left-handed breaks.

Heading northwest to more open coast, waves improve for bodysurfing and boogie boarding along Ixtapa's main beach Playa del Palmar, while usually remaining calm and undertow-free enough for swimming beyond the breakers. As for surfing, good breaks sometimes rise off the Playa Escolleros jetty at the west end of Playa del Palmar.

Along Ixtapa's outer beaches, swimming is great along very calm Playa Quieta; surfing, bodysurfing, and boogie boarding are correspondingly good but hazardous in the sometimes mountainous open-ocean surf of Playa Larga farther north.

Snorkeling and Scuba Diving

Clear offshore waters (sometimes up to 100-foot visibility during the dry winter-spring season) have drawn a steady flow of divers and nurtured professionally staffed and equipped dive shops. Just offshore, good snorkeling and scuba spots, where swarms of multicolored fish graze and glide among rocks and corals, are accessible from **Playa Las Gatas, Playa Hermosa,** and **Playa Carey** (on Isla Ixtapa).

Many boat operators take parties for offshore snorkeling excursions. On Playa La Ropa, contact the aquatics shop at the foot of the hill beneath Hotels Sotavento and Catalina. Playa Las Gatas, easily accessible by boat for $5 from the Zihuatanejo pier, also has snorkel and excursion boat rentals. In Ixtapa, similar services are available at beachside shops at the Hotels Las Brisas, Barceló, NH Krystal, and seasonally at other hotels.

Other even more spectacular offshore sites, such as Morros de Potosí, El Yunque, Bajo de Chato, Bajo de Torresillas, Piedra Soletaria, and Sacramento, are accessible with the help of professional guides and instructors.

A pair of local scuba dive shops stands out. In Zihuatanejo, marine biologist-instructor Juan M. Barnard Avila coordinates **Zihuatanejo Scuba Center** at his Hotel Paraíso Real, on Playa La Ropa, tel./fax 755/554-3873, 755/554-8156, or 755/554-2147, divemexico@email.com, www.divemexico.com. Licensed for instruction through NAUI (National Association of Underwater Instructors), Avila is among the Mexican Pacific coast's best-qualified professional instructors. Aided by loads of state-of-the-art equipment and several experienced licensed assistants, his shop has accumulated a long list of repeat customers. Avila's standard resort dive package, including a morning pool instruction session and an afternoon offshore half-hour dive, runs about $70 per person ($60 with your own gear) complete. Other services for beginners include open-water certification (one week of instruction, $450) and advanced NAUI certification up to assistant instructor. For certified divers (bring your certificate), Avila offers night, shipwreck, deep-water, and marine-biology dives at more than three dozen coastal sites. He's open Mon.–Sat. about noon–8 P.M.

Carlo Scuba, at Playa Las Gatas, also offers professional scuba services. The PADI-trained instructors offer a resort course, including one beach dive, for $60; a five-day open-water certification course, $400; and a two-tank dive trip for certified participants, $75, one-tank $50.It also conducts student referral courses and night dives. Contact the manager-owner, friendly Jean-Claude Duran (known locally as Jack Cousteau), on Las

Gatas beach, tel. 755/554-3570, fax 755/554-2810, zih@carloscuba.com, www.carloscuba.com.

Sailing, Sailboarding, and Kayaking

The tranquil waters of Zihuatanejo Bay, Ixtapa's Playa del Palmar, and the quiet strait off Playa Quieta are good for these low-power aquatic sports. Shops on Playa La Ropa (at Hotels Sotavento and Catalina) in Zihuatanejo Bay and in front of Ixtapa hotels, such as the Las Brisas Ixtapa, the Barceló, and the NH Krystal, rent small sailboats, sailboards, and kayaks hourly.

Fishing

Surf or rock casting with bait or lures, depending on conditions, is generally successful in local waters. Have enough line to allow casting beyond the waves (about 50 feet out on Playa La Ropa, 100 feet on Playa del Palmar and Playa Linda).

The rocky ends of Playas La Ropa, La Madera, del Palmar, and Las Gatas on the mainland and Playa Carey on Isla Ixtapa are also good for casting.

For deep-sea fishing, you can launch your own boat or rent one. *Pangas* are available for rent from individual fishermen on the beach, the boat cooperative at Zihuatanejo pier, or aquatics shops of the Hotel Sotavento on Playa La Ropa or the Hotels Las Brisas Ixtapa, Barceló, NH Krystal, and others on the beach in Ixtapa. Rental for a seaworthy *panga,* including tackle and bait, should run about $20 per hour, depending upon the season and your bargaining skill. An experienced boatman can help you and your friends hook, typically, six or eight big fish in about four hours, which local restaurants are often willing to serve as a small banquet for you in return for your extra fish.

Big-Game Sportfishing

Zihuatanejo has long been a center for billfish (marlin, swordfish, and sailfish) hunting. Most local captains have organized themselves into cooperatives, which visitors can contact either directly or through town or hotel travel agents. Trips begin around 7 A.M. and return 2–3 P.M. Fishing success depends on seasonal conditions. If you're not sure of your prospects, go down to the Zihuatanejo pier around 2:30 P.M. and see what the boats are bringing in. During good times they often return with one or more big marlin or swordfish per boat (although captains are increasingly asking that billfish be set free after the battle has been won). Fierce fighters, the sinewy billfish do not make the best eating and are often discarded after the pictures are taken. On average, boats bring in two or three other large fish, such as *dorado* (dolphinfish or mahimahi), yellowfin tuna, and roosterfish, all more highly prized for the dinner table.

The biggest local sportfishing outfitter is the blue and white fleet of the **Sociedad Cooperativa Teniente Azueta,** tel./fax 755/554-2056, named after the naval hero Lieutenant José Azueta. You can see adjacent to the Zihuatanejo pier many of its several dozen boats bobbing at anchor. Arrangements for fishing parties can be made through hotel travel desks or at its office, open daily 6 A.M.–6 P.M., at the foot of the pier. The largest 36-foot boats, with four or five lines, go out for a day's fishing for about $250 low season, $500 high. Twenty-five-foot boats with three lines run about $120 per day low season, $250 high. Smaller *pangas* go out for about $100 low season, $150 high.

The smaller (18-boat) **Servicios Sociedad Cooperativa Benito Juárez,** tel./fax 755/554-3758, tries harder by offering similar boats for lower prices. Its 36-foot boats for six start around $300; a 25-foot for four, about $150. Contact the office across from the naval compound, near the west end of Paseo del Pescador, open daily 9 A.M.–7 P.M.

On the adjacent corner, next door, at Paseo El Pescador 20, newest and trying even harder, is **Whiskey Water World,** Paseo del Pescador 20, tel./fax 755/554-0147, fax 755/554-0146, whiskey@prodigy.net.mx, www.zihuatanejosportfishing.com and www.ixtapasportfishing.com, which claims to employ only sober captains. Its top-of-the-line-only boats run from 30 feet and $250, including license, bait, and drinks. Jack Daniel's is extra. Captains will take two people fishing, from 7 A.M. to 2 P.M., for $40 apiece (six-person minimum). Proud members of the IGFA (International Game Fishing Association), captains follow sailfish, tuna, and *dorado* catch-and-release policy.

Prices quoted by providers often (but not necessarily) include fishing licenses, bait, tackle, and amenities such as beer, sodas, ice, and on-board toilets. Such details should be pinned down (ideally by inspecting the boat) before putting your money down.

Sportfishing Tournament

Twice a year, usually in May and January, Zihuatanejo fisherfolk sponsor the **Torneo de Pez Vela,** with prizes for the biggest catches of sailfish, swordfish, marlin, and other varieties. Entrance fee runs around $800, and the prizes usually include a new Dodge pickup, cars, and other goodies. For information, contact the local sportfishing cooperative, Sociedad Cooperativa Teniente José Azueta, Muelle Municipal, Zihuatanejo, Guerrero 40880, tel. 755/554-2056, or the fishing tournament coordinator, Crecencio Cortés, tel. 755/554-8423, or Whiskey Water World.

Marina and Boat Launching

Marina Ixtapa, at the north end of Paseo Ixtapa, offers excellent boat facilities. The slip charge runs about $.75 per foot per day, for 1–6 days ($.55 for 7–29 days), subject to a minimum charge per diem. This includes use of the boat ramp, showers, pump-out, electricity, trash collection, mailbox, phone, fax, and satellite TV. For reservations and information, contact the marina daily 9 A.M.–2 P.M. and 4–7 P.M., at the harbormaster's office in the marina-front white building on the right a block before the big white lighthouse, tel./fax 755/553-2180, marina0@prodigy.net.mx, or write Harbormaster, Marina Ixtapa, Ixtapa, Guerrero 40880.

The smooth, gradual Marina Ixtapa **boat ramp,** open to the public for an approximately $10 fee, is on the right-hand side street leading to the water, just past the big white lighthouse. Get your ticket beforehand from the harbormaster.

Sports Equipment Shops

Deportes Náuticos, corner of N. Bravo and Guerrero in downtown Zihuatanejo, tel. 755/554-4411, sells snorkel equipment, boogie boards, tennis racquets, balls, and a load of other general sporting goods. Open Mon.–Sat. 10 A.M.–2 P.M. and 4–9 P.M.

Pesca Deportiva (Sportfishing), on the other hand, specializes in fishing rods, reels, lines, weights, and lures. Open Mon.–Sat. 9 A.M.–2 P.M. and 4–7 P.M., at the far west end of Álvarez, corner of Armada de Mexico.

Other Practicalities

SHOPPING

Zihuatanejo

Every day is market day at the Zihuatanejo **Mercado** on Avenida Benito Juárez, four blocks from the beach. Behind the piles of leafy greens, round yellow papayas, and huge gaping sea bass, don't miss the sugar and spice stalls. There you will find big cones of raw *panela* (brown sugar), thick, homemade golden honey, mounds of fragrant *jamaica* petals, crimson dried *chiles,* and forest-gathered roots, barks, and grasses sold in the same pungent natural forms as they have been for centuries.

For more up-to-date merchandise, go to the nearby **Super de Zihuatanejo,** tel. 755/554-3634, on the side street bordering the market's north side. It's a typical sleepy Mexican country grocery, with shelves of canned vegetables, lots of good in-season fruit, and dusty back aisles piled with bags of sugar, beans, and salt; open Mon.–Sat. 7 A.M.–8 P.M. Next door, you can get about the same thing plus medications at the **Super y Farmacia Rosy,** tel. 755/554-8617.

For convenience shopping, the grocery **Adriana y Pancho,** at the plaza-front corner of Juan Álvarez and Cuauhtémoc, is one of the only stores in downtown Zihuatanejo with any food. Open Mon.–Sat. 9 A.M.–9 P.M.

Zihuatanejo's first supermarket-department store is the big **Comercial Mexicana** behind the Central Bus Station, on Highway 200, about a mile east of downtown, open daily 9 A.M.–9 P.M.

Ixtapa

Ixtapa's **Centro Comercial** mall complex stretches along the midsection of Paseo Ixtapa across from the hotels. It has four viable (of about 10 planned but still not functioning) and attractive subcomplexes, all fronting the boulevard. As you move east to west, first come the Los Patios and Fuentes subcomplexes, where minimarts, T-shirt and trinket shops, and super-expensive designer stores occupy the choice boulevard frontages. Behind them, dozens of mostly small and ordinary crafts and jewelry shops languish along back lanes and inside patios. More of the same occupies the La Puerta subcomplex 100 yards farther on. Next comes the police station, and, after that, the Galerías Ixtapa subcomplex at the corner of Paseo de las Garzas.

Don't miss the sugar and spice stalls at the Zihuatanejo Mercado. There you will find big cones of raw* panela *(brown sugar), thick, homemade golden honey, mounds of fragrant* jamaica *petals, crimson dried* chiles, *and forest-gathered roots, barks, and grasses.

Handicrafts Shopping

Although some stores in the Ixtapa Centro Comercial shopping center and the adjacent tourist market (across from the Hotel Barceló) offer handicrafts, Zihuatanejo offers the best selection and prices.

The Zihuatanejo **tourist market** stalls line the downtown's west side street, Calle 5 de Mayo. Vendors display a flood of crafts brought by families who come from all parts of the Mexican Pacific coast mainland states. Their goods—delicate Michoacán lacquerware, bright Tonalá birds, gleaming Taxco silver, whimsical Guerrero masks, rich Guadalajara leather—although common here, often make treasured souvenirs and gifts back home. Compare prices; although bargaining here is customary, the glut of merchandise makes it a one-sided buyer's market, with many sellers barely managing to scrape by. If you err in your bargaining, kindly do it on the generous side.

Prominent among individual downtown shops nearby is the **Casa Marina** shopping center, tel. 755/554-2373, a family project of late community leader Helen Krebs Posse. Her adult children and spouses own and manage stores in the two-story complex, just west of the beachfront town plaza.

Their original store, **Embarcadero,** on the lower floor, streetside, has an unusually choice collection of woven and embroidered finery, mostly from Oaxaca. In addition to walls and racks of colorful, museum-quality traditional blankets, flower-embroidered dresses, and elaborate crocheted *huipiles,* she also offers wooden folk-figurines and a collection of intriguing masks.

Other stores in the Casa Marina include **La Zapoteca** on the bottom floor, specializing in weavings from Teotitlán del Valle in Oaxaca. Others include **Metzli,** with all-Mexico resort wear, **Arte de la Tradición,** with a trove of lovely Talavera pottery, tel. 755/554-4625. Upstairs are **El Jumil** (silver and masks), **Latzotil** (Maya art), **El Calibria** (leather), and on the ground floor, facing the beach, the Cafe La Marina (pizza and used paperbacks). Local weavers demonstrate in the Embarcadero and La Zapoteca stores mornings and afternoons. The entire complex is open Mon.–Sat. approximately 10 A.M.–2 P.M. and 5–9 P.M.; credit cards are generally accepted.

A block west, toward the pier, **La Tienda de Ropa Típica,** on Paseo del Pescador, across from the naval compound, would be easy to pass because of its mounds of ho-hum T-shirts. But if you look inside, you'll find racks of many fetching hand-crocheted *huipiles* and blouses from backcountry Guerrero and Oaxaca. Open daily 8 A.M.–10 P.M.

Walk away from the beach, along Cinco de Mayo, past the church, to **Nopal** handicrafts, the labor of love of the owner, who likes things from Oaxaca, especially baskets. He fills his shop with an organized clutter, including unique woven goods and ceramics. Open Mon.–Sat. 9 A.M.–3 P.M. and 4:30–9 P.M. low season, Mon.–Sat. 9 A.M.–9 P.M. high season, tel./fax 755/554-7530.

Head back along Álvarez two blocks, past the

plaza, to **Cerámicas Tonalá,** 12B Álvarez, beach side, to view one of the finest Tonalá ceramics collections outside of the renowned source itself. Here, friendly owner Eduardo López's graceful glazed vases and plates, decorated in traditional plant and animal designs, fill the cabinets, while a menagerie of lovable owls, ducks, fish, armadillos, and frogs, all seemingly poised to spring to life, crowd the shelves. Open Mon.–Sat. 9 A.M.–2 P.M. and 4–8 P.M., tel. 755/554-2161; credit cards are accepted.

A few steps up Cuauhtémoc, **Alberto's** pair of shops, on opposite sides of the street, tel. 755/554-2161, offer an extensive silver jewelry collection. As with gold and precious stones, silver prices can be reckoned approximately by weighing, at between $1 and $1.25 per gram. The cases and cabinets of shiny earrings, chains, bracelets, rings, and much more, are products of a family of artists, taught by a master craftsman, now semiretired, in Puerto Vallarta. Many of the designs are original, and, with bargaining, reasonably priced. Open Mon.–Sat. 9 A.M.–8 P.M.; credit cards are accepted.

A block farther, at the corner of Ejido, step into **Rosimar,** the creation of Josefina and Manuel Martínez. Manuel's intriguing outside murals lead you inside to their eclectic, priced-to-sell collection of Tonalá and Tlaquepaque pottery, papier-mâché, and glassware.

At **Galería Maya,** on Cuauhtémoc farther from the beach, past Ejido, on the right, tel. 755/554-4606, owner Tania Scales has accumulated a multitude of one-of-a-kind folk curios from many parts of Mexico. Her wide-ranging, carefully selected collection includes masks, necklaces, sculptures, purses, blouses, *huipiles,* ritual objects, and much more. Open Mon.–Sat. 10 A.M.–2 P.M. and 5–9 P.M. Furthermore, be sure not to miss Tania's labor of love, several regal sculptures that represent a number of indigenous female deities: Ixta Bay, Maya jungle goddess; Coyolxauhqui, Aztec moon goddess; and Cihuateteo, representing all the women of Zihuatanejo.

Photography

In Zihuatanejo, **Foto 30** on Ejido, between Galeana and Guerrero, two blocks from the plaza, tel. 755/554-7610, offers 30-minute develop-and-print service and stocks lots of film and accessories. These include a host of cameras, including SLRs, and film, including 120 print, 35mm slide, and sheet film, plus filters, tripods, and flashes. Open Mon.–Sat. 9 A.M.–8 P.M., Sunday 10 A.M.–2 P.M.

In Ixtapa, **Foto Quick,** in shopping center Galerias Ixtapa, across the boulevard from Hotel Riviera, offers approximately the same products and services.

INFORMATION

Tourist Information Office

The Ixtapa state-federal office of **Turismo,** tel. 755/553-1967 or 755/553-1968, answers questions and dispenses literature and maps Mon.–Fri. 8 A.M.–8 P.M., Saturday 8 A.M.–2 P.M. Find it in the Ixtapa La Puerta shopping complex, across the boulevard from the Hotel Presidente Intercontinental.

Publications

The best local English-language book and magazine selection fills the many shelves of the **Hotel Las Brisas** shop. Besides dozens of new paperback novels and scores of popular U.S. magazines, it stocks *USA Today* and the *News* of Mexico City and a small selection of Mexico coffee table books of cultural and historical interest. Open daily 9 A.M.–9 P.M.

The **newsstand,** west side of the Zihuatanejo plaza, is a customary source of popular U.S. magazines, such as *Vogue, Time,* and *Sports Illustrated,* plus the newspapers *News* of Mexico (around 1 P.M.), the Miami *Herald,* and *USA Today.* Open daily 8 A.M.–8 P.M.

Many used paperbacks fill the bookshelf at friendly **Cafe Marina** adjacent to the beach just west of the plaza; open Mon.–Sat. till 10 P.M., closed June to mid-September.

The small Zihuatanejo **Biblioteca** (public library) also has some shelves of English-language paperbacks. Open Mon.–Fri. 9 A.M.–8 P.M., Saturday 9 A.M.–5 P.M.; on Cuauhtémoc, five blocks from the beach.

Ecological Associations and Humane Society

The grassroots **Asociación de Ecologistas** sponsors local cleanup, tree-planting, save-the-turtles, and other projects. For information, contact the society's president, architect Edgar Morales, tel. 755/553-1858, or Anita Hahner Rellstab, owner of Bungalows Pacífico, tel. 755/554-2112.

In Ixtapa, volunteers of **Eco-Ixtapa** concentrate their efforts on a community recycling project. For information, contact leader Carmen Huras, tel. 755/553-1758.

The family members of the late Helen Krebs Posse are the guiding lights of the **Sociedad Protectora de Animales,** tel. 755/555-7227 or 755/555-6191, fax 755/555-3533, www.zihuatanejo.net/spaz, which is working hard to educate people about animal issues. Contact one of the family members, at the family's shop complex, Casa Marina, just west of the Zihuatanejo plaza, tel. 755/554-2373.

SERVICES

Money Exchange

Several banks, all with ATMs, clustered east of downtown of Juárez, serve customers. Go to **Banamex,** tel. 755/554-7293 or 755/554-7294, at the corner of Guerrero and Ejido, two blocks from the beach, open for money exchange Mon.–Fri. 9 A.M.–5 P.M., Saturday 9 A.M.–2 P.M. If the Banamex lines are too long, use the ATM or walk three blocks east, to **Bancomer,** tel. 755/554-7492 or 755/554-7493, open Mon.–Fri. 9 A.M.–5 P.M., Saturday 10 A.M.–2 P.M., or **Banco Serfin,** tel. 755/554-3941, open Mon.–Fri. 9 A.M.–4 P.M., both near the corner of Bravo and Juárez.

After hours, go around the corner to the **Casa de Cambio Guibal,** tel. 755/554-3522, fax 755/554-2800 (with long-distance telephone and fax), at Galeana and Asencio, two blocks from the beach, to change U.S., Canadian, French, German, Swiss, and other currencies and traveler's checks. For the convenience, it offers you a few percent less for your money than the banks. Open daily 8 A.M.–9 P.M.

In Ixtapa, for long money-changing hours, go to **Banco Internacional,** in front of the Hotel Riviera right on Paseo Ixtapa, tel. 755/553-0641, 755/553-0642, or 755/553-0646. Open Mon.–Fri. 8 A.M.–7 P.M., Saturday 8 A.M.–3 P.M. Alternatively, go to **Bancomer** in the Los Portales complex behind the shops across the boulevard from the Hotel Presidente Intercontinental, tel. 755/553-2112, 755/553-0535, or 755/553-0525, open Mon.–Fri. 8:30 A.M.–4 P.M.

The local **American Express** branch in the Hotel NH Krystal sells and cashes American Express traveler's checks and provides travel agency services to the public. For card-carrying members, it provides full money services, such as check-cashing. Hours are Mon.–Fri. 9 A.M.–6 P.M., Saturday 9 A.M.–1 P.M. Money services hours may be shorter. Call for confirmation, tel. 755/553-0853, fax 755/553-1206.

Communications

The only ***correo*** (post office), tel. 755/554-2192, serving both Zihuatanejo and Ixtapa is in Zihuatanejo at the Centro Federal, in the northeast corner of downtown, five blocks from the beach about three blocks east of the Ixtapa minibus stop at Juárez and Morelos. Open Mon.–Fri. 8 A.M.–3 P.M., Saturday 9 A.M.–1 P.M. Also in the post office is a suboffice of the very reliable government **Mexpost** (like U.S. Express Mail) upgraded, secure mail service.

Next door is **Telecomunicaciones,** which offers long-distance telephone, public fax 755/554-2163, telegrams, and money orders Mon.–Fri. 8 A.M.–7 P.M. Another similar telecommunications office serves Ixtapa, in the La Puerta shopping center (rear side), across Paseo Ixtapa from the Hotel Presidente Intercontinental.

Money-changer Casa de Cambio Guibal is also downtown Zihuatanejo's private ***larga distancia*** telephone and fax office, on Galeana, the lane parallel to Cuauhtémoc, corner of Bravo, tel./fax 755/554-3522. Open daily 8 A.M.–9 P.M.

In both Ixtapa and Zihuatanejo, many streetside public phone booths provide economical national and international long distance service, using Ladatel telephone cards (call the United States for about $1 per three minutes). Cards are readily available in grocery, drug, and liquor stores everywhere. First dial 001 for calls to the United

States and Canada, and 01 for Mexico long distance. Lacking a Ladatel card, use your personal telephone credit card. Dial tel. 001-800/462-4240 for the English-speaking AT&T international operator, 001-800/674-6000 for MCI.

Health and Emergencies

For medical consultations in English, contact U.S.-trained **IAMAT associate** Dr. Rogelio Grayeb, in Zihuatanejo, at Bravo 71A, beach side, between Guerrero and Galeana, tel. 755/554-3334, 755/553-1711, or 755/554-2040, cell tel. 044-755/551-3335, fax 755/554-5041.

Another Zihuatanejo medical option is the very professional **Clínica Maciel,** which has a dentist, pediatrician, gynecologist, surgeon, and general practitioner on 24-hour call, at 12 Palmas, two blocks east, one block north of the market, tel. 755/554-2380 or 755/554-0517.

Neither Ixtapa nor Zihuatanejo has any state-of-the art private hospitals. However, many local people recommend the state of Guerrero ***hospital general,*** on Avenida Morelos, corner of Mar Egeo, just off from Highway 200, tel. 755/554-3965, 755/554-3650, or 755/554-3436, for its generally competent, dedicated, and professional staff.

For medicines and drugs in Ixtapa, ask your hotel desk to put you in contact with a *farmacia.* Alternatively, call one of the many pharmacies in downtown Zihuatanejo, such as the **Farmacia La Principal,** corner of Cuauhtémoc and Ejido, two blocks from the beachfront plaza, tel. 755/554-4217; open Mon.–Sat. 9 A.M.–9 P.M.

For police emergencies in Ixtapa and Zihuatanejo, contact the ***cabercera de policía*** headquarters in Zihuatanejo, on Calle Limón, near Highway 200, tel. 755/554-2040. Usually more accessible are the police officers at the ***caseta de policía*** 24-hour police booth at the Zihuatanejo plaza-front, and in Ixtapa on Paseo Ixtapa, across from the Hotel Presidente Intercontinental. On Playa La Ropa, go to the small police station on the Paseo Costera, at the north-end intersection by the Hotel Villa del Sol.

Immigration and Customs

If you lose your tourist permit, go to **Migración,** on Avenida Colegio Militar, about five blocks north of Plaza Kyoto, on the northeast edge of downtown, tel. 755/554-2795; open Mon.–Fri. 9 A.M.–3 P.M. Bring your passport and some proof of the date you arrived in Mexico, such as your airline ticket, stamped passport, or a copy of your lost tourist permit. Although it's not wise to let such a matter go until the last day, you may be able to accomplish the needed paperwork at the airport Migración office (open daily 8 A.M.–6 P.M.). Call first, however, tel. 755/554-8480.

The **Aduana** (Customs) office, tel. 755/554-3262, is at the airport, off Highway 200 about seven miles south of Zihuatanejo, open daily 9 A.M.–7 P.M. If you have to temporarily leave the country without your car, have someone fluent in Spanish call about the required paperwork, if any.

Tour Guides

A number of reliable local agents arrange and/or guide local excursions. One of the most experienced all-around is **Turismo International del Pacifico,** in downtown Zihuatanejo, corner of Álvarez and Benito Juárez, tel. 755/554-7510, fax 755/554-7509, tipzihua@prodigy.net.mx, www.ixtapa-zihuatanejo.com. In Ixtapa, contact it in the Plaza Los Patios Shopping Center, Local L123, tel. 755/553-1081, fax 755/553-1173.

Off-the-beaten-track adventuring, including bird-watching, archaeological sites, and local culture is the specialty of guides Carlos and Elsa Pérez, of **CarElsy Guided Tours,** in Zihuatanejo. Contact them at tel. 755/554-4684, cell tel. 755/557-0553, email carelsy@prodigy.net.mex, www.zihua.net/carelsy.

Laundry and Dry Cleaning

In Zihuatanejo, take your laundry to the **Laundry Super-Clean** at Gonzáles and Galeana, just off Cuauhtémoc, four blocks from the plaza, tel. 755/554-2347; open Mon.–Sat. 8 A.M.–8 P.M. Alternatively, go to **Lavanderia Express,** on Cuauhtémoc, around the corner, a few doors toward the beach, open daily 8 A.M.–8 P.M.

If you also need something dry-cleaned, take both it and your laundry items to **Lavandería Premium,** on Cuauhtémoc, across the street from Super Clean, open daily 8:30 A.M.–8 P.M.

GETTING THERE AND AWAY

By Air

Four major carriers connect Ixtapa-Zihuatanejo directly with U.S. and Mexican destinations year-round; two more operate during the fall-winter season.

Many **Aeroméxico** flights connect daily with Mexico City, and one with Guadalajara, where connections with U.S. destinations may be made. For reservations, call tel. 755/554-2018 or 755/554-2019; for flight information, call tel. 755/554-2237 or 755/554-2634.

Mexicana Airlines flights connect directly with Mexico City. For reservations, call tel. 755/554-2208 or 755/554-2209; for flight information, call tel. 755/554-2227.

Alaska Airlines connects with Los Angeles, San Francisco, and Seattle. Call a travel agent or toll-free Mex. or U.S. tel. 800/426-0333 for flight information and reservations.

America West Airlines connects with Phoenix. Call a travel agent or toll-free Mex. or U.S. tel. 800/235-9292 for flight information and reservations.

Continental Airlines connects with Houston seasonally during the late fall, winter, and spring. Call a travel agent or toll-free Mex. tel. 800/900-5000 for flight information and reservations.

Canadian World of Vacations charter flights connect with Toronto and perhaps other Canadian gateways during the fall, winter, and spring. Call a travel agent, such as American Express, tel. 755/553-0853, for reservations, or visit www.worldofvacations.com.

Air Arrival and Departure

Ixtapa-Zihuatanejo is quickly accessible, only seven miles (11 km) north of the airport via Highway 200. Arrival is generally simple—if you come with a day's worth of pesos and hotel reservations. Although the terminal does have an ATM (by the exit door near the car rentals), it has neither tourist information booth nor hotel-reservation service. Best arrive with a hotel reservation and not leave the choice up to your taxi driver, who will probably deposit you at the hotel that pays him a commission on your first night's lodging.

Transportation to town is usually by *taxi especial* (private taxi) or *colectivo* van. Tickets are available at booths near the terminal exit. Tariff for a *colectivo* is $6–9 per person (depending on destination); for a taxi, $19–26 for three or four people. Taxis to Troncones run about $48. Mobile budget travelers can walk the few hundred yards to the highway and flag down one of the frequent daytime Zihuatanejo-bound buses (very few, if any, continue to Ixtapa, however). At night, spend the money on *colectivo* or taxi.

Several major **car rental** companies staff airport arrival booths. Avoid problems and save money by negotiating your car rental through the agencies' toll-free numbers before departure. Agents include Hertz, tel. 755/554-3050 or 755/554-2590; Budget, tel. 755/554-4837 or 755/553-0397; and Alamo, tel. 755/553-0206.

Departure is quick and easy if you have your passport, tourist permit (which was stamped on arrival), and $19 cash (or the equivalent in pesos) international departure tax if your air ticket doesn't already cover it. Departees who've lost their tourist permits can avoid trouble and a fine by either getting a duplicate at Zihuatanejo Immigration or (perhaps) by having a stamped passport, a copy of the lost permit, or at least some proof of their date of arrival, such as an airline ticket.

For last-minute postcards and shopping, the airport has a mailbox and a several gift shops and a pretty fair magazine stand.

By Car or RV

Three routes, two easy and one unsafe and not recommended, connect Ixtapa-Zihuatanejo with Playa Azul and Michoacán to the northwest, Acapulco to the southeast, and Ciudad Altamirano and central Guerrero to the northeast.

Traffic sails smoothly along the 76 miles (122 km) of Highway 200, either way, between Zihuatanejo and Lázaro Cárdenas/Playa Azul. Allow about two hours. Several miles before Lázaro Cárdenas the new Highway 37 D *cuota* toll expressway allows easy access to highland central Michoacán (190 miles, 312 km, 4.5 hours to Uruapan, add another hour to Pátzcuaro) from Zihuatanejo. The same is true of the 150-mile

(242-km, allow four hours) Highway 200 southern extension to Acapulco.

The story is much different, however, for the winding, sparsely populated, cross-sierra Highway 134 (intersecting with Highway 200 nine miles north) from Zihuatanejo to Ciudad Altamirano. Rising through vine-hung, jungly foothills, the paved but sometimes potholed road leads over cool, pine-clad heights and descends to the rich Altamirano oasis river valley after about 100 miles (160 km). The continuing leg to Iguala and the Acapulco-Mexico City highway is longer, about 112 miles (161 km), equally winding and often busy. Allow about eight hours westbound and nine hours eastbound for the entire trip. Keep filled with gasoline, and be prepared for emergencies, especially along the Altamirano-Zihuatanejo leg, where no hotels and few services exist. *Warning:* In the past, this route has been plagued by robberies and nasty drug-related incidents. Inquire locally—your hotel, the tourist information office, the bus station—to see if authorities have secured the road before attempting this trip.

By Bus

Zihuatanejo's big, shiny long-distance Estrella Blanca ***Central de Autobús*** bus station is on Highway 200, Acapulco-bound side, about a mile southeast of downtown Zihuatanejo. Travelers have the use of a Sendatel public long-distance phone/fax and hotel reservations agency (for certain hotels only), a left-luggage service and a small snack bar. You should prepare by stocking up with water and goodies before you depart.

Estrella Blanca (EB), tel. 755/554-3477, the major carrier, computer-coordinates the service of its subsidiaries Flecha Roja (FR), Elite (EL), Futura (FU), and Autotransportes Cuauhtémoc. Tickets are available with cash or credit cards for all departures from computer-assisted agents. In total, they offer luxury class (infrequent, super-first-class, reserved), first class (frequent, reserved), and second class (very frequent, unreserved) service.

Most buses run along the Highway 200 corridor, connecting with Lázaro Cárdenas/Playa Azul and northwestern points, and with Acapulco and points south and east.

Several luxury- and first-class buses and many (every half hour) second-class buses connect daily with Acapulco. Several of them continue to Mexico City, and at least one continues east along the Oaxaca coast all the way to Salina Cruz. In the opposite direction, many luxury-, first-, and second-class buses (at least one an hour) connect daily with Lázaro Cárdenas, Playa Azul, and northwest points.

A number of departures also connect, along the Pacific coast Highway 200 corridor, southeast with Acapulco and the Oaxaca coast, and northwest via Manzanillo, Puerto Vallarta, and Mazatlán, to the U.S. border at Mexicali and Tijuana. At least one daily departure connects north with Michoacán points of Uruapan and Morelia, via the new expressway.

Another major bus carrier, **Estrella de Oro,** tel. 755/554-2175, offers a few competing long-distance first-class connections east along the coast via Acapulco, thence inland, via Chilpancingo, Iguala, and Taxco, with Mexico City. Its station is on the highway, next to the Estrella Blanca Central de Autobus.

South of Ixtapa-Zihuatanejo

This trio of pocket paradises, less than a half hour southeast of Zihuatanejo, long known by local people, are now being discovered by a growing cadre of off-the-beaten-track seekers of heaven on earth. Taken together, they offer a feast of quiet south-seas delights: good fishing, beachcombing, camping, wildlife-viewing, and comfortable, reasonably priced lodgings.

Playa Las Pozas, a surf-fishing and seafood haven, is reachable via the Zihuatanejo airport road. A pair of palm-shaded bungalows offers comfortable accommodation. Playa Blanca, a mile farther southeast, is a long, lovely golden-sand beach, decorated by a lovely petite designer hotel and restaurant. A few miles farther, Barra de Potosí village offers the ingredients of a heavenly one-day or one-week tropical excursion: palm-shaded seafood *palapas,* room for tent or RV camping, stores for supplies, a wildlife-rich mangrove lagoon, and a long beach, ripe for swimming, surfing, fishing, and beachcombing. A pair of petite bed-and-breakfast lodgings and a downscale beachfront hotel offer accommodation.

PLAYA LAS POZAS AND PLAYA BLANCA

Playa Las Pozas

Playa Las Pozas rewards visitors with a lagoon full of bait fish, space for RV or tent camping (be careful of soft sand), a wide beach, and friendly beachside *palapa* restaurants. The beach itself is 100 yards wide, of yellow-white sand, and extends for miles in both directions. It has driftwood but not many shells. Fish thrive in its thunderous, open-ocean waves. Consequently, casts from the beach can yield five-pound catches by either bait or lures. Local folks catch fish mostly by net, both in the surf and the nearby lagoon. During the June–Sept. rainy season, the lagoon breaks through the bar. Big fish, gobbling prey at the outlet, can be netted or hooked at the same spot themselves.

Camping is popular here on weekends and holidays. Other times you may have the place to yourself. As a courtesy, ask the friendly Neto family restaurant (on the west end, by the lagoon), the best of the *palapa* restaurants, if it's okay to camp nearby.

Rustic accommodations have arrived at Playa Las Pozas through the ingenuity of builder Jeffry Meyers, who has erected a pair of tropical "Treetops" bungalows beside a beachside swimming pool. Rentals run about $90 per night for two, discounts may be available for longer stays. If you're bringing kids under 15, he asks that you rent both bungalows. For reservations, contact him at tel. 755/554-8278 or treetopsbeach@hotmail.com. For more information, visit www.zihua.net/treetops. He closes approximately June–October.

Get to Playa Las Pozas by following the well-marked airport turnoff road at Km 230. After one mile, turn right before the cyclone wire fence just before entering the terminal complex and follow the bumpy but easily passable straight level road 1.1 miles (1.8 km) to the beach.

Playa Blanca and Hotel Las Palmas

In 2001, friendly but savvy and hardworking owner-builders from Phoenix, Arizona, decided to create heaven on lazy, lovely Playa Blanca. The result was Hotel Las Palmas, replete with precious architecture-as-art, including polished natural tree trunk–beamed ceilings, elegant Mexican hardwood shutters, and massive overhanging thatched *palapa* roofs. A recipe for paradise? Yes, but even more: a big blue pool, good restaurant and bar, all set in cool green grassy grounds overlooking a long, creamy, yellow-white strand. Their six super-comfortable, hand-crafted rooms, four with a/c, two with ceiling fans, rent for $175 d high season, $125 low (June–Oct.), with breakfast, but without TV, phones, credit cards, or kids under 18. Reserve directly at the hotel, tel. 755/557-0634, hotellaspalmas@hotmail.com. Reservations are also possible through the owners' Arizona agent, Gold Coast Travel, fax 602/253-3487, goldcoasttravel@hotmail.com. For more information, visit www.zihuatanejo.net/laspalmas. Get there by continuing about 1.5 miles (2.5 km) along the beach road from Playa Las Pozas to Playa Blanca and Hotel Las Palmas.

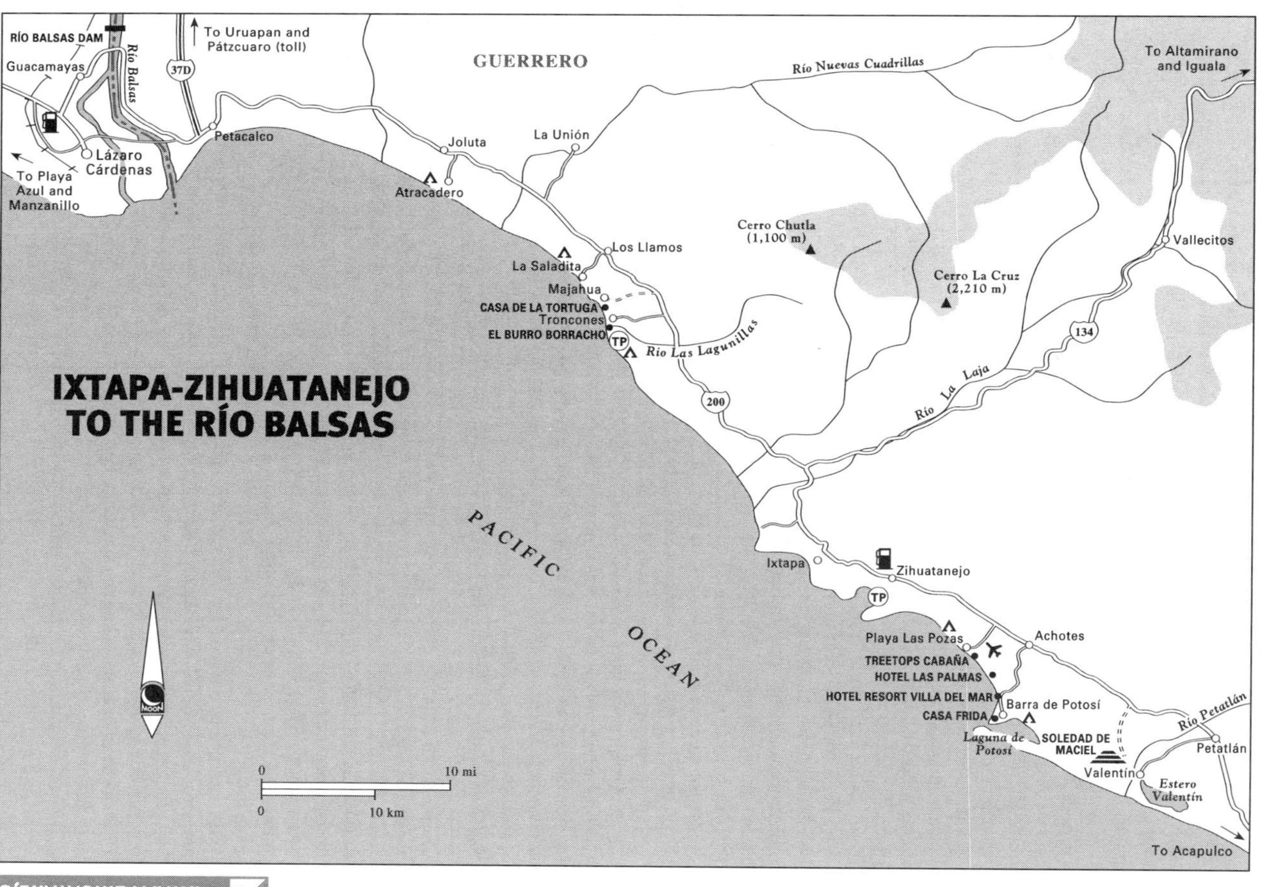
IXTAPA-ZIHUATANEJO
TO THE RÍO BALSAS
RÍO BALSAS DAM
Guacamayas
Río Balsas
To Uruapan and Pátzcuaro (toll)
37D
GUERRERO
Río Nuevas Cuadrillas
To Altamirano and Iguala
Petacalco
Lázaro Cárdenas
To Playa Azul and Manzanillo
Joluta
La Unión
Atracadero
Cerro Chutla (1,100 m)
Los Llamos
Vallecitos
La Saladita
Cerro La Cruz (2,210 m)
Majahua
CASA DE LA TORTUGA
Troncones
EL BURRO BORRACHO
TP
Río Las Lagunillas
134
Río La Laja
200
PACIFIC OCEAN
Ixtapa
Zihuatanejo
Playa Las Pozas
Achotes
TREETOPS CABAÑA
HOTEL LAS PALMAS
HOTEL RESORT VILLA DEL MAR
Barra de Potosí
CASA FRIDA
Laguna de Potosí
SOLEDAD DE MACIEL
Río Petatlán
Petatlán
Valentín
Estero Valentín
To Acapulco
0
10 mi
10 km
MOON

BARRA DE POTOSÍ

At Achotes, on Highway 200, nine miles (15 km) south of Zihuatanejo, a Laguna de Potosí sign points right to Barra de Potosí, a picture-perfect fishing hamlet at the sheltered south end of the Bahía de Potosí. After a few miles through green, tufted groves, the paved road parallels the bayside beach, a crescent of fine white sand, with a scattering of houses and one modest beachfront hotel.

The waves become even more tranquil at the beach's southeast end, where a sheltering headland rises beyond the village and the adjacent broad lagoon. Beneath its swaying palm grove, the hamlet of Barra de Potosí (pop. 1,000) has the ingredients for weeks of tranquil living. Several broad, hammock-hung *palapa* restaurants (here called *enramadas*) front the bountiful lagoon.

Sights and Recreation

Home for flocks of birds and waterfowl and shoals of fish, the **Laguna de Potosí** stretches for miles to its far mangrove reaches. Adventure out with your own boat or kayak, or go with Orlando, who regularly takes parties out for fishing or wildlife-viewing tours. Bring water, a hat, and insect repellent.

Bait fish, caught locally with nets, abound in the lagoon. Fishing is fine for bigger catches (jack, snapper, mullet) by boat or casts beyond the waves. Launch your boat easily in the lagoon, then head, like the local fishermen, past the open sandbar.

Accommodations and Food

In the village, a pair of bed-and-breakfast-style hotels offer lodging. First consider the charming flower-bedecked **Casa del Encanto** (House of Enchantment) on a village side street; ask for owner Laura Nolo. She rents her lovingly decorated rooms for about $65 d, high season (Nov.–May), $45 low, including private hot-water bath and full breakfast. For reservations, contact tel. 755/556-8199 or lauragecko@hotmail.com. For more information, visit www.casdelencanto.com.

Beneath the plumy grove nearby, guests at **Casa Frida,** life project of Mexican-French couple Annabel and François, enjoy fondly decorated rooms within a charmingly compact pool-patio garden. Room furnishings, based on a Frida Kahlo theme, include handcrafted art and furniture, mosquito curtains over the double beds, and bright Talavera-tiled hot-water bathrooms. Rates run about $75 d, including breakfast; adults only, no pets, closed May 1–Nov. 1. For reservations, call cell tel. 755/556-3944 (inside Mexico, first dial 044) or email casa-frida@zihuatanejo.net. For more information, visit www.barra-de-potosi.com/casafrida or www.zihuatanejo.net.

About a mile out of the village, back toward Zihuatanejo, the downscale **Hotel Resort Barra de Potosí,** tel. 755/554-8290, cell tel. 044-755/557-7259, fax 755/554-3445, perches right on the beach. The surf is generally tranquil and safe for swimming near the hotel, although the waves, which do not roll but break rather quickly along long fronts, do not appear good for surfing. The hotel, once neglected, has been largely restored. Rooms have been renovated and the pool has been returned to a brilliant blue. The owner says that the restaurant will be open during the high winter season, but will close during the low summer and fall. The beach, nevertheless, remains inviting year-round. Kitchenette apartments rent for about $50, studios $40, but with only tepid room-temperature water. All lamps are bare-bulb; bring your own lampshade or booklight.

Camping is common by RV or tent along the uncrowded edge of the lagoon.

Village stores can provide basic supplies. Prepared food is available at about a dozen permanent lagoon-side *palapa* restaurants. **Restaurant Teresita** is especially recommended.

For more information about Barra de Potosí, visit www.barra-de-potosi.com.

Getting There and Away

Get to Barra de Potosí by following the signed turnoff road from Highway 200, at Km 225, nine miles (14 km) south of Zihuatanejo, just south of the Los Achotes River bridge. Continue along the good mostly paved road; pass the hotel at Mile 5 (Km 8) and continue to the village at Mile 5.5 (Km 8.9).

(Alternatively, get to Barra de Potosí by continuing east about three miles along the beach road from Hotel Las Palmas at Playa Blanca.)

North of Ixtapa-Zihuatanejo

Visitors to Troncones and Majahua (mah-HAH-wah), in addition to a long, pristine, coral-studded beach, can also enjoy the natural delights of small kingdom of forested, wildlife-rich hinterland that stretches for miles above and behind the beach. While Troncones has acquired a modicum of modern travel amenities, including a number of restful bed-and-breakfast inns and gourmet restaurants, Majahua remains charmingly rustic.

TRONCONES

Troncones (pop. 750) has a little bit of everything: shady seafood *ramadas,* cozy seaside inns, restaurants, a small trailer park, and room to park your RV or set up a tent by the beach. Most folks arriving get there from Ixtapa-Zihuatanejo via the side road off of Highway 200 about 20 miles north of Ixtapa.

© BRUCE WHIPPERMAN

At Troncones, a lush beachfront forest embellishes the already lovely tropical ambience.

But that's just the beginning. Troncones has acquired a growing colony of North Americans, some of whom operate small accommodations for lovers of peace, quiet, and the outdoors. Besides lazing in hammocks and sunning on the sand, guests at all Troncones lodgings share the same luscious shoreline. You can swim, surf, bodysurf, and boogie board the waves, jog along the sand, explore a limestone cave, and thrill to a treetops cable adventure in the adjacent jungle hinterland. Back by the shore, you can beachcomb to your heart's content while enjoying views of the wildlife trove—fish, whales (Dec.–March), dolphins, turtles (Nov.–Jan.), swarms of herons, boobies, egrets, and cormorants—that abounds in the ocean and in nearby lagoons.

Accommodations and Food

Virtually all Troncones accommodations fall into the $50–100 category. As you move northwest (from the entrance road, turn right at the beach) after the bridge, first comes **Casa Ki,** the life project of Ed and Ellen Weston, P.O. Box 405, Zihuatanejo, Guerrero 40880, tel. 755/553-2815, casaki@yahoo.com, www.casa-ki.com. Casa Ki (named after the Japanese word for energy and wholeness), offers three immaculate, charmingly rustic cottages, tucked in the Westons' lovingly tended seaside garden compound. Each cottage sleeps approximately two adults and two children and comes with shower, toilet, fans, and a refrigerator. Guests share a shady outside cooking and dining *palapa.* High-season (Nov. 1–April 30) rentals run $75 s, $85 d (approximately $60, $70 low season) for the three cottages, including full breakfast. Ed and Ellen also rent a lovely two-bedroom, two-bath house that sleeps up to six, with full kitchen and daily maid service, for about $165 high, $130 low. Get your winter reservations in early.

After another quarter mile find **Casa de la Tortuga,** the original Troncones lodging, built by friendly pioneer Dewey McMillin during the late 1980s. Now, his guests enjoy a clean room (some with shared bath) and breakfast in their rustic-modern beach house, a restful patio with plenty of shade, quiet, and opportunities for delighting in the outdoors. During the Nov. 1–April 30 high season, room rentals run about $50 s or d, with shared bath; $75 s or d, with private bath, all with breakfast. A kitchen is available for guest use. No children under 12, unless you rent the whole place. The entire layout (sleeping a dozen or more) rents, high season, for about $350/day, $2,000/week, $7,500/month, with staff; guests supply their own food. Rates during the low May–Oct. season are discounted about 20 percent. Write, fax, or email early for reservations (mandatory during the winter) at P.O. Box 37, Zihuatanejo, Guerrero 40880, tel./fax 755/553-2862, casdelatortuga@yahoo.com. If business is too slow, Casa de la Tortuga closes June, July, and August. For more information, visit www.casadelatortuga.net.

Continuing another half mile, you'll find one of the newer additions to Troncones, the **Inn at Manzanillo Bay,** owner-chef Michael Bensal's plumy haven of eight rustic-style *palapa*-roofed cabanas, comfortably furnished with deluxe amenities, set around a luscious blue swimming pool and leafy patio. Here you can have it all: a gently curving, wave-washed surfable shoreline, with the murmur of the billows at night and plenty of hammock time by day. There's a good restaurant and even TV if you want it. All this from about $88 d high season, $68 low. Reserve by tel./fax 755/553-2883 or manzanillobay@aol.com. For more information, visit www.manzanillobay.com.

Finally, 100 yards farther along the beach, you arrive at the six-room **Eden Beach Hacienda and Caña del Sol Restaurant,** which shares the same luscious tropical forest oceanfront as all the other lodgings. The amenities include 10 immaculate lodgings, six in the main house and four open to the air in the detached beachfront house, all invitingly decorated in stucco and Talavera tile, with king-sized beds and private hot-water bathrooms. High-season rates (Jan.–Oct.) run $65–85 d, in the main house, $85–95 on the beachfront, including breakfast. Rates drop to $65 for all rooms Nov. 1–Dec. 20. Make reser-

© BRUCE WHIPPERMAN

Every day seems to be Sunday along the restful oceanfront of Casa de la Tortuga in Troncones.

vations directly at tel. 755/553-2884, cell tel. 044-755/556-5879, fax 755/553-2883, evaandjim@aol.com, or in the United States by mail at 41 Riverview Dr., Oak Ridge, TN 37830, fax 801/340-9883. For more information, visit www.edenmex.com. Star of the Eden show is chef Christian Shirmer, American graduate of the Baltimore culinary academy, whose menus feature traditional Mexican cuisine with a nouveau flair, focusing on fresh ingredients and seasonal foods. At least, stop in for lunch or dinner and meet Christian and Eva Robbins and Jim Garrity, the builder-owners.

At the opposite, southeast end of the Troncones beach, **El Burro Borracho** (The Drunken Burro) beachfront *palapa* restaurant and inn has become a favorite stopping place for the growing cadre of daytime visitors who are venturing out from Ixtapa and Zihuatanejo. Here, owner Dewey McMillin continues the standard set by former owner/chef Michael Bensal, with spicy shrimp tacos, rum-glazed ribs, jumbo shrimp grilled with coconut-curry sauce, and broiled pork chops with mashed potatoes. Besides the shady ocean-view *palapa* restaurant, Burro Borracho offers six "elegantly simple" airy rooms, each with bath, in three stone duplex beachfront cottages. Extras include king-sized bed, rustic-chic decor, hot water, and fans. Shared cooking facilities are also available. Sports and activities include swimming, surfing, and boogie boarding, plus kayaks, for use of guests. Room rentals run about $60 d high season, $35 low, with continental breakfast. Facilities also include five (shadeless) RV spaces, with all hookups, adjacent to the cottages for about $15 per night. Discounts are negotiable for long-term rentals. Write, telephone, or fax for reservations (mandatory in winter) at P.O. Box 37, Zihuatanejo, Guerrero 40880, tel./fax 755/553-2834, cell tel. 044-755/553-0732.

For more choices, consider some of the platoon of newer bed-and-breakfast inns, hotels, and vacation rental houses that have recently sprouted on the Troncones beachfront. For example, they include a cluster of jointly managed houses—**Casa Alegria, Casa Canela, La Canelita,** and **Santa Benita**—with rentals varying from individual rooms to whole houses, from $25 to $125, tel. 755/553-2800, fax 755/553-2807, www.troncones.com.mx/alegria; **Hotel and Restaurant Atlantis,** deluxe suites, $95–125, tel. 755/553-2889, www.atlantis-troncones.com; **Casa Colorida,** deluxe suites, $175–245, U.S. tel. (Colorado) 303/400-5442, www.casacolorida.com; **Casa de Helen,** luxurious three-bedroom house, $125–225, tel. 755/553-2800, www.tronconeshelen.com. For much more information on the above rentals and many more, see www.troncones.com.mx and the excellent www.zihuatanejo.net.

For **camping or RV parking** spots, turn south (left) at the beach and follow the road half a mile past several likely spots to pull off and camp. At the far southern end, a lagoon spreads beside a pristine coral-sand beach, which curls around a low hill toward a picture-perfect little bay. Stores back by the entrance road can supplement your food and water supplies. El Burro Borracho also provides RV spaces.

Recreation and Shopping

Dewey McMillin and partners Bill and Kat Moore have established **Jaguar Tours** across the road from Casa de Tortuga. Beside surf and boogie-board and bicycle rentals they offer a number of ecoadventure tours. These include bird-watching and wildlife-viewing walks; a not-for-the-faint-of-heart jungle canopy tour along a cable hitched to the treetops; a trip into nearby Majahua limestone cave, replete with rocky gardens of stalagmites and stalactites. For more information, contact tel. 755/553-2862, cell tel. 044-755/557-7189, jaguartours@hotmail.com, or visit www.jaguartours.net.

Michael Bensal at the **Inn at Manzanillo Bay** also arranges sealife-viewing tours and fully equipped launches for four hours of fishing for 2–4 people for about $135.

Michael also runs a shop at his inn, selling fine wines, Taxco silver, and Cuban cigars. Eva Robbins, at Eden Beach Hacienda, has a shop with a charming collection of mostly Guerrero country crafts: baskets, toys, silver jewelry, silk scarves, and much more.

Getting to Troncones

Follow the (signed southbound) paved turnoff to

Playa Troncones from Highway 200, around Km 30, about 18 miles north of Zihuatanejo; or about 42 miles (73 km) south of the Río Balsas dam. Continue 2.2 miles to the Playa Troncones beachfront *ramadas.* Turn left for the camping spots, the main part of the beach and El Burro Borracho; turn right for the other described lodgings, beginning with Casa Ki, about a mile farther along the beachfront forest road. From there, the car-negotiable graveled road continues about 1.5 miles along the beach to Playa Majahua.

Majahua

Here you can enjoy a slice of this beautiful coast as it was before tourism bloomed at Troncones nearby. Instead of cell phones and the Internet, Majahua folks still enjoy plenty of palmy shade, stick-and-wattle houses, and lots of the fresh seafood that they serve in about half a dozen hammock-equipped *ramadas* scattered along the beach. One of the *ramadas* is competently run by a friendly family who calls it **Restaurant of the Angels** (Los Angeles). Also, Troncones longtimers recommend *palapa* Restaurant Las Brisas next door. Camping is safe and welcomed by local folks (although space, especially for RVs, is limited). Water is available, but campers should bring water or purifying tablets and food.

The beach curves from a rocky southeast-end point, past the lagoon of Río Lagunillas, and stretches miles northwest past shoreline palm and acacia forest. The sand is soft and dusky yellow, with mounds of driftwood but only seasonal shells. Waves break far out and roll in gradually, with little undertow. Fine left-breaking surf rises off the southern point. Boats are easily launchable (several *pangas* lie along the beach) during normal good weather.

To get to Playa Majahua directly, follow the signed turnoff at Km 33, 20 miles northwest of Zihuatanejo (just south of the Río Lagunillas bridge), or 44 miles (70 km) southeast of the Río Balsas dam. Continue 2.9 miles (4.7 km) to the beach.

BEYOND TRONCONES: LA SALADITA, ATRACADERO, AND THE RÍO BALSAS

This northwest corner of the Acapulco region hides a few small havens for those who yearn for their fill of fresh seafood, uncrowded beach camping, and plenty of swimming, surfing, fishing, and beachcombing. And finally, those who venture to Guerrero's extreme northwest edge can encounter the great Río Balsas, the Mexican Pacific's mightiest river, whose drainage basin extends over five states: Jalisco, Morelos, Michoacán, Guerrero, and Oaxaca.

This northwest corner of the Acapulco region hides a few small havens for those who yearn for their fill of fresh seafood, uncrowded beach camping, and plenty of swimming, surfing, fishing, and beachcombing.

La Saladita

At La Saladita (The Little Salty Lagoon), the day used to climax when the oyster divers would bring in their afternoon catches. Now, however, the oysters are all fished out. While the oysters recover, divers go for octopus and lobster which, broiled and served with fixings, sell for about $10 for a one-pounder. You can also do your own fishing via rentable (offer $15/hour) beach *pangas,* which go out daily and routinely return with three or four 20-pound fish.

The beach itself is level far out, with rolling waves fine for surfing, swimming, boogie boarding, and bodysurfing. There are enough driftwood and shells for a season of beachcombing. The beach spreads for hundreds of yards on both sides of the road's end. Permanent *palapa* restaurants supply shade, drinks, and seafood.

Beach camping is customary, especially during the Christmas and Easter holidays. Other times, you may have the whole place to yourself. Bring your own food and water; the small stores at the highway village may help add to your supplies.

Although it's popular, camping is no longer necessary to stay overnight at La Saladita. **Indio's Bar and Grill** offers beachfront bungalow rentals, past the gate at the beach.

To get to La Saladita, at Km 40, 25 miles (40 km) northwest of Zihuatanejo, and 39 miles

(63 km) southeast of the Río Balsas, turn off at the village of Los Llanos. At .2 mile, turn right, at the church, and continue another 3.1 miles (5.1 km) to the beach, where a left fork leads you to Indio's, and a right leads you to the "Embarcadero" sector of the beach and Paco's and Ibañez *palapa* restaurants.

Atracadero

A few miles farther northwest, Atracadero is less frequented than La Saladita. Except for the fishing family's house down the beach, you probably would have the entire place to yourself most of the time. The beach *palapa* restaurant appears to operate only seasonally. Crowds must gather sometimes, however: the main *palapa* has, over time, accumulated a five-foot pile of oyster shells.

The beach sand itself is soft and yellow-gray. The waves, with good surfing breaks, roll in from far out, arriving gently on the sand. Boat launching would be easy during calm weather. Little undertow menaces casual swimmers, bodysurfers, or boogie boarders. Lots of driftwood and shells—clams, limpets, snails—cover the sand. The beach extends for at least three miles past palm groves on the northwest. A fenced grove and house occupy the southeast. A grassy lot on the northwest side could accommodate some tents and RVs. Bring your own food and water.

To get to Playa Atracadero, turn off at Highway 200 Km 64, near the hamlet of Joluta, 40 miles (64 km) from Zihuatanejo and 24 miles (39 km) from the Río Balsas. Bear left all the way, 2.1 miles (3.3 km) to the beach.

The Río Balsas

It's hard to remain unimpressed as you follow Highway 200 over the Río Balsas Dam for the first time. The dam, which marks the Michoacán-Guerrero state boundary, is huge and hulking. Behind it a grand lake mirrors the Sierra Madre, while on the opposite, downstream side, Mexico's greatest river spurts from the turbine exit gates hundreds of feet below. The river's power, converted into enough electric energy for a million Mexican families, courses up great looping transmission wires, while the spent river meanders toward the sea.

LÁZARO CÁRDENAS

The newish industrial port city of Lázaro Cárdenas, named for the Michoacán-born president famous for expropriating American oil companies, is an important transportation and service hub for the northwest Acapulco region. Most of its services, including banks, bus stations, post office, hospitals, hotels, and restaurants, are clustered along north-south Avenida Lázaro Cárdenas, the main ingress boulevard, about three miles from its Highway 200 intersection.

Accommodations and Food

Take a break from the sun beneath the shady streetfront awning of the **Restaurant Las Sombrillas,** open daily 8 A.M.–8 P.M., across from Banamex. (Don't be afraid to ask the staff to turn the TV off or at least lower the volume.)

For cheaper but wholesome country cooking, check out the *fondas* (foodstalls) on the side street, Constitución de 1814, adjacent to the Galeana station bus lot, and on side street Corregidora, the next block, north.

If you decide to stay overnight, a number of nearby hotels offer reasonably priced lodging. The most centrally located is the **Hotel Delfín,** 1633 L. Cárdenas, Lázaro Cárdenas, Michoacán 60950, tel. 753/532-1418, fax 753/532-1419, across the street from the Galeana bus station. The approximately 20 rooms with baths, in three stories, cluster around an inner pool and patio. Rates run about $20 d, fan only, $30 with a/c, with hot water, TV, and telephone.

For more class, go to the high-rise **Hotel Casablanca** (on Bravo, a block east from Lázaro Cárdenas, visible behind Bancomer). It offers about six floors of light and comfortable modern-standard deluxe rooms with panoramic, private balcony views. Downstairs, past the lobby, a restaurant overlooks an inviting rear pool and patio. Rooms cost $36 s, $52 d, with a/c, TV, and parking. For reservations, dial 753/537-3480 through 753/537-3480-3484, fax 753/532-4036.

An even fancier hotel option is the **NH Krystal Express,** on the ingress boulevard, Avenida Lázaro Cárdenas, west side, about a quarter mile from the town center. It offers 120 deluxe rooms

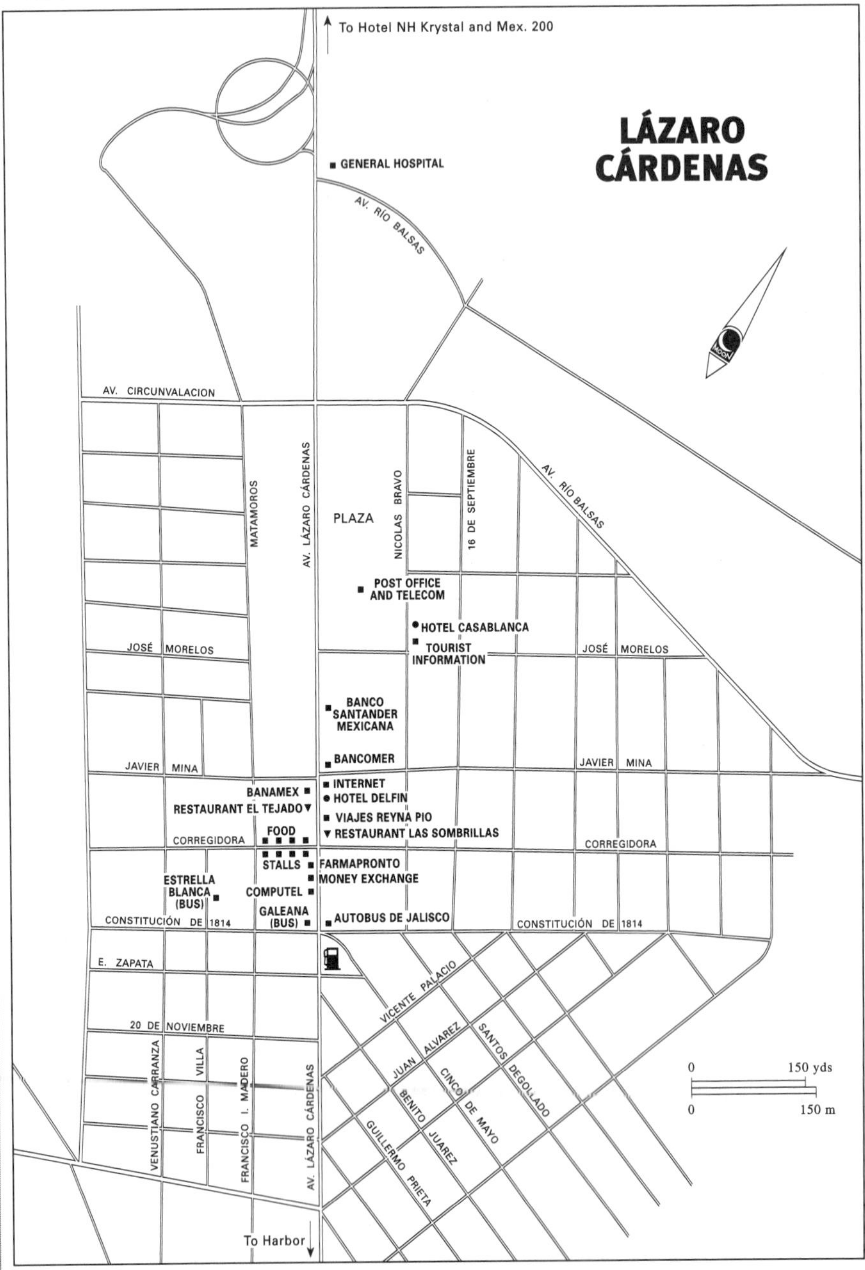

LÁZARO CÁRDENAS

To Hotel NH Krystal and Mex. 200
GENERAL HOSPITAL
AV. RÍO BALSAS
MOON
AV. CIRCUNVALACION
MATAMOROS
AV. LÁZARO CÁRDENAS
PLAZA
NICOLAS BRAVO
16 DE SEPTIEMBRE
AV. RÍO BALSAS
POST OFFICE AND TELECOM
HOTEL CASABLANCA
TOURIST INFORMATION
JOSÉ MORELOS
JOSÉ MORELOS
BANCO SANTANDER MEXICANA
BANCOMER
JAVIER MINA
JAVIER MINA
BANAMEX
RESTAURANT EL TEJADO
INTERNET
HOTEL DELFIN
VIAJES REYNA PIO
RESTAURANT LAS SOMBRILLAS
FOOD STALLS
CORREGIDORA
CORREGIDORA
FARMAPRONTO
MONEY EXCHANGE
ESTRELLA BLANCA (BUS)
COMPUTEL
GALEANA (BUS)
AUTOBUS DE JALISCO
CONSTITUCIÓN DE 1814
CONSTITUCIÓN DE 1814
E. ZAPATA
VICENTE PALACIO
20 DE NOVIEMBRE
JUAN ALVAREZ
SANTOS DEGOLLADO
CINCO DE MAYO
BENITO JUAREZ
GUILLERMO PRIETA
VENUSTIANO CARRANZA
FRANCISCO VILLA
FRANCISCO I. MADERO
AV. LÁZARO CÁRDENAS
0 150 yds
0 150 m
To Harbor

for about $80 d, with continental breakfast, restaurant, exercise gym, and whirlpool tub. Reserve at tel. 753/533-2900 or 753/533-2941, toll-free U.S. tel. 800/231-9860, nhlazaro@nh-hoteles.com.mx. For more information, visit www.nh-hoteles.com.

Tourist Information Office

For information and a selection of excellent maps and brochures, stop by the local branch of Michoacán state tourism, at N. Bravo 475, front of the Casablanca Hotel, open Mon.–Fri. 9 A.M.–6 P.M., Sat.–Sun. 10 A.M.–2 P.M.

Travel Agents

A competent and conveniently situated travel agency (and possible information source) is **Viajes Reyna Pio,** on L. Cárdenas, right across from the Galeana bus station and Banamex, tel. 753/532-3868 or 753/532-3935, fax 753/532-0723. Alternatively, try **Chinameca Viajes,** on N. Bravo, one block east from L. Cárdenas and two blocks north of the Casablanca Hotel, tel. 753/537-0253.

Money Exchange

Change your money at one of three banks, all with ATMs, clustered nearby. **Banamex,** at Av. L. Cárdenas 1646, tel. 753/532-2020, is open for money exchange Mon.–Fri. 9 A.M.–4 P.M., Saturday 10 A.M.–2 P.M. If it's too crowded, try **Bancomer,** open Mon.–Fri. 9 A.M.–4 P.M., Saturday 10 A.M.–2 P.M., a block north and across the street, at 1555 L. Cárdenas, tel. 753/532-3888; or **Banco Santander Mexicano,** tel. 753/532-0032, at 1681 L. Cárdenas, on the same side, half a block farther north.

Communications

The ***correo*** (post office), tel. 753/537-2387, is in the middle of the big grassy town plaza; look for it on the left as you arrive at the town center, two long blocks after the big traffic circle.

Telecomunicaciones, with telegraph, money orders, telephone, and public fax 753/532-0273, is next door to the post office. For telephone, plenty of public street phones accept widely available Ladatel telephone cards. More expensive, but with long hours, **Computel,** the computer-assisted long-distance telephone and fax agency, operates daily 7:30 A.M.–10 P.M., tel./fax 753/532-4806, fax 753/532-4807, next to the Galeana bus terminal, at 1810 L. Cárdenas, corner of Constitución de 1814.

Connect to the **Internet** at the small store, tel. 753/532-1480, corner of Javier Mina, across the street, south of Bancomer; open Mon.–Sat. 9 A.M.–9 P.M. Sunday 10 A.M.–2 P.M.

Health

The **General Hospital,** known locally as "Seguro Social," tel. 753/532-0900 through 753/532-0904, is on the boulevard into town, left side, corner of H. Escuela Naval, a block before the big right-side traffic circle. Alternatively, visit highly recommended Dr. Gustavo Cejos Pérez, at Melchor Ocampo 475, tel. 753/532-3902. For routine medicines and drugs, go to conveniently situated **Farmacia Pronto,** tel. 753/537-5002, open daily 8 A.M.–10 P.M., a few doors north of the Galeana bus station; or **Droguería Moderna,** tel. 753/532-0246, on the main street, across from the Galeana bus station, open daily 7:30 A.M.–9 P.M.

Getting There and Away

By car or RV, the options to and from Lázaro Cárdenas are virtually the same as those for Ixtapa-Zihuatejo. Simply add or subtract the 50 miles (80 km) or 1.25-hour travel difference between Ixtapa-Zihuatanejo and Lázaro Cárdenas.

By bus, a trio of long-distance bus terminals serves Lázaro Cárdenas travelers. From the Galeana (officially, Lineas Unidas del Sur) terminal at 1810 Av. L. Cárdenas, tel. 753/532-0262 or 753/537-3868, **Ruta Paraíso** first- and second-class local-departure buses connect daily north with Apatzingán, Uruapan, Pátzcuaro, and Morelia. Very frequent local departures connect northeast along the coast with La Mira, Playa Azul, and Caleta de Campos. Additionally, several more first- and second-class departures connect northwest with Manzanillo and intermediate points. In an adjacent booth, tel. 753/532-3006, agents sell tickets for **Parhikuni** luxury-class buses (with a/c waiting lounge), connecting north

with Michoacán destinations of Nueva Italia, Uruapan, Pátzcuaro, and Morelia.

Directly across the street, **Autobuses de Jalisco** and associated lines, tel. 753/537-1850, maintains a small streetfront station. It offers four types of departures: executive class "Plus," connecting northeast with Guadalajara via Tecomán and Colima; first-class Autobuses de Jalisco, connecting north, then west, with Uruapan, Zamora, and Guadalajara; first-class Via 2000 buses, connecting north, then east, via Uruapan, Morelia, and Toluca, with Mexico City; and second-class Autobuses Sur de Jalisco connecting northwest with Manzanillo and also with Guadalajara, via Colima and Ciudad Guzmán.

The big **Estrella Blanca** terminal, tel. 753/532-1171, is two short blocks away, directly behind the Galeana terminal, on Fco. Villa, between Constitución de 1814 and Corregidora. From there, one or two daily first-class buses local departures connect north with Michoacán destinations of Uruapan, Pátzcuaro, and Morelia. Three first-class buses stop, en route southeast to Zihuatanejo, Acapulco, and the Oaxaca coast, and northwest to Manzanillo, Puerto Vallarta, Mazatlán, and the U.S. border. In the opposite direction southeast, many first and second-class local departures connect with Zihuatanejo, Acapulco, and intermediate points, in addition to three Futura first-class departures that connect daily with Mexico City.

Guerrero Upcountry

A treasury of surprises await travelers who venture out into Acapulco's pine-tufted sierra hinterland. The discoveries begin in Chilpancingo, Mexico's Home of the Brave, which basks in a banana-belt upland valley, ringed by mighty, cloud-tipped mountains.

From Chilpancingo as a base, explore up-country Acapulco's River Country, and enjoy swimming, kayaking, and camping beside clear, spring-fed rivers and investigating stalagtite-draped limestone caves.

Continue deeper into the sierra, to Acapulco's renowned Handicraft Country of Chilapa and Olinalá. Select from a treasury of soft palm baskets and sombreros, bright pottery, exotic masks, charmingly rustic furniture, and exquisite lacquerware.

Continue north to Iguala, both Independence memorial and Shrine to the Flag. Wonder at Iguala's surrealistically large Mexican flag and later take a bonus side trip to a duo of fascinating ancient indigenous ruins.

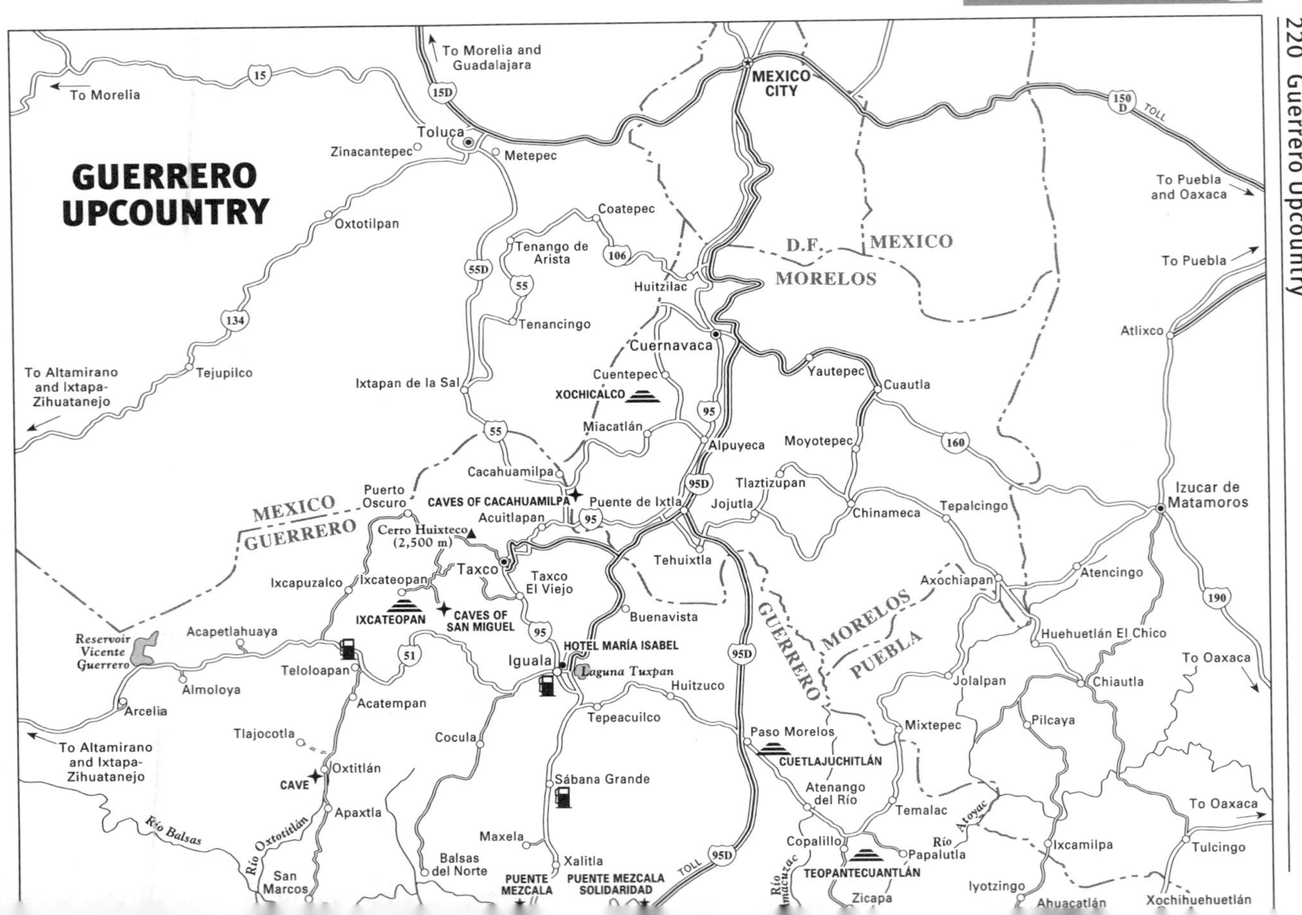
GUERRERO UPCOUNTRY
To Morelia
To Morelia and Guadalajara
To Altamirano and Ixtapa-Zihuatanejo
To Altamirano and Ixtapa-Zihuatanejo
15
15D
134
55D
55
106
95
95D
51
160
190
150 D
TOLL
Toluca
Metepec
Zinacantepec
Oxtotilpan
Tejupilco
Ixtapan de la Sal
Tenancingo
Tenango de Arista
Coatepec
Huitzilac
Cuernavaca
Cuentepec
XOCHICALCO
Miacatlán
Cacahuamilpa
CAVES OF CACAHUAMILPA
Puerto Oscuro
MEXICO
GUERRERO
Cerro Huixteco (2,500 m)
Taxco
Acuitlapan
Taxco El Viejo
CAVES OF SAN MIGUEL
IXCATEOPAN
Ixcateopan
Ixcapuzalco
Acapetlahuaya
Reservoir Vicente Guerrero
Almoloya
Arcelia
Teloloapan
Acatempan
Iguala
HOTEL MARÍA ISABEL
Laguna Tuxpan
Cocula
Tlajocotla
CAVE
Oxtitlán
Apaxtla
Río Oxtotitlán
San Marcos
Río Balsas
Balsas del Norte
Maxela
PUENTE MEZCALA
Xalitla
PUENTE MEZCALA SOLIDARIDAD
Sábana Grande
Tepeacuilco
Huitzuco
Buenavista
Tehuixtla
Puente de Ixtla
Jojutla
Tlaztizupan
Alpuyeca
Moyotepec
Chinameca
Yautepec
Cuautla
Tepalcingo
Axochiapan
MEXICO CITY
D.F.
MORELOS
MEXICO
MORELOS
PUEBLA
GUERRERO
Paso Morelos
CUETLAJUCHITLÁN
Atenango del Río
Copalillo
TEOPANTECUANTLÁN
Río Amacuzac
Zicapa
Río Papalutla
Temalac
Mixtepec
Jolalpan
Río Atoyac
Iyotzingo
Ahuacatlán
Ixcamilpa
Pilcaya
Chiautla
Huehuetlán El Chico
Atencingo
Izucar de Matamoros
To Oaxaca
To Oaxaca
Tulcingo
Xochihuehuetlán
Atlixco
To Puebla
To Puebla and Oaxaca

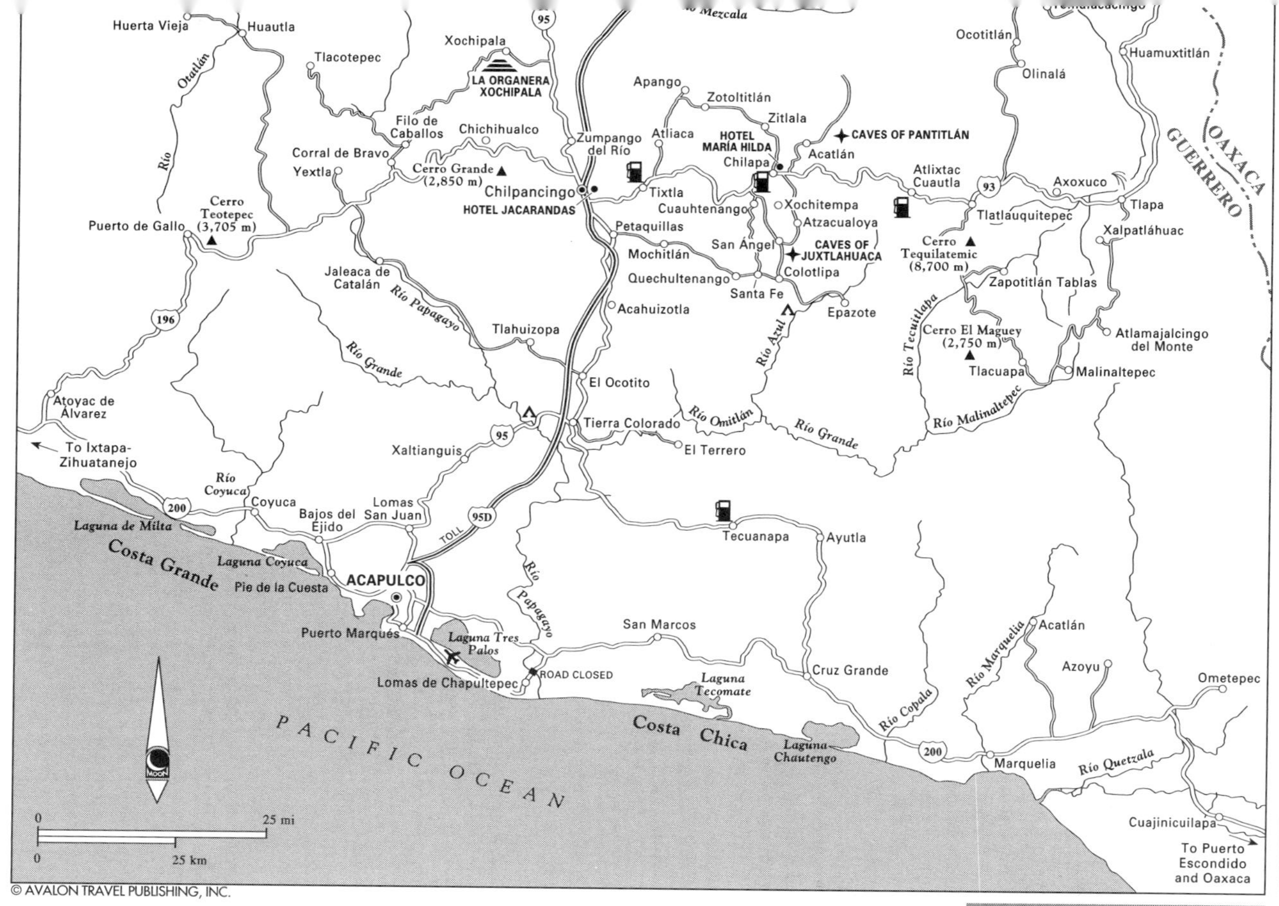

GUERRERO UPCOUNTRY

And finally, be sure to visit Taxco, the silver-rich colonial jewel of the highlands. After exploring its winding lanes and its museums and baroque monuments, visit Taxco's trio of nearby gems—the monumental limestone Caves of Cacahuamilpa, the legendary ruined city of Xochicalco, and Ixcateopan, final resting place of the heroic "Descending Eagle," Cuauhtémoc, the Aztecs' last emperor.

Chilpancingo

The formal name of the Guerrero state capital, **Chilpancingo de los Bravo** (Chilpancingo of the Brave), reflects Mexico's kinship with the United States, "The Home of the Free and Land of the Brave." Historically, in both cases, "the Brave" was more than a mere patriotic turn of phrase. Like the Continental Congress that began meeting in Philadelphia in 1774, the members of the 1813 revolutionary Congress of Anahuac in Chilpancingo did so at the constant risk of their lives.

Chilpancingo, besides being the Guerrero state capital and the cradle of Mexican liberty, is also closely associated with Vicente Guerrero, the Mexican hero most comparable to George Washington in the United States. Probably more than any other, Guerrero, Mexico's second president, battled to win Mexico's 1821 Independence and continued the struggle to ensure Mexico's 1824 constitution and resulting republican government.

Nevertheless, it's still priest-general José María Morelos who holds the hearts of Mexicans eight generations after his death. It was Morelos who convened Mexico's first revolutionary legislature, the Congress of Anahuac, in Chilpancingo, on September 14, 1813.

Morelos had earlier expressed his libertarian ideas, in the celebrated Sentimientos de la Nación, which, with as much force as the ideas of Thomas Jefferson a generation earlier, gave direction to the Congress of Anahuac's work. On November 6, 1813, the Congress declared a manifesto of principles, which notably included the idea that "sovereignty proceeds immediately from the people" and that Mexico should therefore "be free and independent."

It's interesting to note that the Mexican Act of Independence, 37 years after the American Declaration of Independence, took freedom a step farther. Among its principles, the Congress of Anahuac declared that "slavery be prohibited forever," a principle that required 52 more years and a terrible civil war to establish in the United States.

SIGHTS

Arrival and Orientation

Judging from its narrow downtown streets, Chilpancingo (pop. 200,000, elev. 4,000 feet, 1,300 meters) is a little town that grew big. Traveling the 62 toll *(cuota)* expressway miles (100 km) from Acapulco (or 83 miles, 133 km by old Highway 95), arrivees must make an effort not to

The northbound Avenida Vicente Guerrero tunnel beneath the Chilpancingo downtown plaza fortunately renders the plaza free of traffic.

miss the downtown. Both first-class buses and the south-north throughway Avenida Vicente Guerrero bypass the town center completely.

Buses deposit passengers at the Camionera Central (a mile north of the central plaza; taxi or ride a *colectivo* minivan from there).

Drivers, watch carefully for turnoff signs. If you're fortunate, you'll get on to main south-end ingress boulevard Avenida Lázaro Cárdenas, which begins at the Ciudad Universitaria right turnoff. After about half a mile (.8 km) from the turnoff, bear right at a big traffic circle and follow the boulevard, which becomes Bulevar Juan Álvarez and passes, via a one-block tunnel, beneath the Chilpancingo central plaza *(zócalo)*.

Around the Zócalo

Traffic having been diverted from (and beneath) it and the surrounding streets, the Chilpancingo *zócalo* makes an enjoyable strolling ground. The best vantage point is the front steps of the tall Guerrero **Palacio de Gobierno** (statehouse). Face (or imagine you're facing) the plaza, officially the "Plaza of the First Congress of Anahuac," and you're looking east. North is on your left, south on your right. East across the plaza rises the classical facade of the **Museo Regional de Chilpancingo,** and to the left of that, the twin white bell towers of the **Templo de Santa María de la Asunción,** where the Act of Independence was declared on November 6, 1813.

Note the noble gilded statue of Morelos, at the plaza's northeast corner, below and in front of the church. It memorializes his Sentimientos de la Nación, with the pivotal quotation: "No nation has the right to prevent another from the free use of its sovereignty."

At the adjacent, southeast plaza corner, below and in front of the museum, note the grand plaque, placed on September 13, 1985, that honors the 175th anniversary of the opening of the Congress of Anahuac. Its inscription, quoting José María Morelos, commemorates the end of the long period of Spanish dominion from August 12, 1521, until September 14, 1813: "On that day the chains of our servitude to Mexico-Tenochtitlán were broken forever in the brave town of Chilpancingo."

© BRUCE WHIPPERMAN

The Chilpancingo plazafront church is revered as the place where Mexico's independence was declared.

Through art, antiques, artifacts, and displays, the Regional Museum (open daily except Monday, 10 A.M.–6 P.M., tel. 747/472-8088) illustrates Guerrero geology, flora, fauna, archaeology, history, and folkways.

A major attraction is the now-faded but epic historical mural, by Roberto Cueva del Río and Luis Arenal, that wraps around the entire inner patio. The mural begins at the patio's northeast (across the patio, left as you enter) corner and continues clockwise. The first panel shows the infant future emperor Cuauhtémoc (notice his birth sign, the descending eagle above the infant).

Continue to the panel of the encounter of Cuauhtémoc with Cortés, then to the first corner, where another panel depicts the burial of the remains of Cuauhtémoc in Ixcateopan, near Taxco. Farther on, panels represent the independence heroes Morelos, Guerrero, and Hermanegildo

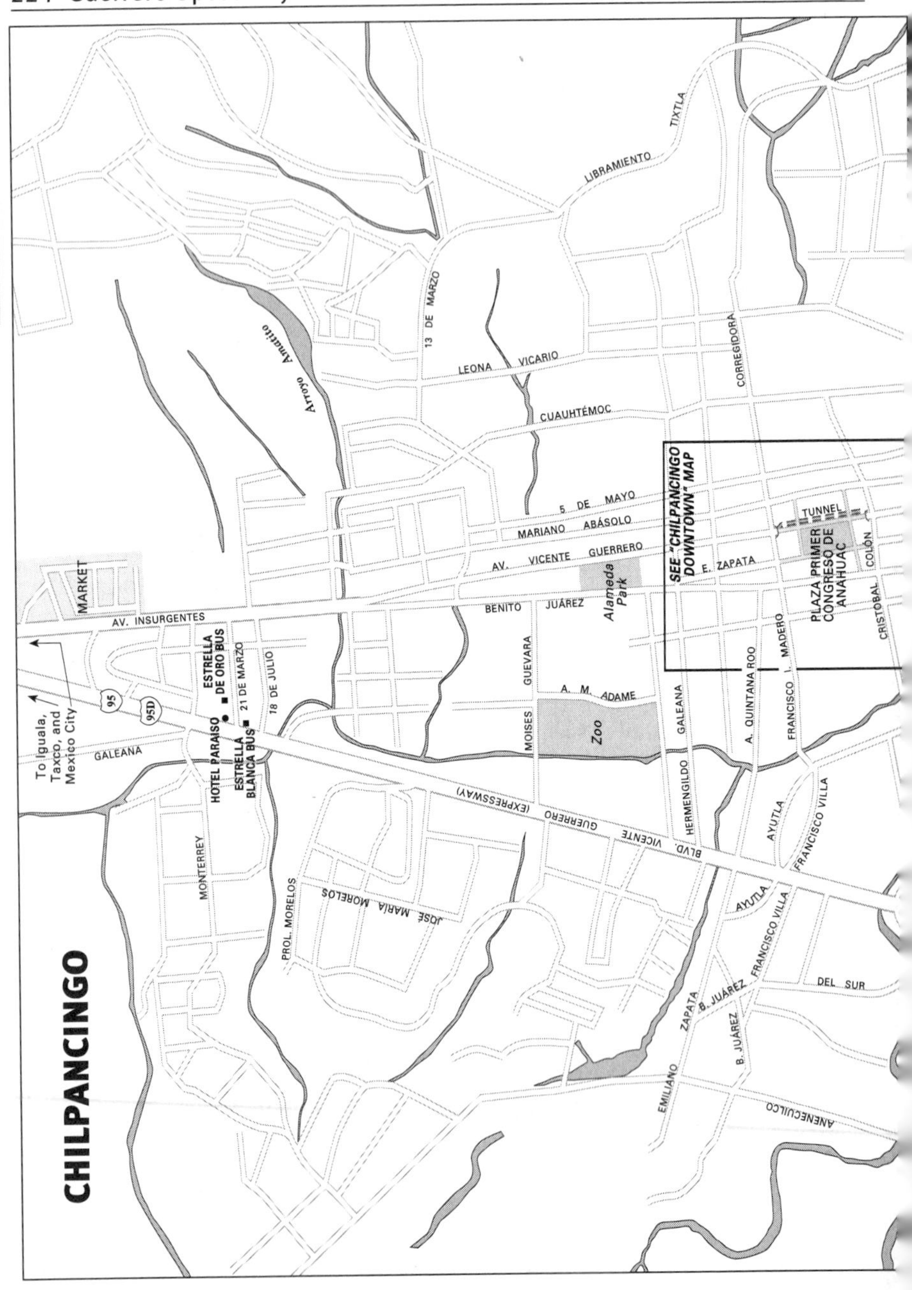
CHILPANCINGO
N
To Iguala, Taxco, and Mexico City
95
95D
GALEANA
AV. INSURGENTES
MARKET
HOTEL PARAISO
ESTRELLA DE ORO BUS
ESTRELLA BLANCA BUS
21 DE MARZO
18 DE JULIO
MONTERREY
PROL. MORELOS
JOSE MARIA MORELOS
BLVD. VICENTE GUERRERO (EXPRESSWAY)
Arroyo Amatitio
13 DE MARZO
LIBRAMIENTO TIXTLA
LEONA VICARIO
CUAUHTÉMOC
5 DE MAYO
MARIANO ABÁSOLO
AV. VICENTE GUERRERO
BENITO JUÁREZ
Alameda Park
MOISES GUEVARA
A. M. ADAME
Zoo
HERMENGILDO GALEANA
CORREGIDORA
SEE "CHILPANCINGO DOWNTOWN" MAP
E. ZAPATA
TUNNEL
PLAZA PRIMER CONGRESO DE ANAHUAC
COLÓN
CRISTÓBAL
A. QUINTANA ROO
FRANCISCO I. MADERO
AYUTLA
FRANCISCO VILLA
DEL SUR
B. JUÁREZ
EMILIANO ZAPATA
ANENECUILCO

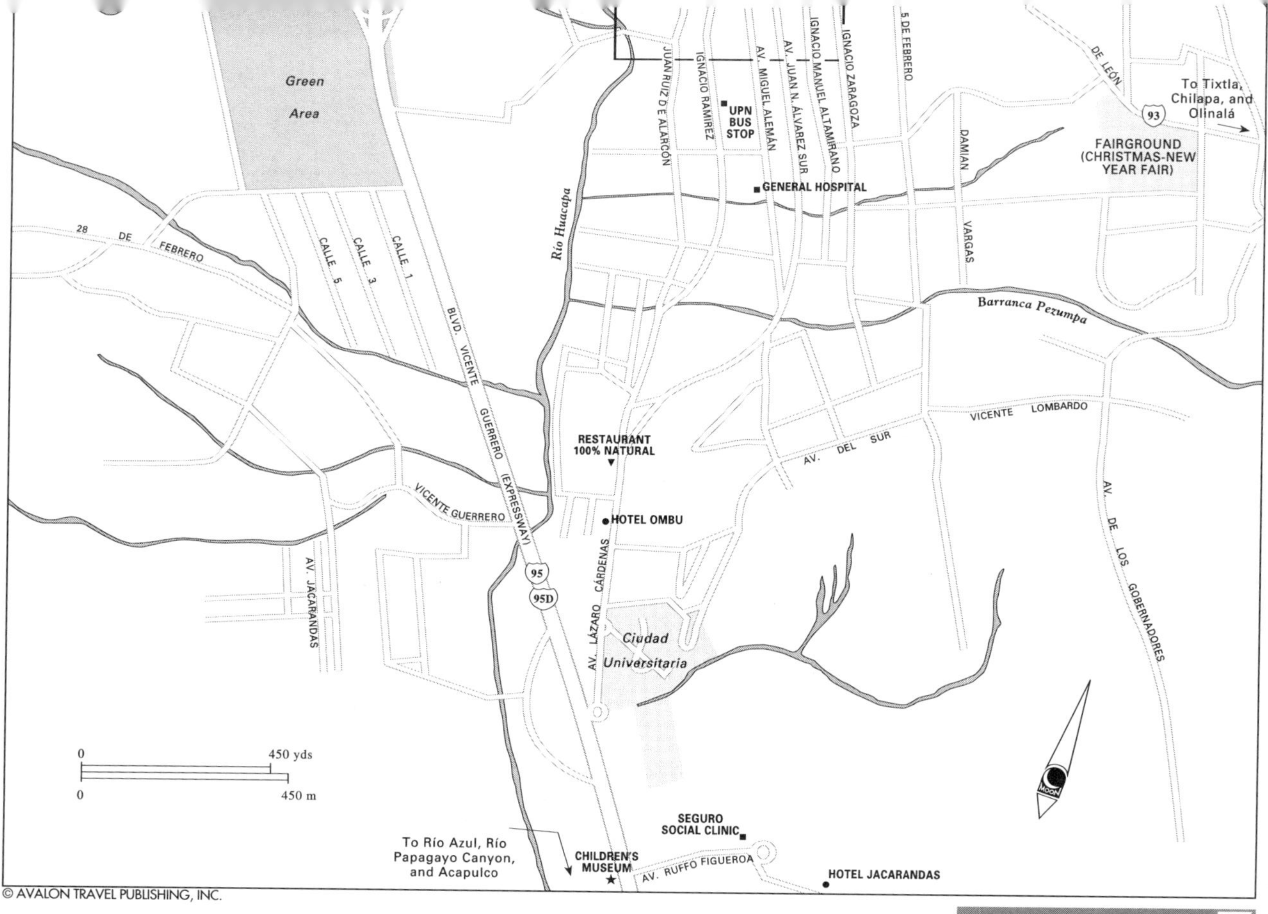
Green Area
JUAN RUIZ D E ALARCÓN
IGNACIO RAMIREZ
UPN BUS STOP
AV. MIGUEL ALEMÁN
AV. JUAN N. ÁLVAREZ SUR
IGNACIO MANUEL ALTAMIRANO
IGNACIO ZARAGOZA
5 DE FEBRERO
DE LEÓN
To Tixtla, Chilapa, and Olinalá
93
FAIRGROUND (CHRISTMAS-NEW YEAR FAIR)
DAMIAN VARGAS
GENERAL HOSPITAL
Río Huacapa
28 DE FEBRERO
CALLE 5
CALLE 3
CALLE 1
BLVD. VICENTE GUERRERO (EXPRESSWAY)
Barranca Pezumpa
VICENTE LOMBARDO
RESTAURANT 100% NATURAL
AV. DEL SUR
VICENTE GUERRERO
HOTEL OMBU
AV. DE LOS GOBERNADORES
AV. JACARANDAS
95
95D
AV. LÁZARO CÁRDENAS
Ciudad Universitaria
0
450 yds
0
450 m
SEGURO SOCIAL CLINIC
To Río Azul, Río Papagayo Canyon, and Acapulco
CHILDREN'S MUSEUM
AV. RUFFO FIGUEROA
HOTEL JACARANDAS
© AVALON TRAVEL PUBLISHING, INC.

JOSÉ MARÍA MORELOS: CHAMPION OF MEXICAN INDEPENDENCE

© BRUCE WHIPPERMAN

The heroic statue of José María Morelos on the Chilpancingo downtown plaza commemorates his celebrated Sentiments of the Nation that formed the basis for the formal Mexican declaration of independence on November 6, 1813.

As did his famous predecessor, George Washington, Mexican Independence General José María Morelos y Pavón convened his nation's first constitutional convention. The First Congress of Anahuac, an assemblage of leaders from all over Mexico, assembled in Chilpancingo on September 14, 1813. It was virtually three years to the day after martyr-priest Miguel Hidalgo had ignited revolution from the balcony in Dolores, Guanajuato. Later, Morelos remembered: "On that day the chains of our servitude to Mexico-Tenochtitlán (Mexico City) were broken forever."

Those early days of revolution were heady times for a poor priest of such obscure origin. José María Morelos y Pavón was born in Valladolid (now Morelia, named in his honor), Michoacán, on September 30, 1765. Among experts, opinion is divided on Morelos's possible African Mexican ancestry. Most historians go along with the major evidence: Morelos's swarthy, dark-eyed complexion and the well-known old legal document certifying that one of his grandmothers was a *"mujer libre,"* a standard legal phrase for an free, nonslave woman of African descent.

Young José no doubt was a devout Catholic. Early on, he wanted to study for the priesthood. While waiting to be admitted to seminary, he supported himself by working as a mule driver until he was admitted to the Valladolid Colegio San Nicolas in the mid-1780s.

While a student, José came under the influence of Father Miguel Hidalgo, who was the rector at San Nicolas. Hidalgo was not the usual role model for a budding acolyte. He was ambitious and much more interested in politics than in his priestly duties. Hidalgo's inner circle, which quickly included Morelos, debated the ideas of the French Enlightenment philosophers Jean-Jacques Rousseau *(The Social Contract),* and Count Montesquieu *(The Spirit of the Laws)* who had strongly influenced the founding fathers of the brand-new United States of America.

Hidalgo, always seeking advancement, got an assignment to a rich Guanajuato parish, while José went west and served in a poor isolated corner of Michoacán.

After igniting revolution on September 15, 1810, Hidalgo led his raggedy peasant army, which grew rapidly to about 100,000 at its peak. Inspired, Morelos offered his services to Hidalgo, who told him to go south, raise an army, and capture Acapulco and the riches of the Manila galleon.

Morelos returned to his Michoacán homeland, raised a scruffy platoon of volunteers, and marched toward the coast. Along the way, Morelos recruited droves of volunteers, many of them African Mexican. They passed Zacatula and followed the coast east to Acapulco, arriving as an eager but ill-equipped 3,000-man guerrilla brigade.

In Acapulco, the only point of resistance (albeit stiff resistance) was the old Fuerte San Diego, where Morelos, after weeks of besieging the fort, divided his force. He left half surrounding the fort and led the remainder north to Chilpancingo, which he captured with the help of Hermanegildo Galeana and Nicolas Bravo.

Next, Morelos marched west, capturing Chilapa. Then, with a buoyantly robust force of 4,000, he continued north to Cuautla, in the present state of Morelos. Although besieged for 73 days by a superior royalist division, Morelos broke out with most of his men and marched southeast, where he captured Oaxaca, the prize of the south.

At Oaxaca, his radical egalitarian views, source of his popularity with his troops, surfaced:

We must eliminate the outdated classifications separating us into black, mulatto, mestizo, and criollo . . . and call ourselves Americans for our origin as do the English, the French, and that other European country that is oppressing us.

The time was mid-1813, and Morelos was riding his crest of success. At 48, he was at his prime, cutting a dashing figure, topped by a colorful bandanna that wrapped his balding head. Napoleon Bonaparte is said to have paid Morelos the ultimate compliment: "With three such men as José Morelos, I could conquer the world."

Although a priest, Morelos, like his mentor Miguel Hidalgo, rejected sexual abstinence. He fathered several children by his indigenous common-law wife, Brigida Almonte, of Necupétaro, Michoacán.

One of Morelos's sons, Juan Almonte, born in 1803, gained fame, paradoxically working for the Mexican conservative cause. He served as President Bustamante's Minister of War during the 1830s, under General Santa Anna at the Alamo in Texas, later as ambassador to the United States and Britain, and finally in Emperor Maximilian's cabinet during the 1860s.

Morelos's signal achievement was the Congress of Anahuac, Mexico's first constitutional convention, that Morelos convened in Chilpancingo on September 14, 1813. Although subsequently driven from Chilpancingo by royalist forces, the Congress reconvened in Apatzingan, Michoacán, where it promulgated Mexico's first constitution on October 22, 1814.

Continually pressed by royalist troops, Morelos fought desperately for the remainder of his days protecting the Congress, which amounted to Mexico's first republican government. Finally, royalist troops captured him and spirited him to Mexico City on November 22, 1815. After a monthlong trial during which Morelos argued eloquently for the justice of the *insurgente* cause, he was defrocked and taken to the city of San Cristóbal Ecatepec, where he was executed for treason by firing squad on December 27, 1815.

Galeana (see sidebars in this and The Costa Grande chapter), the Revolution of 1910, and, finally, the latter-day development of Guerrero state.

Step next door to the church, the site revered in Mexico, not unlike Independence Hall in Philadelphia, as the place where Mexico's independence was declared. Note the polished, hand-carved church doors, with reliefs of Mexico's independence heroes: Morelos, first president Nicolás Bravo, Guerrero, and the magnificent eagle and serpent national symbol.

Sights out of Downtown

Children will most certainly enjoy the small Chilpancingo **zoo,** near the corner of Moises Guevara and Arturo M. Adame, about half a mile northeast of the *zócalo.* The entrance is on the north side of a large park, with plenty of room to run around and spread a picnic.

Another kid-friendly place is the **children's museum,** south of town, a block west of the corner of Bulevar Vicente Guerrero and Avenida Rulfo Figueroa. The museum's mission is to introduce technology with a host of hands-on, child-level (ages 4–12) activities. Find it open approximately 10 A.M.–3 P.M.

ACCOMMODATIONS

Considering its many visitors on government or commercial business, Chilpancingo has relatively few hotels. Be certain to reserve at least a day (better a week) in advance. Few, if any, Chilpancingo hotels accept credit cards.

The best city-center lodging choice is the busy business-style **Hotel del Parque,** a block south of the *zócalo,* at Colón 5, Chilpancingo, Guerrero 39000, tel. 747/472-3491 or 747/472-1364, fax 747/472-2547. Its 28 very clean rooms rise in four floors (but with no elevator) around a small inner lobby-patio. Inside, the rooms are comfortable, modern semideluxe, with hot-water shower baths. Rentals run about $45 s or d, with TV, phone, fans, good restaurant downstairs, but no pool. Parking nearby, about $5, is extra. For more information and reservations, email alarcoma@prodigy.net.mx.

Much more downscale but still recommendable is the homey **Hotel Cárdenas,** a block north of the *zócalo,* at Madero 11, Chilpancingo, Guerrero 39000, tel. 747/471-6153. Rooms in this converted old family home open on to an interior patio with chairs and shade umbrellas for relaxing. The plain but clean enough (I saw only one cockroach, but it was dying) bare-bulb rooms rent for about 12 s, $17 d, and $31 t, with hot-water shower baths.

If nothing else is available, try the bare-bones **Hotel Cuauhtémoc,** a short block south of the plaza's southwest corner, at Miguel Aleman 14, Chilpancingo, Guerrero 39000, tel. 747/472-3223. The 20 drab, bare-bulb rooms with bath rent for about $14 s, $20 d, and $22 t.

Outside of the immediate downtown, visitors have a number of decent hotel choices. About a mile south of the *zócalo,* check out the newish **Hotel Ombu,** at Lázaro Cárdenas 28, tel. 747/472-5382 or 747/471-1173, fax 747/474-9911. Above the small lobby, three floors of 33 walk-up rooms rise around a spartan-chic inner atrium. Rooms themselves are simply but attractively decorated in tile, natural wood, and earth-tone bedspreads and curtains. Tariffs run about $31 for a smallish, double-bed room, and $49 for larger rooms with two double beds, with good cable TV, phone, portable fan available, restaurant downstairs, and parking in the basement.

Farther south, about 1.5 miles (2.5 km) south of the town center is Chilpancingo's best: the government resort-style **Hotel Jacarandas,** on Avenida Jacarandas, Chilpancingo, Guerrero 39300, tel. 747/472-4444, fax 747/472-4987. Guests enjoy a choice of about 100 rooms in a big, curving white jacaranda-decorated hillside block. Inside, rooms, although less than immaculate, are spacious, light, and comfortable and open to airy private balconies overlooking a big blue pool-patio and tropical garden. For such amenities, rates are a reasonable $40 s, $49 d, $63 t, with cable TV, fan, phone, private hot-water shower baths, good restaurant, and parking. Reserve early; this place is often booked completely by conferences.

On the other hand, car travelers interested in an immaculate, well-managed lodging might like the **Parador del Marquez,** at the far south edge of

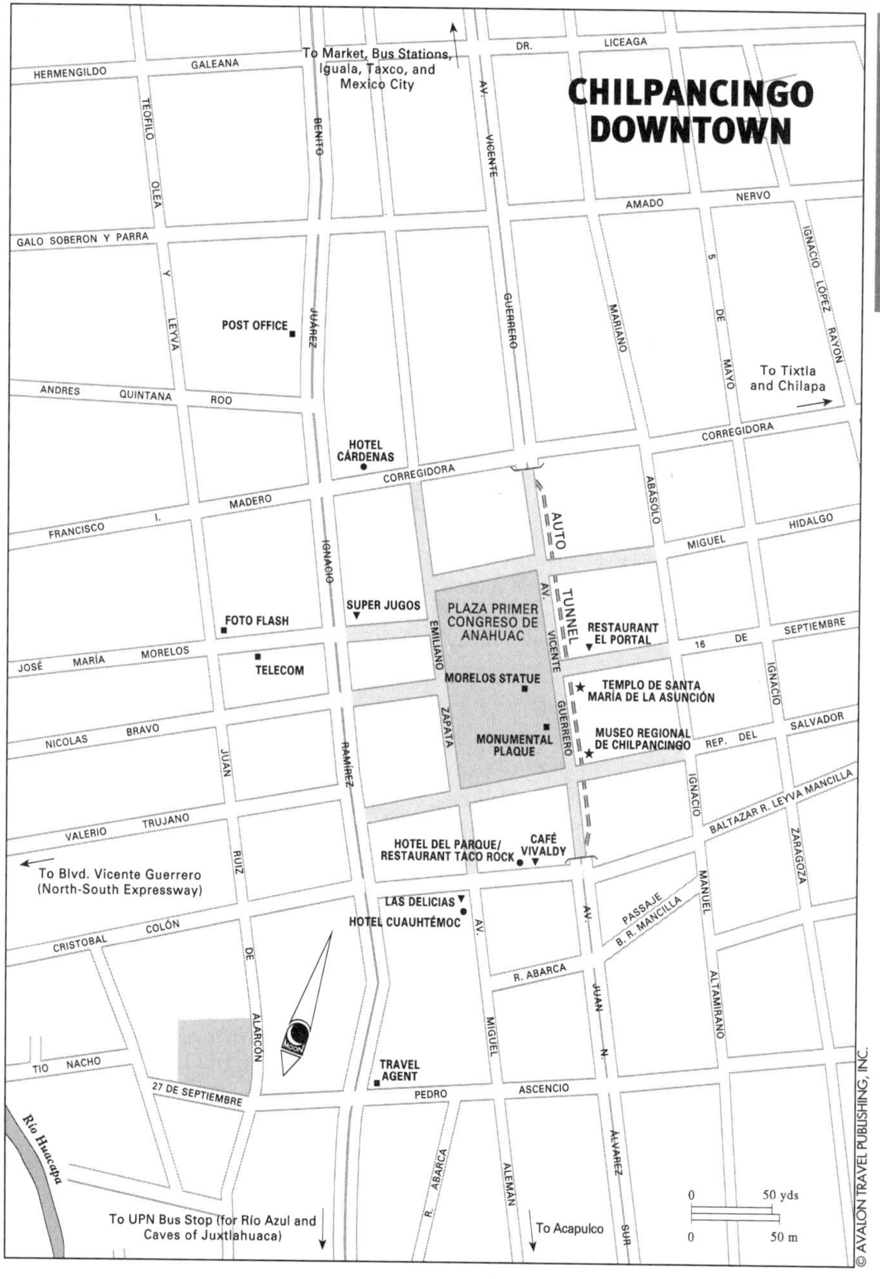
CHILPANCINGO DOWNTOWN
To Market, Bus Stations, Iguala, Taxco, and Mexico City
To Tixtla and Chilapa
To Blvd. Vicente Guerrero (North-South Expressway)
To UPN Bus Stop (for Río Azul and Caves of Juxtlahuaca)
To Acapulco
POST OFFICE
HOTEL CÁRDENAS
SUPER JUGOS
FOTO FLASH
TELECOM
PLAZA PRIMER CONGRESO DE ANAHUAC
MORELOS STATUE
MONUMENTAL PLAQUE
RESTAURANT EL PORTAL
TEMPLO DE SANTA MARÍA DE LA ASUNCIÓN
MUSEO REGIONAL DE CHILPANCINGO
HOTEL DEL PARQUE/ RESTAURANT TACO ROCK
CAFÉ VIVALDY
LAS DELICIAS
HOTEL CUAUHTÉMOC
TRAVEL AGENT
AUTO TUNNEL
HERMENGILDO GALEANA
DR. LICEAGA
AMADO NERVO
GALO SOBERON Y PARRA
ANDRES QUINTANA ROO
CORREGIDORA
FRANCISCO I. MADERO
MIGUEL HIDALGO
JOSÉ MARÍA MORELOS
16 DE SEPTIEMBRE
NICOLAS BRAVO
REP. DEL SALVADOR
VALERIO TRUJANO
BALTAZAR R. LEYVA MANCILLA
CRISTOBAL COLÓN
PASSAJE B. R. MANCILLA
R. ABARCA
TIO NACHO
27 DE SEPTIEMBRE
PEDRO ASCENCIO
TEOFILO OLEA Y LEYVA
BENITO JUÁREZ
IGNACIO RAMÍREZ
AV. VICENTE GUERRERO
EMILIANO ZAPATA
MARIANO ABASOLO
5 DE MAYO
IGNACIO LÓPEZ RAYON
IGNACIO MANUEL ALTAMIRANO
ZARAGOZA
JUAN RUIZ DE ALARCÓN
AV. MIGUEL ALEMÁN
AV. JUAN N. ÁLVAREZ SUR
R. ABARCA
Río Huacapa
0 50 yds
0 50 m
MOON

town, at Km 276, Carretera Mexico-Acapulco, Chilpancingo, Guerrero 39000, tel. 747/472-6773, fax 747/472-9532. The hotel's location, about two miles (3 km) south of the town center, makes it likely to have a room when no other hotel in town does. The 20-odd rooms in an inviting garden are immaculate and impeccably maintained in traditional Mexican tile, stucco, and brick decor. Choose from one king-sized bed or two doubles. Rates run about $33 s or d in one bed; $49 d, t, or q in two beds, with cable TV, phone, parking, breakfast restaurant, but no pool.

On the north side of town, bus or car travelers might appreciate the convenience of the newish **Hotel Paraíso,** across from the bus station, on throughway Bulevar Vicente Guerrero. Find it about a mile north of the *zócalo,* at the corner of 21 de Marzo, Chilpancingo, Guerrero 39010, tel. 474/471-1122 or 474/472-8863, fax 474/471-4591. The 40-odd rooms enclose an inner parking-patio. Inside, they're comfortable and immaculate, with all-white deluxe decor and hot-water shower baths. Rooms begin at about $40 d, with cable TV, phone, a/c, and parking.

FOOD

For snacks, try one of the many very clean street-front *jugerías* and *loncherias* around the downtown plaza. For example, check out **Las Delicias,** which serves plenty of fresh *aguas,* juices, and hot *tortas* and *hamburguesas* (about $2), open 8 A.M.–10 P.M., at the corner of Alemán and Colón, a block south of the plaza's southwest corner. Alternatively, try **Comida Rápida** diagonally south, across Alemán.

A few blocks north, on the plaza's northwest side, an excellent similar choice is **Super Jugos** a block west of the plaza, at the northeast corner of Ramírez and Morelos.

A few sit-down restaurants provide good food in restful settings near the plaza. First choice goes to refined **Restaurant El Portal** just off the main plaza, on the north side of the church, corner of Guerrero and Hidalgo. With open-air seating, in view of the dramatic bust of Morelos across the street, El Portal is ideal for a relaxing snack or meal all day. In addition to a very recognizable menu of professionally prepared and served breakfasts, salads, soups, pastas, poultry, and meats ($2–6), it offers a bountiful three-course *comida corrida* ($3.50), 1–5 P.M. daily. Find it open daily 8:30 A.M.–10 P.M., tel. 747/472-4668.

The class-act **Restaurant Taco Rock** of the Hotel del Parque, at 5 Colón, around the block south of the plaza, is a very popular breakfast and lunch stop for business and professional people. At night it becomes a TV bar and nightclub, featuring Latin "taco rock" music. Food entrées ($5–10), from a long Mexican-style coffee-shop menu, are professionally prepared and presented. Open daily, 8 A.M.–midnight, tel. 747/472-3012 or 747/472-1285.

Although it's not strictly vegetarian-macrobiotic, the menu of **Restaurant 100% Natural,** half a mile south of downtown, features plenty of healthy and tasty food. Choose from fruits and fruit *liquados,* granola, pancakes, eggs, yogurt, avocado, cheese, soya and meat burgers, french fries, and much more, in many styles, from scrumptious sandwiches to hearty entrée plates ($3–8). Service, by a dedicated squad of 20-somethings in white, beneath an open-air *palapa,* is exemplary. Find it at Lázaro Cárdenas 12, open daily 9 A.M.–9 P.M., tel. 747/472-5457.

OTHER PRACTICALITIES

Entertainment and Events

Chilpancingo people unwind during the big year-end fair, **Feria de San Mateo, la Navidad, y el Año Nuevo,** December 24–January 8. The festivities kick off with the *teopancolaquio,* a ritual honoring the birth of God on Earth. Offerings include riots of flowers and regional dances, including Los Tlacololeros, Pescados (Fish), Diablos (Devils), and Manueles. Concurrent with all this is a grand commercial and agricultural fair, bullfights, carnival, fireworks, cockfights, and plenty of hearty Guerrero country food.

In nearby Tixtla (see Excursions from Chilpancingo), folks whoop it up during a couple of unique local fiestas. They celebrate the birthday of their most famous native son, Vicente Guerrero, on August 9, with a feast of cultural events, including music and favorite regional dances.

DANCE OF LOS TLACOLOLEROS

The noise and excitement of the Chilpancingo regional dance Los Tlacololeros remains a favorite of campesinos, who crowd in at fiesta time. The name refers to *tlacolol*, the Aztec word meaning "preparing the fields for planting" by the age-old slash and burn method, still widely used in the Sierra Madre backcountry.

The compelling drama centers on the whips, which the hilariously masked, cotton-and-sombrero-clothed men snap loudly on each others' padded arms, supposedly to imitate the crackle of the burning brush fire. In one version of the dance a she-dog called *la maravilla* makes a madcap chase after a *tigre* that threatens the campesinos.

All of a sudden, without warning, the fire mysteriously goes out, while the dumbfounded dancers flail each other with increased desperation, trying frantically to find the culprit for the fire's failure. Soon, however, all is well that ends well as the loud rattling of chains simulates the fire's return, driving the *tigre* from the campesinos' midst.

Three weeks later, September 1–8, the Tixtla plaza is awash with celebrants for the **Fiesta de la Natividad de María.** Indigenous folks flood into town for the parade of floats, the carnival, fireworks, *jaripeo* bull roping and riding, and favorite traditional dances Los Manueles, Moros, Diablos, Tigres, and Tlacololeros. This is probably the most colorful time all year to visit the Tixtla Sunday market, known for its loads of for-sale native handicrafts.

Shopping

The best supermarket–department store in town is **Comercial Mexicana,** recognizable by the tall orange and white pelican emblem-sign, at Calle Baltazar Leyva, by throughway Bulevar Vicente Guerrero (and McDonald's), about a mile north of downtown. It's open daily 8 A.M.–10 P.M., tel. 747/472-6355.

Although a few vendors sell handicrafts in the municipal market, on Insurgentes, corner of Gardenias, about 1.5 miles north of the *zócalo,* the best source is the big Sunday ***tianguis*** native market in Tixtla. (See Excursions from Chilpancingo.)

For film and photo supplies and services, go to **Foto Flash,** open Mon.–Sat. 9 A.M.–9 P.M., closed Sunday, at the corner of Morelos and Olea y Leyva, two blocks west of the plaza's northwest corner, tel. 747/472-8075.

Services

Banks: A number of bank branches, all with ATMs, cluster around the downtown plaza. The best bet is long-hours Bital (Banco Internacional), open Mon.–Sat. 8 A.M.–7 P.M., at Juárez 2, a block north and a block west of the plaza's northwest corner. Alternatively, go to Banamex, near the plaza's southwest corner, at Alemán 2, open approximately Mon.–Fri. 9 A.M.–4 P.M.; or Bancomer, open similar hours, at Alarcón 20, two blocks west, two blocks south of the plaza's southwest corner.

Communications: Buy stamps and mail letters at the downtown *correo* (post office), on Juárez, a block west and three blocks north of the plaza's northwest corner. Find it open Mon.–Fri. 8 A.M.–6 P.M., Saturday 9 A.M.–3 P.M. For a telephone, buy a widely available Ladatel card and use one of the many street phones scattered around the downtown. For telephone, fax, and money orders, go to Telecom, on Morelos, two blocks west of the plaza, open Mon.–Fri. 8 A.M.–7:30 P.M., Saturday 9 A.M.–12:30 P.M., tel. 747/472-1154 or 747/472-2017.

Travel Agent: Go to Viajes Chilpancingo, at the corner of Ascencio and Ramírez, one block west and three blocks south of the plaza's southwest corner, tel. 474/471-1389, tel./fax 474/472-9394.

Health and Emergencies: Chilpancingo has up-to-date medical facilities. If you get sick, follow your hotel's recommendation. Otherwise, hire a taxi to take you to the Seguro Social Clinic, tel. 474/472-2390 or 474/472-3413, on Avenida Jacarandas, which intersects with throughway Avenida Vicente Guerrero, about a mile south of downtown. Alternatively, go to the general Seguro Social Hospital, on Bulevar Miguel Alemán, about a quarter mile south of the *zócalo.* For fire emergencies, call the

VICENTE GUERRERO: FATHER OF THE MEXICAN REPUBLIC

The 1849 proposal for a new Mexican state to be carved from the states of Mexico, Puebla, and Michoacán would seem improbable, except that the proposed state was to be named Guerrero in honor of Mexico's famously popular independence hero and second president, Vicente Ramón Saldana Guerrero.

Vicente Guerrero, Mexico's first African Mexican president, was born of working-class parents in the village of Tixtla, near Chilpancingo, on August 10, 1782. In 1811, Vicente was working successfully as a gunsmith when, inspired by Father Miguel Hidalgo's *insurgente* cause, he joined with priest-general José María Morelos's ragtag southern rebel forces.

Vicente's valor in battle and natural leadership ability led to his swift promotion. By 1815, however, with most of its original leaders, including Morelos, dead, the *insurgente* cause had lost momentum. Nevertheless, Guerrero grabbed the rebel banner in the south and rallied his men. Guerrero and his *compadre* commanders, Juan Álvarez and Pedro Ascencio, kept royalist brigadier Agustín de Itúrbide's troops in frustrated disarray, chasing their ragtag bands throughout the southern Sierra Madre.

Vicente Guerrero was confronted by a crucial test in 1819. When offered amnesty, the ex-

Youths exercise in front of the great tablet honoring the words of Tixtla's celebrated sons, Vicente Guerrero and Ignacio Altamirano.

hausted Guerrero was tempted to give up. Even his father pleaded with him to surrender. But Guerrero remained resolute. In front of his men, Guerrero answered with the now-hallowed words, "Father, to me your voice is sacred . . . [but] the voice of my country comes first."

In 1821, Mexican royalists, faced with a new unfriendly liberal Spanish government, swallowed hard and joined Guerrero and the rebels. Under the flag (for which Guerrero had personally chosen the colors: red, white, and green) of "Three Guarantees"—independence, Catholicism, equality—Guerrero and Itúrbide rode victoriously into Mexico City.

But quickly, Itúrbide vaulted himself to glory as Emperor Agustín I of Mexico. As could be expected, Guerrero soon revolted, forcing Itúrbide into exile, in February 1823.

Mexican republicans took over and put together a national constitution in 1824. An election elevated liberal Guadalupe Victoria to president and conservative Nícolas Bravo to vice president. Although the restless Bravo revolted in 1827, the breach was temporarily resealed with the election of Vicente Guerrero as Mexico's second president in 1828.

Guerrero, although an able general and enormously popular war hero, was ill at ease among Mexico City's blue bloods. Guerrero left most of the salon politicking to his war minister, Leonardo Zavala (who had organized a popular revolt to get Guerrero elected), and Joel Poinsett, U.S. President Andrew Jackson's savvy American ambassador.

In the last analysis, although Guerrero's egalitarian views were bad news to Mexico's powerful conservative chosen few, his untutored working-class and mixed-race background was the clincher. He simply didn't fit into Mexico City's upper crust. As it turned out, others were more than willing to take Guerrero's place.

One of those was Antonio López de Santa Anna, who became the darling of Mexican conservatives when his regiment batted down a half-hearted Spanish invasion on the Gulf Coast in July 1829. With Santa Anna's backing, conservative General Anastasio Bustamante mounted a revolt, forcing Guerrero to step down from the presidency in December 1829.

Guerrero again retreated to his southern home territory and drummed up yet another guerrilla revolt against the Mexico City *politicos.* As usual, Guerrero was master on his own ground. His irregulars outwitted government troops for a year.

Bustamante decided that trickery was the only way to defeat Guerrero. His agents got Guerrero to board the ship *Colombo,* in Acapulco, by bribing the ship's Genoese captain, archvillain Francisco Pichaluga. He took Guerrero, under custody, to Huatulco and handed him over to Bustamante's operatives on January 20, 1831.

Guerrero was next taken to the Valley of Oaxaca; after a bogus trial, he was executed by firing squad at the old Cuilapan basilica, on February 14, 1831.

Sadly, the old warrior was gone. But his cause was not lost. Others—Juan Álvarez, Benito Juárez, Emiliano Zapata, Alvaro Obregón, Lázaro Cárdenas—and many more, would carry Guerrero's banner for generations to come.

bomberos (fire station), at tel. 474/472-2280. For police, call the *policia municipal,* at tel. 474/472-2062 or 474/472-4115.

Getting There and Away

By Bus: The main bus station, Estrella Blanca, is on side street 21 de Marzo, between throughway Vicente Guerrero and the municipal market, about 1.5 miles north of downtown.

Out front, a platoon of taxis, local buses, and minivans ferry passengers to dozens of nearby destinations. Ladatel card–operated street telephones are available for calls.

Inside the smallish terminal, agents (tel. 474/472-0680) sell long-distance bus tickets. Both first- and second-class direct departures (including intermediate points) connect with Mexico City, Acapulco, Morelia, Guadalajara, Acapulco, Zihuatanejo, Puerto Vallarta, Iguala, Chilapa, Olinalá, Tlapa de Comonfort, Taxco, and the U.S. border at Nogales and Tijuana.

Outside, nearby, a few stands sell snacks, drinks, tacos, and sandwiches. For fresh items, stock up at the market, a block uphill.

Across the street, first-class Estrella de Oro buses connect north and south with Acapulco, Iguala, Taxco, and Mexico City.

By Car: Good roads make connections to and from Chilpancingo easy. To or from Acapulco, follow the toll *(cuota)* expressway a quick 62 miles (100 km) (toll a steep $20) in about an hour and a quarter. Toll-free *libre* Highway 95 (83 miles, 133 km) connects with Acapulco in about twice the time, with much more than twice the hazard and wear and tear.

In the opposite direction, the *cuota* expressway connects Chilpancingo with Mexico City in 148 miles (239 km), toll about $30, but worth it, in about 3.5 hours. Make sure you arrive in Mexico City on a permitted day. (See the sidebar "Mexico City Driving Restrictions" in the Acapulco chapter.) The old Highway 15 connection, via Iguala and Taxco, with Mexico City, adds at least two hours to this under the best of conditions.

Connect north with Iguala in 67 miles (108 km), two hours, via old Highway 15; continue to Taxco in another 24 miles (38 km), one hour, for a total of 91 miles (145 km) and three hours.

For details on the east-west connection with Chilapa, Olinalá, and Tlapa de Comonfort, see Getting There and Away under Chilapa and Olinalá in the Handicrafts Country section.

EXCURSIONS FROM CHILPANCINGO

Roads fan out from Chilpancingo to a number of spots worth visiting. These include Tixtla de Guerrero, the historic and colorful birthplace of Vicente Guerrero, the fascinatingly exotic La Organera Xochipala Archaeological Zone, and the easily accessible great outdoors of the Papagayo River and canyon.

Tixtla de Guerrero

The trip to Tixtla (pop. 20,000) is part of the fun of going there. Although it's only eight miles (12 km), Tixtla is over a mountain, where, at the summit, breezes are refreshing and the view is beautiful. The first glimpse of Tixtla is its green patchwork of orchards and fields, framed by high, pine-tufted ridges.

The place to arrive is the town-center plaza. Bus riders, get off at the adjacent Tixtla market, at the end of the line. Drivers, turn left on to the main north-south town street, several blocks after entering the town. Let the church's bell tower be your guide to the central plaza.

The plaza focuses around the **Monument to Vicente Guerrero,** a bronze likeness of the great general in a heroic cape.

Next, head across the street, south, from the plaza to the **house where Vicente Guerrero lived** and directed Mexico's rebellion against Spain. Although having been the Tixtla Presidencia Municipal since 1978, the house is a virtual shrine to Vicente Guerrero, not unlike Mount Vernon is for George Washington. The house's main attraction is a mural by Jaime A. Gómez de Payan that dramatically portrays major events and players in Mexican history. Moving clockwise: *insurgente* General Ignacio M. Altamirano (also born in Tixtla) with his hand on a jaguar's head; Benito Juárez surrounded by his contemporaries; José María Morelos passing the flame of liberty to Vicente Guerrero, who completes the struggle for independence; Emperor Cuauhtémoc, tortured for resisting Cortés.

From the plaza, head west (away from the church) to an open ceremonial plaza, fringed by market stalls and with a line of busts of eight of Tixtla's favorite sons and daughters. All of the busts are looking west to the adjacent monument, dedicated jointly to Vicente Guerrero and Ignacio M. Altamirano. A large tablet records the words of the two most famous of Tixtla's sons:

Before friendship, stands the homeland!
Before sentiment, stands the idea!
Before compassion, stands justice!

Ignacio M. Altamirano

Your voice, father, is sacred to me;
But the voice of my homeland comes first.

Vicente Guerrero

From the Guerrero-Altamirano monument, walk south along Calle Federico Encarnación about four blocks. Turn right, west, and walk three blocks to the small park, the **Cuna (Cradle) de Vicente Guerrero.** Vicente Guerrero was born in the modest house (occupied) at the rear of the park, on August 9, 1782.

If you get hungry during your Tixtla visit, a few clean plaza-front *torta* and taco *loncherías* supply wholesome snacks. For a further treat, hire a taxi to whisk you to the nearby **Centro Recreativo Tixtla** park, for a swim in the big spring-fed pool (and kiddie pool) and a picnic in the shade beneath a grove of big trees.

Although any day is good, Sunday is the best day to arrive in Tixtla, for the big ***tianguis*** native market, when *campesinos* troop in, loaded with for-sale handicrafts. These include soft palm *tenates* (tumpline baskets), sombreros, leather belts and huaraches, and colorfully embroidered *huipiles,* blouses, and skirts.

Get to Tixtla, by minibus, from the corner of Avenida Insurgentes and 17 de Octubre (near the Chilpancingo market) about 10 blocks (.6 mile, 1 km) north of the Chilpancingo *zócalo.* Drivers, get there from downtown Avenida Juan Álvarez, about eight blocks south of the *zócalo.* Head east, uphill, along Laureles. After two blocks, turn left on Zaragoza; continue three blocks to Heronias del Sur and turn right, uphill. Continue east, going uphill at every intersection, until you arrive at the Tixtla *libramento* highway, where you turn right and follow the traffic.

La Organera Xochipala Archaeological Zone

This half-day (60 miles, 100 km) trip to La Organera Xochipala (named for the zone's giant organ cactuses) is typical of other sites of the Mezcala culture, which were inhabited in the west and central inland areas of the present state of Guerrero for more than 1,000 years, until about A.D. 1400. Xochipala, which means "the flower that paints red" in the Aztec language, comprised an urban ceremonical center and probably

© BRUCE WHIPPERMAN

The name of the Organera Xochipala archaeological zone comes from the surrounding grove of great organ cactuses.

defensive refuge, for a community that probably lived and farmed in an adjacent river valley.

At the present, expertly restored site, archaeologists have partially rebuilt more than two dozen significant constructions, including colonnaded palaces, false-arched passageways, plazas, patios, temples, rooms, tombs, basements, and a ball court. Its forest of towering organ cactuses adds to La Organera Xochipala's invitingly exotic ambience.

Archaeologists have uncovered five stages in La Organera Xochipala's history. The oldest, now covered over by more recent construction, started with walls of cemented blocks, associated with pottery fragments identifiable with the Mexican classic period, A.D. 200–350. During the second stage of construction, around 200 years later, the builders added false arches, one of which formed the dome of a tomb of an adolescent. Most of the visible construction was completed during the third epoch, centering around A.D. 800. Builders completed columned, circular structures that supported flat roofs. The site declined during the fourth, "decadent," stage, in which old buildings were either abandoned or merely maintained. The site was completely abandoned during the fifth stage, around A.D. 1400.

Important clues have been discovered in the trash dumps left by the inhabitants: much pottery, similar to that used today, stone hatchets, metates, tiles, polishing stones, arrow and spear heads, leather, copper greenstone beads, and much more. All this, added to the evidence of trade in cotton, fruit, salt, seeds, and medicinal plants recorded at the time of the conquest, surely indicates a vibrant agricultural and commercial culture, with busy trade ties with both neighboring and distant communities.

Get to La Organera Xochipala by second-class Tlacotepec-bound bus or minivan from the main Chilpancingo bus station. (See Getting There and Away in the Chilpancingo section.) Ask the driver to let you off at the signed Zona Arqueológica side road on the left before Xochipala. The site is another two miles on foot.

Drivers, head north on old Highway 95 about 20 miles (33 km) to the signed Filo de Caballo paved secondary road. Turn left and continue uphill six miles (10 km) to the signed Zona Arqueológica dirt side road on the left. Continue two miles (3 km) to the signed gate on the right.

The Organera Xochipala archaeological zone is open daily except holidays approximately 9 A.M.–5 P.M. Few facilities, except a toilet, are available. Bring drinks, food for a picnic, sturdy walking shoes, and a hat.

River Country

Chilpancingo serves as an excellent jumping-off point to enjoy this trio of uniquely lovely natural attractions, set like gems, beneath the pine-tufted Sierra Madre del Sur.

Closest to Chilpancingo is the Río Azul, a popular Sunday picnic route, decorated along the way by a winding, intimate canyon, a lush green farm valley, colorful, petite market towns, climaxed by an azure ribbon of crystalline springs.

Although all that would be quite enough, a marvelous natural treat hides at the end of the 31-mile road: the Caves of Juxtlahuaca, a pristine wonderland grotto of varicolored limestone formations, underground rivers, prehistoric burial remains, and wall paintings, all culminating in a wondrous garden of flowery, snow-white aragonite (calcium carbonate) crystals.

South of Chilpancingo, the clear green Río Papagayo and its rocky canyon provide plenty of opportunities for swimming, kayaking, hiking, and camping.

THE RÍO AZUL

Heading Out

By bus, this trip could be done from Chilpancingo in one very long day. Start out at dawn, via a Colitlipa-bound bus, from the UPN (Universidad Pedagogical Nacional) streetfront bus terminal, at the corner of Ignacio Ramírez and Niños Héroes, three blocks south of the Chilpancingo main plaza. For more leisure, hire a taxi all day (figure about $50), or stay an extra day, camping or staying in a cabana at Balneario Santa Fe (see Río Azul Balnearios).

Travelers by car could likewise do this 74-mile (119-km) round-trip in a long day. Start off around 7 A.M., drive to the Juxtlahuaca Cave and explore until around 1 P.M. On the return, stop for a leisurely lunch and swim at the Balneario Santa Fe. Fill up with gasoline before you leave; otherwise, gas is customarily available en route at Quechultenango.

Along the Way: Petaquillas, Mochitlán, and Quechultenango

Drivers, follow old Highway 15 (not the expressway) south from Chilpancingo seven miles (11 km) to the signed Petaquillas-Quechultenango crossroad. Mark your odometer and turn left, east.

Immediately pass through **Petaquillas** (pop. 5,000, stores, local-style restaurants, town plaza, post office), known for its Balneario Bugambilias water slide, pool, and restaurant, a block from the town plaza. During the week before August 27, folks will also be celebrating their patronal **Fiesta de San Agustín,** with bullfights, plenty of food, a carnival, and regional dances, including the

Tlacololeros, Moros, Pastoras (Shepherdesses), and Diablos (Devils).

Continue east, winding through the narrow, precipitous canyon of the Río Azul. Although the riverbed will probably be dry during the winter and spring, don't worry; year-round springs keep the downstream delightfully crystal blue (except perhaps during some muddy summer rainy season floods).

At Mile 6 (Km 10) arrive at **Mochitlán** (pop. 4,000, *centro de salud*, post office, street market, taco shops, and stores), presiding over its lush irrigated riverbottom fields. If you have an extra few minutes, take a look inside the town's venerable barrel-nave church. It's the focus of the July 26 **Fiesta de Santa Ana,** when the townsfolk stage a float parade, carnival, fireworks, and enjoy regional dances, including the Tlacoleros, Santiagueros, Diablos, and Huexquitxles.

Continue east to **Quechultenango** (pop. 4,000), the dominant town of the upper Río Azul Valley, at Mile 17, Km 27. As if proclaiming the town's importance, the brilliantly decorated **church** presides over the east side of the plaza. Enter and pass the flowery *retablo* behind the Virgin of Guadalupe on the left. Overhead, paintings of the Stations of the Cross decorate the ceiling, while up front, behind the altar, Santiago, mounted on a silver horse, brandishes a sword while trampling a hapless band of defeated Moors.

Community celebration focuses yearly at that very altar during the eight-day **Fiesta of Santiago,** combined with the unique indigenous rite of Ocozuchil, all of which culminates on the Santiago Feast Day of July 25. People flock in from neighboring communities, among them men decked out in red leather with machetes in hand, to perform the traditional dance Los Santiagueros. Representing Christian warriors, their machetes clash menacingly and repeatedly with the swords of the Moors, whom the Santiagueros finally vanquish and force to accept baptism.

Concurrently other folks journey to the sierra to collect *ocozuchil*, an aromatic wild herb. When cut, the herb oozes a strong medicinal odor, thought to be curative. They walk to Quechultenango with the *ocozuchil* branches draped over their bodies and crowd into the church atrium. Inside, a chosen group of penitents pass, one by one in front of the image of Santiago, with an *ocozuchil* branch in each hand. Afterward, they dance, whirling to the mesmerizing beat of the pre-Hispanic *teponaxtli* drum.

The Source of the Río Azul

The series of *manantiales* (springs) at Coxcamila, one mile farther east of Quechultenango, at Mile 18, are the marvelous main source of the Río Azul. At the Coxcamila village center, go right, south, on to the dirt side road to the springs, called locally **El Borbollon.** Follow the pedestrian file about a quarter mile to a grove of giant old trees, from beneath whose gnarled roots cool crystal-clear water wells, free for everyone to enjoy.

On Sunday, dozens of cars loaded with picnickers gradually arrive in a big lot, where vendors sell corn on the cob, tamales, and soft drinks from wheelbarrows, cows stand around, men fill buckets for washing their trucks, women do laundry and bathe their children, while everyone else seems to be frolicking in the water.

That this is the source is certain. Walk upstream 100 yards, and the river is a mere trickle during the dry season. But downstream, many tens of thousands of gallons a minute of clear water, delightfully cool on a warm day, flow constantly.

Río Azul Balnearios

Farther downstream, activity focuses at three *balnearios* (bathing spots) on the Río Azul. These include **Los Manantiales** (several attractive swimming pools and restaurant at Mile 19, Km 31); **Los Sauces** (at Mile 22, Km 35, but apparently abandoned); and by far the most popular, **Balneario Santa Fe,** reachable by the signed paved side road, right at mile 19.4 (Km 31.2), about half a mile after Los Manantiales.

For Balneario Santa Fe, continue along the side road two miles (3 km), passing through the small but thriving Santa Fe town, to the river overlook, then downhill the last quarter mile to the river.

A dozen shady *palapa* restaurants line the clear, two-foot-deep flowing stream, a welcome marvel, especially during the dry and oft-hot winter and spring.

© BRUCE WHIPPERMAN

The cool, clear spring at Coxcamila forms nearly the entire flow of the Río Azul.

Besides ready food for eating and hammocks for resting, low-tech water sports abound. After taking your fill of swimming, inner-tubing, and rafting, cross the river suspension bridge to the other side, to the best of all possible swimming holes, complete with rope to swing out and plunge into the cool water.

If you decide to linger, the walk-in Campamento Santa Fe, also across the suspension bridge, offers some options. Choose one of the cramped cabanas ($8 for up to four people, $16 for up to eight). For a better choice, if you're equipped, set up your tent in one of the roomy camping spaces, $1.50 per person. Toilets are in shared lavatories. For a bath, jump in the river.

RV campers (with medium to small rigs) can park, in a large riverside lot accessible by driving carefully along the pedestrian walkway, past the riverside food *palapas.*

THE CAVES OF JUXTLAHUACA

The lightly touristed but wondrous Caves of Juxtlahuaca (Grutas de Juxtlahuaca) takes its name from its neighboring village, Juxtlahuaca (hooks-tlah-WAH-kah). The small town of Colotlipa, four miles before the cave, is the jumping-off point for guides, food, and services.

Colotlipa

Reach the town (pop. 4,000), not far past the Río Azul *balnearios,* 23 miles (37 km) east of old Highway 95. If you arrive during the February 18–26 **Fiesta del Señor de las Misericordias** (Lord of Mercy) festival, the plaza might be filled with celebrants, who, at dawn on February 26, climax the festivities by saluting their *patron* with jingle bells and *mañanitas* (birthday songs).

Besides the usual services, such as local-style restaurants, market fruits and vegetables, grocery stores, *centro de salud,* post office, and street telephones, Colotlipa is the place to hire your guide.

A right-side sign, on east-west plaza-front Calle Guerrero, marks the cave guides' at-home office. Up until the late 1990s, the main guide was Profesor Andrés Ortega Covarrubias, who during the 1950s was first to explore the cave thoroughly. Andrés, known locally as El Chivo (The Goat), is now semiretired. He leaves most of the guiding to his heirs: wife, son, and granddaughter, who continue the tradition as Chivo II, Chivo III, and Chivo IV.

EXPLORING THE CAVES OF JUXTLAHUACA

© BRUCE WHIPPERMAN

The Caves of Juxtlahuaca tour climaxes at a garden of crystalline aragonite as delicate as snowflakes on the cave wall and ceiling.

Although the Juxtlahuaca limestone cave complex, 30 miles (50 km) east of Chilpancingo, is not the world's largest, the treasures that it hides are exquisite and unique.

The cave complex, used as a burial ground and sacred site, probably by 400 B.C., was explored by latter-day investigators in 1926 and later more thoroughly by Andrés Ortega Covarrubias during the 1950s. Ortega uncovered a then-unknown entrance and eight underground branches, extending a total of about four miles (6 km).

As in all limestone caves, Juxtlahuaca's extensive limestone stalagmites, stalactites, columns, and curtains result from the slight solubility of limestone (calcium carbonate) in water. Thus groundwater, over eons, gradually dissolved the limestone, forming hollow chambers.

The process continues with water droplets falling from the ceiling, leaving a small wet spot above and a similar wet spot below, which dry and deposit some limestone at top and bottom. The dripping continues, gradually building the deposits into long, massive formations that, after many thousands of years, often merge to form grand columns. Water dribbling down the cave walls can deposit limestone similarly, forming magnificent curtains, lovely enough for a maharaja's palace.

Moreover, variations in mineral content, especially iron, causes color variations in the deposits, from pure white, to cream, dusty rose, and sienna. Explorers have named many of the formations thus created, such as the Enchanted Fountain, the Cathedral, the Salon of the Ghost, and the Tiger.

Bats and insects make up the bulk of the cave's permanent living inhabitants. Thousands of bats roost on the ceilings not far from the entrance; on the cave floor, cockroaches scurry, feasting on the bats' droppings.

Deep in the cave, humans have left their signs on the cave's walls and floors. Several burial sites, including complete petrified skeletons, much pottery, and *El Chaman, El Serpiente,* and *El Jaguar,* a trio of magnificent cave paintings, attest to the human presence that continues to the present day.

The Chivo guides have inherited the exclusive Juxtlahuaca Cave guide franchise, awarded to Andrés by the governor of Guerrero in 1958. They lead individuals and small groups for about $20 per person, or $10 per person in a larger group of four to eight.

Their complete tour (in Spanish), which lasts two to three hours and stretches about two underground miles round-trip, is fascinating, but moderately difficult. If at all possible, try not to miss the climactic conclusion, which requires wading along a knee-to-waist-deep underground river, then crawling 100 feet along a cramped, damp passageway. You'll get wet, but, at the end of the road, a marvelous garden of flowery aragonite crystals will be well worth the effort. Be sure to take along a pair of tennis shoes for wading and a small backpack or camera holster and watertight bags to keep your cameras dry and undamaged. Call at least a day in advance for a reservation, tel. 756/474-7006.

Get to the Caves of Juxtlahuaca from Colotlipa by taxi. By car, drive to the eastern edge of town, where a "Grutas" sign directs you left on to a paved secondary road. After three miles, pass a sugar cane–pressing mill on the left, which squeezes out juice for sweet *tepache* or for fermentation into fiery *aguardiente* white lightning. After four miles, arrive at the cave parking lot. Facilities consist only of a toilet and a sometimes *palapa* restaurant.

© BRUCE WHIPPERMAN

The Shotover Jet boat sits idle during the Papagayo River's late-spring low-water season.

THE RÍO PAPAGAYO

Only about 30 miles (50 km) south of Chilpancingo, both the old Highway 95 and the new toll expressway 95 D cross the clear, green, and wild Río Papagayo. Its cool waters and rocky canyon provide adventurers with plenty of swimming, rafting, canoeing, kayaking, hiking, rock-climbing, and informal camping opportunities.

The Shotover Jet

New Zealand has arrived on the Papagayo River, in the form of the Shotover Jet boat. ("Shotover" has nothing to do with target practice; it's the name of the original New Zealand boat inventor-promoter.) The local franchise, which began during the mid-1990s offering breezy jet boat rides on the Papagayo River, is about 45 minutes by *cuota* expressway south of Chilpancingo (about the same north of Acapulco). The boat ride runs about half an hour and costs about $50. The fee also includes use of the big, blue river-view pool and shady picnic area. A small restaurant also serves wholesome, tasty snacks and sandwiches.

But there's more. From the same base, named "Bravo Town," the staff also offers a menu of adventures, including hiking, camping, caving, rappeling, climbing, and rafting. For more information, contact tel. 744/484-1155, fax 744/484-2648, www.shotoverjet-acapulco.com.

Independent Options

None of this ecotouring hullabaloo prevents travelers from organizing their own Papagayo River adventures. Plenty of sandy riverfront is available, beneath the Papagayo River bridge (at old Highway 95 Km 322), for RV parking and tent camping. Food, water, and supplies are available at stores in nearby Tierra Colorada town.

The river itself is usually a lovely clear green and both swimmable and navigable by kayak, canoe, or rubber boat (except during the muddy June–Sept. flood season).

An option for those not equipped to camp is to go to Tierra Colorada (pop. 15,000), with nearby local-style riverfront swimming pools, bathing beaches, hotels, restaurants, and services.

Get to the Papagayo River from the Chilpancingo main bus station in a hour and a half by second-class bus to either Tierra Colorada or Acapulco via old Highway 95, by way of Tierra Colorada. For the Shotover Jet, ask the driver to let you out at the signed Tierra Colorada crossing. From there, walk, taxi, or thumb a ride along old Highway 95, the paved road southwest (beneath the toll expressway) downhill about four miles (follow the Shotover Jet signs) to the river.

By bus from Acapulco, go by second-class Tierra Colorada–bound bus from the Estrella Blanca Ejido Station. For the Shotover Jet, ask the bus driver to let you off at the Shotover Jet riverfront headquarters a fraction of a mile past the old Highway 15 Papagayo River bridge, at Km 322.

By car, drive about 30 miles (50 km) or 45 minutes south from Chilpancingo (or the same north from Acapulco) via the *cuota* expressway to the Tierra Colorada exit and old Highway 15. For the Shotover Jet, head under the expressway, along old Highway 15, about four miles southwest to the Shotover Jet headquarters, or a fraction of a mile farther, to the Highway 15 bridge, where dirt roads lead downhill to the river.

If instead you're bound for Tierra Colorada, back at the old Highway 15 freeway exit head the opposite direction from the Shotover Jet, downhill a mile or two to Tierra Colorada.

(If you have an extra hour and enjoy handicrafts, stop by **Acahuizotla** two miles off the Acapulco expressway, about 17 miles, 28 km, south of Chilpancingo. Folks make and sell fetching curios carved from the rose-colored wood of the *palo de morado* tree.)

Handicrafts Country

Their renowned handicrafts draw a steady stream of buyers and visitors to these upcountry mountain towns. Be sure to arrive in Chilapa, only an hour's travel east of Chilpancingo, early for the Sunday *tianguis,* native market, where craftspeople from all over the Guerrero Sierra Madre bring their best for sale.

Travel a few hours farther east to Olinalá and visit the workshops of the masters of a preconquest lacquerware tradition whose intriguingly mysterious origins are lost in time.

CHILAPA

Presiding over its rich spring-fed mountain valley, Chilapa de Álvarez (pop. 20,000, elev. 4,300 feet, 1,310 meters) was named in honor of the liberal hero General Juan Álvarez (1810–1867).

History

The other part of the town's name comes from Chilapan, a label that comes from the Aztec—from *chili* (red), *atl* (water), and *pan* (on or above). It translates roughly as "on the red water," or simply, "red river."

An early historical reference to Chilapan comes from the time of Emperor Moctezuma I (Moctezuma Ilhuacamina), who, around A.D. 1450, was expanding his domain. He ordered his subordinate officer, Texcolo Tecutlique, to establish an outpost beneath the mountain Chilapantépetl, which eventually became the town of Chilapan.

In 1522, the Spanish, in the person of Hernán Cortés's lieutenant, conquistador Gonzalo Sandoval, conquered the local people. Soon, Augustinian missionaries arrived and began converting the natives and building a church and convent, which they dedicated to Saint Augustine on October 5, 1533.

The Augustinian friars encouraged the Chilapa people to expand their long-established weaving

Local members of the spiny agave family populate the slopes near Chilapa, along Highway 93.

tradition. For many centuries before the conquest, their elaborately crafted blankets, *huipiles,* and skirts had been traded all over southern Mexico. Under the guidance of the Augustinians, they broadened their skills, eventually crafting the wide variety of baskets and hats, napkins and pottery, that make up the rich Chilapa handicrafts tradition that continues to the present day.

Getting Oriented and Getting Around

The prime orientation point upon Chilapa arrival is the main highway crossing by the crafts market, marked by the permanent stalls behind the fence just east of the crossing. If you arrive on a Sunday, park your car or get off your bus and head for the crafts market. Later, from the crossing, you can reach the downtown plaza either on foot (about half a mile south), or bici-taxi (bicycle rickshaw), taxi, or your own wheels.

Sights

Beginning Saturday afternoon, country folks, loaded with hand-made goods, begin arriving for the renowned **Chilapa Sunday crafts market.** Their wealth of offerings customarily include an array of materials—**leather:** bags, belts, coin purses, wallets, shoes, huaraches; **shell and horn:** bracelets, combs, ashtrays, desk sets, lampshades; **iron:** machetes, hatchets, daggers, swords, knives; **textiles,** many handpainted or embroidered: bags of *ixtle* (agave fiber), shawls *(rebozos),* napkins, tablecloths, *huipiles;* **basketry:** palm sombreros, mats, and baskets, reed baskets; and **wood:** miniature castles and bulls, human tiger-masked figures, pine furniture, musical instruments, and animal figurines.

Many crafts come from outside Chilapa—for example, shawls from Tenancingo; silver from Taxco; huaraches from Iguala and Tixtla; fireworks from Ayahualulco; lacquerware and tiger masks from Olinalá; papier mâché from Mezcala; bright earth-red pottery from Atzcualoya; *amate* (painted bark paper) from Amayaltepec; animal figures from Temalacatzingo; and embroidered blouses and skirts from Acatlán.

You might also stroll through the colorful **main market,** adjacent, east of the crafts market. Here, the double meaning of *tianguis,* the native name for both awning and market, becomes abundantly clear in the seeming acres

© BRUCE WHIPPERMAN

The Chilapa churchfront is a good spot to catch a "bici-taxi" ride.

of colorful awnings. The excitement begins on the market-front steps, where women sell small piles of produce (radishes, corn, small pumpkins, squash, mangoes in the March–July season, beans, and mountain herbs).

For more sights, head south to the downtown plaza and towering neo-Gothic **cathedral,** dedicated to St. Francis and seat of the local bishop. One of the cathedral's main attractions occurs every Sunday at noon, when the miraculous roses of the Virgin of Guadalupe are revealed to mechanical figures of Don Diego and Archbishop Zumárraga at the door on the right bell tower. Inside the cool nave, spectacularly large stained glass windows, each one donated by a Guerrero locality, add daytime cheer to the cavernous interior. Up front, contemplate the image of mother Mary above the altar being lifted to heaven by a band of angels.

Back outside the church, a fleet of bici-taxis (BEE-see), looking every bit like Indian subcontinent bicycle rickshaws, stop and pick up passengers at curbside.

Before leaving the Chilapa plaza, be sure to stop for a drink or snack and admire the marvelous mask collection at the plaza-front Casa Pilla restaurant.

Accommodations and Food

Chilapa visitors enjoy a pair of recommendable hotels. About three blocks north of the plaza is **Hotel María Hilda,** at Av. Revolución 229, Chilapa, Guerrero, tel. 756/475-1840. The hotel's 36 rooms occupy two stairway-accessible floors above street level. Rooms are cool, clean, light, and sparely but comfortably furnished with bedspreads, curtains, and tiled hot-water shower baths. They have no reading lamps, however. Most rooms have all double beds, one, two, or three in a room. A few rooms have king-sized beds. Rates run $14 s, $17 d (one bed); $23 s or d in king; $23 d (two beds); $26 t (two beds); and $30 t (three beds), with cable TV and parking, but no fans or a/c.

"Cleanliness Is Our Rule" at **Hotel Las Brisas** at the Chilpancingo highway intersection, Prolongacion Av. Revolución 2, Chilapa, Guerrero, tel. 756/475-0769. Here you get to choose from 36 clean rooms, comfortably furnished, with double beds, shiny wood furniture, bright bedspreads, and small but tiled hot-water shower baths. Some rooms have bedside reading lamps. Expect to pay about $14 s or d (one bed), 24 d, t, or q (two beds), $33 for 3–6 in three beds, with cable TV and parking, but no fans or a/c. Reserve the quietest rooms (with least highway noise): 5, 6, or 7 on the second and third floors.

Some of Chilapa's best budget food is available at the several permanent *jugerías* (juices, *tortas,* and *hamburguesas,* $1–3) and *fondas* (stews, soups, tacos, *chiles rellenos,* enchiladas, $2–4), at the rear of the main market floor, at the highway crossing north of downtown. One of the best is *fonda* **Doña Lilia,** which specializes in savory chicken or pork *pozole* and steaming *guisado de res* (beef stew), daily 7:30 A.M.–7 P.M.

One of Chilapa's best sit-down eateries is restaurant-bakery **Casa Pilla,** tel. 756/475-0263, open daily 8 A.M.–8 P.M., at the northeast downtown plaza corner. If not for the food, Casa Pilla is unforgettable for the wondrous mask collection that adorns its airy dining room. The menu is nevertheless both recognizable and appetizing: breakfasts (pastries, fruit, omelettes, pancakes, $2–5), lunch and dinner (hamburgers, spaghetti, pork chops, seafood, and *pozole,* $3–7).

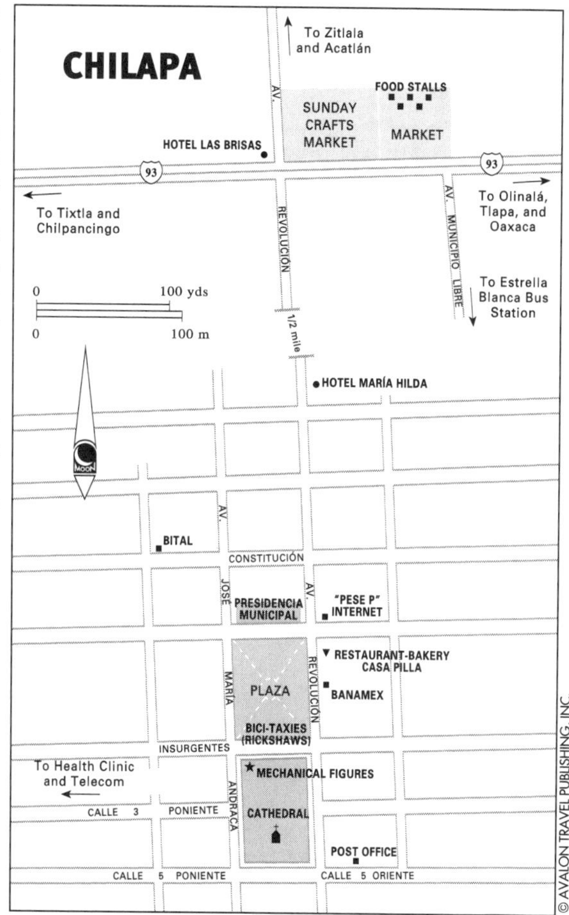

Entertainment and Events

Chilapa takes time out for a pair of colorful yearly fiestas. First comes the **Fiesta de San Juan,** in which, around June 24, folks crowd the plaza to watch a parade of floats, listen to the oompah of country bands, fireworks, and enjoy their favorite regional dances, including the Pescados (Fish) and Moros y Cristianos (Moors and Christians).

Those who didn't get a chance to celebrate earlier get another opportunity when townsfolk parade their patron at the August 15 **Fiesta de la Virgen de la Asunción.**

Services

A number of essential services are available near the downtown Chilapa plaza.

Banks: Find at least two banks, with 24-hour ATMs. Best bet is long-hours Banco Internacional (Bital). From the plaza's northwest corner, walk a block north to Constitución, turn left, west, and continue a block to the bank, open Mon.–Sat. 8 A.M.–7 P.M., tel. 756/475-2396. Alternatively, go to Banamex**,** on the east side of the plaza, open Mon.–Fri. 9 A.M.–4 P.M., tel. 756/465-0010.

Communications: The *correo* (post office) is on the south side of the plaza on Calle 5 Oriente (East). From the plaza's southeast corner, walk south. At Calle 5 Oriente (just past the south end of the church), go left about three doors, to the *correo* at number 394, open Mon.–Fri. 9 A.M.–3 P.M., tel. 756/475-0066. For telephone, either buy a Ladatel phone card and use one of the plaza-front street telephones, or go to Telecom, on Calle 3 Poniente (West), for public telephone, fax, and money orders. From the southwest (church-front) plaza corner, walk south a block to Calle 3 Poniente. Turn right and continue, past the Centro de Salud, three blocks to Telecom, open Mon.–Fri. 9 A.M.–3 P.M., Sat.–Sun. 9 A.M.–1 P.M. Internet connection is available at Pese P

© BRUCE WHIPPERMAN

Flowers are a big seller at the Chilapa market.

Internet store, at the northeast plaza corner, open daily 9 A.M.–9 P.M., tel. 956/475-2400, chelisinc@hotmail.com.

Health: For medical attention, let your hotel desk clerk call a doctor for you. Alternatively, go to the Centro de Salud, with a doctor on call 24 hours, tel. 756/475-0077, at Calle 3 Poniente 703, a block east of the Telecom.

Getting There and Away

By Bus: From Chilpancingo, get to Chilapa via a first- or second-class departure from the Estrella Blanca main bus station. From Acapulco, Chilapa is similarly accessible from the Estrella Blanca Avenida Ejido terminal.

For Chilapa bus departure, go by taxi or bicitaxi to the local Estrella Blanca terminal, at Av. Municipio Libre 1804, tel. 756/475-0032. Find it about a block east of the market to Municipio Libre, then right (south) about a mile. From the terminal, a number of first- and second-class buses connect daily with Chilpancingo and Acapulco. One bus per day connects with Olinalá, and another with Tlapa de Comonfort, where connections are available with Puebla and Oaxaca destinations.

By Car: The good, super-scenic, all-paved but winding Highway 93 connects Chilpancingo with Chilapa in 34 miles (54 km), in about an hour. In the opposite direction, Highway 93 connects Chilapa with Tlapa de Comonfort over three 7,000-foot ridges, in about 75 miles (121 km) of smooth, scenic, but winding highway, in about three hours. In all cases, fill up with gasoline at the Chilapa station on the highway.

Reach Olinalá by starting out driving east toward Tlapa. But after about 57 miles (92 km), 2.5 hours, turn left, north, from Highway 93 at the signed Olinalá junction. Continue north about 30 potholed miles (50 km), an hour and a half, to Olinalá, for a total of about four hours from Chilapa.

OLINALÁ

Reigning over its fertile, mountain-rimmed valley on the edge of the sunny basin of the Río Balsas, Olinalá is famous not only for its renowned lacquerware, but also for its masks and furniture. Most Olinalá families are involved in lacquerware, and a number of artisans welcome visitors into their home factory-stores.

THE ART OF DON CHICO CORONEL

Olinalá's native son Francisco "Don Chico" Coronel is the nationally acknowledged master of the style of lacquerware that has made Olinalá famous. Born in 1941, young Francisco was apprenticed into the traditional craft of lacquerware as it had been learned by nameless generations of Olinalá youths before him.

Originally, Olinalá craftspeople had made an art of lacquer-decorated gourds. Demand extended the original craft to trinket and jewel boxes, then trays and chests, tables and chairs, and more.

But regardless of size and variety, the method has remained constant. First, the wood is collected, cut, carved to shape, and hand-sanded. A base coat of *chia* seed oil, colored with a locally gathered and ground natural mineral pigment, is applied and left to dry. The piece is then burnished to a shine with a smooth stone, and the whole process is repeated many times over. After the last coat of oil has been applied, the piece is left to dry for a month.

Craftspeople next lay out designs, which are engraved into the piece, traditionally with a natural agave needle. Vivid colors are painted into the engraving to create a harmonious animal or floral design.

During the 1970s, Don Chico began adding gold to his colors, creating rich and lovely gilded flowers, birds, rabbits, and much more, in his designs.

Some Olinalá craftspeople, impatient with the time-consuming traditional materials and processes, are using commercial pigments and oils and faster machine methods. In some cases quality has suffered.

But that's not true of Don Chico's art. He continues to work by the traditional methods and materials. He's become so famous that presidents have commissioned him to make gifts representative of Mexican craftsmanship. Don Chico responded by making a magnificent tray for Queen Elizabeth II of Great Britain. And when Pope John Paul came to Mexico in July 2002 to canonize the first Latin American indigenous saint, President Vicente Fox presented John Paul a regal chest made by Francisco "Don Chico" Coronel, of Olinalá.

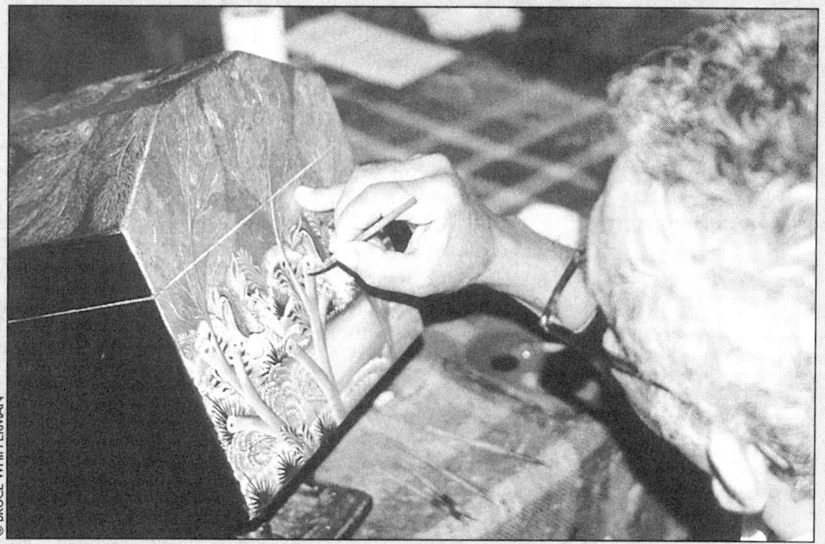

Acknowledged Olinalá lacquerware maestro Francisco "Don Chico" Coronel finishes a finely crafted box.

Arrival and Orientation

Olinalá (pop. 5,000, elev. 4,000 feet, 1,300 meters) is basically a large, easy-to-explore village. As in most Mexican towns, Olinalá's streets run north-south and east-west.

Bus travelers from Chilpancingo-Chilapa arrive at the Olinalá main plaza. Drivers, turn left, west, two or three blocks after the ingress highway bridge. Within about four blocks, you'll likewise arrive at the main town plaza.

Orient yourself by the Presidencia Municipal portals on the plaza's west side, and the church, on the opposite, east side. Olinala's two main streets, Ramón Ibarra and Vicente Guerrero, run east-west along the south and north sides of the plaza, respectively.

Sights and Shopping

For a revealing preview of the finest of all possible Olinalá lacquerwork, head first to the town showplace **Templo de San Francisco,** one of Mexico's unique churches, on the plaza's east side.

Inside, a riot of lacquerware, known locally as *linaoe* (lee-nah-OH-ay), dominates the decorations. Although many local artisans have contributed to the decorations, some features stand out. The nave columns, in contrasting cream and maroon, are the work of the acknowledged Olinalá master *artesano* Francisco Coronel.

Also, don't miss the right front side chapel, dedicated to the Virgin of Guadalupe. And before you leave, be sure to look at the mural by the front door, featuring a unique Trinity. Its deity-trio, all of whom resemble Jesus, rain avenging angels down upon devils and sinners in hell.

Next, go to the source, the workshop-store of maestro **Francisco "Don Chico" Coronel.** He welcomes visitors during the day at Juan Aldama 12, tel. 756/473-0084. From the plaza's southwest corner, walk west, uphill, along Ibarra, a few blocks to Aldama, turn right, and continue a few doors to the maestro's house on the right. Inside, if you're lucky, you'll get to watch him applying the finishing touches to a fine piece of work. The masterfully crafted and detailed treasury—*bateas* (trays), *cajas* (boxes), *arcas* (chests), *calabazas* (gourds)—that decorates his workshop represents the pinnacle of Olinalá craftsmanship. Collectively, the pieces represent the essence of many centuries of experience and practice. Individually, each piece is the prized product of hours of meticulous work, gathering and processing the natural raw materials, sanding, painting, burnishing, engraving, and finally the fine finish painting that maestro Francisco applies. The prices that he asks, typically $40–60 for small-to-medium pieces, are modest indeed.

Several other noted Olinalá artisans welcome visitors. Back at the plaza's southeast corner, walk downhill, east, along Ibarra one block. Turn right, on Matamoros, and continue a few doors to the shop of **Adolfo Escudero Mejia,** at Matomoros 5, tel. 756/473-0075. He specializes in beautiful, meticulously designed and adorned boxes, chests, and trays, many of innovative decoration.

Continue east, downhill, along Ibarra a long

block to Comonfort. Turn right to find, on the left, Cajita Linaloe, the shop of *artesana* **Audelia Rendón Franco,** at Comonfort 3, tel. 756/473-0029. Her factory store and workshop (visitors welcome), in the rear, is the ongoing result of more than 200 years of family tradition. It abounds with a myriad of lacquerware: mirrors, boxes large and small, *calabazas,* picture frames, jaguar masks, and much more. (If you want to see still more, look inside the **Art Olinalá** store back on the southeast corner of Comonfort and Ibarra.)

For yet more fine lacquerware, masks, and much more, visit the even more remote village of **Temalacatcingo** (pop. 2,000), 17 miles (27 km) by bus or minivan via the graveled road north from Olinalá. After about 13 miles (20 km), turn right at the fork to Ahuacatlán, and continue past Ahuacatlán for about two miles.

Accommodations and Food

Olinalá accommodates visitors with at least two acceptable hotels. The best choice is **Hotel Sindi,** at 46 Guerrero, Olinalá, Guerrero, two blocks east of the plaza, tel. 756/473-0114. I arrived at night and nearly missed the place, because its illuminated sign says "Corona Hotel" (for Corona Beer, which installed the sign). This loosely run family establishment offers about 15 rooms (not all in operating condition at this writing) in three exterior corridor-floors overlooking a parking lot-garden. If you make your way past the store-front-desk and the stashes of semitrash along hallways and in corners, you'll find the rooms decently clean and attractive, with pink bedspreads and tiled baths. With the added pluses of hot water, ceiling fan (make sure yours works), TV, parking, and airy upstairs restaurant, you'll have a deal at $12 s, $16 d.

Second choice goes to four-floor **Hotel Coral,** half a block east of the plaza, at Ramón Ibarra s/n, Olinalá, Guerrero, tel. 747/563-0194. A popular stopping place for truck drivers, the Coral offers about 30 plain but clean bare-bulb rooms with colorful tile, fluffy bedspreads, curtains, and hot-water showers. Rates run $7 s, $12 d (in one double bed), $17 d (two double beds), with fan and TV; street parking only.

As for food, economy meals (soups, stews, tacos, enchiladas, *pozole* and more) are the specialties of the several ***fondas*** (food stalls) that set up daily (and nightly) on the north side of the plaza.

For sit-down breakfast, lunch, and supper, the best choice in town is the charming **Pozoleria La Cabaña,** open Mon.–Sat. 8 A.M.–10 P.M., Sunday 8 A.M.–3 P.M., on Ibarra, half a block east of the plaza. Savvy owners have turned a rustic, massive-beamed old house into a restaurant that fits its name perfectly. Part of the fun of La Cabaña is the eclectic old-time collection—masks, *cazuelas* (stewing crocks), gourds, wooden spoons, long-horn cattle skulls, and a yellowed portrait of Emiliano Zapata—that decorates the walls. Although La Cabaña's specialty is savory, country-style *pozole,* your choices are more varied. For breakfast, choose among juice, Nescafé, fruits, eggs, and potatoes ($2–5); for lunch, order either à la carte or a three-course set *comida corrida,* with choice of seafood, stew, chicken ($3–4); for supper, go for *pozole* or *chiles rellenos,* tacos, and enchiladas ($2–5).

Entertainment and Events

If you like old-Mexico color and don't mind crowds, time your visit to coincide with either of Olinalá's big festivals, the **Fiesta de Pascua** (Passover) during the week before Easter Sunday, or the patronal **Fiesta de San Francisco de Asis,** October 2–5.

During the Easter festival, the highlight, besides plenty of food, handicrafts for sale, fireworks, cockfights, and carnival, is the procession of the Stations of the Cross that reenacts the Passion of Jesus.

Later, the San Francisco festival features much of the same, plus a big for-sale handicrafts exposition, *mojigangos* (giant dancing effigies), and favorite traditional dances, including Los Tigres, Los Tecuanes, and the French courtship Danza de los Doce Pares. (Make your hotel reservation early.)

Services

Olinalá provides some essential services within a block of the plaza.

Banks: First try Banco Internacional, on Guerrero, a block west of the plaza, open Mon.–Sat. 8 A.M.–7 P.M. Alternatively, go to Bancomer, beneath the Presidencia Municipal portal, west side of the plaza, open Mon.–Fri. 9 A.M.–4 P.M. Both have ATMs.

Communications: Find the *correo* (post office) and Telecom (fax and money orders) beneath the Presidencia Municipal portal, west of the plaza. The *correo* is open Mon.–Fri. 8 A.M.–3 P.M. Telecom is open Mon.–Fri. 9 A.M.–3 P.M., Saturday 9 A.M.–noon. Longer hours for public telephone and fax are available at the Farmacia Discuento.

Health: Olinalá provides a number of options. For simple medications and advice, try Farmacia Discuento, with Dr. Pardo Guzmán in charge, tel. 756/473-0346, open Mon.–Sat. 8 A.M.–3 P.M. and 4–10 P.M., Sunday 8 A.M.–3 P.M., on the north side of Ibarra, a block west of the plaza, corner of H. Colegio Militar. Doctors are also available for consultations. Drop in to the 24-hour Centro de Salud, tel. 756/473-0040, across the street from Farmacia Discuento. Of Olinalá's private physicians, Dr. Cipriano López Hernandéz is highly recommended, at 85 Guerrero, about three blocks downhill, east of the plaza. Alternatively, visit Doctora Marizela Jiménez, also on Guerrero, half a block east of the plaza.

Getting There and Away

By Bus: To reach Olinalá, bus travelers can connect via Estrella Blanca buses from western destinations of Acapulco (via Chilpancingo) and Chilapa. (See Chilapa and Chilpancingo sections.)

In Olinalá, the plaza kiosk snack bar sells Estrella Blanca bus tickets for the one daily Chilapa-Chilpancingo westbound departure from the plaza.

Bus connections with northern and eastern destinations, including Mexico City and the states of Puebla, Morelos, and Oaxaca, are available at the Sur bus terminal, tel. 747/563-3009, on Ibarra, about three blocks west of the plaza.

By Car: To or from the west, drivers can connect with Olinalá, via Highway 93, to or from Chilpancingo via Chilapa. Westbound, about 57 miles (92 km), 2.5 hours, after Chilapa, head left, north, from Highway 93 at the signed Olinalá junction. Continue north about 30 potholed miles (50 km), 1.5 hours, to Olinalá, for a total of about four hours from Chilapa (or 121 miles, 195 km, about five hours, from Chilpancingo).

To or from the north and east (Mexico City and the states of Morelos, Puebla, and Oaxaca), connect via Highway 190 via Izucar de Matamoros, Puebla, or Huajuapan de León, Oaxaca, at the Highway 190 junction with Highway 92 (37 miles, 59 km) south of Izucar, or 57 miles (92 km) west of Huajuapan. Head south 78 miles (126 km) to the Olinalá junction at Huamuxtitlán. Continue via west-bound secondary road another 17 miles (27 km), via Cuauhlote, Cualac, and Xhiacingo, to Olinalá. For this trip, figure a total of about four hours from Izucar, five from Huajuapan.

Iguala

Only a tiny fraction of the vacationers hurrying south to Acapulco bother to stop in Iguala (pop. 100,000, elev. 2,430 feet, 740 meters). Consequently, Iguala is nearly tourist-free. This is remarkable, since the town's official name, Iguala de la Independencia, is much more than a slogan. Iguala is a major patriotic-historic center of Mexico and cradle of Agustín de Itúrbide's Plan de Iguala, which spelled out Mexican Independence, and his Flag of the Three Guarantees, the red, white, and green tricolor beneath which Itúrbide finally rode triumphantly into Mexico City, on September 27, 1821.

Local folks don't seem to mind the lack of tourist hullabaloo, however. They go about their business, living well from the agricultural bounty—fruit, corn, cattle—of their fertile, spring-fed valley.

They also love their pedestrian-friendly downtown, with not one but three shady plazas, sprinkled with juice and snack stands and cafés.

All this would be easily worth an overnight, but Iguala offers much more: a whole complex of many dozens of shops selling gold jewelry, the fascinating Museum and Sanctuary to the Flag, and, not to be missed, atop a breezy view hillside, a spectacularly large Mexican flag, billowing gracefully above a monument to the Heroes of the Independence.

Excursions nearby lead to Lake Tuxpan, for possible boating and camping, and adjacent lovely Quinta Alegre bathing resort. Farther afield, ruins enthusiasts can visit Teopantecuantlán and Cuetlajuchitlán, a pair of fascinating partly restored pre-Columbian ceremonial centers.

HISTORY

The name Iguala comes from the town's former Aztec-language label, Yohualtépetl, which means, very appropriately, "basin surrounded by mountains." After the conquest, the local Spanish missionaries shifted the name to the more pronounceable Yohuala, and finally, Iguala.

Chontal-speaking people at least as early as A.D. 800 founded the town, which was originally known as Motlacehuatl, an Iguala district still called "old town." During the Aztec expansions of the A.D. 1400s, warriors under direction of Emperor Izcoatl conquered Motlacehuatl and erected a temple. Aztec colonists arrived and prospered on the labor of their Chontal-speaking slaves and servants. According to the 16th-century *Codex Mendocino,* the official Aztec hieroglyph of Yohualtépetl was a star-centered circle with nine stars around its circumference.

The Spanish arrived in 1522 and replaced the Aztec temple, warriors, and settlers with their own church, soldiers, and colonists. They prospered for nearly 300 years until the surrounding region, ignited by Miguel Hidalgo's 1810 cry for independence and led by Generals José María Morelos and Vicente Guerrero, became a focus of anti-Spanish rebellion.

From 1811 to 1821 Spanish troops fought an agressive but losing campaign, battling rebel guerrillas from the cool, pine-tufted high sierra to Acapulco's summery shoreline. Finally, the independence drama climaxed in Iguala on February 24, 1821, when Agustín Itúrbide, former royalist general turned rebel, joined forces with Guerrero.

Their agreement was based on the Plan de Iguala, an independence strategy based on more than two dozen points. The Plan of Iguala was essentially a moderate compromise that both the conservative white elite that Itúrbide represented and Guerrero's indigenous and mestizo campesinos could agree upon. It called for an independent Mexico with a parliament presided over by a constitutional Spanish monarchy, much as the 19th-century English monarchs presided over the Dominion of Canada. The Plan de Iguala even invited King Ferdinand VII of Spain to agree to all of this, which he never did.

The core of the plan that lasted were the Trigarantias (Three Guarantees): independence, Catholicism, and equality of all Mexicans (for men only, however).

Later, on October 27, 1849, Iguala was chosen as the first capital of the new state of Guerrero, with General Juan Álvarez as governor. Soon, in early 1850, the first state legislature met in Iguala. Later, the capital shifted to Tixtla, and finally Chilpancingo, by the end of the 19th century.

SIGHTS

Arrival and Orientation

Most bus passengers arrive at the Estrella Blanca bus station, north side of the main market, corner of Galeana and Salazar. For the center of town, walk seven blocks north along Galeana (to the right as you exit the terminal), or ride a *colectivo* minivan to the *zócalo* (central plaza). (If, however, you arrive at the east-side Estrella de Oro bus station, on Highway 95, do the same by either minivan or walking eight blocks west, away from the highway, along Bandera Nacional to the *zócalo.*)

Drivers arriving via Highway 95 from Taxco heading south, or from Chilpancingo heading north, follow "Centro," or "Zócalo" highway signs west after passing the *periférico* peripheral boulevard (heading south, turn right; heading north, turn left). Continue about eight blocks west to the *zócalo.*

At the Iguala town center you'll find a trio of inviting plazas: from east to west, first comes the **Plaza de Trigarantias,** bordered by Avenida Vicente Guerrero on the north and Avenida Bandera Nacional on the south. Move diagonally southwest, across the corner of Bandera Nacional and north-south Calle Altamirano, to find the broad garden **Plaza y Monumento a la Bandera,** bordered on the south by Calle Aldama.

Finally, move diagonally northwest, across the corner of Calle Juan Álvarez and Avenida Bandera Nacional, to the ***zócalo*** (plaza), the very heart of the town. Its bordering streets are one-block Constitución, on its north side; Juárez, on the west side; Reforma, on the south side; and Álvarez, on the east side. Note the landmarks: the Museum and Sanctuary to the Flag on its west, Juárez side, and the Hotel María Isabel, on its Constitución, north, side.

The Zócalo

The downtown *zócalo,* one of Guerrero's most

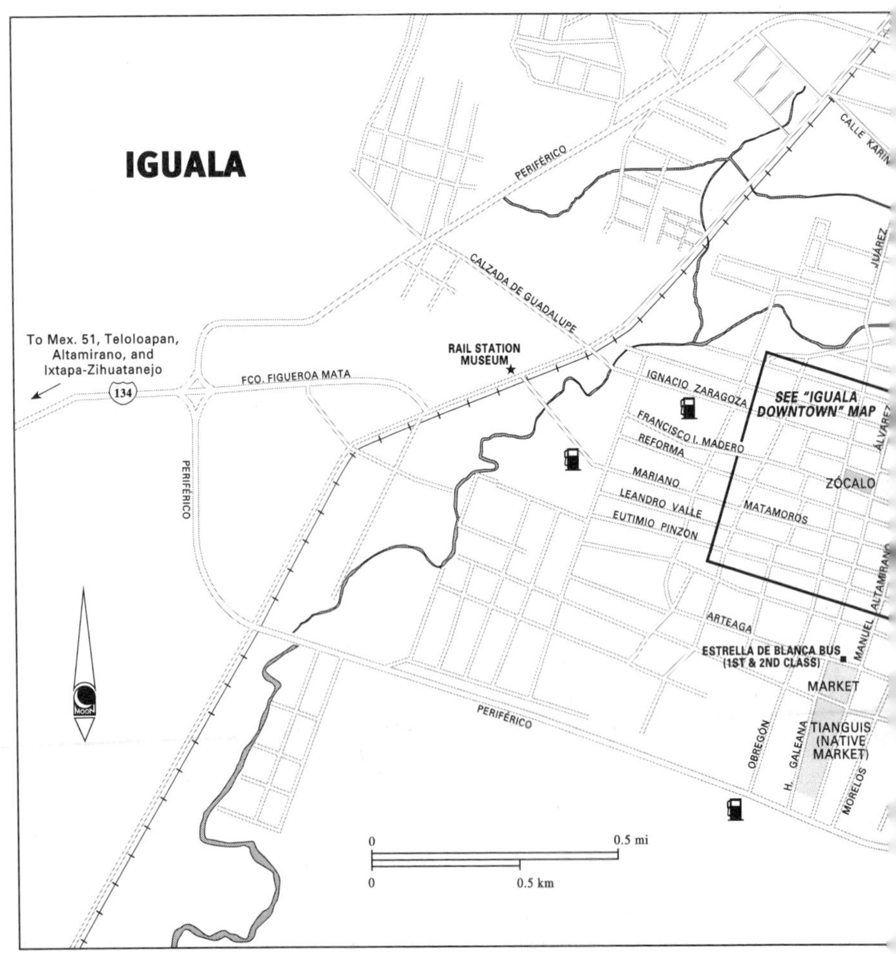

pleasant town plazas, is a relaxing people-watching sight all in itself. Pause for a refreshment at one of the juice bars and enjoy the shade beneath the 32 leafy tamarind trees, planted in 1832, thanks to General Don Luis Gonzaga Vieyra.

Museo y Santuario a la Bandera

From the *zócalo,* walk west, across Juárez, to the Museo y Santuario a la Bandera, open Tues.–Sat. 9 A.M.–6 P.M., Sunday 9 A.M.–3 P.M., tel. 733/333-6765. The museum has three main *salas* (exhibition halls), all worth a visit.

The **Sala de las Banderas** exhibits about two dozen historic Mexican flags, led off by the celebrated tricolor Bandera de las Trigarantias, with its diagonal white, green, and red stripes. They represent the Plan of Iguala's Three Guarantees: pure white, for the Catholic religion, green for independence, and red, representing equality for all the races of Mexico.

Also notable is the eagle-and-serpent Aztec "flag," from the Aztec historical document the *cronica Mexcáyotl,* as preserved in the postconquest record, the *Codex Duran.*

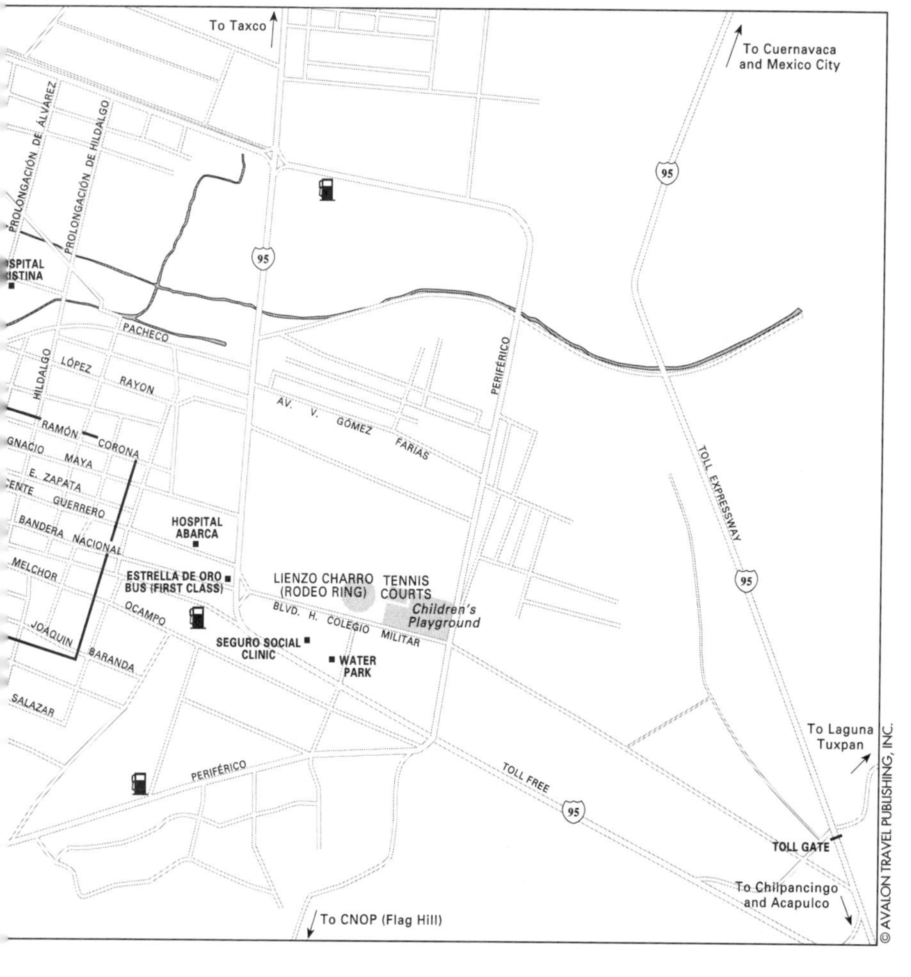

The 20-odd remaining flags are remarkable, partly for their evolutionary linkages to the present Mexican national flag, adopted in 1952, at the end of the hall.

Continue to the **Sala Plan de Iguala,** which exhibits, besides the words of the Mexican national anthem, a copy of the original Plan de Iguala, signed by Agustín de Itúrbide on February 24, 1821, next to a more readable modern copy. The Plan de Iguala is interesting, partly for its comparison with the revolutionary-period documents of the United States. While the Mexican document effectively declares Catholicism to be the religion of the land and all races to be equal, its U.S. counterparts, such as the Declaration of Independence and the Bill of Rights, say nothing about equality of the races and next to nothing about religion, except the freedom to worship (or not to worship) thereof.

© BRUCE WHIPPERMAN

The town-center *zócalo* provides a shady respite during Iguala's many warm spring and summer days.

The third hall is the **Sanctuary to the Mexican Flag,** with a grand, illuminated Mexican flag at one end of a hushed and darkened room.

More Downtown Sights

From the museum, head due east to the *zócalo*'s southeast corner. Diagonally southeast, across the corner of Álvarez and Bandera Nacional, spreads the **Plaza y Monumento a la Bandera** (Monument to the Flag). The plaza's grand central memorial, dedicated in 1942 by then-President Manuel Ávila Camacho, reflects the Socialist Realism style of the day. It depicts an abnormally husky native couple, the woman with torch in hand, guarding the flag. On the monument itself, an inscription translates as: ". . . the city of Iguala, cradle of Mexican Independence, the consummation proclaimed here, on February 24, 1821." Before moving on, you might stroll over to the plaza's northeast (church side) corner for a look at the bronze bust memorializing Francisco Gonzales Bocanegra, author of the words for the Mexican national anthem.

The **Centro Joyero de Iguala** (Jewelry Center) is both a sight and a shopping ground. Find it at the corner of Reforma and Obregón, just one block south of the *zócalo*'s southeast corner. Inside, a swarm of shops sell seemingly everything possible that can be made of gold, daily 9 A.M.–7 P.M. (For more specifics, see the Shopping section.)

The **Rail Station Museum,** in the process of being finished at this writing, will probably be open for visitors by the time you read this. Find it, at the west end of downtown: Taxi or walk (about a mile) beginning along Reforma, a block south of the *zócalo.* Go four blocks and turn left at the dead end (at the library), at Mariano Herrera. Continue one short block and turn right, west, at the fire station, corner of 18 de Marzo. Continue two short blocks to diagonal street Calzada del Ferrocarril; follow it about two blocks to the old rail station, across the railroad track.

Sights out of Downtown

Although initially I didn't plan to climb the hill west of town for a close-up view of **Iguala's big Mexican flag** atop its summit, I changed my mind

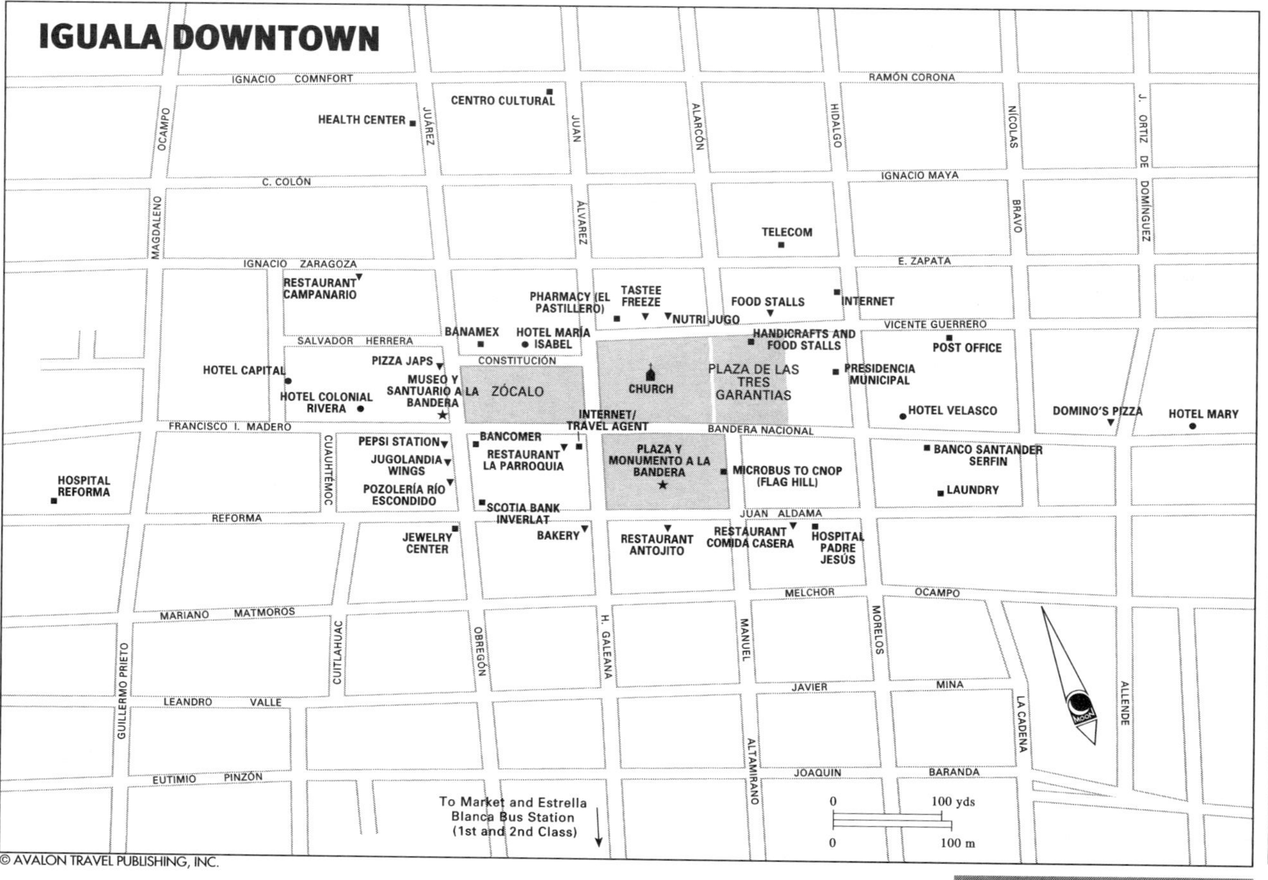
IGUALA DOWNTOWN
IGNACIO COMNFORT
RAMÓN CORONA
C. COLÓN
IGNACIO MAYA
IGNACIO ZARAGOZA
E. ZAPATA
SALVADOR HERRERA
VICENTE GUERRERO
CONSTITUCIÓN
FRANCISCO I. MADERO
BANDERA NACIONAL
REFORMA
JUAN ALDAMA
MARIANO MATMOROS
MELCHOR OCAMPO
LEANDRO VALLE
JAVIER MINA
EUTIMIO PINZÓN
JOAQUIN BARANDA
OCAMPO
MAGDALENO
JUÁREZ
JUAN ÁLVAREZ
ALARCÓN
HIDALGO
NÍCOLAS BRAVO
J. ORTIZ DE DOMÍNGUEZ
CUAUHTÉMOC
CUITLAHUAC
OBREGÓN
H. GALEANA
MANUEL ALTAMIRANO
MORELOS
LA CADENA
ALLENDE
GUILLERMO PRIETO
HEALTH CENTER
CENTRO CULTURAL
TELECOM
RESTAURANT CAMPANARIO
PHARMACY (EL PASTILLERO)
TASTEE FREEZE
NUTRI JUGO
FOOD STALLS
INTERNET
BANAMEX
HOTEL MARÍA ISABEL
HANDICRAFTS AND FOOD STALLS
POST OFFICE
PIZZA JAPS
HOTEL CAPITAL
MUSEO Y SANTUARIO A LA BANDERA
ZÓCALO
CHURCH
PLAZA DE LAS TRES GARANTIAS
PRESIDENCIA MUNICIPAL
HOTEL COLONIAL RIVERA
HOTEL VELASCO
DOMINO'S PIZZA
HOTEL MARY
INTERNET/ TRAVEL AGENT
PEPSI STATION
BANCOMER
RESTAURANT LA PARROQUIA
PLAZA Y MONUMENTO A LA BANDERA
BANCO SANTANDER SERFIN
JUGOLANDIA WINGS
MICROBUS TO CNOP (FLAG HILL)
HOSPITAL REFORMA
POZOLERÍA RÍO ESCONDIDO
LAUNDRY
SCOTIA BANK INVERLAT
JEWELRY CENTER
BAKERY
RESTAURANT ANTOJITO
RESTAURANT COMIDA CASERA
HOSPITAL PADRE JESÚS
To Market and Estrella Blanca Bus Station (1st and 2nd Class)
0
100 yds
0
100 m
© AVALON TRAVEL PUBLISHING, INC.

© BRUCE WHIPPERMAN

The phenomenal size of Iguala's hilltop memorial flag becomes apparent close up, especially when it is lowered before sunset. Notice the tiny figure at the base of the pole, like an ant in comparison to the flag's 200-foot length.

when one day I glanced west across town and noticed the flag for first time. It was so fantastically huge that it dwarfed every tall building and tree (which were much closer) in the town foreground.

The hilltop, known as C.N.O.P., is officially the site of the **Monument to the Heroes of the Independence** (which features a shrine inside a summit building that had closed by the time I arrived around 5:30 P.M.). Nevertheless, it was fortunate that I had arrived during one of Iguala's oft-breezy late afternoons. The noise alone from the flag's graceful, slow-motion rippling was surprisingly powerful, like the repeated rumble and snap of a chorus of minisonic booms (which they in fact are). The flagpole, a monumental stack of welded steel, about eight feet in diameter at the base, is a wonder in itself.

A small platoon of 25 men is required to carry and fold the 550-pound (250-kg) flag, which is brought down daily before sunset and raised around sunrise. To view the spectacle, arrive before approximately 5 A.M. or 6 P.M. summers, 6:30 A.M. or 5:30 P.M. winters.

Get to the flag by either taxi ($4 round-trip) from near the *zócalo* or *colectivo* minivan ($.50 one way) from the east (Avenida Altimirano) side of the Monument to the Flag plaza.

By car, drive to the south side of the *periférico* (peripheral boulevard). Head east until, a block before the old Highway 95 underpass, you see a chapel on the right. Turn right and pass in front of the chapel, uphill. Continue up the all-paved grade, following the red, white, and green signs to the top.

ACCOMMODATIONS

Iguala visitors enjoy a number of good, moderately priced hotels near the town center. Start with the best, **Hotel María Isabel,** at Portal Constitución 5, Iguala, Guerrero 40000, tel. 733/333-3233 or 733/333-3242, fax 733/333-3240. Once Iguala's pride, now a bit worn but still worthy, the hotel offers about 40 clean (but less than immaculate), conservatively but thoughtfully decorated, rooms with bath. The best and quietest are the upper rear rooms, with small balconies overlooking the tree-shaded pool-patio. Rentals cost $36 s, $45 d, $52 t with a/c (mandatory in the hot spring months), $30, $35, and $40 with fan only, with TV, fan, phone, large pool, parking, and reliable sidewalk restaurant downstairs.

Walk west of the *zócalo* for two more recommendable hostelries. On the short north-south street, a block due west of the *zócalo,* find new **Hotel Capital,** at José A. Ocampo 1, Iguala, Guerrero 40000, tel. 733/333-7121. Here, guests have the advantage of a quiet side-street location, a mere block from the downtown action. The 30-odd smallish rooms in three floors are invitingly decorated in color-coordinated shades of blue, with hot-water shower baths, tile floors, and attractive wooden furniture. Rentals (with one double bed only) cost $20 s, $23 d fan only; $34 s, $39 d, with a/c. Two beds cost $25 d, $30 t fan only, $42 d and $47 t with a/c; all include TV, parking, and small pool and patio.

A block south and a block and a half farther west is the classier old-standby hostelry, **Hotel Colonial Rivera,** at Madero 3, Iguala, Guerrero 40000, tel. 733/333-3464 or 733/333-2587, fax 733/333-2547. The hotel's builders have packed a lot of hotel into a small space. Most of the two floors of 49 rooms line a leafy but narrow interior patio-garden. Unfortunately, most rooms are dark, with only one window (which must be covered for privacy) facing the exterior corridor. A few lighter, more private rooms face the street but are consequently noisier. The good news is that the rooms are immaculate and have attractive neocolonial decor. Rates, furthermore, are moderate, at $23 s, $27 d, in a one-double-bed room, fan only; $33 and $38 with a/c. Two-double-bed rooms cost $32 d and $37 t fan only, $40 d and $45 t with a/c; all rooms have TV, phone, security box, parking, with restaurant but no pool.

Shift to the opposite side of the *zócalo* for a pair of good economy hotel choices, well managed by the same savvy owners. Two blocks east of the *zócalo,* find **Hotel Velasco** at Bandera Nacional 3, tel. 733/332-0566 or 733/332-8120, fax 733/332-5714. Clever design has placed the 30 rooms in two floors *above* (rather than beside) the smoggy-noisy parking patio. Another fortunate feature is an airy front breezeway, with tables and soft couches for relaxing. Corridors also have the same. Furthermore, rather than charging for power-hungry a/c, owners have equipped a number of rooms with environmentally friendlier "desert coolers" (with a fan blowing air through dripping water). One-double-bed rentals run a modest $16 s, $18 d, fan only; $19 s, $22 d, with desert cooler, also with ceiling fans. For two double beds, rates are $20 d fan only, $23 d with desert cooler, and $23 t fan only, $26 t, with desert cooler. All rooms have hot-water shower baths, phones, cable TV, and parking. If you must have a room with a/c, add about 20 percent to the fan-only prices above.

Two blocks farther east, find the **Hotel Mary,** at Bandera Nacional 39A, Iguala, Guerrero 40000, tel. 733/332-5020 or 733/332-5320, fax 733/332-5714. The three-floor Mary has the same savvy amenities as its brother, the Velasco: breezeways with soft chairs for relaxing, clean, well-maintained rooms with hot-water shower baths, and a choice of room with fan, desert cooler, or a/c. The Mary has the advantage of an enclosed bottom-floor garage, but the disadvantage of some noisier street-front rooms. Reserve a quieter room in the upper rear. Prices run about the same as the Velasco.

Additional nearby lodging choices are in Tuxpan (see Excursions from Iguala): either RV parking and/or tenting on the Laguna Tuxpan shoreline or the inviting family resort, Quinta Alegre.

FOOD

Snacks, Bakeries, and Food Stalls

Snacks and bakeries are plentiful downtown. For example, on one of Iguala's frequent warm afternoons, beat the heat with a *liquado* (ice, fruit, milk, and sugar, whipped to a milkshakelike froth but minus the calories) at one of the *jugerías* that dot the *zócalo* area. If you want more, they usually always serve fresh fruit, hot dogs, *hamburguesas,* and *tortas.*

For example, on the west side, pull up a stool at **Jugolandia Wings,** open daily 6 A.M.–11 P.M., diagonally across from the *zócalo*'s southwest corner, across Madero from the Museum of the Flag. On the *zócalo*'s east side, enjoy about the same tasty options at **Nutrijugo,** on Vicente Guerrero, across (north) from the church.

For plenty of pastries, muffins, and doughnuts, visit **Panadería San Francisco,** at the corner of Reforma and Galeana, diagonally across from the southwest corner of the Monument to the Flag plaza, open Mon.–Sat. 8 A.M.–9 P.M., Sunday 9 A.M.–3 P.M.

Hearty budget country-style specialties (tacos, tostadas, *tortas, sincronizadas, pinguinos, quemeyes, alambre*) and more are offered by the platoon of *fondas* (food stalls) in the **food market San Francisco Plaza,** on Guerrero, a block and a half east of the *zócalo,* past the church, across from the Plaza de Trigarantias.

Cafés and Restaurants

Of the lineup of sidewalk cafés along the *zócalo*'s north side, best is probably **Restaurant Bambino,** at the front of the Hotel María Isabel. Here you can get your day started right, with a choice of fruit, good espresso coffee, *panes dulces,* eggs any style, hotcakes and much more ($2–5). For lunch and dinner, choose among plenty of sandwiches, salads, and meat, pasta, and poultry platters ($3–9). Open daily 8 A.M.–midnight, tel. 733/333-6389.

Many downtown restaurants accommodate the crowds of Iguala people who have the money to eat out. One of the town center's best is **La Parroquia,** which lives up to its name, made famous by the many good like-named restaurants all over Mexico. Here, breakfasts are the main event. Choose from six, from the simple (but misnamed) "American," actually continental, breakfast, to the hearty "Campesino" breakfast ($3–6). The lunch specialty is a four-course set *comida corrida* (about $4). Otherwise order from a long all-day list of fruit, eggs, poultry, soups, salads, Mexican *antojitos,* and elaborate house specialties, such as Molcajete La Parroquia (roasted meats, cactus leaves, fondue, and much more), served in a stone grinding bowl ($3–13). Find La Parroquia, in the small Plaza San Ángel complex, near the *zócalo*'s southeast corner, open daily 7 A.M.–midnight, tel. 733/333-3400.

Second restaurant choice goes to class-act mod **Tastee Freeze–La Vaca Negra,** on Guerrero, half a block east of the *zócalo,* across from the church, tel. 733/332-0177. Although its name sounds like that of a fast food joint, it's actually a refined coffee shop trying to appeal to the middle- and upper-class young at heart. It does it quite well with a tasty, professionally prepared and served breakfast, lunch, and dinner menu ($4–10). Find it open daily 8 A.M.–11 P.M.

A number of town-center restaurants also serve folk hungering for country fare the way *abuelita haga* (grandma used to make). The best example is **Pozolería Río Escondido,** the place for you to learn even more if you think you already know Mexican food. Start out with appetizer *pata de puerco,* continue with *tacos de longaniza,* then *tostadas de tinga,* all about $2. If, on the other hand, you hanker for something familiar, go for the house specialty *pozole* (savory pork and hominy soup) *con todo* (all the fixin's). Find it on Obregón, half a block south of the southwest *zócalo* corner, open daily 11 A.M.–11 P.M., tel. 733/333-3362.

Finally, get away from old Mexico for a spell and go to **Domino's Pizza.** Enter the cool white dining room, with the lineup of a dozen styles of the usual pizzas, plus half a dozen local favorites you haven't heard of ($5–15). Open daily 9 A.M.–midnight, tel. 733/332-4567, four blocks east of the *zócalo,* at the corner of Ortiz de Domínguez and Bandera Nacional.

ENTERTAINMENT AND EVENTS

For child's play, Iguala has both the kid-friendly west-side park and playground **Parque Infantil del D.I.F.** (Integral Family Development) and its neighboring **CICI Parque Aquatico** water-slide park. Find them on the eastern extension of Vicente Guerrero, on opposite sides of the street, a few hundred yards east of Highway 95, by the *lienzo charro* (rodeo ring).

Sunday afternoons (check with your hotel desk for times) at the *lienzo charro,* riders practice the art of *jaripeo* (bull riding and roping) and show off their skills of horsemanship. Sometimes young women, in colorful *ropa típica,* compete in a daredevil *escaramuza charra* in which they race sidesaddle, with abandon, around the ring. A

THE FLOWER OF CHRISTMAS

Mexican people tell a story of the lovely red poinsettia flower, which they know as the Flower of Christmas:

Once upon a time, on Christmas Eve (Nochebuena) in a village of southern Mexico, a poor girl named Angelita stood outside the village church sadly watching the faithful carrying rich offerings of fruit, candy, and flowers for the infant Jesus. Angelita was weeping, because she had nothing to offer.

At that moment an angel, shining with a brilliant light, appeared and told Angelita to pick some wild plants beside the road. Angelita did this and returned with a large but humble bunch of weeds. Inside, as she approached the altar, Angelita's weeds miraculously transformed themselves into lovely scarlet flowers.

At the same time, the Virgin above the altar lowered her arm in a gesture of love, and gold stars on her blue cape showered the faithful in the nave. Simultaneously, outside in the black night sky a single star glowed a brilliant white over the little pueblo.

From that time forward, Angelita's brilliant red flowers have blossomed all over southern Mexico just before Christmas. For that reason, people have named that gorgeous bloom the *flor de Nochebuena* and always offer bunches of them to the baby Jesus on December 24.

frequent local treat are the noisy "oompah" wind instrument bands, known locally as the Bandas de Chile Frito. (Get to the *lienzo charro* by taxi, on the eastern prolongation of Bandera Nacional, past old Highway 95, about nine blocks east of the *zócalo.*)

Iguala **Semana Santa** celebrations, in addition to the usual processions, *mañanitas,* stations of the cross, food, and carnival games, also feature a procession of dozens of *penitencias* who may be flaying themselves or crawling on hands and knees to the downtown church altar to ask for forgiveness.

The big patronal **Fiesta de San Francisco** features an October 4 parade of crazy *locos* throwing water and eggs and whatever else in honor of St. Francis of Assisi, who's famous for his sense of humor.

The **Day of the Dead,** celebrated November 1 and 2, is big in Iguala. Families go to cemeteries and clean up the grave sites of their loved ones. They rebuild the "house" of the dead people and bring the favorite foods of the departed, thus tempting their relatives to leave the land of the dead and be with the family once again.

If you're in Iguala around the time of Carnaval (the week before Ash Wednesday), consider visiting the important town of Teloloapan (pop. 20,000), about 17 miles (27 km) along the Altamirano highway west of Iguala. The Teloloapan Carnaval (Mardi Gras), locally called the **Paseo de los Agullis,** is unique. Beginning a week before Ash Wednesday, usually in early February, celebrants dance through the streets to the rhythm of drum and tamborine and splash themselves with paint. On Tuesday before Ash Wednesday they climax it all with a dangerous competition, climbing a high tree for valuable prizes in its limbs. The merrymaking continues during the subsequent week, in the **Fiesta of the Second Friday of Lent,** a weeklong (Mon.–Sun. after Ash Wednesday) celebration, including a daily round of traditional dances, a big handicrafts fair, and fireworks.

SHOPPING

Iguala's prime general shopping ground is the main **town market,** at the corner of Salazar and Galeana, six blocks south of the *zócalo.* Everything—from shoes and clothes to produce and hot food—seems to be on sale. Even if you don't buy anything, the market is an interesting place for wandering and enjoying the displays, especially the festoons of old-fashioned goods: flowers, mounds of spices, dried flower petals, cinnamon bark, *cal* (limestone), *panela* (rough brown sugar), and mountain-gathered herbs and remedies.

Iguala's **handicrafts** vendors cluster on the Plaza de Trigarantias, two blocks east of the *zócalo,* behind the church. Customarily about a dozen stands offer a large variety, including soft palm-leaf *tenates* (tumpline baskets) and *petates* (mats), wooden bowls and utensils, colorful pottery, masks, and much more.

Iguala is famous for its **gold market,** the Centro Joyero de Iguala, Mexico's third gold merchandising center after Taxco and Guadalajara. Find its many dozens of shops under one roof at the corner of Obregón and Reforma, a block south of the *zócalo*'s southwest corner. Inside is a budget jewelry lover's paradise, where the gold and silver is genuine, but most of the apparent rubies, diamonds, and emeralds are not. (Nevertheless, a few stores, such as Orovel's and Jeisha, do carry genuine low-to-medium-quality gemstones.)

If you want to check on the reasonableness of a price, ask the prospective seller to weigh it. Ordinary sterling silver pieces customarily sell reasonably for about $1 per gram, 12–22 karat (50–90 percent) gold for about $8–15. The center is open daily 9 A.M.–7 P.M., tel. 733/333-3778. (See Buying Silver and Gold Jewelry under Shopping in the On the Road chapter.)

SERVICES

Banks: All with ATMs, these are plentiful near the *zócalo.* All are open approximately Mon.–Fri. 9 A.M.–4 P.M. Find Banamex at the *zócalo*'s northwest corner and Bancomer across the *zócalo* at the southwest corner. Banco Scotia Inverlat is one block south of that, at the corner of Reforma and Obregón, across from the Centro Joyero. After bank hours, go to the *casa de cambio* (money-exchange office) Dicambios, on the *zócalo*'s north side, next to the Hotel María Isabel, open Mon.–Sat. 9 A.M.–4 P.M.

Communications: Find the *correo* (post office) open Mon.–Fri. 9 A.M.–5 P.M. on the south side of Guerrero, two and a half blocks west of the *zócalo.* For telephone, buy a Ladatel card and use one of the many street telephones. Otherwise, go to Telecom (northeast of the *zócalo,* on Zapata, between Alarcon and Hidalgo), for fax and money orders, open Mon.–Fri. 9 A.M.–8 P.M. Connect to the Internet at Arroba Internet store, northeast of the *zócalo,* on Hidalgo, half a block north of Guerrero. It's open Mon.–Sat. 9 A.M.–9 P.M., Sunday noon–5 P.M., tel. 733/332-4331.

Health and Emergencies: For routine medications and remedies, try one of the many downtown pharmacies, such as El Pastillero (Pill Seller), on Guerrero, half a block east of the *zócalo*'s northeast corner, open daily 8 A.M.–midnight (or 24 hours by phone, tel. 733/333-3208). If you need a doctor, ask your hotel desk to call one for you. Otherwise, a handily situated internist, Dr. Javier Ulises López, tel. 733/333-2113, is available for consultations Mon.–Fri. 9 A.M.–3 P.M. and 5–8 P.M., in the commercial Plaza San Ángel, by the Restaurant Parroquia, near the *zócalo*'s southeast corner. In an emergency, contact him at tel. 733/332-0833. Also in an emergency, a number of good hospitals provide round-the-clock services in the downtown area. Hire a taxi to take you to one of the following: Hospital Reforma, at Reforma 54, tel. 733/333-5892; Sanitorio Padre Jesús, at Aldama 24, tel. 733/332-0801, or Hospital Cristina, at Prolongación Álvarez 153, tel. 733/333-2514 or 733/333-7386.

For police, call tel. 733/332-8005. In case of fire, call the *bomberos* (fire station), tel. 733/332-8955.

Travel Agents: Often willing sources of information, these are available in the downtown area. For example, try Agencia de Viajes María Isabel, next to the Hotel María Isabel, tel./fax 733/333-0506 or 733/333-3192, agencia_mariaisabel@hotmail.com. Hours are Mon.–Fri. 9 A.M.–8 P.M., Sat.–Sun. 9 A.M.–3 P.M.

Laundry: Get your clothes washed at Lavandería Easy, open Mon.–Sat. 9 A.M.–3 P.M. and 4–7 P.M., closed Sunday, tel. 733/332-6189. From the *zócalo*'s southeast corner, walk one block south to Aldama, turn left and walk two and a half blocks west.

GETTING THERE AND AWAY

By Bus: The main bus station, **Central Camionera Estrella Blanca,** is at Galeana and Salazar, six blocks south of the *zócalo*'s southeast corner.

The terminal (for schedule information, call tel. 733/332-3473) has many services, including kept luggage ($1 for 3 hours, $7/day), long-distance telephone and fax office, a/c first-class waiting room, cafeteria, and money exchange. Buy fresh fruits and vegetables across the street at the market.

First- and second-class buses connect with many destinations in all directions, both long-distance and semilocal:

One first-class **Elite** departure connects daily northwest with the U.S. border at Mexicali and Tijuana, via Cuernavaca, Toluca, Guadalajara, Tepic, and Mazatlán, along the Pacific Coast.

One first-class **Futura or Turistar** departure connects daily north with the U.S. border at Nuevo Laredo, via Cuernavaca, Toluca, San Luis Potosí, Saltillo, and Monterrey.

Many first- and second-class buses connect (hourly during the day) north with Mexico City and south with Chilpancingo and Acapulco. Others connect northeast with Puebla via Izucar de Matamoros, where connections southeast with Oaxaca may be made.

Many second-class buses connect east with Altamirano and north with Toluca via Taxco.

A swarm of second-class **Flecha Roja** buses connect with dozens of small regional destinations, such as Huitzuco, Taxco, Zacapalco, Jojutla, and Casahuatlán.

By Car: Connect north 22 miles (36 km), with Taxco via old nontoll Highway 95 in about an hour. Connect north directly with Mexico City via Cuernavaca by *cuota* (toll) expressway Highway 95 D. (Find the expressway entrance along old Highway 95, on the southeast, Acapulco, end of town.) Allow about 2.5 hours for this 80-mile (129-km) trip. Make sure you arrive in Mexico City on a permitted driving day. (See the sidebar "Mexico City Driving Restrictions" in the Acapulco chapter.)

Connect south with Chilpancingo via old Highway 95, about 64 miles (103 km), in about an hour and a half. Continue to Acapulco via the toll expressway 95 D, an additional 62 miles (100 km), in another hour and a quarter.

Connect west with Altamirano from the *periférico's* northwest side, via winding but scenic Highway 51, 114 miles (184 km), in about 3.5 hours.

EXCURSIONS FROM IGUALA

Tuxpan

Nearby Laguna Tuxpan makes an interesting excursion, if not for the lake itself, at least for the country views and the palmy Quinta Alegre family resort.

Along the two-mile road to Tuxpan, the source of Iguala's prosperity becomes immediately apparent. Irrigation has been the key, turning the Iguala valley into an oasis of lush cornfields and a grand orchard of mango trees like the ones you see overhanging the Tuxpan road.

Soon, on the right, pass the refined restaurant *campestre* (country-style) **Villa Los Ocampo,** with plenty of shade and lots of room for kids to run around. The menu includes shrimp tacos, fish fillets, and brochettes, and also breakfast ($4–8).

Continue through the Tuxpan village (with a few small groceries, a post office, and a pharmacy or two) to the restaurants on the north Laguna Tuxpan lakeshore. Two of the most inviting are **El Muelle,** with a pier to walk out on; and farther on, **Restaurant El Arbolito,** shaded by *tabachín* trees (which burst out with lovely red blossoms in season). Both restaurants offer good fish and shrimp dinners beneath airy lakeview *palapas.*

The lake itself is large, about a mile across and spring-fed. Despite continual withdrawing of irrigation water, the lake level remains virtually constant year-round. When I was there, during the dry spring season, the lake was not very inviting. Local folks were dirtying it up washing clothes on the shoreline. Furthermore, people told me that the lake bass were small because fisherfolk are so poor that they take anything, regardless of size.

Nevertheless, the lake would be certainly cleaner and more appealing on the far west side, accessible by the lakeshore dirt road after the restaurants. Amenities include some shade trees, plenty of room for RV parking or tent camping (customary and allowed any time), and easy boat and kayak-launching access.

Much more inviting is the family-friendly **Balneario Quinta Alegre** (from the Tuxpan ingress road, follow the signed Quinta Alegre fork to the right). This is a gorgeous spot for at least a picnic and at most a one-week stay. Amenities include five blue, palm-shaded swimming pools, three kiddie pools, restaurants, basketball, minimarket, tennis, volleyball and squash courts, and a soccer field, all surrounded by a beautiful orchard of palm, orange, *limón,* and mango trees. The Quinta Alegre accommodations are no less than you would expect: about 20 clean, semideluxe rooms around an inviting pool-patio, separated from the oft-noisy day-use area. Room decor is invitingly rustic, embellished with interior brick and hand-hewn wood furnishings. Rates run, for adults, about $30 s or d, $35 t or q; add $5 per kid, with TV, a/c, and parking. For more peace and quiet, reserve a weekday stay, via tel. 733/332-3562.

Get to Tuxpan by local bus or *colectivo* minivan, from the Estrella Blanca main bus station, seven blocks south of the *zócalo.* By car, from the town center, get on to old nontoll Highway 95. For example, from the *zócalo,* via Bandera Nacional, after seven blocks turn right, south, at Highway 95. Continue under the *periférico* overpass. Approximately half a mile after the overpass, at the Rotary Internacional sign on the left, fork left on to the Tuxpan road. Continue to the signed Quinta Alegre fork on the right or straight ahead for Tuxpan village and lakeshore after another mile.

Cuetlajuchitlán Archaeological Site

Adventurous ruins enthusiasts might enjoy a day exploring at least one of a pair of partially restored archaeological sites, about an hour by car, two hours by bus, east of Iguala.

Closest is Cuetlajuchitlán (koo-way-tlah-hoo-chee-TLAN), near the small town of Paso Morelos, just off the Mexico City-Acapulco toll *autopista* expressway. Cuetlajuchitlán, an Aztec (Náhuatl) label, has two possible contrasting translations: either "place of red flowers" or "shriveled place."

Engineers saved the site from destruction by building the expressway tunnel, Los Querendes, under the archaeological zone, which covers about 90 acres (35 hectares). Investigators believe that Cuetlajuchitlán was occupied as early as 600 B.C. and reached its cultural and economic zenith around 200 B.C. Although little is known of the ethnic identity of its founders, archaeologists believe that Cuetlajuchitlán influenced a wide region, stretching north to the Valley of Morelos state, south to the Pacific Coast, and east and west along the Río Balsas basin. The reason is that the cylindrical stone monoliths found extensively at Cuetlajuchitlán are also widespread in so many far-flung regions centering on Cuetlajuchitlán. Consequently, archaeologists have begun to associate Cuetlajuchitlán with what they call the "Culture of the Cylinders."

The most fascinating part of the zone is the **Recinto Ceremonial,** a 100- by 60-foot enclosure, at the heart of the ruins complex, with both a number of the stone cylinders and *tinas ceremoniales* (ceremonial baths), presumably for purification rituals.

Also of great interest, about 100 feet south of the *recinto ceremonial,* is the *taller de cantería* (stonework factory) with a number of the great cylindrical monoliths lying about, apparently finished but unused.

Three **Complejos Habitacionales** (Habitational Complexes), apparently for nobles and priests, can be explored, respectively about 100 feet northeast and about 300 feet west, of the Recinto.

Get to Cuetlajuchitlán by bus, via Huitzuco, an hour southeast, from the Iguala main bus station. From Huitzuco, continue by bus or local minivan east to Paso Morelos, just past (east of) the Mexico City-Acapulco expressway. Continue by taxi or on foot (ask local directions) to the nearby archaeological site.

By car, from Iguala, drive south along Highway 95 about six miles (9 km) to the left, east-bound, turnoff road to Huitzuco. Continue another 14 miles (23 km) to Huitzuco and another 10 miles (16 km) to the expressway and Paso Morelos, just east of it. In Paso Morelos, ask directions to the site, nearby.

Teopantecuantlán Archaeological Site

Equally fascinating, but a bit more more remote, is Teopantecuantlán (tayoh-pahn-tay-kooan-TLAN), in the valley about 20 miles east of Cuetlajuchitlán. The entire archaeological zone, including both the ceremonial center and surrounding former agricultural village, occupies nearly a square mile (about 500 acres or 200 hectares).

The site is especially interesting because of the antiquity of its two main pieces of Olmec-style monumental art, heavy with jaguar symbolism, dating from around 1400 B.C. As a result, archaeologists have inferred connections between Teopantecuantlán and the similar Olmec-style art found in the cave paintings at Juxtlahuaca and Oxtotitlán, 100 miles to the south.

Archaeologists believe Teopantecuantlán reached its zenith around 900 B.C., with irrigation that in turn led to bumper crops, rising population, economic specialization, wealth, and architectural innovation. Massive stone walls were raised, culminating in a pair of grand platforms and arched passageways leading to noble tombs.

Exploration of the site reveals partly restored remains of Teopantecuantlán's grandeur: pyramidal platforms, palaces, plazas, tombs, two ball courts, and an irrigation channel.

Get to Teopantecuantlán via Paso Morelos, by the route described at the end of the Cuetlajuchitlán section. From Paso Morelos, by car or local minivan or bus, continue 22 miles (36 km) southeast to Atenango del Río, and another seven miles (12 km) to the right (south) turnoff to Copalillo village. After two more miles, at Copalillo, ask for local directions to the site nearby.

Taxco

As Acapulco thrives on what's new, Taxco (pop. 150,000) luxuriates in what's old. Nestling beneath forest-crowned mountains and decorated with monuments of its silver-rich past, Taxco now enjoys an equally rich flood of visitors, many of whom who stop en route to or from Acapulco. They come to enjoy its fiestas and clear, pine-scented air and to stroll the cobbled hillside lanes and bargain for world-renowned silver jewelry.

And despite the acclaim, Taxco preserves its diminutive colonial charm *because* of its visitors, who come to enjoy what Taxco offers. They stay in venerable, family-owned lodgings, walk to the colorful little *zócalo,* where they admire the famous baroque cathedral, and wander among the awning-festooned market lanes just downhill.

But Taxco offers even more. Travel an hour north to wander within the colossal limestone fairyland of the renowned Caves (Grutas) of Cacahuamilpa. On the same day, continue another hour north to marvel at the exquisite, untouristed remains of Xochicalco, ruined pre-Columbian capital and internationally acclaimed United Nations World Heritage site.

On yet another day, travel west an hour to Ixcateopan village and visit the revered resting place of Cuauhtémoc, the last Aztec emperor who, at the eventual cost of his life, rallied his people against the Spanish conquest.

HISTORY

The traditional hieroglyph representing Taxco shows athletes in a court competing in a game of *tlatchtli* (still locally played) with a solid, natural rubber *(hule)* ball. "Tlachco," the Náhuatl name representing the place that had become a small Aztec garrison settlement by the eve of the conquest, literally translates as "Place of the Ball Game." The Spanish, more interested in local minerals than in linguistic details, shifted the name to Taxco.

Colonization

In 1524, Hernán Cortés, looking for tin to alloy with copper to make bronze cannon, heard that people around Taxco were using bits of metal for money. Prospectors hurried out, and within a few years they struck rich silver veins in Tetelcingo, now known as Taxco Viejo (Old Taxco), seven miles downhill from present-day Taxco. The Spanish crown appropriated the mines and worked them with generations of native forced labor.

Eighteenth-century enlightenment came to Taxco in the person of José Borda, who, arriving from Spain in 1716, modernized the mine franchise his brother had been operating. José improved conditions and began paying the miners, thereby increasing productivity and profits. In contrast to past operators, Borda returned the proceeds to Taxco, building the monuments that still grace the town. His fortune built streets, bridges, fountains, arches, and his masterpiece, the church of Santa Prisca, which included a special chapel for the miners, who before had not been allowed to enter the church.

Independence and Modern Times

The 1810–1821 War of Independence and the subsequent civil strife, within a generation, reduced the mines to but a memory. They were nearly forgotten when William Spratling, an American artist and architect, moved to Taxco in 1929 and began reviving Taxco's ancient but moribund silversmithing tradition. Working with local artisans, Spratling opened the first cooperative shop, Las Delicias.

Spurred by the trickle of tourists along the new Acapulco highway, more shops opened, increasing the demand for silver, which in turn led to the reopening of the mines. Soon silver demand outpaced the supply. Silver began streaming in from other parts of Mexico to the workbenches of thousands of artisans in hundreds of family- and cooperatively owned shops dotting the still-quaint hillsides of a new, prosperous Taxco.

SIGHTS

Getting Oriented

Although the present city (elev. 5,850 feet, 1,780 meters) spreads much farther, the center of town encompasses the city's original seven hills, wrinkles in the slope of a towering mountain.

For most visitors, the downhill town limit is the *carretera,* the local stretch of old National Highway 95, now named Avenida de los Plateros,

TLATCHTLI: THE BALL GAME

Basketball fever is probably a mild affliction compared to the enthusiasm pre-Columbian crowds felt for *tlatchtli,* the ball game that was played throughout Mesoamerica and is still played in some places. Contemporary accounts and latter-day scholarship have led to a partial picture of *tlatchtli* as it was played centuries ago. Although details varied locally, the game centered around a hard, natural rubber ball, which players batted back and forth across a center dividing line with leg-, arm-, and torso-blows.

Play and scoring was vaguely similar to tennis. Opponents, either individuals or small teams, tried to smash the ball past their opponents into scoring niches at the opposite ends of an I-shaped, sunken court. Players also could garner points by forcing their opponents to make wild shots that bounced beyond the court's retaining walls.

Courts were often equipped with a pair of stone rings fixed above opposing ends of the center dividing line. One scoring variation awarded immediate victory to the team who could manage to bat the *tlatchtli* through the ring.

Like tennis, players became very adept at batting the ball at high speed. Unlike tennis, the ball was solid and perhaps as heavy as two or three baseballs. Although protected by helmets and leather, players were usually bloodied, often injured, and sometimes even killed from opponents' punishing *tlatchtli*-inflicted blows. Matches were sometimes decided like a boxing match, with victory going to the opponent left standing on the court.

As with everything in Mesoamerica, tradition and ritual ruled *tlatchtli.* Master teachers subjected initiates to rigorous training, prescribed ritual, and discipline not unlike the ascetic lifestyle of a medieval monastic brotherhood.

Potential rewards were enormous, however. Stakes varied in proportion to a contest's ritual significance and the rank of the players and their patrons. Champion players could win fortunes in gold, feathers, or precious stones. Exceptional games could result in riches and honor for the winner and death for the loser, whose heart, ripped from his chest on the centerline stone, became food for the gods.

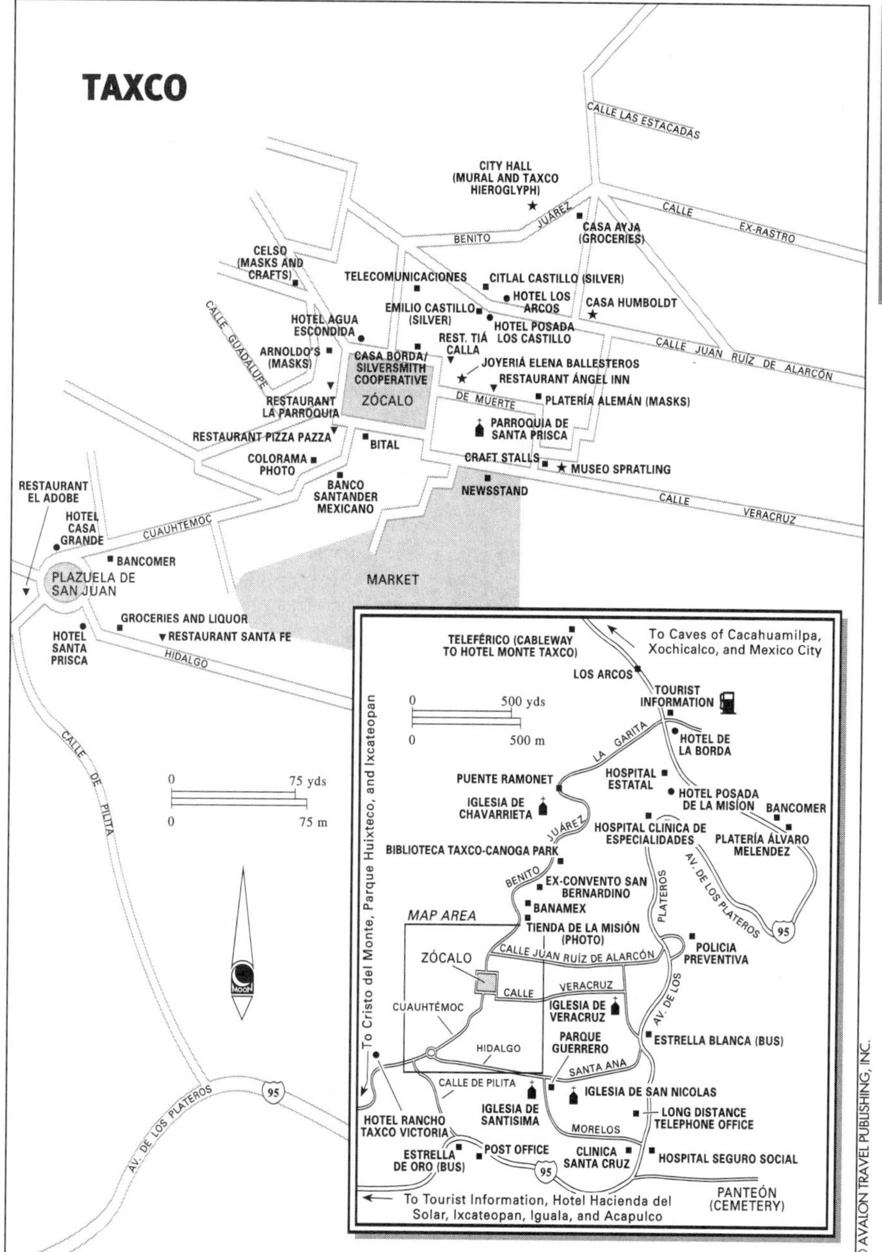
TAXCO
CALLE LAS ESTACADAS
CITY HALL (MURAL AND TAXCO HIEROGLYPH)
BENITO JUÁREZ
CASA AYJA (GROCERIES)
CALLE EX-RASTRO
CELSO (MASKS AND CRAFTS)
TELECOMUNICACIONES
CITLAL CASTILLO (SILVER)
HOTEL LOS ARCOS
CASA HUMBOLDT
CALLE GUADALUPE
EMILIO CASTILLO (SILVER)
HOTEL POSADA LOS CASTILLO
HOTEL AGUA ESCONDIDA
REST. TIÁ CALLA
CALLE JUAN RUÍZ DE ALARCÓN
ARNOLDO'S (MASKS)
CASA BORDA/ SILVERSMITH COOPERATIVE
JOYERIÁ ELENA BALLESTEROS
RESTAURANT ÁNGEL INN
ZÓCALO
DE MUERTE
PLATERÍA ALEMÁN (MASKS)
RESTAURANT LA PARROQUIA
PARROQUIA DE SANTA PRISCA
RESTAURANT PIZZA PAZZA
BITAL
COLORAMA PHOTO
CRAFT STALLS
MUSEO SPRATLING
RESTAURANT EL ADOBE
BANCO SANTANDER MEXICANO
NEWSSTAND
CALLE VERACRUZ
HOTEL CASA GRANDE
CUAUHTEMOC
BANCOMER
PLAZUELA DE SAN JUAN
MARKET
GROCERIES AND LIQUOR
HOTEL SANTA PRISCA
RESTAURANT SANTA FE
HIDALGO
CALLE DE PILITA
0 75 yds
0 75 m
AV. DE LOS PLATEROS
95
TELEFÉRICO (CABLEWAY TO HOTEL MONTE TAXCO)
To Caves of Cacahuamilpa, Xochicalco, and Mexico City
LOS ARCOS
TOURIST INFORMATION
0 500 yds
0 500 m
LA GARITA
HOTEL DE LA BORDA
To Cristo del Monte, Parque Huixteco, and Ixcateopan
PUENTE RAMONET
HOSPITAL ESTATAL
HOTEL POSADA DE LA MISIÓN
BANCOMER
IGLESIA DE CHAVARRIETA
JUÁREZ
HOSPITAL CLÍNICA DE ESPECIALIDADES
PLATERÍA ÁLVARO MELENDEZ
BIBLIOTECA TAXCO-CANOGA PARK
BENITO
EX-CONVENTO SAN BERNARDINO
AV. DE LOS PLATEROS
PLATEROS
BANAMEX
MAP AREA
TIENDA DE LA MISIÓN (PHOTO)
POLICIA PREVENTIVA
ZÓCALO
CALLE JUAN RUÍZ DE ALARCÓN
CALLE VERACRUZ
IGLESIA DE VERACRUZ
CUAUHTÉMOC
AV. DE LOS
ESTRELLA BLANCA (BUS)
HIDALGO
PARQUE GUERRERO
SANTA ANA
CALLE DE PILITA
IGLESIA DE SAN NICOLAS
HOTEL RANCHO TAXCO VICTORIA
IGLESIA DE SANTISIMA
LONG DISTANCE TELEPHONE OFFICE
MORELOS
ESTRELLA DE ORO (BUS)
POST OFFICE
CLINICA SANTA CRUZ
HOSPITAL SEGURO SOCIAL
95
PANTEÓN (CEMETERY)
To Tourist Information, Hotel Hacienda del Solar, Ixcateopan, Iguala, and Acapulco

after the Taxco *plateros* (silversmiths) who put Taxco on Mexico's tourism map. The highway contours along the hillside from Los Arcos (The Arches) on the north, Mexico City, end of town about two miles, passing the Calle Pilita intersection on the south, Acapulco, edge of town. Along the *carretera,* immediately accessible to a steady stream of tour buses, lie the town's plusher hotels and many silver shops.

The rest of the town is fortunately insulated from tour buses by its narrow winding streets. From the *carretera,* the most important of them climb and converge, like bent spokes of a wheel, to the *zócalo*. Beginning with the most northerly, the main streets (and the directions they run) are La Garita (uphill), Alarcón (downhill), Veracruz (downhill), Santa Ana (downhill), Salubridad (uphill), Morelos (downhill), and Pilita (downhill).

© BRUCE WHIPPERMAN

Although only one block long, Calle Los Arcos (marked by the quaint arch in the background) is nevertheless one of Taxco's busiest streets, since it leads directly to the Taxco market.

Getting Around

Although walking is Taxco's most common mode of transport, taxis go anywhere within the city limits for about $2. White *combi* collective vans (fare about $.30) follow designated routes, marked on the windshields. Simply tell your specific destination to the driver. For side trips to nearby towns and villages, a fleet of Flecha Roja second-class local buses and *colectivo* vans leave frequently from their *carretera* terminal near the corner of Veracruz.

Around the Zócalo

All roads in Taxco begin and end on the *zócalo* at **Santa Prisca church.** French architect D. Diego Durán designed and built the church between 1751 and 1758 with money from the fortune of silver king Don José Borda. The facade, decorated with saints on pedestals, arches, and spiraled columns, follows the baroque churrigueresque style (after Jose Churriguera, 1665–1725, the "Spanish Michelangelo"). Interior furnishings include an elegant pipe organ, brought from Germany by muleback (via boat to Veracruz, thence overland) in 1751, and several gilded side altars. The riot of interior elaboration climaxes in the towering gold-leaf main altar, which seems to drip with ornamentation in tribute to Santa Prisca, the Virgin of Guadalupe, and the Virgin of the Rosary, who piously preside above all. Dreamy Bible-story paintings by Miguel Cabrera decorate a chamber behind the main altar, while in a room to the right, portraits of Pope Benedict IV, who sanctioned all this, and Manuel Borda, Santa Prisca's first priest, hang among a solemn gallery of subsequent padres.

Outside, landmarks around the plaza include the **Casa Borda,** open daily except Mon. 10 A.M.–8 P.M., visible (as you face away from the church facade) on the right side of the *zócalo.* This former Borda family town house, built concurrently with the church in typical baroque colonial style, now serves as the Taxco Casa de Cultura, featuring exhibitions by local artists and artisans.

Heading out and down the church steps, you can continue downhill in either of two interesting ways. If you walk left immediately downhill from

A plethora of baroque details decorates Santa Prisca church.

the church, you reach the lane Calle Los Arcos, running alongside and below the church. From there, reach the **market** by heading right before the quaint archway over the street, down the winding staircase-lane, where you'll soon be in a warren of awning-covered stalls.

If, however, you head right from the church steps, another immediate right leads you beside the church along legendary **Calle de Muerte** (Street of Death), so named because of the former cemetery where the workers who died constructing the church were buried. (Note the skeleton on the church-front corner facing Calle de Muerte.)

Continuing downhill, you'll find **Museo Guillermo Spratling,** fronting the little plaza behind the church. On the main and upper floors, the National Institute of Archaeology displays intriguing carvings and ceramics (including unusual phallic examples), such as a ball-game ring, animal masks, and a priestly statuette with knife in one hand, human heart in the other. Basement-floor displays interestingly detail local history from the Aztecs through William Spratling. The museum is open seasonally Tues.–Sat. 9 A.M.–6 P.M., Sunday 9 A.M.–3 P.M., although hours may vary seasonally, tel. 762/622-1660.

Back outside, one block down Alarcón (the downhill extension of Calle de Muerte), stands the **Casa Humboldt,** after the celebrated geographer (who is said to have stayed only one night, however). Now the state maintains it as the Museum of Viceregal (read colonial) Art. Displays feature a permanent collection of historical artifacts, including the Manila galleon, colonial technology, and colonial religious sculpture and painting. Open Tues.–Sat. 10 A.M.–5 P.M., Sunday 10 A.M.–4 P.M., although winter hours may be shorter, tel. 762/622-5501.

Nearby, the **Museo Platería,** 4 Alarcón, third floor, next door to the Hotel Posada, illustrates a history of Taxco silvercraft and displays outstanding pieces by local artisans. Open daily 10 A.M.–6 P.M. (Alternately, you may enter the museum through the *zócalo*-front shopping patio de Las Artesanías, next to the Casa Borda.)

Other In-Town Sights

A short ride, coupled with a walk circling back to the *zócalo,* provides the basis for an interesting half-day exploration. Taxi or ride a *combi* to the Hotel Posada de la Misión, where the **Cuauhtémoc Mural** glitters on a wall near the pool. Executed by renowned muralist Juan O'Gorman with a riot of pre-Columbian symbols—yellow sun, pearly rabbit-in-the-moon, snarling jaguar, writhing serpents, fluttering eagle—the mural glorifies Cuauhtémoc, the last Aztec emperor. Cuauhtémoc, unlike his uncle Moctezuma, tenaciously resisted the conquest, but was captured and later executed by Cortés in 1525. His remains were discovered not long ago in Ixcateopan, about 24 miles west by local bus or car. (See Excursions from Taxco.)

Continue your walk a few hundred yards along the *carretera* (Mexico City direction) from the Hotel Posada de la Misión. There, a driveway leading right just before the gas station heads to the Hotel Borda grounds. Turn left on the road just after the gate and you'll come to an antique brick smelter chimney and cable-hung derrick. These mark an inactive **mineshaft** descending to the mine-tunnel honeycomb thousands of feet beneath the town. The mines are still being worked from another entrance, but for mostly lead rather than silver. You can see the present-day works from the hilltop of the Hotel Hacienda del Solar on the south edge of town.

Now, return to the *carretera,* cross over and stroll the **Calle la Garita** about a mile back to the *zócalo.* Of special interest, besides a number of crafts stores and stalls, are the **Iglesia de Chavarrieta,** the **Biblioteca Taxco–Canoga Park** (library, with many English-language novels and reference books, open Mon.–Fri. 10 A.M.–7 P.M., Saturday 10 A.M.–1 P.M.), and the **ex-Convento San Bernardino.**

Farther on, a block before the *zócalo,* pause to decipher the colored stone mosaic of the **Taxco Hieroglyph,** which decorates the pavement in front of the Palacio Municipal (City Hall). Inside, climb the stairs for a balcony-front view of the hieroglyph and the wall mural for a graphic review of Mexican history. See the main actors, from left to right: stolid Benito Juárez ("Respect for the rights of all is peace"); elderly General Porfirio Díaz gives away church and communal land to foreigners; banderilla-laden Emiliano Zapata declares his Plan de Ayala; President Lázaro Cárdenas in overalls expropriates foreign oil companies; and Aldolfo López Mateos declares free school textbooks, while Juárez, Kennedy, Kissinger, de Gaulle, and Nehru look on.

Cableway (Teleférico) to Hotel Monte Taxco

On the north side of town, where the *carretera* passes beneath Los Arcos, a cableway above the highway lifts passengers to soaring vistas of the town on one side and ponderous, pine-studded mesas on the other. Open daily 7:30 A.M.–7:30 P.M.; round-trip tickets about $4, kids half price; return by taxi if you miss the last car. The ride ends at the Hotel Monte Taxco, where you can make a day of it golfing, horseback riding, playing tennis, eating lunch, and sunning on the panoramic-view pool deck.

Cristo del Monte

Above the opposite, west, side of town, about two miles uphill from the *zócalo,* stands the colossal stone statue of Jesus, where folks enjoy an airy panoramic town view framed by lush, green looming mountains. Get there on foot (if you relish a 1,500-foot climb, wear a hat and carry water) or by taxi (about $2.50), *colectivo* (to Casahuates village), or car, west from the *zócalo* via Calle Cuauhtémoc, past the Hotel Victoria. On foot, after about two miles (3 km); fork right at the Huixteco sign and continue past Casahuates village about 200 yards, where a dirt driveway leads right to the Cristo del Monte park.

In-Town Vistas

You needn't go as far afield as the Hotel Monte Taxco or the Cristo del Monte to get a good view of the city streets and houses carpeting the mountainside. Vistas depend not only on van-

© BRUCE WHIPPERMAN

High above Taxco the Cristo del Monte presides over an airy town, valley, and mountain vista.

tage point but time of day, since the best viewing sunshine (which frees you from squinting) should come generally from *behind.* Consequently, spots along the highway (more or less east of town), such as the patios of the Hotel Posada de la Misión and the *mirador* atop the Hotel Borda, provide good morning views, while afternoon views are best from points west of town, such as the restaurant balcony or the hilltop of the Hotel Rancho Taxco Victoria.

ACCOMMODATIONS

The dry, temperate local climate relegates air-conditioning, ceiling fans, and central heating to frills offered only in the most expensive hotels. All of the hotel recommendations below have hot water and private baths, however.

Taxco's low-end hotels (less than $50, but nevertheless comfortable) cluster in the colorful *zócalo* neighborhood, while the midrange and high-end ($50 and up) lodgings are scattered mostly along the *carretera.*

Under $50

Walk west of the *zócalo* half a block past Plazuela de San Juan to the **Posada Lucy** on the left, at Carlos J. Nibbi 8, Taxco, Guerrero, 40200, tel./fax 762/622-1780. Here, owners offer 32 budget rooms in a rambling complex, fortuitously isolated below and away from street noise. Airy patios with chairs and tables invite quiet relaxation. Inside, rooms are simply but attractively decorated with color-coordinated curtains, bedspreads, and handmade wooden furniture. Prices run a reasonable $20 s or d in one bed; $40 for two to four people in two double beds.

Back by the *zócalo,* on Alarcón just downhill, a pair of former colonial mansions, now popular hotels, face each other across the street. First choice goes to the refined **Hotel Los Arcos,** J. Ruiz de Alarcón 4, Taxco, Guerrero 40200, tel. 762/622-1836, fax 762/622-7982, losarcos hotel@hotmail.com. The 24 rooms rise in three vine-draped tiers around an inner patio, replete with reminders of old Mexico. The rooms, with thoughtfully selected handmade polished wooden furniture, tile floors, rustic wall art, and immaculate hand-painted cobalt-on-white tile bathrooms, rent for about $25 s, $35 d.

The **Hotel Posada,** J. R. Alarcón 7, Taxco, Guerrero 40200, tel./fax 762/622-1396, across the street, is small and intimate, with plants, carved wood, paintings, and sculptures gracing every wall and corner. Rooms, in neocolonial decor, are clean and comfortable. The owners also run a nearby silver boutique, whose displays decorate the downstairs lobby. The 14 rooms rent for about $30 s, $35 d, $40 t; credit cards are accepted.

Taxco's only *zócalo*-front hostelry, the **Hotel Agua Escondida,** stands on the diagonally opposite corner from the church, at Calle Guillermo Spratling 4, Taxco, Guerrero 40200, tel. 762/622-0726 or 762/622-1166, fax 762/622-1306, hotel aguaesc@prodigy.net.mx, www.aguaescondida .com. A multilevel maze of hidden patios, rooftop sundecks, and dazzling city views, the Agua Escondida has dozens of clean, comfortable rooms. The name, which translates as "Hidden Water," must refer to its big swimming pool, which is tucked away in a far rooftop corner. Rooms vary; if you have the choice, look at several. Try to avoid the oft-noisy streetfront rooms. If you don't mind climbing, some of the upper-floor rooms have airy, penthouse views. The 76 rooms run about $33 s, $44 d, $51 t, with limited parking; credit cards are accepted.

Heading past the opposite, west, side of the plaza, follow Cuauhtémoc to the Plazuela de San Juan and the adjacent **Hotel Santa Prisca,** Cena Obscura 1, P.O. Box 42, Taxco, Guerrero 40200, tel. 762/622-0080 or 762/622-0980, fax 762/622-2938. This tranquil, dignified old hostelry was built around an oft-fragrant garden of orange trees; its off-lobby dining room shines with graceful details, such as beveled glass, a fireplace, blue-white stoneware, and ivy-hung portals. Its tile-decorated rooms, in two floors around the garden just outside, are clean and comfortable. Standard rooms go for about $29 s, $44 d; larger superior-grade rooms, $46 s or d, all with private baths, parking, and credit cards accepted.

A short block farther uphill, **Hotel Rancho Taxco Victoria,** Carlos J. Nibbi 5 and 7, Taxco, Guerrero 40200, tel. 762/622-0210 or 762/622-0004, fax 762/622-0010, rambles, in a picturesque state of decay, along its view hillside. Built sometime back in the 1930s, the hotel usually slumbers on weekdays, reviving on weekends and holidays. (Actually, it's two hotels in one—the Victoria uphill and the Rancho Taxco, neglected and returning to the earth across the road, downhill.) The better-maintained Victoria, however, is brimming with rustic, old-world extras—hand-hewn furniture, whitewashed stucco walls, riots of bougainvillea, a spreading top-level view garden—plus a big pool and a relaxed restaurant and bar where guests enjoy the best afternoon vista in town. Some of the spacious, comfortable rooms have luxurious view balconies. If you prefer peace and quiet, ask for one of the rooms away from the road, numbers 22–28, off the upper *terraza mirador* view patio, where, summer nights, you can enjoy the singing of the tree frogs and watch the lightning flicker in the clouds far away. Standard-grade rooms run about $58 s or d holidays and festivals, $45 s or d the rest of the time. Deluxe junior suites cost more, with parking; credit cards are accepted.

$50–100

From a distance, the **Hotel Borda,** off the *carretera* downhill, appears to be the luxury hotel it once was, at Cerro de Pedregal, P.O. Box 483, Taxco, Guerrero 40200, tel. 762/622-0225, fax 762/622-0617. Unenthusiastic management, however, has detracted from the hotel's magnificent assets—grand vistas, spacious garden, and luxurious blue pool and patio. Check to see if your room is clean and in working order before you move in. The 110 rooms rent for about $82 s or d, with restaurant, bar, and parking; credit cards are accepted. (*Note:* The Hotel Borda may be headed for improvement. New owners, who also own the spiffy Hotel Posada de la Misión, may have renovated it by the time you read this.)

Over $100

The luxuriously exclusive **Hotel Hacienda del Solar,** P.O. Box 96, Taxco, Guerrero 40200, tel./fax 762/622-0857, hdadelsolar@prodigy.net.mx, spreads over a tranquil hilltop garden on the southern edge of town. Guests in many of the 22 airy and spacious rooms enjoy private patios, fireplaces, and panoramic valley and mountain views. Rooms, in deluxe and junior suite versions, vary individually but are all artfully furnished with appointments including handwoven rugs, colorful tile, paintings, and folk art. Some rooms share a spacious living area near the lovely view pool and patio; junior suites have huge beds and deep tile bathtubs. Other amenities include a view restaurant, the Ventana (Window) de Taxco, and a cocktail lounge. Rooms for two go for about $120 deluxe, and $150 junior suite.

Vacationers who enjoy plenty of activity and resort amenities stay at the **Hotel Monte Taxco,** Lomas de Taxco, Taxco, Guerrero 40200, tel. 762/622-1300 or 762/622-1301, fax 762/622-1428, www.montetaxco.com, atop a towering mesa accessible by either a steep road or cableway *(teleférico)* from the highway just north of town. On weekends, the hotel is often packed with well-heeled Mexico City families, whose kids play organized games while their parents enjoy the panoramic poolside view or play golf and tennis. The 156 deluxe rooms, many with view balconies, rent from about $130 s or d, with a/c, phones, and TV; facilities include restaurants, shops, a piano bar, disco, weekend live music, parking, a gym, pool, sauna, and spa. The adjacent country club offers a nine-hole golf course, tennis courts, and horseback riding; credit cards are accepted. For more information visit the website.

If you'd like to stay atop Monte Taxco, a more economical alternative to the hotel would be to rent one of the neocolonial-style apartments of the **Country Club Monte Taxco,** tel./fax 762/622-5609, www.montetaxco.com, adjacent to the golf course, 100 yards outside the Hotel Monte Taxco front door. For about $110, you get a deluxe, two-bedroom mountain-view apartment with kitchen, use of the country club's pool, and access to the golf course, tennis courts, horseback riding, mountain trails, and the Hotel Monte Taxco's facilities next door.

Back down on the highway in town, the **Hotel Posada de la Misión** spreads over a hillside, at Cerro de la Misión 32, Taxco, Guerrero 40200, tel. 762/622-0063 or 762/622-0533, fax 762/622-2198, hpmreserva@posadamision.com, www.posadamision.com. Its guests, many on group tours, enjoy cool, quiet patios, green gardens, plant-lined corridors, a sunny pool and deck, a view restaurant, and parking. Many of the luxurious rooms have panoramic city views; some have fireplaces. All rooms have color TV and phones. Standard rooms rent for about $150 d, $200 including dinner and breakfast (Christmas–New Year's prices are higher); credit cards are accepted. Just off the *carretera,* uphill side, 200 yards south of the Pemex gas station. Reserve by email.

FOOD

Stalls and Snacks

The numerous *fondas* (permanent foodstalls) atop the *artesanías* (ar-tay-sah-NEE-ahs) handicrafts section of the market are Taxco's prime source of wholesome country-style food. The quality of their fare is a matter of honor for the proprietors, since among their local patrons word of a little bad food goes a long way. It's very hard to go wrong, moreover, if your selections are steaming hot and made fresh before your own eyes (in contrast, by the way, to most restaurant and hotel fare).

You can choose from a potpourri that might include steaming bowls of *menudo* or *pozole* ($3) or maybe plates of pork or chicken *mole* ($4) or *molcajetes* (big stone bowls) filled with steaming meat and broth and draped with hot nopal cactus leaves ($5).

Stalls offering other variations appear evenings on the *zócalo.* One family sells tacos and *pozole,* while another, which labels itself La Poblana, sometimes arrives in a truck and offers french-fried bananas, *churros,* and potato chips fried on the spot until about 10:30 P.M., next to the church.

Restaurants

Although its restaurants are not what draws Taxco's visitors, Taxco nevertheless offers some recommendable dining options. Of the *zócalo* restaurant choices, the upstairs **La Parroquia,** tel. 762/622-3096, a half block from the church steps, ranks among the best; open 9 A.M.–11 P.M.; credit cards are accepted. The front balcony tables are ideal perches for watching the people parade below while enjoying a good breakfast, lunch, or dinner ($4–8).

Another good bet on the *zócalo* is **Pizza Pazza,** at the corner, right-hand side of the cathedral, upstairs, tel. 762/622-5500. Although the menu offers a little bit of everything, the specialty is good pizza, in about 15 varieties ($5–10). Extras include relaxed ambience, professional service, checkered tablecloths, and airy, plaza-view balcony tables. If the TV bothers you, the staff won't mind turning it down to low volume, if asked. Open daily noon–midnight.

At least recommendable for its refined old-world ambience, the restaurant **Del Ángel Inn** adds an airy view and good food to the reasons for going there. Inside, rustic old-adobe walls, regal stone columns, and baroque statuary enhance the pleasing effect. As for food, choose from a very recognizable, tasty menu of appetizers, soups, salads, pasta, Mexican specialties, meats, and more. Figure about $10–15, plus drinks, per person. Find it at Calle de Muerte (now Celso Muñoz) 4, 2nd floor, a few steps down the *zócalo* churchfront, left corner. Open daily 7 A.M.–10 P.M., tel. 762/622-5525.

A block from the *zócalo,* along Calle Cuauhtémoc overlooking Plazuela de San Juan, try Mexican-style **Restaurant El Adobe,** Plazuela de San Juan 13, tel. 762/622-1416, for breakfast or a lunch break. For breakfast, you can enjoy juice, eggs, and hotcakes; for lunch, hamburgers, tacos, and enchiladas; for dinner, steak Adobe-style and shrimp brochette ($5–12). Open daily 8 A.M.–11 P.M.

Of the restaurant options, best for old-Mexico ambience is the local favorite **Restaurant Santa Fe,** tel. 762/622-1170, on the left a few doors downhill from Plazuela San Juan. Tasty, professionally prepared and served country fare keeps a battalion of faithful patrons happy. Although the long à la carte menu varies from *pozole* and soup to chicken and fish, the main event is the daily four-course *comida* of soup (try *crema de zanahoria*), spaghetti, main dish (try *chiles rellenos*), and dessert, about $5. Good for breakfast, too ($3–5); open daily 8 A.M.–10 P.M.

Uphill a block past the Plazuela San Juan, you're likely to enjoy the **Hotel Rancho Victoria** restaurant, especially for lunch and dinner, where, although the food (plates, $6–12) is quite good, the main attraction is the best afternoon view in town. From the *zócalo,* walk west along Cuauhtémoc; continue two blocks past Plazuela de San Juan. Open daily 7:30 A.M.–8 P.M.; credit cards are accepted.

A classy spot where you can enjoy the view, a swim, and lunch after seeing the Cuauhtémoc Mural is the adjacent **Restaurant El Mural,** at the Hotel Posada La Misión on the *carretera;* open daily for breakfast 7–9:30 A.M. ($5–10), lunch 1–3:30 P.M. ($5–12), and dinner 7–11 P.M. ($7–20). If the place is packed with tour groups, have a drink, enjoy the mural, and go somewhere else.

For good food in an elegant view setting, go to **Restaurant La Ventana de Taxco,** tel. 762/622-0587, at the Hotel Hacienda del Solar two blocks off the highway, south end of town. Open daily for breakfast 8:30–10:30 A.M. ($5–10), lunch 1–4:30 P.M. ($10–20), and dinner 7:30–10:30 P.M. ($15–25), when the whole town appears like a shimmering galaxy through the windows; reservations are recommended. The mostly Italian specialties include salads, lasagna, scallopini, saltimbocca, grilled red snapper, shrimp brochette, and wines.

ENTERTAINMENT AND EVENTS

Taxco people mostly entertain each other. Such spontaneous diversions are most likely around the *zócalo,* which often seems like an impromptu festival of typical Mexican scenes. Around the outside stand the monuments of the colonial past, while on the sidewalks sit the native people who come in from the hills to sell their onions, tamales, and pottery. Kids run between them, their parents and grandparents watching, while young men and women flirt, giggle, and jostle one another until late in the evening.

Three restaurant/bars on the side adjacent to the church provide good perches for viewing the hubbub. Visitors can either join the locals at **Bar Berta,** on the church corner, or take a balcony seat and enjoy the bouncy music with the mostly tourist crowd at **Bar Paco** next door. For more tranquillity, head upstairs to **Restaurant La Parroquia** a few steps farther on.

Later, or another day, continue your Taxco party via the jazzy recorded music pouring out of the speakers at the restaurant/bar **Concha Nostra,** upstairs at Hotel Casa Grande, at Plazuela de San Juan.

For more music, the **Hotel Monte Taxco,** tel. 762/622-1300 or 762/622-1301, offers a piano bar and discotheque and a trio weekends and seasonally. At the **Hotel Posada de la Misión,** tel. 762/622-0063 or 762/622-0533, patrons enjoy a roving trio for lunch and a piano bar nightly. Programs may vary; call to confirm.

Festivals

An abundance of local fiestas provide the excuses for folks to celebrate, starting on January 17 and 18 with the **Festival of Santa Prisca.** On the initial day, kids and adults bring their pet animals for blessing at the church. At dawn the next day, pilgrims arrive at the *zócalo* for *mañanitas* (dawn Mass) in honor of the saint, then head for folk dancing inside the church.

During the year Taxco's many neighborhood churches celebrate their saints' days (such as Chavarrieta, March 4; Veracruz, the four weeks before Easter; San Bernardino, May 20; Santísima Trinidad, June 13; Santa Ana, July 26; Asunción, August 15; San Nicolas, September 10; San Miguel, September 19; San Francisco, October 4; and Guadalupe, December 12) with food, fireworks, music, and dancing.

Religious fiestas climax during Semana Santa (Easter week), when, on the Thursday and Good Friday before Easter, cloaked penitents file through the city, carrying gilded images and bearing crowns of thorns.

On the Monday after the November 2 Día de los Muertos (Day of the Dead), Taxco people head to pine-shaded **Parque Huixteco** (PAR-kay weesh-TAY-koh) atop the Cerro Huixteco behind town to celebrate their unique **Fiesta de los Jumiles.** In a ritual whose roots are lost in pre-Columbian legend, people collect and feast on *jumiles* (small crickets)—raw or roasted—along with music and plenty of beer and fixings. Since so many people go, transportation is easy. Drive or ride a *colectivo*

(Huixteco on windshield) along the west-side road (westward extension of Cuauhtémoc from the *zócalo*) uphill about two miles. Fork right at the Huixteco sign. Continue for several miles to the mountainop Parque Huixteco.

SPORTS AND RECREATION

Stay in shape as local folks do, by walking Taxco's winding, picturesque side streets and uphill lanes. And, since all roads return to the *zócalo,* getting lost is rarely a problem.

For more formal sports, the **Monte Taxco Country Club** has horses ready for riding ($10/hour), three good tennis courts ($10/hour), and a nine-hole golf course available for use by nonguests for $25 per person. Contact the country club sports desk, in the little house about 50 yards away from the Hotel Monte Taxco's front entrance. Informal *sendas* (hiking paths; ask directions from the horse-rental attendant) branch from the horse paths to the surrounding luscious pine- and cedar-forested mesa country. Take sturdy shoes, water, and a hat.

SHOPPING

Market

Taxco's big market day is Sunday, when the town is loaded with people from outlying villages selling produce and live pigs, chickens, and ducks. The market is just downhill from Los Arcos, the lane that runs below the right side of the *zócalo* church (as you face that church). From the lane, head right before the arch and down the staircase. Soon you'll be descending through a warren of market stalls. Pass the small Baptist church on Sunday and hear the congregation singing like angels floating above the market. Don't miss the spice stall, **Yerbería Castillo,** piled with the intriguing wild remedies collected by owner Elvira Castillo and her son Teodoro.

Farther on you'll pass mostly scruffy meat stalls but also some clean juice stands, such as **Liquados Memo,** open daily 7 A.M.–6 P.M., where you can rest with a delicious fresh *zanahoria* (carrot), *toronja* (grapefruit), or *sandía* (watermelon) juice.

Before leaving the market, be sure to ask for *jumiles* (hoo-MEE-lays), live crickets that sell in bags for about a penny apiece, ready for folks to pop into their mouths.

If *jumiles* don't suit your taste, you may want to drop in for lunch at one of the *fondas* above the market's *artesanías* (handicrafts) section.

Handicrafts

The submarket **Mercado de Artesanías** (watch for the white sign above the market staircase) offers items for mostly local consumption, such as economical belts, huaraches, wallets, and inexpensive silver chains, necklaces, and earrings.

As you head out for tonier shops, don't miss the common but colorful handicrafts, such as the host of charming ceramic cats, turtles, doves, fish, and other figurines that local folks sell very cheaply. Find them everywhere, in the market, on street corners, and, especially in front of the Museo Spratling. If you buy, bargain—but not too hard, for the people are poor and have often traveled far.

Masks are the prime attraction at **Arnoldo,** Palma 1, tel. 762/622-1272, upstairs, across the uphill lane next to Hotel Agua Escondida, where the friendly proprietors, Arnoldo Jacobo and his son Raoul, are more than willing and able to explain every detail about their fascinating array of merchandise. Hundreds of masks from all over Guerrero—stone and wood, antique and new—line the walls like a museum. All of the many motifs, varying from black men puffing cigarettes and blue-eyed sea goddesses to inscrutable Aztec gods in onyx and grotesque lizard-humanoids, are priced to sell. Open Mon.–Sat. 9 A.M.–8:30 P.M., Sunday 10 A.M.–5:30 P.M.

Other shops nearby have similar offerings. Arnoldo's neighbor, **Celso,** at 4 Palma, just uphill, tel. 762/622-2848, is open Mon.–Tues. and Thurs.–Sat. 10 A.M.–2 P.M. and 4–8 P.M., and Sunday 10 A.M.–4 P.M., but closed Wednesday.

For a good general Mexico handicrafts selection—Puebla Talavera ceramics, Tonalá papier-mâché, metalwork, pewter—take a look inside the shop, confusingly named "Plaza San Juan," on the Plazuela San Juan, west side, beneath Restaurant Adobe, tel. 762/622-1683. Find it open Mon.–Sat. 10 A.M.–8 P.M., Sunday 10 A.M.–3 P.M.

Silver Shops

Among the many good silver shops that cluster around the *zócalo* and downhill on the highway, one of the most venerable is the family-owned shop of **Emilio Castillo** adjacent to the lobby of the Hotel Posada, downhill from the *zócalo,* to the right of the Hotel Agua Escondida. Run by a branch of the industrious and prolific Castillo family, the shop offers all in-house work, specializing in porcelain and silver, at reasonable prices. Here, unlike at many shops, you can bargain a bit. At J. R. Alarcón 7, tel. 762/622-3471, open Mon.–Fri. 9 A.M.–7 P.M.; Saturday 9 A.M.–6 P.M., Sunday 9 A.M.–4 P.M.; credit cards are accepted.

Be sure not to miss what must be Mexico's most elegantly extravagant silver shop, the Joyería Elena Ballesteros, a virtual shrine to silver, with dining-room tables loaded with enough plate for a maharaja's banquet, 10-pound $50,000 crucifixes, and a solid silver organ.

Step into the shop across the street, and enjoy the offering of another of the Castillo clan, Citlal Castillo, personable owner of Hotel Los Arcos just downhill. Here, she displays many examples of her elegant designs, in addition to a small gallery of large colonial-era paintings. Open Mon.–Sat. 10 A.M.–8 P.M.

One of the more interesting silver shops, if only for a look around, is **Luna Collection,** in the *zócalo*-front complex, Patio de las Artesanías, next to the Casa Borda, tel. 762/622-6447. They say, with a smile, that the Grutas de Cacahuamilpa were modeled after their shop. Inside, plaster stalagmites hang above small mountains of fine silver jewelry. Open daily 9 A.M.–8 P.M.; credit cards are accepted.

While you're on the *zócalo,* be sure to step into the **Casa Borda,** and admire the silver offering of the 60-member silversmithing cooperative, Soc. De Producción José de la Borda. Find them there Mon.–Sat. 9 A.M.–2 P.M. and 4–7 P.M.

For a very fitting silver-shopping finale, be sure not to miss what must be Mexico's most elegantly extravagant silver shop, the **Joyería Elena Ballesteros.** More than just a labor of love, hers is a virtual shrine to silver, beginning with the simply exquisite, moving to dining-room tables loaded with enough plate for a maharaja's banquet, to gleaming, 10-pound $50,000 crucifixes, a solid silver organ, and a huge gold tree of life. At Calle de la Muerte 4, tel. 762/622-3767, fax 762/622-3907, silver@ballesteros.com, www.ballesteros.com.

Photo and Grocery Stores

The small **Colorama** photo shop, at 7 Cuauhtémoc, offers a modest stock of merchandise, such as batteries, point-and-shoot cameras, popular print film (100–1600 ASA), and slide film. Open Mon.–Sat. 10 A.M.–8 P.M., tel. 762/622-3394.

Better-stocked **Tienda la Misión,** formerly on Cuauhtémoc, now at Benito Juárez 215, a few blocks past the City Hall next to Banamex, tel. 762/622-0116, offers some cameras and accessories and Kodak film, including Tri-X Pan, Plus-X, and Ektachrome. It also does photocopying, including enlargement and reduction. Open Mon.–Sat. 10 A.M.–8 P.M., Sunday 10 A.M.–2 P.M.

A grocery store nearby, **Casa Ayja,** at Benito Juárez 7, tel. 762/622-0364, a rarity in silver-rich Taxco, three blocks down Juárez from the *zócalo,* stocks a bit of everything, including wine, cheese, and milk on its clean, well-organized shelves and aisles. Open Mon.–Sat. 9 A.M.–10 P.M., Sunday 10 A.M.–7 P.M. If it's closed, go to the similarly attractive **Super La Gloria,** open daily, on Hidalgo, a block downhill from Plazuela de San Juan.

INFORMATION AND SERVICES

Tourist Information Offices, Guide, and Travel Agent

Taxco has a pair of **tourist information offices,** both beside the highway at opposite ends of town, open daily approximately 9 A.M.–8 P.M. The knowledgeable and English-speaking officers readily answer questions and furnish whatever maps and literature they may have. The north office, tel. 762/622-0798, is next to the north-end Pemex gas station; the south office is about a quarter mile south of the south-end Pemex station.

Personable, veteran Mexico guide **Benito Flores Batalla,** tel./fax 762/622-0542, who staffs the north-side tourist information office, offers his services as a guide. For starters, he offers a 3.5-hour city tour for $30, without car; $60 with car supplied. Longer trips might include the Caves (Grutas) of Cacahuamilpa, Xochicalco, and Ixcateopan. (See Excursions from Taxco.)

One of the most reliable travel agents in town is veteran **Turismo Misión,** at the Hotel Posada de la Misión, tel. 762/622-1125 or 762/622-0063, on the *carretera.*

Publications

English-language books and newspapers are hard to find in Taxco. Nevertheless, the bookstore **Agente de Publicaciones Raoul Domínguez,** tel. 762/622-0794, has used English-language paperbacks. It's open daily 9 A.M.–2 P.M. and 4:30–8 P.M. on the Los Arcos lane adjacent to and below the church. If it doesn't have what you want, try **Casa Domínguez** newsstand, tel. 762/622-0133, at Los Arcos 7, a few doors downhill, open Mon.–Sat. 10:30 A.M.–2:30 P.M. and 4–7:30 P.M., Sunday 10 A.M.–2:30 P.M.

The scarcity of English reading matter makes the collection at the small library **Biblioteca Taxco–Canoga Park** even more precious. Browse its several shelves of English-language novels, nonfiction, magazines, and reference books Mon.–Fri. 9 A.M.–1 P.M. and 3–7 P.M., Saturday 9 A.M.–1 P.M. Most of the collection was donated by volunteers from Taxco's sister city, Canoga Park, California. The library is a five-minute walk downhill from the city hall on the alley off Juárez, on the right, half a block past Banamex.

Money Exchange

Banks near the *zócalo* and their ATMs are Taxco's cheapest source of pesos. The good longest-hours option is **Banco Internacional (Bital),** open Mon.–Sat. 8 A.M.–7 P.M., to the right of the church, tel. 762/622-7300 or 762/622-7506. Alternatively, a few doors along Cuauhtémoc from the *zócalo,* try **Banco Santander Mexicano,** tel. 762/622-3536 or 762/622-3270, open Mon.–Fri. 9 A.M.–4 P.M., or **Bancomer,** tel. 762/622-0287 or 762/622-0288, open Mon.–Fri. 9 A.M.–5 P.M., a few doors farther along Cuauhtémoc.

Communications

The town center ***correo*** (post office) is in the Presidencia Municipal, on Juárez, downhill, east from the *zócalo,* open Mon.–Fri. 8 A.M.–5 P.M., Saturday 9 A.M.–1 P.M. The highway branch downhill is half a block north (Mexico City direction) of the Estrella de Oro bus station, open Mon.–Fri. 8 A.M.–3 P.M. **Telecomunicaciones,** off the *zócalo,* behind the Casa Borda, downhill, tel. 762/622-4885, fax 762/622-0001, offers telex, money orders, and public fax services; open Mon.–Fri. 9 A.M.–3 P.M., Saturday 9 A.M.–noon.

Public street telephones all over the town center allow cheap, easy long-distance direct dialing with widely available Ladatel telephone cards. Get them everywhere, especially at pharmacies and liquor and grocery stores.

Internet access is available at **Plaza de Computación,** in the town market, 200 feet down the steps below the right (west) side of the church. Open Mon.–Sat. 9 A.M.–9 P.M., Sunday 9 A.M.–3 P.M. If Plaza de Computación is closed, go to the hole-in-the-wall Internet store on Cuauhtémoc, half a block west of the *zócalo.* Open daily, 11 A.M.–11 P.M.

Health and Emergencies

Taxco has a pair of respected private hospitals, both on the *carretera.* The **Clínica de Especialidades,** 33 Av. de los Plateros, tel. 762/622-1111 or 762/622-4500, has a 24-hour emergency room, X-rays, a laboratory, a 24-hour pharmacy, and many specialists on call. The **Clínica Santa Cruz,** tel. 762/622-3012, offers similar services, also on Carretera Plateros, at the corner of Morelos, across from the government Seguro Social hospital.

For routine medicines and remedies, go to one of the several good local pharmacies, such as **Farmacia Similares,** on Hidalgo, one block downhill from Plazuela San Juan, tel. 762/627-2214, open Mon.–Sat. 8 A.M.–9 P.M., Sunday 8 A.M.–8 P.M. Alternatively, go to the good

24-hour pharmacy at the Clinica de Especialidades, on the *carretera.*

For police emergencies, contact the ***policía,*** either on duty on the *zócalo;* or at the city hall, two blocks downhill, at Juárez 6, tel. 762/622-0007; or at the substation on the side street Calle Fundaciones, one block below the *carretera* near the corner of Alarcón.

GETTING THERE AND AWAY

By Car or RV

National Highway 95 provides the main connection south with Acapulco in a total of about 148 miles (238 km) of easy driving via Iguala, accessible in 22 miles (36 km) via winding, old Highway 95. From there, continue south via Highway 95, to Chilpancingo (for a total of about 86 miles, 138 km). For Acapulco, continue another 62 miles (100 km) via the *cuota* (toll) *autopista.* Allow about four hours' driving time for the entire Taxco-Acapulco trip, either direction.

Highway 95 also connects Taxco north via Cuernavaca with Mexico City, a total of about 106 miles (170 km). The new leg of the Taxco-Mexico City toll *autopista* splits off from old Highway 95 about two miles north of town. For those in a hurry, it cuts about half an hour off the driving time. Otherwise, follow the scenic curving old Highway 95 about 20 miles (32 km) to its intersection with Highway 95 *cuota* superhighway. Congestion around Mexico City may lengthen the driving time to about three hours in either direction.

Note: Authorities limit driving your car in Mexico City according to the last digit of your license plate. (See the sidebar "Mexico City Driving Restrictions" in the Acapulco chapter.)

Highway 55 (junction at Cacahuamilpa) gives Michoacán- and Jalisco-bound drivers the desirable option of avoiding Mexico City by connecting Taxco directly with Toluca (and thence the fast east-west toll expressway 90 D, five hours to Guadalajara). The two-lane Highway 55 is paved and in good condition for its entire 74 miles (119 km). Fortunately, a faster, safer toll *autopista* along the northern half of Highway 55 shortens the Taxco-Toluca driving time by at least an hour over the old winding, nontoll highway. Northbound, figure about 2.5 hours driving time to Toluca; southbound, allow about two hours.

By Bus

Competing lines **Estrella Blanca,** tel. 762/622-0131, and **Estrella de Oro,** tel. 762/622-0648, operate separate stations on the downhill *carretera* a few blocks apart. Both offer several luxury- and first-class connections north with Mexico City via Cuernavaca and south with Acapulco via Iguala and Chilpancingo.

Additionally, Estrella Blanca offers connections with Puebla, and the very useful option for northwest-bound travelers of bypassing Mexico City via the super-scenic Highway 55 route via Ixtapan del Sal (an interesting spa town) to Toluca. In Toluca, you can connect via Pátzcuaro, Michoacán, or Guadalajara, Jalisco, to the palmy Pacific beach destinations of Troncones, Ixtapa-Zihuatanejo, Playa Azul, Manzanillo, Puerto Vallarta, San Blas, and Mazatlán.

EXCURSIONS FROM TAXCO

The monumental duo of the Caves of Cacahuamilpa and the ruins of ancient Xochicalco makes for a fascinating day trip. Start early; the caves are 15 miles (25 km) north (Mexico City direction) of town and Xochicalco is 25 miles (40 km) farther. On another day, travel west for about 20 miles (32 km) to Ixcateopan to visit the final resting place of the Aztecs' last emperor.

Caves of Cacahuamilpa

They're well worth the effort. The Caves of Cacahuamilpa (kah-kah-ooah-MEEL-pah) are one of the world's great cavern complexes. Forests of stalagmites and stalactites, in myriad shapes—Pluto the Pup, the Holy Family, a desert caravan, asparagus stalks, cauliflower heads—festoon a series of gigantic limestone chambers. The finale is a grand, 30-story hall that meanders for half a mile, like a fairyland in stone. The caves are open daily; hourly three-mile, two-hour walking tours in Spanish are included in the $5 admission and begin at 10 A.M. A few gift shops sell souvenirs; snack bars supply food.

Getting There: *Combi* collective vans leave hourly for the caves, beginning at 8:30 A.M., from just north of the Estrella Blanca bus station on the *carretera.* Watch for "Grutas" (Caves) written on the windshields; expect to pay about $4 for a one-way fare. By car, get to the caves via Highway 95 north from Taxco; after 10 miles (16 km) from the northside Pemex station, fork left onto Highway 55 toward Toluca. Continue five more miles (8 km) and turn right at the signed Grutas de Cacahuamilpa junction. After a few hundred yards, turn right again into the entrance driveway.

Xochicalco Archaeological Zone

Xochicalco (soh-shee-KAHL-koh), an hour farther north, although little publicized, is a fountainhead of Mesoamerican legend. The archaeological zone, officially designated as a United Nations World Heritage site, spreads over a half dozen terraced pyramid hilltops above a natural lake-valley, which at one time sustained a large population. Xochicalco flowered during the late classic period around A.D. 800, partly filling the vacuum left by the decline of Teotihuacán, the previously dominant Mesoamerican classic city-state. Some archaeologists speculate that Xochicalco at its apex was the great center of learning, known in legend as Tamanchoan, where astronomer-priests derived and maintained calendars and where the Quetzalcoatl legend was born.

Exploring the Site: Walk about 100 yards directly west, uphill, from the parking lot, where the **Pyramid of Quetzalcoatl** (The Plumed Serpent) rises on the hilltop. Vermilion paint remnants hint at its original appearance, which was perhaps as brilliant as a giant birthday cake. In bas-relief around the entire base a serpent writhes, intertwined with personages, probably representing chiefs or great priests. Above these are warriors, identified by their helmets and *atlatl,* or lance-throwers.

Most notable, however, is one of Mesoamerica's most remarkable bas-reliefs, flanking the staircase. It shows the 11th week sign, *ozomatli* (monkey), being pulled by a hand (via a rope) to join with the fifth week sign, *calli* (house). Latter-day scholars generally interpret this as describing a calendar correction that resulted from a grand conclave of chiefs and sages from all over Mesoamerica, probably at this very spot.

About 150 feet south rises the **Temple of the Steles,** so named for three large stone tablets found beneath the floor. They narrate the events of the Quetzalcoatl legend, wherein Quetzalcoatl (discoverer of corn and the calendar) was transformed into the morning star (the planet Venus); he continues to rule the heavens as the brightest star and the Lord of Time.

About 100 yards farther south, the **Main Plaza** was accessible to the common people via roads from below. This is in contrast to the sacrosanct **Ceremonial Plaza** nearby. A faintly visible causeway once connected the La Malinche pyramid, 200 yards to the southwest, with the Ceremonial Plaza.

That causeway passed the **Ball Court,** which is strikingly similar to ball courts as far away as Toltec Tula in the north and Maya Copan in Honduras, far to the south. On the opposite side of the causeway from the Ball Court lies the **Palace,** a complex marked by many rooms with luxury features such as toilet drainage, fireplaces, and steam baths.

On the opposite side of the complex is the **Observatory,** a room hollowed into the hill and stuccoed and fitted with a viewing shaft for timing the sun and star transits essential for an accurate calendar.

Getting There: Get to Xochicalco by either tour (for example, Misión Tours, at the Hotel Posada de la Misión, tel. 762/622-1125 or 762/622-0065) or car. Get there by continuing past the Caves (Grutas) of Cacahuamilpa driveway entrance, northeast via Highway 160 toward Alpuyeca. After 25 miles (40 km) from the caves, a signed road heads left uphill to the Xochicalco ruins, which are open daily 10 A.M.–5 P.M. Admission runs about $4, Sunday and holidays free. Since caretakers shoo all visitors out by 5 P.M., arrive early enough to allow a couple of hours to explore the ruins. Bring food, drinks, a hat, and comfortable walking shoes.

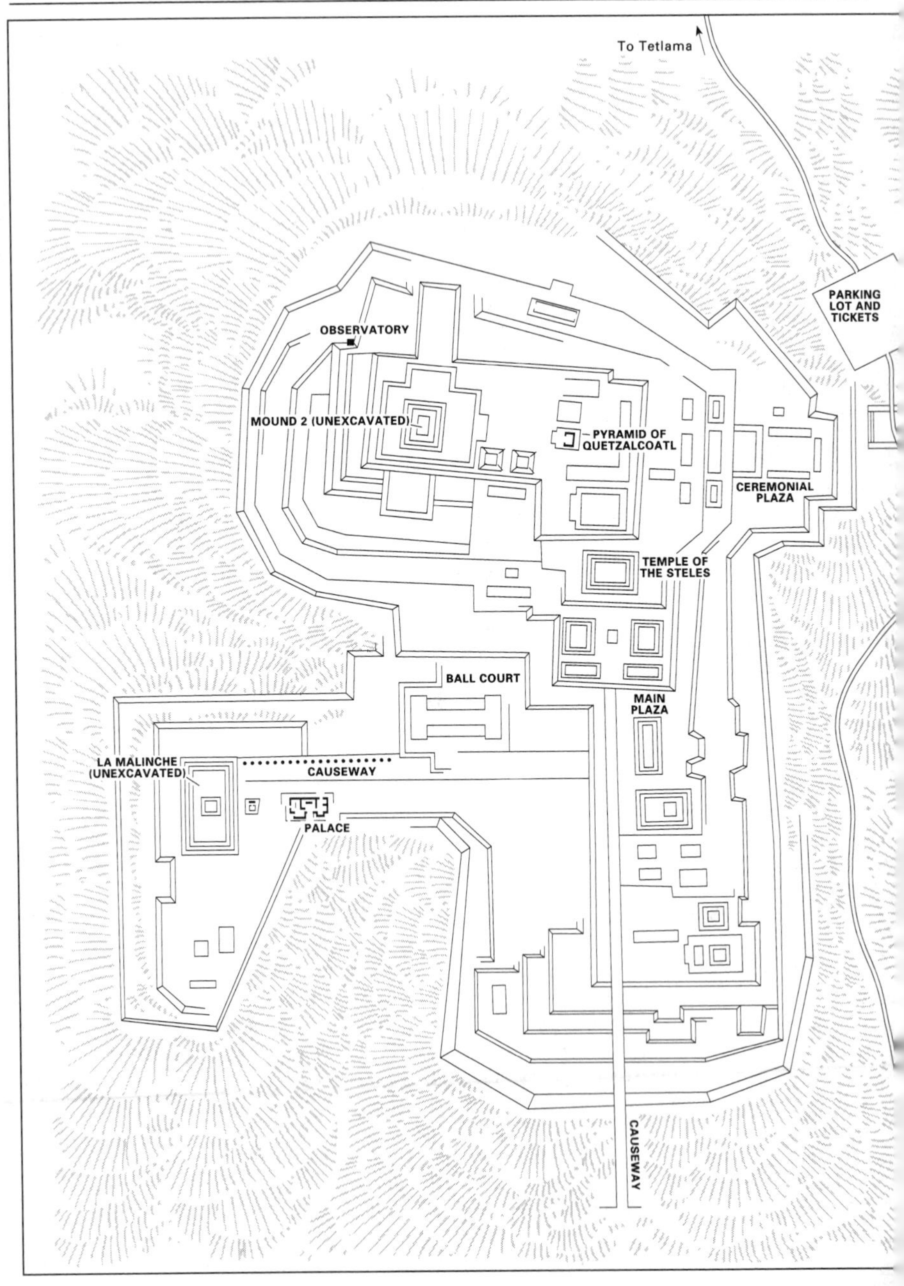
To Tetlama
PARKING LOT AND TICKETS
OBSERVATORY
MOUND 2 (UNEXCAVATED)
PYRAMID OF QUETZALCOATL
CEREMONIAL PLAZA
TEMPLE OF THE STELES
BALL COURT
MAIN PLAZA
LA MALINCHE (UNEXCAVATED)
CAUSEWAY
PALACE
CAUSEWAY

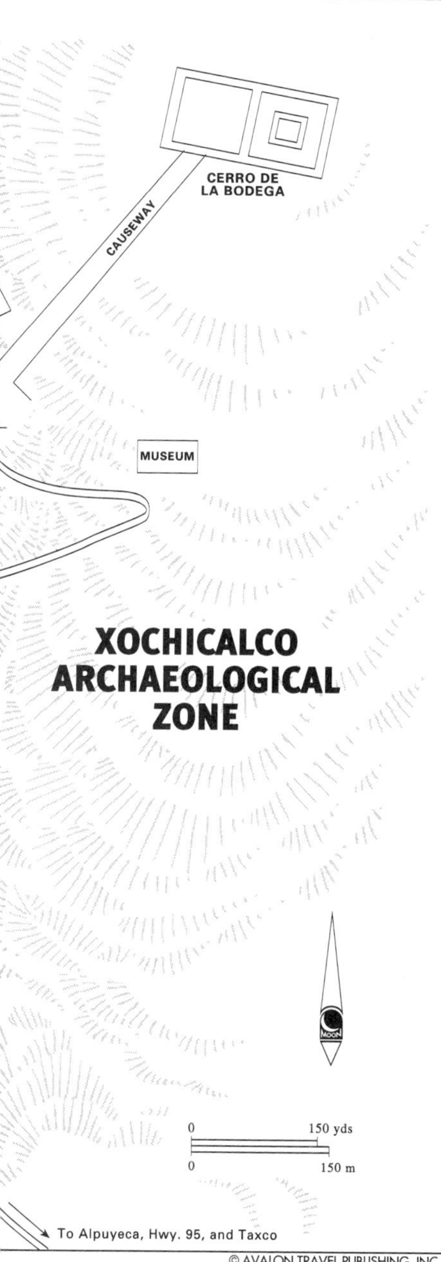

Ixcateopan

The picturesque little furniture-making town of Ixcateopan (eeks-kah-tay-OH-pan—Land of Cotton) has become famous for the remains of the last Aztec emperor, Cuauhtémoc, which archaeologists discovered there on September 26, 1949.

Exploring Ixcateopan: The renown has been beneficial. The town streets and plaza are smartly cobbled with the local white marble, and houses and shops are neatly painted and whitewashed. At the center of all this stands Cuauhtémoc's resting place, the venerable **Iglesia de Santa María de la Asunción**, at the south side of the town plaza. Inside, Jairo Rodríguez, son of the codiscoverer of Cuauhtémoc's remains and lineal descendant of Cuauhtémoc himself, devotes his life to maintaining the sanctuary and its small adjoining museum. Cuauhtémoc's relics themselves, which were subjected to rigorous investigation when they were unearthed, are undoubtedly authentic. The bones lie in a glass case directly over the spot where they were buried beneath the altar stones more than four centuries ago.

The **museum** next door details the story of Cuauhtémoc's heroic defense of the Aztec capital, Tenochtitlán, and his capture, torture, and subsequent execution by Cortés on February 28, 1525. Copies of pictograms, known as codices, such as the *Codex Vatican-Ríos* (1528), displayed in the museum, represent Cuauhtémoc (literally, The Descending Eagle) with an inverted, stylized eagle above his head. The sanctuary and museum hours are Mon.–Sat. 9 A.M.–3 P.M. and 4–5 P.M., Sunday 9 A.M.–3 P.M. Jairo sells an excellent booklet ($3) in Spanish, which details the fascinating story of the discovery and authentication of his ancestor's remains. (*Note:* At this writing, Jairo was seriously ill. I hope he will be recovered by the time you read this.)

Outside, be sure to take a look about three blocks downhill past the church, on main street Calle Guerrero, at the town **archaeological site,** open daily Wed.–Sun. 10 A.M.–5 P.M. The main remains, called the "Temple of Cotton," echoing the name Ixcateopan, reveal a ceremonial complex, including a pair of pedestals,

CUAUHTÉMOC: THE LAST AZTEC EMPEROR

Cuauhtémoc (koo-ah-oo-TAY-mok) is more than just a national hero, he's the celebrated Aztec leader who said no to the Spanish conquistadores and, spitting on the spineless example of his uncle Moctezuma before him, did something about it. Faced with the disastrous reality that most of imperial Tenochtitlán's population of 250,000 was either dead or sick with smallpox, Cuauhtémoc rallied his people to hold out for 75 days against Spanish cannon and their 100,000-strong army of native allies.

That the story of Cuauhtémoc was more than a legend became clear when, on September 26, 1949, official investigators announced the discovery of Cuauhtémoc's long-missing remains, in the small municipality of Ixcateopan, not far from the famous Acapulco region silver town of Taxco, Guerrero.

Cuauhtémoc was born into the comfort and privilege of the Mexican imperial family on February 23, 1501. His father, Ahuitzotl, was the son of the eighth Aztec emperor, also Ahuitzotl. His mother, princess Cuayautitalli, was the daughter of the lord of Zompancuahuitl (now Ixcateopan, Guerrero).

His given name, Cuauhtémoc, translates from the Aztec language as "descending eagle." Cuauhtémoc's traditional hieroglyph is thus marked by a stylized diving eagle.

Orphaned by his father when still an infant, Cuauhtémoc was brought up by his mother. At the age of 15 he entered Calmécac academy for sons of noble military officers and priests. His formal education initiated him into the secrets of the gods and the sciences of astronomy and the calendar.

After completing his schooling, Cuauhtémoc followed his uncle, Moctezuma II, in his infamous "War of the Flowers" conquests. During this time he proved his valor and skill, gaining the high rank of *tlacetechutli,* the command equivalent of a modern colonel.

Moctezuma II, upon returning home in glory, with thousands of captives, presided over the elevation of his nephew, Cuauhtémoc, as governor of the important Tlatelolco and Teotecuhtli districts of the capital Tenochtitlán.

The good times didn't last, however, for soon Hernán Cortés and his small but determined band of armored soldiers and cavalry was entering the gates of Tenochtitlán. Cuauhtémoc's uncle, frozen by fear that Cortés might be the returned god Quetzalcoatl, quickly surrendered himself and all of his golden treasure to the wily Cortés. On July 1, 1520, angered by Spanish brutality and their emperor's fearful acquiescense, the Tenochtitlán populace rebelled, killing Moctezuma II and forcing the Spanish into their disastrous Noche Triste (Sad Night) retreat, at the end of which an exhausted Cortés sat down and cried for the loss of half of his men.

The Aztecs' triumph was short-lived, however. Although they had rid themselves of the Spanish, smallpox, the Spaniards' deadly legacy, began spreading among the people. When the Spanish, in late May 1521 returned to Tenoctitlán reinforced by a vast corps of native allies, Cuauhtémoc, by contrast, ruled a city decimated by smallpox. Nevertheless, with herculean resolve, he united his people, exhorting those who could care for the wounded, gather rocks, or help pile bricks for a barricade.

After a bloody siege two and a half months long, Cortés resorted to leveling the capital to capture it. On August 13, 1521, Cuauhtémoc, desperate for reinforcements, set out to find them, but he was captured and brought before Cortés and his translator-mistress, Malinche. Cuauhté-

© BRUCE WHIPPERMAN

After missing for a dozen generations, the remains of Cuauhtémoc were found on September 26, 1949, in Santa María de la Asunción church, where they still lie.

moc pointed to the dagger that Cortés held in his belt and said to Malinche, "Malintzin, since I've resisted you in the defense of my city and my people, and come by coercion and in chains before you, take that dagger and kill me with it."

Cortés, however, didn't allow Cuauhtémoc such an honorable death. Perhaps hoping that he could convince him to be his puppet emperor, Cortés kept him in captivity for another four years. He even took Cuauhtémoc and a retinue of Aztec nobles along on his ill-fated expedition to Honduras in 1523–1525. Tortured with foreboding that Cuauhtémoc and his compatriots were plotting against him, Cortés had Cuauhtémoc hanged on February 28, 1525.

Cuauhtémoc's grisly remains were still suspended in the hanging tree when Cuauhtémoc's warrior companion, Tzilactzín, rescued them. Afraid that vandals would desecrate the body, he took down Cuauhtémoc's corpse and wrapped it in aromatic leaves. He and a band of about 30 companions, all deserters of Cortés's expedition, carried the remains for 40 days and nights and buried them secretly at Ixcateopan, the home of Cuauhtémoc's mother. There, 424 years later, Cuauhtémoc's lineal descendant, Salvador Rodrigo Juárez, and historian and Professor Eulalia Guzmán announced the discovery of Cuauhtémoc's remains. They are on public display before the altar of Ixcateopan town church, Santa María de la Asunción, in a glass casket above the spot where they were found.

royal rooms, and a former spring leading through what appear to have been wash basins (presumably for the cotton the high priests may have ritually processed there).

Farther afield, you might be able to find a guide to show you the limestone caves, **Grutas de San Miguel,** near neighboring San Miguel village (about an hour by high-clearance jeep, SUV, or truck); off the highway back to Taxco, fork right at the dirt road, at some houses, about seven miles from Ixcateopan.

Festivals: Customarily sleepy Ixcateopan wakes up for three annual fiestas. The fun kicks off in February, when folks celebrate their indigenous roots, with a weeklong party of daily flower processions, indigenous dances, and fireworks, all climaxing around the February 23 birthday of Cuauhtémoc.

The customary arrival of the governor of Guerrero, the Acapulco Symphony, and maybe even the president of Mexico, on September 26, the discovery date of Cuauhtémoc's remains, culminates another week of celebrating.

Finally, townsfolk bring in the New Year in grand style with a combined Christmas-carnival-New Year celebration of their patron Santo Niño de Atocha.

Accommodations and Food: Besides its historic interest, Ixcateopan and its environs—the rustic old church and garden, the tranquil plaza, the surrounding lush oak-forested hills—invite lingering. Moreover, the amiable, frankly curious townsfolk—who are definitely not overwhelmed by tourists—are ready for visitors. They operate some pretty fair plaza-front country restaurants and a homey local hotel, the **Hotel Hernández,** on the main street, at Calle V. Guerrero 14, Ixcateopan, Guerrero, tel. 736/366-2368, a block past the plaza, across the street from the church. The heirs of late founder Sara Hernández offer eight clean rooms around a tranquil inner patio, furnished with attractive, locally crafted wood furniture and homespun bedspreads. Rooms go for about $12 s, $16 d, with private hot-water shower baths.

Getting There: Get to Ixcateopan via *colectivo* van, labeled Ixcateopan. Catch it in front of the Estrella Blanca bus station in Taxco, or at any point on the *carretera* before the south-side, signed turnoff road to Ixcateopan. Expect to pay about $2 per person, one-way.

Drivers, follow the signed fork, west (turn right if traveling south) from the *carretera,* past the Pemex *gasolinera* about a mile south of town. Mark your odometer. Continue about an hour along the very scenic (a pair of waterfalls, good for picnicking and splashing, at Mile 4.5, Km 7.2, and Mile 11, Km 17.7), sometimes potholed, paved road for 23 miles (37 km) to the town plaza.

The Costa Chica

In reality the Costa Chica, the "Little Coast," which traditionally includes the coast of Guerrero east of Acapulco and the adjoining coast of Oaxaca, isn't so little after all. Highway 200, heading out of the Acapulco hubbub, requires 150 miles to traverse the scattered groves, forests, fields, and villages to the Mixtec and Amusgo indigenous country around Pinotepa Nacional, Oaxaca.

To many thousands of Costa Chica indigenous peoples, Spanish is a foreign language. Many of them live in remote foothill villages, subsisting as they always have on corn and beans, without telephones, sewers, schools, or roads. Those who live near towns often speak the Spanish they have learned by coming to market. In the Costa Chica town markets of Ometepec, Xochistlahuaca, and Pinotepa Nacional you will brush shoulders with them—mostly Mixtecs, Amusgos, and Chatinos—men sometimes in pure-white cottons and women in colorful embroidered *huipiles* over wrapped handwoven skirts.

Besides the indigenous people, you will often see African Mexicans—*morenos* (brown ones)—known as *costeños* because their isolated settlements are near the coast. Descendants of African slaves imported hundreds of years ago, the *costeños*

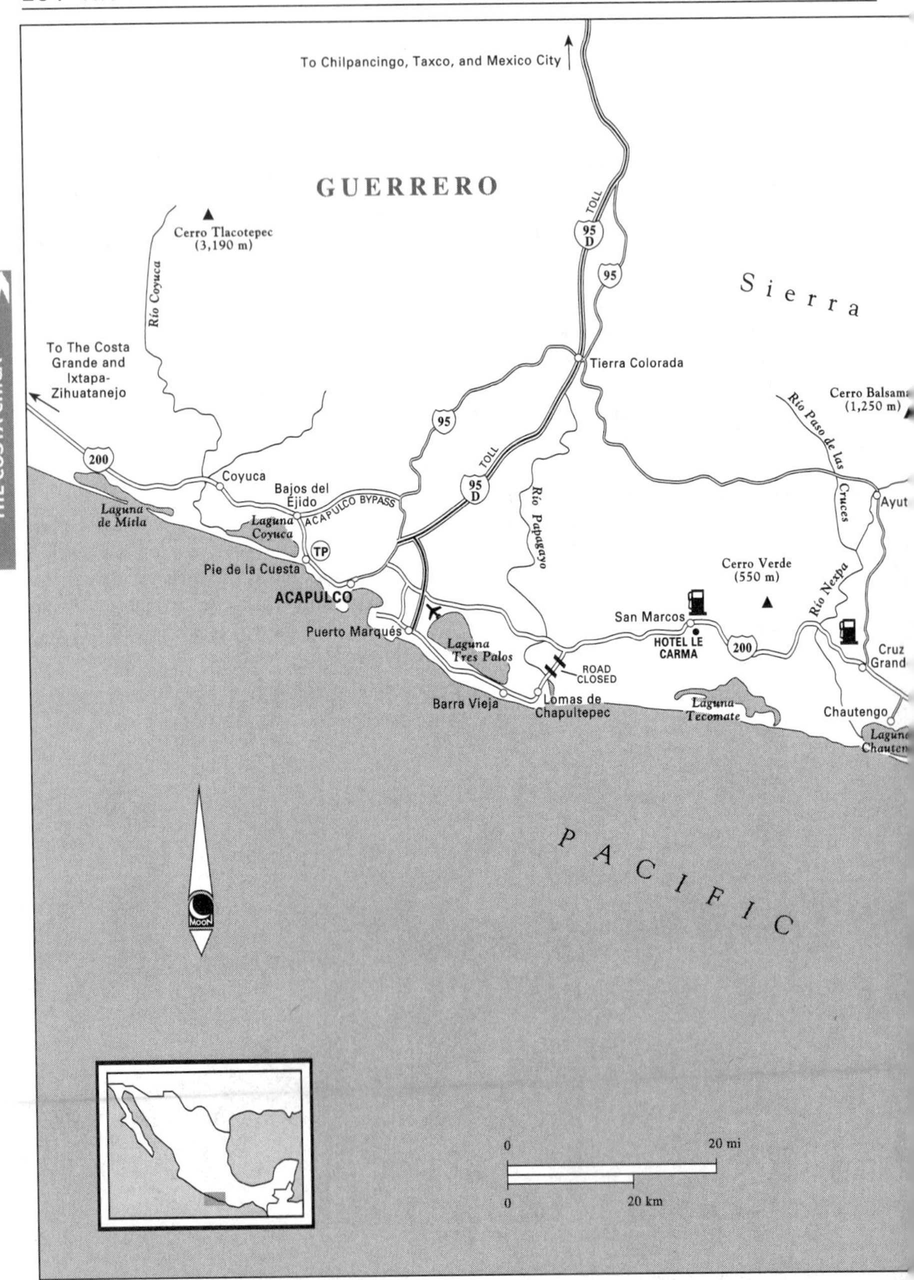
To Chilpancingo, Taxco, and Mexico City
GUERRERO
Cerro Tlacotepec
(3,190 m)
Río Coyuca
TOLL
95
D
95
Sierra
To The Costa
Grande and
Ixtapa-
Zihuatanejo
Tierra Colorada
Cerro Balsam
(1,250 m)
Río Paso de las Cruces
200
Coyuca
Bajos del
Ejido
ACAPULCO BYPASS
Laguna
de Mitla
Laguna
Coyuca
TP
Pie de la Cuesta
ACAPULCO
Río Papagayo
Ayut
Cerro Verde
(550 m)
Río Nexpa
San Marcos
HOTEL LE
CARMA
Puerto Marqués
Laguna
Tres Palos
ROAD
CLOSED
Cruz
Grand
Barra Vieja
Lomas de
Chapultepec
Laguna
Tecomate
Chautengo
PACIFIC
0
20 mi
0
20 km

THE COSTA CHICA
OAXACA
Madre del Sur
Cerro Mexcaltepec (1,950 m)
Cerro Picdra Gris (3,000 m)
Río Quetzala
Río Copala
To Oaxaca
Putla
125
San Cristóbal
Tlacoachistlahuaca
Xochistlahuaca
Acatlán
Igualapa
Santa Maria Zácatepec
Zacualpan
Azoyú
HOTEL VENUS I
HOTEL BELLO NIDO
Ometepec
200
San Pedro Amusgos
Huistepec
Cacahuatapec
HOTEL LA CARACOLA
Marquelia
Copala
Playa Las Peñitas
HOTEL PUERTO PALISADA
TP
Playa Ventura
San Sebastian Ixcapa
Barra de Tecoanapa
Cuajinicuilapa
San Juan Colorado
Tierra Colorada
HOTEL MARÍN
Tlacamama
Pinotepa Don Luis
San Nicolás
Pinotepa Nacional
Armenta
Huaxpaltepec
El Ciruelo
Tetepec
Puerto Maldonado
Llano Grande
Huazolotitlan
Jamiltepec
Corralero
Laguna Corralero
To Puerto Escondido and Oaxaca
Río Arena
Río Verde
OCEAN

subsist on the produce from their village gardens and the fish they catch.

Costa Chica *indígenas* and *costeños* have a reputation for being unfriendly and suspicious. If true in the past (although it's certainly less so in the present), they have had good reason to be suspicious of outsiders, who in their view have been trying to take away their land, gods, and lives for 400 years.

Communication is nevertheless possible. Your arrival, for the residents of a little mountain or shoreline end-of-road village, might be the event of the day. People are going to wonder why you came. Smile and say hello. Buy a soda at the store or *palapa.* If kids gather around, don't be shy. Draw a picture in your notebook. If a child offers to do likewise, you've succeeded.

ALONG THE ROAD

Although you can traverse the Costa Chica in less than a day, linger a while to sample the many interesting towns and relaxing diversions along the way. These include the petite south-seas beach resorts of Playa Ventura and Playa Las Peñitas; a wildlife-rich mangrove lagoon, Laguna Chautengo, and its associated breezy barrier beach village, San José de la Barra; Cuajinicuilapa and its unique Afromestizo museum and cultural center and nearby Puerto Maldonado; and the unmissable indigenous Amusgo (Ometepec, Xochistlahuaca) and Mixtec (Pinotepa Nacional, Jamiltepec) market towns.

Heading Out

If you're going by bus, ride one of the several daily first-class or second-class buses from the Estrella Blanca (Avenida Ejido) terminal in Acapulco. Let the highway kilometer markers (both at roadside and on the asphalt itself) lead you to your chosen destination. A minute ahead of time, let the driver know where to let you off.

If driving from Acapulco, mark your odometer at the traffic circle where Highways 95 and 200 intersect over the hill from Acapulco. If, on the other hand, you bypass that congested point via the Acapulco airport road, set your odometer to zero at the east-side interchange near Puerto Marqués where the airport highway continues along the overpass—but where you exit to the right, and follow the Highway 200 Pinotepa Nacional sign. Mileages and kilometer markers along the road are sometimes the only locators of turnoffs to hidden villages and little beaches.

Fill up with gas before starting out in Acapulco. After that, gas is customarily available at Cruz Grande (56 miles, 91 km), Ometepec (110 miles, 177 km), Pinotepa Nacional (157 miles, 253 km), and Puerto Escondido (247 miles, 398 km).

SAN MARCOS

San Marcos (pop. 10,000), 36 miles (58 km) east of Acapulco, is a frequent first stop for essential services along the Costa Chica. It has a bank (Banamex, tel. 745/453-0036, open Mon.–Fri. 9 A.M.–3 P.M., with 24-hour ATM); Seguro Social health center on the highway; a pharmacy, tel. 745/453-0527; a doctor (Mauricio Ibarra), streetfront Ladatel card–operated telephones, and post and *telecomunicaciones* (long-distance telephone, money orders, and fax, tel. 745/453-0130, open Mon.–Fri. 9 A.M.–3 P.M., Saturday 9 A.M.–noon) offices. Find the pharmacy, bank, doctor and more on the town *jardín,* on main street Hidalgo, about .3 mile (.5 km) north of the highway.

Accommodations and Food

San Marcos's best hotel, the **Le Carma,** tel. 745/453-0037, on the highway, south side, is recommendable for an overnight. Although the hotel's loose management leaves something to be desired, guests enjoy a major plus, cooling off in the hotel's inviting blue pool. The approximately 20 clean rooms rent for about $20 d, with fans and hot-water shower baths.

For food, try **Restaurant Ruth** on the highway, on the same south side and about a block east of the hotel. Although the restaurant is less than spotless, its food is plentiful and good and the dogs and roosters in the back add a homey touch. If that's not your style, check out Restaurant Edith across the highway.

LAGUNA CHAUTENGO AND PLAYA VENTURA

These laid-back havens are attractive for different reasons: Playa Ventura is for those who enjoy civilized south-seas delights, while the broad Laguna Chautengo estuary attracts folks hankering for wild things, such as troves of wildlife for viewing and photographing, pristine beaches for camping, and swarms of good-eating *lisa* (mullet), *sierra* (mackerel), *robalo* (snook), just for the catching.

Laguna Chautengo

Follow the good turnoff road four miles (about 6 km) east of Cruz Grande (43 miles, 69 km east of Acapulco). Continue 3.7 miles (6 km) to the boat dock. Here, the big mangrove lagoon spreads about eight miles in both directions along the coast and four miles across to the barrier sandbar. Most of the year Laguna Chautgengo is a freshwater reservoir of the rivers Nexpa, Jalapa, and Copala. But during the rainy season the lagoon breaks through the sandbar, slicing a channel between the beachfront hamlets of Pico de Monte and San José de la Barra, which beckon far across the lagoon.

Boatmen customarily charge $20 per boat (of up to 10 passengers) for the cross-lagoon roundtrip, which includes waiting for the passengers to enjoy a fish dinner one of the several beachfront *palapas*. If you're going to camp overnight on the beach, let your boatman know when to return and pick you up.

Although road's-end facilities amount to no more than the dock and a snack restaurant, alternatives exist. Rent a boat and captain (figure $10–20 per hour) and mount your own fishing trip. Or do the same with your own boat or kayak. Launching appears doable from the calm, gently sloping shoreline.

Playa Ventura

Three miles east of the small town of Copala, 77 miles (123 km) from Acapulco, a roadside sign points toward Playa Ventura. Four miles down a paved road, which a truck-bus from Copala traverses regularly, you arrive pavement's-end at Ventura village. From there, a mile-long golden-sand beach arcs gently east. Past a lighthouse, the beach leads to a point, topped by a stack of granite rocks known locally as Casa de Piedra (House of Stone).

Playa Ventura can provide nearly everything for a restful day or week in the sun. Several good tent camping or RV (maneuverable medium rigs, vans, or campers) spots sprinkle the inviting, outcropping-dotted shoreline. Shady *palapas* set up by former campers stand ready for rehabilitation and reuse by new arrivals.

Surf fishing (with net-caught bait fish) is fine from the beach, while *pangas* go out for deep-sea catches. Good surfing breaks angle in from the points, and, during the rainy season, the behind-the-beach lagoon is good for fishing, shrimping, and wildlife-viewing. (Bring your kayak or inflatable raft.)

The palm-lined beach stretches southeast for miles. Past the picturesque Casa de Piedra outcropping, an intimate *palapa-* and *panga*-lined sandy cove curves invitingly to yet another palmy point, Pico del Monte. Past that lies still another, even more pristine cove and beach.

Accommodations and Food

Besides the village stores, food is available at a number of *loncherías* and beach *palapa* restaurants. Accommodations are available at a sprinkling of family *posadas,* the foremost of which is the **Restaurant and Ramada Pérez,** cell tel. 744/439-8890. If anyone dispels the rumor that *costeño* folks are unfriendly, it's the hospitable Pérez family team (father Bulmaro, mother Inés, son Luis, and daughter Hortencia), who have put together the modest beginnings of a little resort. Inés and her family invite visitors to park RVs in their small lot, where they offer a friendly word, showers, a homemade swimming pool, kiddie pool, and a bit of shade for a reasonable $6 per party per day. For tenters, they rent spaces beneath their shady beachfront *ramada* for the same price. Furthermore, besides the Perezes' main oceanview *ramada* restaurant, son Luis has added a breezy rooftop *palapa* hamburger restaurant, and Luis's brother Arturo has created his life dream of a petite but elegant Discoteca Pérez.

Others have followed the Pérez example. From

the Pérez compound, move east along the beach to find plumy **Las Palmeras** with a shady, spacious grove for RV parking or tenting. Continue next door to beachfront restaurant and campground **Doña Maura,** with plenty of space for small-to-medium self-contained RVs and tents beneath shady palm-frond *ramadas.* Next come a couple of inviting restaurants, first **El Faro,** with a working lighthouse, and finally the thatched **Jay** restaurant.

Most of Playa Ventura's hotels are on Playa Ventura's west, Acapulco side. Past the Perezes', find the restaurant and hotel **Doña Celsa,** with about 20 clean, modern rooms, with tiled baths and hot-water showers, for about $25 d, $40 holidays. Alternatively, check out the lineup of similar lodgings at **Cabañas Condesa, Hermoso Pacheco,** and **Tomy.**

The best publicized of all these Playa Ventura accommodations appears to be beachfront hotel and restaurant **La Caracola,** aura@cableonline.com.mx, www.playaventura.com, which I found only via the Internet. On her website, the enterprising owner Aura Elena Rodríguez advertises rustic but comfortable beachfront cabanas, rentable for a five-night minimum, no dogs, prices not given (but probably in the $40 range, high-season).

All this development ferment has led to a growing colony of beachfront homes. A number of the original Playa Ventura families are getting rich selling lots. Luis Pérez tells me that the going price is currently about $9,000 for a 60-foot by 60-foot beachfront lot. Before putting your money down, be sure to research the legal details of owning property in Mexico. Go through a reputable real estate agent, such as Century 21 and others (see the Long-Term Rentals section and the sidebar "Owning Paradise" in the Acapulco chapter).

MARQUELIA, PLAYA LAS PEÑITAS, AND BARRA DE TECOANAPA

The small market town of **Marquelia** (pop. 10,000, 91 miles, 146 km, east of Acapulco) offers a number of services and is a jumping-off point for the charming beachfront haven of Playa Las Peñitas and the hardscrabble end-of-the-road fishing village of Barra de Tecoanapa. You can't miss Marquelia, since its market stalls crowd the highway.

Playa Las Peñitas

Just east of Marquelia, turn south (if not driving, catch a truck ride) on the signed Playa Las Peñitas turnoff road. After 3.5 miles (5.7 km) go right at the signed driveway 50 yards to the beach. The main attraction, popular with local holiday vacationers and Sunday picnicking families, is the long, steep, yellow-sand beach, lined with seafood *palapas,* two small lodgings, and Las Peñitas (the Little Rocks), a family of sandstone rocks, picturesquely perched on the shoreline.

Besides its yellow sand, cooling sea breezes, and good seafood, Playa Las Peñitas' main attraction is a venerated, water-sculpted rock, beside gurgling, people-friendly tidepools.

At high tide, one of the Las Peñitas becomes a small islet, where folks have set a pilgrimage cross around which the faithful congregate for devotions on the May 3 (Día de la Cruz) holiday. It provides a perfect playground for kids scampering and splashing in the waves that curl gently around the islet. Moreover, families frolic in a bathtublike tidepool on one side of the islet, dunking themselves in the gentle waves that fill its foamy basin.

Accommodations and Food: A pair of small inviting hotels complete the lovely Las Peñitas picture. Most accessible right on the beach is **Hotel Puerto Palisada,** where enterprising owners offer about five clean, comfortable rooms, with two double beds, fans, and hot-water shower baths, for about $25 for 1–4. Amenities include a shady beachfront yard, with picnic tables and kitchen for guest use. No pool as of this writing, however. For reservations, contact the owners (in Spanish) at tel. 741/412-1662.

Nearby, about 100 yards farther east, just inland from the beach to the right of the road, stands attractive **Hotel Palapa Sol de la Peña,** with about four large rooms. When I arrived, I didn't get to see inside the rooms because they were all occupied. The hotel, however, within an inviting fenced garden compound centering around a big pool, appeared inviting and well maintained. The manager, however, was not welcoming and volunteered very little information, not even a telephone number. He did say, however, that rooms were ordinarily available for rent.

A number of *palapa* restaurants line the Las Peñitas beach. One of them, **Palapa Iris,** occupies an especially scenic perch next to Laguna Colorada, the petite swimming lagoon, perfect for tots, behind the sandbar-beach, a few steps from the rock islet. Take a seat in the shade and enjoy the gorgeous double (lagoon and ocean) view.

Barra de Tecoanapa

Continue 1.5 miles by car (or, if without wheels, by truck; offer to pay), ford a shallow river, immediately pass a store, then bear left, passing through Guadalupe village. Continue another 4.5 miles (7.2 km) to road's end at Barra de Tecoanapa (pop. 1,000).

The village spreads for about a mile along the sandbar of the Río Quetzala, which empties into the sea from its lagoon-estuary about a quarter mile east of town. You can continue (drivers, be careful of soft sand) along the beach track to the embarcadero, decorated with a few dozen fishing *lanchas* pulled up on the lagoon-front. The river channel through the sandbar allows ocean fish (*sierra, robalo, lisa*) to populate the lagoon.

The village appears to owe its existence to fishing and the holiday and weekend visitors who enjoy fresh seafood at its scattering of humble beachfront *palapa* restaurants. Terns and pelicans diving into onshore waves signal ideal conditions for surf fishing.

Although life on the Barra de Tecoanapa is simple and ruled by the unhurried rhythms of sun and tide, local folks, whose houses are primarily of stick and thatch, do enjoy a few 21st-century amenities. These include a basketball court, two or three small stores, a kindergarten, a primary school, and a potable water system.

All this might spell heaven for experienced visitors equipped to enjoy country beachfront living. If you don't mind a few curious townsfolk, plenty of space, especially west of town, is available for beachfront tenting and RV parking. Rent a boat or float your own either at the lagoon or right on the beachfront. Waves, which break gradually about 100 yards out, recede with only slight undertow, fine for wading, splashing, and boogie boarding. Although the waves I saw appeared too mild for surfing, stronger swells, a likely seasonal possibility, might produce ideal surfing conditions.

OMETEPEC AND VICINITY

Ometepec (pop. 15,000) is the principal town of the Guerrero indigenous heartland. In Ometepec's foothill hinterland, Spanish is a foreign language. About half of the Ometepec *municipio* (pop. 50,000) people are native-speaking. In more remote *municipios,* such as Xochistlahuaca (so-chees-tlah-HWAH-kah), more than three-quarters speak native tongues.

Bright markets with their piles of fruit and flowers, old-fashioned handmade goods, and crowds of folks in colorful native dress are the

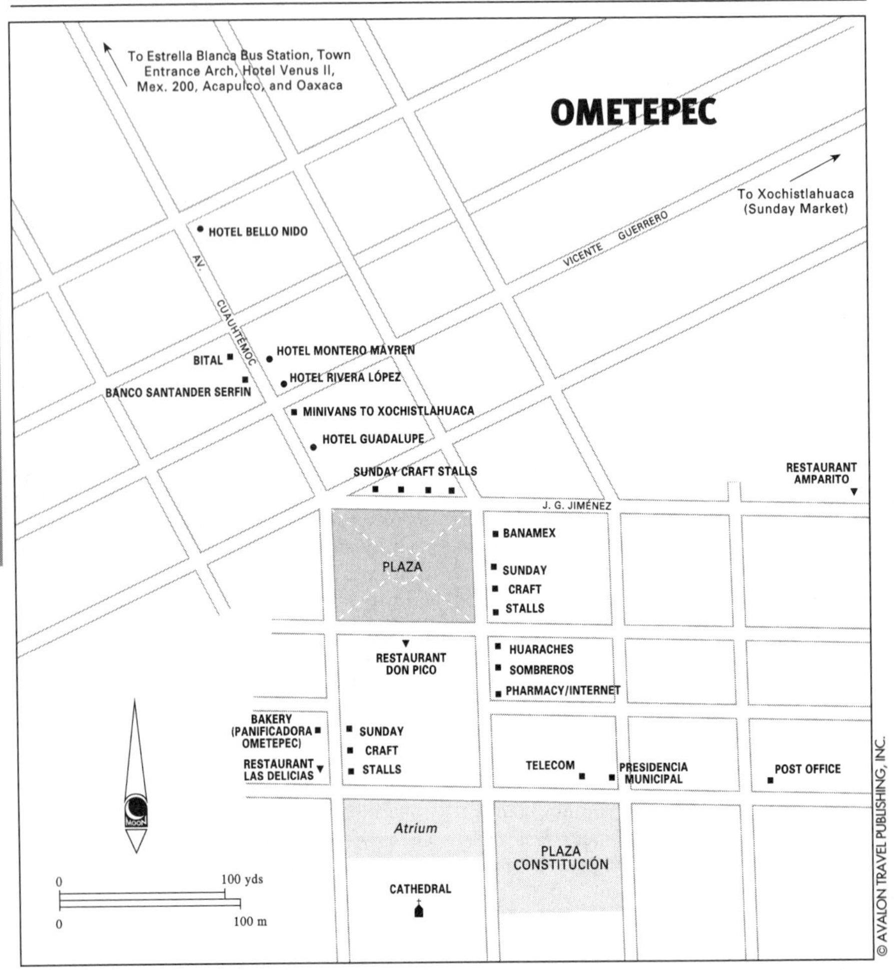

reward for visitors who venture uphill to spend time exploring these vibrant towns.

Access and Orientation

Ometepec, Guerrero's Costa Chica "capital," is accessible via a 10-mile paved road, which branches off Highway 200 at a big signed intersection 110 miles (177 km) east of Acapulco. Besides being an important market and service center, Ometepec (elev. 1,000 feet) enjoys a cooler climate, drawing crowds of native peoples, notably Amusgos and Mixtecs, from outlying villages to its big Sunday market. Reflecting its upland location, the town's name, from the Náhuatl (Aztec) language, combines *ome* (two) and *tepec* (hill), meaning "land between two hills."

Ometepec orients itself along a single street, Avenida Cuauhtémoc. Entering town eastbound, via the ingress highway from the coast, you pass under a big entrance arch. Immediately comes the main market on the right.

Avenida Cuauhtémoc continues east past the main (Estrella Blanca) long-distance bus station. After about half a mile, the thoroughfare angles right (southeast), going through the business district, passing most shops, restaurants, hotels, and banks. Finally, at the petite main plaza on the left, Cuauhtémoc bends due south and ends within a block, in front of the main church, dedicated to Santiago (St. James).

Sights

Ometepec's **church,** although not old, having been built during the 1960s, is both popular and handsome. Evenings, spotlights keep its lovely blue and white facade shining long after dark. During the day, the faithful crowd through its gates and approach the facade, populated with its choir of white-shining saints and angels. Atop this all presides a sculpture of a mounted, sword-brandishing Santiago. Approach even closer and admire the church's grand polished wooden doors, climaxed in the center by yet another Santiago, this time with his horse's hooves trampling the defeated Moors. Inside, swallows swoop beneath the airy nave's ceiling and perch and chirp in the chandeliers. Above the altar rises a grand dome whose paintings depict a vista of heaven so pleasing that it seems as pretty as the view must be through the pearly gates themselves.

Ometepec's other famous attraction, the Sunday ***tianguis*** (tee-AHN-geese) native market, operates in two sections: one, on the west side, just inside the town entrance arch, and the other, around the downtown plaza. At the downtown plaza are most of the handicrafts, including embroidered *huipiles,* huaraches, and sombreros. In the west-side section you'll find a small mountain of everything else: forest-gathered herbs, seeds, and spices, *chiles,* homemade brooms, fruits (mangoes, grapes, and bananas), vegetables (radishes, sweet potatoes, tomatoes), tobacco (in aromatic bunches of big dried leaves), and mounds of dried fish, all in one spreading, semi-organized five-acre area. (For more market sights, see the Excursion to Xochistlahuaca section.)

Accommodations

Ometepec has several hotels, all of which accept cash only. They do a brisk business, accommodating the town's many market, business, and festival visitors.

THE AMUSGO PEOPLE

If not the most numerous, the Amusgos are the most visible of the Acapulco region's indigenous groups. On Sunday, crowds of Amusgo-speaking people flock to easily accessible market towns in the Costa Chica foothills about 100 miles east of Acapulco.

The Amusgo homeland comprises an approximately 30- by 40-mile territory straddling the Oaxaca-Guerrero border. About a third of the 30,000 Amusgo speakers live in Oaxaca, around the small centers of Cacahuatepec and San Pedro Amusgos, while the remaining majority lives on the Guerrero side, near the centers of Ometepec, Xochistlahuaca, and Tlacoachistlahuaca.

Linguists reckon that the Amusgo language, a member of the Mixtec language subfamily, separated from Mixtec between 2000 and 1000 B.C. Around A.D. 1000 the Amusgos came under the domination of the strong coastal Oaxaca Mixtec kingdom of Tututepec. In A.D. 1457 they were conquered by the Aztecs and, not long after, by the Spanish in the 1520s. Decimation of the Amusgo population by disease during the 16th century led to the importation of African slave labor, whose descendants, known locally as *negros* or *costeños,* live along the Guerrero-Oaxaca coastline.

The Amusgo population eventually recovered; many of the old colonial-era haciendas remained intact until modern times and continued to employ Amusgo people as laborers. The Amusgos, isolated from the mainstream of modern Mexican life, retain their age-old corn-bean-squash subsistence farming tradition. Moreover, they have received little attention from anthropologists or archaeologists, although several intriguing archaeological mounds exist near Amusgo villages.

Amusgo women are nevertheless famous for their hand-embroidered *huipiles,* whose colorful floral and animal designs fetch willing customers in the Acapulco region and Oaxaca tourist centers. Even better, Amusgo women often wear their *huipiles,* appearing as heavenly visions of spring on dusty small-town side streets.

The **Hotel Venus II,** at Crucero de Talapa, Ometepec, Guerrero 41700, tel. 741/412-2349, hotel_venus@hotmail.com, stands prominently to the left of the arch as you enter Ometepec. The hotel, at the uncongested edge of town, and with a secure parking lot, is convenient for visitors with cars. Past the reception, the place is modern and clean, with guests in many rooms enjoying balcony vistas (of the parking lot below and hills beyond). The hotel's 20-odd rooms cost about $17 d with fan, $25 with a/c, all with private hot-water shower baths, good cable TV, and a one-block walk to the west-side market. For reservations, call the hotel directly or email.

(The **Hotel Venus I,** the Venus II's comparably good sister hostelry, stands prominently at the Highway 200-Ometepec intersection, 10 miles downhill. Use the same email and telephone number for reservations.)

The remainder of Ometepec's hotels are downtown. Move southwest to first find comfortable **Hotel Bello Nido,** about three blocks from the plaza, at Cuauhtémoc 50, Ometepec, Guerrero 41700, tel. 741/412-0141 or 741/412-0234. Past the small but inviting lobby, the hotel rises in three motel-style floors around an appealing pool-patio. Rooms are clean and furnished with dark bedspreads, drapes, and tiled shower baths, but with no bedside reading lamps. Rentals run about $15 s, $17 d in one double bed, $25 d, t, or q in two double beds, with TV, fans, and parking. Add about $10 for a/c. For more tranquillity, light, and privacy, reserve a room an upper floor room in the back, away from the busy streetfront.

© BRUCE WHIPPERMAN

Ometepec's pride and joy is its church, dedicated to Santiago (St. James).

A trio of cheaper hotel options clusters in the middle of the downtown action, about a block farther east. Best of the three is downscale **Hotel Rivera López,** at Cuauhtémoc 22, Ometepec, Guerrero 41700, tel. 741/412-0028. Choose from 33 sparely furnished rooms in three floors around an inner parking patio. Rooms cost about $15 s or d in one double bed, $19 d, t, q in two double beds, with TV, fans, parking, and hot-water shower bath. Add about $10 for a/c.

Farther down the scale, next door is barebones **Hotel Montero Mayren,** at Cuauhtémoc 23, Ometepec, Guerrero 41700, tel. 741/412-0100. Its 20 plain rooms in three floors each rent for about $14 s or d in one bed, $25 d, t, or q in two beds, with fans and parking, but no hot water. Add about $8 for a/c.

Finally, half a block from the plaza, lovers of old Mexico might appreciate the **Hotel Guadalupe,** at Cuauhtémoc 20, Ometepec, Guerrero 41700, tel. 741/412-2228. The approximately 20 plain but clean rooms surround a leafy interior garden patio. They rent for about $12 s or d, with room-temperature-only private shower baths, and no fans.

Food

Most eating out in Ometepec occurs in one of two locales. The busiest of these is in the west-side main market, where *fondas* (permanent food stalls) offer country-style offerings of savory *guisado* (stews of chicken, pork, beef), piles of *antojitos* (*chiles rellenos, pozole,* tamales, tacos), and much more. (Permanent market *fondas* de-

Tacos *al pastor,* made from spit-barbecued pork or beef, are the specialty of Ometepec's Restaurant Las Delicias.

pend on repeat customers and therefore serve wholesome food. If in doubt, remember that cooked food, if it's steaming, will also be safe.)

Food sources also concentrate downtown, along Cuauhtémoc by the plaza. For fresh baked goods, go to **Panificadora Ometepec,** at Cuauhtémoc 9, open daily 7 A.M.–9 P.M., across the street from the plaza.

Most sit-down eateries downtown specialize in country-style *antojitos.* An excellent such choice near the plaza is sidewalk **Restaurant Las Delicias,** at the end of Cuauhtémoc, in view of the churchfront. Although basically a taco shop, Las Delicias serves breakfasts (pancakes, omelettes, french toast $2–3), *comida,* a set four-course lunch $3–4, noon–6 P.M., and until midnight, tacos *al pastor* (barbecued beef and pork, $2) in a dozen tasty options, with a mound of stuffings served on a plate along with a bottomless supply of hot tortillas. Yum. Moreover, Restaurant Las Delicias offers more than food. After the teen crowd goes home around 8 or 9, it becomes a pleasant spot to spend a balmy hour or two, enjoying the lovely illuminated churchfront view (and if you're lucky the full moon rising above and to the left of it).

The Ometepec downtown restaurant that everyone seems to recommend is **Amparito,** at Juan Garcia Jiménez 11, past Banamex, downhill two blocks east of the plaza. Amparito, named after the grandmotherly owner, although specializing in seafood plates (shrimp, octopus, whole fish, fillets, $4–8), does offer nonseafood specials. These might include *codorniz* (quail, $8) or *guisado de res* (beef stew, $6). For breakfasts ($3–5), it can serve anything from eggs any style and French toast to pancakes or pastries with fresh fruit. If the TV noise bothers you, ask the staff to please lower the volume (*favor de moderar el volumen*—fah-VOR day moh-day-RAHR AYL vo-LOO-mayn). Find Amparito, tel. 741/412-2044, open daily 7 A.M.–7 P.M.

Entertainment and Events

Ometepec is known for a number of festivals, notably the Easter-week **Semana Santa,** which includes, besides the usual religious Masses and processions, also cattle, agricultural, and handicrafts expositions, *jaripeo* (bull riding and roping), and a carnival. Festivities climax with regional folk dance performances, including the favorite, Los Chilenos, said to have originated in Ometepec.

If you arrive in town on certain dates, join the festivities—May 3: Fiesta del Día de la Santa Cruz (Holy Cross); July 24–26: Fiesta de Santiago; Sept. 9–11: Fiesta de San Nicolás Tolentino; Sept. 15–16: Fiestas Patrias, including the 11 P.M. reenactment of Father Miguel Hidalgo's Grito de Dolores at the *presidencia municipal,* and the dances of El Mulo y La Tortuga (Mule and the Turtle) and El Macho.

The region's most popular festival is the **Fiesta del Señor del Perdón** at Igualapa (pop. 3000), half an hour northwest of Ometepec. It may be worthwhile to make a special trip for this important indigenous fiesta, which local folks throw yearly on the third Friday of Lent (two weeks, two days after Ash Wednesday).

The main event is a pilgrimage to pay respects to the Señor del Perdón, visited by thousands. They arrive to ask, at least, for small favors and, at most, for miracles. And judging from the Señor del Perdón's popularity, the wishes are often granted.

The main event is a pilgrimage to pay respects to the Señor del Perdón (Lord of Pardon), visited by thousands, arriving on all fours, on their knees, by foot, or by car or bus. They arrive to ask, at least, for small favors and, at most, for miracles. And judging from the Señor del Perdón's popularity, the wishes are often granted.

Miracles nothwithstanding, merrymaking abounds, especially among the swarm of campesinos—mostly speaking dialects of Amusgo, Mixtec, and Tlapanec languages—decked out in their Sunday best native *traje.* For a feast of scents, sounds, and sights, simply walk among the dozens of stalls around the Igualapa pilgrimage church, the Santuario del Señor del Perdón. Before departing, make sure to enjoy the whirl and flash of regional dances performed by a number of brightly costumed troupes.

From Ometepec, get there, either via taxi or minivan, from the west-side market, or by car. Follow the west exit road toward Highway 200. About a mile from the west edge of town, turn right at the Igualapa turnoff road; continue about 7 miles (11 km) to Igualapa.

Shopping

Handicrafts are mostly sold downtown on Sunday at plaza-front stores and stalls. Get huaraches and sombreros at a pair of stores on the plaza's east side. Women also sell embroidery and embroidered *huipiles* on the plaza, mostly at temporary north-side stalls, on Sunday.

Foto Alfa, tel. 741/412-1245, on Cuauhtémoc, a block northwest of the plaza, offers developing, popular film varieties, some supplies, and point-and-shoot cameras. Find it open Mon.–Sat. 8 A.M.–7 P.M., Sunday 9 A.M.–2 P.M.

The best spot for groceries and fresh fruits and vegetables in town is the main **market,** at the west end of Cuauhtémoc.

Services

Many establishments offer essential services near the downtown plaza. (*Note:* At the plaza, orient yourself by the church, which is *south* of the plaza.)

Banks: Banks, all with ATMs, include Banamex, tel. 741/412-0880 or 741/412-1354, at the plaza's northeast corner, open Mon.–Fri. 9 A.M.–4 P.M.; long-hours Banco Internacional (Bital), open Mon.–Sat. 8 A.M.–7 P.M., at 52 Cuauhtémoc, a couple of blocks northwest of the plaza, tel. 741/412-2878 and 741/412-2879; and neighboring Banco Serfin-Santander, open Mon.–Fri. 9 A.M.–4 P.M., tel. 741/412-0113 or 741/412-0940.

Communications: Mail letters at the *correo* (post office), a block east of Plaza Constitución. For local and long-distance calls, use Ladatel card–operated streetfront phones; and Internet access and copies are available at Super Farmacia Mexicana, southeast plaza corner, open daily 8:30 A.M.–9:30 P.M., tel. 741/412-0224. Money orders and public fax are available at Telecom, at the *presidencia municipal,* on Plaza Constitución, two short blocks south of the plaza, tel. 741/412-0386, open Mon.–Fri. 9 A.M.–3 P.M., Saturday 9 A.M.–12:30 P.M.

Health: If you get sick, consult with highly recommended Dr. Alfredo Yañez Lobato, tel.

741/412-0224. If he's not available, ask a taxi to take you to the private Hospital de la Amistad, tel. 741/412-0985, or Hospital Seguro Social, tel. 741/412-0392.

Getting There and Away

By Bus: Estrella Blanca, tel. 741/412-0035, provides a number of bus departures from its station on Cuauhtémoc, just west of its bend toward the plaza. Several daily departures, most in the morning, connect with Acapulco. Additionally, one daily departure connects directly with upcountry Guerrero, all the way to Chilapa via Chilpancingo.

Although few, if any, long-distance buses from Ometepec connect directly with the very interesting easterly Costa Chica destinations of Cuajinicuilapa and Pinotepa Nacional, Oaxaca, alternatives exist. You can get an early taxi or *colectivo* minivan downhill to the Highway 200 intersection. There, continue by local minivan, or wait for an Estrella Blanca (Elite, Gacela, Flecha Roja) eastbound bus. (*Note:* The Ometepec Estrella Blanca agent may be able to tell you the bus connection times at the Highway 200 intersection.)

By Car or RV: Driving to and from Ometepec is easy. To or from westerly Costa Chica destinations, simply follow Highway 200: one hour to/from Marquelia–Playa Las Peñitas, 33 miles (53 km); 1.5 hours to/from Copala–Playa Ventura, 48 miles (72 km); and 4.5 hours to/from Acapulco, 120 miles (194 km).

Similar good (but winding) road conditions prevail in the easterly direction: three-quarters of an hour to/from Cuajinicuilapa, 25 miles (41 km); and two hours, 58 miles (93 km) to/from Pinotepa Nacional, Oaxaca.

Excursion to Xochistlahuaca

Plan your Ometepec visit for a Friday or Saturday arrival (reserve your hotel room a week early) so you can visit the colorful indigenous Sunday markets at both Ometepec and Xochistlahuaca, about 17 miles (27 km) northeast. On the other hand, the things you find along the road to Xochi (SOH-chee), as Xochistlahuaca is known locally, may persuade you to linger.

The name Xochistlahuaca (pop. 3,000), which in the Náhuatl (Aztec) language means "plain of flowers," is apt, especially during the summer rains, when wildflowers bloom all over

Folks hurry to the Sunday *tianguis* native market at Xochistlahuaca.

the town's foothill *municipio* (township). Although an interesting destination all on its own, Xochi is a jumping-off point for even more remote Amusgo towns such as Chacalapa, Huistepec, and others with even less pronounceable names, such as Tlacoachistlahuaca.

Although the name Xochistlahuaca is of Aztec origin, the town is virtually all Amusgo speaking, and you can be certain that the Xochi folks have their own name for their town. At the Xochi Sunday market you may have to search around for someone who can translate Spanish into Amusgo well enough to help you bargain for one of the prized embroidered *huipiles* for which Amusgo women are renowned.

Although most Xochi young folks learn Spanish in school, and outside vendors descend to sell plastic dishes and transistor radios every Sunday, Xochistlahuaca and its surrounding *municipio* is a domain firmly rooted in tradition. Here, *curanderos* still do much of the healing, women often recuperate from childbirth in a *temascal* ritual heat bath, and campesinos in their milpas (corn, squash, and bean fields) still thank the earth spirits and the Lord of the Mountain for their harvests.

Along the Road to Xochi: Get to Xochi by *colectivo* minivan, from the Ometepec downtown corner of Cuauhtémoc and Vicente Guerrero, a block west of the plaza. If you have only one Sunday to visit, leave early for Xochi to give you time to return to see the Ometepec market by 1 or 2 in the afternoon. Drivers, mark your odometer as you head northeast along Guerrero, from the same corner. Along the 17-mile (27-km) route are a number of interesting stops that you may want to visit on a later day.

After about 3.5 miles (5.6 km), arrive at San José village, marked by a gas station and then a road fork. (The right fork, worth exploring on its own, heads down into the lush Río Catarina river valley, crosses the river, and continues uphill to indigenous Huistepec village and beyond.)

For Xochi, follow the left fork and continue a fraction of a mile to the signed **Cochoapa** left entrance road, four miles (6 km), from Ometepec. (Cochoapa people welcome visitors to their community museum, which exhibits ancient Olmec-style artifacts, along with displays of local costumes and traditions. Regular museum hours are Mon.–Fri. 10 A.M.–4 P.M. If the museum is not open, see if you can get someone—ask for Profesor Lorenzo Coronado—from the municipal office to open it up for you.)

For Xochi, continue past the Cochoapa turnoff. Nearly immediately, a right-side dirt driveway leads about a mile to **Atotonilco** community hot spring. (Two pools, one larger and lukewarm, another small and very hot, can provide a curative and relaxing midday break. Bring a picnic and stay a while. *Note:* In respect of modest local custom, rinse off beforehand, if possible, and *never bathe in the nude.* Lacking a bathing suit, bathe in your clothes as the local folks do.)

Back on the road to Xochi, at about nine miles (15 km) from Ometepec, the road splits. The left fork heads five miles (8 km) to **Tlacoachistlahuaca,** an indigenous market town and *municipio,* comparable to Xochi.

For Xochi, bear right at the fork and continue straight ahead. Pass through Zacualpan village at around Mile 10 (Km 16). Continue to the San Pedro River bridge, at about Mile 15 (Km 24). Feast your eyes on the luscious procession of swimming holes, decorated by giant, friendly, water-sculptured rocks. (During the June–Sept. rainy season, however, the river may be a yucky muddy brown, but it will clear to an inviting jade-green as the rains abate by October.) Although swimming holes near the bridge are sometimes crowded with noisy local teens, spots upstream, via the riverside 4WD-navigable trail, would probably be cleaner, more tranquil, and possible for overnight RV parking and/or tenting.

Xochistlahuaca Market Sunday: Follow the crowd to the Xochi *tianguis* (native market) that spreads over the middle of town, from the intersection of Calles Morelos and Reforma. Along Reforma, a block uphill from the corner, stands the *presidencia municipal* beside the *museo comunitario* (community museum). Although the museum is not ordinarily open Sunday, someone (ask for Profesor Delfino Flores) may be available to open it up for you. Regular museum hours are Mon.–Fri. 10 A.M.–5 P.M.

As in many backcountry areas, some men and most women wear *traje* (indigenous dress) unique to their home towns. Xochi women distiguish themselves with a creamy white, embroidered cotton *huipil,* decorated with a pair of crimson over-the-shoulder ribbons, both front and back.

Women dominate both buying and selling. Buyers bustle about, concentrating on mostly staples, fruit and vegetables and housewares, perhaps pausing to pick out a bit of ribbon or jewelry as a treat. Sellers wait patiently behind their piles of offerings, which vary from flowers and metates to mangoes and mameys.

If you get hungry, head to **Comedor Vele,** Xochi's best and cleanest eatery, on Morelos, half a block west (Ometepec direction) of Reforma. Take a seat in the shade and choose from a very recognizable list of *tortas, hamburguesas,* enchiladas, tacos ($2–4) and fresh seafood ($3–5). Friendly, hardworking owner-chef Aquileo Morales López is *a su servicio* (at your service).

CUAJINICUILAPA AND PUERTO MALDONADO

Astride Highway 200, a few miles before the Oaxaca border, Cuajinicuilapa (kwah-hee-nee-kwee-LAH-pah) (pop. 10,000) is the major market town and cultural center for the scattering of eastern Guerrero *costeño* (African Mexican) communities. These include farming villages Los Hoyos, Montecillos, San Nicolas, and the airy, laid-back local fishing port, Puerto Maldonado.

Cuajinicuilapa

In Cuajinicuilapa, known locally as "Cuaji" (koo-AH-hee), 125 miles (199 km) east of Acapulco, the market hubbub crowds both east and west ends of town. The clutter clears, however, at the town center, marked by a big covered basketball court.

Behind the basketball court stands the **Museo de las Culturas Afromestizos,** open daily except Monday 10 A.M.–2 P.M., 5–7 P.M. The museum is unmissable, being one of the very few Mexican museums dedicated to African Mexican history and culture. Inside, it offers several excellent, professionally prepared displays, plus a library, and dance, theater, guitar, and crafts workshops.

Accommodations: A pair of town-center hotels offer comfortable lodgings. Best is the 30-room **Hotel Marin,** tel. 741/414-0021, a few doors east of the basketball court. It's built along along a shady corridor, interspersed with lush green tropical minipatios. The comfortably decorated rooms run $16 s or d with fan, $20 s or d with a/c.

Second choice goes to the more basic **Hotel Alejim,** tel. 741/414-0310, on the west side of town. The plainly decorated rooms go for $17 s or d with fan, $23 s or d with a/c.

Services: Cuaji has a bank (Banamex, open Mon.–Fri. 9 A.M.–4 P.M.); a Centro de Salud (no phone, open 24 hours); a pharmacy (Santa Isabel, tel. 741/414-0017, open Mon.–Sat. 7 A.M.–2 P.M., 4–8 P.M. and Sunday 7 A.M.–2 P.M.); post office (open Mon.–Fri. 8 A.M.–3 P.M.); Ladatel-operated street telephones, and *telecomunicaciones* for money orders and public fax, tel. 741/414-0337, open Mon.–Fri. 9 A.M.–3 P.M. and Sat.–Sun. 9 A.M.–noon.

Puerto Maldonado

This country coastal fishing village (pop. 1,000), about 20 miles (32 km) south of Cuajinicuilapa, appeared on the map initially because of its lighthouse. A reassuring beacon, the lighthouse perches atop the tip of the point of land called Punta Maldonado, crowning the 100-foot-high bluff that lines this remote coast.

The lighthouse adds a picturesque aspect to the entire scene: a long, breeze-swept beach curving east, while west of the Punta (Point) a few fisherfolks' homes, a couple of stores, a small guesthouse, and a sprinkling of fishing *lanchas* decorate the strand.

Here, life goes on quietly and easily. You can stroll the beach, picking up a bit of driftwood and a shell or two, joke with the locals, play with the kids, watch the fishermen mend their nets, or rent a boat and mount your own fishing excursion.

Along the Road: Get to Puerto Maldonado by minibus from the middle of Cuaji, by the basketball court. Drivers, head east from the town. After only a mile, turn right (south), on to the

© BRUCE WHIPPERMAN

Puerto Maldonado's main source of livelihood is the fish catch of a small fleet of a dozen-odd *pangas* (fishing motorboats).

signed Puerto Maldonado road near Km marker 201. Mark your odometer.

After about 10 miles (16 km) pass through Montecillos village (pop. about 2,000), a mixed mestizo, African Mexican community. Farther along, at around 15 miles (24 km), at Tejastruda village, notice the apparently evangelistic church, decorated with both a Christian cross and the Star of David. Finally, arrive at Puerto Maldonado just after 19 miles (31 km) from Highway 200.

Sights and Recreation: Get oriented at the rustic **Las Brisas Palapa,** perched on the scenic Punta Maldonado beach-tip. From beneath the *palapa,* drink in the gorgeous panorama as the waves curl around the Punta and swish and disappear, into the coral-dotted golden sand of the point's west-side beach.

Use the existing posts in front of the *palapa* for a volleyball game (bring your own ball and net), explore the tidepools, or launch your own boat from the beach. Surfing is a regular pastime here, on the waves that swell inshore past the point and break diagonally along the beach line.

Practicalities: You can park your self-contained RV or set up your tent beneath the point's small but sheltering palm grove. A few village stores can supply essential groceries and water.

Travelers can also stay at the guesthouse **Casa de Huéspedes Valle Encantado,** in the beach fishing village about a quarter-mile west of the point. The three plain but clean rooms rent for about $10 s or d, with private bath (but tepid room-temperature water only). For reservations, leave a message with the long-distance *caseta* operator, tel. 741/412-1224 or 741/412-1301.

For prepared food, visit the airy, oceanview *comedor* that the friendly guesthouse owner also operates, just above the beach.

If you need medical attention, visit the Centro de Salud on the bluff above the beach.

PINOTEPA NACIONAL

Pinotepa Nacional, Oaxaca (pop. about 50,000; 157 miles, 253 km, east of Acapulco; 90 miles, 145 km, west of Puerto Escondido) and its neighboring communities comprise the hub of an important coastal indigenous region. Mixtec, Amusgo, Chatino, and other peoples stream into town for markets and fiestas in their traditional dress, ready to combine business with pleasure. They sell their produce and crafts—pottery, masks, handmade clothes—at the market, then later get tipsy, flirt, and dance.

The Name

So many people asked the meaning of their city's name that the town fathers wrote the explanation on a wall next to Highway 200 on the west side of town. Pinotepa comes from the Aztec-language words *pinolli* (crumbling) and *tepetl* (mountain)—thus "Crumbling Mountain." The second part of the name came about because, during colonial times, the town was called Pinotepa Real (Royal). This wouldn't do after independence, so the name became Pinotepa Nacional, reflecting the national consciousness that emerged during the 1810–1821 struggle for independence.

The Mixtecs, the dominant regional group, disagree with all this, however. To them, Pinotepa has always been Ñií Yo-oko (Little Place). Only within the town limits do the Mexicans (mestizos), who own most of the town businesses, outnumber the Mixtecs. The farther from town you get, the more likely you are to hear people conversing in the Mixtec language, a complex tongue that uses a number of subtle tones to make meanings clear.

POZAHUANCOS

To a coastal Mixtec woman, her *pozahuanco* is a lifetime investment symbolizing her maturity and social status, something that she expects to pass on to her daughters. Heirloom *pozahuancos* are wraparound, horizontally striped skirts of hand-spun thread. Women dye the thread by hand, always including a pair of necessary colors: cotton dyed a light purple *(morada)* from secretions of tidepool-harvested snails, *Purpura patula pansa,* and silk dyed scarlet red with cochineal, a dye extracted from the beetle *Dactylopius coccus,* cultivated in the Valley of Oaxaca. Increasingly, women are weaving *pozahuancos* with synthetic thread, which has a slippery feel compared to the hand-spun cotton. Consider yourself lucky if you can get a traditionally made *pozahuanco* for as little as $100. If someone offers you a look-alike for $20, you know it's an imitation.

Getting Oriented

On Pinotepa's west (Acapulco) side, Highway 200 splits into the town's two major arteries, which rejoin on the east (Puerto Escondido) side. The north, west-bound branch is called Aguirre Palancares; the south, west-bound branch, the more bustling of the two branches, passes between the town-center plaza and church and is called Avenida Porfirio Díaz on the west side and Avenida Benito Juárez on the east. The main north-south street, Avenida Pérez Gasga, runs past both the church front and the *presidencia municipal* (city hall), which faces east, toward the town plaza.

Market

Highway 200 passes a block north of the main town market, by the big, fenced-in secondary school, on the west side, about a mile west of the central plaza. Despite the Pinotepa market's oft-exotic goods—snakes, iguanas, wild mountain fruits, forest herbs, and spices—its people, nearly entirely Mixtec, are its main attraction, especially on the big Wednesday and Sunday market days. Men wear pure white loose cottons, topped by woven palm-leaf hats. Women wrap themselves in their lovely striped purple, violet, red, and navy blue ***pozahuanco***—saronglike, horizontally striped skirts. Many women carry a polished tan *jicara* gourd bowl atop their heads, which, although it's not supposed to, looks like a whimsical hat. Older women (and younger ones with babies at their breasts) go bare-breasted with only their white *huipiles* draped over their chests as a concession to mestizo custom. Others wear an easily removable *mandil,* a light cotton apron-halter above their *pozahuancos.* A few women can ordinarily be found selling beautiful handmade *pozahuancos.* (Alternatively, Artemio López Clavel, in his market shop, local 35, sells *pozahuancos,* both machine- and genuine hand-made.)

Festivals

Although the Pinotepa market days are big, they

don't compare to the week before Easter (Semana Santa). People get ready for the finale with processions, carrying the dead Christ through town to the church each of the seven Fridays before Easter. The climax comes on Good Friday (Viernes Santa), when a platoon of young Mixtec men paint their bodies white to portray Jews, and while intoning ancient Mixtec chants shoot arrows at Christ on the cross. On Saturday, the people mournfully take the Savior down from the cross and bury him, and on Sunday gleefully celebrate his resurrection with a riot of fireworks, food, and folk dancing.

Although not as spectacular as Semana Santa, there's plenty of merrymaking, food, dancing, and processions around the Pinotepa *zócalo* church on July 25, the day of Pinotepa's patron, Santiago (St. James).

Accommodations

The motel-style **Hotel Carmona,** Av. Porfirio Díaz 127, Pinotepa Nacional, Oaxaca 71600, tel. 954/543-2322, fax 954/543-2164, about three blocks west of the plaza, offers three stories of clean, not fancy but comfortable rooms, a big backyard garden with pool and sundeck. For festival dates, make reservations. The 50 rooms run about $16 s, $22 d, $28 t, fan only, $24, $33, and $40 for a/c.

If the Carmona is full, check the two high-profile newer hotels, Pepe's and Las Gaviotas, beside the highway on the west side of town. Of the two, **Pepe's,** at Carretera Pinotepa Nacional-Acapulco Km 1, Pinotepa Nacional, Oaxaca 71600, tel. 954/543-4347, fax 954/543-3602, is the much better choice. It offers 35 spacious, semideluxe rooms for a reasonable $12 s, $15 d fan only, $20 and $26 with a/c, with good TV, hot water, restaurant, and parking. Rooms at emergency-only **Hotel Las Gaviotas,** tel. 954/543-2838, fax 954/54320-56, rent for $14 d with fan, $18 with a/c.

Third choice goes to clean **Hotel Marisa,** downtown on the highway, Av. Juárez 134, north side of street, tel. 954/543-2101, 954/543-2022, or 954/543-3190, $10 d, $13 t with fan, $16 s or d, $20 t with a/c, all with parking.

Campers enjoy a tranquil spot (best during the dry late fall-winter-spring season) on the **Río Arena** about two miles east of Pinotepa. Eastbound, turn left just after the big river bridge. Continue a few hundred yards, past a pumphouse on the left, to a track that forks down to the riverbank. Notice the waterfall cascading down the rocky cliff across the river. You will sometimes find neighbors—in RVs or tents and sand collectors, poor but friendly—set up on the riverside beneath the abandoned Restaurant La Roca (now just a rock-wall ruin), a few hundred yards up the smooth stream, excellent for kayaking (if you have some way of returning back upstream.)

Food

For a light lunch or supper, try the very clean, family-run **Burger Bonny,** at the southeast corner of the main plaza, open daily 11 A.M.–10 P.M. Besides six varieties of good hamburgers, Burger Bonny offers *tortas,* tacos, french fries, hot dogs, microwave popcorn, fruit juices, and *refrescos* at very reasonable prices.

Also worthy is traditional-style **Fonda Toñita,** a block north of the churchfront, at the corner of Aguirre Palancares. Local folks flock here for the hearty afternoon *comida* (pick the entrée, and you get rice and tortillas thrown in free); it's also good for breakfast. Open Mon.–Sat. 7 A.M.–9 P.M.

Third restaurant choice goes to restaurant **Tacos Orientales,** with 15 styles of tacos, from fish to *carnitas,* three for $2.50. Find it on Pérez Gasga, half a block north of the churchfront, open daily 6–11 P.M.

On the other hand, consider *marisquería* **Peñitas** next door, which specializes in fresh seafood however you like it: fried, baked, breaded, *al mojo,* and more. Open daily 8 A.M.–midnight.

For a quick and convenient on-the-road breakfast, lunch, or dinner, stop by the restaurant of high-profile **Pepe's Hotel** west of town, open daily 8 A.M.–10 P.M.

Shopping and Services

Visit the **market** on Wednesday and Sunday. For film and film-processing, step to the **photo shop** next door on the south side of the plaza.

Exchange money over the counter or use the

ATM at all Pinotepa banks. Try **Bancomer** open Mon.–Fri. 8:30 A.M.–4 P.M., corner of Díaz and Progreso, two blocks west of the plaza, tel. 954/543-3022 or 954/543-3190; or **Banamex,** across the street, open Mon.–Fri. 9 A.M.–4 P.M. Alternatively, try the long-hours (open Mon.–Fri. approximately 8 A.M.–7 P.M., Saturday 8 A.M.–3 P.M.) **Banco Internacional,** tel. 954/543-3949 or 954/543-3969, also on Avenida Progreso, but across Porfirio Díaz and uphill a block from Bancomer.

The ***correo*** (post office), tel. 954/543-2264, is open Mon.–Fri. 8 A.M.–7 P.M., by the Estrella Blanca bus station, about two blocks west and across the street from Bancomer. The ***telecomunicaciones*** office (money orders, public telephone, and fax) is one block north of the plaza church, on Avenida Pérez Gasga, open Mon.–Fri. 8 A.M.–7:30 P.M., Sat.–Sun. 9 A.M.–noon. ***Larga distancia*** Lada Central telephone and fax office, on the plaza, south side, is open longer, evening hours.

For a doctor, go to the **Clínica Rodriguez** at 503 Aguirre Palancares, tel. 954/543-2330, one block north, two blocks west of the central plaza churchfront. Get routine medications at one of several town pharmacies, such as the 24-hour **Super Farmacia,** on Díaz, a block west of the central plaza churchfront.

Getting There and Away

By **car or RV,** Highway 200 connects west to Acapulco (160 miles, 258 km) in an easy 4.5 hours driving time. The 89-mile (143-km) eastward connection to Puerto Escondido can be done safely in about 2.5 hours. Additionally, the 239-mile (385-km) Highway 125-Highway 190 route connects Pinotepa Nacional to Oaxaca, via Putla de Guerrero and Tlaxiaco (136 miles, 219 km). Although winding most of the way and potholed at times, the road is generally uncongested. It's safely driveable in a passenger car with caution, from Pinotepa to Oaxaca (follow the toll *autopista* near Oaxaca) in about eight hours (under dry conditions) at the wheel, and seven hours in the reverse, downhill, direction from Oaxaca.

Several long-distance **bus** lines connect Pinotepa Nacional with destinations north, northwest, east, and west. **Estrella Blanca,** via subsidiaries Elite, Gacela, and Flecha Roja, tel. 954/543-3194, offers several daily first- and second-class *salidas de paso* (buses passing through) departures west to Acapulco, Zihuatanejo, Lázaro Cárdenas, and Mexico City; and east to Puerto Escondido, Pochutla (Puerto Ángel), Bahías de Huatulco, and Salina Cruz, from its station on Porfirio Díaz about three blocks west of the *zócalo.*

Smaller, mostly second-class lines **Fletes y Pasajes, Estrella del Valle,** and **Oaxaca Pacífico** operate out of a pair of small stations one block north of the central plaza churchfront, on side street Aguirre Palancares. Fletes y Pasajes, tel. 954/543-2163, connects daily with Oaxaca via Putla, Tlaxiaco, and Nochixtlán, by Highways 125 and 190. Estrella del Valle and Oaxaca Pacífico buses, tel. 954/543-2697, also connect with Oaxaca, but in the opposite direction: first east, through Puerto Escondido to Pochutla (Puerto Ángel), then continuing north over the sierra to Oaxaca via Highway 175.

First-class **Cristóbal Colón** also operates out of a small station on the same street, about one block farther west. A few daily departures connect, via Highways 175 and 190, northeast, via Putla and Tlaxiaco, with Oaxaca (by the fast *autopista* via Nochixtlán), and northwest, with Mexico City (via Puebla). Other departures connect east with Puerto Escondido.

EXCURSIONS NORTH OF PINOTEPA

The local patronal festival year begins early, on January 20, at **Pinotepa Don Luis** (pop. 5,000), about 15 miles, by back roads, northeast of Pinotepa Nacional, with the uniquely Mixtec festival of San Sebastián. Village bands blare, fireworks pop and hiss, and penitents crawl until the finale, when dancers whirl the local favorite dance, Las Chilenas.

Yet another exciting time around Pinotepa Nacional is during Carnaval, when nearby communities put on big extravaganzas. Pinotepa Don Luis, sometimes known as Pinotepa Chica (Little Pinotepa), is famous for wooden masks the people make for their big Carnaval festival. The celebration usually climaxes on the Sunday before Ash Wednesday, when everyone seems to be in costume and a corps of performers gyrates in the traditional dances: Paloma (Dove), Tigre (Jaguar), Culebra (Snake), and Tejón (Badger).

Pinotepa Don Luis bubbles over again with excitement during Semana Santa, when the faithful carry fruit- and flower-decorated trees to the church on Good Friday, explode Judas effigies on Saturday, and celebrate by dancing most of Easter Sunday.

San Juan Colorado, a few miles north of Pinotepa Don Luis, usually appears as just another dusty little town until Carnaval, when its festival rivals that of its neighbors. Subsequently, on November 29, droves of Mixtec people come into town to honor their patron, San Andres. After the serious part at the church, they celebrate with a cast of favorite dancing characters such as Malinche, Jaguar, Turtle, and Charros (Cowboys).

Amusgos are best known to the outside world for their lovely animal-, plant-, and human-motif* huipiles, *which Amusgo women always seem to be hand-embroidering on their doorsteps.

Oaxaca Amusgo Country

Cacahuatepec (pop. about 5,000; on Highway 125 about 25 miles north of Pinotepa Nacional) and its neighboring community San Pedro Amusgos are important centers of the Amusgo people. Approximately 20,000 Amusgos live in a roughly 30-mile-square region straddling the Guerrero-Oaxaca state border. Their homeland includes, besides Cacahuatepec and San Pedro Amusgos, Ometepec, Xochistlahuaca, Zacoalpán, and Tlacoachistlahuaca on the Guerrero side.

The Amusgo language is linguistically related to Mixtec, although it's unintelligible to Mixtec speakers. Before the conquest, the Amusgos were subject to the numerically superior Mixtec kingdoms until the Amusgos were conquered by the Aztecs in A.D. 1457, and later by the Spanish.

Now, most Amusgos live as subsistence farmers, supplementing their diet with occasional fowl or small game. Amusgos are best known to the outside world for their lovely animal-, plant-, and human-motif *huipiles,* which Amusgo women always seem to be hand-embroidering on their doorsteps.

Although **Cacahuatepec** enjoys a big market each Sunday, that doesn't diminish the importance of its big Easter weekend festival, the day of Todos Santos (All Saints' Day), November 1, and Day of the Dead, November 2, when, at the cemetery, people welcome their ancestors' return to rejoin the family.

San Pedro Amusgos celebrations are among the most popular regional fiestas. On June 29, the day of San Pedro, people participate in religious processions, and costumed participants dressed as Moors and Christians, bulls, jaguars, and mules dance before crowds of men in traditional whites and women in beautiful heirloom *huipiles.* Later, on the first Sunday of October, folks crowd into town to enjoy the traditional processions, dances, and sweet treats of the fiesta of the Virgen de la Rosario (Virgin of the Rosary).

Even if you miss the festivals, San Pedro Amusgos is worth a visit to buy *huipiles* alone. Three or four shops sell them along the main street through town. Look for the sign of **Trajes Regionales Elia,** the little store run by Elia Guzmán, tel. 954/582-8697. Besides dozens of beautiful embroidered garments, she stocks a few Amusgo books and offers friendly words of advice and local information.

EXCURSIONS EAST OF PINOTEPA

For 30 or 40 miles east of Pinotepa Nacional, where road kilometer markers begin at zero again near the central plaza, Highway 200 stretches through the coastal Mixtec heartland, intriguing to explore, especially during festival times.

Huaxpáltepec

The population of San Andres Huaxpáltepec (oo-wash-PAHL-tay-payk), about 10 miles east

THE MIXTECS

Sometime during the 1980s, the Mixtecs regained their preconquest population of about 350,000. Of that total, around one-third speak only their own language. Their villages and communal fields spread over tens of thousands of square miles of remote mountain valleys north and west of Oaxaca and east of Acapulco. Their homeland, the Mixteca, is divided into three distinct regions: Mixteca Alta, Mixteca Baja, and the Mixteca Costera.

The **Mixteca Alta** centers in the mountains about 100 road miles due west of Oaxaca city, in the high, cool, roof of Oaxaca, centering on the market towns of Tlaxiaco and Juxtlahuaca.

Mixteca Baja communities, such as San Miguel Tequistepec, Tonalá, and Juxtlajuaca, dot the dry northwestern Oaxaca-eastern Guerrero mountains and valleys, centering roughly on Huajuapan de León on Highway 190.

In the **Mixteca Costera,** important Mixtec communities exist in or near Pinotepa Nacional, Huaxpaltepec, and Jamiltepec, all along Highway 200 in southwestern Oaxaca and southeastern Guerrero.

The Aztec-origin name Mixtecos (People of the Clouds) was translated directly from the Mixtecs' name for their own homeland: Aunyuma (Land of the Clouds). The Mixtecs' name for themselves, however, is Nyu-u Sabi (People of the Rain).

When the conquistadores arrived, the Mixtecs were under the thumb of the Aztecs, who, after a long, bitter struggle, had wrested control of Oaxaca from combined Mixtec-Zapotec armies in 1486. The Mixtecs naturally resented the Aztecs, whose domination was transferred to the Spanish during the colonial period, and, in turn, to the mestizos during modern times. The Mixtecs still defer to the town Mexicans, but they don't like it. Consequently, many rural Mixtecs, with little state or national consciousness, have scant interest in becoming Mexicanized.

In isolated Mixtec communities, traditions still rule. Village elders hold final authority, parents arrange marriages through go-betweens, and land is owned communally. Catholic saints are thinly disguised incarnations of old gods such as Tabayukí, ruler of nature, or the capricious and powerful *tono* spirits that lurk everywhere.

In many communities, Mixtec women exercise considerable personal freedom. At home and in villages, they often still work bare-breasted. And while their men get drunk and carry on during festivals, women dance and often do a bit of their own carousing. Whom they do it with is their own business.

of Pinotepa, sometimes swells from about 4,000 to 20,000 or more during the three or four days before the day of Jesus the Nazarene, on the fourth Friday of Lent (or in other words, the fourth Friday after Ash Wednesday). The entire town spreads into a warren of shady stalls, offering everything from TVs to stone metates. (Purchase of a corn-grinding metate, which, including *mano* stone roller, sells for about $25, is as important to a Mixtec family as a refrigerator is to an American. Mixtec husband and wife usually examine several of the concave stones, deliberating the pros and cons of each before deciding.)

The Huaxpáltepec Nazarene fair is typical of the larger Oaxaca country expositions. Even the highway becomes a lineup of stalls; whole native clans camp under the trees, and mules, cows, and horses wait patiently around the edges of a grassy trading lot as men discuss prices. (The fun begins when a sale is made, and the new owner tries to rope and harness his bargain steed.)

Even sex is customarily for sale within a quarter of very tightly woven no-see-through grass houses, patrolled by armed guards. Walking through, you may notice that, instead of the usual women, one of the houses offers men, dressed in low-cut gowns, lipstick, and high-heeled shoes.

Huazolotitlán

At nearby Santa María Huazolotitlán (pop. 3,000) several resident woodcarvers craft excellent **masks.** Local favorites are jaguars, lions, rabbits, bulls, and human faces. Given a photograph (or a sitting), one of them might even carve your likeness for a reasonable fee. (Figure perhaps $40–60.) Near the town plaza, ask for José Luna, Lázaro Gómez, or the master Idineo Gómez, all of whom are related and live in *barrio* Ñií Yucagua.

Textiles are also locally important. Look for the colorfully embroidered animal and floral motif *huipiles, manteles,* and *servilletas* (native smocks, tablecloths, and napkins). You might also be able to bargain for a genuine heirloom *pozahuanco* (handwoven wrap-around skirt) for a reasonable price.

Besides all the handicrafts, Huazolotitlán people celebrate the important local **Fiesta de la Virgen de la Asunción** around Aug. 13–16. The celebrations customarily climax with a number of favorite traditional dances, in which you can see why masks are locally important, especially in the dance of the Tiger and the Turtle. The finale comes a day later, celebrated with the ritual dance of the Chareos, dedicated to the Virgin.

Get to Huazolotitlán (ooah-shoh-loh-teet-LAN) in about two miles along the paved road that forks south uphill from Highway 200 in Huaxpaltepec. Drive, or hitchhike (with caution), ride the local bus, or hire a taxi for about $3.

Jamiltepec

About 18 miles (at Km 30) east of Pinotepa Nacional is the hilltop town formally known as Santiago Jamiltepec (hah-meel-teh-PAYK, for short). Two-thirds of its 20,000 inhabitants are Mixtec. A grieving Mixtec king named the town in memory of his infant son, Jamilly, who was carried off by an eagle from this very hilltop.

The market, while busy most any day, is biggest and most colorful on Thursday. The town's main fixed-date festivals are celebrated on September 1, January 1, and February 15. In addition, Jamiltepec celebrates its famous pre-Easter (week following Domingo de Ramos, or Palm Sunday) festival, featuring neighborhood candlelight processions accompanied by 18th-century music. Hundreds of the faithful bear elaborate wreaths and palm decorations to the foot of their church altars.

Jamiltepec is well worth a stop if only to visit the handicrafts shops **Yu-uku Cha-kuaa** (Hill of Darkness) of Santiago de la Cruz Velasco. Personable Santiago runs both his home shop and a better stocked one at the Jamiltepec plaza market, because the government cluster of shops (Centro Artesanal de la Costa, on the highway) was closed down, victim of a dispute over control. The local Mixtec artisans wanted to manage their own handicrafts sales, while the regional branch of the INI (Instiotuto Nacional Indigenista) preferred to manage instead. The Mixtecs stuck together and refused to bring their handicrafts, closing the government operation.

Some of their crafts—masks, *huipiles,* carvings, hats—occupy the shelves and racks in Santiago's shop. Find it in the market, signed Artesanía Yu-uku Cha-kuaa, by the north entrance (ask for Santiago by name). He stays open until about 4 P.M. If you don't want to miss him, write Santiago a letter at his shop, Av. Principal, esquina Fco. Madero, Barrio Grande, Sec. 5, Jamiltepec, Oaxaca 71700.

Resources

Glossary

Many of the following words have a social-historical meaning; others you will not find in the usual English-Spanish dictionary.

abarrotes, abarrotería—grocery, grocery store
alcalde—mayor or municipal judge
alfarería—pottery
alfarero, alfarera—potter
andando—walkway or strolling path
antojitos—native Mexican snacks, such as tamales, *chiles rellenos,* tacos, and enchiladas
artesanías—handicrafts, as distinguished from *artesano, or artesana,* a person who makes handicrafts
audiencia—one of the royal executive-judicial panels sent to rule Mexico during the 16th century
ayuntamiento—either the town council or the building where it meets
bienes raices—literally "good roots," but popularly, real estate
birria—goat, pork, or lamb stew, in spiced tomato broth, especially typical of Jalisco
boleto—ticket, boarding pass
cabecera—head town of a municipal district, or headquarters in general
cabrón—literally a cuckold, but more commonly, bastard, rat, or S.O.B.; sometimes used affectionately
cacique—chief or boss
calandria—early 1800s-style horse-drawn carriage, common in Guadalajara
camionera—bus station
campesino—country person; farm worker
canasta—basket of woven reeds, with handle
casa de huéspedes—guesthouse, usually operated in a family home
caballero—literally, "horseman," but popularly, gentleman
caudillo—dictator or political chief
charro, charra—gentleman cowboy or cowgirl
chingar—literally, "to rape," but also the universal Spanish "f" word, the equivalent of "screw" in English
churrigueresque—Spanish baroque architectural style incorporated into many Mexican colonial churches, named after José Churriguera (1665–1725)
científicos—literally, scientists, but applied to President Porfirio Díaz's technocratic advisers
codex—An early Mexican colonial-era document, of preconquest legends, history, and customs, dictated by reputable indigenous witnesses, under the direction of Spanish chroniclers. Many codices are preserved in European museums.
cofradía—Catholic fraternal service association, either male or female, mainly in charge of financing and organizing religious festivals
colectivo—a shared public taxi or minibus that picks up and deposits passengers along a designated route
colegio—preparatory school or junior college
colonia—suburban subdivision/satellite of a larger city
Conasupo—government store that sells basic foods at subsidized prices
correo—post office
criollo—person of all-Spanish descent born in the New World
cuadra—Huichol yarn painting, usually rectangular
cuota—toll, as in *cuota autopista* (toll expressway)
Cuaresma—Lent
curandero(a)—indigenous medicine man or woman
damas—ladies, as in "ladies room"
Domingo de Ramos—Palm Sunday
ejido—a constitutional, government-sponsored form of community, with shared land ownership and cooperative decision making
encomienda—colonial award of tribute from a designated indigenous district
estación de ferrocarril—railroad station
farmacia—pharmacy or drugstore

finca—farm
fonda—foodstall or small restaurant, often in a traditional market complex
fraccionamiento—city sector or subdivision
fuero—the former right of clergy to be tried in separate ecclesiastical courts
gachupín—"one who wear spurs"; a derogatory term for a Spanish-born colonial
gasolinera—gasoline station
gente de razón—"people of reason"; whites and mestizos in colonial Mexico
gringo—once-derogatory but now commonly used term for North American whites
grito—impassioned cry, as in Hidalgo's Grito de Dolores
hacienda—large landed estate; also the government treasury
hidalgo—nobleman; called honorifically by "Don" or "Doña"
indígena—indigenous or aboriginal inhabitant of all-native descent who speaks his or her native tongue. Commonly, but incorrectly, an Indian *(indio)*
jardín—garden
jaripeo—the hazardous art of bull riding and roping, a popular event during *charreadas* (known as "rodeos" in the southwest United States)
jejenes—"no-see-um" biting gnats
judiciales—the federal or state "judicial" or investigative police, best known to motorists for their highway checkpoint inspections
jugería—stall or small restaurant providing a large array of squeezed vegetable and fruit *jugos* (juices)
juzgado—the "hoosegow," or jail
larga distancia—long-distance telephone service, or the *caseta* (booth) where it's provided
licenciado—academic degree (abbrev. Lic.) approximately equivalent to a bachelor's degree
lonchería—small lunch counter, usually serving juices, sandwiches, and *antojitos* (Mexican snacks)
machismo; macho—exaggerated sense of maleness; person who holds such a sense of himself
mañanitas—early morning Masses, usually in honor of a patron saint
mestizo—person of mixed native-European descent
mescal—alcoholic beverage distilled from the fermented hearts of maguey (century plant)
milpa—native farm plot, usually of corn, squash, and beans
mojigango—a comical, often giant effigy, usually performed by a costumed person on stilts as part of a fiesta celebration
molcajete—a sturdy three-legged grinding bowl, often made of lava rock and traditionally used for grinding *chiles;* but in country-style restaurants, a savory stew of nopales (cactus leaves), vegetables, broth, and meat, served in a *molcajete,* and labeled as such on the menu
mordida—slang for bribe; literally "little bite"
palapa—thatched-roof structure, often open and shading a restaurant
panga—outboard launch *(lancha)*
papier-mâché—the craft of glued, multilayered paper sculpture, especially in Tonalá, Jalisco, where creations resemble fine pottery or lacquerware
Pasquas, Semana Santa, Domingo de Pasquas—Easter, Easter week, Easter Sunday
Pemex—acronym for Petróleos Mexicanos, the national oil corporation
peninsulares—the Spanish-born ruling colonial elite
peón—a poor wage-earner, usually a country native
petate—a mat, traditionally woven of palm leaf
piñata—papier-mâché decoration, usually in animal or human form, filled with treats and broken open during a fiesta
plan—political manifesto, usually by a leader or group consolidating or seeking power
Porfiriato—the 34-year (1876–1910) ruling period of President-dictator Porfirio Díaz
pozole—stew, of hominy in broth, usually topped by shredded pork, cabbage, and diced onion
preventiva—municipal (or sometimes state) police
presidencia municipal—the headquarters, like a U.S. city or county hall, of a Mexican *municipio,* county-like local governmental unit

pronunciamiento—declaration of rebellion by an insurgent leader
puente—literally "bridge," but commonly a holiday weekend, when resort hotel reservations are highly recommended
puta—whore, bitch, or slut
pueblo—town or people
quinta—a villa or country house
quinto—the royal "one-fifth" tax on treasure and precious metals
retorno—cul-de-sac
ropa típica—traditional dress, derived from the Spanish colonial tradition (in contrast to *traje,* traditional indigenous dress)
rurales—pre-1910 federal country police force created to fight *bandidos*
taxi especial—private taxi, as distinguished from *taxi colectivo,* or collective taxi
telégrafo—telegraph office, lately converting to high-tech ***telecomunicaciones,*** or *telecom,* offering telegraph, telephone, and public fax services
tenate—soft, pliable basket, without handle, woven of palm leaf
traje—traditional indigenous dress
vaquero—cowboy
vecinidad—neighborhood
vinchuca—"kissing" or "assassin" bug
yanqui—Yankee
zócalo—town plaza or central square

Abbreviations

Av.—*avenida* (avenue)
Blv.—*bulevar* (boulevard)
Calz.—*calzada* (thoroughfare, main road)
Fco.—Francisco (proper name, as in "Fco. Villa")
Fracc.—*Fraccionamiento* (subdivision)
Nte.—*norte* (north)
Ote.—*oriente* (east)
Pte.—*poniente* (west)
s/n—*sin número* (no street number)

Spanish Phrasebook

Your Acapulco adventure will be more fun if you use a little Spanish. Mexican folks, although they may smile at your funny accent, will appreciate your halting efforts to break the ice and transform yourself from a foreigner to a potential friend.

Spanish commonly uses 30 letters—the familiar English 26, plus four straightforward additions: ch, ll, ñ, and rr, which are explained in "Consonants," below.

Pronunciation

Once you learn them, Spanish pronunciation rules—in contrast to English—don't change. Spanish vowels generally sound softer than in English. (Note: The capitalized syllables below receive stronger accents.)

Vowels

a — like ah, as in "hah": *agua* AH-gooah (water), *pan* PAHN (bread), and *casa* CAH-sah (house)

e — like ay, as in "may:" *mesa* MAY-sah (table), *tela* TAY-lah (cloth), and *de* DAY (of, from)

i — like ee, as in "need": *diez* dee-AYZ (ten), *comida* ko-MEE-dah (meal), and *fin* FEEN (end)

o — like oh, as in "go": *peso* PAY-soh (weight), *ocho* OH-choh (eight), and *poco* POH-koh (a bit)

u — like oo, as in "cool": *uno* OO-noh (one), *cuarto* KOOAHR-toh (room), and *usted* oos-TAYD (you); when it follows a "q" the **u** is silent; when it follows an "h" or has an umlaut, it's pronounced like "w"

Consonants

b, d, f, k, l, m, n, p, q, s, t, v, w, x, y, z, and **ch** — pronounced almost as in English; **h** occurs, but is silent—not pronounced at all.

c — like k as in "keep": *cuarto* KOOAR-toh (room), Tepic tay-PEEK (capital of Nayarit state); when it precedes "e" or "i," pronounce **c** like s, as in "sit": *cerveza* sayr-VAY-sah (beer), *encima* ayn-SEE-mah (atop).

g — like g as in "gift" when it precedes "a," "o," "u," or a consonant: *gato* GAH-toh (cat), *hago* AH-goh (I do, make); otherwise, pronounce **g** like h as in "hat": *giro* HEE-roh (money order), *gente* HAYN-tay (people)

j — like h, as in "has": *Jueves* HOOAY-vays (Thursday), *mejor* may-HOR (better)

ll — like y, as in "yes": *toalla* toh-AH-yah (towel), *ellos* AY-yohs (they, them)

ñ — like ny, as in "canyon": *año* AH-nyo (year), *señor* SAY-nyor (Mr., sir)

r — is lightly trilled, with tongue at the roof of your mouth like a very light English d, as in "ready": *pero* PAY-doh (but), *tres* TDAYS (three), *cuatro* KOOAH-tdoh (four).

rr — like a Spanish r, but with much more emphasis and trill. Let your tongue flap. Practice with *burro* (donkey), *carretera* (highway), and Carrillo (proper name), then really let go with *ferrocarril* (railroad).

Note: The single small but common exception to all of the above is the pronunciation of Spanish **y** when it's being used as the Spanish word for "and," as in "Ron y Kathy." In such case, pronounce it like the English ee, as in "keep": Ron "ee" Kathy (Ron and Kathy).

Accent

The rule for accent, the relative stress given to syllables within a given word, is straightforward. If a word ends in a vowel, an n, or an s, accent the next-to-last syllable; if not, accent the last syllable.

Pronounce *gracias* GRAH-seeahs (thank you), *orden* OHR-dayn (order), and *carretera* kah-ray-TAY-rah (highway) with stress on the next-to-last syllable.

Otherwise, accent the last syllable: *venir* vay-NEER (to come), *ferrocarril* fay-roh-cah-REEL (railroad), and *edad* ay-DAHD (age).

Exceptions to the accent rule are always marked with an accent sign: (á, é, í, ó, or ú), such as *teléfono* tay-LAY-foh-noh (telephone), *jabón* hah-BON (soap), and *rápido* RAH-pee-doh (rapid).

Basic and Courteous Expressions

Most Spanish-speaking people consider formalities important. Whenever approaching anyone for information or some other reason, do not forget the appropriate salutation—good morning, good evening, etc. Standing alone, the greeting *hola* (hello) can sound brusque.

Hello. — *Hola.*
Good morning. — *Buenos días.*
Good afternoon. — *Buenas tardes.*
Good evening. — *Buenas noches.*
How are you? — *¿Cómo está usted?*
Very well, thank you. — *Muy bien, gracias.*
Okay; good. — *Bien.*
Not okay; bad. — *Mal* or *feo.*
So-so. — *Más o menos.*
And you? — *¿Y usted?*
Thank you. — *Gracias.*
Thank you very much. — *Muchas gracias.*
You're very kind. — *Muy amable.*
You're welcome. — *De nada.*
Goodbye. — *Adios.*
See you later. — *Hasta luego.*
please — *por favor*
yes — *sí*
no — *no*
I don't know. — *No sé.*
Just a moment, please. — *Momentito, por favor.*
Excuse me, please (when you're trying to get attention). — *Disculpe* or *Con permiso.*
Excuse me (when you've made a boo-boo). — *Lo siento.*
Pleased to meet you. — *Mucho gusto.*
How do you say . . . in Spanish? — *¿Cómo se dice . . . en español?*
What is your name? — *¿Cómo se llama usted?*
Do you speak English? — *¿Habla usted inglés?*
Is English spoken here? (Does anyone here speak English?) — *¿Se habla inglés?*
I don't speak Spanish well. — *No hablo bien el español.*
I don't understand. — *No entiendo.*
How do you say . . . in Spanish? — *¿Cómo se dice . . . en español?*
My name is . . . — *Me llamo . . .*
Would you like . . . — *¿Quisiera usted . . .*
Let's go to . . . — *Vamos a . . .*

Terms of Address

When in doubt, use the formal *usted* (you) as a form of address.

I — *yo*
you (formal) — *usted*
you (familiar) — *tu*
he/him — *él*
she/her — *ella*
we/us — *nosotros*
you (plural) — *ustedes*
they/them — *ellos* (all males or mixed gender); *ellas* (all females)
Mr., sir — *señor*
Mrs., madam — *señora*
miss, young lady — *señorita*
wife — *esposa*
husband — *esposo*
friend — *amigo* (male); *amiga* (female)
sweetheart — *novio* (male); *novia* (female)
son; daughter — *hijo; hija*
brother; sister — *hermano; hermana*
father; mother — *padre; madre*
grandfather; grandmother — *abuelo; abuela*

Transportation

Where is . . . ? — *¿Dónde está . . . ?*
How far is it to . . . ? — *¿A cuánto está . . . ?*
from . . . to . . . — *de . . . a . . .*
How many blocks? — *¿Cuántas cuadras?*
Where (Which) is the way to . . . ? — *¿Dónde está el camino a . . . ?*
the bus station — *la terminal de autobuses*
the bus stop — *la parada de autobuses*
Where is this bus going? — *¿Adónde va este autobús?*

the taxi stand — *la parada de taxis*
the train station — *la estación de ferrocarril*
the boat — *el barco*
the airport — *el aeropuerto*
I'd like a ticket to . . . — *Quisiera un boleto a . . .*
first (second) class — *primera (segunda) clase*
round-trip — *ida y vuelta*
reservation — *reservación*
baggage — *equipaje*
Stop here, please. — *Pare aquí, por favor.*
the entrance — *la entrada*
the exit — *la salida*
the ticket office — *la oficina de boletos*
(very) near; far — *(muy) cerca; lejos*
to; toward — *a*
by; through — *por*
from — *de*
the right — *la derecha*
the left — *la izquierda*
straight ahead — *derecho; directo*
in front — *en frente*
beside — *al lado*
behind — *atrás*
the corner — *la esquina*
the stoplight — *la semáforo*
a turn — *una vuelta*
right here — *aquí*
somewhere around here — *por acá*
right there — *allí*
somewhere around there — *por allá*
street; boulevard — *calle; bulevar*
highway — *carretera*
bridge; toll — *puente; cuota*
address — *dirección*
north; south — *norte; sur*
east; west — *oriente (este); poniente (oeste)*

Accommodations

hotel — *hotel*
Is there a room? — *¿Hay cuarto?*
May I (may we) see it? — *¿Puedo (podemos) verlo?*
What is the rate? — *¿Cuál es el precio?*
Is that your best rate? — *¿Es su mejor precio?*
Is there something cheaper? — *¿Hay algo más económico?*
a single room — *un cuarto sencillo*
a double room — *un cuarto doble*
double bed — *cama matrimonial*
twin beds — *camas gemelas*
with private bath — *con baño*
hot water — *agua caliente*
shower — *ducha*
towels — *toallas*
soap — *jabón*
toilet paper — *papel higiénico*
blanket — *frazada; manta*
sheets — *sábanas*
air-conditioned—*aire acondicionado*
fan — *abanico; ventilador*
key — *llave*
manager — *gerente*

Food

I'm hungry — *Tengo hambre.*
I'm thirsty. — *Tengo sed.*
menu — *lista; menú*
order — *orden*
glass — *vaso*
fork — *tenedor*
knife — *cuchillo*
spoon — *cuchara*
napkin — *servilleta*
soft drink — *refresco*
coffee — *café*
tea — *té*
drinking water — *agua pura; agua potable*
bottled carbonated water — *agua mineral*
bottled uncarbonated water — *agua sin gas*
beer — *cerveza*
wine — *vino*
milk — *leche*
juice — *jugo*
cream — *crema*
sugar — *azúcar*
cheese — *queso*
snack — *antojo; botana*
breakfast — *desayuno*
lunch — *almuerzo*
daily lunch special — *comida corrida* (or *el menú del día* depending on region)
dinner — *comida* (often eaten in late afternoon); *cena* (a late-night snack)

the check — *la cuenta*
eggs — *huevos*
bread — *pan*
salad — *ensalada*
fruit — *fruta*
mango — *mango*
watermelon — *sandía*
papaya — *papaya*
banana — *plátano*
apple — *manzana*
orange — *naranja*
lime — *limón*
fish — *pescado*
shellfish — *mariscos*
shrimp — *camarones*
meat (without) — *(sin) carne*
chicken — *pollo*
pork — *puerco*
beef; steak — *res; bistec*
bacon; ham — *tocino; jamón*
fried — *frito*
roasted — *asada*
barbecue; barbecued — *barbacoa; al carbón*

Shopping

money — *dinero*
money-exchange bureau — *casa de cambio*
I would like to exchange traveler's checks. — *Quisiera cambiar cheques de viajero.*
What is the exchange rate? — *¿Cuál es el tipo de cambio?*
How much is the commission? — *¿Cuánto cuesta la comisión?*
Do you accept credit cards? — *¿Aceptan tarjetas de crédito?*
money order — *giro*
How much does it cost? — *¿Cuánto cuesta?*
What is your final price? — *¿Cuál es su último precio?*
expensive — *caro*
cheap — *barato; económico*
more — *más*
less — *menos*
a little — *un poco*
too much — *demasiado*

Health

Help me please. — *Ayúdeme por favor.*
I am ill. — *Estoy enfermo.*
Call a doctor. — *Llame un doctor.*
Take me to . . . — *Lléveme a . . .*
hospital — *hospital; sanatorio*
drugstore — *farmacia*
pain — *dolor*
fever — *fiebre*
headache — *dolor de cabeza*
stomach ache — *dolor de estómago*
burn — *quemadura*
cramp — *calambre*
nausea — *náusea*
vomiting — *vomitar*
medicine — *medicina*
antibiotic — *antibiótico*
pill; tablet — *pastilla*
aspirin — *aspirina*
ointment; cream — *pomada; crema*
bandage — *venda*
cotton — *algodón*
sanitary napkins — use brand name, e.g., Kotex
birth control pills — *pastillas anticonceptivas*
contraceptive foam — *espuma anticonceptiva*
condoms — *preservativos; condones*
toothbrush — *cepilla dental*
dental floss — *hilo dental*
toothpaste — *crema dental*
dentist — *dentista*
toothache — *dolor de muelas*

Post Office and Communications

long-distance telephone — *teléfono larga distancia*
I would like to call . . . — *Quisiera llamar a . . .*
collect — *por cobrar*
station to station — *a quien contesta*
person to person — *persona a persona*
credit card — *tarjeta de crédito*
post office — *correo*
general delivery — *lista de correo*
letter — *carta*
stamp — *estampilla, timbre*

postcard — *tarjeta*
aerogram — *aerograma*
air mail — *correo aereo*
registered — *registrado*
money order — *giro*
package; box — *paquete; caja*
string; tape — *cuerda; cinta*

At the Border

border — *frontera*
customs — *aduana*
immigration — *migración*
tourist card — *tarjeta de turista*
inspection — *inspección; revisión*
passport — *pasaporte*
profession — *profesión*
marital status — *estado civil*
single — *soltero*
married; divorced — *casado; divorciado*
widowed — *viudado*
insurance — *seguros*
title — *título*
driver's license — *licencia de manejar*

At the Gas Station

gas station — *gasolinera*
gasoline — *gasolina*
unleaded — *sin plomo*
full, please — *lleno, por favor*
tire — *llanta*
tire repair shop — *vulcanizadora*
air — *aire*
water — *agua*
oil (change) — *aceite (cambio)*
grease — *grasa*
My . . . doesn't work. — *Mi . . . no sirve.*
battery — *batería*
radiator — *radiador*
alternator — *alternador*
generator — *generador*
tow truck — *grúa*
repair shop — *taller mecánico*
tune-up — *afinación*
auto parts store — *refaccionería*

Verbs

Verbs are the key to getting along in Spanish. They employ mostly predictable forms and come in three classes, which end in *ar, er,* and *ir,* respectively:

to buy — *comprar*
I buy, you (he, she, it) buys — *compro, compra*
we buy, you (they) buy — *compramos, compran*

to eat — *comer*
I eat, you (he, she, it) eats — *como, come*
we eat, you (they) eat — *comemos, comen*

to climb — *subir*
I climb, you (he, she, it) climbs — *subo, sube*
we climb, you (they) climb — *subimos, suben*

Got the idea? Here are more (with irregularities marked in **bold**).

to do or make — *hacer*
I do or make, you (he she, it) does or makes — ***hago,*** *hace*
we do or make, you (they) do or make — *hacemos, hacen*

to go — *ir*
I go, you (he, she, it) goes — ***voy, va***
we go, you (they) go — ***vamos, van***

to go (walk) — *andar*
to love — *amar*
to work — *trabajar*
to want — *desear, querer*
to need — *necesitar*
to read — *leer*
to write — *escribir*
to repair — *reparar*
to stop — *parar*
to get off (the bus) — *bajar*
to arrive — *llegar*
to stay (remain) — *quedar*
to stay (lodge) — *hospedar*
to leave — *salir* (regular except for ***salgo,*** I leave)
to look at — *mirar*

to look for — *buscar*
to give — *dar* (regular except for ***doy,*** I give)
to carry — *llevar*
to have — *tener* (irregular but important: ***tengo, tiene,*** *tenemos,* ***tienen***)
to come — *venir* (similarly irregular: ***vengo, viene,*** *venimos,* ***vienen***)

Spanish has two forms of "to be." Use *estar* when speaking of location or a temporary state of being: "I am at home." "***Estoy*** *en casa.*" "I'm sick." "***Estoy*** *enfermo.*" Use *ser* for a permanent state of being: "I am a doctor." "***Soy*** *doctora.*"

Estar is regular except for ***estoy,*** I am. *Ser* is very irregular:

to be — *ser*
I am, you (he, she, it) is — ***soy, es***
we are, you (they) are — ***somos, son***

Numbers

zero — *cero*
one — *uno*
two — *dos*
three — *tres*
four — *cuatro*
five — *cinco*
six — *seis*
seven — *siete*
eight — *ocho*
nine — *nueve*
10 — *diez*
11 — *once*
12 — *doce*
13 — *trece*
14 — *catorce*
15 — *quince*
16 — *dieciseis*
17 — *diecisiete*
18 — *dieciocho*
19 — *diecinueve*
20 — *veinte*
21 — *veinte y uno* or *veintiuno*
30 — *treinta*
40 — *cuarenta*
50 — *cincuenta*
60 — *sesenta*
70 — *setenta*
80 — *ochenta*
90 — *noventa*
100 — *ciento*
101 — *ciento y uno* or *cientiuno*
200 — *doscientos*
500 — *quinientos*
1,000 — *mil*
10,000 — *diez mil*
100,000 — *cien mil*
1,000,000 — *millón*
one half — *medio*
one third — *un tercio*
one fourth — *un cuarto*

Time

What time is it? — *¿Qué hora es?*
It's one o'clock. — *Es la una.*
It's three in the afternoon. — *Son las tres de la tarde.*
It's 4 A.M. — *Son las cuatro de la mañana.*
six-thirty — *seis y media*
a quarter till eleven — *un cuarto para las once*
a quarter past five — *las cinco y cuarto*
an hour — *una hora*

Days and Months

Monday — *lunes*
Tuesday — *martes*
Wednesday — *miércoles*
Thursday — *jueves*
Friday — *viernes*
Saturday — *sábado*
Sunday — *domingo*
today — *hoy*
tomorrow — *mañana*
yesterday — *ayer*
January — *enero*
February — *febrero*
March — *marzo*
April — *abril*
May — *mayo*
June — *junio*

July — *julio*
August — *agosto*
September — *septiembre*
October — *octubre*
November — *noviembre*
December — *diciembre*
a week — *una semana*
a month — *un mes*
after — *después*
before — *antes*

Suggested Reading

Some of these books are informative, others are entertaining, and all of them will increase your understanding of Mexico. Some are easier to find in Mexico than at home, and vice versa. Take a few along on your trip. If you find others that are especially noteworthy, let us know. Happy reading.

History

Brunk, Samuel. *Emiliano Zapata, Revolution and Betrayal in Mexico.* Albuquerque: University of New Mexico Press, 1995. A detailed narrative of the renowned revolutionary's turbulent life, from his humble birth in Anenecuilco village in Morelos, through his de facto control of Mexico City in 1914–1915, to his final betrayal and assassination in 1919. The author authoritatively demonstrates that Zapata, neither complete hero nor complete villain, was simply an incredibly determined native leader who paid the ultimate price in his selfless struggle for land and liberty for the campesinos of southern Mexico.

Calderón de la Barca, Fanny. *Life in Mexico, with New Material from the Author's Journals.* New York: Doubleday, 1966. Edited by H. T. and M. H. Fisher. An update of the brilliant, humorous, and celebrated original 1913 book by the Scottish wife of the Spanish ambassador to Mexico.

Casasola, Gustavo. *Seis Siglos de Historia Gráfica de Mexico (Six Centuries of Mexican Graphic History).* Mexico City: Editorial Gustavo Casasola, 1978. Six fascinating volumes of Mexican history in pictures, from 1325 to the present.

Collis, Maurice. *Cortés and Montezuma.* New York: New Directions Publishing Corp., 1999. A reprint of a 1954 classic piece of well-researched storytelling. Collis traces Cortés's conquest of Mexico through the defeat of his chief opponent, Aztec Emperor Montezuma. He uses contemporary eyewitnesses—notably Bernal Díaz de Castillo—to revivify one of histories greatest dramas.

Cortés, Hernán. *Letters From Mexico.* Translated by Anthony Pagden. New Haven: Yale University Press, 1986. Cortés's five long letters to his king, in which he describes contemporary Mexico in fascinating detail, including, notably, the remarkably sophisticated life of the Aztecs at the time of the conquest.

Díaz del Castillo, Bernal. *The True Story of the Conquest of Mexico.* Translated by Albert Idell. Garden City: Doubleday, 1956. A soldier's still-fresh tale of the conquest from the Spanish viewpoint.

Fernández, Miguel Ángel. *The China Galleon.* Translated by Debra Nagao. Photographs by Michel Zabé. Monterrey, Mexico: Vitro Corporativo, S.A. de C.V. This authoritatively researched, masterfully translated, and gorgeously illustrated coffee-table volume traces the colorful history of the Manila galleon, and consequently Acapulco, from the fall of Constantinople in A.D. 1453 to the present day. The author shows how the allure of Asia's aromatic spices, glistening lacquerware, smooth silks, glittering gold and gems, and radiant porcelains propelled the Spanish to realize Columbus's old dream and transform the Pacific into the Spanish lake that it remained for 300 years.

Garfias, Luis. *The Mexican Revolution.* Mexico City: Panorama Editorial, 1985. A concise Mexican version of the 1910–1917 Mexican revolution, the crucible of present-day Mexico.

Gugliotta, Bobette. *Women of Mexico.* Encino, CA: Floricanto Press, 1989. Lively legends, tales and biographies of remarkable Mexican women, from Zapotec princesses to Independence heroines.

León-Portilla, Miguel. *The Broken Spears: The Aztec Account of the Conquest of Mexico.* New York: Beacon Press, 1962. Provides an interesting contrast to Díaz del Castillo's account.

Meyer, Michael, and William Sherman. *The Course of Mexican History.* New York: Oxford University Press, 1991. An insightful, 700-plus-page college textbook in paperback. A bargain, especially if you can get it used.

Novas, Himlice. *Everything You Need to Know About Latino History.* New York: Plume Books (Penguin Group), 1994. Chicanos, Latin rhythm, La Raza, the Treaty of Guadalupe Hidalgo, and much more, interpreted from an authoritative Latino point of view.

Reed, John. *Insurgent Mexico.* New York: International Publisher's Co., 1994. Republication of 1914 original. Fast-moving, but not unbiased, description of the 1910 Mexican revolution by the journalist famed for his reporting of the subsequent 1917 Russian revolution. Reed, memorialized by the Soviets, was resurrected in the 1981 film biography *Reds.*

Ridley, Jasper. *Maximilian and Juárez.* New York: Ticknor and Fields, 1999. This authoritative historical biography breathes new life into one of Mexico's great ironic tragedies, a drama that pitted the native Zapotec "Lincoln of Mexico" against the dreamy, idealistic Archduke Maximilian of Austria-Hungary. Despite their common liberal ideas, they were drawn into a bloody no-quarter struggle that set the Old World against the New, ending in Maximilian's execution, insanity of his wife, and the emergence of the United States as a power to be reckoned with in world affairs.

Ruíz, Ramon Eduardo. *Triumphs and Tragedy: A History of the Mexican People.* New York: W.W. Norton, Inc., 1992. A pithy, anecdote-filled history of Mexico from an authoritative Mexican-American perspective.

Simpson, Lesley Bird. *Many Mexicos.* Berkeley: The University of California Press, 1962. A much-reprinted, fascinating broad-brush version of Mexican history.

Unique Guidebooks and Tip Books

American Automobile Association. *Mexico Travelbook.* Heathrow, FL: American Automobile Association. Short and sweet summaries of major Mexican tourist destinations and sights. Also includes information on fiestas, accommodations, restaurants, and a wealth of information relevant to car travel in Mexico. Available in bookstores, or free to AAA members at affiliate offices.

Church, Mike and Terry Church. *Traveler's Guide to Mexican Camping.* Livingston, TX: Rolling Homes Press (161 Rainbow Drive, #6157, Livingston, TX 77399-1061). This is an unusually thorough guide to trailer parks all over Mexico, with much coverage of the Pacific Coast. Detailed maps guide you accurately to each trailer park cited, and clear descriptions tell you what to expect. The book also provides very helpful information on car travel in Mexico, including details of insurance, border crossing, highway safety, car repairs, and much more.

Franz, Carl. *The People's Guide to Mexico.* Emeryville, CA: Avalon Travel Publishing, 12th edition, 2002. An entertaining and insightful A to Z general guide to the joys and pitfalls of independent economy travel in Mexico.

Freedman, Jacqueline, and Susan Gerstein. *Traveling Like Everybody Else.* Brooklyn, NY: Lambda Publishing. Your disability needn't keep you at home. This book is out of print, but libraries may have copies.

Graham, Scott. *Handle With Care: Guide to Socially Responsible Travel in Developing Countries.* Chicago: The Noble Press, 1991. Should you accept a meal from a family who lives in a grass house? This insightful guide answers this and hundreds of other tough questions for people who want to travel responsibly in the third world.

Howells, John, and Don Merwin. *Choose Mexico.* Guilford, CT: Globe Pequot Press. A pair of experienced Mexico residents provide a wealth of astute counsel about the important questions—health, finance, home ownership, work, driving, legalities—of long-term travel, residence, and retirement in Mexico.

Jeffrey, Nan. *Adventuring with Children.* Avalon House Travel Series, 1995. This unusually detailed book starts where most travel-with-children books end. It contains, besides a wealth of information and practical strategies for general travel with children, specific chapters on how you can adventure—trek, kayak, river-raft, camp, bicycle, and much more—successfully with the kids in tow.

Mader, Ron. *Adventures in Nature Mexico.* Emeryville, CA: Avalon Travel Publishing, 1998. Internationally acknowledged expert on ecotravel in Latin America details dozens of environmentally sensitive adventure tours in Mexico. Destinations vary widely, from scuba diving off Cozumel and exploring lost Maya cities to jeeping through the Copper Canyon to rescuing turtle eggs on Oaxaca beaches.

Sanborn's *Recreational Guide to Mexico.* Sanborn's Insurance (P.O. Box 310, McAllen, TX 78502, tel. 800/222-0158). A compilation of hunting sites and lodges mostly from "Mexico Mike" Nelson's travels for Sanborn's during the 1990s. The latest edition, although still useful, is in many places out of date and/or ambiguous.

Simmonds, David, editor. *The Mexico File.* La Jolla, CA: Simmonds Publications (5580 La Jolla Blvd., #306, La Jolla, CA 92037). A monthly newsletter that, besides featuring pithy stories by Mexico travelers and news updates, offers an opportunity-packed classified section of Mexico vacations rentals, publications, services and much more. Subscribe ($39/year) by writing or dialing U.S. tel./fax 858/456-4419 or toll-free U.S. tel. 800/563-9345 (voice mail), or visiting www.mexicofile.com.

Stillman, Alan Eric. *Kwikpoint.* Alexandria, VA: GAIA Communications (P.O. Box 238, Alexandria, VA 22313-0238, www.kwikpoint.com). Kwikpoint is a super-handy, durable color foldout of pictures to point to when you need something in a foreign country. The pictures, such as a frying pan with fire under it (for "fried"), a compass (for "Which direction?"), a red lobster, and a cauliflower, are imaginative and unmistakable, anywhere between Acapulco and Aruba or San Blas and Santander.

Weisbroth, Ericka, and Eric Ellman. *Bicycling Mexico.* New York: Hunter, 1990. These intrepid adventurers describe bike trips from Puerto Vallarta to Acapulco, coastal and highland Oaxaca, and highland Jalisco and Michoacán.

Werner, David. *Where There Is No Doctor.* Berkeley, CA: Hesperian Foundation (1919 Addison St., Berkeley, CA 94704, toll-free U.S. tel. 888/729-1796, www.hesperian.org). How to keep well in the tropical backcountry.

Whipperman, Bruce. *Moon Handbooks Pacific Mexico.* Emeryville, CA: Avalon Travel Publishing, sixth edition, 2003. A wealth of information for traveling the Pacific Coast route, through Mazatlán, Guadalajara, and Puerto Vallarta, to Acapulco and beyond.

Fiction

Bowen, David, and Juan A. Ascencio. *Pyramids of Glass.* San Antonio: Corona Publishing Co., 1994. Two dozen-odd stories that lead the reader along a month-long journey through the bedrooms, the barracks, the cafés, and streets of present-day Mexico.

Doerr, Harriet. *Consider This, Señor.* New York: Harcourt Brace, 1993. Four expatriates tough it out in a Mexican small town, adapting to the excesses—blazing sun, driving rain, vast, untrammeled landscapes—meanwhile interacting with the local folks while the local folks observe them, with a mixture of fascination and tolerance.

Fuentes, Carlos. *Where the Air Is Clear.* New York: Farrar, Straus and Giroux, 1971. The seminal work of Mexico's celebrated novelist.

Fuentes, Carlos. *The Years with Laura Díaz.* New York: Farrar, Straus, and Giroux, 2000. A panorama of Mexico from independence to the 21st century, through the eyes of one woman, Laura Díaz, and her great-grandson, the author. As one reviewer said, that she ". . . as a Mexican woman, would like to celebrate Carlos Fuentes; it is worthy of applause that a man who has seen, observed, analyzed and criticized the great occurrences of the century now has a woman, Laura Díaz, speak for him." Translated by Alfred MacAdam.

Jennings, Gary. *Aztec.* New York: Atheneum, 1980. Beautifully researched and written monumental tale of lust, compassion, love, and death in pre-conquest Mexico.

Peters, Daniel. *The Luck of Huemac.* New York: Random House, 1981. An Aztec noble family's tale—of war, famine, sorcery, heroism, treachery, love, and finally disaster and death—in the Valley of Mexico.

Porter, Katherine Ann. *The Collected Stories.* New York: Delacorte, 1970.

Rulfo, Juan. *The Burning Plain.* Austin: University of Texas Press, 1967. Stories of people torn between the old and new in Mexico.

Rulfo, Juan. *Pedro Paramo.* Rulfo's acknowledged masterpiece, published last in 1980, established his renown. The author, thinly disguised as the protagonist, Juan Preciado, fulfills his mother's dying request by returning to his shadowy Jalisco hometown, Comala, in search of this father. Although Preciado discovers that his father, Pedro Páramo (whose surname that implies "wasteland"), is long dead, Preciado's search resurrects his father's restless spirit, which recounts its horrific life tale of massacre, rape and incest.

Traven, B. *The Treasure of the Sierra Madre.* New York: Hill and Wang, 1967. Campesinos, *federales,* gringos, and *indígenas* all figure in this modern morality tale set in Mexico's rugged outback. The most famous of the mysterious author's many novels of oppression and justice set in Mexico's jungles.

Villaseñor, Victor. *Rain of Gold.* New York: Delta Books (Bantam, Doubleday, and Dell), 1991. The moving, best-selling epic of the author's family's gritty travails. From humble rural beginnings in the Copper Canyon, they flee revolution and certain death, struggling through parched northern deserts to sprawling border refugee camps. From there they migrate to relative safety and an eventual modicum of happiness in Southern California.

People and Culture

Berrin, Kathleen. *The Art of the Huichol Indians.* Harry N. Abrams Publishing, 1978. Lovely, large photographs and text by a symposium of experts provide a good interpretive introduction to Huichol art and culture.

Castillo, Ana. *Goddess of the Americas.* New York: Riverhead Books, 1996. Here, a noted author has selected from the works of seven interpreters about Mesoameriacan female deities; and whose visions range as far and wide as Sex Goddess, the Broken-Hearted, the Subversive, and the Warrior Queen.

Lewis, Oscar. *Children of Sanchez.* New York: Random House, 1961. Poverty and strength in the Mexican underclass, sympathetically described and interpreted by renowned sociologist Lewis.

Medina, Sylvia López. *Cantora.* New York: Ballantine Books, 1992. Fascinated by the stories of her grandmother, aunt, and mother, the author seeks her own center by discovering a past that she thought she wanted to forget.

Meyerhoff, Barbara. *Peyote Hunt: The Sacred Journey of the Huichol Indians.* Ithaca, NY: Cornell University Press, 1974. A description and interpretation of the Huichol's religious use of mind-bending natural hallucinogens.

Palmer, Colin A. *Slaves of the White God.* Cambridge: Harvard University Press. A scholarly study of why and how Spanish colonial authorities imported African slaves into America and how they were used afterward. Replete with poignant details, taken from Spanish and Mexican archives, describing how the Africans struggled from bondage to eventual freedom.

Riding, Alan. *Distant Neighbors: A Portrait of the Mexicans.* New York: Random House Vintage Books. Rare insights into Mexico and Mexicans.

Toor, Frances. *A Treasury of Mexican Folkways.* New York: Crown Books, 1947, reprinted by Bonanza, 1985. An illustrated encyclopedia of vanishing Mexicana—costumes, religion, fiestas, burial practices, customs, legends—compiled during the celebrated author's 35 years' residence in Mexico.

Wauchope, Robert, editor. *Handbook of Middle American Indians.* Vols. 7 and 8. Austin: University of Texas Press, 1969. Authoritative surveys of important Indian-speaking groups in northern and central (vol. 8) and southern (vol. 7) Mexico.

Flora and Fauna

Goodson, Gar. *Fishes of the Pacific Coast.* Stanford, CA: Stanford University Press, 1988. More than 500 beautifully detailed color drawings highlight this pocket version of all you ever wanted to know about the ocean's fishes (including common Spanish names) from Alaska to Peru.

Howell, Steve N.G. and Sophie Webb. *A Guide to the Birds of Mexico and Northern America.* Oxford: Oxford University Press, 1995. All the serious birder needs to know about Mexico's rich species treasury. Includes authoritative habitat maps and 70 excellent color plates that detail the male and females of about 1,500 species. (For a more portable version of the above, check out Steve Howell's *Bird-Finding Guide to Mexico,* 1999.)

Leopold, Starker. *Wildlife of Mexico.* Berkeley: University of California Press, 1959. Classic, illustrated layperson's survey of common Mexican mammals and birds.

Mason, Jr., Charles T., and Patricia B. Mason. *Handbook of Mexican Roadside Flora.* Tucson: University of Arizona Press, 1987. Authoritative identification guide, with line illustrations, of all the plants you're likely to see in the Puerto Vallarta region.

Morris, Percy A. *A Field Guide to Pacific Coast Shells.* Boston: Houghton Mifflin. The complete beachcomber's Pacific shell guide.

Pesman, M. Walter. *Meet Flora Mexicana.* Delightful anecdotes and illustrations of hundreds of common Mexican plants. Published around 1960, now out of print.

Peterson, Roger Tory, and Edward L. Chalif. *Field Guide to Mexican Birds.* Boston: Houghton Mifflin, 1999. With hundreds of Peterson's crisp color drawings, this is a must for serious birders and vacationers interested in the life that teems in the Acapulco region's beaches, forests, and lagoons.

Wright, N. Pelham. *A Guide to Mexican Mammals and Reptiles.* Mexico City: Minutiae Mexicana, 1989. Pocket-edition lore, history, descriptions, and pictures of commonly seen Mexican animals.

Art, Architecture, and Crafts

Baird, Joseph. *The Churches of Mexico.* Berkeley, CA: University of California Press. Mexican colonial architecture and art, illustrated and interpreted.

Cordrey, Donald, and Dorothy Cordrey. *Mexican Indian Costumes.* Austin: University of Texas Press, 1968. A lovingly photographed, written, and illustrated classic on Mexican Indians and their dress, emphasizing textiles.

Covarrubias, Miguel. *Indian Art of Mexico and Central America.* New York: Knopf, 1957. A timeless work by the renowned interpreter of *indígena* art and design.

Martínez Penaloza, Porfirio. *Popular Arts of Mexico.* Mexico City: Editorial Panorama, 1981. An excellent, authoritative, pocket-sized exposition of Mexican art.

Morrill, Penny C. and Carol A. Berk. *Mexican Silver.* Atglen, PA: Shiffer Publishing Co. (4880 Lower Valley Road, Atglen, PA 19310). Lovingly written and photographed exposition of the Mexican silvercraft of Taxco, Guerrero, revitalized through the initiative of Frederick Davis and William Spratling in the 1920s and 1930s. Color photos of many beautiful, museum-quality pieces supplement the text, which describes the history and work of a score of silversmithing families who developed the Taxco craft under Spratling's leadership. Greatly adds to the traveler's appreciation of the beautiful Taxco silvercrafts widely available in Taxco, Acapulco, and Ixtapa-Zihuatanejo.

Sayer, Chloë. *Arts and Crafts of Mexico.* San Francisco: Chronicle Books, 1990. All you ever wanted to know about your favorite Mexican crafts, from papier-mâché to pottery and toys and Taxco silver. Beautifully illustrated by traditional etchings and David Lavender's crisp black-and-white and color photographs.

Internet Resources

Travel in General

www.travel.state.gov

The U.S. State Department information website. Lots of subheadings and links of varying completeness. Many links furnish plenty of solid information, especially consular advice, such as travel advisories or reaching U.S. citizens arrested overseas. Includes an excellent, informative Mexico section with lots of political, demographic, and economic information.

www.orbitz.com
www.travelocity.com
www.expedia.com

Major sites for airline and hotel bookings.

www.travelinsure.com
www.worldtravelcenter.com

Good for travel insurance and other services.

Specialty Travel

www.elderhostel.org

Site of Boston-based Elderhostel, with a huge catalog of ongoing study tours, including three or four in the Guadalajara region.

www.miusa.org

Site of Mobility International, with a number of services for travelers with disabilities, including many connections in Mexico.

Home Exchange

www.homexchange.com
www.intervacus.com
www.homelink.org

Sites for temporarily trading your home with someone else in dozens of places in the world, including a number of spots in the Acapulco region.

Mexico in General

www.visitmexico.com

The official website of the public-private Mexico Tourism Board; a good general site for official information, such as entry requirements. It has lots of summarily informative subheadings, not unlike an abbreviated guidebook. If you can't find what you want here, try its information number, toll-free U.S. tel. 800/44-MEXICO (800/446-3942), or the regional Mexico Tourism Board offices, listed in the On the Road chapter.

www.ticketbus.com.mx

A good Spanish-language work-in-progress that furnishes schedules and sells tickets for major southeastern (Mexico City, Puebla, Morelos, Veracruz, Oaxaca, Tabasco, Campeche, Chiapas, Yucatan, Quintana Roo) bus lines: Cristóbal Colón, ADO (Autobuses del Oriente), UNO (Lineas Unidos) and associated small carriers. Perhaps by the time you read this other major lines will have joined in.

www.mexconnect.com

An extensive Mexico site, with dozens upon dozens of subheadings and links, especially helpful for folks thinking of traveling, working, living, or retiring in Mexico. A state of Guerrero section features several pithy articles on Acapulco, Ixtapa-Zihuatanejo, and Taxco.

www.mexicodesconocido.com.mx

The site of the excellent magazine *Mexico Desconocido* (Undiscovered Mexico), which mostly features stories of unusual and off-the-beaten-path destinations. Several of its library of hundreds of articles cover a number of untouristed Acapulco region destinations, such as Chilapa, Olinalá, and Petatlán. An excellent internal search engine offers access to hard-to-find cultural, historical, and handicrafts information.

www.planeta.com
Life project of Latin America's dean of ecotourism, Ron Mader, who furnishes a comprehensive clearinghouse of everything ecologically correct, from rescuing turtle eggs in Jalisco to preserving cloud forests in Peru. Contains dozens of subheadings competently linked for maximum speed. For example, check out the Mexico travel directory for ecojourneys, maps, information networks, parks, regional guides, and a mountain more.

Hotel, Condo, and Apartment Rentals

www.choice1.com
A good site for picking a vacation rental house, condo, or villa, with information and reservations links to individual owners. Prices vary from moderate to luxurious. Coverage includes the entire Mexican Pacific coast, from Mazatlán to Oaxaca, including Troncones, Zihuatanejo, Acapulco, and Taxco.

www.go2mexico.com
An aspiring commercial site that covers the Pacific destinations from Mazatlán to Oaxaca, including Zihuatanejo and Acapulco. However, a number of destinations are very incomplete at this writing. A work in progress, potentially good if completed.

www.ownerdirect.com
An extensive vacation rental site with about half a dozen links to mostly Ixtapa condo rentals.

www.acapulcocondo-rental.org
Links to a selection of several good Acapulco condo-style hotels, with many details: photos, amenities, prices, and more.

www.mexicotravelnet.com
Good source of upscale hotel specials in Acapulco and Ixtapa-Zihuatanejo.

www.villaworl
Lists several
pulco and 7

Destina

Acapul

www.acap
The website of
Visitor's Bureau broadly
from sightseeing and shopping
transportation. The information is
however, without much detail and generally lacking links for booking hotel reservations.

www.acabtu.com.mx
Website of the former tourist newspaper *Acapulco Heat* that now has gone electronic. It provides many useful links to many midscale hotels, rental condos, houses, and apartments, real estate agencies, restaurants, community events and organizations, travel activities, and entertainments.

www.allaboutacapulco.com
An extensive professionally managed commercial site that includes everything, mostly upscale, from hotel rooms, sportfishing, and shopping malls to rental cars and real estate. Potentially very helpful for up-to-date information.

Ixtapa-Zihuatanejo

www.zihuatanejo.net
A top-notch, very complete, and well-maintained commercial site, listing nearly everywhere to stay (with reservation and email links) and dine and everything to do and much more in Zihuatanejo, Ixtapa, Troncones, and Barra de Potosí. In English or Spanish. Excellent.

www.zihua.net
Similar to, but smaller than, www.zihuatanejo.net, this site (along with its twin, www.ixtapa.net) nevertheless has lots of useful, mostly commercial, information and links.

-rentals.com
vy local resident Leigh Roth, th gorgeous photos) several high- a few moderately priced) condo, nt, and villa rental options, most near my La Madera and La Ropa beaches. also includes informative sections on taurants, shopping, activities, personal anecdotes ("Who's Been to Huautla de Jiménez?"), and stories.

www.ixtapa-zihuatanejo.com
The official site of Ixtapa-Zihuatanejo government tourism bureaus, with listings (but sparse details) of many hotels, villas, bungalows, restaurants (by food category), tours, sports, and more. At this writing, however, a number of links lead to dead ends. Although it was not generally possible to book hotel reservations directly, hotel email and links to some hotel websites were available.

Taxco

www.hotelestaxco.com
Provides details of the hotels of the mountain silver town, north of Acapulco.

Index

A
abbreviations: 308
abejón: 5
acacias: 6
Acahuizotla: 242
Acapulco: 100–150; accommodations 117–129; climate 4; entertainment and recreation 133–138; food 129–133; history 101–105; information 140–143; maps 102–103, 107, 114–115; shopping 139–140; sights 106–117; transportation 143–145; websites 323
accommodations: 55–60; Acapulco 117–129; Ixtapa-Zihuatanejo 182–193; websites 323; *see also specific place*
aerial tram: 268
African Mexicans: 20, 35–36
Aguas Blancas: 27
air evacuation: 96
air travel: 66–69; Acapulco 143–144; Ixtapa-Zihuatanejo 206
alcohol: 64–65
alders: 9
alebrijes: 53
Alemán, Miguel: 25
all-terrain vehicles: 43
amphibians: 11–12
Amusgo people: 291, 302, 303
anhingas: 11
Anson, George: 173
apartments: 58–59; *see also* accommodations
Àrbol del Fraile: 109
arid tropical scrub vegetation zone: 8–9
armadillos: 10
arts and crafts: *see* handicafts; *specific craft*

Archaeological Sites

Cuetlajuchitlán: 262
Ixcateopan: 279, 282
La Organera Xochipala: 235–237
Palma Sola: 111
Soledad de Maciel: 166–167, 168–169
Teopantecuantlán: 262–263
Xochicalco: 277–279

Asociación de Ecologistas: 204
ATMs: 88
Atotonilco: 296
Atracadero: 215
ATVs: 43
Aztecs: 14–15, 280–281

B
baggage: 67, 78–79
Bahía de Puerto Marqués: 115
Balneario Bugambilias: 237
Balneario Quinta Alegre: 261–262
Balneario Santa Fe: 238
banks: 88; Acapulco 141; Chilapa 245; Chilpancingo 231; Coyuca 154; Iguala 260; Ixtapa-Zihuatanejo 204; Lázaro Cárdenas 217; Olinalá 250; Ometepec 294; Petatlán 168; Pinotepa Nacional 300–301; San Marcos 286; Taxco 275; Tecpán 160; *see also specific place*
bargaining: 65
Barra de Coyuca: 146–147
Barra de Potosí: 210
Barra de Tecoanapa: 289
Barra Vieja: 116–117
barrier beaches: 3
basketweaving: 49, 243
bats: 10–11
beach buggies: 43
beachcombing: 39–40
beverages: 64–65
Biblioteca Taxco–Canoga Park: 268, 275
bicycling: 179, 198–199
billfish: 12
bingo: 134–135
bird of paradise: 5
birds/bird-watching: 11; La Barra 154; Laguna de Ixtapa 179; Laguna de Mitla 156; *see also* wildlife-viewing
Birthday of Benito Juárez: 47
blue whale: 13
boating/boat tours: 44, 46; Acapulco 137, 138; Ixtapa-Zihuatanejo 196, 201; La Barra 154; Laguna de Mitla 156; permits 46; Playa Brisas del Mar: 163–164; Playa La Barrita 165–166; Río Papagayo 241

Beaches

general discussion: 2–3, 39–40
El Carrizal: 155–156
La Saladita: 214–215
Piedra Tlalcoyunque: 161
Playa Angosta: 113
Playa Arroyo Seco: 165
Playa Atracadero: 215
Playa Blanca: 208
Playa Brisas del Mar: 163–164
Playa Caleta: 112
Playa Caletilla: 112
Playa Carey: 181, 199, 200
Playa Cayacal: 165
Playa Cayaquitos: 164
Playa Condesa: 114
Playa Coral: 181
Playa Cuachalatate: 181
Playa Cuata: 179
Playa del Palmar: 178–179, 198, 199, 200
Playa Don Rodrigo: 179
Playa el Almacén: 175
Playa El Calvario: 165
Playa Escolleros: 179
Playa Escondida: 162–163
Playa Hamacas: 112
Playa Hermosa: 177–178, 199
Playa Hornitos: 114
Playa Hornos: 112
Playa Icacos: 114
Playa La Barrita: 165–166
Playa Larga (Acapulco): 116
Playa Larga (Ixtapa-Zihuatanejo): 199
Playa La Ropa: 177, 198, 199, 200
Playa Las Gatas: 177, 199, 200
Playa Las Peñitas: 288–289
Playa Las Pozas: 208
Playa Linda: 179, 198–199
Playa Madera: 175–177, 198, 200
Playa Majahua: 214
Playa Morro: 114
Playa Municipal: 175
Playa Ojo de Agua: 164
Playa Paraíso: 157–158
Playa Pie de la Cuesta: 146
Playa Quieta: 179, 198, 199, 200
Playa Revolcadero: 116
Playa Roqueta: 112–113
Playa San Juan de Dios: 179
Playa Tlacopanocha: 112
Playa Varadero: 181
Playa Ventura: 287
Puerto Maldonado: 298

Boca Chica: 158
Boca de Mitla: 156
boogie boarding: Acapulco 137; Playa Arroyo Seco 165; Playa Brisas del Mar 163–164; Playa La Barrita: 165–166; Troncones 211
books/bookstores: Acapulco 140–141; Ixtapa-Zihuatanejo 203; suggested reading 316–321; Taxco 275
border crossing: 75, 85–88
Border Industrialization Program: 26
botany: *see* flora
bread: 65
bribes: 74–75
bullfighting: 46, 134
bull riding and roping: 258–259
bungalows: 58–59; *see also* accommodations
business visas: 84
bus travel: 67, 70, 78–79, 80–83; Acapulco 144–145; Ixtapa-Zihuatanejo 207; maps 72, 80–81; *see also specific place*

C

cabbage agave: 9
Cacahuamilpa caves: 277
Cacahuatepec: 302
cactuses: 8–9
California gray whale: 13
California Gulf porpoise: 13
Calles, Plutarco Elías: 24–25
Camacho, Manuel Avila: 25
Camalote: 157
camera supplies/repair: Acapulco 139; Ixtapa-Zihuatanejo 203; Taxco 274
Campamento Playa Piedra de Tlalcoyunque: 161
camping: 59–60; Acapulco 129, 149–150; packing checklist 99; *see also specific place*
candelabra cactus: 9
canoeing: 241–242; *see also* kayaking
Cárdenas, Lázaro: 25
Carnaval: 47; Iguala 259; San Juan Colorado 302
car travel: 70–76, 79–81, 85, 97–98; Acapulco

145; Ixtapa-Zihuatanejo 206–207; maps 72, 80–81; repairs 143; restrictions 145; *see also specific place*
Casa Borda: 266
Casa de Dolores Olmedo: 109–111
Casa de la Máscara: 108–109
Casa Humboldt: 267
Catholic church: 18–19, 37–38
Cavendish, Thomas: 104
Caves of Cacahuamilpa: 276–277
Caves of Juxtlahuaca: 239–241
Caves of San Miguel: 282
Centro Cultural Guerrerense: 140
Centro Internacional de Convivencia Infantil: 136
Centro Joyero de Iguala: 254, 260
Centro Recreativo Tixtla: 235
ceramics: *see* pottery
Cerro de las Peñas: 169
Cerro Madera: 177
ceviche: 61
Chagas' disease: 95
Charro Day: 48
Chiapas: 27
Chilapa: 242–246; map 245
children, activities for: 136, 228, 258
children, traveling with: 84–85, 91
Chilpancingo: 222–237; climate 4; maps 224–225, 229
Christmas: 48
CICI: 136
CICI Parque Aquatico: 258
Cinco de Mayo: 48
cinemas: Acapulco 133–134; Ixtapa-Zihuatanejo 196
climate: 4; travel seasons 41
clothing, traditional: 37, 50
cloud forest vegetation zone: 9
coapinol: 5
coatis: 10
Cochoapa: 296
coconut palm: 5
coffee shrubs: 7
colonization: 18–20
Colotlipa: 239–241
communications: 89–91; *see also* Internet access; postal services; telephone services
conduct: 96–98
conquistadors: 15–18
Constitution of 1917: 24, 32
consulates: 142–143
coral: 41
coral snake: 12
Coronel, Francisco "Don Chico": 247, 248
corrida de toros: 46
Cortés, Hernán: 15–17, 101, 172, 280–281
Cortínes, Adolfo Ruíz: 26
Costa Chica: 2, 283–304; map 284–285
Costa Grande: 2, 151–169; map 152–153
Coyuca de Benítez: 153–154
credit cards: 89
criollos: 20, 35–36
Cristo del Monte: 268
crocodiles: 12
cruise ships: 77
Cuajinicuilapa: 297
Cuauhtémoc: 15–16, 267, 279, 280–281
Cuauhtémoc Mural: 267
Cuetlajuchitlán archaeological site: 262
cuisine: *see* food
Cuna de Vicente Guerrero: 235
currency: 88–89
customs, social: 96–98
customs and immigration: 84–88; Acapulco 142; Ixtapa-Zihuatanejo 205

D

Dampier, William: 173
dance, regional: 231
dancing: Acapulco 135–136; Ixtapa-Zihuatanejo 197
Day of the Dead: 48; Cacahuatepec 302; Iguala 259
deep-sea fishing: *see* fish/fishing
de la Madrid, Miguel: 26–27
dengue fever: 95
Día de Candelaria: 47
Día de la Purísima Concepción: 48
Día de la Raza: 48
Día de los Muertos: *see* Day of the Dead
Día de los Reyes: 47
Día de Nuestra Señora de Guadalupe: 48
Día de San Francisco: 48
Día de San José: 47
Día de San Pablo y San Pedro: 48
diarrhea: 94–95
Dias Patrias: 48
Díaz, Porfirio: 23
Díaz Ordaz, Gustavo: 26
Diego, Juan: 37–38

disabled travelers: 91–92
discos: *see* dancing
diving: 42; Acapulco 137; Ixtapa-Zihuatanejo 199–200; Playa Escondida 162–163
doctors: 95–96; *see also* medical care
Drake, Francis: 17, 19, 104, 174
dress, traditional: 37, 50
drinks: 64–65
driving: *see* car travel
drugs: 96–97
duendes: 38
dune buggies: 43

E
Eco-Ixtapa: 204
ecological associations: 204
economy: 26–28, 30–32
eels: 11
egrets: 11
El Borbollon springs: 238
El Carrizal: 155–156
electricity: 91
El Grito de Dolores: 20
embroidery: 50
escorpión: 12
Escudero Mejia, Adolfo: 248
Estero Valentín: 168
European exploration and conquest: 15–18
events: *see* festivals and events
ex-Convento San Bernardino: 268

F
fan palm: 5
fauna: 9–13
Feliz Año Nuevo: 47
Feliz Navidad: 48
fer-de-lance: 12
Feria de la Nao de China: 48
Feria de San Mateo, la Navidad, y el Año Nuevo: 48, 230
ferries: 76–77
Festival of Santa Prisca: 47, 272
festivals and events: 47–48; *see also specific festival*
Fiesta de Jesús el Nazareno: 47
Fiesta de la Natividad de María: 48, 231
Fiesta de la Palmera: 154
Fiesta de la Virgen de la Asunción: 48, 245, 304
Fiesta de la Virgen de la Salud: 47
Fiesta del Día de la Santa Cruz: 47, 294
Fiesta de los Jumiles: 48, 272–273
Fiesta del Padre Jesús: 48
Fiesta del Primer de Mayo: 47
Fiesta del Señor de las Misericordias: 239
Fiesta del Señor del Perdón: 47, 294
Fiesta de Pascua: 249
Fiesta de Ramos: 47
Fiesta de San Agustín: 237–238
Fiesta de San Francisco: 259
Fiesta de San Francisco de Asis: 249
Fiesta de San Juan: 245
Fiesta de San Juan Bautista: 48
Fiesta de San Miguel: 48
Fiesta de San Nicolás Tolentino: 48, 294
Fiesta de San Patricio: 47
Fiesta de San Sebastián: 47
Fiesta de Santa Ana: 238
Fiesta de Santiago: 48, 238, 294
Fiesta de Vicente Guerrero: 48
Fiesta Mexicana: 196–197
Fiesta of St. Isador the Farmer: 47
Fiesta of the Second Friday of Lent: 259
Fiestas Patrias: 294
first aid: 94
fish/fishing: 12–13, 43–46, 61; Acapulco 137–138; Ixtapa-Zihuatanejo 200–201; La Barra 154; Laguna de Mitla 156; Laguna de Potosí: 210; La Saladita 214; licenses 46; Piedra Tlalcoyunque: 161; Playa Brisas del Mar: 163–164; Playa Escondida: 162–163; Playa La Barrita: 165–166; Playa Las Pozas: 208; Playa Paraíso 158; Playa Ventura 287
fishfuddle: 5
flag, Mexican: 254–256
flora: 4–9
folk medicine: 38
food: 60–65; Acapulco 129–133; Ixtapa-Zihuatanejo 193–196; safety 93–94; *see also specific place*
Fox, Vicente: 28–29, 33
Friends of Acapulco: 141
frigate birds: 11
fruit: 61, 64
Fuerte San Diego: 18, 104–105, 108
furniture: 50–51, 247, 279

G
Galeana, Hermanegildo: 159
gambling: 134–135
gasoline: 71–73
geography: 2–4

Gila monsters: 12
glass handicrafts: 51
gold jewelry: 52, 65–66, 168, 254
golf: 43; Acapulco 136; Ixtapa-Zihuatanejo 198; Taxco 273
gourd tree: 5
government: 32–33; *see also* history
Green Angels: 71
green turtle: 12
Grutas de Cacahuamilpa: 276–277
Grutas de Juxtlahuaca: 239–241
Grutas de San Miguel: 282
Guerrero, Vicente: 21, 222, 232–233, 234–235
Guerrero state: 2, 30–31
guesthouses: 56–57; *see also* accommodations

H

handicapped travelers: 91–92
hatmaking: 49
hawksbill turtle: 12
health: 93–98; *see also* medical care
herons: 11
Hidalgo, Miguel: 20
high coniferous forest vegetation zone: 9
high season: 41, 55
hiking: 241
history: 13–29
hitchhiking: 83

Handicrafts

general discussion: 49–55, 65
Acapulco: 139–140
Cacahuatepec: 302
Chilapa: 242–244
Huazolotitlán: 304
Iguala: 260
Ixtapa-Zihuatanejo: 202–203
Jamiltepec: 304
Olinalá: 246–249
Ometepec: 291, 294
Pinotepa Nacional: 299
Taxco: 273–274
Tixtla: 235
Xochistlahuaca: 296–297

see also specific craft

holidays: *see* festivals and events
home exchanges: 59
horseback riding: 116, 179, 198, 273
hospitals: 95–96; *see also* medical care
hotels: *see* accommodations
Huaxpáltepec: 302–303
Huazolotitlán: 304
Huerta, Victoriano: 23–24
Huichol art: 51–52
huipiles: 50, 291, 294, 304
humpback whale: 13

I

Iglesia de Chavarrieta: 268
Iglesia de Santa María de la Asunción: 279
Iguala: 250–261; climate 4; maps 252–253, 255
Igualapa: 294
immunizations: 93
Inauguration Day: 48
independence: 20–22, 105, 159, 222, 226–227, 232–233, 264
indigenous people: 20, 34, 35–37, 291, 302, 303
information and services: 84–92; Acapulco 140–143; Ixtapa-Zihuatanejo 203–205
insurance: car 71–72; flight 67
Internet access: 90; Chilapa 245–246; Iguala 260; Lázaro Cárdenas 217; Taxco 275; *see also specific place*
Internet resources: 322–324
ironwork: 51, 243
Isla Ixtapa: 179–181, 198
Isla Montosa: 146
Isla Roqueta: 112–113, 137
Itúrbide, Agustín de: 21
Ixcateopan: 279, 282
Ixtapa-Zihuatanejo: 170–207; accommodations 182–193; entertainment and recreation 196–201; food 193–196; history 172–174; information and services 203–205; maps 171, 176, 178, 180; shopping 201–203; sights 175–181; transportation 206–207; websites 323–324

JK

jaguars: 10
jaguarundi: 10
jai-alai: 134–135
Jamiltepec: 304
jellyfish: 41, 95

jet-boat rides: 241
jet-skiing: *see* personal watercraft riding
jewelry: 52, 65–66, 168, 254
Juárez, Benito: 22–23
Juxtlahuaca caves: 239–241
kayaking: 42; Ixtapa-Zihuatanejo 200; La Barra 155; Laguna de Potosí 210; Río Papagayo 241–242
King's Point: 177

L
La Barra: 154–155
Labor Day: 47
lacquerware: 51, 247, 248–249
lagoons: 2–3
Laguna Chautengo: 287
Laguna Coyuca: 137, 146
Laguna de Ixtapa: 179
Laguna de Mitla: 156–157
Laguna de Potosí: 210
Laguna Tres Palos: 116–117
Laguna Tuxpan: 261
lakes: 2–3
land: 2–4
land reform: 31
language: 37; glossary 306–308; instruction 141; Mexican food 62; phrasebook 309–315
La Organera Xochipala archaeological zone: 235–237; map 235
La Quebrada: 109
La Saladita: 214–215
Las Salinas: 165–166
laundries: Acapulco 143; Iguala 260; Ixtapa-Zihuatanejo 205
La Virgen Morena: 37–38
Lázaro Cárdenas: 215–218; map 216
leatherback turtle: 12
leather goods: 50, 243, 38, 104, 167, 197, 259
legumes: 5
libraries: Acapulco 141; Ixtapa-Zihuatanejo 203; Taxco 275
lighthouses: 112, 297
lily-walkers: 11
López Mateos, Adolfo: 26
Los Manantiales: 238
Los Sauces: 238
Los Tlacololeros: 231
low season: 41, 55
luggage: 67, 78–79

M
machismo: 97
Madero, Francisco I.: 23–24
Mágico Mundo: 112, 136
Majahua: 214
Majolica pottery: 54
mala mujer: 7
Malinche: 15, 280–281
mangrove trees: 5
Manila galleon: 16–17, 101, 104, 172–174
manta rays: 13
maquiladoras: 26
margays: 9–10
Marina, Doña: 15; *see also* Malinche
Marina Acapulco: 138
Marina Ixtapa: 201
marine mammals: 12–13
Marquelia: 288
masks: 52–53, 109, 273, 304
Maximilian, Emperor: 23
medical care: 95–96; Acapulco 142; Chilapa 246; Chilpancingo 231; Coyuca 154; Iguala 260; Ixtapa-Zihuatanejo 205; Lázaro Cárdenas 217; Olinalá 250; Ometepec 294–295; Petatlán 168; Pinotepa Nacional 301; San Marcos 286; Taxco 275–276; Tecpán 160; *see also* health
medical tags: 96
mestizos: 20, 35
metalwork: 53
Mexican cypress: 9
Mexican elm: 7
Mexican Fiesta: 134
Mexican flag: 254–256
Mexican independence: 20–22, 105, 159, 222, 226–227, 232–233, 264
Mexico Tourism Board: 86–87
mimosas: 6
missionaries: 18–19
Mixtec people: 303
Mochitlán: 238
Moctezuma: 15
money: 88–89
Monte Albán: 13–14
Monument to the Heroes of the Independence: 256
Morelos, José María: 20–21, 222, 226–227
morning glory tree: 6
Mother's Day: 48
motorboating: 42

Museums

Casa de la Máscara: 108–109
Casa Humboldt: 267
Iglesia de Santa María de la Asunción: 279
Museo Arqueología de la Costa Grande: 175
Museo de las Culturas Afromestizos: 297
Museo Guillermo Spratling: 267
Museo Platería: 267
Museo Regional de Chilpancingo: 223, 228
Museo y Santuario a la Bandera: 253–254
Naval Historical Museum of Acapulco: 108
Rail Station Museum: 254
Santa Cruz de Mitla Museo Comunitario: 157

mountain lions: 10
mountains: 3
movies: *see* cinemas
Museo Arqueología de la Costa Grande: 175
Museo de las Culturas Afromestizos: 297
Museo Guillermo Spratling: 267
Museo Platería: 267
Museo Regional de Chilpancingo: 223–228
Museo y Santuario a la Bandera: 253–254
music: 135
musical instruments: 53

N
NAFTA: 27
names: 36
National Silver Fair: 48
Naval Historical Museum of Acapulco: 108
newspapers: 140–141, 203, 275
nightclubs: Acapulco 135–136; Ixtapa-Zihuatanejo 197; Taxco 272
North American Free Trade Agreement: 27
Nuestra Señora La Virgen de Guadalupe: 37–38
nuts: 64

O
oak trees: 7–8
Obregón, Alvaro: 24–25
ocelots: 9
offtrack betting: 134–135
Olinalá: 246–250; map 248
olive Ridley turtle: 12
Olmecs: 13
Ometepec: 289–295; map 290
online resources: 322–324; *see also* Internet access
organ-pipe cactus: 9

P
packing: 98, 99
Palacio de Gobierno: 223
Palma Sola archaeological site: 111
palm leaf hats: 49
palm trees: 5
palo del muerto: 6
Papanoa: 164
paper crafts: 53
papier-mâché: 53
parasailing: 42, 137
Parque Huixteco: 272
Parque Infantil del D.I.F.: 258
Parroquia de Padre Jesús: 167–168
Paseo de los Agullis: 259
passports: 84
pastries: 65
Pax Porfiriana: 23
pelicans: 11
people: 34–38
personal watercraft riding: 42–43, 137, 146
Petaquillas: 237
Petatlán: 166–168
pets, traveling with: 85
pharmacies: *see* medical care
photofinishing: Acapulco 139; Ixtapa-Zihuatanejo 203; Ometepec 294; Taxco 274; *see also specific place*
Pie de la Cuesta: 127, 146–150; map 147
Piedra Tlalcoyunque: 161
pine-oak forest vegetation zone: 7–8
pine trees: 7–8
Pinotepa Don Luis: 301–302
Pinotepa Nacional: 298–301
pirates: 17–18, 104, 173
Plan of Iguala: 21, 250, 251, 254
plants: *see* flora; *specific plant*
Playa Angosta: 113
Playa Arroyo Seco: 165
Playa Atracadero: 215
Playa Blanca: 208
Playa Brisas del Mar: 163–164
Playa Caleta: 112
Playa Caletilla: 112
Playa Carey: 181, 199, 200
Playa Cayacal: 165
Playa Cayaquitos: 164

Playa Condesa: 114
Playa Coral: 181
Playa Cuachalatate: 181
Playa Cuata: 179
Playa del Palmar: 178–179, 198, 199, 200
Playa Don Rodrigo: 179
Playa el Almacén: 175
Playa El Calvario: 165
Playa Escolleros: 179
Playa Escondida: 162–163
Playa Hamacas: 112
Playa Hermosa: 177–178, 199
Playa Hornitos: 114
Playa Hornos: 112
Playa Icacos: 114
Playa La Barrita: 165–166
Playa Larga (Acapulco): 116
Playa Larga (Ixtapa-Zihuatanejo): 199
Playa La Ropa: 177, 198, 199, 200
Playa Las Gatas: 177, 199, 200
Playa Las Peñitas: 288–289
Playa Las Pozas: 208
Playa Linda: 179, 198–199
Playa Madera: 175–177, 198, 200
Playa Majahua: 214
Playa Morro: 114
Playa Municipal: 175
Playa Ojo de Agua: 164
Playa Paraíso: 157–158
Playa Pie de la Cuesta: 146
Playa Quieta: 179, 198, 199, 200
Playa Revolcadero: 116
Playa Roqueta: 112–113
Playa San Juan de Dios: 179
Playa Tlacopanocha: 112
Playa Varadero: 181
Playa Ventura: 287–288
Plaza de Trigarantias: 252
Plaza y Monumento a la Bandera: 252, 254
poinsettias: 8, 259
politics: 32–33; *see also* history
population: 34–36; colonial 20
porpoises: 13
postal services: 90; Acapulco 141; Chilapa 245; Chilpancingo 231; Iguala 260; Ixtapa-Zihuatanejo 204; Lázaro Cárdenas 217; Olinalá 250; Ometepec 294; Petatlán 168; Pinotepa Nacional 301; San Marcos 286; Taxco 275; Tecpán 160; *see also specific place*
pottery: 54–55
pozahuancos: 50, 299, 304
Pozo de la Nación: 109
precipitation: 4
Puerto Maldonado: 297–298
Puerto Marqués: 116
Puerto Mío: 198
Puerto Vicente Guerrero: 161–162

QR

Quechultenango: 238
rafting: 241–242
Rail Station Museum: 254
rainfall: 4
rattlesnakes: 12
real estate trusts: 118–119
recreation: 39–46; *see also specific activity*
red mangrove: 5
religion: 37–38
Rendón Franco, Audelia: 249
rental cars: 79
repairs, auto: 73–74, 143
reptiles: 11–12
resorts: 57–58; *see also* accommodations
restaurants: *see* food
Revolution Day: 48
Río Azul: 237–239
Río Balsas: 3–4, 215
Río Balsas Dam: 215
Río Papagayo: 4, 241–242
Rivera, Diego: 109–110
rivers: 3–4
rock-climbing: 241–242
royal poinciana: 5
RV parks: *see specific place*
RV travel: 60, 70–76, 79, 85; *see also* car travel

S

sacred firs: 9
safety: 93–98; money 88–89; road 73, 74; water 40–41
sailboarding: 42; Acapulco 137; Ixtapa-Zihuatanejo 200
sailing: 42, 77; Acapulco 137; Ixtapa-Zihuatanejo 200
Salinas de Gortari, Carlos: 27
salt harvesting: 166
sand box tree: 5
San Jerónimo: 158
San Juan Colorado: 302
San Luis de la Loma: 160

San Marcos: 286
San Miguel caves: 282
San Pedro Amusgos: 302
Santa Anna, Antonio López de: 21–22
Santa Cruz de Mitla Museo Comunitario: 157
Santa Prisca church: 266
savanna vegetation zone: 5
Schapenham, Hugo: 173
scorpions: 95
scuba diving: *see* diving
seafood: 61
sea turtles: *see* turtles
sea urchins: 41, 95
Semana Santa: 47; Iguala 259; Ometepec 293–294; Pinotepa Nacional 300
senior citizens, travel tips for: 92
services: 84–92
sharks: 12–13
shellfish: 61
shopping: 65–66; Acapulco 139–140; Chilapa 243–244; Chilpancingo 231; Iguala 259–260; Ixtapa-Zihuatanejo 201–203; Olinalá 248–249; Taxco 273; *see also* handicrafts; *specific place*
Sierra Madre del Sur: 3
silver jewelry and crafts: 52, 65–66, 267, 274
Sinfonia del Sol: 113
snakes: 11–12, 95
snorkeling: 42; Acapulco 137; Ixtapa-Zihuatanejo 199
Sociedad Protectora de Animales: 204
Soledad de Maciel Archaeological Zone: 166–167, 168–169

Surfing

general discussion: 42
Acapulco: 137
Ixtapa-Zihuatanejo: 199
Piedra Tlalcoyunque: 161
Playa Arroyo Seco: 165
Playa Brisas del Mar: 163–164
Playa Cayaquitos: 164
Playa El Calvario: 165
Playa Escondida: 162
Playa La Barrita: 165–166
Playa Ventura: 287
Puerto Maldonado: 298
Troncones: 211

Spanish language: *see* language
spelunking: 239–241, 276–277, 282
spider monkeys: 9
sportfishing: *see* fish/fishing
sports and recreation: 39–46; *see also specific activity*
stingrays: 13, 41, 95
stone handicrafts: 51
stoneware: 54–55
strangler fig: 7
student visas: 84
sunburn: 93
surf fishing: *see* fish/fishing
surfing: 42
swimming: Acapulco 137; safety 41; *see also specific beach*

T

Talavera pottery: 54
tattoos: 95
Taxco: 263–276; climate 4; map 265; websites 324
Taxco Hieroglyph: 268
taxis: 79, 82
Tecpán: 158–160; map 158
telegraph services: 90; Acapulco 141–142; *see also specific place*
telephone services: 89–90; Acapulco 141–142; Chilapa 245; Chilpancingo 231; Coyuca 154; Iguala 260; Ixtapa-Zihuatanejo 204–205; Lázaro Cárdenas 217; Olinalá 250; Ometepec 294; Petatlán 168; Pinotepa Nacional 301; San Marcos 286; Taxco 275; Tecpán 160; *see also specific place*
Teloloapan; 259
Temalacatcingo: 249
Templo de San Francisco: 248
Templo de Santa María de la Asunción: 223
tennis: 43; Acapulco 136; Ixtapa-Zihuatanejo 198; Taxco 273
Tenochtitlán: 14–15
Teopantecuantlán archaeological site: 262–263
Teotihuacán: 13–14
textiles: 55, 243, 304
thorn forest vegetation zone: 5
Tierra Colorada: 242
time-shares: 118–119
time zone: 91
tipping: 89
Tixtla de Guerrero: 234–235

Tlacoachistlahuaca: 296
tlatchtli: 264
Todos Santos: 48, 302
Topiltzín: 14–15
Torneo de Pez Vela: 201
tourism board: 86–87
tourist cards: 84–85
tourist information offices: Acapulco 140; Ixtapa-Zihuatanejo 203; Taxco 274–275
tours: 77, 82; *see also specific place*
trailer parks: 60; Acapulco 129, 149–150; *see also specific place*
transportation: 66–83; air 66–69; bus 67, 70, 78–79; car/RV 70–76, 79; cruise ship 77; ferry 76–77; hitchhiking 83; sailboat 77; taxi 79, 82; tour 77, 82; *see also specific place*
travel agents: Acapulco 140; Chilpancingo 231; Iguala 260; Ixtapa-Zihuatanejo 205; Lázaro Cárdenas 217; Taxco 275
traveler's checks: 88
travel seasons: 41, 55
Troncones: 211–214
tropical deciduous forest vegetation zone: 7
Tsunenaga, Hasekura: 110–111
turtles: 12, 116, 161, 162–163, 168
Tuxpan: 261

UV

vaccinations: 93
vegetarian food: 61
vegetation zones: 4–9; map 6
Villa, Francisco (Pancho): 23
Villafuerte, Juan Rodriguez de: 16, 101
villas: 58–59; *see also* accommodations
Virgin of Guadalupe: 37–38
Virgin of Guadalupe fiesta: 150
visas: 84
Vivero, Rodrigo de: 110–111

W

water, drinking: 93–94
water parks: 112, 136, 237, 238–239, 258
water-skiing: 42, 115, 137, 146
water sports: 40–42; *see also specific activity*
wave-running: *see* personal watercraft riding
weather: 4; travel seasons 41
weaving, basket: 49
weaving, textile: 55, 243, 304
whales: 13
wheelchair accessibility: 91–92
wildlife: 9–13; *see also specific animal;* wildlife-viewing
wildlife-viewing: 40; Estero Valentín 168; La Barra 154; Laguna Chautengo 287; Laguna Coyuca 146; Laguna de Potosí: 210; Laguna Tres Palos 116; Playa Ventura 287; Troncones 211
woodcarving: 52–53, 243, 304

XYZ

Ximalcota: 168
Xochicalco: 14, 277–279; map 278–279
Xochistlahuaca: 295–297
yellow-bellied sea snake: 11
Zapata, Emiliano: 23–24
Zapatistas: 27
Zedillo, Ernesto: 27, 33
Zihuatanejo: *see* Ixtapa-Zihuatanejo
Zihuatanejo Bay: 198
zoos: 113, 228

Acknowledgments

This book could not have been written without the kind help of hundreds of people who patiently answered my questions, at street corners, by roadsides, at market stalls, and behind counters and desks all over the Acapulco region.

In Acapulco itself, I give a load of thanks to Adolfo Santiago Gonzales, owner of the lovely Hotel Los Flamingos, my Acapulco home-away-from-home. Also, many thanks are due to Lilian Lobata, formerly of Acapulco city tourism, who took time to recommend many excellent restaurants. I owe the same always to Étel Alvarez Sutter, owner of Étel Suites, for her gracious welcome every time I appear at her doorstep. I also owe much to mechanic Hugo Wilson, whose dogged persistence restored my car to health.

In Zihuatanejo, I am especially grateful to scuba *maestro* Juan Barnard Ávila and his charming wife, Margo, owners of Hotel Paraíso Real, for their warmth and hospitality. Also, nearby, in Troncones, I owe a debt of gratitude to Dewey McMillin, owner of Casa Tortuga, for his welcoming hospitality; likewise, I owe the same to Eva Robbins and Jim Garrity, coowners of Eden Beach Hacienda.

At Playa Ventura, on the Costa Chica, I am in debt for the kindness and and warm welcome that I always receive from the Pérez family—Bulmaro, Inés, Hortencia, Luis, and Arturo. Likewise, I am deeply grateful to community leaders Elia Guzman of San Pedro Amusgos, and Santiago de la Cruz Velasco, of Jamiltepec.

Farther afield, I owe many thanks to Victoria Pratt, of Mexico Boutique Hotels in Puerto Vallarta, for her hard work on my behalf. Furthermore, I am deeply in debt to former travel writer, now restauranteur, Memo Barroso, whose early guidebook to the Mexican Pacific coast inspired my first published book, *Moon Handbooks Pacific Mexico*. Moreover, I owe a huge debt to my colleagues of the Mexico Writers Alliance, and especially president Bob Brooke, whose reserves of energy and cheer are an inspiration to all of us.

Likewise, back in California, I am deeply grateful to the Mexico Tourism Board, especially to Jorge Gamboa Patrón, chief of the Los Angeles office, and his associates, for their many years of kind efforts on my behalf. Furthermore, this book is much richer for the kindness of my friends Cecilia Morfín Reid and her husband, Art Reid, also of Los Angeles.

Still nearer to home, I continue to owe a debt of thanks to Avalon Travel Publishing publisher Bill Newlin and his excellent staff, for first placing their faith in me, and finally, their hard work and persistence in completing the job.

In my hometown, thanks to the understanding workers at my office-away-from-home, the Espresso Roma, whose luscious café lattes get my working days off to a good start.

This book could not have been written if not for Halcea Valdés, my friend and business partner, to whom I owe a load of thanks for managing without me while I was away.

Finally, a heap of credit is due to my loving wife, Linda, who kept the home fires burning while I was on the road, and who was patient about everything I had to neglect back home while finishing this book.

U.S.~Metric Conversion

1 inch = 2.54 centimeters (cm)
1 foot = .304 meters (m)
1 yard = 0.914 meters
1 mile = 1.6093 kilometers (km)
1 km = .6214 miles
1 fathom = 1.8288 m
1 chain = 20.1168 m
1 furlong = 201.168 m
1 acre = .4047 hectares
1 sq km = 100 hectares
1 sq mile = 2.59 square km
1 ounce = 28.35 grams
1 pound = .4536 kilograms
1 short ton = .90718 metric ton
1 short ton = 2000 pounds
1 long ton = 1.016 metric tons
1 long ton = 2240 pounds
1 metric ton = 1000 kilograms
1 quart = .94635 liters
1 US gallon = 3.7854 liters
1 Imperial gallon = 4.5459 liters
1 nautical mile = 1.852 km

To compute Celsius temperatures, subtract 32 from Fahrenheit and divide by 1.8. To go the other way, multiply Celsius by 1.8 and add 32.

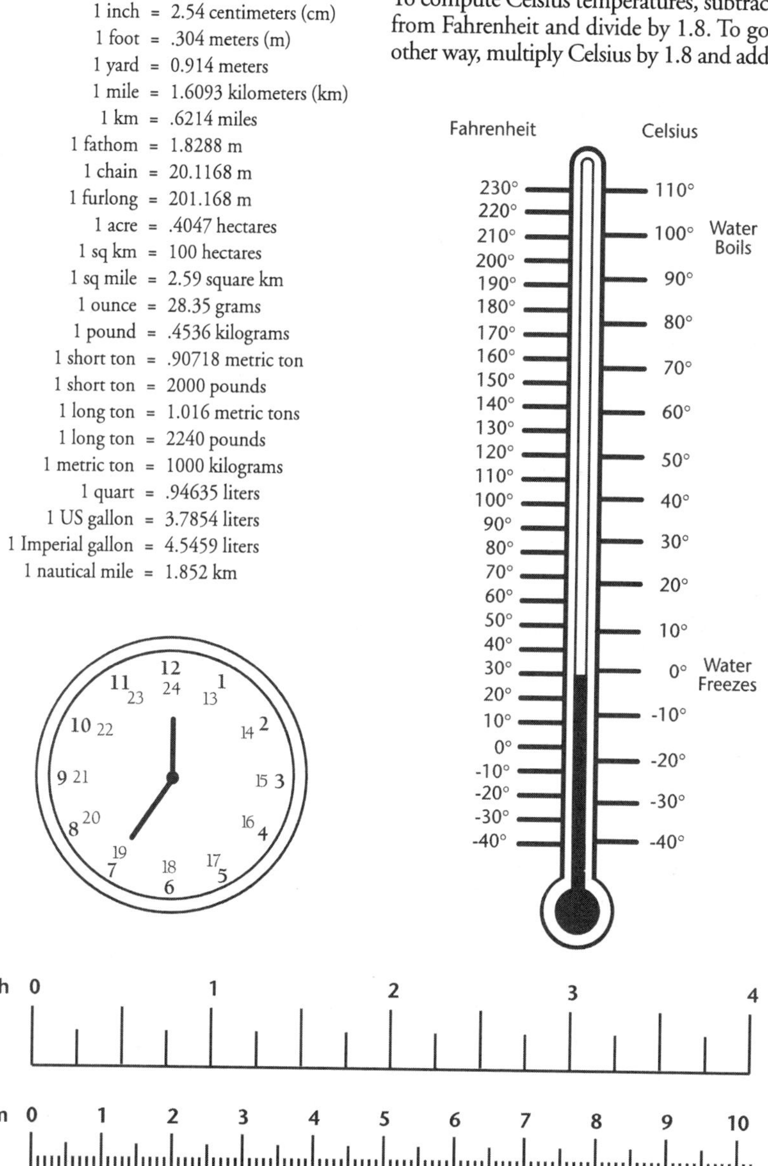

Keeping Current

Although we strive to produce the most up-to-date guidebook humanly possible, change is unavoidable. Between the time this book goes to print and the moment you read it, a handful of the businesses noted in these pages will undoubtedly change prices, move, or even close their doors forever. Other worthy attractions will open for the first time. If you have a favorite gem you'd like to see included in the next edition, or see anything that needs updating, clarification, or correction, please drop us a line. Send your comments via email to atpfeedback@avalonpub.com, or use the address below.

Moon Handbooks Acapulco
Avalon Travel Publishing
1400 65th Street, Suite 250
Emeryville, CA 94608, USA
www.moon.com

Editor: Kathryn Ettinger
Series Manager: Kevin McLain
Acquisitions Editor: Rebecca K. Browning
Copy Editor: Karen Gaynor Bleske
Graphics Coordinator: Deb Dutcher
Production Coordinator: Darren Alessi
Cover Designer: Kari Gim
Interior Designers: Amber Pirker, Alvaro Villanueva, Kelly Pendragon
Map Editor: Olivia Solís
Cartographers: Mike Morgenfeld, Suzanne Service, Kat Kalamaras
Proofreader: Kay Elliott
Indexer: Deana Shields

ISBN: 1-56691-632-1
ISSN: 1548-8012

Printing History
1st Edition—September 2004
5 4 3 2 1

Avalon Travel Publishing
An Imprint of
Avalon Publishing Group, Inc.

Printed in the United States by Malloy, Inc.